Beginning J2EE 1.4

Kevin Mukhar
James L. Weaver

with

James P. Crume
Ron Phillips

Wrox Press Ltd. ®

Beginning J2EE 1.4

First Printed March 2003

Published by Wrox Press Ltd
Arden House, 1102 Warwick Road, Acocks Green, Birmingham, B27 6BH, UK
Printed in the United States
ISBN 1-86100-833-3

Trademark Acknowledgments

Credits

Authors
Kevin Mukhar
James L. Weaver
Ron Phillips
James P. Crume

Additional Material
Rick Leander
Jim MacIntosh
Andrew Watt

Technical Reviewers
Henry Bequet
Chris Crane
Rick Leander
Brad Maiani
Steve Parker
Larry Schoeneman
David Schultz
Ranga Raghunathan
Radha Narayanan
Andrew Watt

Managing Editors
Louay Fatoohi
Liz Toy

Technical Editors
Mankee Cheng
Michelle Everitt
Chris Hart
Robert FE Shaw
Julian Skinner

Commissioning Editor
Ian Blackham

Project Manager
Darren Murphy

Production Coordinator
Sarah Hall

Production Assistant
Paul Grove

Cover
Natalie O'Donnell

Indexer
John Collin

Proofreader
Dev Lunsford

Foreword

I often get questions from readers of my *Beginning Java* series of books asking for recommendations as to which book they should buy next. Generally, I recommend that server-side programming is a logical next step, especially for people who see Java programming as important to their career. However, this is a broad area involving several important topics and technologies. Consequently, it has been hard to come up with a single book that does justice to this topic – until now, that is.

This book provides an excellent introduction to server-side programming using the Java 2 Platform, Enterprise Edition, J2EE. In a single book package, it covers all of the key capabilities provided by the J2EE that you are most likely to need in a real-world Java development context. It starts by carefully explaining what J2EE is all about and how it relates to the Java 2 Platform, Standard Edition. This means that, from the outset, you have an appreciation of the inter-relationships between the specific topics that you will need for effective server-side programming in Java. As you get into the detail you are better able to see how the various technologies involved can be combined.

After guiding you through the process of setting up a development environment for web applications, it continues with introductory tutorials on the core topics in server-side programming, JSP and servlets. It doesn't end there. A whole range of supportive web programming technologies are discussed, each with working examples that show you how they, can be applied. These include JDBC for database access, Enterprise JavaBeans, XML of course, SOAP, WDSL, and many others.

The book is the product of a cooperative effort by several authors who are each experts in their field. Each topic has the benefit of being explained by the author who is best equipped to provide an effective tutorial on that subject. The diverse topics are welded into a coherent whole by the efforts of the excellent editorial staff at Wrox Press.

The aspiring professional Java programmer needs to be conversant with the key Java technologies that are necessary for the development of Web applications as well as an overall perspective on J2EE. This is precisely what you get in this book.

Ivor Horton, author of the acclaimed Beginning Java books by Wrox Press

About the Authors

Kevin Mukhar

Kevin Mukhar is a software developer in Colorado Springs, Colorado. On his most recent project, he was the only man on a team with five other women (hi to Karen, Judy, Sondra, Jennifer, and Vui!). In the world of software development that's like the 500 year flood, or winning the Irish Sweepstakes. For the past five years he has worked on various software systems using different J2EE technologies. He has co-authored three other Wrox Press books, including *Beginning Java Databases* (ISBN 186100-437-0), which is the most popular of the JDBC books available today. He is currently working on a Masters degree in Computer Science and learning to play the saxophone. He recently passed the exam for the Java Web Component Developer Certification, and his web page is at http://home.earthlink.net/~kmukhar/.

Software is magic; I hope this book puts a little magic into your life. I would like to thank my wife and daughter for letting me disappear from their lives while writing this book.

Jim Weaver

Jim Weaver (jim.weaver@jmentor.com) is the Chief Scientist at *Learning Assistant Technologies*, a company that specializes in developing learner-centric tools. He is also the President of *JMentor*, which is a Java mentoring, training, and consulting practice.

This book is dedicated to my wife Julie, daughters Lori and Kelli, and "son" Marty. Thanks for your constant love and support. Thanks to Merrill and Barbara Bishir, Ken and Marilyn Prater, and Walter Weaver for being such wonderful examples. Thanks also to Dan Wright and David Wright for being great business partners and "brothers". Thanks to Ian Blackham, Darren Murphy, Chris Hart, and Mankee Cheng for the opportunity and great experience of writing for Wrox. Psalms 37:4

Ron Phillips

Ron Phillips has been designing and developing commercial software tools for over 10 years, with commercial IDEs, languages, compilers, and software design tools to his credit. At *Rational Software* he lead the team responsible for Rational Rose's core technology, and was one of the leader on the Rational XDE modeling tool. He is a software architect for *Serlio Software*, where he heads up all Java-based projects. He is active in the IT community and has spoken at numerous industry conferences in the USA and Europe. His current research efforts focus on architectural pattern mining and automated intellectual capital mining in legacy systems.

My thanks and love to Lynn for her patience while I was busy with this project. To my parents Joe and Eve, who have always been there.

Jim Crume

Jim Crume (jim.crume@lat-inc.net) is a Java/Web Developer at *Learning Assistant Technologies*, a company that develops applications that empower the learner. Jim has spent many years as a consultant, and specializes in architecting and developing web-based systems, but particularly enjoys Java.

> *This book is dedicated to my wife Cindy, the light of my life, who has been more than patient; my son Chris and daughter Liz who gave up my time for this project; my future daughter-in-law Michelle who helped me laugh when it got stressful; and my "daughter" Yuki, who came to America just in time for me to be immersed in this book. Thanks can't even come close to expressing my appreciation. I love you all! Thanks to Ian Blackham, Darren Murphy, Chris Hart, and Mankee Cheng for the help and guidance. And thanks to Jim Weaver for trusting me enough to ask me to help. Joshua 24:15*

Rick Leander

Rick Leander has worked in software development as a programmer, analyst, IT manager, and consultant doing everything from mainframe COBOL to J2EE. He is currently the owner of *Zeno Street Software*, a Denver-based consulting firm and has his Masters degree in information management from Webster University. His technical interests include EAI, XML, databases and distributed business application development. He lives in the Denver, Colorado area with his wife Barb and their new dog Annabelle. He can be reached through his web site at http://www.zenostreet.com.

> *Thanks again to all the great people at Wrox Press for their help and support in this project and most of all, special thanks to my wife Barb for 25 years of love and encouragement.*

Jim MacIntosh

Jim is a recycled broadcast journalist, currently working with technical support for *ClientLogic* in Saint John, NB, Canada. After spending 30 years crafting the English language into useful creations, he launched into Java as a second language in 1998, and has worked as a technical reviewer on more than two dozen Wrox Press publications. He has also spent some time developing tutorial material and has also done a bit of teaching. In addition to his interest in writing, Jim dabbles in web development, baking, and trout fishing.

> *My thanks to Judy for her encouragement and love.*

Andrew Watt

Andrew Watt is an independent consultant and author with wide-ranging interests in Java, XML, and other web technologies. He is astounded by the progress in computing since he wrote his first programs 18 years ago, enjoys the successive improvements in successive versions of Java and J2EE and hopes to contribute to further progress in years to come.

> *To those who choose peace rather than war, civilization rather than selfishisation.*

TABLE OF CONTENTS

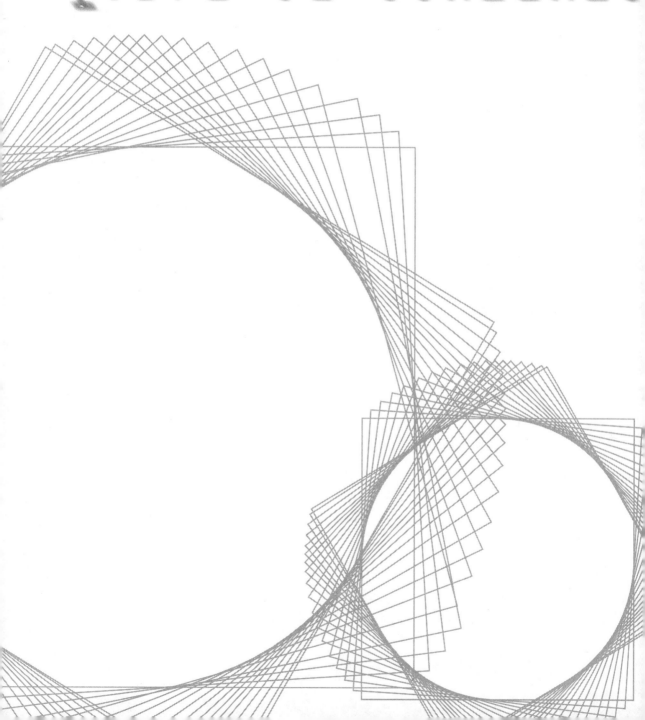

Table of Contents

Introduction   **1**

Who is This Book For?...2

What Does This Book Cover?...2

What You Need to Use this Book..4

Style Conventions...4

Customer Support and Feedback...6

How to Download the Online Package for the Book.................................... 6

Errata 7

Technical Support.. 7

p2p.wrox.com.. 8

Chapter 1: J2EE Essentials   **11**

What is J2EE?..12

How J2EE Relates to J2SE 12

Why J2EE? 13

Multi-Tier Architecture 14

Vendor Independence 19

Scalability.. 20

Features and Concepts in J2EE..20

Containers 21

Java Servlets... 23

JavaServer Pages 24

Enterprise JavaBeans 26

XML Support 29

Web Services 29

Transaction Support... 30

Security 31

Sample J2EE Architectures...31

n-Tier Architecture... 31

Application Client with EJB 32

JSP Client with EJB 32

Applet Client with JSP and Database 33

Using Web Services for Application Integration 33

Summary 34

Table of Contents

Chapter 2: Getting Set   37

Installing the J2EE 1.4 SDK... 37
Problems and Solutions...38

Testing the J2EE 1.4 SDK Installation 41
Starting the database server...41
Starting the J2EE server...42
Problems and Solutions...45

Compiling and Deploying "Hello J2EE World"................... 46
Problems and Solutions...60

Summary 61

Chapter 3: JavaServer Pages   63

Introduction to JSP 63
Developing JSP Pages 64
Basic JSP Lifecycle..64

Writing JSP Pages 65
JSP Elements..66
Directive Elements..66
Scripting Elements..68
Comments...70
Template Data 71
Action Elements..85
JSP Initialization and End-of-Life..88
Implicit Objects...89
The Request Object...89
The Response Object...90
The out Object 91
The session Object 91
The config Object 92
The exception Object...93
The application Object...93
Scope 93

Translation and Compilation 102
The Servlet API...102
The JSP API 102
A Translated JSP 103

Errors and Exceptions 105
The page Directive..105
The Deployment Descriptor 105

Including and Forwarding from JSP Pages 112
include Action 112
forward Action 113
Using include and forward..113
Summary 118

Exercises 120

Chapter 4: Advanced JSP Topics — 123

Expression Language **124**
Syntax of EL 125
Literals 126
Operators 126
Implicit Objects 128
Using EL Expressions 130
Errors and Default Values 130

Custom Actions and Tag Libraries **139**
Custom Actions 140
Tag Handlers 141
Simple Tag Handlers 141
JspFragment 143
Tag Library Descriptor 143
Packaging Tag Libraries 146
Application Structure 146
Deployment Descriptor 146
Importing a Taglib into a Page 147
Classic Tag Handler Design 152
Tag 153
IterationTag 154
BodyTag 155

JavaServer Pages Standard Tag Library (JSTL) **166**
Getting an Implementation 166
What's in the JSTL? 167
Core actions 167
General-Purpose Actions 167
Conditional Actions 168
Iterator Actions 169
Formatting Actions 169
SQL Actions 170

Other Tag Libraries **175**

Summary **176**

Exercises **176**

Chapter 5: Servlets — 179

HTTP and Server Programs **180**
Request Methods 180
GET 181
POST 184
How a Server Responds to Requests 184

Table of Contents

The Servlet Model and HttpServlets..**185**

Basic Servlet Design 186

The service() Method..186

The doPost() and doGet() Methods...187

Request and Response Objects...187

Using the request Object 196

Using the response Object..199

Deployment Descriptors..199

The <context-param> Element...202

The <servlet> Element...202

The <servlet-mapping> Element...203

Servlet Lifecycle...204

Loading and Instantiation...205

Initialization...205

Request Handling..207

End of Service..207

The Login Servlet..208

Event Logging in Servlets...208

Servlets are Multi-Threaded...208

How to Make your Servlets Thread-Safe..214

How Not to Make your Servlets Thread-Safe...215

Handling Exceptions **216**

Poor Exception Handling 216

Error Pages...218

Session Management...**219**

Creating and Using Sessions...219

Session Tracking with Cookies 220

Session Tracking with URL Rewriting..220

What can you do with a Session?...220

Session Management with Cookies 221

Filters **227**

Why you Need Filters 227

Implementing a Filter..227

The Filter API 227

The Deployment Descriptor 229

The MVC Architecture...**237**

Model 1 vs. Model 2 237

MVC..238

Forwarding and Including Requests..239

Getting a RequestDispatcher..239

Using a Request Dispatcher 240

Adding Parameters to the Request 241

Summary **252**

Exercises **253**

iv

Chapter 6: Working with Databases 257

Connecting to Databases **258**
Drivers 259
Driver Types 259
Type 1 Driver 259
Type 2 Driver 260
Type 3 Driver 260
Type 4 Driver 261
Choosing a Driver 261
The DriverManager Class 262
Loading a Driver 262
Using Class.forName() 262
Using a System Property 263
Connections 264
Getting a Connection 264
Releasing Connections 266
Setting the Login Timeout 268
SQLException 268
Logging with the DriverManager 274

Statements **275**
Creating and Using Statement Objects 275
Single Statement Execute 276
Batch Updates 277
Releasing Statements 278

Resultsets **284**
Moving Through the Results 284
Reading Data from the Resultset 285
Working with Null Values 287
Updateable ResultSets 292
Holdable ResultSets 294

Summary **295**

Exercises **295**

Chapter 7: Advanced Topics in JDBC 297

Prepared Statements **298**
Creating a Prepared Statement 299
Using a Prepared Statement 301
Setting Placeholders 301
Setting Null Values 302
Reusing a Prepared Statement 302
Batch Updates 303

Callable Statements **306**
Using Placeholders 308

Data Sources and Connection Pools **310**
Data Source Overview...310
Using a DataSource Object 311
Connection Pool Overview 311

Transactions **320**
Connection Methods for Transaction Control 322
Transactions and Stored Procedures..325
Introduction to Distributed Transactions..331

Locking and Isolation.. **334**
Isolation 335
Locking...336
Pessimistic Locking...337
Optimistic Locking..344

Summary **349**

Exercises **350**

Chapter 8: EJB Fundamentals   **353**

Understanding EJBs **353**
Why Use EJBs?...354
The Three Kinds of EJBs 356
Session Beans 356
Entity Beans 357
Message-Driven Beans...358
Decisions, Decisions 358

A Closer Look at Session Beans **358**
The Anatomy of a Session Bean 359
The Home Interface..359
The Bean Interface...359
The Bean Class 359
The Home and Bean Stubs..360
Developing Session Beans..360
Stateful vs. Stateless Session Beans 377
Choosing Between Stateful and Stateless...377

Summary **385**

Exercises **386**

Chapter 9: EJB Entity Beans   **389**

A Closer Look at Entity Beans **389**
The Anatomy of an Entity Bean...390
The Home Interface..391
The Bean Interface...392
The Bean Class 392
Other Features of Entity Beans 393

Container-Managed Persistence 393
Primary Keys 395
Container-Managed Relationships 395
EJB Query Language 395

Developing CMP Entity Beans **395**

Developing BMP Entity Beans **415**
EJB Local Interfaces 422
Understanding EJB Local Interfaces.. 423
The EJB Query Language 434
EJB-QL Find vs. Select Methods 434

Summary **444**

Exercises **445**

Chapter 10: More EJB Topics   **447**

Container-Managed Relationships **447**
Creating an EJB-QL Select Method 449

Using JDBC with Enterprise JavaBeans **478**

Summary **485**

Exercises **485**

Chapter 11: Design Patterns and Message-Driven Beans   **487**

Using Design Patterns in EJB Applications **487**

Using JSP and Servlets with EJBs **507**

Developing Message-Driven Beans **514**
Introduction to the Java Message Service API 515
Introduction to the EJB Timer Service 516

Summary **528**

Resources **528**

Exercises **529**

Chapter 12: Web Services and JAX-RPC   **531**

Understanding Web Services **531**
Why Use Web Services?.. 534
The Web Services Protocol Stack 535
Transport Layer 535
Encoding Layer 535

Messaging Layer 535
Service Description Layer 536
Service Discovery Layer 536
Emerging Layers 536

Developing Web Services in Java **537**
Understanding JAX-RPC 537
Developing Web Services Using JAX-RPC 538
The Essential Steps for Building and Deploying Web Services 543

Summary **561**

Resources **562**

Exercises **562**

Chapter 13: More J2EE Web Services Topics   **565**

Implementing a Session Bean as a Web Service **565**

Implementing a Stateful Web Service **580**
Can Web Services be Stateful? 580
The JAX-RPC Service Endpoint Model 580
The Service Lifecycle 581
The Endpoint Context 581

Summary **597**

Exercises **597**

Chapter 14: Further J2EE Topics   **601**

The J2EE Roadmap **602**
Web and Internet Technologies 603
HTTP & Web Server Standards 603
JavaServer Pages (JSP) & Servlets..604
JavaMail 604
Data Access 604
JDBC (Java DataBase Connectivity)..604
Java Data Objects (JDO) 604
XML APIs 604
Distributed Computing 605
Web Services 605
Enterprise JavaBeans (EJBs) 605
Remote Method Invocation (RMI) 605
Java Message Services (JMS)..605
Connectors 606
Java IDL and CORBA 606
Management and Administration 606
Java Naming and Directory Interface (JNDI) 606
ECperf..606
J2EE Management and Deployment Specifications..607
Other Technologies and APIs..607

Paths to Knowledge **607**
e-Commerce 608
Review J2SE APIs 608
Performance and Optimization 608
Web Design and Human/Computer Interaction 609
Workflow Automation 609
Messaging 610
Distributed Computing 610
Object-Oriented Analysis and Design 610
Application Service Providers (ASP) 610
Database Technologies 611
Management and Deployment APIs 611
Web Services 611
EDI and Supply Chain Management 612
XML 612
JavaMail 613
Enterprise Application Integration (EAI) 613
Java IDL & CORBA 613
Connectors 613
Other Technologies 614
Other Applications 614

J2EE Resources **614**
SDKs, Documentation, and Specifications 615
Books and Reference Manuals 615
Java Periodicals 616
Other Sources 616

Summary **617**

Resources **617**

Chapter 15: J2EE in the Real World   **619**

Reasons for Using Industrial-Strength J2EE **620**
Performance 620
Fault-Tolerance 621
Scalability 621
Security 622
Administration 622
Developer Productivity 623
Getting to Know the Players 623

The Application Server Market **623**
Fully-Featured Servers 624
BEA's WebLogic Server 624
IBM's WebSphere Application Server 625
Oracle's 9i Application Server 625
Other Choices 626
JSP Servers 626
Apache's Tomcat 627
MacroMedia's JRun 627

Table of Contents

HTTP Servers 627
Apache Web Server 627
Microsoft's Internet Information Services (IIS) 627
Getting to Know the Servers 627

Supporting Roles **628**
J2EE Integrated Development Environments (IDEs) 628
IDE Features 629
Commercial IDEs 631
Testing and Performance Tools 631
Configuration Management (CM) 632
Database Servers 633
Service Providers 634
Adjusting to the Real World 634

Competing Technologies **634**

Summary **635**

Resources **635**

Chapter 16: First Steps in Your Java Career   **639**

Web Resources **639**
Java and J2EE 640
Non-Java Web Resources 642

Java Certification **642**

The Jobs **644**

Books from Wrox Press **645**
Professional Java Server Programming J2EE 1.3 Edition 645
Professional J2EE EAI 646
Expert One-on-One: J2EE Design and Development 647
J2EE Design Patterns Applied 648
Professional Java Servlets 2.3 649
Professional JSP Tag Libraries 650
Professional Java Web Services 651
Professional Web Services Security 652
Professional Apache Tomcat 653

Appendix A: Installing Tomcat   **655**

Getting Tomcat **655**

Binary Installation to Windows **656**

Binary Installation to Linux/Unix **657**

Source Installation **658**

Running Tomcat **658**

Appendix B: SQL and EJB QL — 661

SQL 661
SQL Data Types 663
String Data Types 663
Numeric Data types 664
Date and Time Data Types 664
Binary Data Types.. 664
Working with Tables 665
Creating a Table 665
Specifying Default Values.. 665
Updating the Structure of a Table 666
Deleting Tables... 666
Handling Null Values 667
Selecting Data from Tables 667
Filtering Data in Queries.. 668
Sorting Data from Queries.. 669
Wildcards and Regular Expressions 670
Calculated Fields 671
SQL Functions 672
Inserting New Rows into a Table.. 673
Updating Data in Tables... 674
Deleting Data from a Table 675
Joins 675

EJB QL... 677
The SELECT Clause 679
Navigation Operator 680
Input Parameters 680
Wildcards 680
Functions 681
Aggregate Functions 681
Using Relationships 681

Appendix C: J2EE Glossary — 685

Index — 693

INTRODUCTION

Who is This Book For?   2

What Does This Book Cover?   2

What You Need to Use this Book   4

Style Conventions   4

Customer Support and Feedback   6

Introduction

First things first before we dive in. We, the authors, have read a lot of books on designing and developing software – some better than others – and spent a lot of time and money in the process. We had some very specific thoughts as we put this book together.

First and foremost, the focus of this book is on the *practical* aspects of getting started with developing distributed software for the J2EE platform. J2EE is a broad and deep subject, and getting started can be like getting a drink from a fire hose. We wanted to put together a practical approach to getting started, and spend most of our time talking about the topics that you'll use 90% (or more) of the time. We are serving up meat and potatoes here.

When we pick up a book on software development, we like to have the option of reading straight through, or to skip around and pick up the topics that we're interested in at a given time. As an introduction into J2EE, you'll learn the most if you first read through each chapter in order. Later, as you go back to particular sections, you'll find it easy to skip back to refresh your memory, so feel free to skip around in this book – we hope that we've done a good job of making each topic stand on its own, and provided examples that are straightforward and relevant.

The authors of this book are software engineers first. Like you, we have more projects than time to do them in, and we understand that you don't have extra time to waste when it comes to learning new technologies. We hope the result is a book that you will pick up frequently, highlight, bookmark, and consider a valued addition to your development resources.

Like J2SE, J2EE is comprised of several packages containing classes and interfaces that define the J2EE framework. You're already familiar with J2SE, and you got that expertise by taking the J2SE framework one topic at a time. We'll take J2EE the same way – one topic at a time.

Who is This Book For?

This book is mainly aimed at people who already have knowledge of basic Java, and have been developing small, client-side applications for the desktop. If you have read and absorbed the information contained in an entry-level book such as *Beginning Java 2* written by Ivor Horton, then you will be well placed to begin your journey to developing server-side applications using J2EE.

If you are coming from another object-oriented language, such as C++ or C#, and you wish to begin developing enterprise-level applications with Java, then you will also benefit greatly from this book. The coding concepts, principles, and constructs are similar; you just need to watch out for the syntax differences and, obviously, the different code architecture for the different technology areas of J2EE.

What Does This Book Cover?

This book will take you from having a good grip of the basic Java language to being able to create reusable and scaleable components of J2EE, such as JavaServer Pages, Enterprise JavaBeans, and web services. At the end of the book, we will also point you in which direction go to find out more information on your chosen areas of interest, and how you could land yourself the perfect job developing enterprise applications.

Here's a rundown of what you can expect to see as you work through the book.

- ❑ **Chapter 1: J2EE Essentials** – This chapter will lay out a roadmap of what J2EE is and how it is used as an application foundation. You'll get an introduction to the primary components of J2EE and how they fit together.

- ❑ **Chapter 2: Getting Set** – Having your machine configured correctly is essential if you want to be able to run the sample code presented in this book. This chapter walks through the installation, configuration, and testing of the core components of J2EE.

- ❑ **Chapter 3: JavaServer Pages** – An introduction to the world of server-side web programming using JSP pages. This chapter covers how to write simple JSP pages, covering the fundamentals of the technology and how they can be very useful in your web applications.

- ❑ **Chapter 4: Advanced JSP Topics** – In this chapter, we follow on from the basics of JSP, and look at some deeper features of the technology, such as the expression language, custom actions, and the JSP Standard Tag Library.

- ❑ **Chapter 5: Servlets** – Next, we cover another highly used component in J2EE web applications – servlets, which are designed to be extensions to servers and to extend the capabilities of servers and provide dynamic behavior.

❑   **Chapter 6: Working with Databases** – At some point in developing a J2EE application, you will very likely need to store and manipulate data stored in a data source. This is where JDBC comes in, and this chapter introduces this functionality where we access the Cloudscape database.

❑   **Chapter 7: Advanced Topics in JDBC** – After learning the basic data access functionality in the previous chapter, you will see deeper topics of JDBC in this chapter, covering prepared statements and stored procedures, transactions, and locking.

❑   **Chapter 8: EJB Fundamentals** – In this part of the book, we begin to look at a feature of J2EE dedicated to expressing the business logic of an application – Enterprise JavaBeans or EJBs. This chapter mainly focuses on an overview of EJB technology and looks at session beans in detail.

❑   **Chapter 9: EJB Entity Beans** – This second chapter on EJBs looks at another type of EJB, entity beans, and how they relate and fit in with other types of bean. We cover two different types of persistence and take a look at the EJB Query Language.

❑   **Chapter 10: More EJB Topics** – Creating container-managed relationships and combining the use of JDBC and EJBs are the two topics of this chapter. We also build on the EJB-QL knowledge gleaned from the previous chapter by looking at EJB-QL select methods.

❑   **Chapter 11: Design Patterns and Message-Driven Beans** – In the final EJB chapter of the book, we look at what design patterns are, and how they can be applied to your EJB applications and what benefits they bring. We also cover the final type of bean – message-driven beans.

❑   **Chapter 12: Web Services and JAX-RPC** – The next major topic in the book covers concepts of enabling distributed applications via the magic of web services. We will look at topics such as the fundamentals, guidelines and good practices, and other issues that you should be aware of when creating web services.

❑   **Chapter 13: More J2EE Web Services Topics** – In the second web services chapter of this book, we move on to combining different J2EE technologies. You will see how to implement a session bean as a web service, and also how to implement a stateful web service.

❑   **Chapter 14: Further J2EE Topics** – Now that we have covered the most commonly used features of J2EE, this chapter looks at parts of J2EE that have not been covered already. The chapter's purpose is to give you a brief, descriptive taster of what we haven't covered in the book – it is not meant to be an exhaustive guide.

❑   **Chapter 15: J2EE in the Real World** – Working through the concepts and code in this book has seen you develop in a relatively safe environment. However, real world J2EE development is much more than the closed confines of the reference implementation. This chapter looks at issues you will encounter in real life J2EE.

❑ **Chapter 16: First Steps in your Java Career** – After reading through the whole book, you will no doubt be raring to go out there and get your first J2EE job and kick start your career. This chapter gives you some more resources from which to find out information and ideas on how to extend your J2EE knowledge in the direction you want it to go.

What You Need to Use this Book

The prerequisite system and software requirements for this are very small. Since you already have a background in Java, then you will no doubt have a version of the J2SE SDK installed on your machine already. In this book, we've used the latest version of the Standard Edition software development kit, which was J2SE 1.4.1_01. Throughout the book, we have used Windows 2000 as our operating system but since Java has a "write once, run anywhere" motto, you can use another platform such as Solaris or Linux without any major changes to the code you see.

The only other piece of software you need to download and install to run the examples and follow the discussions in this book is J2EE 1.4. At the time of writing of this book, the final release of J2EE 1.4 is expected to be in the summer of 2003. As a result, we have based all the material contained here on the relatively stable beta version of J2EE 1.4. Where appropriate, we have highlighted any differences or bugs you may come across when using the beta.

Style Conventions

We have used certain layout and font styles in this book that are designed to help you to differentiate between the different kinds of information. Here are examples of the styles that are used, with an explanation of what they mean.

As you'd expect, we present code in two different ways: code used inline with text, and code that is displayed on its own. When we need to mention keywords and other coding specifics within the text (for example, in discussion relating to an `if...else` construct or the `beans` package) we use the single-width font as shown in this sentence. If we want to show a more substantial block of code, then we display it like this:

```
package beans;
import java.rmi.RemoteException;
import javax.ejb.EJBHome;
import javax.ejb.CreateException;

public interface SimpleSessionHome extends EJBHome {
  // The create() method for the SimpleSession bean
  public SimpleSession create()
    throws CreateException, RemoteException;
}
```

Sometimes, you will see code in a mixture of gray and white backgrounds, like this:

```
package beans;

import java.rmi.RemoteException;
import javax.ejb.EJBObject;

public interface SimpleSession extends EJBObject {
  // The public business method on the SimpleSession bean
  public String getEchoString(String clientString)
    throws RemoteException;
}


  private void Page_Load(object sender, System.EventArgs e)
  {
    HeaderIconImageUrl = Request.ApplicationPath + "/Images/winbook.gif";
    HeaderMessage = "Informative Page";
  }
```

In cases like this, we use the gray shading to draw attention to a particular section of the code – perhaps because it is new code, or it is particularly important to this part of the discussion.

Sometimes, you will need to type in commands on the command line. We will display situations like that using the following style:

```
> set classpath=.;C:\j2sdkee1.4\lib\j2ee.jar
> javac -d . client/*.java
```

We show the prompt using a > symbol and then highlight in the **bold** the commands you need to type.

Advice, hints, and background information come in this type of font.

> **Important pieces of information come in boxes like this.**

Bullets appear indented, with each new bullet marked as follows:

❑ **Important Words** are in a bold type font.

❑ Words that appear on the screen, or in menus like File or Window, are in a similar font to the one you would see on a Windows desktop.

❑ Keys that you press on the keyboard like *Ctrl* and *Enter*, are in italics.

Customer Support and Feedback

We value feedback from our readers, and we want to know what you think about this book; what you liked, what you didn't like, and what you think we can do better next time. You can send us your comments, either by returning the reply card in the back of the book, or by e-mail to feedback@wrox.com. Please be sure to mention the book's ISBN and title in your message.

How to Download the Online Package for the Book

When you visit the Wrox web site, http://www.wrox.com/, simply locate the title through our search facility or by using the book list button on the left-hand side. Then you simply need to click on Download Code on the book's detail page to obtain all the code for the book.

When you click to download the code for this book, you are presented with a page that has three options:

❑　If you are already a member of the Wrox Developer Community (in other words. if you have already registered on ASPToday, C#Today, or Wroxbase), you can log in with your usual username and password combination to download the code.

❑　If you are not already a member, you have the option of registering for free code downloads. By registering, you will be able to download several free articles from Wrox Press. It will also enable us to keep you informed about updates and new editions of this book.

❑　The third option is to bypass registration completely and simply download the code.

Registration for code download is *not* mandatory for this book, but if you *do* register for the code download, your details will not be passed to any third party. For more details, you can review our terms and conditions, which are linked from the download page.

When you reach the code download section, you will find that the files that are available for download from our site have been archived using WinZip. When you have saved the files to a folder on your hard drive, you will need to extract the files using a de-compression program such as WinZip or PKUnzip. When you extract the files, the code is extracted into chapter folders, so you need to make sure that your extraction software (WinZip, PKUnzip, and so on) is set to use folder names.

There is an important file included in the code download, ReadMe.htm, which includes more information on how to set up the samples in this book. We strongly recommend you read this file to better understand how the examples are structured.

Errata

We've made every effort to make sure that there are no errors in the text or in the code. However, no one is perfect and mistakes do occur. If you find an error in one of our books, like a spelling mistake or a faulty piece of code, we would be very grateful for feedback. By sending in errata you may save another reader hours of frustration, and of course, you will be helping us provide even higher quality information. Simply e-mail the information to support@wrox.com, where your information will be checked and, if correct, posted to the errata page for that title, or used in subsequent editions of the book.

To find errata on the web site, go to http://www.wrox.com/, and simply locate the title through our search engine or title list. Click on the Errata link, which is below the cover graphic on the book's detail page.

Technical Support

If you would like to make a direct query about a problem in the book, you need to e-mail support@wrox.com. A typical e-mail should include the following things:

- ❑ In the Subject field, tell us the **book name**, the **last four digits of the ISBN** (8333 for this book), and the **page number** of the problem.

- ❑ In the body of the message, tell use your **name**, **contact information**, and the **problem**.

We *won't* send you junk mail. We need these details to save your time and ours. When you send an e-mail message, it will go through the following chain of support:

1. **Customer Support** – Your message is delivered to one of our customer support staff – they're the first people to read it. They have files on most frequently asked questions and will answer anything general about the book or the web site immediately.

2. **The Editorial Team** – Deeper queries are forwarded to the technical editor responsible for the book. They have experience with the programming language or particular product, and are able to answer detailed technical questions on the subject. Once an issue has been resolved, the editor can post the errata to the web site.

3. **The Authors** – Finally, in the unlikely event that the editor cannot answer your problem, he or she will forward the request to the author. We do try to protect the author from any distractions to their writing; however, we are quite happy to forward specific requests to them. All Wrox authors help with the support on their books. They will mail the customer and the editor with their response, and again all readers should benefit.

> Note that the Wrox support process can only offer support to issues that are directly pertinent to the content of our published title. Support for questions that fall outside the scope of normal book support is provided via the community lists of our **http://p2p.wrox.com/** forum.

p2p.wrox.com

For author and peer discussion join, the **P2P mailing lists**. Our unique system provides **programmer to programmer**™ contact on mailing lists, forums, and newsgroups, all *in addition* to our one-to-one e-mail support system. Wrox authors and editors and other industry experts are present on our mailing lists.

At p2p.wrox.com you will find a number of different lists that will help you, not only while you read this book, but also as you develop your own applications. You will find all of the lists in the Java category very useful, including:

- ❑ beginning_jsp
- ❑ enterprise_java_beans
- ❑ expertj2ee_with_rodjohnson
- ❑ j2ee
- ❑ java_certification
- ❑ java_ecommerce
- ❑ pro_java_server
- ❑ pro_jsp
- ❑ servlets

To subscribe to a mailing list just follow these steps:

1. Go to http://p2p.wrox.com/

2. Choose the appropriate category from the left menu bar

3. Click on the mailing list you wish to join

4. Follow the instructions to subscribe and fill in your e-mail address and password

5. Reply to the confirmation e-mail you receive

6. Use the subscription manager to join more lists and set your e-mail preferences

CHAPTER 1

What is J2EE?	**12**
Features and Concepts in J2EE	**20**
Sample J2EE Architectures	**31**
Summary	**34**

J2EE Essentials

The word 'enterprise' has magical powers in computer programming circles. It can increase the price of a product by an order of magnitude, and double the potential salary of an experienced consultant. Your application may be free of bugs, and cleanly coded using all the latest techniques and tools, but is it enterprise ready? What exactly is the magic ingredient that makes enterprise development qualitatively different from run-of-the-mill development?

Enterprise applications solve business problems. This usually involves the safe storage, retrieval, and manipulation of business data: customer invoices, mortgage applications, flight bookings, and so on. They might have multiple user interfaces: a web interface for consumers, and a GUI application running on computers in the branch offices, for example. They have to deal with communication between remote systems, co-ordination of data in multiple stores, and ensure the system always follows the rules laid down by the business. If any part of the system crashes, the business loses part of its ability to function, and starts to lose money. If the business grows, the application needs to grow with it. All this adds up to what characterizes enterprise applications: robustness in the face of complexity.

When we set out to build a GUI application, we don't start out by working out how to draw pixels on the screen, and build our own code to track the user's mouse around the screen; we rely on a GUI library, like Swing, to do that for us. Similarly, when we set out to create the components of a full-scale enterprise solution, we'd be crazy to start from scratch. Enterprise programmers build their applications on top of systems called **application servers**. Just as GUI toolkits provide services of use to GUI applications, application servers provide services of use to enterprise applications – things like communication facilities to talk to other computers, management of database connections, the ability to serve web pages, and management of transactions.

Just as Java provides a uniform way to program GUI applications on any underlying operating system, nowadays Java can provide a uniform way to program enterprise applications on any underlying application server. The set of libraries developed by Sun Microsystems and the Java Community Process that represent this uniform application server API is what we call the **Java 2 Platform, Enterprise Edition**, and is the subject of this book.

This chapter provides a high-level introduction to J2EE, and an introduction to how to get the most benefit from this book. After reading this chapter, you will:

❑ Have an understanding of the reasons that the concepts underlying J2EE are compelling and enabling technologies for large-scale applications

❑ Understand how J2EE relates to J2SE

❑ Be introduced to the cornerstone technologies of J2EE

❑ Be introduced to some of the essential architectural patterns that J2EE facilitates

So, without further ado, let's get started!

What is J2EE?

Since you're reading this book you've got some interest in J2EE, and probably have some notion of what you're getting into. For many fledgling J2EE developers, J2EE equates to Enterprise Java Beans. J2EE is a great deal more than just EJBs, though.

While perhaps an oversimplification, J2EE is a suite of specifications for application programming interfaces, a distributed computing architecture, and definitions for packaging of distributable components for deployment. It's a collection of standardized **components**, **containers**, and **services** for creating and deploying distributed applications within a well-defined distributed computing architecture.

As its name pretty much spells out, Java 2 Enterprise Edition is targeted at large scale business systems. Software that functions at that level doesn't run on a single PC – it requires significantly more computing power and throughput than that. For that reason, the software needs to be partitioned into functional pieces and deployed on the appropriate hardware platforms to provide the necessary computing power. That is the essence of distributed computing. J2EE provides a collection of standardized components that facilitate software deployment, standard interfaces that define how the various software modules interconnect, and standard services that define how the different software modules communicate.

How J2EE Relates to J2SE

J2EE isn't a replacement for the Java 2 Standard Edition. The J2SE provides the essential language framework that the J2EE builds upon. It is the core upon which J2EE is based. As you'll see, J2EE consists of several layers, and J2SE is right at the base of that pyramid for each component of J2EE.

As a Java developer, you've probably already learned how to build user interfaces with the JFC/Swing and AWT components. You'll still be using those to build the user interfaces for your J2EE applications, as well as HTML, based user interfaces. Since J2SE is at the core of J2EE, everything that you've learned so far remains useful and relevant.

In fact, J2EE provides pretty much nothing in the way of user interfaces. You'll also see that the J2EE platform provides the most significant benefit in developing the "middle tier" portion of your application – that's the business logic and the connections to back-end data sources. You'll use familiar J2SE components and APIs in conjunction with the J2EE components and APIs to build that part of your applications.

Why J2EE?

J2EE defines a number of services that, to someone developing enterprise-class applications, are as essential as electricity and running water. Life is simple when you simply turn the faucet and water starts running, or flip the switch and lights come on. If you have ever been involved with building a house, you'll know that there is a great deal of effort, time, and expense in building in that infrastructure of plumbing and wiring that is then so nicely hidden behind freshly painted walls. At the points where that infrastructure is exposed, there are standard interfaces for controlling (water faucets and light switches, for example) and connecting (power sockets, lamp sockets, and hose bibs, for example).

In the same vein, there is a great deal of infrastructure required to write enterprise-class applications. There are a bunch of different system-level capabilities that you need in order to write distributed applications that are scaleable, robust, secure, and maintainable. Some vital pieces of that infrastructure include security, to ensure that a user is who they claim to be, and can only access the parts of the application that they're entitled to access. Database access is also a fundamental component so that your application can store and retrieve data. Transaction support is required to make sure that the right data is updated at the right time. If you're not familiar with some of these concepts, don't worry – you'll be introduced to them one at a time throughout this book.

Suppose, though, that the wiring and plumbing in your home wasn't there. You'd need to put in your own plumbing and electricity. Without standard components and interfaces, though, you'd have to fabricate your own pipes, wiring, and so on – it'd be terrifically expensive and an awful lot of work.

Putting in a distributed computing infrastructure – the plumbing and wiring of an architecture that supports enterprise applications – is no simple feat. That's why J2EE-based architectures are so compelling – the hard system-level infrastructure is already in place. But why not custom build (or pay someone to custom build) an infrastructure that is designed around your particular application? Well, for starters, it would take a fantastic amount of time, money, and effort. And even if you were to build up that infrastructure, it would be different from anyone else's infrastructure, so you'd not be able to share components or interoperate with anyone else's distributed computing model. That's a lot of work for something that sounds like a dead end. Even if you were lucky enough to find a vendor that could sell you a software infrastructure, you should be wary about any solution that would lock you into any single vendor's implementation that would preclude you from switching vendors at some point in the future.

The good news is, no surprise, that J2EE defines a set of containers, connectors, and components that fill that gap. J2EE not only fills the gap, but it's based on well-known, published specifications. That means that applications written for J2EE will run on any number of J2EE-compliant implementations. The reference implementation supplied with the J2EE Software Development Kit from Sun (J2SDKEE) provides a working model that we'll use throughout this book, since it's the implementation that Sun has built from the specification, and is freely available. In the next chapter you'll get an introduction to installing and testing the J2SDKEE.

It's important to note that the reference implementation is a working *model* but it's not designed to be used for enterprise-level deployment. It doesn't provide some of the enterprise-level features that are outside of the scope of the J2EE specification, such as clustering (the ability to have multiple servers handling requests at the same time) or failover (the ability to have a group of servers that can recover when one crashes). Working with the reference implementation, though, ensures that you'll get exposure to the core J2EE concepts that apply to ALL vendor implementations, and you won't get bogged down with vendor-specific details.

For production deployment, you'll want to select one of a number of J2EE solutions available from a number of different vendors, which have been optimized for high volume throughput and are designed for your particular application. Sun (http://www.sun.com/software), IBM (http://www.ibm.com/websphere), Borland (http://www.borland.com/besappserver) and BEA (http://www.bea.com/products/weblogic/server) are high-profile examples – but certainly not all – of the commercial implementations. JBoss (http://www.jboss.org) is an open source implementation that has a huge following. You get to choose which one works best for you – that's an exercise that's beyond the scope of this book.

> **Building a J2EE application for one J2EE implementation and deploying it on another is cheap, but it's not free, nor is each vendor's implementation of J2EE completely free of defects and operational quirks. Although Java and J2EE go a long way towards providing platform independence, that isn't a guarantee that you can develop on one platform and deploy on another without any hiccups or surprises. Bugs, differences in performance, and other little "gotchas" can seriously delay or derail your project. When you are developing systems that will be deployed in a production environment, it is always a good idea to do your development and staging using the same platforms and technologies that the production environment is based upon. This will help to avoid unnecessary surprises during and after the rollout.**

Multi-Tier Architecture

One of the recurring themes that you'll run into with J2EE is the notion of supporting applications that are partitioned into several levels, or **tiers**. That is an architectural cornerstone of J2EE and merits a little explanation. If you are already familiar with n-tier application architectures, feel free to skip ahead. Otherwise, the overview presented here will be a good introduction or review that will help lay the foundation for understanding the rationale behind much of J2EE's design and the services it provides.

If you think about what a software application is composed of, you can break it down into three fundamental concerns, or logical layers. The first area of concern is displaying stuff to the user and collecting data from the user. That user interface layer is often called the **presentation** layer, since its job is to present stuff to the user and provide a means for the user to present stuff to the software system. The presentation layer includes the part of the software that creates and controls the user interface and validates the user's actions.

Underlying the presentation layer is the logic that makes the application work, and handles the important processing. The logic in a payroll application that, for example, multiplies the hours worked by the salary to determine how much to pay someone, is one example of this kind of logic. This logical layer is called the **business rules** layer, or more informally the **middle tier**.

All non-trivial business applications need to read and store data, and the part of the software that is responsible for reading and writing data – from whatever source that might be – forms the **data access** layer.

Simple software applications are written to run on a single computer. All of the services provided by the application – the user interface, the persistent data access, and the logic that processes data that's input by the user and read from storage – all exist on the same physical machine and are often lumped together into the application. That monolithic architecture is called "single tier" because all of the logical application services – the presentation, the business rules, and the data access layers – exist in a single computing layer.

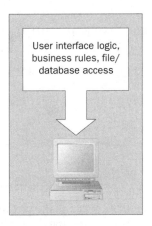

User interface logic,
business rules, file/
database access

More significant applications may take advantage of a database server and access persistent data by sending SQL commands to a database server to save and retrieve data. In this case, the database runs as a separate process from the application, or even on a different machine than the machine that runs the rest of the program. The components for data access are segregated from the rest of the application logic. The rationale for this approach is to centralize data to allow multiple users to simultaneously work with a common database, and to provide the ability for a central database server to share some of the load associated with running the application. This architecture is usually referred to as "client-server".

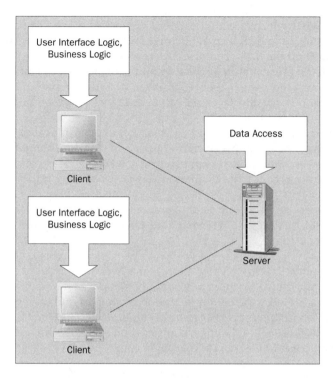

It's convenient and more meaningful to conceptualize the division of the responsibility into layers, or tiers. This software architecture can be shown in two tiers:

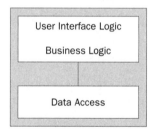

One of the disadvantages of two-tier architecture is the fact that the logic that manipulates the data and applies specific application rules concerning the data is lumped into the application itself. This poses a problem when multiple applications are needed to use a shared database. Consider, for example, a database that contains customer information that is used for order fulfillment, invoicing, promotions, and general customer resource management. Each one of those applications would have to be built with all of the logic and rules to manipulate and access customer data. For example, there might be a standard policy within a company that any customer whose account is more than 90 days overdue will be subject to a credit hold. It seems simple enough to build that rule into every application that's accessing customer data, but when the policy changes to reflect a credit hold at 60 days, updating each application becomes a real mess.

You might be tempted to try to solve this problem by building a reusable library that encapsulates the business rules, and when the rules change just replace that library, rebuild the application and redistribute it to the computers running the application. There are some fundamental problems with that strategy though. First, that strategy assumes that all of the applications have been created using the same programming language, run on the same platform, or at least have some strategy for gluing the library to the application. Next, the applications may have to be recompiled or reassembled with the new library. Moreover, even if the library is a drop-in replacement without recompiling, it's still going to be a royal pain to make sure that each installation of the application has the right library installed simultaneously (it wouldn't do to have conflicting business rules being enforced by different applications at the same time).

In order to get out of that mess, the logical thing to do is to physically separate those business rules out from the computers running the applications onto a separate server so that the software that runs the business rules only needs to be updated once, not for each computer that runs the application. This adds a third tier to our two-tier client-server model:

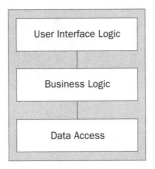

In this model, all of the business logic is extracted out of the application running at the desktop. The application at the desktop is responsible for presenting the user interface to the end user, and for communicating to the business logic tier. It is no longer responsible for enforcing business rules or accessing databases – its job is solely as the presentation layer. Bear in mind that at this point we're talking somewhat abstractly and theoretically. In a perfect world without performance and other implications, the division of responsibility would be very clear-cut. You'll see throughout this book that you will make practical, balanced implementation decisions about how responsibilities are partitioned in order to create an application that is flexible and performs well.

Typically, in a deployed application, the business logic tier executes on a server apart from the workstation (you'll see shortly that this isn't absolutely required, though). The business logic tier provides the logical glue to bind the presentation to the database. Since it's running on a server, it's accessible to any number of users on the network running applications that take advantage of its business rules. As the number of users demanding those services increases, and the business logic becomes increasingly complex and processor-intensive, the server can be scaled up, or additional servers added. Scaling a single server is a lot easier – and cheaper – than upgrading everyone's workstations.

One of the really great things that this architecture makes possible is the ability to start to build application models where the classes defined in the business logic tier are taken directly from the application domain. The code in the business logic layer can work with classes that model things in the real world (like Customers) rather than working with complex SQL statements. By pushing implementation details into the appropriate layer, and designing applications that work with classes modeled from the real world, applications become much easier to understand and extend.

It's possible to continue the process of partitioning the application functionality into increasingly thin functional layers. You'd reach a point of diminishing returns fairly quickly, since the performance penalty for the network communication between the layers would start to chew up any gains in performance. There are some very effective application architectures based on "n-tier" architecture – the application architect is free to partition the application into as many layers as appropriate – based on the capabilities of the computing and network hardware that the system will be deployed on.

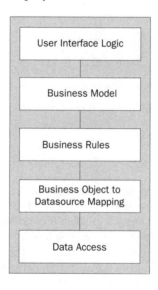

The J2EE architecture is based on the notion of n-tier applications. J2EE makes it very easy to build industrial-strength applications based on 2, 3, or n application layers, and provides all of the plumbing and wiring to make that possible.

I should mention that n-tier architecture does not demand that each of the application layers run on separate machines. It's certainly possible to write n-tier applications that execute on a stand-alone machine, as you'll see. The merit of the application design, however, is that the layers can be split apart and deployed on separate machines, as the application requires.

Labeling a particular architecture as "three-tier", "five-tier", etc. is almost guaranteed to spur some academic debate. Some insist that tiers are defined by the physical partitioning, so if the application components live on client workstations, an application server and a database server machine, it's definitely a three-tier application. Others will classify applications by the logical partitioning where the potential exists for physical partitioning. For the discussions in this chapter, I'll take the latter approach with apologies in advance for those who subscribe to the former.

Vendor Independence

Sun Microsystems – the company that created the Java platform and plays a central role in Java technologies including the J2EE specification – has promoted the Java platform as a solid strategy for building applications that aren't locked into a single platform. In the same way, the architects of J2EE have created it as an open specification that can be implemented by anyone. To date, there are scores of J2EE-based "application servers" that provide a platform for building and deploying scaleable n-tier applications. Any application server that bills itself as J2EE compliant must provide the same suite of services using the interfaces and specifications that Sun has made part of J2EE.

This provides the application developer with a number of choices when implementing a project, and down the road as more applications are added to an organization's suite of solutions. Building an application atop the J2EE architecture provides substantial decoupling between the application logic that you write, and the "other stuff" – transaction support, security, database access – all the distributed computing infrastructure software of the J2EE server that supplies the plumbing and wiring that makes multi-tier applications tick. Remember that all J2EE servers have to support the same interfaces defined in the J2EE specification – that means you can design your application on one server implementation and deploy it on a different one. You can decide later that you want to change which J2EE server you use in your production environment. Moving your application over to the new production environment can be almost trivial.

The vendor and platform independence is something that you can take advantage of in your development. I find myself away from the office quite a bit, and will often use my notebook computer running Windows to do development. It's pretty easy to use that configuration to build, test, and debug (J2EE has great support for pool-side computing). When I am back in the office and happy with a particular component, I can deploy it to the Linux-based servers with little effort, despite the fact that those servers are running a different operating system and different J2EE implementation (after gratuitous testing, of course!).

Bear in mind that each J2EE vendor provides some added value to its particular J2EE implementation. After all, if there weren't market differentiators, there'd be no competition. The J2EE specification covers a lot, but there is also a lot that is not specified in J2EE. Performance, reliability, and scaleability are just a few of the areas that aren't part of the J2EE spec but are areas where vendors have focused a great deal of time and attention. That added value may be ease of use in its deployment tools, highly optimized performance, support for server clustering (which makes a group of servers able to serve application clients as if it were a single super-fast super-big server), and so on. The key point here is to keep two issues in mind: first, your production applications can potentially benefit from capabilities not supported in the Sun J2EE reference implementation. Just because your application's performance stinks on the reference implementation running on your laptop doesn't mean that J2EE is inherently slow. The second issue is that any vendor-specific capabilities that you take advantage of in your production applications may impact the vendor-independence of your application.

Scaleability

Defining throughput and performance requirements is a vital step in requirements definition. Even the best of us get caught off-guard sometimes, though. Things can happen down the road – unanticipated numbers of users that will use a system at the same time, increased loading on hardware, unsatisfactory availability in the event of server failure, and so on – that can throw a monkey wrench into the works.

The J2EE architecture provides a lot of flexibility to accommodate changes as the requirements for throughput, performance, and capacity change. The n-tier application architecture allows software developers to apply additional computing power where it's needed. Partitioning applications into tiers also enables refactoring of specific pain points without impacting adjacent application components.

Clustering, connection pooling, and failover will become familiar terms to you as you build J2EE applications. Several providers of J2EE application servers have worked diligently to come up with innovative ways to improve application performance, throughput, and availability – each with its own special approach within the J2EE framework.

Features and Concepts in J2EE

Getting your arms around the whole of J2EE will take some time, study, and patience. There are a lot of concepts that you'll need to get started, and these concepts will be the foundation of more concepts to follow. The journey through J2EE will be a bit of an alphabet soup of acronyms, but hang tough – you'll catch on, and we'll do our best on our end to help you make sense of it.

Up to this point, I've been using terms like "client" and "server" fairly loosely and liberally. These terms represent fairly specific concepts in the world of distributed computing and J2EE.

A J2EE client can be a console (text) application written in Java, or a GUI application written using JFC/Swing or AWT. These types of clients are often called "fat" clients because they tend to have a fair amount of supporting code for the user interface.

J2EE clients may also be "web-based" clients. That is, they are clients that live inside a browser. Because these clients offload much of their processing to supporting servers, these clients have very little in the way of supporting code. This type of client is often called a "thin" client. A thin client may be a purely HTML-based interface, a JavaScript-enriched page, or may contain a fairly simple applet where a slightly richer user interface is needed.

It would be an oversimplification to describe the application logic called by the J2EE clients as the "server". While it is true that from the perspective of the developer of the client-side code, that illusion is in no small way the magic of what the J2EE platform provides. In fact, the J2EE application server is the actual "server" that connects the client application to the business logic.

The server-side components created by the application developer can be in the form of web components and business components. Web components come in the form of **Java Server Pages (JSPs)** or **servlets**. Business components, in the world of J2EE, are **Enterprise Java Beans (EJBs)**.

These server-side components, of course, rely on the J2EE framework. J2EE provides support for the server-side components in the form of "containers."

Containers

Containers are a central theme in the J2EE architecture. Earlier in this chapter I talked about application infrastructure in terms of the plumbing and electricity that a house provides for its inhabitants. Containers are where those infrastructure services interface with, and provide a host for, application logic.

In the same way that application developers can partition application logic into tiers of specific functionality, the designers of J2EE have partitioned the infrastructure logic into logical tiers. They have done the work of writing the application support infrastructure – things that you'd otherwise have to build yourself. These include things like security, transaction handling, naming, and resource location, and of course the guts of network communications that connect the client to the server. J2EE provides a set of interfaces that allow you to plug your application logic into that infrastructure and access those services. Those interface layers are the J2EE containers.

Think of containers as playing a role much like a video gaming console that you plug game cartridges into. The gaming console provides a point of interface for the game, a suite of services that lets the game be accessed by the user and allows the game to interact with the user. The game cartridge itself needs only be concerned with itself – it doesn't need to concern itself with how the game is displayed to the user, nor what sort of controller is being used, or even if the household electricity is 120VAC or 220VAC – the console provides a container that abstracts all of that stuff out for the game, allowing the game programmer to focus solely on the game and not the infrastructure:

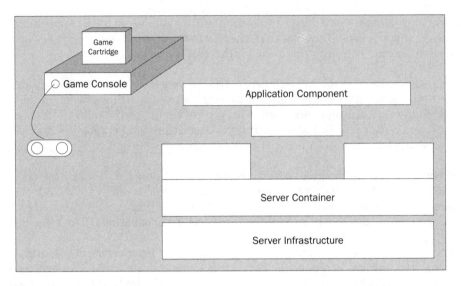

If you've ever created an applet, you're already familiar with the concept of containers. Most web browsers provide a container for applet components. The browser's container for applets provides a defined site for your application component in the form of the `java.applet.Applet` class interface. That site provides services through the `AppletContext` interface. When you develop applets, you are relieved of the burden of interfacing with a web browser and are free to spend your time and effort on the applet logic – not the issues associated with making your application appear to be an integral part of the web browsers.

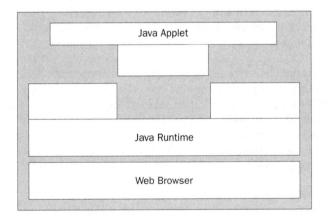

J2EE provides server-side containers in the same vein: they provide a well-defined interface, along with a host of services that allow application developers to focus on the business problems they're trying to solve, and alleviating the need to worry about the plumbing and electricity. Containers handle all of the monkey motion involved with starting up services on the server side, activating your application logic, and cleaning up after you.

J2EE and the Java platform provide containers for web components and business components. These containers – like the gaming console – provide an interface site for components that conform to the container's established interfaces. The containers defined in J2EE include a container for EJBs, Java Server Pages, Servlets, and J2EE clients.

Java Servlets

You are no doubt familiar with accessing simple, static HTML pages using a browser that sends a request to a web server, which in turn sends back a web page that's stored at the server. In that role, the web server is simply being used as a virtual librarian that returns a document based on a request.

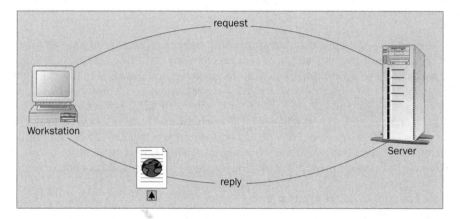

That model of serving up static web pages doesn't provide for dynamically generated content, though. For example, suppose that the web client wants the server to return a list of HTML documents based on some query criteria. In that case, some means of generating HTML on the fly and returning it to the client is needed.

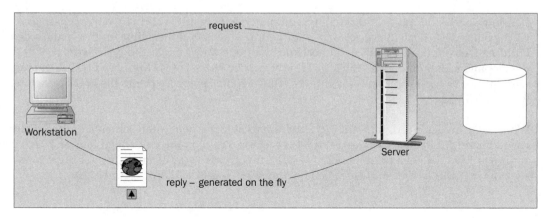

A servlet is a Java component implementing the `javax.servlet.Servlet` interface. It gets invoked as a result of a client request for that particular servlet. The servlet model is pretty generic and not necessarily bound to the Web and HTTP, but nearly all of the servlets that you'll encounter will fall into that category. The web server receives a request for a given servlet in the form of an HTTP query. The web server in turn invokes the servlet and passes back the results to the requesting client. The servlet can be passed parameters from the requesting web client. The servlet is free to perform whatever computations it cares to, and spits out results in the form of HTML back to the client.

The servlet itself is managed and invoked by the J2EE servlet container. When the web server receives the request for the servlet, it notifies the servlet container, which in turn will load the servlet as necessary, and invoke the appropriate `javax.servlet.Servlet` interface service method to satisfy the request.

If you've done any web application programming using CGI (common gateway interface), you'll be familiar with the limitations of that mechanism including lack of portability and no intrinsic support for session management (a much-overused example is the ability to maintain a list of items in a virtual shopping cart). If you've not done any development using CGI, consider yourself lucky and take my word for it – life with J2EE is a whole lot better! Java Servlets are portable, and as you will see in later chapters, the Servlet containers provide support for session management that allows you to write complex web-based applications. Servlets can also incorporate JavaBean components (which share little more than a name with Enterprise JavaBeans) that provide an additional degree of application compartmentalization.

Servlets are covered in detail in Chapter 5.

JavaServer Pages

Java Server Pages, like servlets, are concerned with dynamically generated Web content. These two web components comprise a huge percentage of the content of real-world J2EE applications.

Building servlets involves building Java components that emit HTML. In a lot of cases that works out well, but isn't very accessible for people who spend their time on the visual side of building web applications but don't necessarily care to know much about software development. Enter the Java Server Page. Java Server Pages are HTML-based text documents with Java code with **scriptlets** – or chunks of Java code – embedded into the HTML document within XML tags.

When JSPs are deployed, something pretty remarkable happens – the contents of the JSP are rolled inside out like a sock, and a servlet is created based on the embedded tags and Java code scriptlets. This happens pretty much invisibly. If you care to, you can dig under the covers and see how it works (which makes learning about servlets all the more worthwhile):

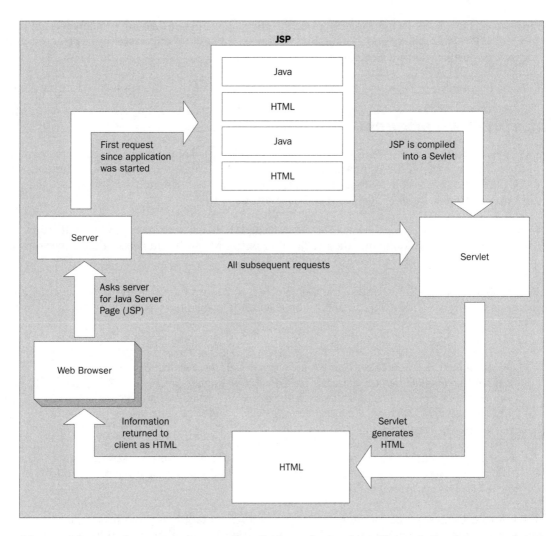

You may have had some exposure to JavaScript – that's a Java-like scripting language that can be included within a web page, and is executed by the web browser when a page containing JavaScript code is browsed to by the user. JSP is a little like that, but the code is compiled and executed at the *server*, and the resulting HTML is fed back to the requesting client. Java Server Pages are lightweight and fast (after the initial compilation to the servlet), and provide a lot of scaleability for web-based applications.

The developer of a Java Server Page can create both static and dynamic content in a JSP. Because content based on HTML, XML, etc. forms the basis of a JSP, a non-technical person can create and update that portion of a page. A more technical Java developer can create the snippets of Java code that will interface with data sources, perform calculations, and so on – the dynamic stuff.

Since an executing JSP is a servlet, JSP provides the same support for session management as servlets. JSPs can also load and call methods of JavaBean components, access server-based data sources, or perform complex calculations at the server.

JSPs are introduced in detail in Chapter 3. Chapter 4 continues with more advanced JSP concepts.

Enterprise JavaBeans

Enterprise JavaBeans are to J2EE what Mickey Mouse is to Disney – it's the flagship technology of the platform. When J2EE is mentioned, EJB is what immediately comes to mind. I mentioned earlier that J2EE is a whole lot more than EJB, but my intention isn't to trivialize EJBs – the attention that the technology gets is certainly merited.

In order to better understand what EJBs are and do, it helps to start out with Java's Remote Method Invocation. If you're not already familiar with RMI, or if you need a quick overview or a refresher, you may want to refer to http://java.sun.com/rmi.

RMI is Java's native means of allowing a Java object to run on one computer, and have its methods called by another object running on a separate computer across a network.

> *In order to create a remote object with RMI, you'd first design an interface that extends the* `java.rmi.Remote` *interface. This interface defines the operations that you want to expose on your remote object. The next step is to design the remote object as a Java class that implements the interface you've defined. This class extends the* `java.rmi.server.UnicastRemoteObject` *class, which will provide the necessary network communications between this object and the objects that call it. Finally, you'd write an application that creates an instance of this class and registers that instance with the RMI registry. The registry is a simple lookup service that allows remote computers to find the remote object using a name-based lookup. The same service is used by the client application, which requests a named object from the registry and casts it into the remote interface designed in the first step.*

What RMI provides is a bare-bones client-server implementation. It provides the basic stuff: a registry for lookup, the guts of network communication for invoking operations and passing parameters to and from remote objects, and a basic mechanism for managing access to system resources as a safeguard against malicious code running on a remote computer.

RMI is lightweight, though. It's not designed to satisfy the requirements of enterprise-class distributed applications. It lacks the essential infrastructure that enterprise-class applications rely on, such as security, transaction management, and scaleability. While it supplies base classes that provide networking, it doesn't provide a framework for an application server that hosts your server-side business components and scales along with your application – you have to write the client and the server applications.

Enter Enterprise Java Beans. EJBs are Java components that implement business logic. This allows the business logic of an application (or suite of applications) to be compartmentalized into EJBs and kept separate from the front-end applications that use that business logic.

The J2EE architecture includes a server that is a container for EJBs. The EJB container loads the bean as needed, invokes the exposed operations, applies security rules, and provides the transaction support for the bean. If it sounds to you like the EJB container does a lot of work, you're right – the container provides all of the necessary plumbing and wiring needed for enterprise applications. As you'll see in Chapter 7, building Enterprise Java Beans follows the same basic steps as creating an RMI object, but since the EJB container provides all of the enterprise plumbing, you get to spend more time building your application and less time messing around with trying to shoehorn in services like security and transaction support.

Enterprise Java Beans come in a few different flavors: session beans, entity beans, and message beans. Session beans, like the name implies, live only as long as the conversation or "session" between the client application and the bean lasts. The session bean's primary reason for being is to provide application services, defined and designed by the application developer, to client applications. Depending on the design, a session bean may maintain state during the session (that is, it keeps its internal member variables' values so it can maintain sort of a conversation with the client), or it may be "stateless", meaning that it provides business rules through its exposed operations but doesn't provide any sense of "state" – that responsibility is delegated to the client.

Entity beans represent business objects – such as customers, invoices, and products – in the application domain. These business objects are persisted so they can be stored and retrieved at will. The J2EE architecture provides a lot of flexibility for the persistence model that allows you to defer all of the work of storing and retrieving the bean's state information to the container, or lets you control it all (very useful when you're dealing with interfacing your J2EE system to a legacy application!).

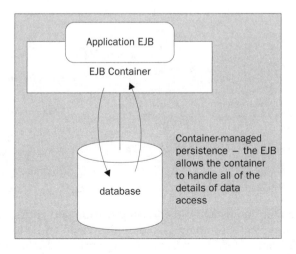

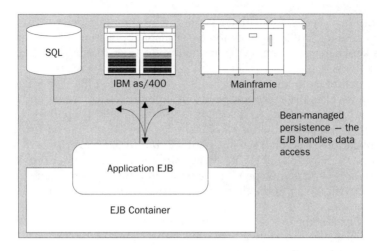

The third type of EJB, the message bean, provides a component model for services that listen to Message Service messages. The J2EE platform includes a messaging queue that allows applications to post messages to a queue, as well as to "subscribe" to queues that get messages. The advantage to this particular way of doing things is that the sender and the receiver of the message really need know nothing about each other – they only need to know about the message queue itself.

One example use of a message queue is an automated stock trading system. Stock prices are sent as messages to a message queue, and things that are interested in stock prices consume those messages.

With message-driven EJBs, it is possible to create an EJB that responds to messages concerning stock prices and makes automatic trading decisions based on those messages.

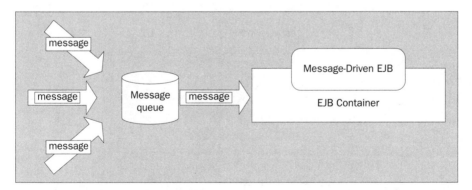

You will learn a lot about the ins and outs of using session and entity beans in Chapter 7. Your J2EE applications will typically be comprised of both session and entity beans. Message beans will come later in the book – they're not used as frequently as the other flavors in most applications, but they're still pretty darn cool!

XML Support

Extensible Markup Language (XML) is a significant cornerstone for building enterprise systems that provide interoperability and are resilient in the face of changes. There are several key technologies in J2EE that rely on XML for configuration and integration with other services.

J2EE provides a number of APIs for developers working with XML. Java API for XML Processing (JAXP) provides support for generating and parsing XML with both the Document Object Model (DOM), which is a tree-oriented model, and SAX (Simple API for XML), which is a stream-based event-driven processing model.

The Java API for XML Binding (JAXB) provides support for mapping XML to and from Java classes. It provides a compiler and a framework for performing the mapping so you don't have to write custom code to perform those transformations.

The Java API for XML Registries (JAXR), Java API for XML Messaging (JAXM), and Java API for XML-based Remote Procedure Calls (JAX-RPC) round out the XML API provisions. These sets of APIs provide support for SOAP and web services (discussed in the following section).

This book assumes that you've got a basic familiarity with XML. If you need a refresher on XML, you might want to review Chapter 21 and 22 of *Beginning Java 2* (*Wrox Press, ISBN 1-86100-569-5*).

Web Services

The World Wide Web is becoming an increasingly prevalent backbone of business applications. The end points that provide web applications with server-side business rules are considered "web services." The W3C consortium, in an effort to unify how web services are published, discovered, and accessed, has sought to provide more concrete definitions for web services:

> *"A web service is a software system identified by a URI, whose public interfaces and bindings are defined and described using XML. Its definition can be discovered by other software systems. These systems may then interact with the web service in a manner prescribed by its definition, using XML-based messages conveyed by internet protocols."*
>
> [Web Services Architecture, Working Draft 14: *http://www.w3.org/TR/ws-arch*]

This specifies some specific requirements:

❑   XML is used to publish the description of the services

❑   Those descriptions are discoverable through some form of registry

❑   XML messages are used to invoke those services and to return the results to the requestor

The W3C has established Web Service Description Language (WSDL) as the XML format that is used by web services to describe their services and how clients access those services. In order to call those services, clients need to be able to get their hands on those definitions. XML registries provide the ability to publish service descriptions, search for services, and obtain the WSDL information describing the specifics of a given service.

There are a number of overlapping XML registry service specifications, including ebXML and Universal Description, Discovery, and Integration (UDDI). The JAXR API provides an implementation-independent API for accessing those XML registries.

Simple Object Access Protocol (SOAP) is the lingua franca used by web services and their clients for invocation, parameter passing and obtaining results. SOAP defines the XML message standards and data mapping required for a client application to call a web service and pass it parameters. The JAX-RPC API provides an easy-to-use developer interface that masks the complex underlying plumbing.

Not surprisingly, the J2EE architecture provides a container that hosts web services, and a component model for easily deploying web services. Chapter 12 and 13 in the book cover SOAP and web services.

Transaction Support

One of the basic requirements of enterprise applications is the ability to allow multiple users of multiple applications to simultaneously access shared databases and to absolutely ensure the integrity of that data across those systems. Maintaining data consistency is no simple thing.

Suppose that your application was responsible for processing bank deposits, transfers, and withdrawals. Your application is processing a transfer request from one account to another. That process seems pretty straightforward: deduct the requested amount from one account and add that same amount to the other account. Suppose, however, that immediately after deducting the sum from the source account, something went horribly wrong – perhaps a server failed or a network link was severed – and it became impossible to add the transfer to the target account. At that point, the data's integrity has been compromised (and worse yet, someone's money is now missing).

Transactions can help to address this sort of problem. A transaction represents a set of activities that collectively will either succeed and be made permanent, or fail and be reverted. In the situation described above, we could define the transaction boundaries to start as the transfer amount is withdrawn from the source account, and end after the target account was updated successfully. When the transaction had been made successfully, the changes are committed. Any failure inside of the transaction boundary would result in the changes being rolled back and the account balances restored back to the original values that existed before the start of the transaction.

J2EE – and EJB in particular – provides substantial transaction support. The EJB container provides built-in support for managing transactions, and allows the developer to specify and modify transaction boundaries without changing code. Where more complex transaction control is required, the EJB can take over the transaction control from the container and perform fine-grained or highly customized transaction handling.

Security

Security is a vital component in enterprise applications, and J2EE provides built-in security mechanisms that are far more secure than home-grown security solutions that are typically added as an afterthought.

J2EE allows application resources to be configured for anonymous access where security isn't a concern. Where there are system resources that need to be secured, however, it provides authentication (making sure your users really are who they say they are) and authorization (matching up users with the privileges they are granted).

Authorization in J2EE is based on roles of users of applications. You can classify the roles of users who will be using your application, and authorize access to application components based on those roles. J2EE provides support for declarative security that is specified when the application is deployed, as well as programmatic security that allows you to build in fine-grained security into the Java code. These security mechanisms are discussed in the online chapter that comes as part of the download package for this book, available from the Wrox web site at http://www.wrox.com.

Sample J2EE Architectures

There is no such thing as a single software architecture that fits all applications, but there are some common architectural patterns that reappear frequently enough to take note of. The following architectures are ones that you're likely to run into as you examine and develop J2EE-based systems.

Each one of these has its own merits and strong points. I present them here to illustrate that there are a number of ways to put together applications and as a short "field guide" for identifying these architectures as you spot them in the wild.

n-Tier Architecture

n-Tier application architecture is intended to address a number of problems, including:

- ❑ High cost of maintenance when business rules change

- ❑ Inconsistent business rule implementation between applications

- ❑ Inability to share data or business rules between applications

- ❑ Inability to provide web-based front ends to line-of-business applications

- ❑ Poor performance and inability to scale applications to meet increased user load

- ❑ Inadequate or inconsistent security across applications

plications address sharing of data between applications and, to a lesser degree, performance scalability, but do not address any of the other concerns. The business still must be coded into the client applications, leaving the problems of high maintenance and inconsistency in business rules and security.

J2EE provides a platform that enables developers to easily create n-tier applications in a number of different configurations. The following examples illustrate some typical J2EE application configurations.

Application Client with EJB

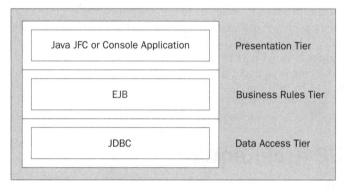

The client application is built as a stand-alone (JFC/Swing or console) application. The application relies on business rules implemented as EJBs running on a separate machine.

JSP Client with EJB

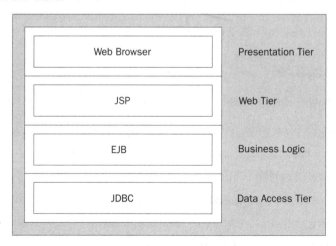

The client in this architecture is a web browser. Java Server Pages access business rules and generate content for the browser.

Applet Client with JSP and Database

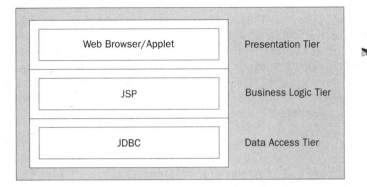

Again, the client application is a web browser, but in this case a Java applet is used within a web page to provide a more interactive, dynamic user interface for the user. That applet accesses additional content from JSPs. Data is accessed from the JSP via the JDBC API.

Using Web Services for Application Integration

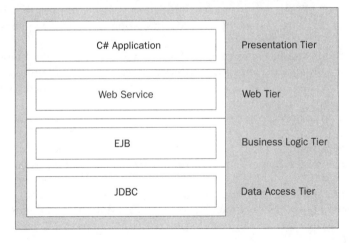

In this final example, a client application implemented in C# accesses data from a web service implemented in Java.

Summary

In this opening chapter to the book, we have covered an overview of the J2EE and how all the various bits fit together to enable you to create powerful business components. We first looked at what *exactly* J2EE is and tackled the obvious issue of moving from creating desktop applications with Java 2 Platform, Standard Edition (J2SE) to building enterprise-level applications and dynamic, data-driven web sites using the Enterprise Edition of the Java 2 Platform, J2EE. We covered how the two relate to each other and how they differ from each other, as well as looking at how applications are built using J2EE.

Next we looked at what makes up a J2EE application. J2EE architecture is based on the idea of building applications around multiple tiers of responsibility. The application developer creates components, which are hosted by the J2EE containers. Containers play a central theme in the J2EE architecture.

Servlets are one type of J2EE web component. They are Java classes that are hosted within, and invoked by the J2EE server by requests made to, a web server. These servlets respond to those requests by dynamically generating HTML, which is then returned to the requesting client.

JavaServer Pages (JSPs) are very similar in concept to servlets, but differ in that the Java code is embedded within an HTML document. The J2EE server then compiles that HTML document into a servlet, and that servlet generates HTML in response to client requests.

Enterprise Java Beans are the centerpiece of J2EE and are the component model for building the business rules logic in a J2EE application. EJBs can be designed to maintain state during a conversation with a client, or can be stateless. They can also be designed to be short-lived and ephemeral, or can be persisted for later recall. EJBs can also be designed to listen to message queues and respond to specific messages.

The J2EE platform provides a number of services beyond the component hosting of servlets, JSPs, and EJBs. Fundamental services include support for XML, web services, transactions, and security.

Extensive support for XML is a core component of J2EE. Support for both document-based and stream-based parsing of XML documents forms the foundation of XML support. Additional APIs provide XML registry service, remote procedure call invocation via XML, and XML-based messaging support.

Web services, which rely heavily on XML, provide support for describing, registering, finding, and invoking object services over the Web. J2EE provides support for publishing and accessing J2EE components as web services.

Transaction support is required in order to ensure data integrity for distributed database systems. This allows complex, multi-step updates to databases to be treated as a single step with provisions to make the entire process committed upon success, or completely undone by rolling back on a failure. J2EE provides intrinsic support for distributed database transactions.

J2EE provides configurable security to ensure that sensitive systems are afforded appropriate protection. Security is provided in the form of authentication and authorization.

After reading through the chapter, you might think that J2EE is *just* about EJBs. The truth is that it is about a lot more than EJBs, although EJBs do play a prominent role within J2EE. J2EE provides a platform for developing and deploying multi-tiered, distributed applications that are designed to be maintainable, scaleable, and portable.

Just as an office building requires a lot of hidden infrastructure of plumbing, electricity, and telecommunications, large scale applications require a great deal of support infrastructure. This infrastructure includes database access, transaction support, and security. J2EE provides that infrastructure and allows you to focus on application.

Building distributed applications (software with components that run as separate processes, or on separate computers) allows you to partition the software into layers of responsibility, or tiers. Distributed applications are commonly partitioned into three primary tiers: presentation, business rules, and data access. Partitioning applications into distinct tiers makes the software more maintainable and provides opportunities for scaling applications up as the demand on those applications increases.

That's it for your first taster of how J2EE works and why it is so popular. In the next chapter, you'll see the extra steps required to set up your environment, ready for developing powerful J2EE applications.

CHAPTER 2

Installing the J2EE 1.4 SDK   37

Testing the J2EE 1.4 SDK Installation   41

Compiling and Deploying "Hello J2EE World"   46

Summary   61

Getting Set

Since this is a book for developers by developers, you'll get the most from this book by running the examples and experimenting. This chapter will help you to make sure that you've properly installed the J2EE 1.4 SDK and will walk you through the steps of setting up the environment and writing a simple application. This is vital to ensuring that you don't encounter needless frustration as you work through the examples. You'll also get a taste of the essential steps of creating a J2EE application, what those steps do, and why they're needed.

In this chapter, you will learn:

- ❑ What the exact prerequisites for installing the J2EE 1.4 SDK are, and how to configure your system to run enterprise Java applications

- ❑ How to construct a simple JSP application, and how to deploy and run this application

Even if you already have your environment set up, it's probably a good idea to read through the development steps in this chapter not only to ensure that your environment is set up correctly, but also to give you some essential insight into the fundamentals of building a J2EE application.

All of the installation files are available from the Sun web site. Both the J2EE SDK and the J2SE SDK (required to run the J2EE SDK) are freely available at http://java.sun.com.

Installing the J2EE 1.4 SDK

> This chapter assumes that you're running Windows 2000 Professional or XP Professional. The J2EE 1.4 SDK does not support earlier versions of Windows. The Sun web site (http://java.sun.com/j2ee) has installation details of other supported operating systems (Solaris SPARC 8 & 9, and RedHat Linux 7.2).

Installing the J2EE 1.4 SDK couldn't be much easier. As we saw in Chapter 1, the J2EE environment is based on the Java 2 Standard Edition platform, so you need to have that installed before following the steps described in this chapter. You'll need to ensure that you've got the Java Development Kit for J2SE (Java Standard Edition) 1.4 (or later) installed. If you've got an earlier JDK, you need to update it. If you're not certain which version of Standard Edition you have, you can try running the J2SDKEE 1.4 installation anyway. If you don't have the correct version of J2SE installed, you'll see a warning message, and have to abort the installation. You should then install the correct version of the J2SE SDK and run the J2EE SDK installation again.

Alternatively, you can simply go to a command line prompt and type `java -version` at the command prompt. The Java interpreter should print out the version information:

```
> java -version
java version "1.4.0"
Java(TM) 2 Runtime Environment, Standard Edition (build 1.4.0-b92)
Java HotSpot(TM) Client VM (build 1.4.0-b92, mixed mode)
```

The version listed in the first line should be at least "1.4.0".

Problems and Solutions

Problem	Solution
Java version is lower than 1.4.0	Obtain and install the latest version of the J2SE SDK. You may want to uninstall the older version before installing the newer version. (You don't have to, but unless you have some compelling reason to keep it around, it's just dead weight).
`java -version` returns the message: 'java' is not recognized as an internal or external command, operable program or batch file.	The J2SE SDK is not installed, or the PATH environment variable does not include the path to the java executables. Check the PATH, and correct the problem, or reinstall the J2SE SDK.

Once you've done that, installing J2EE is a breeze – just run the installation program. The installation program will firstly check to make sure you've got the right version of the J2SE SDK. Then, make a note of where you're installing the J2EE SDK to on your system – you'll need to know the path to the `j2sdkee` directory after the installation is complete in order to update and add some environment variables.

Environment variables are used by the Windows operating system as a shortcut to selected directories on your system You can set either user-specific environment variables, or (provided you're logged in as a user with administrative rights) system-wide environment variables. Once you set an environment variable for your Java installation, you will find it much quicker and easier to compile and run your Java applications from the command line, as you'll see shortly.

Once the installation is complete, it's time to set up the environment variables you'll need to run the examples in this book. You can check and set these from the System properties. From the **Control Panel,** choose the **System** applet. Select the **Advanced** tab and click on **Environment Variables:**

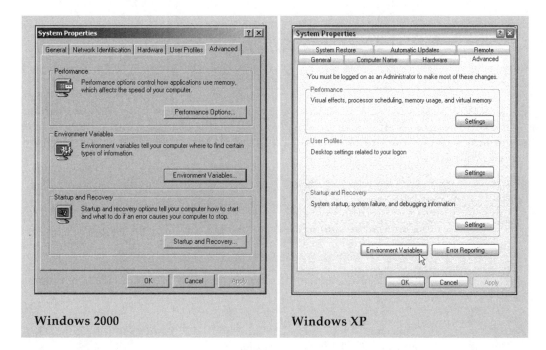

When you click the **Environment Variables** button, a dialog will allow you to check and set the values for environment variables:

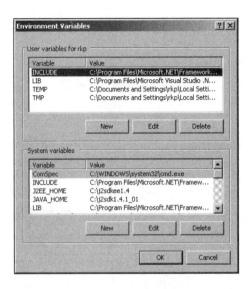

Make sure that the following environment variables are set either in your local user variables, or in the system variables. If they don't already appear in the list, you can add them by clicking the New button. If they need to be modified, edit them by clicking the Edit button. Click OK when you've finished.

Variable name	Settings
JAVA_HOME	Contains the path to the directory where J2SE is installed, for example: `c:\j2sdk1.4.1_01`
J2EE_HOME	Contains the path to the directory where J2EE SDK is installed, for example: `c:\j2sdkee1.4`

PATH	This should include the path to the `bin` directories of the J2SE SDK and the J2SDKEE. For example:
	
	`c:\j2sdk1.4.0\bin;c:\j2sdkee1.4\bin;...`
	
	You can alternatively use the `JAVA_HOME` and `J2EE_HOME` environment variables in your path to make things a little simpler, for example:
	
	`%JAVA_HOME%\bin;%J2EE_HOME%\bin;...`
	
	Note that the system will search through for executable files using the `PATH` variable, starting with the directories that appear first in the path. In order to ensure that there aren't other versions of the J2SE or J2EE interfering on this machine, make sure that these new entries go at the front of the `PATH` variable.

Testing the J2EE 1.4 SDK Installation

If everything went according to plan, your system should be set up and ready to use, so we're now going to walk through some quick tests to ensure that you're ready to run the code in this book.

Starting the database server

When you install the J2EE 1.4 SDK, a sample database called Cloudscape is also installed. We'll be using this database later on in the book, so we need to ensure that the database is ready for use by starting it and testing it out.

Open a command window and enter:

```
> cloudscape -start
```

and hit *Enter*. After a second or two you should see a response message:

```
Redirecting application output to C:\j2sdkee1.4\logs\launcher.cloudscape.log
```

This indicates that the database server has started. The next step is for you to work with the database server from the interactive SQL tool for the Cloudscape database. At the command line enter:

```
> cloudscape -isql
```

To start the interactive SQL tool. After a second or two you will see the interactive tool's command prompt:

```
> cloudscape -isql
ij version 4.0 (c) 1997-2001 Informix Software, Inc.
CONNECTION0* -  jdbc:cloudscape:CloudscapeDB;create=true
* = current connection
```

We'll create a database table and test it. At the `ij>` prompt, carefully type in the following SQL command to create a table, and press *Enter*. Make sure that the line ends with a semicolon – that tells the interactive tool that the command is complete. You'll see a response message as soon as you press *Enter*:

```
ij> create table zootable (animal varchar(12) primary key, legcount int);
0 rows inserted/updated/deleted
```

The message says 0 rows inserted/updated/deleted, which may seem a bit odd. What is happening here is that the table is created successfully, but as yet, we've not yet added any rows to the table.

Next, add a few rows of data to the newly created table by typing in the following SQL commands and pressing *Enter* after each command. Again, make sure that a semicolon ends each command. As before, you'll see a response message as soon as you press *Enter*:

```
ij> insert into zootable values ('duck',2);
1 row inserted/updated/deleted
ij> insert into zootable values ('horse',4);
1 row inserted/updated/deleted
ij> insert into zootable values ('aardvark',4);
1 row inserted/updated/deleted
```

Finally, run a SQL query to see the data that you've added. Type the following SQL query and press *Enter* to execute the query:

```
ij> select * from zootable;
```

The interactive tool will query the database and print the results of the query:

```
ANIMAL          |LEGCOUNT
---------------------------
duck            |2
horse           |4
aardvark        |4

3 rows selected
```

One last step – we need to delete the table before we exit. Type the SQL command, followed by a semicolon, and press *Enter*:

```
ij> drop table zootable;
0 rows inserted/updated/deleted
```

Exit the interactive tool by typing the following and pressing *Enter*:

```
> exit;
```

When you are finished with Cloudscape, you can stop the Cloudscape server by typing the following:

```
> cloudscape -stop
```

Starting the J2EE server

The next step to verifying that your installation is working correctly is to start the J2EE server. The server can be launched from menus that are automatically created during installation, or from a command line. We'll use the command line and start the J2EE server in the "verbose" mode so we can watch as it initializes.

Open a new command window, and enter j2ee -verbose. After a couple of seconds, you should see initialize messages appearing:

```
> j2ee -verbose
J2EE server listen port: 1050
Naming service started: 1050
Binding DataSource, name = jdbc/Cloudscape, url =
jdbc:cloudscape:rmi:CloudscapeDB;create=true
Binding DataSource, name = jdbc/EstoreDB, url =
jdbc:cloudscape:rmi:CloudscapeDB;create=true
Binding DataSource, name = jdbc/InventoryDB, url =
jdbc:cloudscape:rmi:CloudscapeDB;create=true
Binding DataSource, name = jdbc/DB1, url =
jdbc:cloudscape:rmi:CloudscapeDB;create=true
Binding DataSource, name = jdbc/DB2, url =
jdbc:cloudscape:rmi:CloudscapeDB;create=true
Binding DataSource, name = jdbc/_ejb_container, url = jdbc/_ejb_container__xa
Binding DataSource, name = jdbc/_ejb_container__xa, dataSource =
COM.cloudscape.core.XaDataSource@6
42bd6
Binding DataSource, name = jdbc/XACloudscape, url = jdbc/XACloudscape__xa
Binding DataSource, name = jdbc/XACloudscape__xa, dataSource =
COM.cloudscape.core.RemoteXaDataSour
ce@80b22e
Starting JMS service...
Initialization complete - waiting for client requests
Starting JMS via Resource Adapter
Deploying jmsra.rar in C:\j2sdkee1.4\lib\system_apps\jmsra.rar
ResourceAdapter jmsra.rar started...
Initializing Coyote HTTP/1.1 on port 8000
Initializing Coyote HTTP/1.1 on port 7000
Loaded registry information 721 ms
Starting service J2EE(TM) Web Server
Apache Tomcat/5.0
Missing application web.xml, using defaults only StandardEngine[Standard-
engine].StandardHost[local
host].StandardContext[]
Added certificates -> request attribute Valve
Starting Coyote HTTP/1.1 on port 8000
Starting Coyote HTTP/1.1 on port 7000
JACC:Policy Repository set to C:\j2sdkee1.4\repository\policy
Added certificates -> request attribute Valve
Configured an authenticator for method FORM
J2EE Web Admin Tool started
JAXR:Installing JAXR RA
Deploying jaxr-ra.rar in C:\j2sdkee1.4\lib\system_apps\jaxr-ra.rar
Binding Connection Factory, name = jms/QueueConnectionFactory
Binding Connection Factory, name = QueueConnectionFactory
Binding Connection Factory, name = eis/JAXR
Binding Connection Factory, name = TopicConnectionFactory
Binding Connection Factory, name = jms/TopicConnectionFactory
```

```
Cannot create Destination jms/Queue since it already exists
Binding Administered Object, name = jms/Queue
Cannot create Destination jms/Topic since it already exists
Binding Administered Object, name = jms/Topic
Starting EJB Timer Service...
J2EE server startup complete.
```

At this point the J2EE server is started. You might be a little curious about these messages that are displayed during startup. These can be pretty useful if you run into problems. Some of the more interesting and significant messages are:

```
Naming service started: 1050
```

The naming service is used to be able to reference objects by names – this is a type of directory service that is used by J2EE

```
Binding DataSource, name = jdbc/Cloudscape, url =
jdbc:cloudscape:rmi:CloudscapeDB;create=true
...
```

There is a series of messages that indicate that the name service is being used to register data sources by name. Cloudscape, which we looked at a moment ago, is a relational database that is bundled with the J2EE SDK.

```
Starting JMS service...
Starting JMS service...
Initialization complete - waiting for client requests
Starting JMS via Resource Adapter
Deploying jmsra.rar in C:\j2sdkee1.4\lib\system_apps\jmsra.rar
ResourceAdapter jmsra.rar started...
```

You should recall from Chapter 1 that message queues are used to post and retrieve messages in systems where the sender and receiver of those messages need not know much about the other. This series of messages indicates the progress of starting and initializing the Java Messaging Service that's part of the J2EE SDK.

```
Initializing Coyote HTTP/1.1 on port 8000
Initializing Coyote HTTP/1.1 on port 7000
Loaded registry information 721 ms
Starting service J2EE(TM) Web Server
Apache Tomcat/5.0
Missing application web.xml, using defaults only StandardEngine[Standard-
engine].StandardHost[local
host].StandardContext[]
Added certificates -> request attribute Valve
Starting Coyote HTTP/1.1 on port 8000
Starting Coyote HTTP/1.1 on port 7000
```

These messages show the servlet container, along with the connectors that allow it to function as a web server. This step creates services to listen on port 8000 for regular connections, and on port 7000 for Secure Sockets connections.

When you see the following message, the J2EE server is initialized and ready for requests:

```
J2EE server startup complete.
```

The server is now running inside that command shell (the instance of the command console window), so if you close that command shell, it will shut down the J2EE server. Don't close the shell just yet – you'll need the server to be running for the next step!

Next, open a browser, and go to the following URL:

http://localhost:8000

The web browser should display the default J2EE web page:

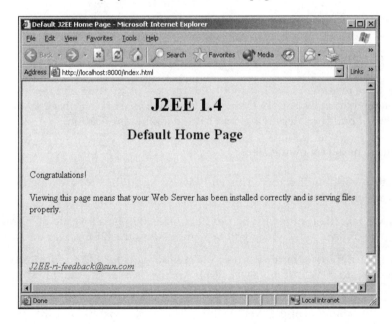

Pat yourself on the back for a job well done. Let's go shred a little code for a final test.

Problems and Solutions

Here are some possible problems you might come up against when running through the previous steps to test your J2EE 1.4 SDK installation:

Problem	Solution
`j2ee -verbose` returns the message: 'java' is not recognized as an internal or external command, operable program or batch file.	You haven't properly set the `PATH` variable to include the `bin` directory of the J2SDKEE install.
The web browser reports "Page cannot be displayed" when trying to open the URL http://localhost:8000	Make certain that there weren't any errors reported when starting the J2EE server. If you see messages indicating that the server couldn't start because TCP ports were in use by other processes, you may either have another web server using port 8000, or have another instance of the J2EE server running. Make certain that you've specified the port "8000" in the URL (this is the default port used by the J2EE server).

Compiling and Deploying "Hello J2EE World"

As a final test, we're going to walk through the process of creating and deploying a Java Server page. This is going to make certain that the J2EE server is working properly first, and give you your first taste of building, deploying, and testing a J2EE application.

This will consist of the following steps:

- ❏ Create a working directory. This will give us a sandbox for creating the application files and editing them.
- ❏ Create a text file for the Java Server Page. This will be a text file of HTML with snippets of Java code, which will be compiled by the J2EE server into a Servlet.
- ❏ Using the deploytool utility, select the components for the application and package them up into a Web Archive. The Web Archive is a jar file that bundles all of the application components into a single file for easy deployment.
- ❏ Verify the contents of the Web Archive. The deploytool has a utility that will test the contents of the Web Archive before it's distributed to catch problems beforehand.
- ❏ Distribute the Web Archive to the J2EE server. Once this is done, the application is available and ready to be run.
- ❏ Test the application.

So, let's get started!

Try It Out   Hello J2EE World

1. Create a directory on your machine that will be your sandbox for this exercise. I'll use `C:\8333\Ch02` for mine.

2. Create a new file in that directory called `index.jsp` using your favorite text editor. Here's the code for that file:

```
<%--

    file: helloworld.jsp
    desc: test installation of j2sdkee
--%>

<html>
<head>
  <title>Hello World - test the J2SDKEE installation</title>

<%
  for (int i = 1; i < 5; i++)
  {
%>
   <h<%=i%>>Hello World</h<%=i%>>
<%
  }
%>
</head>
<body>
```

3. Start up the J2EE server if it's not already running, by following the instructions given above. It will appear as an icon in your task bar if it's running.

4. Start the J2EE deploytool application that comes with the J2EE SDK. This tool is a utility that is used to assemble application components into distributable archives, and also to distribute the application to the J2EE server. You'll find a menu for it under Start I Programs I Java 2 SDK, Enterprise Edition 1.4 I Deploytool. Alternatively, if you've correctly set up your environment variables, you can start the application by entering `deploytool` at a command prompt. When deploytool has finished initializing you'll see its main window:

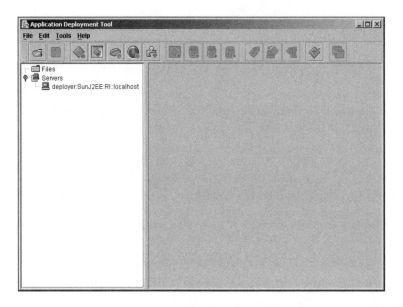

5. We need to create a new **Web Ar**chive (WAR). A WAR file is an archive file that will contain the web components of a J2EE application, along with a descriptor or "table of contents" that describes what is in the archive. Web applications frequently consist of many more files than our simple application, and the WAR is a very convenient means of bundling up all of those files into a single file for deployment. Select File | New | Web Application WAR from the menu. This will start the New Web Application wizard:

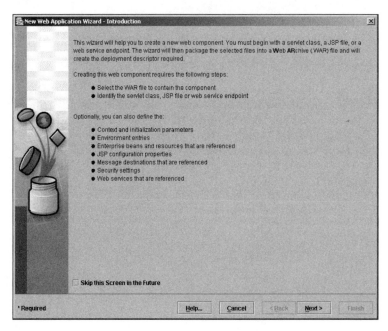

After reading the introduction, click the **Next >** button:

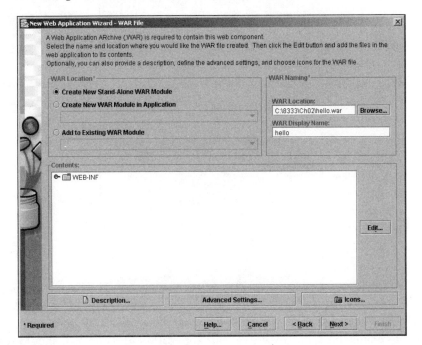

Make certain that the radio button labeled "Create New Stand-Alone WAR Module" is checked.

6. In the WAR location text field, enter the path to your working directory, followed by `hello.war` (in my case, `C:\8333\ch02hello.war`). This tells the deploytool what to name the WAR file.

Next, click the "Edit..." button on the right hand side of the dialog. This will open a dialog to select files to add to the Web Archive:

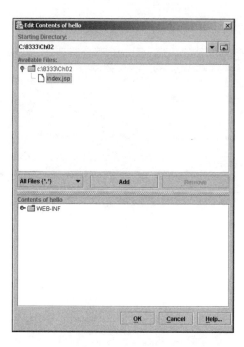

7. Set the starting directory (using the top textbox) to your working directory. This simply points the dialog to where your application files are. You should see a folder tree with index.jsp appearing below your working directory folder. Select index.jsp and click the Add button. You should now see index.jsp in the Contents tree at the bottom of the dialog. Click the OK button to close this dialog. Click the Next button to go to the next page of the wizard:

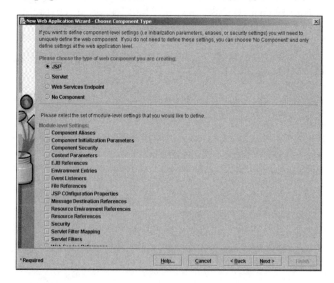

8. You learned in Chapter 1 that there are several different kinds of components in J2EE. This particular application includes a Java Server Page component – this is where we tell the deploytool what kind of component we're building. Select the radio button labeled "JSP" to indicate that you are creating a JavaServer Page component. Click on the **Next** button to go to the next page of the wizard:

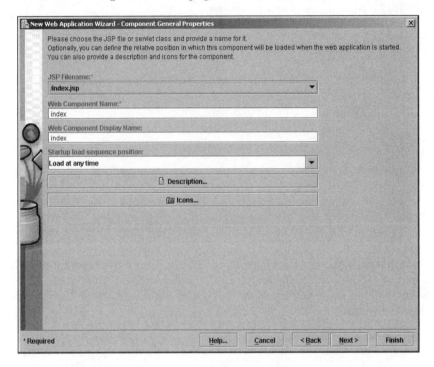

9. This dialog allows you to set run-time properties on the components of the WAR. Click the combo box labeled **JSP Filename** and select /index.jsp (it's the only choice in the combo box list – if we had provided more files to be part of this WAR they would appear in the list as well). The next two text fields will fill in automatically when you select the file in the combo box. Click the **Next** button to go to the final page of the wizard:

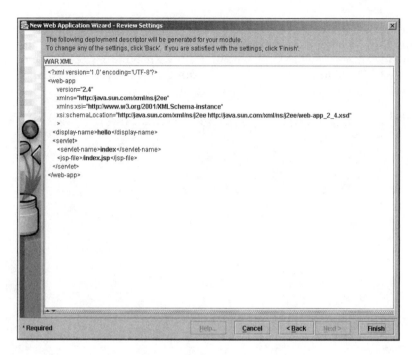

This final page shows you what you've just created – a **deployment descriptor**. The deployment descriptor tells the J2EE server about the contents of the WAR file. You'll learn all about these in the next few chapters. For now, click on the Finish button to close the wizard:

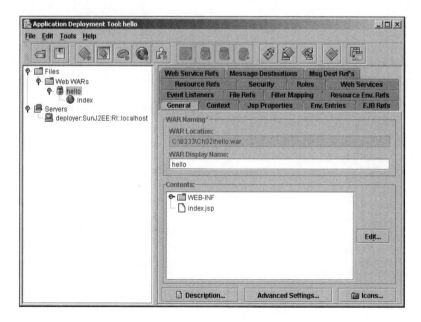

The deploytool's tree navigator now displays the Web Archive you've just created, and its contents.

10. Next, we set the context root for deployment. Make sure that the hello archive is selected, and select File I Deployment Settings I Create New File... from the menu. That will bring up the deployment settings dialog:

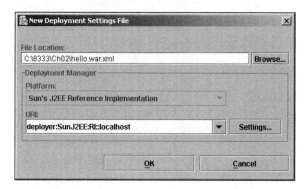

11. Accept these settings by clicking the OK button. You'll see the tree navigator has updated, and your hello WAR has an icon underneath it showing that it contains a deployment setting for the Sun J2EE Reference Implementation server (see the screen shot that follows this paragraph). Select it by clicking on that icon. This will bring up a property page for setting what's called the "context root" (kind of a "home base") for your WAR when it gets deployed to the server.

You can think of the context root as sort of like a logical directory that's part of the URL. For example, a web application that's available at www.wrox.com/codesamples/index.jsp has a root context of "codesamples". Note that this doesn't necessarily correspond to a directory on the server called "codesamples" – it's a name that the server recognizes and maps to a specific application.

12. We've created a WAR that's called hello, and out of convenience we'll create a context root called "hello" too. Type "hello" at the context root text field to create a context root called `hello`:

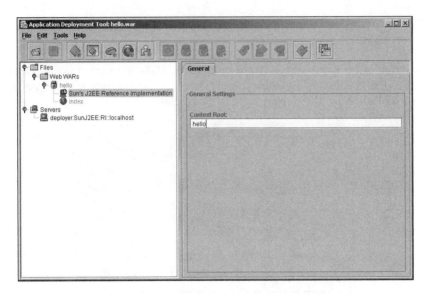

From the menu, select File I Deployment Settings I Close File. That will invoke the Save Deployment Settings dialog. Click Save to save your context root:

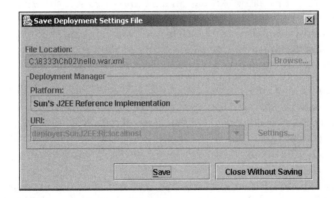

Save your work now. With the hello WAR highlighted, select File ISave.

13. The next step is to verify the WAR. This step will catch problems with bad code in the JSP, problems with the deployment descriptor, and in general make sure that the WAR doesn't have obvious problems before it's deployed to the server. Make sure the "hello" WAR is still highlighted, and select Tools I Verifier... from the menu. This will bring up a window that will help you verify that your WAR complies with the J2EE specification.

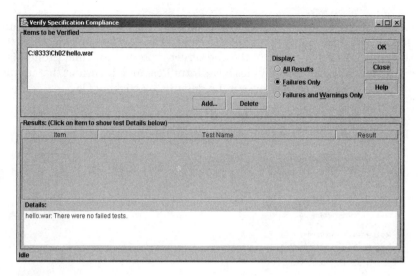

The Display group of radio buttons lets you select how much detail you care to see about the tests that are run. If you want to only see messages about failures, select the radio button labeled Failures Only (try not to take it personally – it's not the best phrasing in the world). Click the OK button.

If all went well, you should see a message at the bottom indicating that no tests failed. If your JSP had problems with its code, you will get compilation error messages. If you see compilation errors, go back to your JSP file and check it carefully to make sure it matches the code in the book.

14. We're almost done. Next, we need to deploy the WAR to the J2EE server. With the hello WAR selected in the tree navigator, select Tools | Deploy... from the menu. This will bring up the Deploy Module dialog:

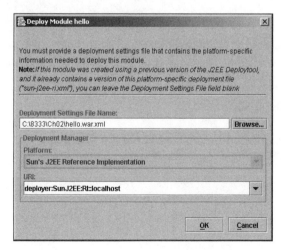

15. The deployment settings are written into a file. The first prompt will be automatically filled in with a file name that will be created. The next prompt identifies the server platform (since we've only got the one server type running, that prompt is disabled). Finally, the URI prompt provides a Uniform Resource Identifier that uniquely identifies the target server. Accept the defaults by clicking OK.

When the dialog closes, a window will appear and will show the status of the deployment process. You should see something like:

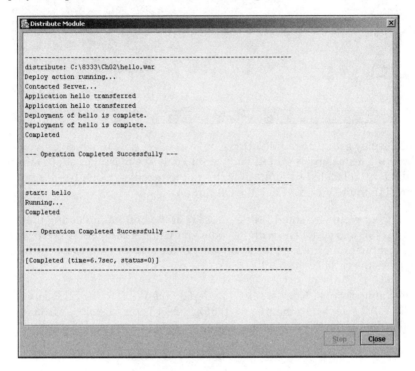

Wait until you see the Completed message, and click Close.

16. It's time to test your first JSP. Start a web browser and open the following URL:

http://localhost:8000/hello

After a couple of seconds, you should see the web page:

Congratulations! Your first JSP is a success!

17. Before we look at what we've done in this example, you should stop the J2EE and Cloudscape servers:

To stop the J2EE server, you can either:

❑   Select **Stop J2EE** from the **Java 2 Enterprise Edition** menu, or

❑   Enter `j2ee -stop` from a command line, in a different command window

To stop the Cloudscape database server, you can either:

❑   Select **Stop Cloudscape** from the **Java 2 Enterprise Edition** menu, or

❑   Enter `cloudscape -stop` from a command line window

How It Works

The JSP file that you created is a text file that consists of HTML and embedded snippets of code. Notice in this file that there are tags with enclosed Java code, as we discussed in Chapter 1:

```
<%--

    file: helloworld.jsp
    desc: test installation of j2sdkee
--%>

<html>
<head>
  <title>Hello World - test the J2SDKEE installation</title>
```

```
<%
  for (int i = 1; i < 5; i++)
  {
%>
    <h<%=i%>>Hello World</h<%=i%>>
<%
  }
%>
</head>
<body>
```

When the JSP is compiled into a Servlet, that Servlet code expands the JSP's code snippets and HTML into code that writes HTML to an output stream:

```
out.write("\n\n");
out.write("<html>\n");
out.write("<head>\n   ");
out.write("<title>Hello World - test the J2SDKEE installation");
out.write("</title>\n\n");
for (int i = 1; i < 5; i++)
{
  out.write("\n   ");
  out.write("<h");
  out.write(String.valueOf(i));
  out.write(">Hello World");
  out.write("</h");
  out.write(String.valueOf(i));
  out.write(">\n");
}
out.write("\n");
out.write("</head>\n");
out.write("<body>\n");
```

That code, when executed, will write the following HTML code to the stream that is sent back to the requesting browser:

```
<html>
<head>
  <title>Hello World - test the J2SDKEE installation</title>

  <h1>Hello World</h1>

  <h2>Hello World</h2>

  <h3>Hello World</h3>

  <h4>Hello World</h4>

</head>
<body>
```

That's how the JSP code works. The process of packaging and deployment has a few more steps. Let's dig in a bit and see what's happening:

In order to deploy a J2EE application to a server, it has to be bundled up into an archive – that's a single file that packages up all the requisite files. The Web Archive (WAR) has to contain the components that we've created for the application (the JSP file), as well other support files. Those support files include a deployment descriptor that tells the server what's contained in the WAR and how to run it, a manifest for the archive, which is an application table of contents, and a file containing deployment information specific to the J2EE reference implementation server:

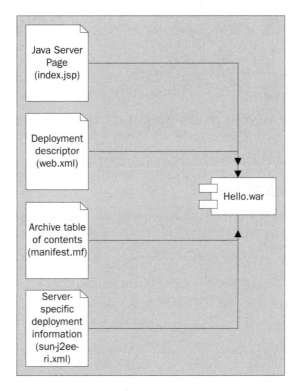

Once those contents have been assembled into a WAR file, that WAR can then be deployed to the J2EE server. That process sends the archive to the server, which then reads the deployment descriptor to determine how to unbundle the contents. In the case of this application, it sees that the WAR contains a JSP, and so it compiles that JSP into a servlet.

In order to run the application once it is deployed, you have to request the JSP by requesting an URL with your web browser. Notice that the URL consists of the protocol (`http`), the server name (`localhost`), the root context of the application (`hello`) and the requested resource (`index.jsp`):

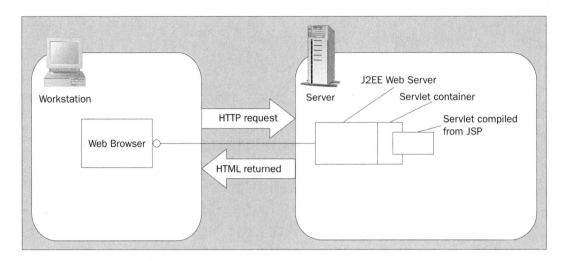

The server receives the incoming HTTP request, and uses the deployment information to invoke the appropriate servlet in a servlet container. The servlet writes HTML to an output stream, which is returned to the web browser by the server.

Problems and Solutions

If you run into any difficulties, the following table lists some common problems and how to fix them:

Problem	Solution
Deploytool won't start from the command line.	Check that the PATH variable is set correctly to include the bin directory of the J2EE SDK.
Verifier reports errors.	Carefully retrace your steps and ensure that the steps are followed correctly as described.
When testing the JSP, the web browser reports "Page cannot be displayed" when trying to open the URL http://localhost:8000.	Make certain that there weren't any errors reported when starting the J2EE server. Make certain that you've specified the port "8000" in the URL (this is the default port used by the J2EE server).
When testing the JSP, it reports a compilation error in the web browser.	Double-check the code in index.jsp. If you've mistyped something, the server won't be able to compile the JSP. The message in the web browser should give you a hint where to look.

Summary

This chapter described how to get the J2EE SDK installed, and to verify that the installation was successful. You also got your first taste of creating and running a J2EE application, as well as looking at some of the core concepts involved in building J2EE applications:

❏   Java Server Pages (JSPs) consist of HTML, with embedded snippets of Java code. The JSP is compiled into a servlet by the J2EE server which, when executed, emits HTML back to the requesting client.

❏   WARs (Web Archives) are deployment components that contain the Web components of a J2EE application. The WAR contains the components themselves (such as JSPs), and the deployment descriptor that defines the contents of the WAR. The WAR can also contain server-specific deployment information.

At this point in the book, you should now be familiar with the following procedures:

❏   How to install and configure the J2EE environment

❏   How to start and stop the Cloudscape database server

❏   How to start the interactive SQL tool for Cloudscape

❏   How to start and stop the J2EE server

❏   How to start the deploytool

❏   The essential steps of building a J2EE application:

    ❏   Create the application components

    ❏   Bundle the components into an archive

    ❏   Verify the contents of the archive to catch problems before deploying

    ❏   Distribute the archive to the J2EE server

    ❏   Test the application

If you've been able to get through this exercise, you're more than ready to dive into more detail. The next chapter will take you deeper into the details of Java Server Pages – you'll learn the essential structure of JSPs, and how to enable users to interact with your JSPs.

CHAPTER 3

Introduction to JSP	**63**
Writing JSP Pages	**65**
Translation and Compilation	**102**
Errors and Exceptions	**105**
Including and Forwarding from JSP Pages	**112**
Exercises	**120**

JavaServer Pages

In the previous chapters, we briefly introduced the J2EE and JavaServer Pages (JSP) technologies; in this chapter, we'll start to take a much more detailed look at JSP.

JSP pages are components in a web, or J2EE, application that consist of HTML with Java code added to the HTML. You might ask, "What's so different about that? I've been putting JavaScript into my HTML for years." The difference is that JavaScript runs on the client, whereas the code in a JSP runs on the server. JavaScript can only affect the particular page in which it is embedded; code in a JSP can access data across the entire web application.

In this chapter we will begin to look at how to create JSP pages for your web application. We will look at:

- ❑ The basic structure of JSP pages, and how to write a JSP page
- ❑ How to use directive, scripting, and action elements
- ❑ How to access the implicit objects of the page
- ❑ How servers translate and compile JSP pages
- ❑ How to handle errors and exceptions
- ❑ How to forward and include pages from a JSP page

Introduction to JSP

As components in a J2EE application, JSP pages run on a server and respond to requests from clients. These clients are usually users accessing the web application through a web browser. The protocol used by clients to call the HTML and JSP pages in our J2EE application is HTTP, the same protocol used by browsers to get HTML pages from a web server.

> *For the moment we'll concentrate on the basics of creating JSP pages, but we'll look at the underlying HTTP protocol in Chapter 5.*

Developing JSP Pages

In order to create a JSP page that can respond to client requests, there are a number of things we need to do. Firstly, of course, we need to write the JSP page. At some point, this page is translated and compiled into a Java class. This can happen before the page is loaded to a server, or it can happen at the time the client makes a request. The page executes inside a JSP container. A container is a piece of software that loads and manages J2EE components, in this case JSP pages. This container can be part of the web server, or it can run separately from the web server.

We can divide this process into three steps:

❑ Creation – The developer creates a JSP source file that contains HTML and embedded Java code.

❑ Deployment – The JSP is installed into a server. This can be a full J2EE server or a standalone JSP server.

❑ Translation and compilation – The JSP container translates the HTML and Java code into a Java code source file. This file is then compiled into a Java class that is executed by the server. The class file created from the JSP is known as the JSP page implementation class.

Note that this last step can actually occur at various times. Even though it is listed last here, you can translate and compile the JSP prior to deployment, and deploy the class file directly. Compiling first allows us to catch and fix syntax errors in our code prior to deployment. Alternatively, the JSP container can compile the JSP when it is deployed to the server. Finally, the usual process is that when the first request is made for the JSP, the server translates and compiles the JSP. This is known as translation at request time.

Basic JSP Lifecycle

Once compilation is complete, the JSP lifecycle has these phases:

❑ Loading and instantiation – The server finds the Java class for the JSP page and loads it into the Virtual Machine. After the class is loaded, the JVM creates one or more instances of the page. This can occur right after loading, or it can occur when the first request is made.

❑ Initialization – The JSP page is initialized. If you need to execute code during initialization, you can add a method to the page that will be called during initialization.

❑ Request processing – The page responds to a request. After performing its processing, a response is returned to the client. The response consists solely of HTML tags or other data; none of the Java code is sent to the client.

❏   End of life – The server stops sending requests to the JSP. After all current requests are finished processing, any instances of the class are released. If you need code to execute and perform any cleanup actions, you can implement a method that will be called before the class instance is released.

When a client sends a request for a JSP, the web server gives the request to the JSP container, and the JSP container determines which JSP page implementation class should handle the request. The JSP container then calls a method of the JSP page implementation class that processes the request and returns a response through the container and web server to the client:

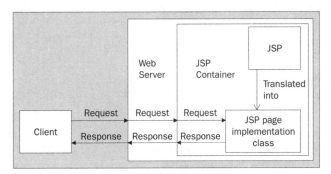

Although we've seen how JSP works, we haven't yet addressed the question of *why* we need JSP. The JSP home page (http://java.sun.com/products/jsp/) says, "Web developers and designers use JavaServer Pages technology to rapidly develop and easily maintain information-rich, dynamic web pages that leverage existing business systems." JSP pages can be rapidly developed and easily maintained because they are based on HTML and XML. Documents with markup such as HTML are easy to understand and there are many automated tools for dealing with HTML and XML documents. JSP pages are dynamic because they can contain Java code, which can process the request and tailor the response based on the request. All the power of Java sits behind every JSP page.

Writing JSP Pages

So, now that we've seen how JSP pages work, let's look at what they contain, and how we go about writing them. Take a look at the following line of code:

```
<html><body><p>Hello, World!</p></body></html>
```

Admittedly, this example is not a very good JSP example. However, these HTML tags do form a correct and valid JSP file. You could save the above file as HelloWorld.jsp, install it into a web application, and the server would access it as a JSP resource. The point I want to make is that JSP pages tend to look a lot like HTML pages. To make these pages dynamic, you can embed special tags and Java code in them. You can think of JSP pages as web pages with little bits of Java embedded in them.

The reason the example above is not very good is that it isn't dynamic in any way. If your JSP pages don't contain Java code, you might as well just make them static HTML pages. JSP pages are intended to have dynamic behavior; they are supposed to change in response to specific client requests. You give the page dynamic behavior by embedding Java code into the page.

JSP Elements

You can't just write Java code wherever you want in the page, though. You need some way to tell the server which bits are code, and which bits are regular HTML. To do this, the JSP specification defines HTML-like or XML tags that enclose the code in the JSP. Those tags come in three categories:

❑   Directive elements

❑   Scripting elements

❑   Action elements

The original JSP specification used tag formats for these elements that were not compatible with XML; that is, they were not well-formed according to the XML specification. With the JSP 1.2 specification, alternative XML-compliant versions of all the above tags were introduced. You will see both formats in this book, with the original style referred to as JSP style, and the newer as XML style.

Directive Elements

Directive elements provide information to the JSP container about the page. There are three directives available: `page`, `include`, and `taglib`. We will look at `page` and `include` here, deferring discussion of `taglib` to the next chapter. The `page` and `include` directives have these forms:

JSP Style	XML
`<%@ page` `attributes %>`	`<jsp:directive.page` `attributes />`
`<%@ include` `attributes %>`	`<jsp:directive.include` `attributes />`

You can find the complete list of attributes and their meanings in the JSP specification, which you can download at http://java.sun.com/products/jsp. Shown below are the attributes you are most likely to be using as you start developing JSP pages:

Directive	Attribute	Description
page	import	Lists the Java packages to be imported into the page. Just as with a Java source file, the Java code embedded in a JSP page must import the packages of the classes used with the code. Multiple package statements are delimited by commas, for example `import="java.io.*,java.util.*"`.
	session	The valid values are `"true"` or `"false"`. The default value is `"true"`. If `"true"`, the page participates in a session; if `"false"`, then it does not, and cannot access any session information. Sessions are covered later in the chapter.
	isThreadSafe	Whether the page is thread-safe or not. If `"true"`, the container can use the JSP for multiple concurrent request threads. The default is `"true"`.
	info	An arbitrary string. This can have any value. It is provided so that the JSP can provide information to a management tool about its contents, purpose, name, etc.
	errorPage	The URL of the web page that should be sent to the client if an error occurs in a page.
	isErrorPage	Whether the current page is an error page. The default is `false`.
	contentType	Defines the content type of the page. The content type can appear as a simple type specification, or as a type specification and a charset. The default value is `"text/html"` for JSP-style JSP tags and `"text/xml"` for XML-style JSP tags. When including the charset, the syntax for the attribute is `contentType="text/html;charset=char_set_identifier"`. Whitespace can follow the semicolon in the attribute value. Charsets indicate how written characters are encoded, so that pages can support languages that use different scripts. Information about charsets can be found at http://www.w3.org/TR/REC-html40/charset.html.
	pageEncoding	The charset of the current page. The default is ISO-8859-1 (Latin script) for JSP-style and UTF-8 (an 8-bit Unicode encoding) for XML-style tags.
include	file	The file to be included at the current position in the file. The included file can be any HTML or JSP page or fragment of a page. The file is specified using a URI to a file within the web application.

A single JSP page can have multiple instances of the page directive.

The include directive is used, as stated in the table, to include another page within the current page. This might typically be a standard header or footer, but it can include any content. You would use this when you have standard data that you want to include in multiple JSP pages. The file is included when the page is translated into its Java form. Later we will see a function that allows you to include content at request time.

Scripting Elements

The scripting elements are the elements in the page that include the Java code. There are three subforms of this element: declarations, scriptlets, and expressions. Their forms are:

JSP Style	XML
`<%! declaration %>`	`<jsp:declaration>declaration</jsp:declaration>`
`<% scriptlet code %>`	`<jsp:scriptlet>code fragment</jsp:scriptlet>`
`<%= expression %>`	`<jsp:expression>expression</jsp:expression>`

Declarations

A declaration is used to declare, and optionally define, a Java variable or a method. It works just like any declaration within a Java source code file. The declaration only appears within the translated JSP page, but not in the output to the client. For example, to declare a Vector in your JSP, you would use one of these forms:

```
<%! Vector v = new Vector(); %>
<jsp:declaration>Vector v = new Vector()</jsp:declaration>
```

This JSP fragment declares a variable v of type Vector and initializes it by calling the Vector constructor. Any variable you declare within a declaration element becomes an instance variable of the JSP page implementation class, and thus is global to the entire page. Thus, you must take care when initializing variables with a declaration, because instance variables are not thread-safe. By default, the server can send multiple requests to the same page simultaneously. You don't want one thread to change the variable while another thread is using the variable.

You can also declare and define methods within a declaration element:

```
<%!
public int void countTokens(String s) {
   StringTokenizer st = new StringTokenizer(s);
   return st.countTokens();
}
%>
```

```
<jsp:declaration>
public int countTokens(String s) {
  StringTokenizer st = new StringTokenizer(s);
  return st.countTokens();
}
</jsp:declaration>
```

Variables or methods in a declaration element can be called by any other code in the page.

Scriptlets

Scriptlets contain Java code statements. The code in the scriptlet appears in the translated JSP, but not in the output to the client. Any legal Java code statements can appear within a scriptlet. For example, to repeat the phrase "Hello, World!" ten times in the output page, you could use this scriptlet:

```
<%
   for (int i = 0; i < 10; i++) {
%>
Hello, World!
<%
   }
%>
```

As in this code snippet, we can freely interleave Java code and HTML and/or text data. Everything between the scriptlet markers (<% and %>) is script code; everything outside the markers is template data, which is sent to the client as written. Notice that in the above example the Java code block does not need to begin and end within the same scriptlet element. This allows you complete freedom to mix Java code and HTML elements as needed within the page.

The above example is relatively simple. However, as your application gets more complicated and involved, you'll get more and more code mixed in with the HTML and the page will tend to get complicated. In the next chapter, we will see how tag libraries can give the same rich behavior as above, but using only XML tags.

Since scriptlets can contain Java statements, the following is a legal scriptlet:

```
<%
Vector v = new Vector();
// more code...
%>
```

This looks very similar to the code snippet in the declaration section that preceded this section. This might lead you to wonder what the difference between scriptlets and declarations is, since they appear to be the same. Despite that seeming similarity, they are different in the following ways:

❑ Scriptlets cannot be used to define a method; only declarations can be used for that.

❑ Variables declared in a declaration are instance variables of the JSP page implementation class. These variables are visible to all other code statements or methods in the page.

❑ Variables declared in a scriptlet are local to a method in the JSP page implementation class. They are visible only within their defining code block.

Expressions

Expressions are used to output the value of a Java expression to the client. For example, this code fragment in a JSP:

```
The number of tokens in this statement is <%= countTokens("The number of
tokens in this statement is n") %>.
```

would result in the text **"The number of tokens in this statement is 9."** being displayed in the browser. The code snippet above calls the hypothetical `countTokens(String)` method that was shown in the declaration section previously. To count the number of tokens in the statement, a literal copy of the statement is passed to the method. In the code snippet above, the method call returned an `int` value, which was printed to the client's browser. Here is the same expression using XML style:

```
The number of tokens in this statement is
<jsp:expression>
    countTokens("The number of tokens in this statement is n")
</jsp:expression>.
```

Any legal Java expression can be used with an expression element. An expression could contain a method call, as shown above, or a literal expression such as '2 + 2', or an expression using Java variables or keywords such as 'v instanceof Vector', or any combination of these. Notice also that because declarations and scriptlets contain Java code, the lines of Java code must be terminated with a semicolon. Expressions, however, will not necessarily be legal code statements (but they will be valid expressions), so they do not need a terminating semicolon.

Comments

You can use standard HTML comments within the JSP and those comments will appear in the page received by the client browser. Standard HTML comments have this form:

```
<!-- This comment will appear in the client's browser -->
```

You can also include JSP-specific comments that use this syntax:

```
<%-- This comment will NOT appear in the client's browser --%>
```

JSP comments will not appear in the page output to the client.

Template Data

Everything that is not a directive, declaration, scriptlet, expression, or JSP comment (usually all the HTML and text in the page) is termed **template data**. This data is output to the client as if it had appeared within a static web page.

Try It Out   **Creating a JSP Web Application**

OK, now we really will develop an example JSP page using the information seen so far. This page will provide a welcome page to an application that manages a Frequently Asked Questions (FAQ) forum. Once we've written the code, we will use this example to show how to deploy a JSP application to the J2EE reference implementation server and to a standalone Tomcat server.

1. Start by creating a directory structure to match the web application. If you are planning to deploy this application to Tomcat standalone, you can create this directory directly in the Tomcat /webapps directory. Here is the directory structure, with the files that will be created:

```
8333/
  Ch03/
    welcome.jsp
    WEB-INF/
      web.xml
      footer.jspf
      errorPage.jsp
      classes/
        Ch03/
          FaqCategories.java
          FaqCategories.class
```

As you go through the following steps and create each file, refer to the directory structure above to determine where to save each file.

2. Let's start with the page that welcomes users to the web application. This is the welcome.jsp file:

```
<%@ page errorPage="/WEB-INF/errorPage.jsp"
         import="java.util.Iterator,Ch03.FaqCategories" %>

<!DOCTYPE HTML PUBLIC "-//W3C//DTD HTML 4.01 Transitional//EN">
<html>
  <head>
    <title>Java FAQ Welcome Page</title>
  </head>

  <body>
```

```
    <h1>Java FAQ Welcome Page</h1>
    Welcome to the Java FAQ

<%! FaqCategories faqs = new FaqCategories(); %>
Click a link below for answers to the given topic.
<%
  Iterator categories = faqs.getAllCategories();
  while (categories.hasNext()) {
    String category = (String) categories.next();
%>
    <p><a href="/<%= replaceUnderscore(category) %>"><%= category %></a></p>
<%
  }
%>

<%@ include file="/WEB-INF/footer.jspf" %>
  </body>
</html>

<%!
public String replaceUnderscore(String s) {
  return s.replace(' ','_');
}
%>
```

3. The `welcome.jsp` page above has a JSP `include` directive to add a standard footer. Because the include file is just a fragment and not a complete JSP file, we use the convention of naming the file with a `.jspf` extension as recommended by the JSP specification. Here is the `footer.jspf` file:

```
<hr>
Page generated on <%= (new java.util.Date()).toString() %>
```

4. Now create `errorPage.jsp`:

```
<%@ page isErrorPage="true" import="java.io.PrintWriter" %>

<!DOCTYPE HTML PUBLIC "-//W3C//DTD HTML 4.01 Transitional//EN">
<html>
  <head>
    <title>Error</title>
  </head>
  <body>
    <h1>Error</h1>
    There was an error somewhere.
    <%@ include file="/WEB-INF/footer.jspf" %>
  </body>
</html>
```

5. And finally, we have a helper file that will be used by `welcome.jsp`. This file is `FaqCategories.java`. After entering the source, compile the file into a class file.

```java
package Ch03;

import java.util.Iterator;
import java.util.Vector;

public class FaqCategories {
  private Vector categories = new Vector();

  public FaqCategories() {
    categories.add("Dates and Times");
    categories.add("Strings and StringBuffers");
    categories.add("Threading");
  }
  public Iterator getAllCategories() {
    return categories.iterator();
  }
}
```

How It Works

The `welcome.jsp` file demonstrates many of the features that have been introduced in this chapter so far. It begins with the `page` directive. This directive has two attributes, as shown below. First, an `errorPage` is defined, to which the browser will be redirected if an error occurs on the page. The other attribute used with the page directive is the `import`. The page imports two Java classes: the `Iterator` class from the Java API and the `FaqCategories` class that is part of this application:

```
<%@ page errorPage="/WEB-INF/errorPage.jsp"
         import="java.util.Iterator,Ch03.FaqCategories" %>
```

Note that the page can also use this syntax for the `import`:

```
<%@ page errorPage="/WEB-INF/errorPage.jsp"
         import="java.util.*,Ch03.*" %>
```

This is followed by some straight HTML. Further down in the page is a declaration scripting element. This element declares a variable called `faqs` and initializes it by calling the constructor of the `FaqCategories` helper class. You can see that declaration elements must follow Java coding rules, including the use of a semicolon to terminate the statement:

```
<%! FaqCategories faqs = new FaqCategories(); %>
```

JSP element in the page is a scriptlet. This scriptlet gets an `Iterator` from the ~~~egories instance. We use this `Iterator` to loop through each of the categories ~~~~~ in the `FaqCategories` class. Each category is loaded into a `String` variable called `category`, and this is used to create an HTML link. Each category is printed out twice using expression elements – first within the `href` attribute of the `<a>` tag to set the page that the link refers to, and then within the body of the link. The first expression element calls the `replaceUnderscore()` method (defined later in the page) and prints the result; the other expression element simply prints the `category` value:

```
<%
   Iterator categories = faqs.getAllCategories();
   while (categories.hasNext()) {
   String category = (String)categories.next();
%>
     <p><a href="/<%= replaceUnderscore(category) %>"><%= category %></a></p>
<%
   }
%>
```

Notice that with the scriptlet, Java syntax must be used. However, within an expression element, you only need to use the expression itself, without a semicolon to end the statement.

At the bottom of the page, an `include` directive includes a standard footer:

```
<%@ include file="/WEB-INF/footer.jspf" %>
```

The last thing in the file is another declaration element. This element, shown below, declares the `replaceUnderscore()` method, which replaces the spaces in a string with underscores. It was called by the scriptlet earlier in the file:

```
<%!
public String replaceUnderscore(String s) {
   return s.replace(' ','_');
}
%>
```

The next file is `footer.jspf`:

```
<hr>
Page generated on <%= (new java.util.Date()).toString() %>
```

You will see that this is not a complete JSP file. This file uses an expression element to print out the current date and time at the server when the page is served to the user. I used the extension `.jspf` as recommended by the specification to indicate that this file is a fragment. Also, because it is a fragment and is not meant to be publicly available, the file was put into the **WEB-INF** directory. Files in this directory are not publicly available. This means that you cannot enter an address into a browser to access this file. Only code within the application can access files within the **WEB-INF** directory.

The errorPage.jsp is meant to be used when an uncaught exception occurs in the welcome.jsp page. It includes the standard footer. However, assuming everything in the page is correct, it will not be called in this application. This page is not meant to be publicly available, so it too resides in the **WEB-INF** directory:

```
<%@ page isErrorPage="true" import="java.io.PrintWriter" %>

<!DOCTYPE HTML PUBLIC "-//W3C//DTD HTML 4.01 Transitional//EN">
<html>
  <head>
    <title>Error</title>
  </head>
  <body>
    <h1>Error</h1>
    There was an error somewhere.
    <%@ include file="/WEB-INF/footer.jspf" %>
  </body>
</html>
```

Since this is an error page, notice that we set the isErrorPage attribute of the page directive to true. Apart from that directive, this page contains just straight HTML and an include directive to include our footer.jspf file.

The final source file is FaqCategories.java. This is a helper class that supplies three categories to the welcome.jsp page. In a real-world application, the categories would come from some persistent store such as a database or a directory. For this example, we use the helper class to "hard-code" the categories for welcome.jsp:

```
package Ch03;

import java.util.Iterator;
import java.util.Vector;

public class FaqCategories {
  private Vector categories = new Vector();

  public FaqCategories() {
    categories.add("Dates and Times");
    categories.add("Strings and StringBuffers");
    categories.add("Threading");
  }
  public Iterator getAllCategories() {
    return categories.iterator();
  }
}
```

The categories are stored in a Vector object, which is an instance member of the class. In the class constructor, we just add our hard-coded categories to this Vector. Finally, we define a getAllCategories() method, which simply returns the Iterator for our Vector. Our JSP page uses this Iterator to loop through each of the categories in turn.

Deploying the Web Application in J2EE

That finishes the code for our application, but before it can actually be accessed by clients, we need to deploy our application to an application server. We'll look at two application servers in this book – the reference implementation server that comes with the J2EE SDK, and the Tomcat stand-alone server. In fact, the J2EE server is itself nothing other than Tomcat, but since it comes with its own utility for deploying applications, we'll look at the two ways of deploying JSP web apps separately. First, let's see how we do it with the J2EE server.

1. Ensure the J2EE server is running, and start up the J2EE Deploytool that we looked at in the previous chapter.

2. Select File | New | Application EAR from the menu to create a new Application EAR file. EAR stands for Enterprise Archive.

3. In the dialog that results, enter a filename for the application. I used JavaFAQ.ear for this example:

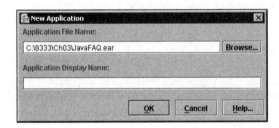

4. Select File | New | Web Application WAR from the menu to create a new web application. This will start the Web Application Wizard:

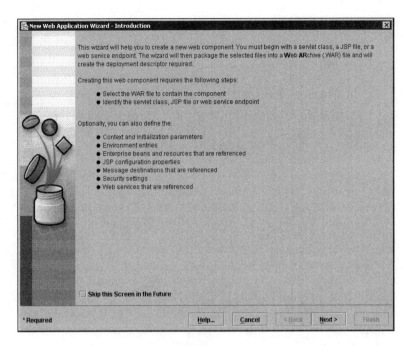

5. At the first screen of the wizard, shown below, ensure the correct application is selected in the **Create New WAR Module in Application** drop-down box. Click the **Edit** button in the **Contents** panel and add these files to the WAR:

❑ `FaqCategories.class`

❑ `errorPage.jsp`

❑ `footer.jspf`

❑ `welcome.jsp`

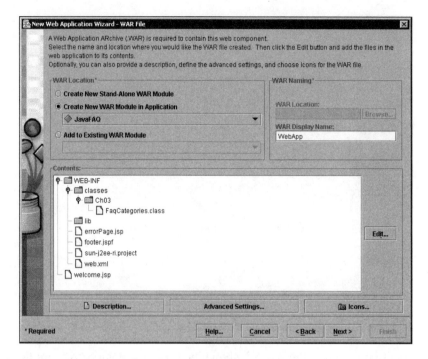

Make sure that the `errorPage.jsp` and `footer.jspf` files appear in the correct location underneath the **WEB-INF** directory. If they are not, you can drag and drop them into the correct location. Note that the wizard will create the deployment descriptor, `web.xml`, for you. You do not need to add `web.xml` to the application.

6. At the next dialog, select the **JSP** radio button and click the **Next** button:

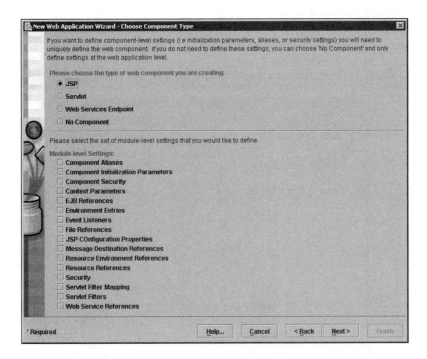

7. In the JSP Filename drop-down box, select /welcome.jsp as the JSP to define. The Web Component Name and Web Component Display Name fields will be automatically filled. Click the Finish button:

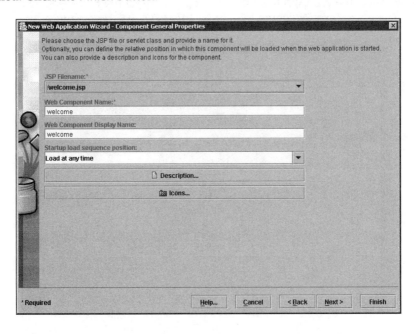

8. In the navigation pane on the left, ensure the application is selected. In the screenshot below, the web application has been named JavaFAQ, and you can see it is selected. In the right pane, select the **Web Context** tab, and double-click in the **Context Root** field. Enter **Ch03** as the context root and press *Enter*:

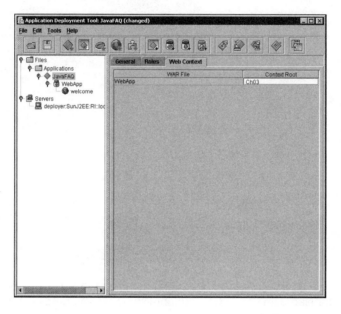

9. Now select the **WebApp** label in the left pane. Select the **File Refs** tab in the right pane. Add an entry for a **Welcome File**. Enter the welcome.jsp page.

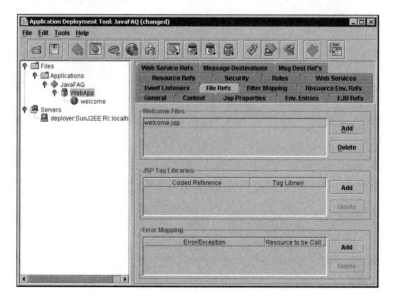

10. Ensure the JavaFAQ application is selected in the left-hand pane, and select File I Save As to save the Application EAR. The location doesn't matter, as long as you remember where you save it.

11. On the main menu, select File I Deployment Settings I Create New File. In the dialog that follows, the File Location should already be set to the location where you saved the application `.ear` file, and the filename should already be set to `{application_name}.ear.xml`. If this is not so, set the File Location to match the location of the saved `.ear` file, and set the name to `{application_name}.ear.xml`. Click OK:

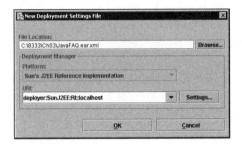

12. Select File I Deployment Settings I Close File. Select the Save option at the dialog that results.

13. Select Tools I Deploy from the menu. The correct `.ear.xml` file should already be selected. Click OK. The Deploytool will deploy your web application.

14. When the tool is finished, open a browser window. Enter the address http://localhost:8000/Ch03. The `welcome.jsp` page will automatically load:

| **Try It Out** | **Deploying the Web Application in Tomcat** |

Deploying applications to a Tomcat stand-alone server is simpler, but it does require us to write a special XML file, known as a **deployment descriptor**. This file is also required by the J2EE server, but the Deploytool creates it for us, so we don't need to write it by hand.

1. Firstly, then, if you are deploying to Tomcat standalone, you need to write a deployment descriptor for the web application. Development descriptors are XML files that contain configuration information about the entire web application. We will look at development descriptors in more detail in Chapter 5. Here is the deployment descriptor for our `JavaFAQ` application. This file is called `web.xml` and is placed in the application's **WEB-INF** directory:

```
<?xml version="1.0" encoding="ISO-8859-1"?>

<!DOCTYPE web-app
  PUBLIC "-//Sun Microsystems, Inc.//DTD Web Application 2.3//EN"
  "http://java.sun.com/dtd/web-app_2_3.dtd">

<web-app>
  <!-- this is the deployment descriptor for Chapter 3
      Try It Out example 1                            -->

  <welcome-file-list>
    <welcome-file>welcome.jsp</welcome-file>
  </welcome-file-list>
</web-app>
```

2. If the J2EE server is running, shut it down.

3. If you created the directory structure we described earlier in the chapter (when we looked at the source code for the application) within the Tomcat /webapps directory, then you are finished. Go to step 5.

4. If the application directory is not under the Tomcat /webapps directory, you can do one of two things:

Either copy the directory structure to Tomcat /webapps.

Or navigate to the top-level directory of the web application. For example, if the highest directory of the application is /Ch03, you would navigate into that directory.

Now create the Web Archive manually:

```
> jar cf Ch03.war *
```

Copy the .war file to the Tomcat /webapps directory.

5. Start the Tomcat server. When it is started, open a browser window and enter the address http://localhost:8080/Ch03. The `welcome.jsp` file will load as shown in the J2EE example.

How It Works

Since you'll need to write a deployment descriptor for any web applications you want to deploy to Tomcat stand-alone, let's take a moment to look at the `web.xml` file in this example. First come the standard XML declaration and document type declaration, which you can use for any JSP deployment descriptors:

```
<?xml version="1.0" encoding="ISO-8859-1"?>
<!DOCTYPE web-app
    PUBLIC "-//Sun Microsystems, Inc.//DTD Web Application 2.3//EN"
    "http://java.sun.com/dtd/web-app_2_3.dtd">
```

Next, comes the XML content of the file. The root XML element is called `<web-app>`, and in this case contains only a single child element, `<welcome-file-list>`:

```
<web-app>
  <welcome-file-list>
    <welcome-file>welcome.jsp</welcome-file>
  </welcome-file-list>
</web-app>
```

This element lists the files that will be served to any client that simply enters the application context from a browser. These files are referred to as welcome files. For example, an address like http://localhost:8080/Ch03 does not reference any resource within the web application root context, /Ch03. Anyone who enters a URL like this will be served a welcome file from the list. If multiple files are listed in the welcome file list, the server will respond with the first file in the welcome file list that it finds.

I will cover specific elements of the deployment descriptor as they apply, but we will look at deployment descriptors in more detail in Chapter 5. You can also find more information about the deployment descriptor in the documentation for Tomcat, and the JSP and Servlet specifications.

When you load the welcome page, you probably saw that the links in that page do not reference actual resources within the application. If you clicked on one of the links, you probably received an HTTP 404 error in the browser. You did not see the error page, because the problem was a Resource Not Found in the server, not an uncaught exception in the page.

> The elements in the deployment descriptor must follow a particular order specified by a Document Type Definition (DTD) (JSP 1.2 and earlier), or an XML Schema (JSP 2.0). If the elements are not in the correct order, the server will not start the application. In Chapter 5 in this book, we'll look at the correct order as defined by the DTD in the Servlet 2.3 specification.

To actually deploy the application to Tomcat, we need to copy the files to Tomcat's /webapps directory. If you don't want to store the application's files directly in this directory, you can deploy the application by packaging all the files into a web archive, or WAR, file. The WAR is a convenient way to package all the files and components that make up a web application into one archive. All JSP containers know how to read and deploy web applications from the WAR. Thus, deploying a web application is as simple as creating the archive with the correct application directory structure and putting it into the correct directory location for the container. The directory structure of the web application, and thus the WAR, is defined in the servlet specification. Likewise, the deployment descriptor is defined by the specification. When you use a tool like the J2EE Deploytool, it takes care of creating the correct directory structure and deployment descriptor for you, but you need to create it manually if you're deploying to Tomcat stand-alone.

In general, the structure of your application will look like this:

```
app_context/
  public web resources
  WEB-INF/
  web.xml
  tlds/
    tld files
  lib/
     archives used by application
  classes/
    class files used in application
```

The directory at the top of the structure defines the web application context. The application context provides a separation between different web applications. Under the application context directory are the public files of the application. This will generally include the HTML and JSP pages of the application. Under the application context is the **WEB-INF** directory. This directory contains the deployment descriptor web.xml and other files that are not publicly accessible by clients of the application. There can be any number of directories under **WEB-INF**, but three common ones are shown above. The **tlds** directory is not required, but is a commonly used directory for keeping tag library descriptor files (see Chapter 4). The **lib** directory is used for Java archives (.jar files) that are used by the web application. Finally, the **classes** directory is used for class files in the web application.

Action Elements

The last set of JSP elements we will look at are the action elements. These elements are also known as **Standard Actions**. Standard actions are defined by the JSP specification (which is one reason why they are called standard).

As we will see in the next chapter, we can define our own actions that can be used in a JSP page.

The JSP 2.0 specification defines these standard actions:

- ❑ `<jsp:useBean>`
- ❑ `<jsp:setProperty>`
- ❑ `<jsp:getProperty>`
- ❑ `<jsp:param>`
- ❑ `<jsp:include>`
- ❑ `<jsp:forward>`
- ❑ `<jsp:plugin>`, `<jsp:params>`, `<jsp:fallback>`
- ❑ `<jsp:attribute>`
- ❑ `<jsp:body>`
- ❑ `<jsp:invoke>`
- ❑ `<jsp:doBody>`

We will look at `<jsp:include>`, `<jsp:forward>`, and `<jsp:param>` later in the chapter.

The `<jsp:plugin>`, `<jsp:params>`, and `<jsp:fallback>` elements are used to include applets or Java Beans in the HTML page generated by a JSP page. Using these over hand-coding the HTML allows the server to create browser-specific HTML from the JSP tags. These tags are not discussed further in this book.

The elements `<jsp:attribute>` and `<jsp:body>` are used with standard and custom actions. The elements `<jsp:invoke>` and `<jsp:doBody>` are only valid in tag libraries, which we will cover in the next chapter.

The <jsp:useBean> Action

This element makes a JavaBean available to the page. A JavaBean (which is not the same as an Enterprise JavaBean, or EJB) is simply a Java class that follows certain requirements. The two requirements that are important for our purposes are:

- ❑ The JavaBean class has a no-argument constructor.
- ❑ Every property of the bean that is provided for client use has a method to set the value of the parameter, and a method to get the value of the parameter. The methods have this form:

```
public type getSomeParameter() { return someParameter; }
public Boolean isSomeParameter() { return someParameter; }
public void setSomeParameter(type someParameter) {
  // Set the parameter
}
```

The name of every setter and getter uses the name of the parameter, with the first letter capitalized, appended to the token set, get, or is. The getter method has the form isXXX() for Boolean properties, and getXXX() otherwise.

The <jsp:useBean> element has these attributes:

Attribute	Description
id	The name used to access the bean in the rest of the page. It must be unique. It is essentially the variable name that references the bean instance.
scope	The scope of the bean. Valid values are page, request, session, or application. The default is page. See the *Scope* section below for more information.
class	The fully qualified class name of the bean class.
beanName	The name of a bean, as expected by the instantiate() method of the java.beans.Beans class. Most often you will use the class attribute, rather than beanName. Refer to the JavaBeans specification at http://java.sun.com/products/javabeans for more information on how to supply a name to the instantiate() method.
type	The type to be used for the variable that references the bean. This follows Java rules, so it can be the class of the bean, any parent class of the bean, or any interface implemented by the bean or by a parent class.

The <jsp:useBean> element causes the container to try to find an existing instance of the object in the specified scope and with the specified id. If no object with the specified id is found in that scope, and a class or bean name is specified, the container will try to create a new instance of the object. You can use the class, beanName, and type attributes in these combinations:

❑   class – creates an instance of the class that can be referred to by the given id

❑   class, type – creates an instance of the given class; the bean will have the given type

❑   beanName, type – creates an instance of the given bean; the bean will have the given type

❑   type – if an object of the given type exists in the session, the id will refer to that object

You must create a reference to a JavaBean using the <jsp:useBean> element before you can use <jsp:setProperty> or <jsp:getProperty>.

The <jsp:setProperty> Action

Sets the property for a JavaBean. The <jsp:setProperty> element has these attributes:

Attribute	Description
name	The id of the bean.
property	The name of the property to set.
	The value can explicitly name a property of the bean, in which case the setXXX() method for the property will be called.
	The value can also be "*", in which case, the JSP will read all the parameters that were sent by the browser with the client's request, and set the properties in the bean that have the same names as the parameters in the request. We will see an example of this in the next *Try It Out* section.
param	The parameter name in the browser request whose value will be used to set the property. Allows the JSP to match properties and parameters with different names.
value	The value to assign to the property.

The name and property attributes are always required. The param and value elements are mutually exclusive. If neither param nor value are used, the jsp:setProperty element attempts to use the request parameter with the same name as the property attribute. I will show examples of request parameters in the next section.

Suppose we have a JavaBean that holds information about a user of the system. This bean might look like this:

```
public class User {
    private String id;
    private String surname;
    public void setId(String id) { this.id = id; }
    public String getId() { return id; }
    public void setSurname(String surname) { this.surname = surname; }
    public String getSurname() { return surname; }
}
```

Here is one simple example of using the <jsp:setProperty> element with a literal value, and an expression:

```
<jsp:useBean id="userA" class="User" />
<jsp:setProperty id="userA" property="surname" value="Smith" />
<jsp:setProperty id="userA" property="id"
                 value="<%= validateId("86753") %>" />
```

After this code in the compiled JSP executes, the surname property of the instance of User has a value of "Smith" and the id property has whatever value is returned by the hypothetical validateId() expression. What occurs is that the JSP translator takes the elements above and translates them into code that creates an instance of the User class, and then calls the setSurname() and setId() methods of the object.

The <jsp:getProperty> Action

This element retrieves the value of a property from a JavaBean. The <jsp:getProperty> element has these attributes:

Attribute	Description
name	The id of the bean.
property	The name of the property to get.

The name and property attributes are always required. When used within a JSP, the value of the property will be output as part of the response. Given the example in the previous section, you could write template data that used <jsp:getProperty> like this:

```
The user with id <jsp:getProperty id="userA" property="id" />
has a surname of <jsp:getProperty id="userA" property="surname" />
```

When the JSP page is translated into Java code, this will result in calls to the getSurname() and getId() methods of the object. The return values are then output with the template data to the response, so that the client sees this in his browser:

The user with id 86753 has a surname of Smith

JSP Initialization and End-of-Life

In the JSP lifecycle section above, I mentioned that you can add methods to your JSP that will be called when the JSP is initialized and when the JSP is destroyed. These methods are declared using the declaration scripting element.

When you need to perform one-time initialization of the JSP, you would add this method to the JSP:

```
<%!
public void jspInit() {
   // ...perform one time initialization.
   // ...this method is called only once per JSP, not per request
}
%>
```

If you need to clean up any resources used by the JSP, you would add this method to the JSP:

```
<%!
public void jspDestroy() {
   // ...perform one time cleanup of resources
}
%>
```

If you don't need to perform initialization or cleanup, you do not need to add these methods to the JSP.

Implicit Objects

The previous section stated that the properties of a JavaBean can be set from the parameters in the request sent by the client browser. Your JSP can also access the client's request directly. You access the client's request through an object named `request`. In addition to the `request` object, the JSP model provides you with a number of other implicit objects. These objects are implicit because a JSP has access to and can use them without needing to explicitly declare and initialize the objects. Implicit objects are used within scriptlet and expression elements. In this section, we will look at these implicit objects:

- `request`
- `response`
- `out`
- `session`
- `config`
- `exception`
- `application`

In this section, I will show the methods of these objects that you will be using the most. You should consult the Javadoc for the complete list and explanation of all the available methods.

The Request Object

JSP pages are web components that respond to and process HTTP requests. The `request` implicit object represents this HTTP request. Through the `request` object, you can access the HTTP headers, the request parameters, and other information about the request. You will most often use this object to read the request parameters.

When a browser submits a request to a server, it can send information along with the request in the form of request parameters. These take two forms:

- URL-encoded parameters – These are parameters appended to the requested URL as a query string. The parameters begin with a question mark, followed by the name-value pairs of all the parameters, with each pair delimited by an ampersand (&):

```
http://www.myserver.com/path/to/resource?name1=value1&name2=value2
```

❏ Form-encoded parameters –These parameters are submitted as a result of a form submission. They have the same format as URL-encoded parameters, but are included with the body of the request and not appended to the requested URL.

These parameters can be read through various methods of the `request` object:

```
String request.getParameter(String name);
String[] request.getParameterValues(String name);
Enumeration request.getParameterNames();
Map getParameterMap();
```

The `getParameter(String)` method returns the value of the parameter with the given name. If the named parameter has multiple values (for example, when a form submits the value of checkboxes), this method returns the first value. For multi-valued parameters, `getParameterValues(String)` returns all the values for the given name. The `getParameterNames()` method returns all the parameter names used in the request, while `getParameterMap()` returns all the parameters as name-value pairs.

Information can also be passed to the server using extra path information. This data is appended to the requested URL. For example, suppose /Ch03/MyComponent were the context and name of a web application component; additional information could be appended to the path like this: Ch03/MyComponent/extraPathInfo. With the correct configuration, the server would send the request to `MyComponent`, and `MyComponent` would get the extra path information using this method:

```
String request.getPathInfo();
```

The `request` object has request scope. That means that the implicit request object is in scope until the response to the client is complete. It is an instance of `javax.servlet.HttpServletRequest`. For further information about the methods of `request`, see Chapter 5.

The Response Object

The `response` object encapsulates the response to the web application client. Some of the things you can do using the response are set headers, set cookies for the client, and send a redirect response to the client. You can perform those functions with these methods:

```
public void addHeader(String name, String value)
public void addCookie(Cookie cookie)
public void sendRedirect(String location)
```

It is an instance of `javax.servlet.HttpServletResponse` and it has page scope.

The out Object

The out implicit object is a reference to an output stream that you can use within scriptlets. Using the out object, the scriptlet can write data to the response that is sent to the client. For example, we could rewrite the earlier welcome.jsp to use the out object like this:

```
<%
  Iterator categories = faqs.getAllCategories();
  while (categories.hasNext()) {
    String category = (String)categories.next();
    out.println("<p><a href=\"" + replaceUnderscore(category) + "\">" +
                category + "</a></p>");
  }
%>
```

The scriptlet above would cause the same HTML to be sent to the client as was sent in the original version of welcome.jsp. Note that one of the purposes of JSP is to separate the HTML from the Java code, so the above example is not the best use of the out object.

The out object is an instance of javax.jsp.JspWriter. It has page scope.

The session Object

HTTP is a stateless protocol. As far as a web server is concerned, each client request is a new request, with nothing to connect it to previous requests. However, in web applications, a client's interaction with the application will often span many requests and responses. To join all these separate interactions into one coherent conversation between client and application, web applications use the concept of a session. A session refers to the entire conversation between a client and a server.

The JSP components in a web application automatically participate in a given client's session, without needing to do anything special. Any JSP page that uses the page directive to set the session attribute to false does not have access to the session object, and thus cannot participate in the session.

Using the session object, the page can store information about the client or the client's interaction. Information is stored in the session, just as you would store information in a Hashtable or a Hashmap. This means that a JSP page can only store objects in the session, and not Java primitives. To store Java primitives, you need to use one of the wrapper classes such as Integer, or Boolean. The methods for storing and retrieving session data are:

```
Object setAttribute(String name, Object value);
Object getAttribute(String name);
Enumeration getAttributeNames();
void removeAttribute(String name);
```

When other components in the web application receive a request, they can access the session data that was stored by other components. They can change information in the session or add new information to it. Also, be aware that sessions are not inherently thread-safe. You should consider the possibility that two or more web components could access the same objects from the same session simultaneously. If this could be a problem for your application, you must synchronize access to the objects stored in the session.

Normally, you don't need to write code in your page to manage the session. The server creates the `session` object, and associates client requests with a particular session. However, this association normally happens through the use of a cookie that is sent to the client. The cookie holds a session ID; when the browser sends the cookie back to the server, the server uses the session ID to associate the request to a session. When the browser does not accept cookies, the server falls back to a scheme called **URL rewriting** to maintain the session. If there is the possibility that the server will be using URL rewriting, your page needs to rewrite any embedded URLs. This is actually done with a method of the `response` object:

```
response.encodeURL(String);
response.encodeRedirectURL(String);
```

The second method is used when the URL will be sent as a redirect to the browser using the `response.sendRedirect()` method. The first method is used for all other URLs.

The `session` object has session scope, and all the objects stored in the `session` object also have session scope. The session object is an instance of `javax.servlet.http.HttpSession`.

The config Object

This object is used to obtain JSP-specific `init` parameters. These initialization parameters are set in the deployment descriptor, but are specific to a single page. JSP `init` parameters are set in the `<servlet>` element of the deployment descriptor. This is because the page implementation class of the JSP (the Java class which is compiled from the JSP page) is a servlet class. The `<servlet>` element with the `<init-param>` element will look like this:

```
<servlet>
  <servlet-name>StockList</servlet-name>
  <servlet-class>web.StockListServlet</servlet-class>
  <init-param>
    <param-name>name</param-name>
    <param-value>value</param-value>
  </init-param>
</servlet>
```

See Chapter 5 for more information on how to use the `<servlet>` element.

If JSP initialization parameters are defined in the deployment descriptor, you can access them using:

```
config.getInitParameter(String name);
```

The exception Object

This implicit object is only available within error pages. It is a reference to the
java.lang.Throwable object that caused the server to call the error page.

The application Object

This object represents the web application environment. You will use this object to get
application-level configuration parameters. Within the deployment descriptor, you can set
application parameters using this element:

```
<webapp>
  <context-param>
    <param-name>name</param-name>
    <param-value>value</param-value>
  </context-param>
</webapp>
```

The value of the parameter can be accessed using:

```
application.getInitParameter(String name);
```

Scope

Objects that are created as part of a JSP have a certain scope, or lifetime. That scope varies with
the object. In some cases, such as the implicit objects, the scope is set and cannot be changed.
With other objects (JavaBeans for example), you can set the scope of the object. Valid scopes are
page, request, session, and application.

- ❑ **page** – Page scope is the most restrictive. With page scope, the object is only accessible
  within the page in which it is defined. JavaBeans created with page scope and objects
  created by scriptlets are thread-safe. (Recall, though, that Java objects created by
  declaration elements are not thread-safe.)

- ❑ **request** – With request scope, objects are available for the life of the specific request. This
  means that the object is available within the page in which it is created, and within pages
  to which the request is forwarded or included. Objects with request scope are thread-
  safe. Only the execution thread for a particular request can access these objects.

- ❑ **session** – Objects with session scope are available to all application components that
  participate in the client's session. These objects are not thread-safe. If multiple requests
  could use the same session object at the same time, you must synchronize access to
  that object.

- ❑ **application** – This is the least restrictive scope. Objects that are created with
  application scope are available to the entire application for the life of the application.
  These objects are not thread-safe and access to them must be synchronized if there is a
  chance that multiple requests will attempt to change the object at the same time.

Try It Out   Using JavaBeans in JSP Pages

In this example, we will expand the earlier example. This example will add a registration page to the application. Using the registration page, we will see some examples of using a JavaBean in the page. This example will also use the implicit `request` object to read request parameters.

1. Here is the application structure for this example:

```
Ch03/
   registration.jsp
   registrationform.html
   welcome.jsp
   WEB-INF/
     errorPage.jsp
     footer.jspf
     web.xml
     classes/
       Ch03/
         FaqCategories.java
         User.java
         FaqCategories.class
         User.class
```

2. Start by creating the JavaBean. This bean consists of a class called `User`, and represents a user of our application. After entering the source, compile it into a class file:

```java
package Ch03;

public class User {
  private String firstName;
  private String surname;
  private String loginName;
  private int age;

  public String getFirstName() { return firstName; }
  public void setFirstName(String newFirstName) {
    this.firstName = newFirstName;
  }

  public String getSurname() { return surname; }
  public void setSurname(String newSurname) {
    this.surname = newSurname;
  }

  public String getLoginName() { return loginName; }
  public void setLoginName(String newLoginName) {
    this.loginName = newLoginName;
  }
```

```
public int getAge() { return age; }
public void setAge(int newAge) {
  this.age = newAge;
}
}
```

3. Next, we'll modify `welcome.jsp` from the earlier example. This page will ask users to register, if they haven't already done so:

```
<%@ page errorPage="/WEB-INF/errorPage.jsp"
    import="java.util.Iterator,Ch03.*" %>
```

```
<!DOCTYPE HTML PUBLIC "-//W3C//DTD HTML 4.01 Transitional//EN">
<html>
  <head>
    <title>Java FAQ Welcome Page</title>
  </head>

  <body>
    <h1>Java FAQ Welcome Page</h1>
```

```
<%
  User user = (User) session.getAttribute("user");
  if (user == null) {
%>
    You are not yet registered, please
    <a href="registrationform.html">register</a>.
<%
  } else {
%>
    Welcome to the Java FAQ

<%! FaqCategories faqs = new FaqCategories(); %>
Click a link below for answers to the given topic.
<%
    Iterator categories = faqs.getAllCategories();
    while (categories.hasNext()) {
      String category = (String) categories.next();
%>
      <p><a href="<%= replaceUnderscore(category) %>.jsp"><%= category
%></a></p>
<%
    }
%>

<%@ include file="/WEB-INF/footer.jspf" %>
<%
  }
%>
  </body>
</html>
```

```
<%!
public String replaceUnderscore(String s) {
  return s.replace(' ','_');
}
%>
```

4. Next, create the `registrationform.html` page that collects the user information:

```html
<!DOCTYPE HTML PUBLIC "-//W3C//DTD HTML 4.01 Transitional//EN">
<html>
  <head>
    <title>Registration Page</title>
  </head>
  <body>
    <h1>Registration Page</h1>

    <form action="registration.jsp" method="POST">
      <table>
        <tr>
          <td align="right">First name:</td>
          <td align="left"><input type="text"
              name="firstName" length="30"/></td>
        </tr>
        <tr>
          <td align="right">Surname:</td>
          <td align="left"><input type="text"
              name="surname" length="30"/></td>
        </tr>
        <tr>
          <td align="right">Login Name:</td>
          <td align="left"><input type="text"
              name="loginName" length="30"/></td>
        </tr>
        <tr>
          <td align="right">Age:</td>
          <td align="left"><input type="text"
              name="age" length="5"/></td>
        </tr>
      </table>

      Which topics are you interested in?
      <br><input type="checkbox" name="topics"
              value="Dates and Times">
        Dates and Times</input>
      <br><input type="checkbox" name="topics"
              value="Strings and StringBuffers">
          Strings and StringBuffers</input>
      <br><input type="checkbox" name="topics"
              value="Threading">
          Threading</input>
```

```
        <p><input type="submit" value="Submit"/></p>
      </form>
    </body>
</html>
```

5. This form submits to a JSP page that gathers the form data and populates the User bean. This page is registration.jsp:

```
<!DOCTYPE HTML PUBLIC "-//W3C//DTD HTML 4.01 Transitional//EN">
<html>
  <head>
    <title>Register User</title>
  </head>
  <body>
    <h1>Register User</h1>

    <jsp:useBean id="user" scope="session" class="Ch03.User">
      <jsp:setProperty name="user" property="*" />
    </jsp:useBean>

    Welcome new user, these are the values you submitted:
    <p>Your first name is <%= user.getFirstName() %>.</p>
    <p>Your last name is
        <jsp:getProperty name="user" property="surname" />.</p>
    <p>Your user id is
        <jsp:getProperty name="user" property="loginName" />.</p>
    <p>Your age is
        <jsp:getProperty name="user" property="age" />.</p>
    You selected these topics:

<%
  String[] topics = request.getParameterValues("topics");
  if (topics == null) { topics = new String[] {"No topics"}; }
  for (int i = 0; i < topics.length; i++) {
%>
    <br><%= topics[i] %>
<%
  }
%>
    <p>Go to <a href="welcome.jsp">Topic List Page</a></p>
    <%@ include file="/WEB-INF/footer.jspf" %>
  </body>
</html>
```

6. The other files for this application remain the same as before.

7. Deploy this application to the server of your choice, using the same steps as in the first example in this chapter. If you want to update an existing EAR using the Deploytool, there are a couple of things you can do. Update the existing files by selecting the specific application in the left pane, and then selecting **Tools | Update Files** from the menu. If you also need to add new files, select the web application entry in the left pane, then click the **Edit** button on the **General** tab in the right pane, and add the new files (`registration.jsp`, `registrationform.html`, and `User.class`). Now update the deployment descriptor by selecting **File | Deployment Settings | Edit Existing File**, ensuring that the correct `.ear.xml` file is selected, and then clicking on **OK**, choosing to overwrite the existing file. Close the file by selecting **File → Deployment Settings | Close File**, choosing to save the changes. Finally, redeploy the application by selecting **Tools | Deploy**.

8. If you're using Tomcat standalone and the application files are stored in the Tomcat **/webapps** directory, you just need to update the files and add the extra ones in this directory structure. If they're stored outside this directory, delete the existing `.war` file and the **/Ch03** directory in **/webapps**, recreate the `.war` file by calling `jar cf Ch03.war *` from the application's root directory as before, and copying this file to **/webapps**.

9. Enter the URL for the `welcome.jsp`. You should see this page in your browser:

10. Click on the **register** link to load the registration page.

11. Fill out the fields and check one or more of the boxes. Click the Submit button.

12. Clicking the Submit button will cause the registration information to be passed to registration.jsp. That JSP will display this page:

13. Finally, clicking the link in this page will send you to `welcome.jsp` again. This time, `welcome.jsp` will display the topic list:

How It Works

As in the first example, the entry into the application is the `welcome.jsp` page. However, this time, the page checks for the existence of a `User` object in the session using this code:

```
User user = (User)session.getAttribute("user");
```

Recall that all JSP pages have access to the implicit `session` object, unless specified otherwise with the `page` directive. Using the `getAttribute()` method, the page attempts to get the named object from the session. Notice that `getAttribute()` returns a reference of type `Object`, which must be cast to the proper type to assign it to the `user` variable.

If there is no `user` object in the session (that is, if `user` is `null`), `welcome.jsp` outputs the HTML with a link for the `registrationform.html` page. Later, when returning to this page, the `user` object will exist, and the welcome page displays the topic list. The remainder of this page is unchanged.

The `registrationform.html` page is a standard web page with a form that submits form data to the server. The resource that it submits to is given in the `<form>` tag:

```
<form action="registration.jsp" method="POST">
```

The `action` attribute contains the URI for the server resource that should receive the data. This URI can be relative as shown, or absolute. The `method` attribute indicates which HTTP method should be used for the submission. The form includes some text fields and some checkboxes. The form submits all its data to `registration.jsp`.

The first interesting thing about `registration.jsp` is the `<jsp:useBean>` tag shown here:

```
<jsp:useBean id="user" class="Ch03.User">
  <jsp:setProperty name="user" property="*" />
</jsp:useBean>
```

This tag creates an instance of the class given by the `class` attribute. Throughout the rest of the page, the object can be referred to using the variable `user`. Enclosed within the `<jsp:useBean>` element is a `<jsp:setProperty>` element. This element uses the `property="*"` attribute, which causes the page to find each `setXXX` method of the given bean, and call each method with the same named parameter in the request. If you look at the `User` class, you will see it has four public `setXXX` methods: `setFirstName(String)`, `setSurname(String)`, `setLoginName(String)`, and `setAge(int)`. These methods must be matched by four request parameters. If you examine `registrationform.html`, you will see that it does have four form fields with the correct names: `firstName`, `surname`, `loginName`, and `age`. The value from each of these request parameters is used to set the properties of the `User` bean.

You may recall that the `<jsp:setProperty>` tag also has an attribute named `param`. This attribute is used when the names in the request do not match the names in the bean. For example, suppose that the web page from had a field `lastName` instead of `surname` and that you were not allowed to change the web form or the bean. The JSP could not use the `property="*"` syntax, because the JSP is not able to match request parameters to bean properties in this case. The way to set the properties would be to use this syntax:

```
<jsp:useBean id="user" class="Ch03.User">
  <jsp:setProperty name="user" property="surname" param="lastName"/>
</jsp:useBean>
```

Using this syntax, the page knows that it can set the bean's `surname` property using the value of the request parameter called `lastName`.

Although it is shown enclosed within the `<jsp:useBean>` element, you can use `<jsp:setProperty>` any time after the bean is created.

Next, `registration.jsp` stores the newly created bean in the implicit `session` object. This makes it available to every component in the application. Thus, when the `welcome.jsp` is called again, it will find the bean object.

Then the page prints out the values of the `User` bean's properties. For the first property, a JSP expression is used to print the property. For the remainder of the properties, the `<jsp:getProperty>` element is used:

```
<p>Your first name is <%= user.getFirstName() %></p>
<p>Your last name is
    <jsp:getProperty name="user" property="surname" />.</p>
```

The page then prints out the remainder of the request parameters. These are the values of the checkboxes that were checked in the form. The page calls the `request.getParameterValues()` method and then prints every element in the `String` array returned by the method. Notice that the web browser only submits values for the boxes that were checked. Finally, the JSP prints a link to the `welcome.jsp` page.

When `welcome.jsp` is called this time, the `User` object exists in the session, so the JSP outputs the topic list.

Translation and Compilation

As you develop and test JSP pages, you may have noticed that the first time you access a new page, there is some delay before the page is sent to the browser. This is a result of the server translating and compiling the page at request time. After the page has been translated and compiled, subsequent requests to the page are processed more quickly.

The Servlet API

When a page is translated, whether at request time, or earlier, it is translated into a Java source file. This Java class is known as a **servlet**. You may have noticed the term "servlet" earlier in the chapter. Much of what a JSP does is based on the Servlet API, another API within J2EE. In fact, the Servlet API predates the JSP API.

Servlets were developed to allow a server's capabilities to be extended by Java code that ran inside the server. `HttpServlets` are servlets that run inside an HTTP server. A servlet accepts HTTP requests from clients, and creates dynamic responses to those requests. It sends response data to the client through an `OutputStream`. The servlet uses a `session` object to store data about a client and the client's interactions with the server. The servlet has access to the application through a `ServletContext` object, and it can access servlet parameters through a `ServletConfig` object. In fact, all the features of JSP pages that we will see in this chapter are based on the servlet model.

The JSP API

So, if servlets can do everything JSP pages can do, why do we need JSP?

If a JSP page is an HTML page with bits of embedded code, a servlet is Java code with bits of HTML. However, the larger the web application, the more HTML tends to be in the Java code. This becomes very hard to maintain, especially if your team has web experts who are not programmers.

Servlets tend to be good at computations and processing, while JSP pages tend to be good at data presentation. If only there were a way to get all the HTML out of servlets, and all the Java code out of JSP pages. That way, programmers could work on the servlets, and web designers could develop the JSP pages. In the next chapter, we will see one way to move the code out of JSP pages.

So, although you don't need to be a servlet expert to work with JSP, if you know how servlets work it can help to understand what is happening with the page. We'll look at servlets in detail in Chapter 5.

A Translated JSP

Let's take a quick look at a translated JSP to see how the JSP page is translated into code that implements a Java servlet. Most servers will keep the translated .java source file in the file system, so you can examine it if you need to. For J2EE, that location is *J2EE_HOME*\web\repository\Standard-Engine\localhost*application_context* where *J2EE_HOME* is the appropriate location of the J2EE installation on your system. For Tomcat standalone, that location is *TOMCAT_HOME*\work\Standalone\localhost*application_context*, where *TOMCAT_HOME* is the appropriate location of the Tomcat installation on your system. If you have deployed the examples in this chapter, navigate to the appropriate directory and open the source file for the welcome.jsp page. We will not look at every line in the file, but only some of the lines that show the relation between the JSP source and the Java source. For this section, I looked at the welcome_jsp.java source file created by Tomcat 5.0 for the last *Try It Out* example. Your Java source file may differ, depending on which server you have and which source file you are looking at.

One of the first things you will notice is that the import attribute of the page directive has been turned into import statements:

```
import java.util.Iterator;
import ch3.*;
```

This is followed by the class statement:

```
public final class welcome_jsp
    extends org.apache.jasper.runtime.HttpJspBase
    implements javax.servlet.jsp.el.FunctionMapper,
            org.apache.jasper.runtime.JspSourceDependent {
```

Notice that the class extends HttpJspBase. In the servlet chapter, we will see that servlets in a web application extend HttpServlet.

Next, you will see that the two declarations in the JSP page have been turned into a variable declaration and a public method declaration in the Java source. Note that the variable is declared as a member variable of the class, and so is accessible from all the methods in the class:

```
FaqCategories faqs = new FaqCategories();

public String replaceUnderscore(String s) {
  return s.replace(' ','_');
}
```

The main body of the JSP is contained in the _jspService() method as shown here. In the Servlet API, the analogous method is service(). This method starts by declaring the implicit objects that are used when servicing a request. Of course, they are not so implicit now that the translator has added the code to declare and initialize them:

```
public void _jspService(HttpServletRequest request,
                        HttpServletResponse response)
            throws java.io.IOException, ServletException {

    JspFactory _jspxFactory = null;
    javax.servlet.jsp.PageContext pageContext = null;
    HttpSession session = null;
    ServletContext application = null;
    ServletConfig config = null;
    JspWriter out = null;
    Object page = this;
    JspWriter _jspx_out = null;
```

Following the code above is code that initializes all the implicit objects. Although we will not explicitly look at all the code in this chapter, I do want to show one last snippet from the _jspService() method:

```
out.write("<body>\n      ");
out.write("<h1>Java FAQ Welcome Page");
out.write("</h1>\n\n");

User user = (User) session.getAttribute("user");
if (user == null) {
    out.write("\n    You are not yet registered, please \n    ");
    out.write("<a href=\"registrationform.html\">register");
    out.write("</a>.\n");
```

This is part of the code that outputs the template data to the client. Notice that the translated code uses the same implicit out object that the JSP can use. Also, notice that the whitespace from the JSP source file is preserved in the Java source file. A servlet implementing the same page would similarly output the HTML template data using print statements. However, with a servlet, you would need to code those statements manually. With a JSP page, it is much easier to write the template data as HTML, and let the container perform the translation to Java code.

Earlier in the chapter, I stated that you could declare and define a jspInit() method and a jspDestroy() method. If you define those methods in the JSP, they will appear as additional methods in the Java source file.

Errors and Exceptions

If you've typed in any of the examples in this chapter, or if you have created any JSP pages of your own, you have probably run into the situation where you've had bugs in your page. Whether these bugs occur at translation time or at request time affects the response that you see in the browser when you attempt to test your page. Sometimes you see a very ugly stack trace. Well, maybe not ugly to you, as the developer, but you don't want any of the users of your application to see anything so unfriendly.

Java web applications can deal with exceptions in a number of ways. Obviously, some exceptions can be handled as you develop the web application by adding data validation and try-catch blocks into the code. This technique avoids the exceptions. However, you need a way to deal with unexpected exceptions. Two ways to deal with unexpected exceptions are through:

❑ The page directive
❑ The deployment descriptor

The page Directive

We have already seen how to include a page directive in your JSP page. The page directive can have an attribute named errorPage. Whenever an uncaught exception occurs in that particular page, the server sends the specified error page to the client. This allows you to use different error pages for different components in the application. The errorPage attribute looks like this:

```
<%@ page errorPage="/WEB-INF/errorPage.jsp" %>
```

where the value of the errorPage attribute is the path to the error page file. The drawback is, of course, that you can only specify a single error page for all exceptions in the JSP page.

The Deployment Descriptor

The deployment descriptor allows you to specify application-wide error handlers for errors in the application. This provides a way to specify different error pages for exceptions that might occur within a single page. If a given exception or HTML error occurs anywhere in the application, the deployment descriptor identifies an error page that can be served to the client. Of course, a specific error page identified in a JSP page takes precedence over the error page identified in the deployment descriptor.

You can specify error pages for Java exceptions, and error pages for HTML errors. Error page elements come immediately after the <welcome-file-list> element in the deployment descriptor.

To specify an error page for a Java exception, use this element in the deployment descriptor:

```
<error-page>
  <exception-type>java.lang.NumberFormatException</exception-type>
  <location>/WEB-INF/BadNumber.html</location>
</error-page>
```

To specify an error page for an HTML error, use this element:

```
<error-page>
  <error-code>404</error-code>
  <location>/WEB-INF/NoSuchPage.html</location>
</error-page>
```

A complete list of the HTML error codes can be found in the HTTP specification at http://www.w3.org/Protocols/rfc2616/rfc2616-sec10.html.

Try It Out   Exception Handling in JSP Pages

In this example, we will add error handling to the Java FAQ application.

1. The structure of the web application looks like this:

```
Ch03/
  welcome.jsp
  Dates_and_Times.jsp
  registration.jsp
  registrationform.html
  Threading.jsp
  WEB-INF/
    footer.jspf
    errorPage.jsp
    web.xml
    BadNumber.html
    NoSuchPage.html
    classes/
      Ch03/
        FaqCategories.java
        FaqCategories.class
        User.java
        User.class
```

2. Add this page to the JavaFAQ application. This page is Threading.jsp, and it is located in the root directory of the application (the same directory in which welcome.jsp is located):

```
<%@ page errorPage="/WEB-INF/errorPage.jsp" %>

<!DOCTYPE HTML PUBLIC "-//W3C//DTD HTML 4.01 Transitional//EN">
<html>
  <head><title>Threading FAQs</title></head>
  <body>
<% Integer i = new Integer("string"); %>
  </body>
</html>
```

3. Modify `errorPage.jsp` as shown here:

```
<%@ page isErrorPage="true" import="java.io.PrintWriter" %>

<!DOCTYPE HTML PUBLIC "-//W3C//DTD HTML 4.01 Transitional//EN">
<html>
  <head>
    <title>Error</title>
  </head>
  <body>
    <h1>Error</h1>
    There was an error somewhere.
    <p>Here is the stack trace
    <p><% exception.printStackTrace(new PrintWriter(out)); %>
<%@ include file="/WEB-INF/footer.jspf" %>
  </body>
</html>
```

4. Create the JSP `Dates_and_Times.jsp` in the root directory:

```
<!DOCTYPE HTML PUBLIC "-//W3C//DTD HTML 4.01 Transitional//EN">
<html>
  <head>
    <title>Dates and Times FAQ</title>
  </head>

  <body>
    <h1>Dates and Times FAQ</h1>
<% Integer i = new Integer("string"); %>
<%@ include file="/WEB-INF/footer.jspf"%>
  </body>
</html>
```

5. Create two HTML pages that will be used as error pages. The first is `NoSuchPage.html`, and it is located in the **WEB-INF** directory:

```
<!DOCTYPE HTML PUBLIC "-//W3C//DTD HTML 4.01 Transitional//EN">
<html>
  <head>
```

```
      <title>Resource Not Found</title>
  </head>

  <body>
    <h1>Resource Not Found</h1>
    You are attempting to go to a page that does not exist
    or is not available. If you entered the address by hand,
    please go to the <a href="welcome.jsp">Welcome Page</a>.

    <p>If you clicked on a link on this site, the page is
       temporarily unavailable. Try again later.
<%@ include file="/WEB-INF/footer.jspf"%>
  </body>
</html>
```

6. The second error page is `BadNumber.html`. It too is located in the **WEB-INF** directory:

```
<!DOCTYPE HTML PUBLIC "-//W3C//DTD HTML 4.01 Transitional//EN">
<html>
  <head>
    <title>Invalid Number</title>
  </head>

  <body>
    <h1>Invalid Number</h1>
    You entered a number that is incorrect.
    Only digits are allowed. Please press the
    back button and try again.
<%@ include file="/WEB-INF/footer.jspf"%>
  </body>
</html>
```

7. Modify the deployment descriptor. If you are using J2EE, go to step 8. If you are using Tomcat, edit the `web.xml` file as shown here:

```
<?xml version="1.0" encoding="ISO-8859-1"?>

<!DOCTYPE web-app
    PUBLIC "-//Sun Microsystems, Inc.//DTD Web Application 2.3//EN"
    "http://java.sun.com/dtd/web-app_2_3.dtd">

<web-app>

  <!-- this is the deployment descriptor for Chapter 3
       Try It Out example 3                            -->

  <welcome-file-list>
    <welcome-file>welcome.jsp</welcome-file>
  </welcome-file-list>
```

```
<error-page>
  <exception-type>java.lang.NumberFormatException</exception-type>
  <location>/WEB-INF/BadNumber.html</location>
</error-page>

<error-page>
  <error-code>404</error-code>
  <location>/WEB-INF/NoSuchPage.html</location>
</error-page>

</web-app>
```

8. If you are using the J2EE Deploytool, modify the **File Refs** tab for the **WebApp** as shown below. You need to add two entries to the **Error Mapping** list. Add the same mappings that are shown in the web.xml file in step 4:

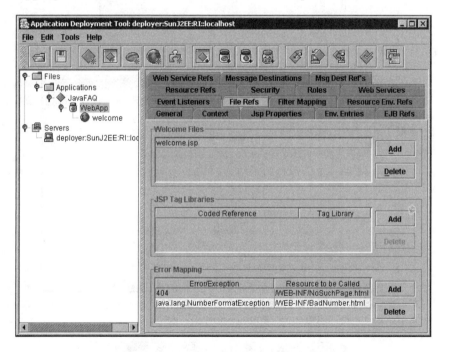

9. Deploy the application.

10. Open a browser and navigate through the screens until you reach the topic list page as shown below:

11. Click the link for Threading. The browser should look something like this:

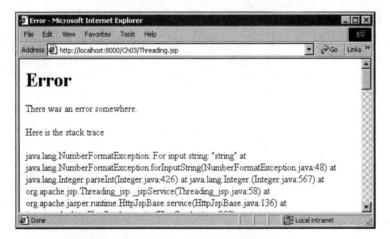

12. Click the link for Dates and Times. You will see this:

13. Click the link for **Strings and StringBuffers**. You will see this:

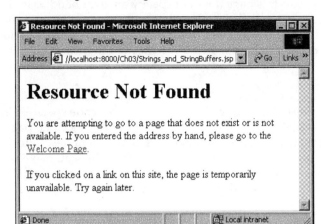

How It Works

We've added three pages to the application, each of which causes a different error-handling mechanism to control the page flow.

The `Threading.jsp` page included a `page` directive that specified the error page. Since `Threading.jsp` attempts to create an `Integer` object with an invalid argument to the constructor, an exception is thrown, and the page does not have an error handler to catch the exception. This causes the server to call the error page specified by the `page` directive, and that page is sent to the client.

The error page, `errorPage.jsp`, has access to the implicit `exception` object. This is because the page includes the `page` directive with the `isErrorPage` attribute set to `true`. Pages that don't have this attribute do not have access to the `exception` object. We can use this object together with the implicit `out` object to print out the stack trace to the response like this:

```
<p><% exception.printStackTrace(new PrintWriter(out)); %>
```

This works because the `java.lang.Throwable` interface defines a `printStackTrace(PrintWriter)` method. The `PrintWriter` constructor can take an `OutputStream` instance, which is exactly the type of the implicit `out` object. The method prints the stack trace to the given `PrintWriter`. (Keep in mind that you wouldn't print a stack trace in a live page meant for a user of the application. It provides no useful information for users, and just gives them a bad feeling about your application. The example above is used to show that you can access the implicit `exception` object in an error page.)

The Date_and_Times.jsp also uses an Integer object to cause an exception to be thrown from the page. However, this page does not specify an error handler in the page directive. In this case, the server matches the exception thrown to an exception specified in an <error-page> element in the deployment descriptor. The server sends the BadNumber.html page to the client. If the exception did not match a specification in the deployment descriptor, the server would probably have sent an HTTP 500 error to the client.

Finally, the Strings_and_StringBuffer.jsp page does not exist. This creates an HTTP 404 error in the server. Since this error code matches an error code specified in an <error-page> element in the deployment descriptor, the server sends the specified page to the client. If the error code had not matched a specification in the deployment descriptor, the server would have taken some server-specific action. Some servers, such as Tomcat, may send a server-specific page back to the client with the error; other servers might simply send the error code to the browser and let the browser decide how to display the error to the user.

Including and Forwarding from JSP Pages

JSP pages have the ability to include other JSP pages or servlets in the output that is sent to a client, or to forward the request to another page or servlet for servicing. This is accomplished through the standard actions <jsp:include> and <jsp:forward>.

include Action

Including a JSP page or servlet through a standard action differs from the include directive in the time at which the other resource is included, and how the other resource is included. Recall that an include directive can be used in either of the two formats below, anywhere within the JSP:

```
<%@ include file="/WEB-INF/footer.jspf">
<jsp:directive.include file="/WEB-INF/footer.jspf"/>
```

When the JSP container translates the page, this directive causes the indicated page to be included in that place in the page, and become part of the Java source file that is compiled into the JSP page implementation class. That is, it is included at translation time. Using the include directive, the included file does not need to be a complete and valid JSP.

With the include standard action, the JSP file stops processing the current request and passes the request to the included file. The included file passes its output to the response. Then control of the response returns to the calling JSP, which finishes processing the response. The output of the included page or servlet is included at request time. Components that are included via the include action must be valid JSP pages or servlets.

The included file is not allowed to modify the headers of the response, nor to set cookies in the response.

forward Action

With the `forward` action, the current page stops processing the request and forwards the request to another web component. This other component completes the response. Execution never returns to the calling page. Unlike the `include` action, which can occur at any time during a response, the `forward` action must occur prior to writing any output to the `OutputStream`. In other words, the `forward` action must occur prior to any HTML template data in the JSP, and prior to any scriptlets or expressions that write data to the `OutputStream`. If any output has occurred in the calling JSP, an exception will be thrown when the `forward` action is encountered.

Using include and forward

The format of the `include` action is:

```
<jsp:include page="URL" flush="true|false">
  <jsp:param name="paramName" value="paramValue"/>
</jsp:include>
```

For the `include` element, the `page` attribute is required, and its value is the URL of the page whose output is included in the response. The `flush` attribute is optional, and indicates whether the output buffer should be flushed before the included file is called. The default value is `false`.

If the JSP needs to pass parameters to the included file, it does so with the `<jsp:param>` element. One element is used for each parameter. This element is optional. If it is included, both the `name` and `value` attributes are required. The included JSP can access the parameters using the `getParameter()` and `getParameterValues()` methods of the `request` object.

The format of the `forward` element is similar:

```
<jsp:forward page="URL">
  <jsp:param name="paramName" value="paramValue"/>
</jsp:forward>
```

The meaning and use of the attributes and of the `<jsp:param>` element are the same as for the `include` action.

Try It Out	Including and Forwarding to JSP Pages

In this last example of the chapter, we will modify the `JavaFAQ` application to use `forward` actions to control the application flow. Here is the application structure:

```
Ch03/
  welcome.jsp
  Dates_and_Times.jsp
  registration.jsp
```

```
registrationform.html
Threading.jsp
WEB-INF/
  footer.jspf
  errorPage.jsp
  web.xml
  BadNumber.html
  NoSuchPage.html
  formatStackTrace.jsp
  classes/
    Ch03/
      FaqCategories.java
      FaqCategories.class
      User.java
      User.class
```

1. Start by modifying `welcome.jsp` as shown here:

```jsp
<%@ page errorPage="/WEB-INF/errorPage.jsp"
  import="java.util.Iterator,Ch03.*" %>
```

```jsp
<%
  User user = (User)session.getAttribute("user");
  String reqType = request.getParameter("reqType");
  if (user == null && reqType == null) {
%>
    <jsp:forward page="registrationform.html"/>
<%
  } else if (user == null && reqType != null) {
%>
    <jsp:forward page="registration.jsp">
        <jsp:param name="submitTime"
                   value="<%=(new java.util.Date()).toString()%>" />
    </jsp:forward>
<%
  }
%>

<!DOCTYPE HTML PUBLIC "-//W3C//DTD HTML 4.01 Transitional//EN">
<html>
  <head>
    <meta name="Cache-control" content="no-cache">
    <title>Java FAQ Welcome Page</title>
  </head>

  <body>
    <h1>Java FAQ Welcome Page</h1>
    Welcome to the Java FAQ
```

```jsp
<%! FaqCategories faqs = new FaqCategories(); %>
Click a link below for answers to the given topic.
```

```
<%
    Iterator categories = faqs.getAllCategories();
    while (categories.hasNext()) {
      String category = (String) categories.next();
%>
      <p><a href="<%= replaceUnderscore(category) %>.jsp">
        <%= category %></a></p>
<%
    }
%>

<%@ include file="/WEB-INF/footer.jspf" %>
  </body>
</html>

<%!
public String replaceUnderscore(String s) {
  return s.replace(' ','_');
}
%>
```

2. The next modified file is `registrationform.html`. Only the single line that contains the form tag needs to be modified as shown here:

```
<!DOCTYPE HTML PUBLIC "-//W3C//DTD HTML 4.01 Transitional//EN">
<html>
  <head>
    <title>Registration Page</title>
  </head>
  <body>
    <h1>Registration Page</h1>

    <form action="welcome.jsp?reqType=register" method="POST">
      <table>

<!-- The remainder of registrationform.html is the same as before,
    so it is not shown here -->
```

3. A single new line of code has been added to the `registration.jsp` file; only the applicable snippet is shown here:

```
<%    String[] topics = request.getParameterValues("topics");
      if (topics == null) { topics = new String[] {"No topics"}; }
      for (int i = 0; i < topics.length; i++) {
%>
        <br><%= topics[i] %>
<%
      }
%>
```

```
        <p>This request was submitted at
          <%= request.getParameter("submitTime") %>
      <p>Go to <a href="welcome.jsp">Topic List Page</a></p>
    <%@ include file="/WEB-INF/footer.jspf" %>
  </body>
</html>
```

4. This next file is `errorPage.jsp`. This file now has an `include` action in addition to the `include` directive for the standard footer:

```
<%@ page isErrorPage="true" import="java.io.PrintWriter" %>

<!DOCTYPE HTML PUBLIC "-//W3C//DTD HTML 4.01 Transitional//EN">
<html>
  <head>
    <title>Error</title>
  </head>
  <body>
    <h1>Error</h1>
    There was an error somewhere.
    <p>Here is the stack trace
    <p>
      <% request.setAttribute("ex", exception); %>
      <jsp:include page="formatStackTrace.jsp" />
<%@ include file="/WEB-INF/footer.jspf" %>
  </body>
</html>
```

5. The JSP page included by the `include` action in `errorPage.jsp` is shown here. It is named `formatStackTrace.jsp`:

```
<%@ page import="java.io.PrintWriter" %>
<%
  out.println("<pre>");
  Throwable t = (Throwable) request.getAttribute("ex");
  if (t != null) {
    t.printStackTrace(new PrintWriter(out));
  }
  out.println("</pre>");
%>
```

6. Create the web application with these new files, and the files developed in previous examples. Deploy the application to the J2EE server or the Tomcat stand-alone server. For the J2EE server, use the same web application settings as in the previous *Try It Out* example. For Tomcat, you can use the same deployment descriptor as in the previous *Try It Out* example.

7. Open a browser and enter the appropriate address for the `welcome.jsp` page. The browser will display the registration form page.

8. Enter the appropriate parameters, and click the **Submit** button. The browser will display the registration page.

9. Click the link in the registration page, and the browser will display the welcome page with the topic list. If the topic list is not displayed, your browser has probably cached the welcome page. Click the refresh button to get the correct page.

10. Click the **Threading** topic link. The browser will display the **errorPage.jsp** with a nicely formatted stack trace:

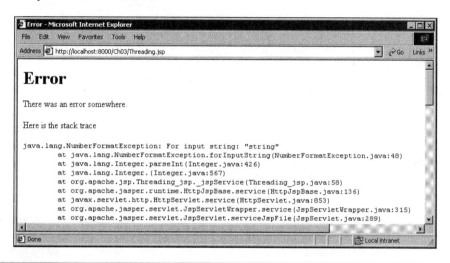

How It Works

The first thing the `welcome.jsp` does now is to check for the existence of the `user` object, as previously, and for a request parameter with the name `reqType`. As before, the `user` object is put into the session by the `registration.jsp`; the `reqType` parameter will be added to the request by the `registrationform.html` page. If both of these are `null`, neither the `registrationform.html` nor `registration.jsp` pages has been called, so the `welcome.jsp` forwards the request to the `registrationform.html` page:

```
<%
  User user = (User)session.getAttribute("user");
  String reqType = request.getParameter("reqType");
  if (user == null && reqType == null) {
%>
    <jsp:forward page="registrationform.html"/>
```

If you look at the registrationform.html, you will see that the action attribute of the <form> tag has been modified to add a request parameter to the URL. When the Submit button is clicked, the form submits to welcome.jsp. This method of submitting request parameters in the URL is known as URL encoding. This time, welcome.jsp finds that the user object is still null, but that the reqType has a value. Since this indicates that the registrationform.html page has been visited, but the registration has not been submitted, welcome.jsp forwards the request to registration.jsp; it includes another request parameter with the request using the <jsp:param> element:

```
<%
  } else if (user == null && reqType != null) {
%>
    <jsp:forward page="registration.jsp">
        <jsp:param name="submitTime"
                   value="<%=(new java.util.Date()).toString()%>" />
    </jsp:forward>
<%
  }
%>
```

This flow is artificially complicated, because it probably makes more sense to have
registrationform.html submit directly to registration.jsp. The main
reason for submitting to welcome.jsp is to provide several different examples of the
use of the <jsp:forward> action. However, there is a little justification for having all
requests go through the welcome.jsp page: this is a very simple example of something
known as a Model 2, or Model View Controller, architecture. With a Model 2
architecture, one component acts as a controller, directing the requests to the component
that is set up to handle a particular request. We will look at the Model 2 architecture in
more detail in the Chapter 5.

The registration.jsp page performs the same actions as in previous examples, with the addition of reading the new request parameter added by welcome.jsp, and displaying the value of that parameter. When the user clicks the link, the request is again sent to welcome.jsp. This final time, both user and reqType are not null, so welcome.jsp does not forward the request, but completes the response itself.

Clicking the **Threading** topic link again calls Threading.jsp, which still causes a NumberFormatException. This time, however, errorPage.jsp includes formatStackTrace.jsp. The formatStackTrace.jsp outputs the stack trace as older versions of errorPage.jsp did, but it wraps it in a <pre> tag, so that the stack trace is nicely formatted.

Summary

In this chapter, we've taken a tour of many of the basic features of JSP pages. With the information in this chapter, you should be able to easily begin creating JSP web applications of your own. After completing this chapter you should have learned:

- ❏ JSP pages consist of HTML data, also known as template data, and Java code.

- ❏ You can specify an error page for a JSP using `<%@page errorPage="" %>`. Error pages are used to provide a meaningful error page to a user when something bad happens to the web application.

- ❏ You can import Java packages for the page using `<% page import="" %>`.

- ❏ Java code is included in the page using a declaration `<%! declaration %>`, a scriptlet `<% scriptlet %>`, or an expression `<%= expression %>`. These elements allow you to mix Java code with the template data in the page.

- ❏ JavaBean instances can be created using the `<jsp:useBean>` standard action; properties of the bean can be set using `<jsp:setProperty>`; and the value of a bean's properties can be obtained using `<jsp:getProperty>`. JavaBeans are one way to encapsulate business or domain logic so that JSP pages can be used primarily for presentation.

- ❏ Various implicit objects such as `request`, `response`, `out`, `session`, and so on, are always available to the JSP to help process a request. The `session` object is particularly useful because it enables the web application to keep track of user information. One example of the usefulness of this is an e-commerce application that needs to keep track of a user's shopping cart.

- ❏ Servers translate and compile JSPs into Java classes that behave like servlets.

- ❏ You can specify error handlers for the entire application using the `<error-page>` element in the deployment descriptor.

- ❏ A JSP can include the output of other JSPs or servlets in the response to clients. This is done through the `<jsp:include>` standard action.

- ❏ A JSP can forward a request to another JSP or servlet for processing. This is done through the `<jsp:forward>` standard action.

That's quite a lot. All these features put together allow application developers to create dynamic and powerful web applications that can be used for many purposes from chat rooms to e-commerce, from virtual communities to business applications. However, you may have noticed that as the examples in this chapter became more dynamic, more featured, they also tended to have more and more Java code interspersed in the JSP pages. This tends to be a problem because web page developers are often not Java developers.

What would be ideal is a way to create JSP pages that hide the Java code from the page developers. This would allow the page developer to concentrate on the format and structure of the markup, and leave Java developers free to work on only the Java code. There are several ways to do this, and we will see some of them in the next chapter, where we explore some of the new JSP features introduced in the latest version of the JSP specification.

Exercises

1. Declare an init and a destroy method in a JSP. Include some debug output so that you can see when these methods are called. Deploy the JSP and determine when these methods are called. (You may not see the output from the destroy method.)

2. Write additional JSP pages for the `JavaFAQ` application that allow a user to submit a question, and answer a question.

3. Create a JSP web application that presents a quiz to the user. Use a JSP page to present each question one at a time to the user. Use the same page to accept the answer submitted by the user. (That is, the HTML created by the page should submit the answer to the same `.jsp` page.) The page should determine whether the answer is correct or not, compute the current score of the user, and select a graphic that illustrates the current status, and select the next question; this is all put into the response back to the client.

CHAPTER 4

Expression Language   **124**

Custom Actions and Tag Libraries   **139**

JavaServer Pages Standard Tag Library (JSTL)   **166**

Other Tag Libraries   **175**

Summary   **176**

Exercises   **176**

Advanced JSP Topics

The previous chapter introduced you to JSPs and provided enough information to enable you to begin writing and using those web components. However, the previous chapter only scratched the surface of what can be done with JSP.

In this chapter, we'll stretch our JSP wings a little further and explore some more advanced topics. Some of the material in this chapter has been in use for a while as part of earlier JSP specifications. Other material, though, comes from the JSP 2.0 specification, and so is quite new. For the examples in this chapter that rely on new JSP 2.0 features, you will need to use a server that supports JSP 2.0, such as J2EE 1.4 or Tomcat 5.0.

We won't cover every aspect of JSP, because that would take up a whole book in itself, and would mean going into details that you'll probably never need to know. Instead, we'll focus on learning some of the new or advanced features that will help you the most when writing real-world JSP pages.

The topics we'll look at in this chapter are:

- ❑ **Expression language** – Expression language was developed as a way to simplify expressions in a JSP. It provides a way to use run-time expressions outside JSP scripting elements. Expression language is a new feature of JSP 2.0.

- ❑ **Custom actions** – Standard actions were introduced in the previous chapter. Standard actions provide a way to encapsulate Java code so that the page designer only has to know the syntax of the tag. JSP provides a way for Java developers to create their own actions, known as **custom actions** or **tag extensions**. We'll look at both **classic** and **simple** custom actions and how to use them in JSPs. Classic tag extensions are from JSP 1.2 and prior; Simple tag extensions are a part of JSP 2.0.

- ❑ **JSTL** – To avoid multiple developers creating conflicting tag libraries for basic actions, the **JSP Standard Tag Library** specification was developed. It doesn't stop multiple developers creating the same tag extensions, but if they follow the specification, at least the libraries will work the same. The JSTL is compatible with JSP 1.2. We'll look at what it is and how to use it in your JSPs.

Expression Language

In the previous chapter, we saw how we can create scripting elements that can be used to embed Java code in the JSP file. Scripting elements included JSP tags for declarations, scriptlets, and expressions:

```
<%! int a = 5; %> <%-- declaration --%>
<% while (x < 10) { out.write("x=" + x); } %> <%-- scriptlet --%>
<%= user.getFirstName() %> <%-- expression --%>
```

JSP 2.0 adds **Expression Language** (EL) statements to the JSP toolkit. Expression language statements provide a somewhat simpler syntax for performing some of the same actions as the JSP elements above. Further, you can use EL expressions in scriptless JSP pages. Scriptless JSP pages are those pages that, for whatever reason, are not allowed to use JSP declarations, scriptlets, or scripting expressions.

You can, of course, write any JSP page without using any declarations, scriptlets, or expressions. We saw an example of one such page at the beginning of the previous chapter: `HelloWorld.jsp`. That page was scriptless by choice. You can also force a page to be scriptless. One reason for doing this is to enforce a separation between display elements and business logic. By enforcing scriptless pages, the dynamic behavior of JSP pages must be provided through other elements such as JavaBeans (see the previous chapter), EL expressions, custom actions, and standard tag libraries (we will see custom actions and standard tag libraries later in this chapter). By encapsulating business logic in JavaBeans and custom actions, the page designers do not need to learn any Java code. Whether or not your application should have scriptless JSP pages is a decision you must make based on the requirements and needs of your application.

There are two ways to ensure a page doesn't contain any scripting elements: through a `page` directive, or through an element of the deployment descriptor. You can also specify whether EL expressions are allowed or not through the same two mechanisms. The `page` directive looks like this:

```
<%@ page isScriptingEnabled="true|false" isELEnabled="true|false" %>
```

The default for `isScriptingEnabled` is `true`. The container sets the default `isELEnabled` value to `true` for JSP 2.0; `false` for JSP 1.2 or earlier. The container determines the JSP version based on the deployment descriptor. Descriptors that have a `DOCTYPE` declaration that includes `"web-app_2_3.dtd"` imply JSP 1.2. Descriptors with a `web-app` attribute of `version="2.4"` are JSP 2.0.

Under JSP 2.0 you can also specify JSP configuration information in the deployment descriptor. Where the `page` directive applies to a single page, the deployment descriptor can apply to whole sets of pages. For example:

```
<web-app xmlns="http://java.sun.com/xml/ns/j2ee"
    xmlns:xsi="http://www.w3.org/2001/XMLSchema-instance"
    xsi:schemaLocation="http://java.sun.com/xml/ns/j2ee/web-app_2_4.xsd"
    version="2.4">

  <welcome-file-list>
    <welcome-file>TopicList.jsp</welcome-file>
  </welcome-file-list>

  <jsp-config>
    <jsp-property-group>
      <url-pattern>*.jsp</url-pattern>
      <el-enabled>true</el-enabled>
      <scripting-enabled>true</scripting-enabled>
    </jsp-property-group>
  </jsp-config>
</web-app>
```

Within the `<web-app>` element of the deployment descriptor, the `<jsp-config>` element supplies configuration information for the JSP pages in a web application. This element only applies in a deployment descriptor where the `web-app` version is 2.4.

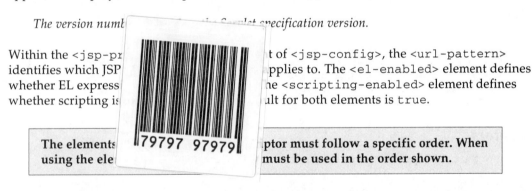

The version numb_____ _____ specification version.

Within the `<jsp-pr`_____ t of `<jsp-config>`, the `<url-pattern>` identifies which JSP _____ pplies to. The `<el-enabled>` element defines whether EL express _____ he `<scripting-enabled>` element defines whether scripting is _____ lt for both elements is `true`.

The elements _____ ptor must follow a specific order. When using the ele _____ must be used in the order shown.

You can have multiple `<jsp-property-group>` elements within the `<jsp-config>` element. If a resource matches more than one group, the pattern that is most specific applies.

Syntax of EL

The basic syntax for an EL expression is:

```
${expr}
```

where *expr* is a valid expression. Valid expressions can include literals, operators, object references (variables), and function calls.

Literals

The EL syntax provides for a number of literal values that can be used in expressions. These literal values are:

- ❏ Boolean literals – `true`, `false`

- ❏ String literals – any string delimited by single or double quotes. The backslash is used as an escape character for quotes and backslashes. For, example, `'This string\'s value has an escaped single quote'` or `"the directory is c:\\My Documents\\wrox"`. You need to escape quotes only when they are enclosed by a quote of the same kind (in other words `'\''` or `"\""`). If double quotes had been used around the string example earlier in this paragraph, the single quote would not need to be escaped: `"This string's value has a single quote"`.

- ❏ Integer literals – any positive or negative integer number (`-13, 45, 2374`, and so on).

- ❏ Floating-point literals – any positive or negative floating-point number (`-1.3E-30`, `3.14159, 2.00000000000001, .45, .56e2`, etc.)

- ❏ Null literal – `null`

Here are some examples:

```
${true} <%-- evaluates to true --%>
${"Single quotes inside 'double quotes' do not need to be escaped"}
   <%-- evaluates to Single quotes inside 'double quotes'
         do not need to be escaped --%>
${2*4} <%-- evaluates to 8 --%>
```

Operators

Most of the usual operators available in Java are available in Expression Language:

Type	Operator
Arithmetic	`+, -, *, /,` div, `%,` mod
Relational	`==` and eq
	`!=` and ne
	`<` and lt
	`>` and gt
	`<=` and le
	`>=` and ge

Type	Operator
Logical	`&&` and `and`
	`||` and `or`
	`!` and `not`
Other	`()`, `empty`, `[]`, `.`

You should be familiar with most of the operators in the table above. In the next few paragraphs, we will look at the last four "other" operators in the list. However, note that many of the operators have both symbolic and word variants (such as `/` and `div`, or `<` and `lt`). These equivalents are provided so that if your JSP page needs to be XML-compliant, you can avoid using entity references (such as `&lt;` for `<`). Within an XML document, an EL expression for "less than" could be coded `${2 lt 3}` rather than `${2 < 3}`.

As with most expressions, the parentheses can be used to change the precedence of the expression:

```
${ (2 * 4) + 3 } <%-- evaluates to 11 --%>
${ 2 * (4 + 3) } <%-- evaluates to 14 --%>
```

The `empty` operator can be used to test for various conditions. An expression such as:

```
${empty name}
```

will return `true` if `name` references a `null` object or if `name` references an empty `String`, `List`, `Map`, or array. Otherwise `empty` returns `false`. The object referenced by `name` is an object stored in the `page`, `request`, `session`, or `application` implicit objects. For example:

```
<% Vector vec = new Vector();                // Create empty vector
pageContext.setAttribute("someName", vec); %> // Store vector in pageContext
${empty someName}   // Evaluates to true; notice the operator acts on the
                    // attribute name someName, not the variable name vec
```

Keep in mind that this works for any object in one of the contexts, not just objects you explicitly add using `setAttribute()` or some other method. For example, as we will see later, custom actions can create variables that are accessible through EL expressions. The `empty` operator can be applied to these variables. Another way to add objects to a context is by creating a JavaBean; JavaBeans are stored in a context based on the `scope` attribute of the `<jsp:useBean>` action. The point is that the empty operator can be applied to any object that can be referenced by name in one of the contexts.

The final two operators are the dot operator (`.`) and the operator `[]`. These are used to access the attributes of an object in the page. The left-value (`lvalue`) of the operator is interpreted to be an object in the page; the right-value (`rvalue`) is a property, key, or index. For example, if you have defined a bean in the page using the `<jsp:useBean>` standard action, you can access the properties of the bean using either notation. Given a bean with the properties `firstName` and `surname`, you could access its properties using either notation like this:

```
${user.firstName}
${user[surname]}
```

The two notations are equivalent when accessing the properties of an object in the page. Either expression above results in the page attempting to find the given object in the page and call the `getXXX()` method for the given property.

The two operators can also be used for `Maps`, `Lists`, or arrays. When either operator is applied to a `Map` (such as `Hashtable` or `HashMap`) the page class attempts to access the `Map` attribute with the key given by the `rvalue`. That is, given:

```
${myObject[name]} <%-- myObject is a Hashtable or HashMap --%>
```

the equivalent code statement is:

```
myObject.get("name");
```

If the operator is applied to a `List` or array, the page attempts to convert the `rvalue` into an index and access the value using:

```
myObject.get(name);         // myObject is a List
Array.get(myObject, name);  // myObject is an array
```

When `myObject` is an object that implements `List`, the page class uses the `get(int)` method of `List` to get the value of the expression. When `myObject` references an array, the `get(Object, int)` method of `Array` is used.

Implicit Objects

EL expressions also have implicit objects available to them. Many of these implicit objects are the same implicit objects that are available in JSP scriptlets and expressions. Through the implicit objects, the EL expression can perform many of the actions that can be performed through scriptlets and JSP expressions. In the *Try It Out* section, we will see examples of how to use some of these objects. The implicit objects are:

❑ pageContext – the `javax.servlet.jsp.PageContext` object for the page. Can be used to access the JSP implicit objects such as `request`, `response`, `session`, `out`, etc. For example, `${pageContext.request}` evaluates to the `request` object for the page.

❏ pageScope – a `Map` that maps page-scoped attribute names to their values. In other words, given an object, such as a bean, that has page scope in the JSP, an EL expression can access the object with `${pageScope.`*objectName*`}` and an attribute of the object can be accessed using `${pageScope.`*objectName*`.`*attributeName*`}`. In this code snippet, the bean has been given `page` scope, and it has a property named `topic`:

```
<jsp:useBean id="questions" scope="page" class="Ch04.Questions">
  <jsp:setProperty name="questions" property="topic"/>
</jsp:useBean>
${pageScope.questions.topic} <%-- Evaluates to the topic property of the
                                bean referenced by the id 'questions' --%>
```

❏ requestScope – a `Map` that maps request-scoped attribute names to their values. This object allows you to access the attributes of the `request` object.

❏ sessionScope – a `Map` that maps session-scoped attribute names to their values. This object is used to access the session objects for the client. For example, if you've added an object to the session, you can access it as shown here:

```
<% session.put("address", "123 Maple St."); %>
${sessionScope.address}          <%-- evaluates to 123 maple St. --%>
<%= session.get("address"); %>   <%-- equivalent scripting expression --%>
```

❏ applicationScope – a `Map` that maps application-scoped attribute names to their values. Use this object to access objects with application scope.

❏ param – a `Map` that maps parameter names to a single `String` parameter value (obtained by calling `ServletRequest.getParameter(String name)`). Recall that a `request` object contains data sent by the client. The `getParameter(String)` method returns the parameter with the given name. The expression `${param.`*name*`}` is equivalent to `request.getParameter(`*name*`)`. (Note that *name* is not the literal string `'name'`, but the name of the parameter.)

❏ paramValues – a `Map` that maps parameter names to a `String[]` of all values for that parameter (obtained by calling `ServletRequest.getParameterValues(String name)`). Similar to the previous implicit object, but it retrieves a `String` array rather than a single value. For example, the expression `${paramValues.`*name*`}` is equivalent to `request.getParameterValues(`*name*`)`.

❏ header – a `Map` that maps header names to a single `String` header value (obtained by calling `ServletRequest.getHeader(String name)`). Requests always contain header information such as the content type and length, cookies, the referring URL, and so on. The expression `${header.`*name*`}` is equivalent to `request.getHeader(`*name*`)`.

❏ headerValues – a `Map` that maps header names to a `String[]` of all values for that header (obtained by calling `ServletRequest.getHeaders(String)`). Similar to the `header` implicit object. The expression `${headerValues.`*name*`}` is equivalent to `request.getHeaderValues(`*name*`)`.

❑   cookie – a Map that maps cookie names to a single Cookie object. A client can send one or more cookies to the server with a request. The expression ${cookie.*name*.*value*} returns the value of the first cookie with the given name. If the request contains multiple cookies with the same name, you should use ${headerValues.*name*}.

❑   initParam – a Map that maps context initialization parameter names to their String parameter value (obtained by calling ServletContext.getInitParameter(String name)). To access an initialization parameter, use ${initParam.*name*}.

Using EL Expressions

EL expressions can be used as attribute values in standard and custom actions. They can also be used anywhere there is template text (such as HTML or non-JSP elements) in the JSP file.

This next code snippet shows the use of an EL expression in the attribute value of the <jsp:forward> standard action:

```
<jsp:forward page="${param.nextPage}" />
```

In this example, the <jsp:forward> action will forward the request to the URL specified by the request parameter named nextPage. If the request parameter does not exist, or if its value is not a valid URL, an error will occur in the page.

Errors and Default Values

Because of their use in display-oriented JSP pages, EL expressions do not throw the same exceptions that you might expect from the equivalent Java expression. For example, given this expression:

```
${user.surname}
```

The analogous Java expression is:

```
user.getSurname();
```

Now, if you were writing this Java code manually, and you had not defined the user variable, or did not provide a getSurname() method, the compiler would warn you of this situation. Before the code was ever executed, you would be able to correct the problem. If you did not initialize the variable user at run-time, the code would throw a NullPointerException.

However, in a JSP page, many of these requirements cannot be checked until run-time. Since the JSP page is usually used for presentation, many EL expressions result in **default values** rather than thrown exceptions. For example, in the expression above, if `user` is `null`, the value of the EL expression is `null`. With many of the operators, if either the `lvalue` or the `rvalue` is `null`, the default value of the expression is `null` (rather than a thrown exception). You should consult the JSP specification for the full list of default values. When an EL expression does result in an exception, the exception is handled via the normal JSP exception-handling mechanisms.

Try It Out	Using EL Expressions

In this example, we'll create a few JSPs that use EL expressions. Note that you must deploy this example to a server that supports JSP 2.0. If you are trying this example with J2EE or Tomcat, you will need to use J2EE 1.4 or Tomcat 5.0. Here is the directory structure of the application:

```
Ch04/
    TopicList.jsp
    Questions.jsp
    WEB-INF/
        web.xml
        EL_1.jsp
        classes/
            Ch04/
                Questions.java
```

We will be creating the files `TopicList.jsp`, `Questions.jsp`, `EL_1.jsp`, and `Questions.java`. If you are deploying to Tomcat, you will also need to create a `web.xml` deployment descriptor. The basic flow of the application is shown below. In fact, we will use this same flow for several examples in this chapter:

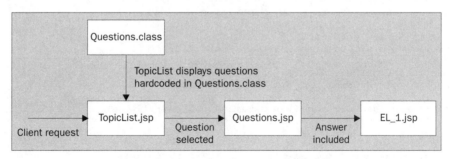

1. Although this example builds on the Java FAQ example application from the previous chapter, you will not need to use any of the files from previous examples. Since we're not using the `welcome.jsp` from the previous chapter, we need another entry point into this part of the Java FAQ application. That entry point is this file, `TopicList.jsp`:

```
<!DOCTYPE HTML PUBLIC "-//W3C//DTD HTML 4.01 Transitional//EN">
<html>
  <head><title>Topic Questions</title></head>
  <body>
    <h1>Topic Questions</h1>

    <jsp:useBean id="questions" class="Ch04.Questions">
      <jsp:setProperty name="questions" property="topic" />
    </jsp:useBean>

The number of questions in topic ${questions.topic} is ${questions.numTopics}
<%
  for (int i = 1; i <= questions.getNumTopics(); i++) {
    pageContext.setAttribute("count", ""+i);
%>
<p>Question <a href="Questions.jsp?qid=${questions.topic}_${count}">
    ${questions.topic}_${count}</a>:
    ${questions.questions[count]}
<%
  }
%>
  </body>
</html>
```

2. The `TopicList.jsp` above displays a list of questions for a given topic. These questions are hard-coded into the `Questions.java` class:

```
package Ch04;

import java.util.Map;
import java.util.HashMap;

public class Questions {
  private String topic;
  private int numTopics;
  private Map questions = new HashMap();

  public String getTopic() { return topic; }
  public void setTopic(String t) { topic = t; }

  public int getNumTopics() { return numTopics; }
  public void setNumTopics(int n) { numTopics = n; }

  public Map getQuestions() { return questions; }
  public void setQuestions(Map m) { questions = m; }

  public Questions() {
    questions.put("1", "How do I use implicit objects?");
    questions.put("2", "How do I use the JSTL?");
    questions.put("3", "How do I use the 'empty' operator?");
    setNumTopics(questions.size());
  }
}
```

3. Compile this file into `Questions.class`.

4. After displaying the list of questions, the user can click a link for a particular question. The request is posted to the `Questions.jsp` file, shown here (yes, this really is the whole file!):

```jsp
<jsp:include page="/WEB-INF/${param.qid}.jsp" />
```

5. As you can see, `Questions.jsp` simply includes the appropriate question file based on the user's selection. For this example, we will only create the JSP page for the first question. In a later example, we will see `EL_2.jsp`; `EL_3.jsp` will not be presented here, but it is included with the code download for this book at **www.wrox.com**. Here is `EL_1.jsp`:

```jsp
<!DOCTYPE HTML PUBLIC "-//W3C//DTD HTML 4.01 Transitional//EN">
<html>
  <head>
    <title>Expression Language Q1</title>
  </head>

  <body>
    <h1>Expression Language Question 1</h1>
    <h2>How do I use implicit objects?</h2>

    <p>The explicit objects are</p>
    <ul>
      <li>pageContext</li>
      <li>pageScope</li>
      <li>requestScope</li>
      <li>sessionScope</li>
      <li>applicationScope</li>
      <li>param</li>
      <li>paramValues</li>
      <li>header</li>
      <li>headerValues</li>
      <li>cookie</li>
      <li>initParam</li>
    </ul>

    <p>Implicit objects form the lvalue of an EL expression, and their
properties are accessed using the . or [] operator. Here are some
examples:</p>
<%-- The four lines after this comment contain special expression syntax
        needed to display a literal ${} in the output of a JSP. This is done
        by using an expression to evaluate the literal '${'. That is, the
        expression ${ '${' } evaluates to ${, and whatever follows the
        expression is treated as normal template text.              --%>
    <p>${'${'}pageContext.request.requestURI} evaluates to
      "${pageContext.request.requestURI}"</p>
    <p>${'${'}param.qid} evaluates to "${param.qid}"</p>
```

```
   <p>${'${'}header.referer} evaluates to "${header.referer}"</p>
   <p>${'${'}cookie.JSESSIONID.value} evaluates to
      ${cookie.JSESSIONID.value}</p>
 </body>
</html>
```

6. Finally, if you are deploying to Tomcat, or some other stand-alone JSP container, you will need a deployment descriptor. Here is a very simple web.xml file that will do the job:

```xml
<?xml version="1.0" encoding="ISO-8859-1"?>

<web-app xmlns="http://java.sun.com/xml/ns/j2ee"
    xmlns:xsi="http://www.w3.org/2001/XMLSchema-instance"
    xsi:schemaLocation="http://java.sun.com/xml/ns/j2ee web-app_2_4.xsd"
    version="2.4">

  <!-- This is the deployment descriptor for Chapter 4 -->

  <!-- Expression Language example, welcome file list  -->

  <welcome-file-list>
    <welcome-file>TopicList.jsp</welcome-file>
  </welcome-file-list>
</web-app>
```

7. If you are deploying to Tomcat 5.0, you can copy the entire directory structure into the Tomcat /**webapps** directory. Alternately, you can create a .war file and place that into /webapps. You create the .war file by navigating to the top-level directory of the application (/Ch04 in this example) and executing this command:

```
> jar cvf Ch04.war *
```

After deploying, go to step 15.

8. If you are deploying to J2EE, start the J2EE server. After the server has started, run the Deploytool.

9. Create a new Application EAR by selecting File | New | Application EAR from the menu. Enter a name for the EAR and click OK.

10. Create a new Web Application Archive in the EAR by selecting File | New | Web Application WAR from the menu.

11. Add the files TopicList.jsp, Questions.jsp, EL_1.jsp, and Questions.class to the WAR. Ensure you place the EL_1.jsp file into the /**WEB-INF** directory. Click Next. Select the JSP radio button, and click Next. At the screen that follows, select TopicList.jsp as the component to create. Click Finish.

12. In the main Deploytool window, select the application in the left pane, and select the Web Context tab in the right pane. Set the context root for the EAR to be Ch04.

13. Save the EAR file. Then select File | Deployment Settings | Create New File to create a new deployment settings file. Select File | Deployment Settings | Close File to close and save the settings file.

14. Deploy the application using Tools | Deploy from the menu.

15. After the application is deployed, open a web browser and enter the address http://localhost:8000/Ch04/TopicList.jsp?topic=EL (or, if you are using Tomcat standalone as the server, use port 8080)

16. Note that because this is an example, not all the links will work correctly. Additionally, you must enter the correct value for the topic (EL) for it to work correctly. When you enter the correct URL, you will see this display:

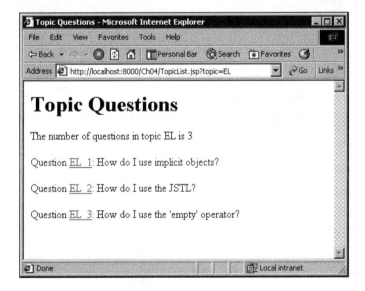

17. Click on the EL_1 link, and you will see this display:

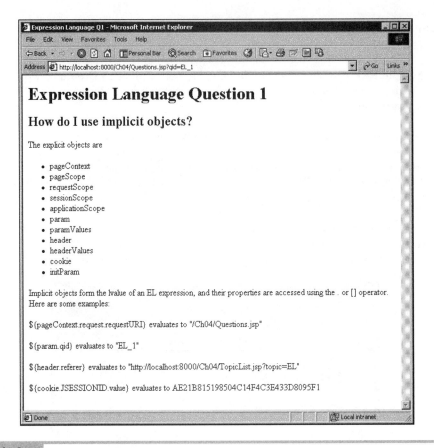

How It Works

Let's take a quick look at the deployment descriptor first. One big change between JSP 2.0 and previous JSP versions is that you no longer need the DOCTYPE declaration. If you use a DOCTYPE declaration that specifies version 2.2 or 2.3 of the DTD, as we did in the previous chapter, the container will not allow EL expressions or other JSP 2.0 features to be used. To activate JSP 2.0 support, you need to include the web-app attributes shown in the example here:

```
<web-app xmlns="http://java.sun.com/xml/ns/j2ee"
    xmlns:xsi="http://www.w3.org/2001/XMLSchema-instance"
    xsi:schemaLocation="http://java.sun.com/xml/ns/j2ee/web-app_2_4.xsd"
    version="2.4">
```

The questions that are displayed on the page for each topic are hard-coded into the Questions JavaBean. This class has a member called questions, of type Map, which is used to store the individual questions together with a name that holds the number for each question.

```
public class Questions {
  private String topic;
  private int numTopics;
  private Map questions = new HashMap();
```

This property has standard JavaBean setter and getter methods. This means that in an EL expression, we can access the property using the dot notation:

```
${questions.questions}
```

When the bean is instantiated, we add our questions to this Map, together with its name – a String literal that has an integer value:

```
questions.put("1", "How do I use implicit objects?");
questions.put("2", "How do I use the JSTL?");
questions.put("3", "How do I use the 'empty' operator?");
```

Since the property is actually a data structure that stores name-value pairs, we can access any particular value if we know the name.

TopicList.jsp is similar to the welcome.jsp page we used in the previous chapter. It begins by using the <jsp:useBean> standard action to create an object in the page:

```
<jsp:useBean id="questions" class="Ch04.Questions">
  <jsp:setProperty name="questions" property="topic" />
</jsp:useBean>
```

Because this object automatically has page context, we can reference it in an EL expression. That is the next thing the file does, accessing the topic and numTopics properties using this template data with EL expressions:

```
The number of questions in topic ${questions.topic} is ${questions.numTopics}
```

The EL expression references the bean using its id from the <jsp:useBean> action. It accesses the properties using the dot notation. The expression ${questions.topic} evaluates to the value of the topic property of the bean, which happens to be "EL". The expression ${questions.numTopics} evaluates to the value of the numTopics property, which is "3". Next, the page uses a scriptlet to perform a loop. Notice that each time through the loop, it stores the current index as a pageContext attribute using the name count. This allows another EL expression to access the current index using ${count}.

```
for (int i = 1; i <= questions.getNumTopics(); i++) {
  pageContext.setAttribute("count", ""+i);
%>
<p>Question <a href="Questions.jsp?qid=${questions.topic}_${count}">
  ${questions.topic}_${count}</a>:
```

Not only does the page access the value of count to create a link in the page, it uses count to access the value of the question stored by the Questions object:

```
${questions.questions[count]}
```

Since we can access any particular value if we know the name, we can retrieve a particular question held by the questions object like this:

```
<p>Question <a href="Questions.jsp?qid=${questions.topic}_${count}">
    ${questions.topic}_${count}</a>:
    ${questions.questions[count]}
```

Because the value of count is a String that has an integer value, the code ${questions.questions[count]} is equivalent to:

```
Map m = questions.getQuestions();
String q = (String)questions.get(count);
```

The value of the expression after evaluation is simply the question string stored by the class. This is output to the response.

When you click one of the links in the page created by TopicList.jsp, the request is sent to the Questions.jsp page. This is a very simple page consisting of a single standard action, the <jsp:include> action:

```
<jsp:include page="/WEB-INF/${param.qid}.jsp" />
```

Notice that this file has no template text in it. JSP files can consist solely of JSP elements and still be valid JSP pages. The include action uses an EL expression in the page attribute to determine which JSP page to include. It does this using the implicit param object and the name of the parameter that is being accessed. The TopicList.jsp page outputs a link that looks like this:

```
<a href="Questions.jsp?qid=EL_1">EL_1</a>
```

This link sends the request to the Questions.jsp file with a request parameter of qid=EL_1. The Questions.jsp page can access the value of that parameter with the EL expression:

```
${param.qid}
```

What we want to do is to use this value to include the answer to the selected question in the response to the user. In this case, the answer is found in a page called EL_1.jsp in the **WEB-INF** directory, so the page directive for our <jsp:include> action is set to "/WEB-INF/${param.qid}.jsp".

This answer page also uses EL expressions. One interesting thing to note is that the specification provides a way to have a literal ${expr} in the output of a page. This is done by placing the quoted expression '${' in an EL expression. The EL expression ${'${'} evaluates to ${ in the page, and the rest of the string is output without evaluation. For example, the line:

```
<p>${'${'}param.qid} evaluates to "${param.qid}"</p>
```

will generate the HTML:

```
<p>${param.qid} evaluates to "EL_1"</p>
```

The remainder of the page uses various EL expressions to show how to use some of the implicit objects available in an EL expression.

Custom Actions and Tag Libraries

Several times in the previous chapter, we talked about removing Java code from the JSP to further separate the display elements from the business logic. In reality, the Java code is not removed from the page, but it is hidden from the page developer. For example, in the previous chapter, we saw some standard actions defined by the JSP specification. Standard actions are actions that must be implemented by every JSP container. A standard action appears in a JSP page as an XML-style tag. Here is the tag for a useBean standard action with an enclosed setProperty action:

```
<jsp:useBean id="questions" class="Ch04.Questions">
  <jsp:setProperty name="questions" property="topic"/>
</jsp:useBean>
```

At the start of the tag is the namespace prefix, jsp (a namespace is analogous to a Java package). This is followed by the action name. The standard action can have attributes, and some actions have bodies between the start and end tag. Tag bodies can include other tags (as shown above) and/or template data. To anyone familiar with XML, this looks like a standard XML tag (but even though the tag looks like an XML tag, it is used in a JSP file, which does not have to be an XML document).

However, the JSP translator "sees" the tag a little differently. The translator sees the tag as a token that is to be replaced by Java code. This Java code implements the functionality specified by the tag. Thus, the Java code is not removed from the page, but it is "encapsulated" within the tag. For example, when the JSP translator for Tomcat 5.0 sees the tag above, it generates the code below:

```
questions = (Ch04.Questions)java.beans.Beans.instantiate(
              this.getClass().getClassLoader(), "ch04.Questions");
```

Now, if the only actions you had available were the standard actions, you would still need to use Java code embedded in your JSP. Fortunately, the JSP specification provides a way for developers to create their own actions. These actions are known as **custom actions**. Custom actions are deployed to the web application using a **tag library**. The mechanism for defining, implementing, deploying, and executing custom actions is known as **tag extension**. Using standard and custom actions, a web designer can build a dynamic web page without needing to know how to program in Java.

Custom Actions

When we use the term **custom action** (or standard action), we are generally referring to the tag in the JSP file. Custom actions, like standard actions, can be used just like any other tag in a JSP file. Custom actions are identified by a prefix and a name:

```
<prefix:name />
```

The prefix is used to avoid name collisions between tags with the same name. The *prefix* is selected and used by the page developer, although the tag developer can suggest a prefix, as we will see later. The *name* is the name of the action. This is specified by the tag developer.

Custom actions can be empty (they have no body):

```
<x:MyCustomAction />    <%-- Start and end tags combined into single tag --%>
<x:MyCustomAction></x:MyCustomAction>   <%-- Separate tags --%>
```

Or they can have bodies:

```
<x:MyCustomAction>
  Body content
</x:MyCustomAction>
```

The Java code that implements the tag can direct the page to evaluate the body or skip the body. Actions can be nested. Here is an example using the `<jsp:useBean>` and `<jsp:setProperty>` standard actions:

```
<jsp:useBean id="user" class="Ch03.User">
  <jsp:setProperty name="user" property="*"/>
</jsp:useBean>
```

Also, as shown with the `<jsp:useBean>` and `<jsp:setProperty>` actions, an action can have attributes that customize the action. Actions can access the implicit objects of JSPs (`request`, `response`, and so on), and use these objects to modify the response to the client. Objects can be created by a custom action, and these objects can be accessed by other actions or scriptlets in the JSP.

The actual behavior of a custom action is provided at run-time by an instance of a Java class. This Java class is also known as a **tag handler**.

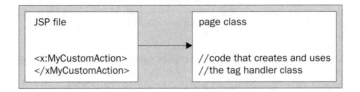

Tag Handlers

The tag handler is the Java class that implements the behavior of a custom action. The tag handler class follows the requirements of a JavaBean, and it will implement one of the tag extension interfaces. There are several tag handler interfaces available.

JSP 1.1 had two interfaces, `Tag` and `BodyTag`, for tag handlers. `Tag` handles a simple action with no iteration and no need to process the body of the tag; `BodyTag` is used when the body of the tag is processed (rather than simply output) as part of the action. JSP 1.2 introduced the `IterationTag` to deal with iteration (JSP 1.1 used `BodyTag` to handle iteration). These three interfaces – `Tag`, `IterationTag`, and `BodyTag` – are known as **classic tag handlers**. JSP 2.0 adds the `SimpleTag` interface to make tag handling easier, and the `JspFragment` interface to encapsulate the body content of a tag in an object. `SimpleTag` and `JspFragment` are known as **simple tag handlers**.

JSP Specification	Reference Implementation	JSP Interfaces
JSP 1.1	Tomcat 3, J2SDKEE 1.2	`Tag, BodyTag`
JSP 1.2	Tomcat 4, J2SDKEE 1.3	`IterationTag`
JSP 2.0	Tomcat 5, J2SDKEE 1.4	`SimpleTag, JspFragment`

Simple tag handlers are called simple, because they simplify the process of developing a tag handler. They are no less capable than classic tag handlers in dealing with iteration and processing of body content. You are more likely to be using simple tag handlers than the more complicated classic tag handlers in your development, so we will look at those first.

Simple Tag Handlers

The tag extension mechanism of JSP 1.2 was powerful, but it was also relatively complicated to use, as we will see later. JSP 2.0 introduces the `SimpleTag` interface and a base class, `SimpleTagSupport` that implements this interface:

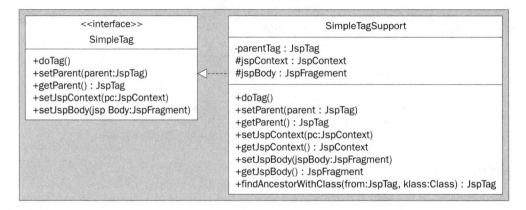

We can use this interface and base class to implement any tag handlers in JSP 2.0, regardless of whether the tag needs to be processed multiple times, or whether it has a body that needs to be processed. To create a custom action, you would create a tag handler class that extends the `SimpleTagSupport` base class, overriding the methods as necessary to provide the behavior for a custom action. Usually, all you will need to do is override the `doTag()` method. This method provides all the behavior of the custom action, including tag logic, iterations, and body evaluation. As we will see later, classic tag handlers used three methods to do everything that is done within the single `doTag()` method of `SimpleTag`.

When the tag appears in a JSP file, the translator creates code that:

❑ Creates an instance of the tag handler

❑ Calls `setJspContext()` and `setParent()`

❑ Initializes the tag handler attributes

❑ Creates a `JspFragment` object and calls `setJspBody()`

For the page implementation code to be able to create the tag handler instance and initialize its properties, all tag handlers follow the JavaBean conventions. You may recall that for our purposes, this means two things:

❑ The tag handler class must have a no-argument constructor.

❑ Properties of the class that can be used by clients must be exposed through public `setXXX` methods to set the value; and must have `getXXX` or `isXXX` methods to retrieve the value.

This provides a standard way for JSP containers to create instances of tag handlers and set the properties of tag handlers from attributes of the custom action element in the JSP. Each attribute in the custom action tag must correspond to a property of the tag handler that can be set using some `setXXX()` method.

After the tag handler class is created and initialized, the page class calls doTag(). This method is called only once for the tag; if the body content needs to be evaluated, it does that through the JspFragment object that was passed to the class through setJspBody().

JspFragment

Like SimpleTag, JspFragment is also an interface, but the implementation of the interface is left entirely to the JSP container to implement. As a developer, you only need to know how to call a fragment to evaluate its contents. If your SimpleTag tag handler needs to evaluate the body of the tag, it calls the invoke() method of JspFragment:

```
public void invoke(java.io.Writer out, java.util.Map params)
```

As you can see, invoke() takes two arguments. If the Writer argument is null, the fragment will write its output to the current output stream of the client response; otherwise, the fragment will write its output to the given Writer. The Map argument is used to pass parameters to the fragment. Recall that a Map stores name-value pairs, so the fragment can access the values in the map by using the name in an expression.

Tag Library Descriptor

After creating one or more classes that implement a tag, you need to inform the container which tag handlers are available to the JSP pages in an application. This is done through a descriptor file called a **Tag Library Descriptor** (TLD). The TLD is an XML-compliant document that contains information about the tag handler classes in a tag library.

A TLD for JSP 2.0 will provide information about the tag library using a <taglib> element as shown here:

```xml
<?xml version="1.0" encoding="UTF-8" ?>

<taglib xmlns="http://java.sun.com/xml/ns/j2ee"
        xmlns:xsi="http://www.w3.org/2001/XMLSchema-instance"
        xsi:schemaLocation="http://java.sun.com/xml/ns/j2ee web-
                                         jsptaglibrary_2_0.xsd"
        version="2.0">

  <tlib-version>1.0</tlib-version>
  <short-name>simplefaq</short-name>

  <tag>
     <name>simplelist</name>
     <tag-class>Ch04.SimpleList</tag-class>
     <body-content>JSP</body-content>
     <attribute>
       <name>topic</name>
       <required>yes</required>
```

```
        <rtexprvalue>true</rtexprvalue>
      </attribute>
    </tag>
  </taglib>
```

The `<taglib>` element can have a number of sub-elements. The mandatory elements are:

Element	Meaning
tlib-version	The version number of the library.
short-name	A simple default name. It may be used as the preferred prefix value in `taglib` directives.
tag	Information about a tag handler.

The `<tag>` element has several sub-elements. The mandatory sub-elements are:

Element	Meaning
name	The name of the tag handler.
tag-class	The fully qualified class name of the tag handler class.

In addition, you will often need to use these optional sub-elements of the `<tag>` element:

Element	Meaning
body-content	Whether the body of the tag can have content. Valid values are `tagdependent`, `JSP`, or `empty`. The default is `JSP`. If the value is `empty`, the tag is not allowed to have a body.
variable	Defines the scripting variables created by this tag handler and made available to the rest of the page. This element must contain one of two sub-elements: `name-given` or `name-from-attribute`. If `name-given` is used, the value of this element defines the name that other JSP elements can use to access the created scripting variable. If `name-from-attribute` is used, the value of the attribute with the name given by this element defines the name of the scripting variable.

Element	Meaning
`attribute`	Defines attributes for the tag. This element has three sub-elements: `name`, `required`, and `rtexprvalue`. The value of the `name` element will be the name of the attribute. The element named `required` is optional, and must be one of `true`, `false`, `yes`, or `no`. The default value is `false`. The `rtexprvalue` element is optional, and must be one of `true`, `false`, `yes`, or `no`. The default value is `false`, which means that the attribute can only be set using a static value known at compile time. If the element contains `true` or `yes`, the attribute can be set using a runtime expression.

This may be a bit daunting, especially near the end of that last table, so let's look at an example.

```xml
<?xml version="1.0" encoding="UTF-8" ?>

<taglib xmlns="http://java.sun.com/xml/ns/j2ee"
        xmlns:xsi="http://www.w3.org/2001/XMLSchema-instance"
        xsi:schemaLocation="http://java.sun.com/xml/ns/j2ee web-
                                        jsptaglibrary_2_0.xsd"
        version="2.0">
  <tlib-version>1.0</tlib-version>
  <short-name>wrox</short-name>

  <tag>
    <name>example</name>
    <tag-class>Ch04.Example</tag-class>
    <body-content>empty</body-content>
    <variable>
      <name-given>script1</name-given>
    </variable>
    <variable>
      <name-from-attribute>attr1</name-from-attribute>
    </variable>
    <attribute>
      <name>attr1</name>
      <required>yes</required>
      <rtexprvalue>true</rtexprvalue>
    </attribute>
    <attribute>
      <name>attr2</name>
      <required>no</required>
      <rtexprvalue>false</rtexprevalue>
    </attribute>
  </tag>
</taglib>
```

The TLD above is for a tag library that the developer has identified as version 1.0. It relies on JSP 2.0. The suggested prefix for tags from the library is wrox. However, note that page developers can use whatever prefix they desire. This is so that name conflicts between libraries with the same suggested prefix can be avoided.

The TLD defines one tag with the name "example". The tag handler class for the tag is Ch04.Example. The tag must have an empty body, because the value of the <body-content> element is empty.

The tag creates two objects that are made available to the rest of the page as scripting variables. The JSP accesses the first object using the name script1 (from the <name-given> element). The second object is accessed by the name given in the attr1 attribute of the tag.

The tag takes two attributes. The attribute attr1 is required, and can be set by a run-time expression. The attribute attr2 is optional, and cannot be set at run-time from an expression.

Packaging Tag Libraries

After creating the tag handler classes and the TLD, there are a few final steps that need to be accomplished to use the tags in a JSP.

Application Structure

Although some parts of the structure of a web application are not specified, locations for tag libraries and TLDs are specified.

```
context-root
  META-INF/
    jar_that_contains_TLD.jar
  WEB-INF/
    lib/
      taglib.jar
    tlds/
      descriptor.tld
    classes/
      path/to/tag/handler.class
```

Tag handler classes must be placed in the /classes subdirectory of WEB-INF or in a .jar file in the /lib subdirectory of WEB-INF. TLD files must be placed under WEB-INF, although the actual location under WEB-INF is unspecified. In the example above, a TLD is located in the /tlds directory of WEB-INF. If a TLD is in a .jar file, it must be in the META-INF directory of the application.

Deployment Descriptor

Within the web.xml deployment descriptor, you can create a mapping from a URI to a TLD location. This is done through the <taglib> element. For example, this element:

```
<taglib>
  <taglib-uri>/examples</taglib-uri>
  <taglib-location>/WEB-INF/tlds/descriptor.tld</taglib-location>
</taglib>
```

maps the URI **/examples** to the TLD `descriptor.tld`. This mapping can then be used in the JSP files, as we will see next.

> **The order of elements in the deployment descriptor must follow the order specified by the DTD. See Chapter 5 for the correct order.**

Importing a Taglib into a Page

To use a custom action, you need to "import" the tag library into the JSP. This is done with the `taglib` directive. The `taglib` directive has this form:

```
<%@ taglib uri="URI_of_library" prefix="tag_prefix"%>
```

This element must appear in the JSP file prior to any custom action that uses a tag from the tag library.

The `uri` attribute is either an absolute or relative path to the TLD file. Alternately, if the `web.xml` deployment descriptor has a `<taglib>` element, you can refer to the TLD using the value of the `<taglib-uri>` element from `web.xml` like this:

```
<%@ taglib uri="/examples" prefix="ex"%>
```

Combined with the `<taglib>` element of the previous section, this directive would "import" the tag library defined by `descriptor.tld`. Within the particular JSP file that used this `taglib` directive, the custom actions would be referenced using the prefix given. For example, the TLD above defined a tag handler named `example`. With the taglib directive above, the action would be referenced in a JSP as

```
<ex:example />
<%-- or as --%>
<ex:example></ex:example>
```

Try It Out   Defining a Simple Tag Handler

In this example, we'll develop a tag handler using the simple tag handler interfaces of JSP 2.0. This tag handler will perform iteration and process the body content of the tag. When this example is complete, you will see that custom actions and simple tag handlers can make your JSP files extremely easy to develop. This example has the following structure:

```
Ch04/
  TopicList2.jsp
  Questions.jsp
  WEB-INF/
    web.xml
    EL_1.jsp
      tlds/
        simplefaq.tld
      classes/
        Ch04/
          SimpleList.java
          Questions.java
```

1. Start with a new tag handler class that extends `SimpleTagSupport`. This file is called `SimpleList.java`, and is located in the **/WEB-INF/classes/Ch04** directory. Since this class uses the JSP API, when you compile the class, your `classpath` will need to include the correct libraries. If you are using J2EE, your `classpath` must include `J2EE.jar`. If you are using Tomcat 5.0, your `classpath` must include `jsp-api.jar`. If you are using some other JSP container, check your documentation for the correct `.jar` file to include on the `classpath`.

```java
package Ch04;

import java.util.*;
import javax.servlet.jsp.tagext.*;
import javax.servlet.jsp.*;
import java.io.*;

public class SimpleList extends SimpleTagSupport {
  private String topic;
  private Iterator faqs;
  private int count;
  public void setTopic(String s) { topic = s; }
  public String getTopic() { return topic; }

  public void doTag() throws JspException {
    Questions questions = new Questions();
    questions.setTopic(getTopic());

    // Get list of questions, TreeMap will sort them by key
    Map qmap = new TreeMap(questions.getQuestions());
    faqs = qmap.values().iterator();
    count = 1;
    Map params = new HashMap();

    while (faqs.hasNext()) {
      // Store the parameters for invoke()
      params.put("question", faqs.next());
      params.put("qid", topic + "_" + count);
      count++;
```

```
        try {
          // Process the body
          getJspBody().invoke(null, params);
        } catch (IOException e) {
          throw new JspException("Exception processing body");
        }
      }
    }
  }
```

2. Now we need to create a TLD for this tag handler. This is `simplefaq.tld`, and in this example, it will be saved to the **/WEB-INF/tlds** directory.

```xml
<?xml version="1.0" encoding="UTF-8" ?>

<taglib xmlns="http://java.sun.com/xml/ns/j2ee"
        xmlns:xsi="http://www.w3.org/2001/XMLSchema-instance"
        xsi:schemaLocation="http://java.sun.com/xml/ns/j2ee web-
                                              jsptaglibrary_2_0.xsd"
        version="2.0">

  <tlib-version>1.0</tlib-version>
  <short-name>simplefaq</short-name>

  <tag>
    <name>simplelist</name>
    <tag-class>Ch04.SimpleList</tag-class>
    <body-content>JSP</body-content>
    <attribute>
      <name>topic</name>
      <required>yes</required>
      <rtexprvalue>true</rtexprvalue>
    </attribute>
  </tag>
</taglib>
```

3. If you are using Tomcat, you'll need to edit `web.xml` as shown here:

```xml
<?xml version="1.0" encoding="ISO-8859-1"?>

<web-app xmlns="http://java.sun.com/xml/ns/j2ee"
    xmlns:xsi="http://www.w3.org/2001/XMLSchema-instance"
    xsi:schemaLocation="http://java.sun.com/xml/ns/j2ee web-app_2_4.xsd"
    version="2.4">

  <!-- this is the deployment descriptor for Chapter 4 -->

  <welcome-file-list>
    <welcome-file>TopicList2.jsp</welcome-file>
  </welcome-file-list>
```

```
<jsp-config>
  <!-- This element is for the simple tag handler example -->
  <taglib>
    <taglib-uri>/simplequestions</taglib-uri>
    <taglib-location>/WEB-INF/tlds/simplefaq.tld</taglib-location>
  </taglib>

  <jsp-property-group>
    <url-pattern>*.jsp</url-pattern>
    <el-enabled>true</el-enabled>
    <scripting-enabled>false</scripting-enabled>
  </jsp-property-group>
</jsp-config>

</web-app>
```

If you are using the J2EE Deploytool, the mapping shown above between the URI
/simplequestions and the TLD simplefaq.tld is set in the **JSP Tag Libraries** section
of the **File Refs** tab for the Web Application.

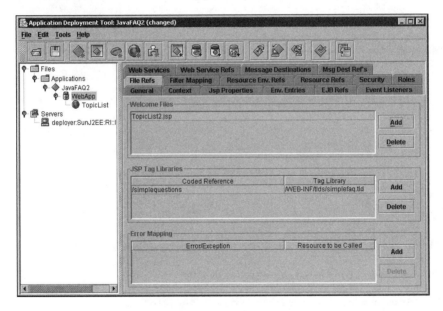

4. Finally, we'll create a new version of TopicList.jsp that uses this new tag. This is
TopicList2.jsp:

```
<!DOCTYPE HTML PUBLIC "-//W3C//DTD HTML 4.01 Transitional//EN">
<%@ taglib uri="/simplequestions" prefix="faq"%>
<html>
  <head><title>Topic Questions 2</title></head>
  <body>
```

```
      <h1>Topic Questions 2</h1>

      <faq:simplelist topic="${param.topic}">
        <p>Question <a href="Questions.jsp?qid=${qid}">${qid}</a>
            ${question}</p>
      </faq:simplelist>
      <p>Click a link to get the answer.</p>
    </body>
</html>
```

5. Deploy these new files and access `TopicList2.jsp` from a browser. Don't be shocked when you see that it looks the same as the first example of this chapter. (Or it should, assuming everything is correct.)

> **If you encounter problems running this example after updating the previous example using the Deploytool, try creating a new application from scratch.**

How It Works

As stated earlier, all the processing for a `SimpleTag` happens in the `doTag()` method. The `doTag()` method starts by instantiating our `Questions` bean, and setting its `topic` property to the value of the `topic` property of our tag handler:

```
      Questions questions = new Questions();
      questions.setTopic(getTopic());
```

As we'll see shortly, this value is set through an attribute in our `<jsp:simplelist>` tag.

Next, we set up the `Iterator` that will be used to step through the questions. We do this by calling the `getQuestions()` method and passing the returned set of questions to a `TreeMap` constructor. A `TreeMap` sorts a collection based on the name in the name-value pairs stored in the map. If you look at the `Questions` class, you will see that the names are the strings `"1"`, `"2"`, and `"3"`. After the `TreeMap` is constructed, the `iterator()` method is called to get an `Iterator`:

```
    Map qmap = new TreeMap(questions.getQuestions());
    faqs = qmap.values().iterator();
```

The class then iterates over each question in the collection. For each question, two pieces of data used by the body of the tag are put into a `HashMap` (called `params`). First, the question itself is put into the `HashMap` using the name `"question"`. Then an ID is put into the `HashMap`. The ID is stored with the name `"qid"`, and is constructed by appending `"EL"`, an underscore, and a digit based on a counter:

151

```
params.put("question", faqs.next());
params.put("qid", topic + "_" + count);
```

We will see shortly how the JSP page uses the names to get the values. After the parameters for a single question are added to the `HashMap`, the `doTag()` method gets a reference to the `JspFragment` for the tag and calls its `invoke()` method:

```
getJspBody().invoke(null, params);
```

Since `null` is passed as the first argument, the body content is passed to the client's output response stream. That is, it is sent directly to the client. The objects in the other argument are made available to the body content. After the body content is processed, the `doTag()` method does the same for another question.

Now let's look at the tag as it is used in `TopicList2.jsp`. This page uses the `taglib` directive to specify the TLD. The URI **/simplequestions** is mapped by the deployment descriptor to `simplefaq.tld`. The prefix used for the tag is `faq`. Notice that this is not the `short-name` used in the TLD. As has been mentioned several times, the page developer chooses the prefix. The name of the tag is the name given in the TLD, and the tag has a single attribute, called `topic`. This attribute was specified in the TLD as a required attribute that could be set using an expression. In our `TopicList2.jsp` page, the value of the attribute is indeed set with an expression, `${param.topic}`. This is the attribute that is used to set the `topic` property of our tag handler:

```
<faq:simplelist topic="${param.topic}">
  <p>Question <a href="Questions.jsp?qid=${qid}">${qid}</a>
      ${question}</p>
</faq:simplelist>
```

The tag has a body, which is allowed by the TLD. The body content is represented by the `JspFragment` instance in the `doTag()` method. When the `invoke()` method is called, the body is evaluated and sent as part of the response to the client. You can see that the body of the tag includes two EL expressions. The value of these expressions comes directly from the parameters that the `doTag()` method added to the `HashMap` that was passed to the `JspFragment invoke()` method. The `doTag()` method placed data into the `HashMap` using the names `question` and `qid`; that data is accessed using EL expressions that use the same names as the expression body.

Classic Tag Handler Design

Prior to JSP 2.0, three interfaces and two implementing classes provided the basic design for tag handlers. As you will see here, using classic tag handlers is somewhat more involved than using simple tag handlers. For that reason, you will probably always use simple tag handlers. However, you may be working a project that still uses a server that only supports JSP 1.2, or you may need to work with tag handlers that were written under JSP 1.2. For that reason we will look at how to use classic tag handlers.

The `javax.servlet.jsp.tagext.Tag` interface is the primary interface for classic tag handlers. It provides an interface for simple tag handler classes that do not need to manipulate their body content. `IterationTag` extends `Tag` to provide an interface for tag handlers that need to perform some iteration or looping. Finally, `BodyTag` extends `IterationTag` for tag handlers that manipulate their body content. These interfaces are shown in the class diagram below:

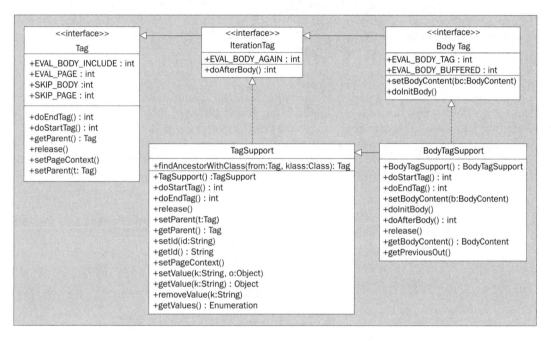

The tag extension API includes two classes that implement the interfaces above. `TagSupport` implements `IterationTag`; `BodyTagSupport` implements `BodyTag`.

Tag

`Tag` is the interface to implement when the tag handler does not need to process multiple times and does not need to manipulate its body. As an alternative to implementing the `Tag` interface, your tag handler can extend `TagSupport` (since `TagSupport` implements `IterationTag`, which extends `Tag`). In fact, this is the usual way you will implement a tag handler for a simple tag. When you extend `TagSupport`, you will only need to override `doStartTag()` or `doEndTag()`. So a simple tag handler class that has no properties will look like this:

```
public class MySimpleTag extends TagSupport {
  public int doStartTag() { // method body }
  public int doEndTag() { // method body }
}
```

The doStartTag() method is called by the page class at the point where the start tag appears in the JSP file. When you implement a tag handler, you implement the doStartTag() method with code that you want to have executed before the body of the tag is processed. When your code is finished, it returns one of two values defined by the Tag interface. If it returns Tag.SKIP_BODY, the body of the tag, which can include template (HTML) data, JSP elements, or other tag extensions, is not evaluated. Earlier, we saw that a descriptor file contains information about the tag extensions. If the <body-content> element of the descriptor has the value empty, this indicates that a tag *must* be empty, and SKIP_BODY is the only allowed return value. If your doStartTag() method returns Tag.EVAL_BODY_INCLUDE, the body of the tag is evaluated.

The doEndTag() method is called by the page class at the point where the end tag appears in the JSP file. When you implement a tag handler, you implement the doEndTag() method with code that you want to have executed after the body of the tag is processed. After your doEndTag() completes, it returns Tag.SKIP_PAGE or Tag.EVAL_PAGE. The value SKIP_PAGE indicates that the remainder of the JSP should not be evaluated; EVAL_PAGE indicates the opposite.

This execution flow is illustrated below:

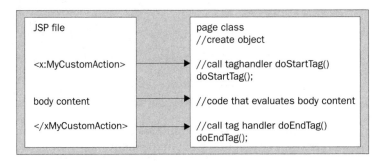

Note that when extending TagSupport, you can, but do not need to, implement both doStartTag() and doEndTag(). If the tag handler does not need to perform any action prior to the body, and the tag must have an empty body, you do not need to implement doStartTag(). However, because the TagSupport implementation of doStartTag() returns SKIP_BODY, if the tag can have a body you should implement a minimal doStartTag() that returns EVAL_BODY_INCLUDE. If the tag handler does not need to perform any action after the body, you do not need to implement doEndTag(). The TagSupport implementation of doEndTag() returns EVAL_PAGE.

IterationTag

When you need a tag handler class to iterate or loop its actions, your tag class will implement IterationTag. Of course, as with Tag, you will usually just extend TagSupport. IterationTag adds one method and one property, which are used to provide the looping behavior. Here is a simple tag handler class without any properties:

```
public class ListQuestions extends TagSupport {
  public int doStartTag() throws JspTagException { // method body }
  public int doAfterBody() throws JspTagException { // method body }
  public int doEndTag() throws JspTagException { // method body }
}
```

This time, the example includes the new method: `doAfterBody()`.

After calling `doStartTag()` and after evaluating the body of the tag, the page class calls the `doAfterBody()` method. The `doAfterBody()` method allows the tag handler class to determine whether the page class should evaluate the body another time. If so, `doAfterBody()` should return a value of `IterationTag.EVAL_BODY_AGAIN`, which indicates that the page class should evaluate the body of the tag again; if not, it returns `Tag.SKIP_BODY`. The page class then calls `doEndTag()` and proceeds as with a `Tag`.

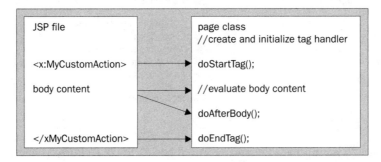

BodyTag

With `Tag` and `IterationTag`, the implementing class can indicate whether the body of the tag should be evaluated by the page class; However, the tag handler classes that implement `Tag` or `IterationTag` have no way of actually manipulating the contents of the tag body. This is possible through the `BodyTag` interface and its implementing class, `BodyTagSupport`:

```
public class ListQuestionsInBody extends BodyTagSupport {
  public int doStartTag() throws JspTagException { // method body }
  public void setBodyContent(BodyContent bc) { // method body }
  public void doInitBody() { // method body }
  public int doAfterBody() throws JspTagException { // method body }
  public int doEndTag() throws JspTagException { // method body }
}
```

For the most part, the doStartTag() method is the same as for Tag or IterationTag. The difference is that the BodyTag interface defines an additional return value for the method. That return value is BodyTag.EVAL_BODY_BUFFERED. When your code returns EVAL_BODY_BUFFERED, the page class calls the setBodyContent() and doInitBody() methods. This makes the body content available to your code in the doAfterBody() and doEndTag() methods. When the return value of doStartTag() is EVAL_BODY_BUFFERED, the page class evaluates the tag body and stores the result in an instance of BodyContent. (Thus, an instance of BodyContent will not contain actions, scriptlets, and so on – only the results of those elements.) The page class then needs to pass the BodyContent instance to the tag handler so that it can manipulate the body content. It does this by calling setBodyContent(); the page class then calls doInitBody(). Inside the doInitBody() method, the tag handler class can perform any initialization that depends on the body of the tag:

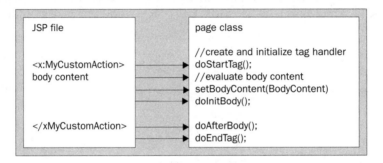

Normally, you will manipulate the body content in the doAfterBody() method. However, the BodyContent object is also available to the doEndTag() method, so you can use the BodyContent object there. The BodyContent class defines various methods for getting the body content, and writing the body content to an output stream. For example, this code snippet shows how to write the body content to the response:

```
public void doAfterBody() {
    // bodyContent is an instance variable of BodyTagSupport
    // Call the getEncloseingWriter() method to get the enclosing JspWriter
    Writer writer = bodyContent.getEnclosingWriter();
    // Call the writeOut(Writer) method to send the body content
    // to the writer
    bodyContent.writeOut(writer);

    if (need_to_eval_body_again) {
        return EVAL_BODY_AGAIN;
    } else {
        return SKIP_BODY;
    }
}
```

The page class will evaluate the body again if the doAfterBody() method returns EVAL_BODY_AGAIN; otherwise, if doAfterBody() returns SKIP_BODY, then the page class calls doEndTag().

In this example, we'll create a custom action using classic tag handlers to list the FAQ questions in the TopicList.jsp page. As with the simple tag handler example previously, by putting the iteration into the custom action, all the Java code will be eliminated from the JSP page and encapsulated in the tag handler. This will make the page simpler than the version introduced in the first example of the chapter. Encapsulating the Java code in beans and tag handlers also makes the page easier for page developers to develop and maintain. Here's the application structure:

```
Ch04/
   Questions.jsp
   TopicList3.jsp
   WEB-INF/
     EL_1.jsp
     web.xml
     tlds/
        faq.tld
     classes/
        Ch04/
           Questions.java
           Questions.class
           ListQuestions.java
           ListQuestions.class
```

Most of the files above are the same as in the previous example. The new files are TopicList3.jsp, faq.tld, and ListQuestions.java.

1. Here's the tag handler, ListQuestions.java. The tag handler will need to iterate over a collection of questions, so it extends TagSupport. Since this class uses the JSP API, when you compile the class, your classpath will need to include the correct libraries. If you are using J2EE, your classpath must include J2EE.jar. If you are using Tomcat 5.0, your classpath must include jsp-api.jar. If you are using some other JSP container, check your documentation for the correct .jar file to include on the classpath. Also, you will need to ensure that Questions.class either exists or is compiled at the same time. You can do that by using javac *.java (assuming the classpath is set):

```
package Ch04;

import java.util.*;
import javax.servlet.jsp.tagext.*;
import javax.servlet.jsp.*;
import java.io.*;

public class ListQuestions extends TagSupport {
  private String topic;
  private Iterator faqs;
  private int count;
```

```
public void setTopic(String s) { topic = s; }
public String getTopic() { return topic; }

public int doStartTag() throws JspTagException {
  Questions questions = new Questions();
  questions.setTopic(getTopic());
  Map qmap = new TreeMap(questions.getQuestions());

  // Get an Iterator for the questions
  // The Iterator is an instance variable because we will access
  // it in the doAfterBody()method
  faqs = qmap.values().iterator();
  count = 0;
  try {
    // Write some preliminary data to the response
    pageContext.getOut().write("<h2>Questions for Topic</h2>");
    pageContext.getOut().write("\nThe number of questions in topic " +
                            getTopic() + " is " + qmap.size());

  } catch (IOException e) {
    throw new JspTagException("Error writing to out");
  }
  return EVAL_BODY_INCLUDE;
}

public int doAfterBody() throws JspTagException {
  // Create the link for a single question
  // Each time this method is called by the page class,
  // the Iterator advances to the next question
  if (faqs.hasNext()) {
    String question = (String) faqs.next();
    String s = "<p>Question <a href=\"Questions.jsp?qid=" + getTopic() +
      "_" + ++count + "\">" + getTopic() + "_" + count + "</a>: " +
      question + "</p>";
    try {
      pageContext.getOut().write(s);
    } catch (IOException e) {
      throw new JspTagException("Error writing to out");
    }
    // Tell the page class to evaluate the body again
    return EVAL_BODY_AGAIN;
  } else {
    // faqs.next() was false, so no more questions
    return SKIP_BODY;
  }
}

public int doEndTag() throws JspTagException {
  try {
    pageContext.getOut().write("<p>Click a link to see the answer</p>");
  } catch (IOException e) {
    throw new JspTagException("Error writing to out");
```

```
      }
      return EVAL_PAGE;
   }
}
```

2. The tag library descriptor (`faq.tld`) for this tag is next:

```xml
<?xml version="1.0" encoding="UTF-8" ?>

<taglib xmlns="http://java.sun.com/xml/ns/j2ee"
        xmlns:xsi="http://www.w3.org/2001/XMLSchema-instance"
        xsi:schemaLocation="http://java.sun.com/xml/ns/j2ee web-
                                           jsptaglibrary_2_0.xsd"
        version="2.0">

   <tag>
     <name>listFaqs</name>
     <tag-class>Ch04.ListQuestions</tag-class>
     <body-content>JSP</body-content>
     <attribute>
       <name>topic</name>
       <required>yes</required>
       <rtexprvalue>true</rtexprvalue>
     </attribute>
   </tag>
</taglib>
```

3. If you are deploying to Tomcat, you will need to add a `<taglib>` element to the deployment descriptor. Here is the modification to `web.xml`:

```xml
<?xml version="1.0" encoding="ISO-8859-1"?>

<web-app xmlns="http://java.sun.com/xml/ns/j2ee"
    xmlns:xsi="http://www.w3.org/2001/XMLSchema-instance"
    xsi:schemaLocation="http://java.sun.com/xml/ns/j2ee web-app_2_4.xsd"
    version="2.4">

  <!-- this is the deployment descriptor for Chapter 4 -->

  <welcome-file-list>
    <welcome-file>TopicList3.jsp</welcome-file>
  </welcome-file-list>

  <!-- this element is for the custom action -->
  <taglib>
    <taglib-uri>/questions</taglib-uri>
    <taglib-location>/WEB-INF/tlds/faq.tld</taglib-location>
  </taglib>
</web-app>
```

4. If you are deploying to J2EE using the Deploytool, you will need to set the `<taglib>` element of the deployment descriptor through the J2EE Deploytool. This is done in the **File Refs** tab of the right pane when the web application is selected in the left pane:

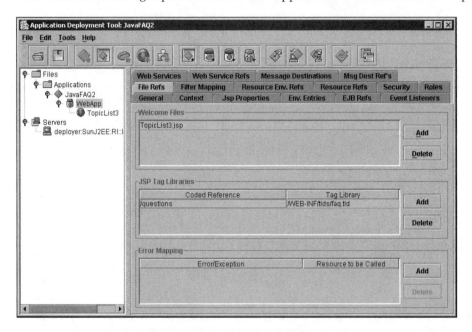

The section where you need to add the taglib mapping is in the **JSP Tag Libraries** section as seen above. Enter **/questions** for the **Coded Reference** and **/WEB-INF/tlds/faq.tld** for the **Tag Library**.

5. Finally, here is the JSP page. Save this as `TopicList3.jsp`:

```
<!DOCTYPE HTML PUBLIC "-//W3C//DTD HTML 4.01 Transitional//EN">
<%@ taglib uri="/questions" prefix="faq"%>
<html>
  <head><title>Topic Questions</title></head>
  <body>
    <h1>Topic Questions</h1>

    <faq:listFaqs topic="${param.topic}">
    </faq:listFaqs>

  </body>
</html>
```

6. Deploy the application to your server. Open a browser window and enter the address http://localhost:8000/Ch04/TopicList3.jsp?topic=EL (use port 8080 for Tomcat). If everything is correct, you will see the same display as in the previous two examples of this chapter.

How It Works

The tag handler class, `ListQuestions`, extends the `TagSupport` class. Since that class implements `IterationTag`, the tag handler can perform iterations, but it can't manipulate the body of the tag. Thus, the tag handler class needs to perform all the output to the response itself. `ListQuestions` provides implementations for the `doStartTag()`, `doAfterBody()`, and `doEndTag()` methods.

The `doStartTag()` creates an instance of the `Questions` class, and gets the `Map` consisting of the list of questions. This `Map` is used to create a `TreeMap` instance. We use `TreeMap` because that provides a sorted collection. Since the keys used in `Questions` are strings representing numbers, this means the `TreeMap` will sort the data with `"1"` first, followed by `"2"`, and so on. Finally, it sets up an iterator for the values (the questions), and prints out some preliminary text. Notice that to do this, it gets an output stream from the `pageContext` object:

```
Map qmap = new TreeMap(questions.getQuestions());
faqs = qmap.values().iterator();
count = 0;
try {
   // Write some preliminary data to the response
   pageContext.getOut().write("<h2>Questions for Topic</h2>");
   pageContext.getOut().write("\nThe number of questions in topic " +
                              getTopic() + " is " + qmap.size());
```

The `doAfterBody()` method actually uses the `Iterator` to create the links and text of each question. As it iterates through each question, it returns a value of `EVAL_BODY_AGAIN`. This signals that the page class should call `doAfterBody()` again. When it has iterated through all the values, `doAfterBody()` returns `SKIP_BODY`:

```
if (faqs.hasNext()) {
   String question = (String) faqs.next();
   String s = "<p>Question <a href=\"Questions.jsp?qid=" + getTopic() +
     "_" + ++count + "\">" + getTopic() + "_" + count + "</a>: " +
     question + "</p>";
   try {
      pageContext.getOut().write(s);
   } catch (IOException e) {
      throw new JspTagException("Error writing to out");
   }
   // Tell the page class to evaluate the body again
   return EVAL_BODY_AGAIN;
} else {
   // faqs.next() was false, so no more questions
   return SKIP_BODY;
}
```

The TLD tells the application about the tag handler class. This TLD only has one <tag> element in it. This <tag> element provides the name of the custom action, listFaq, and the name of the class that implements the action. As in the previous example, the action has one attribute named topic, which is required and which can be set through an expression:

```
<tag>
  <name>listFaqs</name>
  <tag-class>Ch04.ListQuestions</tag-class>
  <body-content>JSP</body-content>
  <attribute>
    <name>topic</name>
    <required>yes</required>
    <rtexprvalue>true</rtexprvalue>
  </attribute>
</tag>
```

We also added a <taglib> element to the deployment descriptor. This <taglib> element specified that a URI of /questions referred to the TLD at /WEB-INF/tlds/faq.tld.

And now we get to the JSP page. Because all of the work is now done by the tag handler, the JSP has become incredibly simple. Notice that there is no Java scriptlet in the page at all. At the top of the page, the tag library is "imported" using the taglib directive. The taglib directive specifies that the TLD is at the URI /questions. Because of the mapping in the web.xml file, this resolves to the file faq.tld.

```
<%@ taglib uri="/questions" prefix="faq" %>
```

The taglib directive specifies that the prefix for custom actions from that library would be faq. In this case, the prefix is the same as the short name, but remember that the page developer can set the prefix to any value regardless of the short name of the library. The single custom action that causes the tag handler to be called is:

```
<faq:listFaqs topic="${param.topic}">
</faq:listFaqs>
```

We have the prefix, faq, followed by the tag name, and the topic attribute. Notice that we set this attribute using an EL expression. This is allowed because the TLD specified that the attribute could be set by a run-time expression.

So, the JSP has become much simpler, and that's good, but at what cost? The ListQuestions class now has HTML tags and data in it. This could become a maintenance problem. Recall that one of the reasons for JSP pages was to remove template data from code. Although it's nice that TopicList3.jsp is so simple, it would be better to put presentation data back into the JSP, and leave the tag handler to do non-presentation tasks. One way to do that is through the BodyTag interface.

Classic Tag Handler with Body Tag Support

1. Here's a revised version of the tag handler; this time it's called
   `ListQuestionsInBody`. Add this class to the /WEB-INF/classes/Ch04 directory.

```java
package Ch04;

import java.util.*;
import javax.servlet.jsp.tagext.*;
import javax.servlet.jsp.*;
import java.io.*;

public class ListQuestionsInBody extends BodyTagSupport {
  private String topic;
  private Iterator faqs;
  private int count;
  public void setTopic(String s) { topic = s; }
  public String getTopic() { return topic; }

  public int doStartTag() throws JspTagException {
    Questions questions = new Questions();
    questions.setTopic(getTopic());
    Map qmap = new TreeMap(questions.getQuestions());
    faqs = qmap.values().iterator();
    count = 1;

    if (faqs.hasNext()) {
      setVariables();
      return EVAL_BODY_INCLUDE;
    } else {
      return SKIP_BODY;
    }
  }

  public int doAfterBody() throws JspTagException {
    if (faqs.hasNext()) {
      setVariables();
      return EVAL_BODY_BUFFERED;
    } else {
      return SKIP_BODY;
    }
  }

  public int doEndTag() throws JspTagException {
    return EVAL_PAGE;
  }

  void setVariables() {
    pageContext.setAttribute("question", faqs.next());
    pageContext.setAttribute("qid", topic + "_" + count);
    count++;
  }
}
```

163

2. We need to add another entry to the TLD for this new tag handler. Modify the `faq.tld` file as shown here:

```xml
<?xml version="1.0" encoding="UTF-8" ?>

<taglib xmlns="http://java.sun.com/xml/ns/j2ee"
        xmlns:xsi="http://www.w3.org/2001/XMLSchema-instance"
        xsi:schemaLocation="http://java.sun.com/xml/ns/j2ee web-
                                             jsptaglibrary_2_0.xsd"
        version="2.0">

  <tag>
    <name>listFaqs</name>
    <tag-class>ch04.ListQuestions</tag-class>
    <body-content>JSP</body-content>
    <attribute>
      <name>topic</name>
      <required>yes</required>
      <rtexprvalue>true</rtexprvalue>
    </attribute>
  </tag>

    <tag>
      <name>faqData</name>
      <tag-class>ch04.ListQuestionsInBody</tag-class>
      <body-content>JSP</body-content>
      <variable>
        <name-given>qid</name-given>
      </variable>
      <variable>
        <name-given>question</name-given>
      </variable>
      <attribute>
        <name>topic</name>
        <required>yes</required>
        <rtexprvalue>true</rtexprvalue>
      </attribute>
    </tag>
</taglib>
```

3. And we need a new version of the topic list page. This is `TopicList4.jsp`:

```jsp
<!DOCTYPE HTML PUBLIC "-//W3C//DTD HTML 4.01 Transitional//EN">
<%@ taglib uri="/questions" prefix="faq"%>
<html>
  <head><title>Topic Questions 4</title></head>
  <body>
```

```
   <h1>Topic Questions 4</h1>

   <faq:faqData topic="${param.topic}">
     <p>Question <a href="Questions.jsp?qid=${qid}">${qid}</a>
       ${question}</p>
   </faq:faqData>
   <p>Click a link to get the answer.</p>
 </body>
</html>
```

4. Modify `web.xml` so that the value for `<Welcome-File>` is now `TopicList4.jsp`.
No other additions or modifications are needed to the existing files in the application.
After deploying the new files, enter the URL
http://localhost:8000/Ch04/TopicList4.jsp?topic=EL (again, use port 8080 for Tomcat).

5. You should see the same behavior as occurred with the previous examples.

How It Works

The `ListQuestionsInBody` class does not have any more template data in it, and does not
need to output anything to the response. All it does is process the collection of questions,
exposing each one to the rest of the page through the `setVariables()` method. This method
adds two attributes to the page context. This makes the variables accessible to the rest of the
page. Within the page, these variables are accessed using the EL expressions `${question}` and
`${qid}`. To cause the body of the tag to be evaluated, `doStartTag()` returns
`EVAL_BODY_INCLUDE` and `doAfterBody()` returns `EVAL_BODY_BUFFERED`. These return
values cause the page class to call the `setBodyContent()` and `doInitBody()` methods of
the class. Since our tag handler didn't need to do anything special with the body content, the
default implementations of these methods in the parent class were sufficient.

To make the variables created by the tag handler accessible to the page, the TLD specifies that
the tag handler should create two scripting variables that are then available to the rest of the
page (although they are only used within the body of the tag). It did this through the
`<variable>` element:

```
   <variable>
     <name-given>qid</name-given>
   </variable>
   <variable>
     <name-given>question</name-given>
   </variable>
```

Each of these elements used the `<name-given>` element to specify the name by which the
scripting variables could be accessed. These are the same names that the tag handler class must
use when adding the attributes to the page context.

165

Finally, there is the topic page. Our new tag is called in the same way as the simple tag example, so `TopicList4.jsp` is simpler than the original `TopicList.jsp`, but not quite as simple as `TopicList3.jsp`. The body of the tag consists of template data and EL expressions:

```
<faq:faqData topic="${param.topic}">
  <p>Question <a href="Questions.jsp?qid=${qid}">${qid}</a>
      ${question}</p>
</faq:faqData>
```

The EL expressions access the scripting variables created by the custom action. Each time the page class evaluates the body, it gets the current values of these variables from the page context and inserts them into the response.

This allows page designers to easily change the presentation of the data without needing to edit and recompile the tag handler.

JavaServer Pages Standard Tag Library (JSTL)

Much of this chapter has been devoted to information about creating your own custom actions and tag libraries. However, you are not limited to using just the tags you create. You can use any tag library that is available. While there are many such libraries distributed, in this section we will look at the JavaServer Pages Standard Tag Library, or JSTL.

The JSTL grew out of the realization that with many developers creating tag libraries, many actions would be duplicated among the various libraries. Because these libraries were developed separately, the duplicated actions would probably have different names, syntaxes, or behaviors. The JSTL standardizes a number of common actions. In theory, then, if you use one implementation of a standard tag library, switching to another standard tag library should be as easy as adding the `.jar` files to your application and changing the `web.xml` file to map the `taglib-uri` to the new different TLD. In this section, we will look at some of the actions in the JSTL.

Getting an Implementation

If you want to experiment with the JSTL, one place where you can get an implementation of the library is the Jakarta project. You can get a copy of the latest version at http://jakarta.apache.org/taglibs/index.html.

Using the JSTL is as simple as:

1. Unpacking the distribution into your application. The `.jar` files containing the tag handlers should go into /WEB-INF/lib, and the TLDs into a directory under /WEB-INF/.

2. Changing the `web.xml` file to map `taglib-uris` to the location of the TLDs.

3. Adding the `taglib` directive to the pages that will use the JSTL tags.

What's in the JSTL?

The JSTL tags have been divided into four categories. These categories with their associated TLDs are:

- ❑ Core actions (`c.tld` and `c-rt.tld`)

- ❑ XML processing (`x.tld` and `x-rt.tld`)

- ❑ Internationalization-capable formatting (`fmt.tld` and `fmt-rt.tld`)

- ❑ Relational database access (`sql.tld` and `sql-rt.tld`)

To simplify the support for both EL expressions and JSP scripting expressions, there are two TLDs for each of the categories above. If your page uses JSP scripting expressions (`<%! %>`, `<%= %>`, or `<% %>`), then you will use the `rt` version of each TLD (`rt` is short for `rtexprvalues`, which is short for "run-time expression values"). If your page uses EL expressions, then you will use the other version. If your page uses both, then you will need both TLDs. You can freely mix actions from either library in the same JSP.

Core actions

The core actions provide tag handlers for manipulating variables and dealing with errors, performing tests and conditional behavior, and executing loops and iterations.

General-Purpose Actions

The general-purpose actions provide support for dealing with variables and errors.

Tag	Meaning
`<c:out value="" default="">`	Sends the value to the response stream. We can specify an optional default value so that if the value attribute is set with an EL expression, and the expression is `null`, the default value will be output.
`<c:set var="" value="">`	Sets the JSP-scoped variable identified by `var` to the given value.
`<c:set target="" property="" value="">`	Sets the property of the given JavaBean or `Map` object to the given value.

Table continued on following page

Tag	Meaning
`<c:remove var="" scope="">`	Removes the object identified by `var` from the given scope. The `scope` attribute is optional. If the `scope` is not given, each scope will be searched in the order `page`, `request`, `session`, `application`, until the object is found or all scopes are searched. If `scope` is given, the object is removed only if it is in the given scope. If the object is not found, an exception will be thrown.
`<c:catch var="">`	Encloses a block of code that might throw an exception. If the exception occurs, the block terminates but the exception is not propagated. The thrown exception can be referenced by the variable named by `var`.

Conditional Actions

Conditional actions allow you to test expressions and evaluate tags based on the result of the test.

Tag	Meaning
`<c:if test="" var="">`	Used like a standard Java if block. The `var` attribute is optional; if present, the result of the test is assigned to the variable identified by var. If the test expression evaluates to true, the tag is evaluated; if false, it is not.
`<c:choose>,` `<c:when test="">,` `<c:otherwise>`	The analog to a Java if...elseif...else block. The `<c:choose>` action starts and ends the block. The test in each `<c:when test="">` tag is evaluated; the first test that evaluates to true causes that tag to be evaluated. If no `<c:when>` action evaluates to true, the `<c:otherwise>` tag is evaluated.

Iterator Actions

Iterator actions allow you to loop over a set of values:

Tag	Meaning
`<c:forEach var="" items="">`	Iterates over each item in the collection identified by `items`. Each item can be referenced by `var`. When `items` is a `Map`, the value of the item is referenced by `var.value`.
`<c:forEach var="" begin="" end="" step="">`	The tag for a `for` loop. The `step` attribute is optional.
`<c:forTokens items="" delims="">`	Iterates over the tokens in the `items` string.

Formatting Actions

Formatting actions are part of the I18N library. As you might guess, they provide support for formatting output. Among the actions for setting locales and time zones, are actions for formatting numbers. Here are two of them:

Tag	Meaning

`<fmt:formatDate value="date"`
`    [type="{time|date|both}"]`
`    [dateStyle="{default|short|medium|long|full}"]`
`    [timeStyle="{default|short|medium|long|full}"]`
`    [pattern="customPattern"]`
`[timeZone="timeZone"]`
`    [var="varName"]`
`    [scope="{page|request|session|application}"]/>`
	Only the `value` attribute is required. The other attributes define how to format the data. The `pattern` attribute can contain a custom pattern for formatting the date string.

Tag	Meaning
```<fmt:formatNumber value="numericValue" [type="{number|currency|percent}"] [pattern="customPattern"] [currencyCode="currencyCode"] [currencySymbol="currencySymbol"] [groupingUsed="{true|false}"] [maxIntegerDigits="maxIntegerDigits"] [minIntegerDigits="minIntegerDigits"] [maxFractionDigits="maxFractionDigits"] [minFractionDigits="minFractionDigits"] [var="varName"] [scope="{page|request|session|application}"]/>```	Formats the number given by value. Various styles are possible, including currency formats and custom formatting styles. You can also use this tag without the `value` attribute, in which case the number to be formatted is passed in the body of the tag.

SQL Actions

The JSTL SQL actions allow page authors to perform database queries, access query results, and perform inserts, updates, and deletes. We will look at just one of the actions `<sql:query>`.

Tag	Meaning
```<sql:query var="" dataSource=""> SQL Command </sql:query>```	Queries the database given by the `dataSource` attribute. The query that is performed is given in the body of the tag. The results of the query can be accessed by `var.rows`. You can use the `<c:forEach>` tag to iterator over the collection of rows.

The `dataSource` attribute can identify the database in two ways. It can use the JDBC URL to access the database, or it can use the JNDI Data Source Name to look up the database. See Chapters 6 and 7 for more information on these techniques. |

Try It Out   Using the JSP Standard Tag Library

In this example, we will finally add another FAQ answer to the FAQ application we have been developing in this chapter. This JSP will show various uses of the JSTL. Here is the structure of the web application:

```
Ch04/
  Questions.jsp
  TopicList.jsp
  WEB-INF/
    EL_1.jsp

    EL_2.jsp
    web.xml
    lib/
      jstl.jar
      standard.jar
    tlds/
      simplefaq.tld
      c-rt.tld
      fmt.tld
    classes/
      SimpleList.class
      Questions.class
```

For the most part, this example will use the files created for the example used earlier to demonstrate simple tag handlers. The new files are EL_2.jsp and the .jar and .tld files from the JSTL.

1. Download the JSTL from the Jakarta web site http://jakarta.apache.org/taglibs/doc/standard-doc/intro.html. Extract all the TLDs into the /tlds directory you've been using for the examples in this chapter. Extract the following .jar files into the lib directory: standard.jar and jstl.jar. You can add the others if you like, but they are not needed for this example.

2. Create the following EL_2.jsp file. Save this file in the same place as EL_1.jsp:

```
<!DOCTYPE HTML PUBLIC "-//W3C//DTD HTML 4.01 Transitional//EN">
<%@ taglib uri="http://java.sun.com/jstl/core_rt" prefix="c_rt" %>
<%@ taglib uri="http://java.sun.com/jstl/format" prefix="fmt" %>

<html>
  <head>
    <title>JSTL Q2</title>
  </head>

  <body>
    <h1>JSTL Question 2</h1>
    <h2>How do I use the JSTL?</h2>

    <jsp:useBean id="questions" class="Ch04.Questions">
      <jsp:setProperty name="questions" property="topic" value="EL"/>
    </jsp:useBean>

    <table border="1">
      <!-- the literal JSTL tag will be in left column of table -->
      <!-- the evaluated JSTL tag will be in right column of table -->
      <tr><th>tag</th><th>result</th></tr>

      <!-- This tag uses c_rt:out to send the value of an EL
           to the response -->
```

```
    <tr>
      <td>&lt;c_rt:out value="${'${'}questions.topic}"/&gt;</td>
      <td><c_rt:out value="questions.topic=${questions.topic}"/></td>
    </tr>

    <!-- this tag uses c_rt:set to set the property of a Java Bean -->
    <tr>
      <td>
        &lt;c_rt:set target="${'${'}questions}" property="topic"
                  value="JSTL" /&gt;
        <c_rt:set target="${questions}" property="topic" value="JSTL" />
      </td>
      <td><c_rt:out value="questions.topic=${questions.topic}"/></td>
    </tr>

    <!-- This tag uses c_rt:if to determine whether to create
         another row -->
    <c_rt:if test="${questions.topic} == 'EL'">
      <tr><td>This row will not be created</td><td></td></tr>
    </c_rt:if>

    <c_rt:if test="${questions.topic == 'JSTL'}">
      <tr>
        <td>This row was created because the c_rt:if tag result was true</td>
        <td></td>
      </tr>
    </c_rt:if>
</table>

<p>Multiplication table, 1 - 5</p>

<!-- Use the forEach tag to create a table -->
<table border="1">
  <tr>
    <td></td><td>1</td><td>2</td><td>3</td><td>4</td><td>5</td>
  </tr>
  <c_rt:forEach var="i" begin="1" end="5">
    <tr>
      <td><c_rt:out value="${i}"/></td>
      <c_rt:forEach var="j" begin="1" end="5">
        <td><c_rt:out value="${i*j}"/></td>
      </c_rt:forEach>
    </tr>
  </c_rt:forEach>
</table>

<h2>Formatting numbers</h2><br>
&lt;fmt:formatNumber value="23.456" type="number" /&gt;
results in <fmt:formatNumber value="23.456" type="number" /><br>
```

```
&lt;fmt:formatNumber type="currency"&gt;23.456&lt;/fmt:formatNumber&gt;
results in <fmt:formatNumber type="currency">23.456</fmt:formatNumber>

<br>&lt;fmt:formatNumber value=".23456" type="percent"/&gt;
results in <fmt:formatNumber value=".23456" type="percent"/><br>

&lt;fmt:formatNumber value=".23456" type="percent"
                 minFractionDigits="2" /&gt;
results in <fmt:formatNumber value=".23456" type="percent"
                            minFractionDigits="2" />

</body>
</html>
```

3. If you are using Tomcat, modify the web.xml file as shown below. If you are using the J2EE Deploytool, set the taglib mapping through the Deploytool.

```
<?xml version="1.0" encoding="ISO-8859-1"?>

<web-app xmlns="http://java.sun.com/xml/ns/j2ee"
    xmlns:xsi="http://www.w3.org/2001/XMLSchema-instance"
    xsi:schemaLocation="http://java.sun.com/xml/ns/j2ee web-app_2_4.xsd"
    version="2.4">

  <!-- this is the deployment descriptor for Chapter 4
      Expression Language example                     -->

  <welcome-file-list>
    <welcome-file>TopicList.jsp</welcome-file>
  </welcome-file-list>

  <!-- this element is for the custom action example -->
  <taglib>
    <taglib-uri>/questions</taglib-uri>
    <taglib-location>/WEB-INF/tlds/faq.tld</taglib-location>
  </taglib>

  <!-- this element is for the simple tag handler example -->
  <taglib>
    <taglib-uri>/simplequestions</taglib-uri>
    <taglib-location>/WEB-INF/tlds/simplefaq.tld</taglib-location>
  </taglib>

  <!-- these elements are for the JSTL example -->
  <taglib>
    <taglib-uri>http://java.sun.com/jstl/core</taglib-uri>
    <taglib-location>/WEB-INF/tlds/c.tld</taglib-location>
  </taglib>
  <taglib>
    <taglib-uri>http://java.sun.com/jstl/format</taglib-uri>
```

```
            <taglib-location>/WEB-INF/tlds/fmt.tld</taglib-location>
        </taglib>

    </web-app>
```

4. That should be all that's required to make the tags available. Deploy the new files and enter the URL http://localhost:8000/Ch04/TopicList.jsp?topic=EL in a browser. Click the link for **EL_2** and you should see this:

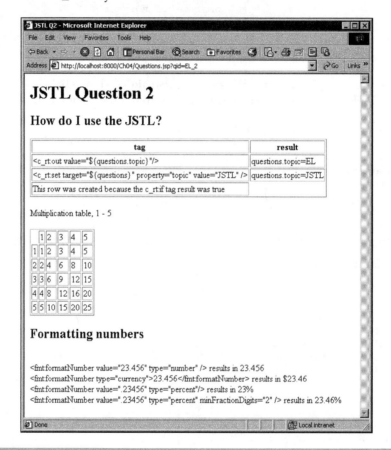

How It Works

This page demonstrates a few of the JSTL tags available to you. We've seen the TLD and the web.xml entries several times now, so I won't cover those at all. The EL_2.jsp file begins by "importing" the tag library:

```
<%@ taglib uri="http://java.sun.com/jstl/core_rt" prefix="c_rt" %>
<%@ taglib uri="http://java.sun.com/jstl/format" prefix="fmt" %>
```

I am using the `rt` version of the core library and the EL version of the format library. The prefix follows the JSTL suggestion; however, recall that I can make the prefix any value I want. The prefix is set by the page designer.

The page then creates a JavaBean from the `Questions` class and prints out the value of its `topic` property. It then sets the `topic` property to a different value and prints that out. Next it uses two `<c:if>` tags to control the creation of another row in the table.

The next part of the page uses nested `<c:forEach>` tags to create a two-dimensional table and to fill the table with the result of multiplying the numbers one through five against themselves.

This example should give you a fair idea of how to start using some of the other tags in the JSTL. There is, of course, much more information in the JSTL specification, available at the Jakarta web site and at java.sun.com.

Other Tag Libraries

The JSTL is certainly not the only tag library available to you. There are many more commercial and free tag libraries available. Here is a short listing of a few:

❑ Struts – This is another tag library from the Jakarta web site. The struts taglib provides tags that are useful in building Model View Controller (MVC) applications. (We saw a simplistic MVC at the end of the last chapter, and we'll see MVC again in the next chapter.)

❑ JNDI – This library is also available from Jakarta. It provides tags for using the Java Naming and Directory Interface API. As we will see throughout this book, you will often use JNDI to look up resources in your web applications.

❑ BEA WebLogic Portal JSP Tag Libraries – This tag library from BEA provides standard tags for working with BEA's web portal.

❑ Coldjava Bar Charts – This is one of many tag libraries available from http://www.servletsuite.com/jsp.htm. This library provides tags for creating horizontal and vertical bar charts.

❑ Orion EJB – Available at http://www.orionserver.com/tags/ejbtags/, this library provides tags for using Enterprise Java Beans.

❑ `jsptags.com` – Not a taglib, but a whole collection of taglibs, can be found at http://jsptags.com/tags/index.jsp. If you can't find what you need here, you will probably need to develop it yourself.

We could spend an entire book just looking at the different tag libraries out there. We obviously don't have room for that here. However, with the information in this chapter on deploying custom actions and using the JSTL, you should have enough information to be able to tackle any taglibs you find.

Summary

So that's the nickel tour of advanced topics in JSPs. We spent some time getting to know Expression Language in some detail, and we spent a lot of time with custom actions and seeing how to implement tag extensions. After that, we took a quick look at the JSP Standard Tag Library.

By no means, though, did we cover everything on those topics. There are many other features of Expression Language, Tag Extensions, and the JSTL that we just didn't have time to cover. What we did look at, though, was the fundamental information, the information that will allow you to sit down and start using these technologies. After you have spent a little time writing tag extensions or EL expressions, you can start delving into the really advanced material.

So, what should you know after having read this chapter?

- ❏ EL expressions provide a simple syntax for using expressions with attributes and template text.

- ❏ EL expressions are very Java-like in their syntax.

- ❏ Custom actions provide a way to hide the Java code from the page designer.

- ❏ Tag handlers are the Java classes that implement a custom action. You will usually extend `SimpleTagSupport`, `TagSupport`, or `BodyTagSupport` when creating a tag handler.

- ❏ Deploying a tag library is as easy as 1, 2, 3 (copy `jars` and `tlds`, add mapping to `web.xml`, add a `taglib` directive to the JSP page).

- ❏ JSTL provides a library of standard tags that can be used for many basic functions.

Exercises

1. When using a classic tag handler, investigate if there is any difference in how the tag handler methods are called for the two different forms of the empty tag: `<empty/>` and `<empty></empty>`.

2. Develop a JSP that uses the `sql` taglib of JSTL to talk to a database.

CHAPTER 5

HTTP and Server Programs	180
The Servlet Model and HttpServlets	185
Handling Exceptions	216
Session Management	219
Filters	227
The MVC Architecture	237
Summary	252
Exercises	253

Servlets

Along with JSPs, servlets are the other highly used component in J2EE web applications. Servlets are server-side applications in much the same way that way applets are client-side applications. Like JSP pages, servlets are Java classes that are loaded and executed by a servlet container that can run standalone or as a component of a web server or a J2EE server. In fact, as we saw in Chapter 3, JSP pages are actually compiled by the container into a servlet class that is then executed by the container. However, while JSP pages are usually HTML pages with bits of embedded Java code, servlets are Java classes with bits of embedded HTML.

Servlets are designed to be extensions to servers, and to extend the capabilities of servers. Notice that I say "servers" rather than "web servers". Servlets were originally intended to be able to extend any server such as an FTP server, or an SMTP (e-mail) server. However, in practice, only servlets that respond to HTTP requests have been widely implemented. Servlets extend the capabilities of a web server and provide dynamic behavior for web applications. Servlets are designed to accept a response from a client (usually a web browser), process that request, and return a response to the client. Although all the processing can occur within the servlet, usually helper classes or other web components such as Enterprise JavaBeans (EJBs) will perform the business logic processing, leaving the servlet free to perform the request and response processing.

After JDBC, servlets were the second J2EE technology invented. Since they were also developed before JSP, early servlets had to handle display processing. This mixture of page design mixed into code was one of the reasons JSP was introduced. When servlets were first introduced, if you were developing a web application in Java, you were using just servlets in the middle tier, and JDBC if you had a database. Now, of course, servlets are just one aspect of the whole J2EE architecture.

In this chapter, we'll introduce you to servlets and show you how to use them correctly in your web application. Specifically, we will look at:

- ❏ How HTTP requests are made to servers
- ❏ How servlets are designed to respond to HTTP requests

❑ The phases in the servlet lifecycle

❑ Ways to make your servlet thread-safe

❑ Handling exceptions in your servlet

❑ How to create and use sessions

❑ How to use filters in your web application

❑ What the Model View Controller (MVC) architecture is, and how it makes better applications

HTTP and Server Programs

Although servlets were originally intended to work with any server, in practice servlets are only used with web servers, so in a J2EE application, you will only be developing servlets that respond to HTTP requests. As we will see later, the Servlet API provides a class named HttpServlet specifically for dealing with these requests. The HttpServlet class is designed to work closely with the HTTP protocol. This protocol was developed years before servlets were designed, and the basic HTTP protocol has been very stable. The HTTP protocol defines the structure of the requests that a client sends to a web server, the format for the client to submit request parameters, and the way the server responds. HttpServlets use the same protocol to handle the service requests they receive and to return responses to clients. So understanding the basics of HTTP is important to understanding how to use servlets.

Request Methods

The HTTP specification defines a number of requests that a web client, typically a browser, can make upon a web server. These are called methods, and there are seven methods defined. They are:

❑ GET – Retrieves information identified by a request Uniform Resource Identifier (URI).

❑ POST – Requests that the server pass the body of the request to the resource identified by the request URI for processing.

❑ HEAD – Returns only the header of the response that would be returned by a GET request.

❑ PUT – Uploads data to the server to be stored at the given request URI. The main difference between this and POST is that the server should not further process a PUT request, but simply store it at the request URI.

❑ DELETE – Deletes the resource identified by the request URI.

❑ TRACE – Causes the server to return the request message.

❑ OPTIONS – Asks the server for information about a specific resource, or about the server's capabilities in general.

These methods are defined in the HTTP specification at
http://www.ietf.org/rfc/rfc2068.txt?number=2068. When developing web applications, we are
concerned primarily with GET and POST requests.

GET

Simply stated, the GET method means that the browser sends a formatted string to the server,
and the server returns the content identified by that string. This string is known as a Uniform
Resource Identifier (URI). One specific type of URI is a string that specifies the location of a
resource in relation to the server. This is a Uniform Resource Locator (URL). The resource can
be a static web page, or the result of a web application. A GET request usually results when a
user clicks a link in a web page, or enters a URL in the address bar of the browser. However,
there are other ways this can occur. For example, you can send a GET request through a telnet
session or programmatically send a GET request to a server; you can even create a web page
form that uses GET for its requests.

When sending a GET request, additional information can be passed to the web server. For GET
requests, this usually takes the form of request parameters that are appended to the URL. For
example, when you perform a web search using the web site **www.google.com**, the search
parameters are passed to the search engine using request parameters as shown here:

   http://www.google.com/search?hl=en&q=Beginning+Java+Server

The request parameters are prefixed by a question mark (?), the parameters are passed as
name-value pairs (hl=en, for example), and each pair is delimited by an ampersand (&). This
format is also known as **URL encoding**.

Another way to pass parameters to a server is by appending the data as additional path
information to the URL. The additional information looks like a continuation of the URL, but
the web application interprets the path information as parameters that it can act upon. For
example, suppose we had a stock brokerage application identified by the URL /stock/StockList.
We could append additional information to the URL, which the StockList application would
interpret as a parameter. It might look like this:

   http://localhost:8000/stock/StockList/AddRating

The /AddRating part of the URL appears to be part of the URL for the web application;
however, it does not identify any resource installed on the server. The resource is StockList,
and the StockList application knows how to interpret the additional path information.

Try It Out   Sending an HTTP request via Telnet

1. You can create a GET request from the command line to see the basic structure of such a request. Start by ensuring that the J2EE server or Tomcat is running. If you need to start the server, use the appropriate script file in the J2EE bin or Tomcat bin directories, or select the Start J2EE shortcut from the Start menu if you are using Windows.

2. Start a telnet client. On Windows, open a command window. For Unix, open a terminal or console window. Then enter the following command to connect to the J2EE server on the default port:

```
> telnet localhost 8000
```

or this command to connect to Tomcat on its default port:

```
> telnet localhost 8080
```

You can replace localhost with an IP address or a hostname, and the port number should be replaced with the correct port for your system, as necessary.

3. For J2EE, enter the following command followed by two *Return* characters:

```
> GET /index.html HTTP/1.0
>
```

If you are attempting to connect to Tomcat, use:

```
> GET /index.jsp HTTP/1.0
>
```

If you wait too long before entering the request, the connection will be automatically closed. Try again, but type more quickly.

4. Don't forget to press the *Return* key twice. The second *Return* creates a blank line; this tells the server that the request is complete. The server should respond with the appropriate information. Here is what was returned when I connected to the J2EE server:

```
HTTP/1.1 200 OK
ETag: W/"1406-1035567554000"
Last-Modified: Fri, 25 Oct 2002 17:39:14 GMT
Content-Type: text/html
Content-Length: 1406
Date: Sun, 05 Jan 2003 19:14:53 GMT
Server: Apache Coyote/1.0
Connection: close
```

```
<!doctype html public "-//w3c//dtd html 4.0 transitional//en">
<html>
<head>
<meta http-equiv="Content-Type" content="text/html; charset=iso-8859-1">
<meta name="GENERATOR" content="Mozilla/4.51 [en] (X11; I; SunOS 5.6 sun4u)
[Netscape]">
    <title>Default J2EE Home Page</title>

...remainder of response not shown...
```

How It Works

The telnet command line includes the name of the telnet program (which just happens to be `telnet`), followed by the hostname for the connection, and the port.

The actual request consists of the method (`GET`) followed by the relative URI of the desired resource, followed by the HTTP identifier for the HTTP version that the telnet program supports. The URI is just /index.html (or /index.jsp), which is the URI for the root resource of the server. Press *Enter* to complete the request line, and then press *Enter* again. The blank line tells the server that the header is complete. Since a `GET` request has no body, the request is sent to the server.

A general HTTP message has this format:

```
Request-Line
Headers
<Carriage Return/Line Feed>
[ message-body ]
```

Each request begins with the request line. In our example, that was `GET /index.html HTTP/1.0`. This is followed by header data. In our example, we did not use any header data. A blank line created by entering just a carriage return/line feed sequence signals the end of the headers. This is followed by an optional message body. Since our example was a `GET` request, there was no message body. `POST` requests will have message bodies.

You can see this entire structure in the response from the server, which has the same message format as a request. The first line of the response is the status line, which consists of the HTTP version, a response code (200), and a response message (OK). This is followed by the response headers: the date, content length, and other information added by the server. The headers, whether part of the request or response, are in the format *name : value*. This is followed by the actual body of the resource. In the example above, the server returns the J2EE home page.

So, whether you are clicking a link, entering an address in a browser address bar, using telnet, or connecting to a server programmatically (using code), the request that is sent to the server must ultimately follow the format prescribed by the HTTP specification. Most of the time, however, formatting the request is handled for you.

183

POST

If the request is sent using the POST method, the request can include a message body, and the server should pass this message body to the resource in the URI for processing. POST requests are typically generated by users submitting a form through their web browser. Forms can be used with either GET or POST requests, although they tend to be used with POSTs. Additionally, like GET requests, POST requests can be generated manually using a program such as telnet, or programmatically using classes in the java.net package.

Also, while data can be passed to the server using the same techniques as with GET requests (appending parameters or adding additional path information), a POST request usually submits data to the server in the body of a request. For example, using the hypothetical StockList application, the POST request to submit stock ratings might look like this:

```
POST /stock/servlet/StockList/AddRating HTTP/1.0
Content-type: application/x-www-form-urlencoding
Content-length: 39

analysts=3&stocks=DDC&ratings=Smashing!
```

Now, if a browser had submitted the above POST request, it would pass more information than I have shown above. However, the commands shown above are sufficient for sending data to a web application. The request starts with the method and URL, and the head of the request includes Content-type and Content-length parameters. This is followed by two pairs of <CRLF> characters, followed by the request data in the message-body. In this example, the POST data consists of 39 characters, formatted using URL-encoding. The data does not need to be URL-encoded, however. POST data can be in any format that the web application understands. The point is that request data for a POST request is usually included in the body of the request, rather than appended to the URL.

How a Server Responds to Requests

We already know how a server responds when the GET request is for a static HTML web page. When you enter an address or click a link, the server locates the resource identified by the URI and returns that resource as part of an HTTP message to the web browser. In the case of a web page, the browser displays the web page for you.

What happens, however, when the resource is a server-side program? In this case, the server needs to interpret the URI as a request for a server-side program, format the request parameters in a form the program recognizes, and pass the request to that program. In the early days of the web, a standardized format for doing this was developed called Common Gateway Interface, or CGI; whenever you see a URL that has /cgi/ as part of the address, you are creating a request to a server-side program of that type. The program must interpret the request parameters, execute the appropriate processing, and return a response to the server, which returns it to the client.

In the early days of the Web, the server program was usually a program written in a language such as C or Perl, which executed in a separate process from the server. Every request caused a new process to be spawned; when the program completed processing the request, it was terminated. This was usually resource intensive.

A process is a running program and all the data associated with it.

Java servlets, and specifically `HttpServlets`, provide several advantages over CGI programs for server-side applications:

❑ They can run in the same process as the server, so new processes don't need to be spawned for every request.

❑ They are portable between servers (as long as they don't use any platform-specific code). CGI programs written and compiled in C, for example, would need to be recompiled for a different operating system.

The Servlet Model and HttpServlets

The following diagram presents a slightly simplified view of what happens when a client makes a request that is processed by a servlet:

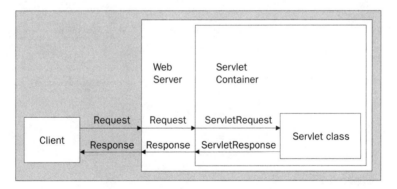

When a client (usually, but not necessarily, a web browser) makes a request to the server, and the server determines the request is for a servlet resource, it passes the request to the servlet container. The container is the program responsible for loading, initiating, calling, and releasing servlet instances. The servlet container takes the HTTP request, parses its request URI, the headers, and the body, and stores all of that data inside an object that implements the `javax.servlet.ServletRequest` interface. It also creates an instance of an object the implements `javax.servlet.ServletResponse`. The response object encapsulates the response back to the client. The container then calls a method of the servlet class, passing the request and response objects. The servlet processes the request, and sends a response back to the client.

If you read the JSP chapters of this book, you will realize that this request-response flow is very similar to the request-response flow for JSP pages. In fact, since JSP pages are translated into servlets, it is almost identical. Is there any difference between the two? Or put another way, when should we use servlets, and when JSP pages? In general, JSP pages are better suited for web components that contain a large amount of presentation logic. Servlets are better suited for web components that perform processing or business logic. Servlets can send display data directly through the response as shown above, but in many web applications the servlet will accept and process the request, using some other component to generate the response back to the client. In the next few sections, we'll look at how a servlet receives the request and returns a response.

Basic Servlet Design

Like CGI programs, HTTP servlets are designed to respond to GET and POST requests, along with all the other requests defined for HTTP, although you will probably never need to respond to anything other than GET or POST. When writing servlets, you will usually extend a class named `javax.servlet.http.HttpServlet`. This is a base class provided by the servlet API that provides support for HTTP requests. The `HttpServlet` class, in turn, extends `javax.servlet.GenericServlet`, which provides some basic servlet functionality. Finally, `GenericServlet` implements the primary servlet API interface, `javax.servlet.Servlet`. It also implements an interface called `ServletConfig`, which allows it to provide easy access to servlet configuration information. This is shown in the class diagram below:

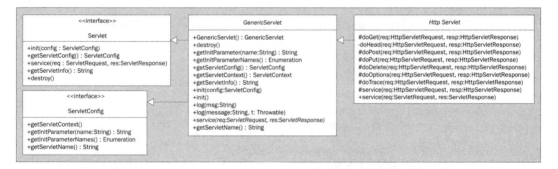

The service() Method

Notice that `Servlet` only defines only a small number of methods. You can probably guess that `init()` and `destroy()` don't handle any requests. We'll look at these methods later when we discuss the servlet lifecycle in more detail. Likewise, `getServletConfig()` and `getServletInfo()` don't handle requests either. That leaves only `service()` to handle requests. When a servlet container receives a request for a servlet, it calls the `service()` method of the servlet. So a servlet that implements the `Servlet` interface must implement the `service()` method to handle requests.

The doPost() and doGet() Methods

HttpServlet is intended to respond to HTTP requests, and it has to handle requests for GET, POST, HEAD, etc. Thus HttpServlet defines additional methods. It defines a doGet() to handle GET requests; doPost() to handle POST requests, and so on: there is a doXXX() method for every HTTP method. What these methods really do, rather than processing the request, is to return an error message to the client saying the method is not supported. You, as the developer, are expected to write your servlet to extend HttpServlet and override the methods you want to support. Usually this will be doPost() and/or doGet().

You will often see servlet examples in books or tutorials that show a servlet class that extends HttpServlet and overrides the service() method to process an HTTP request. This is acceptable for simple example servlets, and you really won't cause any problems if you do this in a real J2EE application. However, HttpServlet already implements a service() method and it determines the correct doXXX() method to call for the HTTP request. In a real-world application, you should avoid overriding service() in your servlet, and instead override doPost() and/or doGet().

When the servlet container receives the HTTP request, it maps the URI to a servlet. It then calls the service() method of the servlet. Assuming the servlet extends HttpServlet, and only overrides doPost() or doGet(), the call to service() will go to the HttpServlet class. The service() method determines which HTTP method the request used, and calls the correct doXXX() method. If your servlet has that method, it will be called because it overrides the same method in HttpServlet. Your doXXX() method processes the request, generates an HTTP response, and returns it to the client. Here is an illustration of that process, with an HTTP GET request:

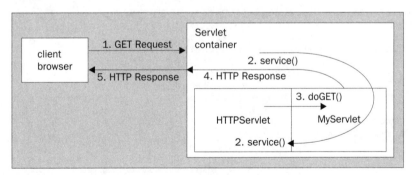

In this illustration, note that even though HttpServlet and MyServlet are shown in separate boxes, together they constitute a single object in the system, an instance of MyServlet.

Request and Response Objects

The actual signature of all of the doXXX() methods is:

```
public void doXXX(HttpServletRequest req, HttpServletResponse res)
```

Each method – `doPost()`, `doGet()`, etc. – accepts two parameters. The `HttpServletRequest` object encapsulates the request to the server. It contains the data for the request, as well as some header information about the request. Using methods defined by the `request` object, the servlet can access the data submitted as part of the request. The `HttpServletResponse` object encapsulates the response to the client. Using the response object and its methods, you can return a response to the client.

Since we know the basic objects at this point, let's look at a simple example servlet. We'll use some of the methods of `HttpServletRequest` and `HttpServletResponse`, even though they have not been introduced yet. We'll look at those methods in more detail after the example.

Try It Out — Creating a Servlet

1. In this example, we'll create a servlet that can respond to HTTP POST requests. Start by creating the simple servlet shown here:

```java
package web;

import javax.servlet.*;
import javax.servlet.http.*;
import java.io.*;

public class Login extends HttpServlet {
  public void doPost(HttpServletRequest request,
                     HttpServletResponse response)
  {
    String username = request.getParameter("username");
    try {
      response.setContentType("text/html");
      PrintWriter writer = response.getWriter();
      writer.println("<html><body>");
      writer.println("Thank you, " + username +
                     ". You are now logged into the system.");
      writer.println("</body></html>");
      writer.close();
    } catch (Exception e) {
      e.printStackTrace();
    }
  }
}
```

2. Compile the servlet. You will need to include the correct library for the compilation. There are two possible libraries to choose from, depending on whether you are using the J2EE reference implementation or the Tomcat server. It doesn't matter which one you use. If you have the J2EE SDK, you can use the `j2ee.jar` library; if you have Tomcat you can use `servlet.jar`. Assuming `J2EE_HOME` is the environment variable for the location of the J2EE SDK, then compile the servlet with the appropriate command line below:

```
> javac -classpath %J2EE_HOME%\lib\j2ee.jar Login.java    # For Windows
> javac -classpath $J2EE_HOME/lib/j2ee.jar Login.java     # For Linux/UNIX
```

If you're using Tomcat, then assuming CATALINA_HOME is the location of the Tomcat installation, compile the servlet with the appropriate command below:

```
> javac -classpath %CATALINA_HOME%\common\lib\servlet.jar Login.java # Windows
> javac -classpath $CATALINA_HOME/common/lib/servlet.jar Login.java  # Linux
```

3. The root of this application will be named Ch05. So, to call the servlet above, the path will be Ch05/Login. Create the HTML page below (login.html), which has a form that posts to the servlet:

```html
<!DOCTYPE HTML PUBLIC "-//W3C//DTD HTML 4.01 Transitional//EN">
<html>
  <head>
    <title>Login</title>
  </head>

  <body>
    <h1>Login</h1>

    Please enter your username and password
    <form action="/Ch05/Login" method="POST">
      <p><input type="text" name="username" length="40">
      <p><input type="password" name="password" length="40">
      <p><input type="submit" value="Submit">
    </form>
  </body>
</html>
```

How It Works

The Login servlet illustrates some of the main points developed in this chapter so far. The class itself is just like any other Java class. In this case, it is a subclass of HttpServlet. As a subclass of HttpServlet, the Login class only needs to override the methods of HttpServlet that it needs to implement its behavior, or alternately, add new methods for new behavior. In this example, Login only needs to override the doPost() method of HttpServlet.

When you click the Submit button of the login.html static page, the web browser submits a POST request to the Tomcat server. Web forms can be used to submit either GET or POST requests. The <form> tag in the web page has a method attribute that has the value POST. This tells the browser to submit a POST request to the resource indicated by the action attribute of the <form> tag. If no method attribute is used, the form defaults to the GET method.

When the Tomcat server receives the POST request, it parses the URL to determine which resource to send the request to. The /Ch05 portion tells Tomcat that this is a resource in the Ch05 application; the /Login portion maps to the web.Login class. Tomcat constructs instances of HttpServletRequest and HttpServletResponse, and calls the service() method of Login. Since Login does not implement service(), the parent class method is called; the service() method of HttpServlet determines that the request is a POST request and calls the doPost() method. Since Login does define doPost(), it is that method which is used to process the request.

Within the doPost() method, the Login servlet reads a request parameter from the HttpServletRequest object. The method that it uses to do this is getParameter(String), which returns a String that has the value of the request parameter with the given name. If no such parameter exists, then null is returned. The name used by the servlet:

```
String username = request.getParameter("username");
```

is the same as the name used in the web form:

```
<p><input type="text" name="username" length="40">
```

There are several other methods used to retrieve the request parameters from the request object. I will cover these methods later in the chapter.

The Login servlet then uses the response object to return a response to the client. It starts by setting the Content-type of the response to "text/html":

```
response.setContentType("text/html");
```

> **The content type must be set before getting an** OutputStream **or** Writer
> **object from the response object, since the content type is used to create the**
> OutputStream **or** Writer.

After setting the content type, the servlet gets a Writer object from the response object. This Writer is used to send the strings that constitute the response to the client:

```
try {
  response.setContentType("text/html");
  PrintWriter writer = response.getWriter();
  writer.println("<html><body>");
  writer.println("Thank you, " + username +
                 ". You are now logged into the system");
  writer.println("</body></html>");
  writer.close();
} catch (Exception e) {
  e.printStackTrace();
}
```

Because writing to a stream can throw an `IOException`, the whole block is wrapped in a `try...catch` block. However, this `try...catch` block just prints out the stack trace for any exception thrown. While this is OK for this example, it is generally a bad practice to ignore exceptions in the servlet. I will show why this is so in the *Handling Exceptions* section later in the chapter. Also, as with the `request` object, I will show the other methods of the `response` object later in the chapter.

<table>
<tr><td>**Try It Out**</td><td>**Deploying a Servlet to the J2EE Server**</td></tr>
</table>

At this point, we are ready to deploy the servlet. The next set of steps will show how to deploy the servlet with the J2EE SDK. These steps are virtually identical to the steps used in the previous JSP chapters. If you want to deploy to Tomcat, go to the next *Try It Out* section. Make sure the J2EE server is running, and open the Deploytool from the **Start** menu (for Windows) or by typing `deploytool` at a command prompt.

1. Create a new Application EAR. Select **File | New | Application EAR** as shown below. Alternatively, you can click the toolbar button for creating a new EAR.

2. In the dialog that results, enter a filename for the EAR. I used `StockBrokerage.ear`. The Deploytool will set the display name automatically:

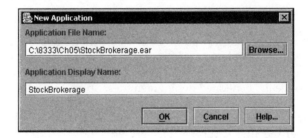

3. Next select **File | New | Web Application WAR** (alternatively, you can click the toolbar button for creating a new Web Application WAR).

4. The New Web Application Wizard will now run. Click **Next** on the opening splash screen. In the **Contents** pane of the next screen, click the **Edit** button and add the `login.html` and `Login.class` files to the application. Click the **Next** button:

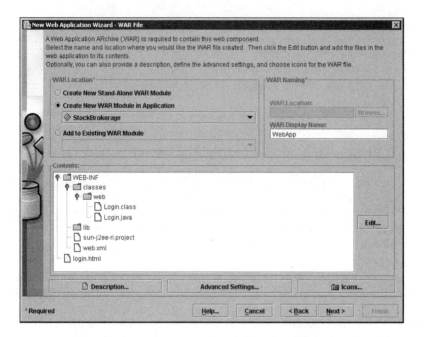

5. The following dialog selects the component to create. Servlet should already be selected, so click Next.

6. The dialog that follows allows you to select the Servlet Class and the Web Component Name. There should only be one selection in the class drop-down box, web.Login, so select this. The wizard will automatically fill in the component name to be Login. Click Finish (or, if you want to see the generated deployment descriptor, select Next, then Finish).

7. With the Login WebApp selected, click on the Aliases tab. Click on Add to add a new alias, and enter the alias /Login for the servlet:

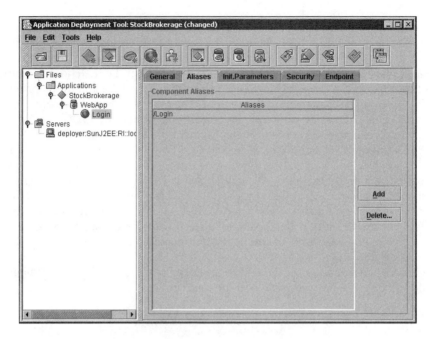

8. You will now see the main Deploytool window. Ensure the StockBrokerage EAR entry is selected in the left navigation pane, and select the tab named Web Context in the right pane. Enter Ch05 for the Context Root as shown below:

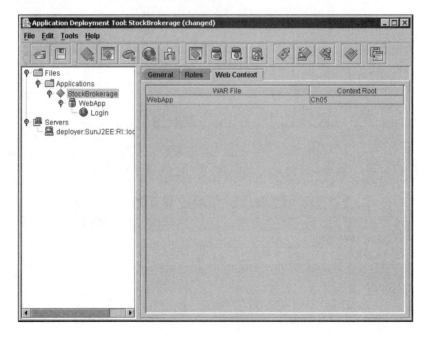

9. Save the application using File | Save As. Put the EAR into a location you can remember, such as the directory where you have the Login.java or Login.class file.

10. Select File | Deployment Settings | Create New File. In the file chooser dialog that follows, select the same location that you used for the EAR file in the previous step. Now select File | Deployment Settings | Close File. Select the Save option in the dialog. This will create a deployment file. If you named the EAR StockBrokerage.ear, then the deployment file will be named StockBrokerage.ear.xml.

11. You are now ready to deploy the servlet. Select Tools | Deploy. The dialog box that follows asks you to select the correct ear.xml file. The file that was created in the previous step should already be selected. If it is not, used the file chooser to select that file. Click the OK button. As the deployment process proceeds, the progress is reported in a new dialog box. After the deployment is complete, close the progress dialog.

12. Open a browser and enter the URL http://localhost:8000/Ch05/login.html into the address bar. The browser will load the login page:

13. Enter a username and password into the dialog and click the Submit button. The servlet will process the request and return this to the browser:

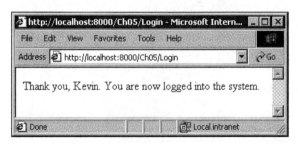

Deploying a Servlet to Tomcat Standalone

1. In the next few steps, I will show how to manually deploy the `Login` servlet to Tomcat standalone. To deploy to Tomcat, the application needs an appropriate directory structure. Start by creating this directory structure:

```
Ch05/
  login.html
  WEB-INF/
    web.xml
    classes/
      web/
        Login.class
```

This is the same directory structure created automatically by the Deploytool in step 4 above. You can create this directory structure anywhere in your file system, but if you create it in the /webapps directory of your Tomcat installation, you'll be one step ahead of the game.

2. The `web.xml` file shown in the directory structure above is also known as the deployment descriptor. For this example, it will look like this:

```
<?xml version="1.0" encoding="ISO-8859-1"?>

<!DOCTYPE web-app
    PUBLIC "-//Sun Microsystems, Inc.//DTD Web Application 2.3//EN"
    "http://java.sun.com/dtd/web-app_2_3.dtd">

<web-app>
  <display-name>Beginning J2EE Ch 5</display-name>
  <servlet>
    <servlet-name>Login</servlet-name>
    <servlet-class>web.Login</servlet-class>
  </servlet>
  <servlet-mapping>
    <servlet-name>Login</servlet-name>
    <url-pattern>/Login</url-pattern>
  </servlet-mapping>
</web-app>
```

3. If you created the directory structure above in the /webapps directory of Tomcat, you can go to the next step. Otherwise, you need to install the application in one of two ways:

Copy the entire directory structure to the /webapps folder of the Tomcat installation.

Create a Web Application Archive (WAR) file and copy the WAR file to Tomcat. Navigate into the /stock directory and create the WAR file using the `jar` tool:

```
C:\8333\Ch05\stock\>jar cf stock.war *
```

Copy the WAR file to the Tomcat **/webapps** directory.

4. Start the Tomcat server. If it is already running, you will need to stop and restart it.

5. Open a browser and enter the URL http://localhost:8080/Ch05/login.html into the address bar. The browser will load the login page as shown in Step 12 above. Enter a username and password and click the Submit button. The web browser will display a welcome message returned by the servlet as shown in Step 13 above.

How It Works

The deployment descriptor for this application has two important elements under the <web-app> element:

```
<servlet>
  <servlet-name>Login</servlet-name>
  <servlet-class>web.Login</servlet-class>
</servlet>
<servlet-mapping>
  <servlet-name>Login</servlet-name>
  <url-pattern>/Login</url-pattern>
</servlet-mapping>
```

The <servlet> element tells the container the class that is used for a given servlet name, and the <servlet-mapping> element maps a URL to a servlet name. Thus, when the servlet container receives a URL that matches the given pattern, it will know which class to send the request to.

Using the request Object

In the example above, the servlet got information from the request object by calling the getParameter() method:

```
String username = request.getParameter("username");
```

The getParameter() method is unique in that it is the only method ever undeprecated by Sun. In the second version of the specification, getParameter() was deprecated and replaced by getParameterValues(). Enough developers expressed the opinion that the method was in fact still useful, and Sun undeprecated the method.

The ServletRequest interface defines a few other methods for getting and using request data from the client's request. Those methods are:

```
public Enumeration getParameterNames()
public String[] getParameterValues(String name)
public Map getParameterMap()
```

The getParameterValues() method returns the request parameters with the given name. The getParameterValues() method is used when the named parameter may have multiple values. For instance, if an HTML form contains a <select> list that allows multiple selections, the request will contain all the selected values keyed by a single name, the name of the <select> list. If you call getParameter() on a parameter with multiple values, the value returned is the same as the first element returned by getParameterValues(). If you call either getParameter() or getParameterValues() and the name does not exist in the request, null is returned. Also, keep in mind that web browsers only send non-null values. In other words, if an HTML form has a checkbox, and the user does not select the checkbox, the checkbox name is not sent in the request.

The getParameterNames() returns an enumeration of all the names in the request.

The getParameterMap() method returns all the parameters stored in a Map object. Each parameter name is a key in the Map; the value can be either a String or a String[] array, depending on whether the parameter has multiple values.

You can also get information about the request using ServletRequest methods. Here is a listing of a few of the more useful methods:

❑   public String getProtocol() – The protocol used by the request; this will usually be "HTTP".

❑   public String getServerName() – The host name of the server that received the request. This is useful if the server uses virtual servers.

❑   public String getRemoteAddr() – The IP address of the client that made the request.

❑   public String getRemoteHost() – The host name of the client that made the request.

You can also get access to the request stream containing the unparsed request parameters. There are two methods available for accessing the request stream:

```
public BufferedReader getReader()
public ServletInputStream getInputStream()
```

You can only use one of the methods with a single request. Once you access the request input stream using one of these methods, the stream cannot be accessed again. Attempting to call either of them for the same request will result in an exception being thrown. Also, note that if you use one of these methods, and the request has a message body, the getParameter() and getParameterValues() methods may not work.

Earlier, we looked at the format of an HTTP message. Recall that it looked like this:

```
Request-Line
Headers
<Carriage Return/Line Feed>
[ message body ]
```

The `HttpServletRequest` object provides a number of methods for reading the header data from the HTTP message:

```
long getDateHeader(String name)
String getHeader(String name)
Enumeration getHeaders(String name)
Enumeration getHeaderNames()
int getIntHeader(String name)
```

Two special methods are provided for getting a header value as a date or an `int`. Headers that are not dates or `int`s can be accessed using the general `getHeader(String)` method. The name argument passed to any of these methods should be the name of the header. Here again is part of the header portion of the response we got from the J2EE server in the first example of the chapter:

```
Last-Modified: Fri, 25 Oct 2002 17:39:14 GMT
Content-Length: 1406
Server: Apache Coyote/1.0
```

A servlet could get the value of the `Last-Modified` header by calling `getDateHeader("Last-Modified")`. It could get the `Content-Length` by calling `getIntHeader("Content-Length")`. A header like `Server`, neither date nor `int`, would be obtained by calling `getHeader("Server")`.

Earlier in the chapter, I mentioned that browsers can append request parameters to the URL. The servlet can obtain those parameters by calling `getQueryString()`.

```
public String getQueryString()
```

Thus, suppose you have a request URL that looks like this:

```
http://localhost/ch05/Login?name=Kevin
```

In this case, calling `getQueryString()` will return `"name=Kevin"`.

I also mentioned that information could be added to the URL that looks like a continuation of the path. This extra path information can be obtained by calling `getPathInfo()`:

```
public String getPathInfo()
```

For example, suppose you have a request URL like this:

```
http://localhost/ch05/Login/extra/path/info
```

In this case, `getPathInfo()` will return `"/extra/path/info"`.

Using the response Object

In the previous example, we used two methods of the `response` object:

```
response.setContentType("text/html");
PrintWriter writer = response.getWriter();
```

Using the `Writer` obtained from the `response`, the servlet sent HTML data to the client browser for it to display. There is another object that can be used to send response data. You will normally use the `Writer` to send character data, but you can also send data to the client using an output stream obtained through this method:

```
public ServletOutputStream getOutputStream()
```

While the `OutputStream` can be used for text data, its primary purpose is to send binary data to the response. However, that topic is beyond the scope of this chapter. Briefly, the servlet would get binary data (an image, for example) and store it in a byte array, then set the content type (`"image/jpeg"`, perhaps), set the content length, and then write the binary data to the output stream.

The three methods above are defined by the `ServletResponse` interface. The `HttpServletResponse` interface adds methods that are useful for responding to HTTP requests. These methods allow the servlet to add or set header data in the response:

```
void addDateHeader(String name, long date)
void addHeader(String name, String value)
void addIntHeader(String name, int value)
void setDateHeader(String name, long date)
void setHeader(String name, String value)
void setIntHeader(String name, int value)
```

Deployment Descriptors

Throughout the last couple of chapters, we've seen several examples of deployment descriptors for our web applications contained in a file called `web.xml`. However, we've postponed a full coverage of deployment descriptors until now, because many of the elements involved relate to servlets rather than JSP pages. So, now you know what a servlet is, we can take a deeper look at the deployment descriptor.

As well as the application-specific deployment descriptors that we've been using so far, Tomcat also has a default web.xml file used for applications that do not provide their own deployment descriptor. This file is located in the Tomcat /conf directory. Note that the servlet specification only requires an application web.xml. Servlet containers other than Tomcat may or may not support a global web.xml file; you should consult the documentation for your servlet container or server to see if it has such a feature.

Your servlet container probably has a tool that automates the process of creating the deployment descriptor. For example, the Deploytool that comes with J2EE can automatically create the deployment descriptor for a web application. In this section we will look at some of the more important elements of the deployment descriptor. This will be useful if you need to understand a deployment descriptor, or if you need to manually create one.

Because the deployment descriptor is contained in an XML file, it must conform to the XML standard. This means it should start with the XML declaration (<?xml version="1.0"?>) and a DOCTYPE declaration, as shown here:

```
<?xml version="1.0" encoding="ISO-8859-1"?>

<!DOCTYPE web-app
    PUBLIC "-//Sun Microsystems, Inc.//DTD Web Application 2.3//EN"
    "http://java.sun.com/dtd/web-app_2_3.dtd">

<web-app>
</web-app>
```

The root element of the deployment descriptor is the <web-app> element. The Servlet 2.3 specification defines these subelements that make can be used within the <web-app> element:

Element	Description
icon	Contains a path to icons that can be used by a graphical tool to represent the web application
display-name	A name that can be used by an application management tool to represent the web application
description	A description of the web application
distributable	Describes whether the web application can be distributed across servers; the default value is false
context-param	Contains parameter values that are used across the application
filter	Defines filter classes that are called prior to the servlet
filter-mapping	Defines aliases for filters

Element	Description
listener	Defines listener classes that are called by the container when certain events occur
servlet	Defines a servlet by name and class file
servlet-mapping	Defines aliases for servlets
session-config	Defines a timeout value for sessions
mime-mapping	Defines a mapping for the public files of the web application to mime types
welcome-file-list	Defines the file to return to the client when no resource is specified in the URL
error-page	Defines the error page returned to the client when a particular error occurs
taglib	Defines the location of tag libraries
resource-env-ref	Configures an external resource that can be used by the servlet
resource-ref	Configures an external resource that can be used by the servlet
security-constraint	Describes the roles or users that can access the web application
login-config	Configures the authentication method
security-role	Defines a security role for the application
env-entry	Defines the name of a resource that be accessed through the JNDI interface
ejb-ref	Defines a remote reference to an Enterprise Java Bean (EJB)
ejb-local-ref	Defines a local reference to an EJB

Note that the servlet container will expect the elements above to be given in the same order as defined in the DTD (for version 2.3 or earlier of the Servlet specification) or the XML Schema (Servlet 2.4). That order is the same as shown in the table above. Let's take a brief look at some of those elements. I will not cover all the elements, or all the options for each element, but rather enough to get you going. We'll look at a couple of these later on in the chapter: in the *Filters* section we will look at <filter> and <filter-mapping>, and in the *Handling Exceptions* section, we will look at <error-page>.

The <context-param> Element

The <context-param> element allows you to define context parameters. These parameters specify values that are available to the entire web application context. The element is used like this:

```
<web-app>
  <context-param>
    <param-name>debug</param-name>
    <param-value>true</param-value>
  </context-param>
</web-app>
```

The deployment descriptor can contain zero or more of these elements. Each web component that has access to the servlet context can access these parameters by name. I will show how this is done later in the chapter. Notice that because the web.xml file is in text format, you can only pass parameters to the application as strings.

The <servlet> Element

The <servlet> element is the primary element for describing the servlets in your web application. The <servlet> element can have the following sub-elements:

- ❑   <icon>
- ❑   <servlet-name>
- ❑   <display-name>
- ❑   <description>
- ❑   <servlet-class>
- ❑   <jsp-file>
- ❑   <init-param>
- ❑   <load-on-startup>
- ❑   <run-as>
- ❑   <security-role-ref>

The only required sub-elements are <servlet-name> and one of the sub-elements <servlet-class> or <jsp-file>. The <servlet-name> sub-element defines a user-friendly name that can be used for the resource. The <servlet-class> or <jsp-file> sub-elements define the fully qualified name of the servlet class or JSP file. In the previous example, we used this for the <servlet> element:

```
<servlet>
  <servlet-name>Login</servlet-name>
  <servlet-class>web.Login</servlet-class>
</servlet>
```

By defining the servlet name as `Login`, and using the `<servlet-mapping>` element to map URLs such as **/Login** to the name `Login`, we were able to access the servlet using the simple URL **/stock/Login**. Okay, that's not such a big deal when the servlet-name and class name are both `Login`; but suppose your class name were `com.mycompany.subdivision.MyServletWithAReallyReallyLongName`. Then it makes much more sense to be able to access the servlet using `SimpleName`.

The `<servlet-class>` sub-element told the servlet container that all requests for `Login` should be handled by the `web.Login` class.

The other elements of servlet that you will often use are `<load-on-startup>` and `<init-param>`.

```
<load-on-startup>5</load-on-startup>
```

The `<load-on-startup>` element, if used, contains a positive integer value that specifies that the servlet should be loaded when the server is started. The relative order of servlet loading is determined by the value; servlets with lower values are loaded before servlets with higher values; servlets with the same value are loaded in an arbitrary order. If the element is not present, the servlet is loaded when the first request for the servlet is made.

The `<init-param>` element is similar to the `<context-param>` element. The difference is that `<init-param>` defines parameters that are only accessible to the given servlet.

```
<init-param>
  <param-name>jdbc.name</param-name>
  <param-value>jdbc/CloudscapeDB</param-value>
</init-param>
```

The `<servlet-mapping>` Element

This element is used to define mappings from a particular request URI to a given servlet name. For example, in the `Login` servlet, I defined this mapping:

```
<servlet-mapping>
  <servlet-name>Login</servlet-name>
  <url-pattern>/Login</url-pattern>
</servlet-mapping>
```

This told Tomcat that if it received any URI that matched the pattern `/Login`, it should pass the request to the servlet with the name `Login`.

*There is a standard mapper that you can use in Tomcat for all servlets. This mapping sends all requests that match **/servlet/*** to a Tomcat-specific servlet named* `invoker`. *The* `invoker` *servlet reads the URL and sends the request to the correct application servlet. The mapping is defined in the default* `web.xml` *file, but is commented out. This means that individual web applications must explicitly decide how to map servlet requests. You can easily make the* `invoker` *servlet the default for all Tomcat web applications by uncommenting the servlet mapping for* `invoker` *in the* `web.xml` *file in the Tomcat* **/conf** *directory.*

Servlet Lifecycle

In the previous example, we looked at a simple servlet that processed a POST request. This processing encompassed just a small portion of a servlet's lifecycle (although that's the most important portion from the client's point of view). Now, let's look at the complete lifecycle of a servlet.

The servlet specification defines the following four stages of a servlet's lifecycle:

❑ Loading and instantiation

❑ Initialization

❑ Request handling

❑ End of life

These four stages are illustrated below, along with the methods that correspond to the change between each stage. It is through these methods that the servlet lifecycle is realized:

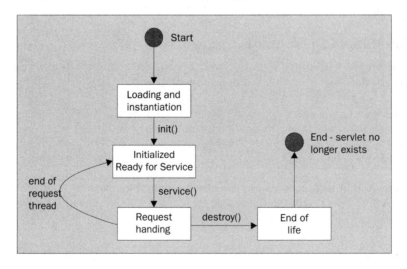

Loading and Instantiation

In this stage of the life cycle, the servlet class is loaded from the classpath and instantiated. The method that realizes this stage is the servlet constructor. However, unlike the other stages, you do not need to explicitly provide the method for this stage. I will show why in a moment.

How does the servlet container know which servlets to load? It knows by reading the deployment descriptors from a well-known location. For example, for Tomcat, that location is the **webapps** directory. Each subdirectory under **webapps** is a web application. Within each subdirectory that uses servlets will be a **WEB-INF** directory that contains a web.xml file. The servlet container reads each web.xml file, and loads the servlet classes identified in the deployment descriptor. Then it instantiates each servlet by calling its no-argument constructor.

Since the servlet container dynamically loads and instantiates servlets, it does not know about any constructors you create that might take parameters. Thus, it can only call the no-argument constructor and it is useless for you to specify any constructor other than one that takes no arguments. Since the Java compiler provides this constructor automatically when you do not supply a constructor, there is no need for you to write any constructor at all in your servlet. This is why your servlet class does not need to define an explicit constructor.

If you do not provide a constructor, how does your servlet initialize itself? This is handled in the next phase of the lifecycle, servlet initialization.

Initialization

After the servlet is loaded and instantiated, the servlet must be initialized. This occurs when the container calls the init(ServletConfig) method. If your servlet does not need to perform any initialization, the servlet does not need to implement this method. The method is provided for you by the GenericServlet class. That is why the Login servlet class earlier in the chapter did not have an init() method. The init() method allows the servlet to read initialization parameters or configuration data, initialize external resources such as database connections, and perform other one-time activities. GenericServlet provides two overloaded forms of the method:

```
public void init() throws ServletException
public void init(ServletConfig) throws ServletException
```

As I mentioned above, the deployment descriptor can define parameters that apply to the servlet through the <init-param> element. The servlet container reads these parameters from the web.xml file and stores them as name-value pairs in a ServletConfig object. Because the Servlet interface only defines init(ServletConfig), this is the method the container must call. GenericServlet implements this method to store the ServletConfig reference, and then call the parameterless init() method that it defines. Therefore, to perform initialization, your servlet only needs to implement the parameterless init() method. If you implement init(), your init() will be called by GenericServlet; and because the ServletConfig reference is already stored, your init() method will have access to all the initialization parameters stored in it.

If you do decide to implement init(ServletConfig) in your servlet, the method in your servlet must call the superclass init(ServletConfig) method:

```
public class LoginTUS extends HttpServlet {

    public void init(ServletConfig config) throws ServletException {
        super.init(config);

      // ...Remainder of init() method
    }

    //...Rest of servlet
}
```

> If you implement **init(ServletConfig)** without calling
> **super.init(ServletConfig)**, the **ServletConfig** object won't be saved,
> and neither your servlet nor its parent classes will be able to access the
> **ServletConfig** object during the remainder of the servlet lifecycle.

The servlet specification requires that init(ServletConfig) successfully complete before any requests can be serviced by the servlet. If your code encounters a problem during init(), you should throw a ServletException, or its subclass UnavailableException. This tells the container that there was a problem with initialization and that it should not use the servlet for any requests. Using UnavailableException allows you to specify an amount of time that the servlet is unavailable. After this time, the container could retry the call to init(). You can specify the unavailable time for the UnavailableException using this constructor:

```
public UnavailableException(String msg, int seconds)
```

The int parameter can be any integer: negative, zero, or positive. A non-positive value indicates that the servlet cannot determine when it will be available again. For example, this could occur if the servlet determines that an outside resource is not available; obviously, the servlet cannot estimate when the outside resource will be available. A positive value indicates that the server should try to initialize the servlet again after that number of seconds.

How the container handles the ServletException is container-dependent. Tomcat, for example, will return an HTTP 500 error to the client if init() throws a ServletException when it is called as a result of a client request. Subsequent client requests will receive an HTTP 404 (resource unavailable) error.

After the servlet successfully initializes, the container is allowed to use the servlet to handles requests.

Request Handling

As we saw in the chapter, the primary method defined for servicing requests during this phase of the servlet lifecycle is the service() method. As each request comes to the servlet container, the container calls the service() method to handle the request. Since you will almost always be subclassing HttpServlet, however, your servlet only needs to override doPost() and/or doGet() to handle requests. Here are the signatures of those two methods:

```
protected void doGet(HttpServletRequest req, HttpServletResponse res)
    throws ServletException, IOException
protected void doPost(HttpServletRequest req, HttpServletResponse res)
    throws ServletException, IOException
```

As with init(), the servlet can throw a ServletException or UnavailableException during the processing of a request. If your servlet throws either exception, then the servlet container is required to stop sending requests to the servlet. For a ServletException or for an UnavailableException that indicates a permanent unavailability (it was created with no value for seconds unavailable), the servlet container must end the servlet's lifecycle. If the servlet throws an UnavailableException with some value for seconds unavailable (see the *Initialization* section above), the servlet specification permits the container to keep or destroy the servlet at its choosing. If it keeps the servlet, it must not route any requests to the servlet until it is again available; if it destroys the servlet, it will presumably create a new servlet instance when the servlet is estimated to be available again.

End of Service

When the servlet container needs to unload the servlet, either because it is being shut down, or for some other reason such as a ServletException, the servlet container will call the destroy() method. However, prior to calling destroy(), the container must allow time for any request threads that are still processing to complete their processing. After they are complete, or after a server-defined timeout period, the container is allowed to call destroy(). Note that destroy() does not actually destroy the servlet or cause it to be garbage collected. It is simply an opportunity for the servlet to clean up any resources it used or opened. Obviously, after this method is called, the container will not send any more requests to the servlet. The signature of the destroy() method is:

```
public void destroy()
```

The destroy() method allows the servlet to release or clean up any resources that it uses. For example, it can close database connections or files, flush any streams, or close any sockets. If there is no cleanup that your servlet needs to perform, your servlet does not need to implement this method. After the destroy() method completes, the container will release its references to the servlet instance, and the servlet instance will be eligible for garbage collection.

Although this method is public, it is meant only to be called by the servlet container. You should never call the destroy() method from within your servlet, and you should not allow other code to call this method.

The Login Servlet

Even though we did not explicitly see it, the Login servlet in the last example followed all the steps of the servlet lifecycle. Since the deployment descriptor did not have a <load-on-startup> element, the servlet was loaded when the first request for the Login servlet was made. After the class was loaded, the init() method was called. Since the Login.class did not have an init() method, this call was handled by the GenericServlet class, the parent class of HttpServlet. After initialization completed successfully, the request was sent to the service() method of HttpServlet, which called the doPost() method of Login. When and if you stop the server, the destroy() method is called, again to be handled by GenericServlet.

Event Logging in Servlets

In addition to the methods of GenericServlet that were presented earlier, you will find two other methods useful:

```
public void log(String)
public void log(String, Throwable)
```

Although you can use the poor man's debug tool (System.out.println()) with servlets, GenericServlet provides two log() methods. Rather than sending their output to System.out, these methods write the log information to the servlet's log. This provides a more convenient and permanent logging mechanism than System.out.println(). We will use these methods in the next example, and the remainder of the examples in this chapter.

Servlets are Multi-Threaded

This statement may seem obvious – or maybe it doesn't. It's obvious because all Java classes are inherently multi-threaded. That is, whether you use them as such or not, they have the potential to have multiple threads executing their methods. (Unless, of course, a method is marked as synchronized.) On the other hand, it's not obvious because most of the time, you don't think about multi-threading when you are writing your Java classes. Think about your first "Hello, World!" class (or whatever you wrote as your first Java class). You probably wrote it with a single static main() method, in which all the processing occurred. When you ran the class, the JVM created a single thread of execution, and this thread executed the main() method. Even today, unless you are writing GUI applications with Swing or AWT or web applications, most of the classes you write are usually executed by only a single thread.

With servlets, you need to change that mindset. Since servlets are firmly in the web world of HTTP protocol, where concurrent requests are the norm and not the exception, you need to plan for multiple concurrent requests being sent to your servlet.

Try It Out   **A Thread-Unsafe Servlet**

In this example, we will see how a servlet that is not thread-safe can cause problems for a web application. This application will be very similar to the previous example; the difference between the two is that we will use a different servlet class for this example.

1. With some simple changes to the Login servlet, we can easily demonstrate the danger of not making your servlet thread-safe. Create this new class, LoginTUS (for Thread-UnSafe), based on the previous Login class:

```java
package web;

import javax.servlet.*;
import javax.servlet.http.*;
import java.io.*;

public class LoginTUS extends HttpServlet {
  private String username;
  private String password;

  public void init(ServletConfig config) throws ServletException {
    super.init(config);
  }

  public void doPost(HttpServletRequest request,
                     HttpServletResponse response)
  {
    String username = request.getParameter("username");
    String password = request.getParameter("password");

    this.username = username;
    this.password = password;

    try {
      String sleeptime = getInitParameter("sleep.time");
      int sleep = Integer.parseInt(sleeptime);
      Thread.sleep(sleep);
    }catch(Exception e){
      log("", e);
    }

    try {
      response.setContentType("text/html");
      PrintWriter writer = response.getWriter();
      writer.println("<html><body>");
      writer.println("<p>METHOD LOCAL");
      writer.println("<br>username=" + username);
      writer.println("<br>password=" + password);
      writer.println("<p>SERVLET MEMBER VARIABLES");
      writer.println("<br>username=" + this.username);
```

```
        writer.println("<br>password=" + this.password);
        writer.println("</body></html>");
        writer.close();
    } catch (Exception e) {
        e.printStackTrace();
    }
  }
}
```

2. Compile this class.

3. If you used the J2EE deploytool and the J2EE server, use the same steps as in the original Login example to create and deploy the stock web application. Create this new web application by removing the Login.class from the web application created in the previous example and replacing it with LoginTUS.class; alternately, you can create an entirely new web application using LoginTUS.class and login.html. Use the same alias (/Login) for the servlet, and don't forget to set the context root. Add an initialization parameter to the servlet through the Init.Parameters tab of the servlet window. The parameter's name is **sleep.time** and the value is 10000:

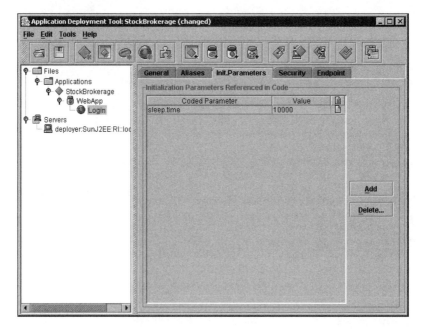

4. If you used Tomcat standalone, you need to add the class file to the web application that was created in the earlier example. If you created the /Ch05 context directly in **webapps**, simply copy the new servlet class to that directory. If you created a WAR package and copied it to **webapps**, you will need to delete the /Ch05 context in /webapps and add the new class file to the WAR.

5. For Tomcat, edit the `web.xml` deployment descriptor as shown here:

```xml
<?xml version="1.0" encoding="ISO-8859-1"?>

<!DOCTYPE web-app
     PUBLIC "-//Sun Microsystems, Inc.//DTD Web Application 2.3//EN"
     "http://java.sun.com/dtd/web-app_2_3.dtd">

<web-app>
  <display-name>Beginning J2EE Ch 5 Thread-UnSafe Login</display-name>
  <servlet>
    <servlet-name>Login</servlet-name>
    <servlet-class>web.LoginTUS</servlet-class>
    <init-param>
      <param-name>sleep.time</param-name>
      <param-value>10000</param-value>
    </init-param>
  </servlet>
  <servlet-mapping>
    <servlet-name>Login</servlet-name>
    <url-pattern>/Login</url-pattern>
  </servlet-mapping>
</web-app>
```

6. Add this deployment descriptor to the /Ch05 context or to the WAR.

7. If you are using Tomcat, stop the server if it is running, and then restart it. If you are using J2EE, that server should already be running.

8. Open two browser windows. Load the `login.html` page into each browser. Enter usernames and passwords into both windows, but do not click Submit.

9. After entering data into both web pages, click the Submit button in one browser; wait approximately four to five seconds and then click the Submit button in the other browser. This screenshot shows the two browser windows on my system prior to clicking the Submit button:

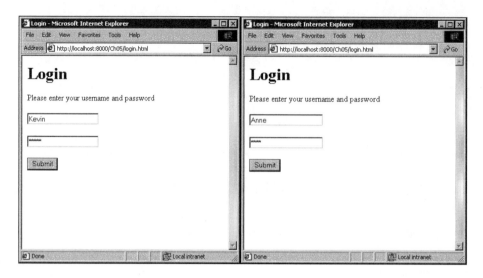

10. Here is my output. Looks like there's a problem: some data from Anne's request is mixed up with the response to Kevin's request:

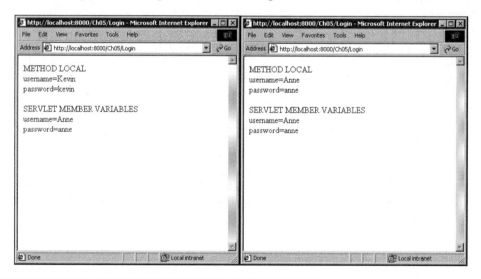

How It Works

In this servlet, I've created a situation that allows multiple concurrent request threads to interfere with each other. This was done by using member variables in the servlet class. Member variables, also known as instance variables, are inherently not thread safe. Each thread that enters a Java class has access to the same instance variables. Our servlet has two instance variables, `username` and `password`:

```
public class LoginTUS extends HttpServlet {
    private String username;
    private String password;
```

The `LoginTUS` class defines two instance variables, `username` and `password`. The `doPost()` method also defines two local variables with the same names. When a thread is inside `doPost()`, the local variables hide the instance variables of the same name if you use the simple names `username` and `password`. You can access the member variables by using the `this` keyword: `this.username` or `this.password`.

```
public void doPost(HttpServletRequest request,
                   HttpServletResponse response)
{
    // These variables are local to the method. Because they have the same
    // name as the instance variables, they hide the instance variables
    // inside the method
    String username = request.getParameter("username");
    String password = request.getParameter("password");

    // Here we use the keyword this. By using this we can access the instance
    // variable of the class. These lines assign the value of the local
    // variables to the instance variables.
    this.username = username;
    this.password = password;
```

Inside `doPost()`, the code reads the `username` and `password` parameters from the request and assigns the strings to both the member variables and the local variables. It then sleeps by calling the `Thread.sleep()` method.

To determine how long to sleep for, the servlet reads an init parameter by calling the `getInitParameter(String)` method. The init parameter is set through the deployment descriptor:

```
<servlet>
  <servlet-name>Login</servlet-name>
  <servlet-class>web.LoginTUS</servlet-class>
  <init-param>
    <param-name>sleep.time</param-name>
    <param-value>10000</param-value>
  </init-param>
</servlet>
```

You can define any number of init parameters for a servlet using one or more `<init-param>` elements. The `<param-name>` is the name that the servlet will use in the `getInitParameter(String)` method. The `<param-value>` element is the value for the init parameter. Each init parameter is servlet-specific; this means that no servlet can access the init parameters defined for anther servlet. Notice that parameter values can only be passed as `Strings` to the servlet. So, if you need to pass a number to the servlet, the servlet will have to convert the string to a numeric type:

```
String sleeptime = getInitParameter("sleep.time");
int sleep = Integer.parseInt(sleeptime);
```

By sleeping, the two requests that you generate, one from each browser window, have a chance to interact with each other. The first request sets the instance variables to a certain value. The second request then changes the same instance variables. The first request sees those changes because it shares the instance variables with every other request thread.

Now this example was pretty simple. We simply read some strings from the request and changed some `String` variables. Imagine what would happen, however, if you used member variables for a more important resource. One problem I've seen is servlet developers who use a member variable to hold a database connection. Concurrent requests end up writing data with the same connection and the database gets corrupted with bad data. That is why it is so important not to use instance variables for request-specific data.

How to Make your Servlets Thread-Safe

In the example above, I showed one way to make servlets thread-unsafe: I used a member variable for data that was specific to a request. What you need to know, however, is how to make your servlet thread-safe. Here is the list of techniques that I use:

❑ Use method variables for request-specific data. Whenever you need to access data from a request, that data should be stored in method variables, also known as local variables. These are variables defined within the scope of a method. Each thread that enters a method gets its own copy of the method variables. Thus, no thread can change the member variables of any other thread.

❑ As far as possible, use the member variables of the servlet only for data that does not change. (However, there are exceptions: see the next two bullets.) Usually you would use member variables for data that is initialized at startup, and does not change for the life of the servlet. This might be data such as lookup names for resources such as database connections (see the *Data Source* section of the JDBC chapter), paths to other resources, or paths to other web components, etc. In the example, I could have made the sleep time a member variable, because this value will not change during the lifetime of the servlet.

❑ Protect access to member variables that may be changed by a request. Occasionally, you may need to use a member variable for data that could be changed by a request. Or, you may have a context attribute that can be changed by a request. For example, I once worked on a web application that allowed an administrator to pause the application via a servlet request. Information about how the application was paused needed to persist across requests. So I saved the data in objects that were instance variable of the servlet. Since I didn't want two administrators trying to pause or unpause the application at the same time, I synchronized access to the objects; thus, while one administrator was pausing or unpausing the application, no other request could use those objects, and therefore could not pause or unpause the application at the same time. When you are using member variables or context attributes that can be changed by a request, you need to synchronize access to that data so that different threads aren't changing the data simultaneously.

❑   If your servlet accesses outside resources, consider protecting access to that resource. For example, suppose you decide to have your servlet read and write data to a file in the file system. One request thread could be reading or writing to that file while some other request thread is writing or reading the file. File access is not inherently thread-safe, so you must include code that manages synchronized access to this resource.

How Not to Make your Servlets Thread-Safe

In addition to the above list, you may see two other suggestions for making your servlet thread-safe, which we'll look at next. However, do *not* follow them. They will either not solve your problem, or will be too unpractical for a real-world application.

1.   Use `SingleThreadModel`

This is a common, but incorrect, solution attempted by servlet developers. `SingleThreadModel` is a marker interface. You use it like this:

```
public class MyServlet implements SingleThreadModel
```

Marker interfaces, such as `Serializable`, have no methods to implement. What `SingleThreadModel` does is signal to the servlet container that only a single thread should be allowed in the class at a time. There are various ways for the servlet container to do this. The usual way to do this is to create a pool of servlet instances. The servlet specification allows the servlet container to create multiple instances of any servlet that implements `SingleThreadModel`.

As each request comes to the container, an instance of the servlet from the pool is used to satisfy the request. While any request thread is executing in a servlet instance, no other thread is allowed to execute in the same instance.

However, this does not guarantee that your servlet is thread-safe. Remember that static member variables are shared by all instances of a servlet; moreover, external resources, such as files, may be accessed concurrently by request threads. If your servlet uses static member variables, uses outside resources, or uses context attributes, using `SingleThreadModel` does not make your servlet thread-safe. You would still need to synchronize access to these resources.

An even more important reason not to use `SingleThreadModel` is because it is not scaleable. There is a limit to the number of servlet instances that can be created. All those instances need to be managed. The larger the number of concurrent requests, the more unusable this solution becomes. It is always easier to create new threads rather than to create new objects. Again, I don't recommend it, but if you must use `SingleThreadModel`, you should only use it where the number of concurrent requests is relatively small (but remember, you still need to make the servlet thread-safe).

2.   Synchronize `service()`, `doPost()`, or `doGet()`

This attempt at making the servlet thread-safe is even worse than attempting to use `SingleThreadModel`. If you override `service()` and make it synchronized at the same time, you have limited your servlet to handling only a single request at a time (remember that the specification allows only a single instance of servlet per JVM for non-`SingleThreadModel` servlets). That may be fine while you are reading this book, and you are the only client of the servlets you write, but as soon as you move to any real-world application this will become totally unworkable. As the number of requests increases, your clients are more and more likely to spend their time watching the little progress icon go around and around. As you probably know, it won't take much of that for users to abandon your web site.

Synchronizing `doPost()` and `doGet()` is just as bad. Since the `service()` method of `HttpServlet` almost always calls `doPost()` or `doGet()`, synchronizing `doPost()` and `doGet()` has the same effect as if you had synchronized `service()`.

Of course, as I mentioned in the previous section, you must sometimes synchronize access to resources used by your servlet. If you must synchronize code within your servlet, you should attempt to synchronize the smallest block of code possible. The less code that is synchronized, the better your servlet will execute.

Handling Exceptions

This chapter has tried to concentrate on how to use the various features of the Servlet API, so exception handling has consisted simply of logging the exception stack trace. In a real-world application, though, you will need to be more vigilant in the way you handle exceptions.

Poor Exception Handling

Look at this code for a very simple servlet:

```java
package web;

import java.io.*;
import javax.servlet.http.*;

public class BadServlet extends HttpServlet {
  public void doPost(HttpServletRequest req, HttpServletResponse res)
    throws IOException
  {
    res.setContentType("text/html");
    PrintWriter writer = res.getWriter();

    writer.println("<html><body>");
    String num = req.getParameter("number");
    Integer i = new Integer(num);
    writer.println("You entered the number " + i.intValue());
```

```
        writer.println("</body></html>");
        writer.close();
    }
}
```

Can you see the problem in the code above? Try creating an HTML form that includes a field named `number`, and which calls the servlet. Deploy the application and test various values.

What happened when you entered anything other than a non-numeric value? If a non-numeric value is entered, the `Integer` constructor throws an exception. What happens on the client side depends on the exception and the server. Sometimes the user might get an ugly (from the user's point of view) stack trace; other times the user might get no response from the server. To the client, it appears as though your application is broken (which it is). You probably should have checked the request parameters to ensure they were valid.

This brings up the question: where should data validation be done, the client side or the server side? The answer to this question depends in part on the requirements of your application. However, you will probably need to do data validation on both sides. You need to validate some data on the client side so that errors can be corrected prior to making the HTTP request. You need to validate data on the server side in case the user bypasses client-side validation.

Your servlet also needs to attempt to provide error handling for every error that could occur. Let's look at a common attempt at error handling and why it is not the best solution. Suppose we take the example above and add a `try...catch` block:

```
try {
    res.setContentType("text/html");
    PrintWriter writer = res.getWriter();

    writer.println("<html><body>");
    String num = req.getParameter("number");
    Integer i = new Integer(num);
    writer.println("You entered the number " + i.intValue());
    writer.println("</body></html>");
    writer.close();
} catch (Exception e) {
    log("", e);
}
```

Looks OK, right? No, there is still a problem. What happens when the `Integer` constructor throws an exception? No output is sent back to the client, because the exception causes the thread of execution to immediately jump to the `catch` block. The client gets to stare at a blank screen.

Unless the exception is an `IOException` thrown while writing the response, you should always attempt to return some kind of response to the client. That could mean putting `try...catch` blocks around the code that you anticipate could throw exceptions, or adding output statements that would be called from the `catch` block to send a response back to the client.

Error Pages

One other way to make your application more robust is to define error pages for your application. For example, given the `BadServlet` above, we might create a web page or JSP that tells the user that they must enter digits only. Then we can specify that the application serve this page whenever a `NumberFormatException` occurs. This is done with the `<error-page>` element of the deployment descriptor:

```
<web-app>
  <!-- This is the deployment descriptor for the BadServlet example -->

  <servlet>
    <servlet-name>BadServlet</servlet-name>
    <servlet-class>web.BadServlet</servlet-class>
  </servlet>
  <servlet-mapping>
    <servlet-name>BadServlet</servlet-name>
    <url-pattern>/BadServlet</url-pattern>
  </servlet-mapping>

  <error-page>
    <exception-type>java.lang.NumberFormatException</exception-type>
    <location>/BadNumber.html</location>
  </error-page>
</web-app>
```

Using this deployment descriptor, the `BadNumber.html` page will be sent to the client whenever the servlet container catches a `NumberFormatException`. You can also specify error pages for HTTP error codes. The `<error-page>` element in the deployment descriptor looks like this:

```
<error-page>
  <error-code>404</error-code>
  <location>/NoSuchPage.html</location>
</error-page>
```

When a user attempts to access a page or resource that does not exist, the server generates a 404 error. Because the deployment descriptor says to send the `NoSuchPage.html` page whenever a 404 error occurs, this is what will be sent to the client. You can find the complete list of error codes at http://www.w3c.org/Protocols/HTTP/HTTPRESP.html.

The one error page you should specify for every application is for error code 500. An error code of 500 indicates an error in the server that the server was unable to deal with. This could be anything from a JSP page that can't be compiled to an uncaught exception in a servlet. By specifying a page to be sent to the client for a 500 error, you can be sure that if an error of this type occurs, the client will get a nicely formatted error page, rather than an ugly stack trace.

Session Management

There's one big challenge with relying on HTTP for web applications. HTTP is a stateless protocol. Each request and response stand alone. Without session management, each time a client makes a request to a server, it's a brand new user with a brand new request from the server's point of view.

To deal with that issue, web applications use the concept of a session. A session refers to the entire interaction between a client and a server from the time of the client's first request, which generally begins the session, to the time the session is terminated. The session could be terminated by the client's request, or the server could automatically close it after a certain period of time. A session can last for just a few minutes, or it could last days or weeks or months (if the application were willing to let a session last that long).

The Servlet API provides classes and methods for creating and managing session. In this section, we'll look in detail at session creation and management.

Creating and Using Sessions

Two methods of the `HttpServletRequest` object are used to create a session. They are:

```
HttpSession getSession();
HttpSession getSession(boolean);
```

If a session already exists, then `getSession()`, `getSession(true)`, and `getSession(false)` will all return the existing session. If a session does not exist, then `getSession()` and `getSession(true)` will cause one to be created; `getSession(false)` will return `null`. Note that you must call one of these methods before writing any data to the response. This is because the default technique for session tracking is to use cookies. Cookies are sent in the header part of an HTTP message, so they must be set in the response prior to writing any data to the response.

In addition, `HttpServletRequest` provides a few other methods for dealing with sessions:

Method	Description
`String getRequestedSessionId()`	Gets the ID assigned by the server to the session
`Boolean isRequestedSessionIdValid()`	Returns `true` if the request contains a valid session ID
`Boolean isRequestedSessionIdFromCookie()`	Returns `true` if the session ID was sent as part of a cookie
`Boolean isRequestedSessionIdFromURL()`	Returns `true` if the session ID was sent through URL rewriting (we'll look at URL rewriting very shortly)

Session Tracking with Cookies

All the data for the session, and all the data stored with the session, is maintained on the server. The server therefore needs some way to associate a client's request with a session on the server. The primary technique for doing this is to use cookies. When the server creates a session, it sends a session ID to the client in the form of a cookie. When the client makes another request and sends the cookie with the session ID, the server can select the correct session for the client based on the session ID.

When the client is accepting cookies, there is nothing your servlet needs to do as far as session tracking is concerned. The servlet container and the server handle all the session tracking for you.

Session Tracking with URL Rewriting

Some users don't like cookies. If you are working with a public web application, you can accept as fact that some users of your application will not accept the cookies sent to them by the server. When that occurs, the server resorts to another technique to track a user's session: URL rewriting. With this technique, the server appends the session ID to the URLs of the pages it serves.

When that occurs, the servlet does need to do something. In this case, the URLs embedded within the HTML pages of the application need to be modified for each client by rewriting the URL. This can be done with these methods of the `HttpServletResponse`:

```
encodeURL(String)
encodeRedirectURL(String)
```

These methods will rewrite the URL given by the `String` argument when the client is not accepting cookies. If the client does accept cookies, then the URLs are returned unchanged. You use `encodeRedirectURL()` for URLs that will be used with the `sendRedirect()` method of `HttpServletResponse`. Use `encodeURL()` for all other URLs.

What can you do with a Session?

All kinds of stuff, it turns out. Primarily, though, sessions are useful for persisting information about a client and a client's interactions with an application. To do that, the `HttpSession` interface defines a number of methods.

The methods you will probably use most often are methods for setting and getting attributes from the session. You would store information in the session using the `setAttribute(String, Object)` method. Since the session is common to the entire application, this data then becomes available to every component in the application (and you therefore need to consider synchronizing access to the session and session data). The stored data is retrieved with the `getAttribute(String)` method.

```
public Object getAttribute(String name)
public Enumeration getAttributeNames()
public void setAttribute(String name, Object value)
public void removeAttribute(String name)
```

You can store anything at all in the session. You could store text information about the user or the user's preferences. If you were working on an e-commerce application, you could store the user's shopping cart in the session.

The next set of methods deal with session creation and lifecycle:

```
public long getCreationTime()
public String getId()
public long getLastAccessedTime()
public boolean isNew()
public void setMaxInactiveInterval(int interval)
public int getMaxInactiveInterval()
public void invalidate()
```

The isNew() method returns true when the client has refused the session (usually by rejecting the cookie with the session ID), or when the session ID has not been sent to the client yet. The setMaxInactiveInterval(int) method is used to tell the servlet container how long a session can be inactive before it is invalidated. When that time limit is reached without activity, the session is invalidated. Using a negative value for the argument tells the container never to expire a session. A session is considered active when a client makes a request and sends the session ID with the request. Finally, the servlet can actively expire the session by calling the invalidate() method.

Lastly, there is a method that returns the ServletContext for the session:

```
public ServletContext getServletContext()
```

Session Management with Cookies

Using the session object provided through the servlet API is the preferred method for using and managing sessions. However, there is another method for session management that can be used in conjunction with, or in place of, session objects. That method is to use cookies for session management.

Cookies are strings of text that a server can send to a client. The client can either accept and store the cookie, or reject the cookie. Cookies should contain information relevant to the client. When the client makes a request to a given server, it sends the cookies it has from the server back with the request.

The session object has two advantages over cookies. First, as I mentioned earlier, clients can reject cookies sent by a server; session objects live on the server, and can always be created, either by setting the session ID in a cookie, or through URL rewriting. Second, cookies can only store text data, so you are limited to storing text information, or information that can be represented by text. Using a session object, you can store any Java object in a session. For these reasons, you should always use the Session API for session management.

However, there is one place where cookies make sense. Have you ever registered at a web site, and then the next time you went back to the site, the site logged you in automatically? This was probably accomplished by sending a cookie to your browser. The cookie contained an ID that the server could use to identify you. When your browser sends the request, it sends the cookie, and the server is able to identify you, retrieve your personalization information from some persistent store, and preload a `session` object with your data before your browser has actually joined the session.

Let's look briefly at how a cookie might be used to do this. Using the `Cookie` object in the Servlet API is straightforward. Cookie data comes in name-value pairs, so the `Cookie` constructor takes a name and a value:

```
Cookie(String name, String value)
```

You could then set a number of properties of the cookie. The two that you are most likely to use are:

```
public void setMaxAge(int expiry)
public void setValue(String newValue)
```

The `setMaxAge(int)` method specifies how long, in seconds, the cookie should be kept by the client. If you do not set a maximum age, the cookie is discarded when the client exits the browser. The `setValue(String)` method allows you to change the value held by the cookie.

After creating a cookie, you can add it to the response using the `addCookie()` method of the `HttpServletResponse` class:

```
void addCookie(Cookie cookie)
```

Cookies are added to the header of the response message, so the servlet must call the `addCookie()` method before any message body data is written to the response.

When a client sends a request to the servlet, the servlet can access the cookies using the `HttpServletRequest`'s `getCookies()` method:

```
Cookie[] getCookies()
```

This returns an array containing `Cookie` objects for all the cookies sent by the client. Note that the client only sends the name-value pairs of the cookies, and not any other information such as maximum age. The servlet can access the names and values of each `Cookie` using the `Cookie` methods `getName()` and `getValue(String name)`.

Finally, even though we have discussed the `Cookie` object and its methods in terms of session management, cookies can be used to send any text data to the client browser, regardless of whether it is used for session management or not.

Try It Out   **Maintaining State with the session Object**

In the first servlet example in this chapter, we created a simple `Login` servlet. That `Login` servlet did not really validate the user credentials, did not use a secure connection for receiving the username and password, and did not store the `Login` information. In a real application, all those things would probably be done. We still won't perform a real validation, but we can show how to store login credentials in a session.

1. Modify the `Login` servlet from the beginning of the chapter:

```java
package web;

import javax.servlet.*;
import javax.servlet.http.*;
import java.io.*;

public class LoginSES extends HttpServlet {
   public void doPost(HttpServletRequest request,
                      HttpServletResponse response)
   {
      String username = request.getParameter("username");
      String password = request.getParameter("password");

      HttpSession session = request.getSession(true);
      session.setAttribute("username", username);
      session.setAttribute("password", password);

      try {
         response.setContentType("text/html");
         PrintWriter writer = response.getWriter();
         writer.println("<html><body>");
         writer.println("Thank you, " + username +
                        ". You are now logged into the system");
         String newURL = response.encodeURL("/Ch05/GetSession");
         writer.println("Click <a href=\"" + newURL +
                        "\">here</a> for another servlet");
         writer.println("</body></html>");
         writer.close();
      } catch (Exception e) {
         e.printStackTrace();
      }
   }
}
```

2. Create a new servlet that will check for the session:

```java
package web;

import javax.servlet.*;
import javax.servlet.http.*;
import java.io.*;
import java.util.*;
```

223

```java
public class GetSession extends HttpServlet {
  public void doGet(HttpServletRequest request,
                    HttpServletResponse response)
  {
    HttpSession session = request.getSession(false);
    try {
      response.setContentType("text/html");
      PrintWriter writer = response.getWriter();
      writer.println("<html><body>");

      if (session == null) {
        writer.println("You are not logged in");
        writer.println("<a href=\"/Ch05/login.html\">Return" +
                       "</a> to the login page");
      } else {
        writer.println("Thank you, you are already logged in");
        writer.println("Here is the data in your session");
        Enumeration names = session.getAttributeNames();
        while (names.hasMoreElements()) {
          String name = (String) names.nextElement();
          Object value = session.getAttribute(name);
          writer.println("<p>name=" + name + " value=" + value);
        }
        writer.println("<a href=\"/Ch05/login.html\">Return" +
                       "</a> to login page");
      }
      writer.println("</body></html>");
      writer.close();
    } catch (Exception e) {
      e.printStackTrace();
    }
  }
}
```

3. Compile these servlets.

4. Here is the deployment descriptor for Tomcat:

```xml
<?xml version="1.0" encoding="ISO-8859-1"?>

<!DOCTYPE web-app
    PUBLIC "-//Sun Microsystems, Inc.//DTD Web Application 2.3//EN"
    "http://java.sun.com/dtd/web-app_2_3.dtd">

<web-app>
  <display-name>Beginning J2EE Ch 5</display-name>
  <servlet>
    <servlet-name>Login</servlet-name>
    <servlet-class>web.LoginSES</servlet-class>
  </servlet>
  <servlet>
```

```
        <servlet-name>GetSession</servlet-name>
        <servlet-class>web.GetSession</servlet-class>
    </servlet>
    <servlet-mapping>
        <servlet-name>Login</servlet-name>
        <url-pattern>/Login</url-pattern>
    </servlet-mapping>
    <servlet-mapping>
        <servlet-name>GetSession</servlet-name>
        <url-pattern>/GetSession</url-pattern>
    </servlet-mapping>
</web-app>
```

5. If you are using Deploytool and J2EE, ensure that both the servlets have aliases as shown in the deployment descriptor above. Through the New Web Application WAR wizrd (File | New | WebApplication WAR) create components for both servlets. Make sure that you add both servlet `.class` files to the first WAR module, and for the second component, select Add to Existing WAR Module on the second screen, instead of creating a new WAR module. Select each component in the left pane, and select the Aliases tab in the right pane to set the alias.

6. Create and deploy the application using the two servlets and the `login.html` page that was created earlier in the chapter. You can either create a new EAR with a new application context, or modify the earlier application. You may need to edit both servlets and the HTML page so that they use the correct application context.

7. Open a browser and ensure that it is accepting cookies. Enter the URL http://localhost:*port*/Ch05/GetSession (assuming that you set the context root to Ch05). Use the correct value (8000 or 8080) for *port*. Because you do not have a session yet, this servlet should respond with a page that tells you to go to the `login.html` page.

8. On the login page, enter a username and password and click Submit. The next page prints a short message that includes a link to the `GetSession` servlet. If you examine the link, you will see that it has the session ID embedded in it. Click the link.

9. On the next page, the `GetSession` servlet printed out the value of the attributes in your session. If you look at the address bar, you will see a URL with the session ID. Click the link to return to the login page:

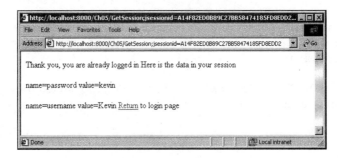

10. Enter a username and password and click **Submit** again. This time, the link on the welcome page does not include the session ID. If you click the link, the URL for the page generated by `GetSession` does not have the session ID either:

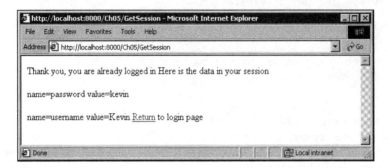

How It Works

Our new version of the login servlet starts by trying to access any existing session by calling the `request.getSession()` method. Since we pass in `true` as the parameter, a new session will be created if one doesn't already exist. Once we've got the session, we store the username and password in it that the user entered in `login.html`:

```
HttpSession session = request.getSession(true);
session.setAttribute("username", username);
session.setAttribute("password", password);
```

A client does not have a session until the server creates a session for the client, the server has sent the session ID to the client, *and* the client has returned the session ID in a cookie or URL. Because the `LoginSES` servlet is the first web component to create the session, the session has not been joined when `LoginSES` generates the page that has the link for the `GetSession` servlet. The `LoginSES` servlet calls `encodeURL()` for the link, and since the client has not joined the session, the URL is rewritten to append the session ID:

```
String newURL = response.encodeURL("/Ch05/GetSession");
writer.println("Click <a href=\"" + newURL +
            "\">here</a> for another servlet");
```

This is the session ID that appears in the browser address window for the page generated by `GetSession` servlet. When you click the link that sends the request to `GetSession`, you have finally joined the session.

When you link back to the `login.html` page again, you have joined the session, and the server knows that the browser accepts cookies. That is why the second time you log in, the server does not rewrite the URL.

Filters

So, you've finished writing the `Login` servlet for your application, and it's working great. When users submit their credentials, your code checks them against the user information stored by the application. The servlet creates a session for the user, so that other components in the application know that the user has logged in properly. Everything's great.

Until the customer comes to you and asks you to log each login attempt to the file system. So you edit the servlet code and redeploy it. Then the customer asks you to log the attempt to a database table. Edit the code and redeploy. Then the customer...

Pretty soon your servlet is filled with lots of code that's useful but is outside the scope of the core job of a servlet: receiving and responding to requests. There's got to be an easier way.

Why you Need Filters

Filters are a way to provide a plug-in capability to your web application. Using filters you can encapsulate different behaviors needed to help process a request. Filters also make it easy to change the functionality of a web application with just a change to the deployment descriptor.

The Javadoc for `Filter` suggests a number of situations in which you might use filters. Some of these include:

- ❑ Authentication filters
- ❑ Logging and auditing filters
- ❑ Data compression filters
- ❑ Encryption filters

The primary job of a servlet is to accept requests and provide responses to clients. Anything outside that scope is the candidate for other classes. So, whether you need the functionality suggested by the list in the Javadoc, or you have some other functionality your application needs to provide, filters provide an excellent way to encapsulate functionality. Further, by encapsulating that functionality in a filter, the same filter can easily be used with several servlets.

Implementing a Filter

To implement a filter for your web application, you need to do two things. The first is to write a class that implements the `Filter` interface; the second is to modify the deployment descriptor to tell the container when to call the filter.

The Filter API

The Filter API consists of three interfaces: `Filter`, `FilterChain`, and `FilterConfig`. `javax.servlet.Filter` is the interface you will use to implement a filter. It has three methods:

Method	Description
void init(FilterConfig filterConfig)	Called by the web container to indicate to a filter that it is being placed into service.

void doFilter(
    ServletRequest request,
    ServletResponse response,
    FilterChain chain)
	The doFilter() method is called by the container each time a request/response pair is passed through the chain due to a client request for a resource at the end of the chain.

void destroy()	Called by the web container to indicate to a filter that it is being taken out of service.

You can see that this interface is very similar to the Servlet interface. Based on this interface, you won't be surprised to learn that a filter lifecycle is very similar to a servlet lifecycle. When the filter is created, the container will call the init() method. Inside the init() method, you can access init parameters through the FilterConfig interface. However, unlike a servlet, if you need to access the FilterConfig in the doFilter() method, you will need to save the reference yourself. To service requests, the container calls the doFilter() method. When the container needs to end the filter lifecycle, it will call the destroy() method.

javax.servlet.FilterConfig is fairly straightforward and almost identical to ServletConfig. If you need to use init parameters or other features of the FilterConfig, you can get more details from the Javadoc.

The javax.servlet.FilterChain interface represents a chain of filters. It defines a method that each filter can use to call the next filter in the chain:

Method	Description

void doFilter(
    ServletRequest request,
    ServletResponse response)
	Causes the next filter in the chain to be invoked, or if the calling filter is the last filter in the chain, causes the resource at the end of the chain to be invoked.

If you look above at the `Filter` interface, you can see that when a filter's `doFilter()` method is called, one of the arguments passed is a reference to a `FilterChain`. When the filter calls `chain.doFilter()`, the next filter in the chain is called. Filter code before the `chain.doFilter()` method call is executed prior to the servlet processing. Thus, any processing that the filter needs to do to the request should occur prior to the call to `chain.doFilter()`. Code that occurs after the `chain.doFilter()` method returns executes after the servlet, so that code performs processing on the response. If you need to do processing both before and after the servlet, then you put code both before and after the `chain.doFilter()` call. On the other hand, if any of the filters needs to abort processing (think of a filter that provides user authentication), it can easily abort the processing by not calling `doFilter()`. If all this sounds a little confusing, the illustration below should make it clearer:

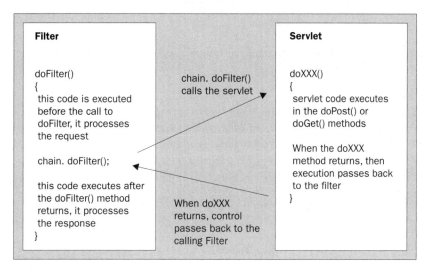

The Deployment Descriptor

The deployment descriptor is used to tell the container which, if any, filters to call for each servlet in the application. Two tags within the deployment descriptor describe the filters and indicate to which servlet requests the filters should be applied.

The first element is `<filter>`. A `<filter>` element including all sub-elements looks like this:

```
<filter>
  <icon>path to an icon file</icon>
  <filter-name>the name of the filter for the application</filter-name>
  <display-name>named for use by management tool</display-name>
  <description>a description</description>
  <filter-class>fully qualified class name</filter-class>
  <init-param>
    <param-name>some_name</param-name>
    <param-value>a_value</param-value>
  </init-param>
</filter>
```

Only two of these sub-elements are required: the <filter-name> and the <filter-class>. If you use an <init-param>, then <param-name> and <param-value> are required. These init values can be accessed through the FilterConfig object.

The second element is the <filter-mapping> element. It looks like this:

```
<filter-mapping>
  <filter-name>same name as filter element</filter-name>
  <url-pattern>URL pattern that the filter applies to</url-pattern>
</filter-mapping>
```

or like this:

```
<filter-mapping>
  <filter-name>Same name as filter element</filter-name>
  <servlet-name>Name of servlet from servlet element</servlet-name>
</filter-mapping>
```

Recall that the order of tags in the deployment descriptor must follow the DTD. All the <filter> tags must occur prior to any <filter-mapping> tags. The <filter-mapping> tags must occur prior to the <servlet> tags.

If multiple filters are needed for a request, then each filter is listed in separate <filter-mapping> elements. The filters are applied in the same order that the <filter-mapping> elements appear in the deployment descriptor. For example, if you had this deployment descriptor:

```
<filter-mapping>
  <filter-name>FilterD</filter-name>
  <servlet-name>Login</servlet-name>
</filter-mapping>

<filter-mapping>
  <filter-name>FilterA</filter-name>
  <servlet-name>Login</servlet-name>
</filter-mapping>

<filter-mapping>
  <filter-name>FilterW</filter-name>
  <servlet-name>Login</servlet-name>
</filter-mapping>
```

Then any request for the Login servlet would first be sent to FilterD, since the filter-mapping element for that filter appears first in the deployment descriptor. When FilterD calls chain.doFilter(), FilterA would be called. After that, FilterW is called. Finally, when FilterW calls doFilter(), the Login servlet would be invoked.

Actually, the claim that filters are called in order of their appearance in the deployment descriptor may not be totally correct. At the time this was written, Tomcat 4.1.18 calls all filters that use `<url-pattern>` for `<filter-mapping>` before it calls the filters that use `<servlet-name>` in the `<filter-mapping>` element. Your server may or may not do this, but since Tomcat is the reference implementation, its behavior is by definition the correct behavior. You should take care to use the same style for the `<filter-mapping>` element for every filter.

> **When defining the** `<filter-mapping>` **chain, use the same** `<servlet-name>` **or** `<url-pattern>` **elements for every filter in the chain.**

Try It Out   Using Filters

1. Create the following filter. This filter will perform request logging for the `Login` servlet:

```
package web;

import javax.servlet.*;
import java.io.*;

public class LogB implements Filter {
  public void init(FilterConfig filterConfig) {}

  public void doFilter(ServletRequest request,
                       ServletResponse response,
                       FilterChain chain)
  {
    System.out.println("Entered LogB doFilter()");
    System.out.println("protocol is" + request.getProtocol());
    System.out.println("remote host is " + request.getRemoteHost());
    System.out.println("content type is " + request.getContentType());
    System.out.println("content length is " + request.getContentLength());
    System.out.println("username is " + request.getParameter("username"));

    try {
      chain.doFilter(request, response);
    } catch (Exception e) {
      e.printStackTrace();
    }
  }

  public void destroy() {}
}
```

2. Create this second filter. This filter will do its processing after the servlet has responded to the request (we've deliberately called the `LogB` filter before `LogA`, just to prove that the filters are called in the order in which they appear in the deployment descriptor, not in alphabetical or some other order):

```
package web;

import javax.servlet.*;
import java.io.*;

public class LogA implements Filter {
  public void init(FilterConfig filterConfig) {}

  public void doFilter(ServletRequest request,
                       ServletResponse response,
                       FilterChain chain)
  {
    System.out.println("LogA passing request to next filter");

    try {
      chain.doFilter(request,response);
    } catch (Exception e) {
      e.printStackTrace();
    }

    System.out.println("The servlet has processed the request");
    System.out.println("LogA filter is now working to process");
    System.out.println("the response");
  }

  public void destroy() {}
}
```

3. If you are using Tomcat, you will need to modify the web.xml file as shown here. You need to add the <filter> and <filter-mapping> elements. If you are using J2EE, skip to step 4:

```
<?xml version="1.0" encoding="ISO-8859-1"?>

<!DOCTYPE web-app
    PUBLIC "-//Sun Microsystems, Inc.//DTD Web Application 2.3//EN"
    "http://java.sun.com/dtd/web-app_2_3.dtd">

<web-app>

<!-- this is the deployment descriptor for the Filter example -->

  <display-name>Beginning J2EE Ch 5</display-name>
  <filter>
    <filter-name>LogA</filter-name>
    <filter-class>web.LogA</filter-class>
  </filter>

  <filter>
    <filter-name>LogB</filter-name>
```

```
        <filter-class>web.LogB</filter-class>
    </filter>

    <filter-mapping>
        <filter-name>LogA</filter-name>
        <url-pattern>/Login</url-pattern>
    </filter-mapping>

    <filter-mapping>
        <filter-name>LogB</filter-name>
        <url-pattern>/Login</url-pattern>
    </filter-mapping>

    <servlet>
        <servlet-name>Login</servlet-name>
        <servlet-class>web.Login</servlet-class>
    </servlet>

    <servlet-mapping>
        <servlet-name>Login</servlet-name>
        <url-pattern>/Login</url-pattern>
    </servlet-mapping>

</web-app>
```

4. If you are using Tomcat, skip to step 10.

5. Start by opening the `StockBrokerage` application that was created earlier in this chapter. If you did not create that application earlier, use the Deploytool to create it now, adding `Login.class`, `LogA.class`, `LogB.class` and `login.html` to the EAR. Refer to the earlier `Login` example for further instructions on how to create the application. Don't forget to alias the `Login` servlet as **/Login**.

6. When creating the application with the Deploytool, you need to specify the filter mappings through the **Filter Mapping** tab of the **WebApp** window. Start by clicking the **Edit Filter List** button:

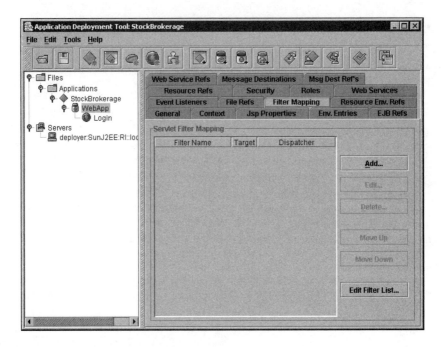

7. Clicking the Edit Filter List button will bring up a dialog through which you specify the available filter classes. Click the Add button and add each of the filter classes, `LogA` and `LogB`, to the list:

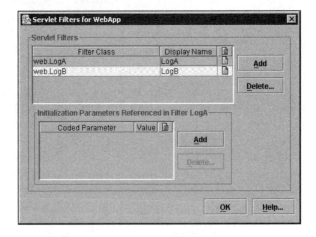

8. When both the classes have been added, click the OK button. When you are back in the main window, you can add filter mappings by clicking the Add button in the Filter Mapping tab. In the Add Servlet Filter Mapping dialog, you specify the filter name, and the target using either a URL pattern or a servlet name. In the Dispatcher Options section, choose Request:

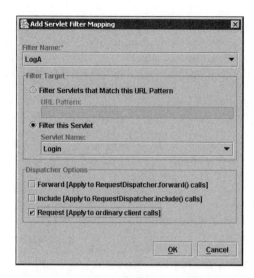

9. When complete, the list of filter mappings should look like this:

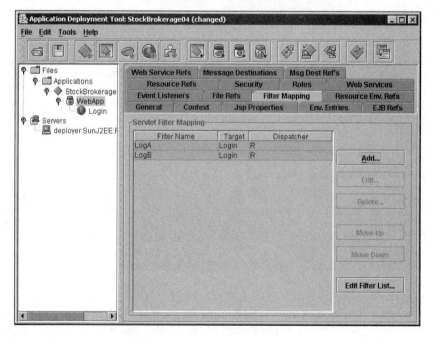

10. Now deploy the application.

11. To see the output in J2EE, you need to have the server in verbose mode. If it is not, rerun the J2EE server in verbose mode by running the `j2ee` script file from the command line and passing the command line parameter `-verbose`. If you start Tomcat from the command line with the script file, you should be able to see the output in the Tomcat console window. Open a browser window. For J2EE, use the address http://localhost:8000/Ch05/login.html. For Tomcat, use http://localhost:8080/Ch05/login.html. Enter a username and password, and click the Submit button. You will see the output from the filters. Here is what I saw on my system:

```
LogA passing request to next filter
Entered LogB doFilter()
protocol is HTTP/1.1
remote host is 127.0.0.1
content type is application/x-www-form-urlencoded
content length is 21
username is k
The servlet has processed the request
LogA filter is now working to process the response
```

How It Works

The `LogA` filter calls the `chain.doFilter()` method almost immediately. This calls the next filter in the chain, `LogB`. The `LogB` filter reads some of the request headers and request parameter from the request and prints them to the console. Then `LogB` calls `chain.doFilter()`. Since it is the last chain in the filter, this calls the servlet, which performs its processing of the request. The code in `LogB` executes before the `doFilter()` method is called, so it executes before the servlet is called:

```
System.out.println("Entered LogB doFilter()");
System.out.println("protocol is" + request.getProtocol());
System.out.println("remote host is " + request.getRemoteHost());
System.out.println("content type is " + request.getContentType());
System.out.println("content length is " + request.getContentLength());
System.out.println("username is " + request.getParameter("username"));

try {
  chain.doFilter(request, response);
} catch (Exception e) {
  e.printStackTrace();
}
```

When the `doPost()` method of the servlet completes, the thread of execution returns to the caller, which in this case is the `LogB` filter. The thread of execution returns to the `doFilter()` method of `LogB`; however, `LogB` performs no other processing. Its `doFilter()` method completes, and execution returns to `LogB`'s caller, `LogA`. When the thread of execution returns to `LogA`, execution continues from the method call `chain.doFilter()`. Since there is code following that method call, it now executes. In a real filter, the code would perform some processing on the response. In the example, all that the filter does is write some strings to `System.out`:

```
System.out.println("The servlet has processed the request");
System.out.println("LogA filter is now working to process");
System.out.println("the response");
```

The MVC Architecture

In the previous JSP chapters, and previously in this chapter, we used an architectural model known as Model 1. In a Model 1 architecture, HTTP requests are handled primarily by web components, which process the request and then return a response to a client. That is, a single web component (or small number of components) handles both the business logic and display logic. There is a second model used for J2EE applications. Unsurprisingly, this model is known as Model 2; it is also known as **Model-View-Controller**, or MVC. In a Model 2 architecture there is a division of functionality: the business data is separated from the display logic, and components that process the data do not manage the display of the data, and vice versa.

Model 1 vs. Model 2

A Model 1 system mixes both application and business logic with display logic. While this is probably OK for small applications, this becomes more and more of a problem as your application grows. This model leads to JSP pages interspersed with a lot of Java code, or servlets that have a lot of `print` statements that output HTML text to the client. While the examples we've used previously aren't too bad (the first `Login` servlet example in this chapter only had three `println` statements), imagine an HTML-heavy application written entirely with servlets, or a code-intensive application written with JSP pages. Your application will become less maintainable as changes to display logic affect business logic and vice versa.

There are various solutions to this problem. On one of the systems I worked on, before the days of JSPs, we solved this problem by creating template files for all the web pages in the application. The template files contained HTML with special place markers for request-specific data. When a servlet needed to send a response to a client, it used a utility class that had methods for reading a template, and replacing the markers with strings. The `toString()` method of the utility class returned a `String` that contained the entire HTML web page. Then it was just a simple matter of one `println` statement to send the response to the client. While this solution was workable, it starts to break down when you have lists, tables, or combo boxes in the web page. You don't know ahead of time how many list items or table rows you might have. Thus, HTML strings start appearing in your servlet code again.

Model 2, or MVC, separates the display from the business logic in another way. In an MVC application, separate components handle the business logic and the display logic. As long as the interface between the two is stable and well defined, the business logic can be changed without affecting the view components, and vice versa.

237

MVC

In an MVC application, the components of the application are divided into three categories: the model, the view, and the controller.

❑ **Model** – The model includes both the data and the business logic components that operate on that data. Again, any class can act as a model component, and many web applications use only JSPs or servlets with regular (not J2EE API) classes providing business logic. As we will see from Chapter 8 onwards, EJBs make excellent components for the model category.

❑ **View** – After the request is processed, the controller determines which view component should be used to display the data to the user. In simpler applications, the controller component may also act as the view component. In more complex systems, view and controller objects are separate. JSP pages tend to make good view components.

❑ **Controller** – Components in this category receive the client requests, process the request, or forward the request to other components that process the data, and then direct the request to a view component. Any web application component, such as a JSP, a servlet, or an EJB, could be a controller component. However, servlets tend to make good controllers due to their basic structure. A servlet is intended to receive requests from clients and return responses to clients, and that matches the purpose of the controller.

Let's take a quick look at an example design that uses MVC. Imagine that you are working on an application that displays stock market analysts and the ratings they have made on certain stocks.

In this example, we would probably want to have a web page that shows the names of the stock market analysts, with actions to add or delete an analyst. We also would want to have a page that showed the different stocks and the ratings given to them by an analyst, with an action to add a new rating. That's the view side of our simple application.

What about the controller side? For this application, we'll use a servlet to be the controller. The primary job of the controller servlet is to route requests to the appropriate JSP page or to another servlet. The other servlet in this application will be a servlet that responds to the "add rating" request from a JSP page.

Finally, for the model side, in a real application, we would probably use a robust data persistence tier. This might include both a database and objects such as EJBs to access the data. Here's a simple diagram illustrating what this application might look like:

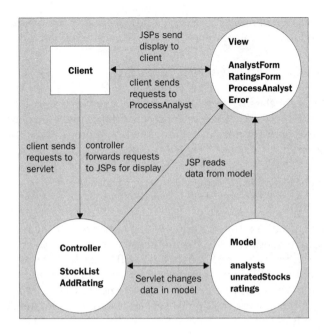

Forwarding and Including Requests

If a servlet is going to be a controller in an MVC application, it needs some way to forward requests to the display components of the application, since the display components create the response back to the client. This is accomplished by getting an object called a `RequestDispatcher`. Through a request dispatcher, a servlet can forward the request to another web component or include the response of another web component in the current response. This is the same as the JSP standard actions `<jsp:forward>` and `<jsp:include>`, which we looked at in Chapter 4.

Getting a RequestDispatcher

You can get a `RequestDispatcher` from the `ServletRequest` object or from the `ServletContext` object. The method signature for the `ServletRequest` method is:

```
RequestDispatcher getRequestDispatcher(String path)
```

This method returns a `RequestDispatcher` for the web component at the given location. The `path` argument is the path to the web application resource. This path can be a relative path or an absolute path. For example, the path to the `Login` servlet earlier in the chapter was /Login. This path starts with a forward slash (/), so it is interpreted as an absolute path that is relative to the application context. For example, if the application context is /Ch05, then /Login would be the resource at /Ch05/Login. If the path does not start with a slash, it is a relative path that is interpreted relative to the current web component location. For example, if the web component were /Ch05/reports/DisplayReport, then the path `PrintReport` would be the resource /Ch05/reports/PrintReport. If the resource does not exist, the method returns `null`.

You can also get a `RequestDispatcher` using a `ServletContext` object. The `GenericServlet` class defines a method to get a reference to the `ServletContext` object for your servlet:

```
ServletContext getServletContext()
```

Since your servlet is a subclass of `GenericServlet`, you can just call this method directly from your servlet. The `ServletContext` represents the application context in which the servlet executes. Next, your servlet can call one of two methods of the `ServletContext` to get a `RequestDispatcher`:

```
RequestDispatcher getNamedDispatcher(String name)
RequestDispatcher getRequestDispatcher(String path)
```

Either method can be used to return a `RequestDispatcher` for the resource at the given path or name. If the resource does not exist, the methods return `null`. The `path` argument for `getRequestDispatcher(String)` must begin with a slash ("`/`"), and is interpreted relative to the application context. The name argument for `getNamedDispatcher(String)` must be the same name used in the `<servlet-name>` sub-element of `<servlet-mapping>` in the deployment descriptor. So, using the `Login` servlet example again, the deployment descriptor for this servlet had this entry:

```
<servlet-mapping>
  <servlet-name>Login</servlet-name>
  <url-pattern>/Login</url-pattern>
</servlet-mapping>
```

The call to `getNamedDispatcher("Login")` would return a `RequestDispatcher` for the web resource /Ch05/Login (remember /Login is interpreted relative to the application context).

Using a Request Dispatcher

Request dispatchers can be used either to forward a request to another resource, or to include another resources' response in the current response. To forward a request, use this method:

```
void forward(ServletRequest request, ServletResponse response)
        throws ServletException, java.io.IOException
```

Since this method relies on another resource to generate the response output, the calling servlet should not write any data to the response stream before calling this method. If response data is sent to the client before this method is called, this method will throw an exception. Also, since the response stream will be complete when the other resource is finished, the calling servlet should not attempt to use the response object after the `forward()` method returns.

Alternatively, you can call another resource and include its response data in the current response. This is done with the method:

```
void include(ServletRequest request, ServletResponse response)
        throws ServletException, java.io.IOException
```

Since this method includes another response in the current response, you can safely write response data to the client both before and after calling this method.

Adding Parameters to the Request

At times, you may need to add additional information to the request object that you use in a `forward()` or `include()` method call. The `ServletRequest` interface defines a number of methods for adding, getting, and removing data from the request object:

```
Object getAttribute(String name)
Enumeration getAttributeNames()
void setAttribute(String name, Object o)
void removeAttribute(String name)
```

The calling servlet can add attributes to the request using `setAttribute(String name, Object o)`. Take care not to duplicate names already used for attributes; if you use a duplicate name, the new attribute will replace the previous attribute. The receiving servlet will use the `getAttribute(String name)` method to get the attribute, using the same name that the calling servlet used to set the attribute.

Try It Out   Using the MVC Architecture

Let's take the simple design above and turn it into a working web application. We will develop view and controller segments as described above. For the model layer, we will simply use some `ArrayList` and `Vector` objects to store the data.

1. Start by creating a directory structure for the web application:

```
stock/
  WEB-INF/
    classes/
      web
```

2. We'll start with one view component not shown above – a static HTML page that will be the entry point into the application. Save this file into the /stock directory with the name `index.html`. This web page provides two links into the application:

```
<!DOCTYPE HTML PUBLIC "-//W3C//DTD HTML 4.01 Transitional//EN">
<html>
  <head>
    <title>Stocks and Analysts</title>
  </head>
```

```
  <body>
    <h1>Stocks and Analysts</h1>
    <p>
      <a href="/stock/StockList/AnalystForm">See all Analysts</a>
    <p>
      <a href="/stock/StockList/RatingsForm">See all Ratings</a>
    <hr>
  </body>
</html>
```

3. Now we'll create the controller for this application. Name this code
StockListServlet.java. Notice that it is in a package named web. Save it into the
/classes/web directory:

```
package web;

import javax.servlet.*;
import javax.servlet.http.*;
import java.io.*;
import java.util.*;

public class StockListServlet extends HttpServlet {
  static ArrayList analysts = new ArrayList();
  static ArrayList unratedStocks = new ArrayList();
  static ArrayList ratings = new ArrayList();

  public void init() {
    analysts.add("Fred");
    analysts.add("Leonard");
    analysts.add("Sarah");
    analysts.add("Nancy");
    unratedStocks.add("ABC");
    unratedStocks.add("DDBC");
    unratedStocks.add("DDC");
    unratedStocks.add("FBC");
    unratedStocks.add("INT");
    unratedStocks.add("JIM");
    unratedStocks.add("SRI");
    unratedStocks.add("SRU");
    unratedStocks.add("UDE");
    unratedStocks.add("ZAP");
    Vector v = new Vector();
    v.add("Fred");
    v.add("ZZZ");
    v.add("Smashing!");
    ratings.add(v);
  }

  public void doPost(HttpServletRequest request,
                     HttpServletResponse response)
```

```
{
  doGet(request, response);
}

public void doGet(HttpServletRequest request,
                  HttpServletResponse response)
{
  try {
    ArrayList data = null;
    RequestDispatcher dispatcher;
    ServletContext context = getServletContext();
    String name = request.getPathInfo();
    name = name.substring(1);

    if ("AnalystForm".equals(name)) {
      data = analysts;
      request.setAttribute("data", data);
    } else if ("RatingsForm".equals(name)) {
      request.setAttribute("data", ratings);
      request.setAttribute("analysts", analysts);
      request.setAttribute("unrated", unratedStocks);
    } else if ("AddRating".equals(name)) {
      request.setAttribute("data", ratings);
      request.setAttribute("analysts", analysts);
      request.setAttribute("unrated", unratedStocks);
    } else {
      name = "Error";
    }

    dispatcher = context.getNamedDispatcher(name);
    if (dispatcher == null) {
      dispatcher = context.getNamedDispatcher("Error");
    }
    dispatcher.forward(request, response);
  } catch (Exception e) {
    log("Exception in StockListServlet.doGet()");
  }
}
}
```

4. We're now ready for the first JSP view component. This is a page that will show all the analysts in the application. Name this file `AnalystForm.jsp`, and save it into the **/stock** directory:

```
<!DOCTYPE HTML PUBLIC "-//W3C//DTD HTML 4.01 Transitional//EN">
<html>
  <head>
    <title>Analyst Management</title>
  </head>
```

243

```
<body>
  <%@ page import="java.util.*" %>
  <h1>Analyst Management Form</h1>
  <form action="/stock/ProcessAnalyst" method="POST">
    <table>
    <%
    ArrayList analysts = (ArrayList)request.getAttribute("data");
    if (analysts == null) {
    %>
      <h2> Attribute is null </h2>
    <%
    } else {
      for (int i = 0; i < analysts.size(); i++) {
        String analyst = (String)analysts.get(i);
    %>
      <tr>
        <td>
          <input type="checkbox" name="checkbox" value="<%= analyst %>"
        </td>
        <td>
          <%= analyst %>
        </td>
      </tr>
    <%
      }
    }
    %>
    </table>
    <input type="submit" value="Delete Selected" name="delete"><p>
    <input type="text" size="40" name="addname">
    <input type="submit" value="Add New Analyst" name="add">
  </form>
</body>
</html>
```

5. When the user attempts to add or delete an analyst from `AnalystForm.jsp`, the request is sent directly to another JSP. That JSP is `ProcessAnalyst.jsp`, although you will see it does not really add or delete an analyst. Save this file into the **/stock** directory too:

```
<!DOCTYPE HTML PUBLIC "-//W3C//DTD HTML 4.01 Transitional//EN">
<html>
  <head>
    <title>Process Analyst Request</title>
  </head>

  <body>
    <h1>Process Analyst Request</h1>
```

```
Adding or deleting an analyst from the database is not currently
implemented. Implementation of this feature is left as an exercise
for the reader.
  </body>
</html>
```

6. The other functionality provided by this application is to show the ratings the analysts have given to certain stocks. This view of the data is handled by the RatingsForm.jsp. Again, since this is a JSP, save it to the **/stocks** directory:

```
<!DOCTYPE HTML PUBLIC "-//W3C//DTD HTML 4.01 Transitional//EN">
<html>
  <head>
    <title>Stock Ratings</title>
  </head>

  <body>
    <h1>Stock Ratings</h1>

    <%@ page import="java.util.*" %>
    <%
    ArrayList stocks = (ArrayList) request.getAttribute("data");
    if (stocks != null && stocks.size() > 0) {
    %>
    <form action="/stock/StockList/AddRating" method="post">
      <table border="1">
          <tr>
            <th>Ticker</th>
            <th>Analyst</th>
            <th>Rating</th>
          </tr>
        <%
        for (int i = 0; i < stocks.size(); i++) {
          Vector v = (Vector) stocks.get(i);
          String ticker = (String)v.elementAt(0);
          String analyst = (String)v.elementAt(1);
          String rating = (String)v.elementAt(2);
        %>
        <tr>
          <td><%= ticker %></td>
          <td><%= analyst %></td>
          <td><%= rating %></td>
        </tr>
        <%
        }
        %>
      </table>
      <table>
          <tr>
            <td>
```

```
            <select name="analysts">
              <%
              ArrayList analysts =
                (ArrayList) request.getAttribute("analysts");
              for (int i = 0; i < analysts.size(); i++) {
                String analyst = (String)analysts.get(i);
              %>
              <option value="<%= analyst %>">
                <%= analyst %>
                <%
                }
                %>
            </select>
          </td>
          <td>
            <select name="stocks">
              <%
              ArrayList unratedStocks =
                (ArrayList) request.getAttribute("unrated");
              for (int i = 0; i < unratedStocks.size(); i++) {
                String ticker = (String)unratedStocks.get(i);
              %>
              <option value="<%= ticker %>">
                <%= ticker %>
                <%
                }
                %>
            </select>
          </td>
          <td>
            <select name="ratings">
              <option value="Run away! Run away!">Run away! Run away!
              <option value="Could be worse!">Could be worse!
              <option value="A bit of OK!">A bit of OK!
              <option value="Take a chance!">Take a chance!
              <option value="Smashing!">Smashing!
            </select>
          </td>
        </tr>
        <tr>
          <td>
            <input type="submit" value="Submit Rating">
          </td>
        </tr>
      </table>
    </form>
    <%
    } else {
    %>
    No stock information found
    <%
    }
    %>
  </body>
</html>
```

7. Now, we need a servlet to process the request to add a stock rating from an analyst. After adding the rating, the servlet will send the request back to the `RatingsForm.jsp` to display the new model of the data. This servlet needs to be saved to the **/web** directory:

```java
package web;

import javax.servlet.*;
import javax.servlet.http.*;
import java.util.*;

public class AddRating extends HttpServlet {
  public void doPost(HttpServletRequest request,
                     HttpServletResponse response)
  {
    try {
      String analyst = request.getParameter("analysts");
      String ticker = request.getParameter("stocks");
      String rating = request.getParameter("ratings");

      Vector v = new Vector();
      v.add(analyst);
      v.add(ticker);
      v.add(rating);

      ArrayList ratings = (ArrayList)request.getAttribute("data");
      ratings.add(v);

      ArrayList unratedStocks =
        (ArrayList)request.getAttribute("unrated");
      unratedStocks.remove(unratedStocks.indexOf(ticker));

      ServletContext context = getServletContext();
      RequestDispatcher dispatcher =
        context.getNamedDispatcher("RatingsForm");
      dispatcher.forward(request, response);
    } catch (Exception e) {
      log("Exception in AddRating.doPost()", e);
    }
  }
}
```

8. Create a simple `Error.jsp` page to handle bad request URLs. If you are using Tomcat stand alone, you need to change the port number shown below from 8000 to 8080. Save this page in the root directory of the web application:

```html
<!DOCTYPE HTML PUBLIC "-//W3C//DTD HTML 4.01 Transitional//EN">
<html>
  <head>
    <title>Error!</title>
```

```
    </head>

    <body>
      <h1>Error!</h1>
      The URL you submitted was not recognized. Please go to the
      <a href="http://localhost:8000/stock/index.html">start page</a>
      and try again.
    </body>
</html>
```

9. Lastly, if you plan to deploy this application to Tomcat stand-alone, you need to create the deployment descriptor. The `web.xml` file I used is shown below. Save this file into the /WEB-INF directory. If you are deploying this application to the J2EE server, you can skip this step because the J2EE Deploytool will create an appropriate deployment descriptor for you:

```xml
<?xml version="1.0" encoding="ISO-8859-1"?>

<!DOCTYPE web-app
    PUBLIC "-//Sun Microsystems, Inc.//DTD Web Application 2.3//EN"
    "http://java.sun.com/dtd/web-app_2_3.dtd">

<web-app>
  <display-name>Beginning J2EE Ch 5</display-name>
  <servlet>
   <servlet-name>StockList</servlet-name>
   <servlet-class>web.StockListServlet</servlet-class>
  </servlet>

  <servlet>
    <servlet-name>AddRating</servlet-name>
    <servlet-class>web.AddRating</servlet-class>
  </servlet>

  <servlet>
    <servlet-name>ProcessAnalyst</servlet-name>
    <jsp-file>/ProcessAnalyst.jsp</jsp-file>
  </servlet>

  <servlet>
    <servlet-name>Error</servlet-name>
    <jsp-file>/Error.jsp</jsp-file>
  </servlet>

  <servlet>
    <servlet-name>AnalystForm</servlet-name>
    <jsp-file>/AnalystForm.jsp</jsp-file>
  </servlet>

  <servlet>
```

```
      <servlet-name>RatingsForm</servlet-name>
      <jsp-file>/RatingsForm.jsp</jsp-file>
   </servlet>

   <servlet-mapping>
      <servlet-name>StockList</servlet-name>
      <url-pattern>/StockList/*</url-pattern>
   </servlet-mapping>

   <servlet-mapping>
      <servlet-name>ProcessAnalyst</servlet-name>
      <url-pattern>/ProcessAnalyst</url-pattern>
   </servlet-mapping>

</web-app>
```

10. Compile the servlet classes.

11. The directory structure of your application should now look like this:

```
stock/
   AnalystForm.jsp
   Error.jsp
   index.html
   ProcessAnalyst.jsp
   RatingsForm.jsp
   WEB-INF/
      web.xml
      classes/
         web/
            AddRating.java
            AddRating.class
            StockListServlet.java
            StockListServlet.class
```

12. Deploy the application.

Tomcat – Copy the entire directory structure into the /webapps directory of the Tomcat installation; or create the WAR file, and copy the WAR file into the /webapps directory.

J2EE – Use the J2EE Deploytool as shown earlier in this chapter and in the JSP chapter. Create a web component for each of the JSP pages and servlet classes. Alias the `StockListServlet` to /StockList/*, and set the context root for the EAR to stock.

> As this chapter was written, the Deploytool for J2EE 1.4 appears to have a bug. As you create each web component through the New Web Application WAR Wizard, the deployment descriptor becomes corrupted. Hopefully, this bug will be fixed before the final release of J2EE 1.4; if not, the `web.xml` file will need to be created by hand and added to the EAR before it is deployed. We will explain how to do this in the code download for the book.

13. If you are using Tomcat, start, or restart, the server.

14. Fire up the browser and start playing with your new little MVC application.

Use this URL for J2EE:

http://localhost:8000/stock/index.html

Or this URL for Tomcat:

http://localhost:8080/stock/index.html

Use the links or buttons to navigate around and try different requests. Here's a screenshot of the RatingsForm.jsp web page after adding a rating:

How It Works

Although a simple example, there is a lot of code here. Rather than go over each servlet and JSP line by line, I'll cover some of the more interesting points of each.

The index.html static HTML page contains links that create two slightly different requests. Each link goes to the same servlet, StockListServlet, but each link uses the additional path technique to pass information to the controller servlet. In the first link, /AnalystForm is the additional path information; in the other link it is /RatingsForm:

```
<a href="/stock/StockList/AnalystForm">See all Analysts</a>
<a href="/stock/StockList/RatingsForm">See all Ratings</a>
```

When StockListServlet is initialized, it populates the various ArrayLists and Vectors that are being used as the model in this MVC application. When it gets a request, it parses the extra path information using the request.getPathInfo() method. It uses this information to determine what model data to add to the request using the setAttribute() method. Then it uses the extra path information to forward the request to the appropriate view or other controller servlet:

```
String name = request.getPathInfo();
//.....some code not shown
dispatcher = context.getNamedDispatcher(name);
//.....some code not shown
dispatcher.forward(request, response);
```

The dispatcher is obtained with a getNamedDispatcher() call; the name used to obtain the dispatcher is the same name assigned to the component in the deployment descriptor. Notice also that the doPost() method in this servlet simply calls doGet(). This is a common technique when you want to support both GET and POST with the same processing. You could also have doGet() call doPost().

The AnalystForm.jsp view component reads the data from the model and displays it to the user. The controller servlet (StockListServlet) added the model data to the request with setAttribute(). The data is obtained in the JSP page by calling the getAttribute() method. The JSP page creates a form, and when the user clicks one of the buttons on the page, a request is sent directly to ProcessAnalyst.jsp (which does nothing in this example):

```
<%
ArrayList analysts = (ArrayList)request.getAttribute("data");
if (analysts == null) {
%>
   <h2> Attribute is null </h2>
<%
} else {
   for (int i = 0; i < analysts.size(); i++) {
      String analyst = (String) analysts.get(i);
%>
   <tr>
     <td>
       <input type="checkbox" name="checkbox" value="<%= analyst %>"
     </td>
     <td>
       <%= analyst %>
     </td>
   </tr>
<%
   }
}
%>
```

The RatingsForm.jsp view component displays the analyst, stock ticker, and rating for all stocks that currently have ratings. It gets the model data from the request by calling the getAttribute() method of the request object. Then it lists all the analysts, all unrated stocks, and the valid ratings. This allows the user to select a stock and assign it a rating. Clicking the Submit button sends the request to StockListServlet, which forwards the request to the AddRating servlet.

`AddRating` is the controller servlet that adds a rating to the model. The servlet gets the model components from the request, and calls a method to change their data. Notice that it does not need to add the model components back to the request. The request already holds a reference to the model; calling the `add()` or `remove()` methods of `ArrayList` does not change the reference held by the request – it only changes the state of the object. After changing the model, this servlet forwards the request back to `RatingsForm.jsp`, so that it can display the new model:

```
String analyst = request.getParameter("analysts");
String ticker = request.getParameter("stocks");
String rating = request.getParameter("ratings");

Vector v = new Vector();
v.add(analyst);
v.add(ticker);
v.add(rating);

ArrayList ratings = (ArrayList) request.getAttribute("data");
ratings.add(v);

ArrayList unratedStocks =
   (ArrayList) request.getAttribute("unrated");
unratedStocks.remove(unratedStocks.indexOf(ticker));

ServletContext context = getServletContext();
RequestDispatcher dispatcher =
   context.getNamedDispatcher("RatingsForm");
dispatcher.forward(request, response);
```

Finally, the `Error.jsp` page handles the case of a user typing an incorrect address into the browser.

You should see now the basics of a simple MVC application. You would not want to use this example directly, though. For one thing, because the data is held in member variables in the servlet – there is no persistence. As soon as the servlet is destroyed, any changes to the model are lost. In later chapters, we will extend the example here with a more robust model.

Summary

We've covered quite a lot of information in this chapter. After reading this chapter, you should have learned:

- ❏ Servers respond to requests and specifically that web servers respond to HTTP requests such as `GET` and `POST`.

- ❏ Servlets extend a server's functionality by providing a server-side program that can respond to HTTP requests. `HttpServlets` live inside servlet containers.

❏ A servlet lifecycle consists of four phases: loading and creating, initialization, request handling, and end of service. For each of those phases, specific servlet methods realize those phases. The servlet will spend most of its lifecycle in the request-handling phase.

❏ You can make your servlet thread-safe: use local variables for request data, and use instance variables for constant data. If you need to change instance variables or outside resources, synchronize access to them. Making your servlet implement `SingleThreadModel` does not guarantee that your server is thread-safe. Synchronizing `service()`, `doGet()`, or `doPost()` will make your servlet thread-safe, but doing this is very, very impractical.

❏ You should always handle exceptions and never allow an exception to bypass the servlet's response (unless it is an `IOException` that occurs during the response).

❏ The Servlet API facilitates session tracking, which allows you to create a web application that can keep track of a client's interactions with the application.

❏ Filters provide a pluggable architecture for processing requests and responses. They encapsulate processing that is outside the scope of the servlet.

❏ The Model-View-Control architecture can help create more easily maintainable applications. Code is kept away from JSPs; HTML is kept away from servlets.

With the information above, you should be able to tackle most of the servlet challenges that you will face as you begin to develop web applications. As usual, though, there is so much more that just could not be covered within the chapter. If you will be doing extensive work with servlets, you may want to obtain a copy of *Professional Java Servlets 2.3* (ISBN 1-86100-561-X) from Wrox Press. In addition, there are several online forums that cover servlet technology. Sun's developer forum hosts a servlet forum at http://forum.java.sun.com/. Wrox Press also has a servlet forum at http://p2p.wrox.com.

Exercises

1. Using one of the servlet examples in this chapter that accepts a POST request, experiment with sending a POST request using a telnet client. Hint: you need to set the `content-length` header.

2. In the section on *Using the response Object*, we very briefly outline the basic steps for using a servlet to send binary data to a client. Create a servlet that accepts a request from a client for an image file. The name of the image file can be passed as a form parameter, part of the URL, or as extra path information. Write the servlet to load the named image into a byte array, set the content type for an image, set the content length (the number of bytes in the array), and write the image to the response.

3. In the session tracking example, remove the code that performs the URL rewriting, set your browser to reject cookies, and experiment with the example to see how it behaves in this situation.

4. Expand the session tracking example to write a cookie with the user ID to the client browser. Use this cookie to "recognize" the user and initialize some session data.

5. If you have read the JSP chapters, rewrite the final example to use custom actions in the JSP pages.

CHAPTER 6

Connecting to Databases   **258**

Statements   **275**

Resultsets   **284**

Summary   **295**

Exercises   **295**

Working with Databases

Many J2EE applications that you work on will be dependent on a **database**. Search engines use databases to store information about web resources, e-commerce sites use databases to store information about customers and orders, geo-imaging sites that provide photographic images of the world from space use databases to store images and information about those images... the list goes on and on.

In this chapter, we will be using the Cloudscape database that comes with the J2EE SDK as our example database. Cloudscape is an example of a **relational database**. Data in a relational database is stored in a series of **tables**. Each table consists of **rows** and **columns**. For example, you can use a table to store information about customers of an e-commerce web application. Each row in the table represents a user; each column in the row represents a particular piece of data about that user. You might also have a separate table that records data about customer orders. Rather than repeating the information about a customer in the orders table, the orders table will have a column that identifies the customer from the customer table. This creates a relationship between the two tables, and thus is why the database is called a relational database.

Java has an API for working with databases, and this technology is known as **JDBC**. JDBC provides the developer with tools that allow clients to connect to databases, and send commands to the database. These commands are written in the **Structured Query Language**, or **SQL**. (For more on SQL, see Appendix B.) Relational databases are not the only kind of database, but they are the most common. However, JDBC can be used with any kind of database. That is because JDBC abstracts common database functions into a set of common classes and methods. Database-specific code is contained in a code library, commonly called a driver library. If there is a driver library for a database, you can use the JDBC API to send commands to the database and extract data from the database.

There is a lot of information about JDBC that can be covered. Clearly, we can't cover everything in this single chapter, but what we will attempt to cover is enough topics to get you started. In the next chapter, we will look at some advanced topics that you need to be aware of as you begin to develop J2EE applications.

Here are the topics we'll cover in this chapter:

❑ How to specify which **driver** your code will use so that you can communicate with the correct database

❑ How your Java code can get a **connection** to a database server

❑ How to use a `Statement` object to insert, update, and delete data from a database

❑ How to read the results of a query from a **resultset**

❑ How to use `PreparedStatements` and `CallableStatements`

If you want to take your understanding of databases beyond that which is presented in these two chapters, you should consider, as your next step, reading Professional Java Data, by Wrox Press, 1-86100-410-9. This book is very comprehensive, and is aimed more at those developers who are looking to work with data day-to-day as professional developers.

Connecting to Databases

The first step in being able to work with a database is to connect to that database. It's a process that's analogous to a web browser making a connection to a web server. The browser makes a connection to a server, sends a specially formatted message to the server, and receives a response back from the server. When working with a database, your code will use the JDBC API to get a connection to a database server, send a specially formatted message to the server, and receive a response back from the server. As mentioned in the introduction, the JDBC API is an abstraction, and it uses a database-specific code library to communicate with a particular database. A high-level diagram of that process is shown here:

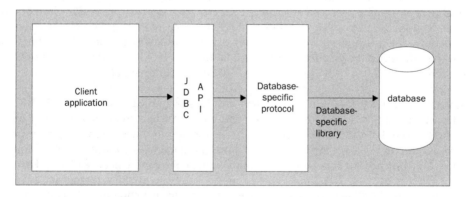

When making a database connection, your code does not need to open any sockets, or use any classes of the `java.net` package to make a connection to the database. All the connection details are handled primarily by a class in the database-specific library. This class is known as a driver. Your code simply tells a class known as the DriverManager that it needs a connection, and the DriverManager works with the driver to create a connection to the database that your code can use.

Drivers

JDBC provides a database-neutral set of classes and interfaces that can be used by your Java class. The database-specific code is included in a driver library that is developed by the database vendor or third parties. The primary advantage of using a driver library is that your code can use the same JDBC API to talk to many different databases simply by changing the library used by your code. Also, by using a driver library, your code is simpler to develop, debug, and maintain, since the lower-level networking details are handled by the driver.

Driver Types

The JDBC specification identifies **four** types of drivers that can be used to communicate with databases. We will briefly look at each of the four types in this section:

Type 1 Driver

This driver provides a mapping between JDBC and some other data access API. The other data access API then calls a native API library to complete the communication to the database. Since native APIs are platform specific, this type of driver is generally less portable. One of the most common Type 1 drivers you will see is the JDBC-ODBC bridge because this driver comes as a standard part of the Java SDK. Like JDBC, ODBC is an API for talking to databases. The JDBC-ODBC Type 1 driver provides a translation layer between your application and the ODBC driver. Thus, if an ODBC driver exists for a database, you can use the JDBC-ODBC bridge driver to communicate with that database. Here is what the communication between client and database looks like using the JDBC-ODBC bridge driver.

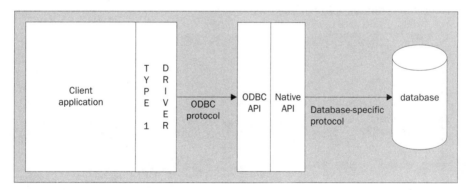

Note that Sun's web site says that the JDBC-ODBC driver should not be used for production applications. Specifically, they say:

"The JDBC-ODBC Bridge driver is recommended for use in prototyping efforts and for cases where no other JDBC technology-based driver exists. If a commercial, all-Java JDBC driver is available, we recommend that it be used instead of the Bridge."

This is taken from http://java.sun.com/j2se/1.3/docs/guide/jdbc/getstart/bridge.doc.html.

259

Type 2 Driver

This type of driver is similar to the Type 1 driver because it communicates to the database through a native API. However, because it makes calls directly to the native API and bypasses the additional data access layer, this type of driver tends to be more efficient than Type 1. Like a Type 1 driver, it is dependent upon the existence of the native API library. The communication between client and database looks like this:

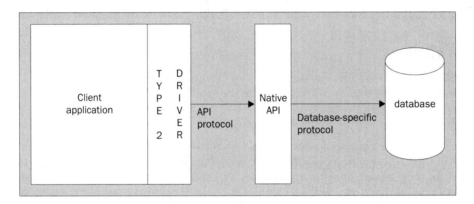

Type 3 Driver

This type of driver sends database calls to a **middleware component** running on another server. This communication uses a database-independent net protocol. The middleware server then communicates with the database using a database-specific protocol. The communication between client and database looks like this:

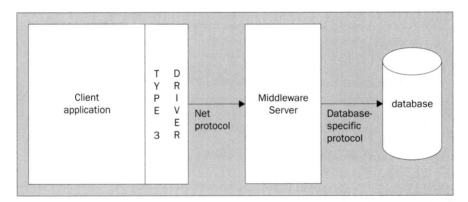

Note that for this driver, the middleware server usually resides on a different computer from the client application, but it may or may not be on a different computer from the database. Also, this driver does not imply that the middleware server uses a native library. The middleware server could be an all-Java piece of code. All that is required is that it translates the JDBC call received from the client into a database call.

Type 4 Driver

The type 4 driver, also commonly known as a **thin driver**, is *completely* written in Java. It communicates directly with a database using the database's native protocol. Since it is written completely in Java without any platform-specific code, it can be directly used on any platform with a Java virtual machine. The driver translates JDBC directly into the database's native protocol without the use of ODBC or native C APIs. The communication between client and database looks like this:

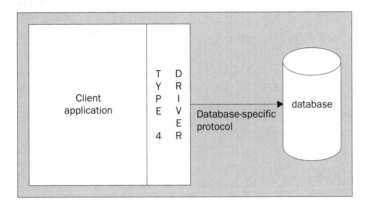

Thus, the thin driver makes an excellent choice for distributed database applications. If you are developing a client application that must communicate with a database, and the client could be installed on various platforms (Windows, Unix, Mac), then you would almost certainly use a Type 4 driver. Using a Type 4 driver, you could deploy the same client code (including the driver) to each platform and the client would work without any other modifications. If, however, you were using the Type 2 driver with this client, you would need to ensure that the native library used by the driver was installed to each client platform. You can see that deploying an application with a Type 4 driver is easier than deploying an application that uses one of the other drivers.

Choosing a Driver

In general you will want to choose either a Type 2 or a Type 4 driver for your web application. Type 1 and Type 3 drivers add a communication layer between the JDBC driver and the database, so they tend to be less efficient. The difference between a Type 2 and a Type 4 driver depends on whether you need to support a single platform or multiple platforms. If you must support multiple platforms, and native libraries do not exist for all platforms, then you will have to use a Type 4 driver. If a native library exists for all platforms, then there is no great difference between a Type 2 and a Type 4 driver. I have seen tests for Oracle's drivers that show the Type 2 performs better in some situations, and the Type 4 performs better in other situations. If performance is an important requirement for your system, you should conduct tests using all the drivers available to you, and then choose the driver that performs best.

The DriverManager Class

The `DriverManager` class is responsible for managing the JDBC drivers available to an application. The other important job of the driver manager is to hand out connections to client code. When you need a connection to a database, you hand the driver Manager a URL, and the driver manager returns a connection to you. To do this, the driver manager maintains a reference to an instance of each driver class that is available. When you ask for a connection, it polls each driver to determine if the driver can handle the URL. As soon as it finds a driver that can handle the URL, it asks the driver for a connection, and returns that connection to you.

For all this to work, two things need to happen:

❑   The driver manager needs to know which drivers are available

❑   You need to provide a valid URL to the `DriverManager` class

We'll look at loading driver classes in the next section, and how to provide a URL in the *Connections* section of the chapter.

Loading a Driver

Before the driver manager can provide connections, a driver class must be loaded by your application and registered with the driver manager. There are various ways to accomplish this:

❑   You can load and register the class dynamically using `Class.forName()`

❑   You can let the system load and register the class automatically using a system property

The first technique is the one you will see most often. The second technique is the one I recommend. Interestingly, even though the driver manager needs to know about the driver class, you do not need to interact directly with it when loading the driver class. Regardless of which technique you use, when the driver class is loaded, the driver class will register itself with the driver manager.

Using Class.forName()

This technique uses the method `forName(String)` from `java.lang.Class`. Calling `forName(String)` instructs the JVM to find, load, and link the class file identified by the `String` parameter. As part of initialization, the driver class will register itself with the driver manager. Thus, your code does not need to create an instance of the class, nor does it need to call the `registerDriver(Driver)` method. The JVM creates the instance for you, and the driver itself does the registration. The code to do this will look like this:

```
try {
  Class.forName("COM.cloudscape.core.JDBCDriver");
} catch (Exception e) {
  e.printStackTrace();
}
```

Note that with the code above, you do not need to `import` any driver-specific packages at the top of your class. The name of the class is given as a literal `String`, so the driver class does not need to be present as compile time. The other step you could take to make your class more database-independent would be to replace the literal `String` with a `String` variable. Then, you just need to pass the string to the application. For example, you could pass it on the command line:

```
> java JDBCClient COM.cloudscape.core.RmiJdbcDriver
```

In the command line above, the `RmiJdbcDriver` class is passed as a command line parameter to the JDBCClient class. To change the driver, and thus the database, used by your application, you simply change the string that is passed to the application. When you hard-code the driver name into the class, you must edit and recompile the class to change the driver. By specifying the driver from *outside* the class, there is no need to edit and recompile the class to change the driver.

However, using `Class.forName()` is a technique that I do not recommend. If there are many developers working on a major J2EE application, they each tend to put the `Class.forName()` method call into their code to ensure the driver is loaded. This leads to code duplication, which reduces the maintainability of your application.

Using a System Property

The other way to load the driver is to put the driver name into the `jdbc.drivers` system property. When any code calls one of the methods of the driver manager, the driver manager looks for the `jdbc.drivers` property. If it finds this property, it attempts to load each driver listed in the property. You can specify multiple drivers in the `jdbc.drivers` property. Each driver is listed by full package specification and class name. A colon is used as the delimiter between each driver.

> *Properties, as you may recall, are name-value pairs that allow you to associate a value with a given name. They are usually stored in an instance of `java.util.Properties`. System properties can be set and read through the `java.lang.System` class.*

So, for example, you can specify system properties on the command line of a Java application. You do this with the `-D` command line option. You probably already know this, but to use it, you put `-D` on the command line, followed immediately by the name of the property to be set, then the assignment operator =, and finally the value of the property. It might look something like this:

```
> java -Djdbc.drivers=COM.cloudscape.core.RmiJdbcDriver MyApplication
```

In the line above, `jdbc.drivers` is the name of the property, and `COM.cloudscape.core.RmiJdbcDriver` is the value of the property. The first time any code calls a driver manager method, such as `getConnection()`, the `DriverManager` class will load and link the drivers specified by the `jdbc.drivers` property and then execute the method. Note that there are other ways of setting a system property, such as reading a property file or resource bundle, but the DriverManager only loads driver classes once, so the system property must be set before any DriverManager method is called. Setting the system property from the command line guarantees the property is set before any code is executed.

Of the two techniques for loading a driver, this is the best for any non-trivial application. Using this technique, the driver classes are automatically loaded. No code needs to create an instance of the driver or call `Class.forName()`. If the driver needs to be changed, it's a simple change in only one place in the application, on the command line, with no need to edit or recompile code. In the next section, we will use this technique to load the driver and get a connection to a database.

Connections

Once we have loaded our driver, the next step is to create a connection to the database. In this section we look at the methods for getting a connection.

Getting a Connection

You get connections from the driver manager, as we mentioned earlier. One of the few times you need to interact with the driver manager is when you need a connection to a database. The driver manager acts as a **factory** for `Connection` objects. The method used to get a `Connection` object is `getConnection()` and there are three overloaded forms of this method:

- ❑ `getConnection(String url)`
- ❑ `getConnection(String url, String username, String password)`
- ❑ `getConnection(String url, Properties properties)`

Common to each of the methods is the `url` parameter. Just as with an HTTP URL, the JDBC URL provides a means to identify a resource (the database) that the client wishes to connect to.

The URL for each database will vary depending on the database and the driver. However, all URLs will have the general form `jdbc:<subprotocol>:<subname>`, with the `<subprotocol>` usually identifying the vendor and `<subname>` identifying the database and providing additional information needed to make the connection.

Here is one example of a Cloudscape URL:

```
jdbc:cloudscape:mydatabase.db;user=username;password=password
```

The subprotocol is `cloudscape` and the subname consists of the name of the database (the name can be relative, as shown above, or absolute), then we specify the name of the user, and the user's password. Notice that Cloudscape uses a semicolon as the delimiter between the parts of the subname. (The Cloudscape URL has another form that we will see later on. It can also contain other parameters besides name and password. You can find these other parameters in the Cloudscape documentation at http://www-3.ibm.com/software/data/cloudscape/pubs/collateral.html.)

Be aware that the driver for a database might be able to accept different URLs. Cloudscape, for example, recognizes seven URLs. You can consult the documentation that comes with your driver to find the various forms of the URL to use with that driver.

The example above used a URL that passed the username and password as part of the URL. You would use this URL with the `getConnection(String)` method. The other two forms of `getConnection()` allow you to pass parameters without including them in the URL. Those two forms are:

```
DriverManager.getConnection(sourceURL, myUserName, myPassword);
DriverManager.getConnection(sourceURL, myProperties);
```

Both methods have a parameter for the URL. The URL parameter has the same form as above (but without the username, password, or other parameters). The method that takes username and password as method arguments is pretty straightforward, so we will not look at it in detail. Rather, let's examine the last form of the `getConnection()` method:

```
getConnection(String url, Properties properties)
```

This method is used when you want to pass additional information to the driver (which can also include username and password), but you don't want to use the URL to pass this information.

The additional information is passed as a property in a `java.util.Properties` object. To supply the properties required by your JDBC driver, you can create a `Properties` object, and then set the properties that you need by calling its `setProperty()` method.

The properties that can be set are dependent on the database. For example, Cloudscape lists the following attributes that can be set with a `Properties` object:

- ❑ autocommit
- ❑ bootPassword
- ❑ create
- ❑ current
- ❑ databaseName
- ❑ dataEncryption

- ❑ encryptionProvider
- ❑ encryptionAlgorithm
- ❑ locale
- ❑ logDevice
- ❑ Password
- ❑ Shutdown
- ❑ Unicode
- ❑ Upgrade
- ❑ user

The documentation for your particular driver will list the properties it accepts. In general, you need to set the user name and password at a minimum. The code fragment below illustrates using a `Property` object to create a connection to a database named `CloudscapeDB`:

```
String sourceURL = "jdbc:cloudscape:CloudscapeDB";
Properties prop = new Properties();
prop.setProperty("user", "cloudscape");
prop.setProperty("password", "cloudscape");
Connection conn = DriverManager.getConnection(sourceURL, prop);
```

Now in real code, you wouldn't hard-code the username and password as shown above. The point is to show how to use a properties file to pass parameters to the driver.

Releasing Connections

I was working on a web application recently where the application locked up every time we stress tested it with thousands of database transactions. We were getting very frustrated because we couldn't release the application to production until it could reliably handle thousands of transactions per hour.

The database vendor included a management utility for their system that showed how many database connections had been opened, and how many had been released. Whenever we tested our application, the utility would show that the number of opened connections slowly but steadily diverged from the number of released connections. It turned out that the developer who had written the JDBC code hadn't understood how to release connections properly. Sometimes the connections were not released; sometimes the same connection was released more than once. Whenever we tested the code, it didn't take long for the defects in the code to cause the system to be starved for connections. After enough time, the application just locked up, waiting for connections that were no longer available.

By now you should see the importance of releasing connections. The `Connection` class has a method for releasing the connection:

```
public void close() throws SQLException
```

Many beginners will try to use it like this:

```
Connection conn = DriverManager.getConnection(url);
// Then some JDBC code that works with the database
conn.close();
```

This is a mistake! Almost all JDBC methods throw SQLExceptions (which are discussed in the next section). If the JDBC code between the getConnection() method call and the close() method call throws a SQLException, the call to close() is completely skipped.

The correct way to use close() is to put it inside the finally block of a try...catch...finally exception handler. Thus, you are ensured that close() will be called no matter what happens with the JDBC code. And since close() also throws an SQLException, it needs to be inside a try...catch block as well. So, JDBC code begins to look something like this:

```
try {
  conn = DriverManager.getConnection(url);
  // Then some JDBC code that works with the database
} catch (SQLEXception e) {
  // Handle the exception
} finally {
  try {
    conn.close();
  } catch (SQLException e2) {
    // Usually this is ignored
  }
}
```

And of course, this needs to be in every class that uses a connection. Pretty soon, you have finally blocks with enclosed try...catch blocks all over the place, and things are starting to look pretty cluttered!

That's the situation I faced with that web application I just spoke of; the developer had written many long methods inside a gigantic class, and all of these methods were opening connections at the top of a try block, and many hundreds of lines later closing them inside their own try...catch blocks (if they were getting closed at all).

To fix this code, I wrote one *single* method inside the class that was responsible for closing a connection. Whenever there was a try...catch block with conn.close(), I replaced it with a call to the new method. This eliminated all the duplicate code that closed connections. Then I went through the class line-by-line and ensured that every time a connection was opened inside a try block, there was a corresponding finally block that called the new method to close the connection.

When we tested the new code, I paid a lot more attention to that system diagnostic that compared open and released connections. When the code was finally correct, the two numbers were always equal when all the transactions were completed. Next time we sent the code to test, the system did not lock up. Mission successful!

Setting the Login Timeout

One other way we might have narrowed down the problem above is by setting a **login timeout**. Our application appeared to lock up because the code was waiting for a connection that never became available. It waited and it waited... and it would have waited forever if we let it.

There is a way to tell the driver manager to wait only a certain amount of time for a connection. To do this, the `DriverManager` class provides the following method:

```
public static void setLoginTimeout(int)
```

The `int` parameter indicates the number of seconds that the driver manager should wait for a connection. If the driver does not return a connection in that amount of time, then the manager throws a `SQLException`.

SQLException

Earlier I mentioned that almost all JDBC methods declare that they throw `SQLExceptions`. In most respects, `SQLExceptions` are the same as the other exception objects that you encounter in your Java code. Your methods that use JDBC code will either need to handle these exceptions in `try...catch...finally` blocks, or declare that they throw `SQLExceptions`.

However, `SQLExceptions` are different from other exceptions in that they can be **chained**. What this means is that the `SQLException` you catch in your code, may contain a reference to another `SQLException`, which in turn may contain a reference to another `SQLException`, and so on, and so on. It's a linked list of exceptions. The `SQLException` class adds a method for dealing with chained exceptions:

```
public SQLException getNextException()
```

Another difference is that the `SQLException` can contain additional information about the error that occurred *inside* the database. Databases have their own error codes that identify the problem that occurred. These error codes are returned inside the `SQLException` object, and you can get the error code with a call to this method:

```
public int getErrorCode()
```

Here is a small snippet of code showing these two methods:

```
try {
  // Some JDBC code
} catch (SQLException e) {
  while (e != null) {
    System.out.println("The error code is " + e.getErrorCode());
    e = e.getNextException();
  }
}
```

Inside the `while` loop, the error code from the database is printed, then `getNextException()` is called. The reference returned by `getNextException()` is assigned back to the variable e. When the last exception is reached, `getNextException()` returns null and the `while` loop will terminate.

Try It Out   Talking to a Database

At this point, we have enough information to start building some classes that communicate with database. We'll create two classes here. The first class will be a utility class that manages JDBC resources for clients. We will use the system property technique for loading the driver, and we will use the Cloudscape demonstration database that comes with the J2EE SDK. We will run Cloudscape as a server that executes separately from your application. The second class is simply the client class that uses the first to get a connection to the database.

1. The first class is the utility class that manages our JDBC resources, which is called `DriverLoader.java`:

```
package Ch06;

import java.sql.*;
import java.util.*;

public class DriverLoader {
  private DriverLoader() {}

  public static Connection getConnection(String url)
    throws SQLException
  {
    DriverManager.setLoginTimeout(10);
    return DriverManager.getConnection(url);
  }

  public static Connection getConnection(
    String url, String user, String password) throws SQLException
  {
    return DriverManager.getConnection(url, user, password);
  }
```

```
public static Connection getConnection(String url, Properties props)
  throws SQLException
{
  return DriverManager.getConnection(url, props);
}

public static void close(Connection conn) {
  if (conn != null) {
    try {
      conn.close();
    } catch (Exception e) {
      e.printStackTrace();
    }
  }
}
}
```

You might notice something unusual about the class above: its one and only constructor is private. I'll explain why this is so in the *How It Works* section later.

2. Now we need a client that will use the DriverLoader class to get a connection to a database. Here's our client code, in a file called JDBCClient.java:

```
package Ch06;

import java.sql.*;

public class JDBCClient {
  public static void main(String[] args) {
    Connection conn = null;
    try {
      String url =
        "jdbc:cloudscape:rmi://localhost:1099/cloudscapeDB;create=true";
      conn = DriverLoader.getConnection(url);
      DatabaseMetaData dbmd = conn.getMetaData();

      System.out.println("db name is " + dbmd.getDatabaseProductName());
      System.out.println(
        "db version is " + dbmd.getDatabaseProductVersion());
      System.out.println("db driver name is " + dbmd.getDriverName());
      System.out.println("db driver version is " + dbmd.getDriverVersion());
    } catch (SQLException e) {
      e.printStackTrace();
    } finally {
      DriverLoader.close(conn);
    }
  }
}
```

3. Compile both the `DriverLoader` and `JDBCClient` classes using this simple line at the command prompt located in the directory you are currently working in:

```
> javac *.java
```

4. Before you can test out the client, you need to start the database server. In server mode, the database runs separately from the client application. The server uses Java Remote Method Invocation (RMI) to accept requests from your client. In this mode, the database is started before your program runs, and continues to run after your program ends. You can find scripts for running the Cloudscape RMI server in the /bin directory of your J2EE installation. To run the server in Windows, you would use the following command line in that directory:

```
> cloudscape -start
```

For Unix/Linux, use:

```
> cloudscape.ksh -start
```

If this works correctly, you should see a simple one-line response from the server like this:

```
C:\j2sdkee1.4\bin> cloudscape -start
Redirecting application output to C:\j2sdkee1.4\logs\launcher.cloudscape.log
```

5. Now that the server is running, you can run the client. First, you need to ensure your classpath is set correctly. The classpath must be set to include the directory structure up to the start of the package for the `JDBCClient` class. It also needs to include the `cloudclient.jar` and `RmiJdbc.jar` libraries. On my system, I've put the class files into `C:\8333\Ch06` and Cloudscape is installed in `C:\j2sdkee1.4\lib\cloudscape`. So, assuming that we're working in the directory `C:\8333`, my classpath statement looks like this:

```
> set classpath=C:\j2sdkee1.4\lib\cloudscape\RmiJdbc.jar
> set classpath=%classpath%;C:\j2sdkee1.4\lib\cloudscape\cloudclient.jar
> set classpath=%classpath%;C:\8333
```

6. If you are trying this code with a different database, you will need to change the lines above so that they are correct for your setup. In general, your classpath needs to include the `.jar` file that contains the JDBC driver for your database, and the path to the top of the package structure for your class files.

7. Now you are ready to run the client. Remember that we will pass the driver class name as a system property on the command line for the application. The command you need to type looks like this:

```
> java -Djdbc.drivers=COM.cloudscape.core.RmiJdbcDriver Ch06.JDBCClient
```

Again, if you are using a different database, you would pass a different driver name on the command line.

8. Here is an example of the output you should see:

```
C:\8333> java -Djdbc.drivers=COM.cloudscape.core.RmiJdbcDriver
Ch06.JDBCClient
db name is DBMS:cloudscape
db version is 4.0.6
db driver name is Cloudscape Embedded JDBC Driver
db driver version is 4.0
```

```
Select Command Prompt                                              _ □ x
C:\8333\Ch06>javac *.java

C:\8333\Ch06>cloudscape -start
Redirecting application output to C:\j2sdkee1.4\logs\launcher.cloudscape.log
C:\8333\Ch06>cd ..

C:\8333>set classpath=C:\j2sdkee1.4\lib\cloudscape\RmiJdbc.jar

C:\8333>set classpath=%classpath%;C:\j2sdkee1.4\lib\cloudscape\cloudclient.jar

C:\8333>set classpath=%classpath%;c:\8333

C:\8333>java -Djdbc.drivers=COM.cloudscape.core.RmiJdbcDriver Ch06.JDBCClient
db name is DBMS:cloudscape
db version is 4.0.6
db driver name is Cloudscape Embedded JDBC Driver
db driver version is 4.0

C:\8333>_
```

How It Works

Let's start by looking at the `DriverLoader` class. This is a class that manages JDBC resources for us. We'll actually modify it several times in the course of this chapter. In developing the `DriverLoader`, I've started to apply some of the practices I recommended earlier. The class uses the system property technique for loading the driver. It also provides a central location for handing out and releasing resources.

Now, like the driver class, you really only need one instance of `DriverLoader` in the entire application. You don't need other developers creating instances of `DriverLoader` in their code; they just need to call the static methods we've provided. So, how do you prevent just anyone from creating instances of `DriverLoader`? The way to do that is to create one *private* constructor. Recall that if you don't provide any constructor, the compiler provides a public no-argument constructor for you. So, you have to provide at least one constructor to stop the compiler from adding a constructor, and make it `private` so that no other code can call the constructor. Now, anyone who wants a JDBC resource can get it from your class, and they cannot create an instance of this class, but can only call the static methods.

The class then has three methods that return connection objects to the caller. At the moment, these three methods are simply a pass-through to the similar methods of `java.sql.DriverManager`. Although they have no behavior of their own at this time, we will modify these methods later in the chapter to give them a little behavior.

Finally, the class includes the `close()` method for the connection. As I mentioned above, it is important to release database resources as soon as you no longer need them. Usually, what you will see in an application is that there are `try...catch` blocks surrounding method calls to the `close()` method of the connection in every class that does some JDBC work. Again, we want to avoid code duplication, so we put a `close(Connection)` method inside the `DriverLoader` class. This way, there is one central class that can close connections, it tests for null before attempting to close the connection, and when used properly, the application code does not need to be littered with duplicate `try...catch` blocks.

The `DriverLoader` class is simple to use. Assuming the system property `jdbc.drivers` is set, you call one of the `getConnection()` methods to get a connection, and call `close(Connection)` when you are finished with the connection. `getConnection()` calls the same named method in driver manager, and driver manager automatically loads the driver before it returns the first `Connection` object.

The `JDBCClient` class shows how to use the `DriverLoader` class. It consists of a single static `main()` method in which all the code executes. We start by assigning the URL string to a variable. Note that for a real application, you should not hard-code the URL into the class, but rather pass it in as a `String` using the command line, or prompt the user for it, or some other technique. Here is the URL:

```
String url =
   "jdbc:cloudscape:rmi://localhost:1099/cloudscapeDB;create=true";
```

The URL is one that is used when the Cloudscape RMI server is on a different computer from the client, although in this case they are actually on the same machine. You can still use this URL, though.

❑   `jdbc:cloudscape` is the JDBC protocol and subprotocol.

❑   `rmi://{host}:{port}/` is the RMI URL (notice that it ends with a forward slash). The port 1099 is the standard RMI port used by Cloudscape.

❑   `cloudscapeDB` is the name of the database.

❑   `create=true` is a property that tells the server to create the database if it doesn't exist yet.

Next, we use `getConnection(String)` to get a connection.

```
conn = DriverLoader.getConnection(url);
```

273

Next, we wanted to show that we actually had connected to the database, so we made a call to a method of `conn` that returns an object that contains data about the database. This object is an instance of `DatabaseMetaData`. From the `DatabaseMetaData` object, we were able to get the name and version of both the database and the driver:

```
DatabaseMetaData dbmd = conn.getMetaData();

System.out.println("db name is " + dbmd.getDatabaseProductName());
System.out.println(
  "db version is " + dbmd.getDatabaseProductVersion());
System.out.println("db driver name is " + dbmd.getDriverName());
System.out.println("db driver version is " + dbmd.getDriverVersion());
```

The `DatabaseMetaData` object contains many other methods that return information about the database. However, since it's not often that you'll be in a situation where you need to use this class, we'll not look at it in detail in this book. If you are interested in the other methods available, you can check the Javadoc for `DatabaseMetaData`.

The last part of the client class is the `finally` block. Remember that you want to ensure that you always release JDBC resources when you are finished with them. Since several of the methods that we called in the client class could have thrown a `SQLException`, if we had put the call to `close()` at the end of the `try` block, it would have been skipped over when an exception is thrown. Putting the `close()` call into the `finally` block ensures that it will always be called before the method terminates. Generally, you will always want to close the JDBC resources in a `finally` block.

Notice also, that we closed the connection in the same method in which we obtained the connection. In general, you should attempt to have the object that gets the connection be responsible for releasing the connection, preferably within the same method. When you obtain the connection and close the connection in the same method, it is much easier to verify you are releasing all your resources, than if you obtain the connection in one method, and release it in some other method.

Logging with the DriverManager

In the code example above, we used a `System.out.println()` to display the database information. This prints directly to the console. If you've done much development with Java, you probably know the problem that can happen with this. You'll have so many `System.out.println()` commands, that what is printed scrolls right off the screen, or is lost among the hundreds of lines of debug.

The `DriverManager` class provides a method that can be used to redirect debug output, and a method to send strings to the output through the driver manager. These methods are

```
public static void setLogWriter(PrintWriter)
public static void println(String)
```

Using `setLogWriter()`, you can direct the `DriverManager` object's debug statements to an instance of `PrintWriter`. The `PrintWriter` can be a wrapper for any `Writer` or `OutputStream`, such as a file, a stream, or a `PipedWriter`. You can also send your own debug statements to the log by calling the `println()` method. Here is a snippet of code showing how we could have used this feature in the example above:

```
// At the top of the try block
FileWriter fw = new FileWriter("mydebug.log");
PrintWriter pw = new PrintWriter(fw);
DriverManager.setLogWriter(pw);

// After getting the Connection and the DatabaseMetaData objects
DriverManager.println("db name is " + dbmd.getDatabaseProductName());
```

Statements

In the previous section, you saw how to get a connection to a database. However, the connection does *not* provide any methods that allow us to do anything to the database. To actually create, retrieve, update, or delete data from the database, we need the `Statement` class.

`Statement` objects are your primary interface to the tables in a database. We will look at using statements to insert new rows into a table, update a row in a table, and delete a row from a table. In the next section on resultsets, we will see how to use a statement to query tables in a database.

Creating and Using Statement Objects

`Statement` objects are creating from methods of the `Connection` class:

Connection Method	Description
`public Statement createStatement()`	Creates a `Statement` object. If the statement is used for a query, the resultset returned by the `executeQuery()` method is a non-updateable, non-scrollable resultset.
`public Statement createStatement(int, int)`	Creates a `Statement` object. If the statement is used for a query, the two parameters determine whether the resultset returned by the `executeQuery()` method is updatable or scrollable.
`public Statement createStatement(int, int, int)`	JDBC 3.0 – creates a `Statement` object. If the statement is used for a query, the two parameters determine whether the resultset returned by the `executeQuery()` method is updateable or scrollable and the third parameter determines holdability.

For now, don't worry what **updateable**, **scrollable**, and **holdable** mean. These apply to statements used to execute an SQL SELECT command. We will cover those topics in the *Resultsets* section. When executing any other SQL command, we only need a statement created with the createStatement() method that takes no parameters.

Once you have a Statement object, you use it to send SQL to the database with one of three four methods:

Statement Method	Description
public int executeUpdate(String)	Used to any execute SQL that is not a query. Those will primarily be create, insert, update, and delete SQL operations.
public ResultSet executeQuery(String)	Used for querying database tables.
public int[] executeBatch()	Used for sending multiple SQL commands in a single operation.
public boolean execute(String)	Used for executing unknown SQL or SQL that could return either ints or resultsets.

We will look at executeQuery(String) in the section on resultsets. The execute(String) method is rarely used – when the SQL could return either a resultset (as from a query) or an int (as from some kind of update) or both, and you don't know which it will return. Since you are not as likely to encounter this situation day-to-day, we'll not be covering this in detail in this book. If you're interested in learning more, you may consider reading *Professional Java Data*, byWrox Press, ISBN 1-86100-410-9.

Single Statement Execute

The executeUpdate(String) method is fairly straightforward. It is used to execute a *single* SQL command. The String parameter is the SQL that you want to execute in the database. It can be any SQL *except* for a query. The return value of the method is the number of rows affected by the SQL. This value can range from 0 to the number of rows in the database table. The number of rows returned by various types of SQL commands is shown below:

SQL type	Number of rows affected
Statements such as CREATE, ALTER, and DROP that affect tables, indexes, and so on.	0
INSERT statements	1...n where n is any number

SQL type	Number of rows affected
DELETE statements	0...n where n is the number of rows in the table
UPDATE statements	0...n where n is the number of rows in the table

If you attempt to execute a SQL query through the `executeUpdate(String)` method, an `SQLException` will be thrown.

Batch Updates

One way that you can improve the performance of your JDBC application is to execute a number of SQL commands in a **batch**. With batch execution, you add any number of SQL commands to the statement. The statement holds these SQL commands in memory until you tell it that you are ready for the database to execute the SQL. When you call `executeBatch()`, the statement sends the entire batch of SQL in one network communication. In addition to the `executeBatch()` method listed above, two other methods are needed for batch execution:

Statement Method	Description
`public void addBatch(String)`	Adds a SQL command to the current batch of commands for the `Statement` object
`public void clearBatch()`	Makes the set of commands in the current batch empty

The use of batch updating is straightforward. You add SQL commands to the statement with the `addBatch(String)` command. When you are ready for the commands to be executed, you call the `executeBatch()` method. This causes the statement to send all the SQL commands to the database for execution. In code, it would look like this:

```
// Each variable in the method call is an SQL command
stmt.addBatch(sqlCreateTable);
stmt.addBatch(sqlInsert);
stmt.addBatch(sqlUpdate);
stmt.addBatch(sqlDelete);
int[] results = stmt.executeBatch();
```

As you can see in the snippet above, the `executeBatch()` method returns an `int` array which contains the number of rows affected by each of the commands. The result of the first SQL command that was added to the statement is returned in the first element of the array, the result of the second SQL command is in the second element, and so on. Since the `executeBatch()` methods returns an `int` array, the one type of SQL command that cannot be executed by batching is a SQL `SELECT` command, which returns a `ResultSet` object, not an `int`.

277

Releasing Statements

Just as with `Connection` objects, it is equally important to release `Statement` objects when you are finished with them. This does not mean that you must immediately release the statement after executing an SQL command – you can use the same `Statement` object to execute multiple SQL commands. However, when you no longer need the statement to execute SQL, you should release it. The `Statement` class has its own `close()` method.

If you're near a computer, take a moment to read the JavaDoc for the `Statement` class (http://java.sun.com/j2se/1.4.1/docs/api/). You'll see that for the `close()` method, the JavaDoc states:

> *"Releases this Statement object's database and JDBC resources immediately instead of waiting for this to happen when it is automatically closed."*

This means that when the `Statement` object goes out of scope or is otherwise no longer reachable, it is eligible for garbage collection; when the object is garbage collected, its resources will be released. However, there's always the potential that objects that you think are out of scope are still reachable. In addition, even if an object is eligible for garbage collection, it may not be collected immediately.

> *Garbage collection of objects relies on the **reachability** of objects. An object is **reachable** if there is a chain of references that reach the object from some root reference. More information can be found at http://java.sun.com/docs/books/performance/ 1st_edition/html/JPAppGC.fm.html.*

Even different databases may handle closing resources differently. For the Cloudscape database, the documentation says that the garbage collector does not close resources. Finally, since database resources are limited, it's never a good idea to hold onto them longer than you need. That is why the Javadoc for `close()` also states:

> *It is generally good practice to release resources as soon as you are finished with them to avoid tying up database resources.*

Just as with the `Connection` objects, the `close()` method call for `Statement` objects should be in a `finally` block, and since it too throws a `SQLException`, it needs to be wrapped inside its own `try...catch` block. And since developers usually close the connection right after the statement, this usually leads to code that looks something like this:

```
    . . .
} finally {
  try {
    stmt.close();
    conn.close();
  } catch (Exception e) {}
}
```

Can you see the potential problem here? There is the possibility that the `stmt.close()` method call will throw an exception. When that occurs, the call to `conn.close()` will be skipped, and now your application has unclosed connections lying around.

The solution is to create a method similar to the `close(Connection)` method in the `DriverLoader` class. This method will have its own try...catch block, but any exception thrown in the new method will not prevent the `close(Connection)` method from being called. We'll look at the code for doing that in the next example.

Try It Out — Using Statements

1. In this example, we will modify the `DriverLoader` class from the previous example. Make a copy of the `DriverLoader.java` source code, which we created in the previous example, and make the following modifications to it:

```
package Ch06;

import java.sql.*;
import java.util.*;

public class JDBCManagerV1 {
  private JDBCManagerV1() {}

// Several methods are not shown in this listing (they are
// the same as the ones used in the DriverLoader class):
// getConnection(String url)
// getConnection(String url, String user, String password)
// getConnection(String url, Properties props)
// close(Connection conn)

  public static void close(Statement stmt) {
    if (stmt != null) {
      try {
        stmt.close();
      } catch (Exception e) {
        e.printStackTrace();
      }
    }
  }
}
```

Notice that I have changed the name of the class – since it is providing some significant methods to manage our database resources, I have decided to call this class JDBCManagerV1. The V1 is because this version will be modified later in the chapter to produce our final JDBCManager class. Don't forget to save your new code in a file named JDBCManagerV1.java.

2. Now enter the client class below that will use the JDBC manager class to get a connection to a database, use the connection to create a `Statement` object, and finally use the statement to insert, update, and delete data in a database. The code should be placed in a file called `JDBCClient2.java`:

```
package Ch06;

import java.sql.*;

public class JDBCClient2 {
  static Connection conn = null;
  static Statement stmt = null;

  static String sqlCreateTable = "create table COUNTRIES " +
    "(COUNTRY VARCHAR(26), COUNTRY_ISO_CODE VARCHAR(2) NOT NULL, " +
    "REGION VARCHAR(26))";
  static String sqlInsert = "insert into COUNTRIES " +
    "(COUNTRY, COUNTRY_ISO_CODE, REGION) " +
    "values ('Kyrgyzstan', 'KZ', 'Asia')";
  static String sqlUpdate = "update COUNTRIES set COUNTRY_ISO_CODE='KG'" +
    " where COUNTRY='Kyrgyzstan'";
  static String sqlDelete = "delete from COUNTRIES " +
    "where COUNTRY='Kyrgyzstan'";
  static String sqlDropTable = "drop table COUNTRIES";

  public static void main(String[] args) {
    try {
      String url =
        "jdbc:cloudscape:rmi://localhost:1099/CloudscapeDB;create=true";
      conn = JDBCManagerV1.getConnection(url);
      stmt = conn.createStatement();

      createTable();
      doInsert();
      doUpdate();
      doDelete();
      dropTable();
      doBatch();
    } catch (SQLException e) {
      e.printStackTrace();
    } finally {
      JDBCManagerV1.close(stmt);
      JDBCManagerV1.close(conn);
    }
  }

  public static void createTable() throws SQLException {
    int result = stmt.executeUpdate(sqlCreateTable);
    System.out.println("Create affected " + result + " rows (expected 0)");
  }
```

```
public static void doInsert() throws SQLException {
  int result = stmt.executeUpdate(sqlInsert);
  System.out.println("Inserted " + result + " rows (expected 1)");
}

public static void doUpdate() throws SQLException {
  int result = stmt.executeUpdate(sqlUpdate);
  System.out.println("Updated " + result + " rows (expected 1)");
}

public static void doDelete() throws SQLException {
  int result = stmt.executeUpdate(sqlDelete);
  System.out.println("Deleted " + result + " rows (expected 1)");
}

public static void dropTable() throws SQLException {
  int result = stmt.executeUpdate(sqlDropTable);
  System.out.println("Drop affected " + result + " rows (expected 0)");
}

public static void doBatch() throws SQLException {
  stmt.addBatch(sqlCreateTable);
  stmt.addBatch(sqlInsert);
  stmt.addBatch(sqlUpdate);
  stmt.addBatch(sqlDelete);

  int[] results = stmt.executeBatch();
  for (int i = 0; i < results.length; i++) {
    System.out.println("result[" + i + "]=" + results[i]);
  }
}
}
```

3. Compile the two classes. This shouldn't require any special classpath and a simple command in execute in the diretory in which the two `.java` files live should suffice:

```
> javac *.java
```

4. If it is not already running, run the Cloudscape RMI server as shown in the previous example. To do this, open a command line window and run the `cloudscape` script located in the `/bin` directory of your J2EE installation:

```
> cloudscape -start
```

5. Set the classpath to include the `RmiJdbc.jar` and `cloudclient.jar` libraries. These libraries are contained in the `/lib/cloudscape` directory of the J2EE installation.

```
> set classpath=c:\j2sdkee1.4\lib\cloudscape\RmiJdbc.jar
> set classpath=%classpath%;c:\j2sdkee1.4\lib\cloudscape\cloudclient.jar
> set classpath=%classpath%;C:\8333\Ch06
```

6. After setting the classpath, run the JDBCClient2 class using the following command line:

```
> java -Djdbc.drivers=COM.cloudscape.core.RmiJdbcDriver Ch06.JDBCClient2
```

This is the output you should see when you run the code:

```
> java -Djdbc.drivers=COM.cloudscape.core.RmiJdbcDriver Ch06.JDBCClient2
Create affected 0 rows (expected 0)
Inserted 1 rows (expected 1)
Updated 1 rows (expected 1)
Deleted 1 rows (expected 1)
Drop affected 0 rows (expected 0)
result[0]=0
result[1]=1
result[2]=1
result[3]=1
```

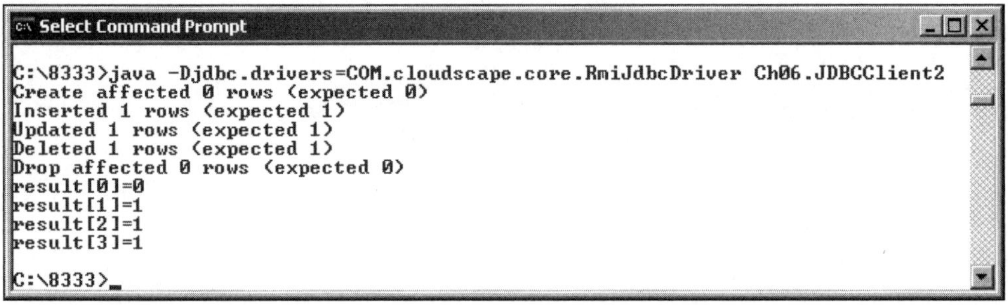

How It Works

The JDBCManager class (previously known as the DriverLoader class) has only one new method, the close(Statement) method. Putting this method here provides a central location for closing statements, and provides a way to avoid putting try...catch blocks in every bit of code that needs to close a statement.

The JDBCClient2 class demonstrates many of the features of statements that were presented in this section. It starts by defining variables for the connection and statement, and then defines a number of strings that contain SQL commands. The main() method gets the connection, and creates a statement, as shown below. You will notice that even though we don't use the connection after the statement is created, we cannot close the connection yet. The connection must remain open as long as you are working with the Statement object:

282

```
String url =
  "jdbc:cloudscape:rmi://localhost:1099/CloudscapeDB;create=true";
conn = JDBCManagerV1.getConnection(url);
stmt = conn.createStatement();
```

You can also see that we're using the same URL as we used with JDBCClient, with the create=true parameter. Recall that this instructs the Cloudscape RMI server to create the given database if it does not exist. If you created the database with JDBCClient, you do not need to include this parameter with the URL.

Next, the main() method calls various other methods. These other methods create the table, insert a row, update the row, and then delete the row. Notice that the CREATE TABLE command and the DROP TABLE command do not directly affect any rows, so the executeUpdate() returns a 0 as the result. The other commands affect a single row, so the return value from executing the INSERT, UPDATE, and DELETE commands is 1. Each of these methods execute the SQL command as *single* statements (that is, *without* batch update). Then, the code calls a method that drops the table, so that it can do the same actions, this time with batching. Here's the method that performs the batch update:

```
public static void doBatch() throws SQLException {
  stmt.addBatch(sqlCreateTable);
  stmt.addBatch(sqlInsert);
  stmt.addBatch(sqlUpdate);
  stmt.addBatch(sqlDelete);

  int[] results = stmt.executeBatch();
  for (int i = 0; i < results.length; i++) {
    System.out.println("result[" + i + "]=" + results[i]);
  }
}
```

Each SQL command is added to the Statement object with the addBatch() method. When all the commands have been added, the code calls the executeBatch() command. The results are returned in an int array. Each element in the array contains the number of rows affected by the corresponding SQL command (first command added is the first element, and so on.) The first command was again the CREATE TABLE – this returns a 0, as expected. The other commands each return 1, which you can see in the screen output above.

Lastly, in a finally block, we release the Statement and Connection objects:

```
} finally {
  JDBCManagerV1.close(stmt);
  JDBCManagerV1.close(conn);
}
}
```

Notice that we close the objects in the opposite order from which they were created. The object created first is closed last, and vice versa. Notice how clean this looks – you don't have to put a try...catch block inside the finally block and you don't have to worry about the close(Statement) method throwing an exception that prevents close(Connection) from executing.

The last method of Statement object that we're going to look at is the executeQuery() method. Unlike the executeUpate() or executeBatch() methods, executeQuery() does not return a simple int value. The method is used to execute a SQL SELECT command, and the SELECT command returns zero or more rows of data from one or more tables. These rows are returned in an object known as ResultSet, which is the subject of the next section.

Resultsets

When you perform a query of a table in a database, the results of the query are returned in a ResultSet object. The ResultSet object allows you to scroll through each row of the results, and read the data from each column in the row.

Moving Through the Results

The ResultSet interface defines a number of methods that can be used for moving through the results returned. However, not all methods are available for every resultset. Here again are the three methods that create Statement objects:

- ❑   public Statement createStatement()
- ❑   public Statement createStatement(int, int)
- ❑   public Statement createStatement(int, int, int)

When you use the first method to create a Statement object, the ResultSet object that is returned by executeQuery() is a nonscrollable ResultSet, or one that is of type forward-only. This means that you can only move from the first row to the last row, and cannot scroll backwards through the results. The only method for moving through the ResultSet object that can be used is:

```
public boolean next()
```

Assuming no problems with the SQL command, the executeQuery() method will always return a non-null ResultSet. When the executeQuery() method returns the ResultSet, the **cursor** is positioned *prior* to the first row of data.

> *Cursor is a database term. It generally refers to the set of rows returned by a query. When a cursor is positioned at a row, we mean that we are accessing a particular row in the set.*

To get to the first row of data, you must call the next() method. Each time you need to get the following row of data, you call next() again. The next() method returns a boolean value. If there is another row of data, the cursor is positioned at that row and the method returns true; if there are no more rows of data, the cursor is positioned after the last row and the next() method returns false. If there are no results at all in the resultset, then next() will return false the first time it is called. If you use any of the other movement methods (which we will see shortly), the resultset will throw a SQLException.

Now, let's take a look at the other two forms of createStatement(). These two forms have method parameters, and the first parameter sets the type. The type refers to whether you can move backwards through the resultset. The second parameter defines whether you can update the table through the resultset. We'll talk about **updateable** resultsets later in the chapter. For the first parameter, you can pass one of these three arguments:

❑ ResultSet.TYPE_SCROLL_SENSITIVE

❑ ResultSet.TYPE_SCROLL_INSENSITIVE

❑ ResultSet.TYPE_FORWARD_ONLY

The first two values create a **scrollable resultset**, a resultset through which you can move forwards or backwards. If changes occur to the database while you are going through a ResultSet, TYPE_SCROLL_SENSITIVE means you will see those changes; TYPE_SCROLL_INSENSITIVE means you will not see the changes. The third value creates a non-scrollable resultset. With a scrollable resultset, you can use these methods for moving the cursor:

boolean next()	boolean previous()	boolean first()
boolean last()	void afterLast()	void beforeFirst()
boolean absolute(int)	boolean relative(int)	
boolean isFirst()	boolean isBeforeFirst()	boolean isLast()
boolean isAfterLast()	int getRow()	
void moveToInsertRow()	void moveToCurrentRow()	

Because these methods are fairly self-explanatory, and since the use of these methods is documented in the JavaDoc (http://java.sun.com/j2se/1.4.1/docs/api/), we will not cover them here, but we'll use them in the next example.

Reading Data from the Resultset

The resultset also contains a number of methods for reading the data in a query result. These methods allow you to reference the column by number or by name, and to retrieve just about any data type. Here are two of the methods:

```
double getDouble(int)
double getDouble(String)
```

These methods allow you to read a double from the ResultSet. The first method gets a double from the column with the index given by the int parameter. The second method gets the double from the column with the name given by the String parameter. There are getXXX() methods for every Java primitive, and for several objects. Here is a short list of some of the methods:

Array getArray(int i)	float getFloat(int columnIndex)
BigDecimal getBigDecimal (int columnIndex)	int getInt(int columnIndex)
boolean getBoolean (int columnIndex)	long getLong(int columnIndex)
byte getByte(int columnIndex)	short getShort(int columnIndex)
Date getDate(int columnIndex)	String getString(int columnIndex)
double getDouble (int columnIndex)	Time getTime(int columnIndex)

You should consult the JavaDoc for the complete list of available methods.

Like the getDouble() methods above, each getXXX() method comes in two overloaded forms. One form takes an int argument. The parameter you pass to the method is the column number of the column you wish to retrieve. One important point to know here is that columns returned from a table are numbered starting from one, *not* zero. If you call one of these methods, and pass a zero as the argument, or pass a column number that is too great, a SQLException is thrown.

> Note that the first column is index 1. With SQL, all column numbering begins at 1 and not 0. Likewise, row numbering starts with 1. So, the first column is 1 and the first row is 1.

The second form takes a String parameter. The argument you pass is the name of the column you wish to retrieve. If you pass an invalid name, a SQLException will be thrown.

Whether you use the int parameter or the String parameter depends on your application. Using the int parameter is more efficient. However, the String parameter is more flexible. This is because column indexes sometimes change but column names rarely do. If you hard-code the column number into your code, you'll have problems as soon as the database analysts change the schema of the database tables so that the column numbers change.

Working with Null Values

NULL is a special value in the world of SQL. NULL is not the same thing as an empty string for text columns, nor is it the same thing as zero for a numeric field. NULL means that no data is defined for a column value within a relation. However, for primitive types and for Booleans, the JDBC driver cannot return a null. When the column data for a row is a SQL NULL, the getXXX() method returns a value that is appropriate for the return type. For all the methods that return an object, getDate() for example, the methods return a Java null for SQL NULL. All of the getXXX() numeric methods, getFloat() for example, return the value 0 for SQL NULL. The getBoolean() method returns false for SQL NULL.

This creates a potential problem. If you call getFloat(), and the return value is 0, how do you know if the column value is really 0 or NULL? The ResultSet instance provides a method that can give you this information. Here is its signature:

```
public Boolean wasNull()
```

It does not take a column number or a column name. It provides its answer based on the most recently read column.

Try It Out   Using ResultSet Objects

1. The ResultSet object is yet another JDBC resource that we need to manage. Here is version 2 of the JDBCManager. This one contains the method for releasing ResultSet objects. Note that to conserve space the methods that have not changed are not shown:

```
package Ch06;

import java.sql.*;
import java.util.*;

public class JDBCManagerV2 {
  private JDBCManagerV2() {}

// The following methods are not shown in this listing:
// getConnection(String url)
// getConnection(String url, String user, String password)
// getConnection(String url, Properties props)
// close(Connection conn)
// close(Statement stmt)

    public static void close(ResultSet rset) {
      if (rset != null) {
        try {
          rset.close();
        } catch (Exception e) {
          e.printStackTrace();
        }
```

```
        }
    }
}
```

2. The client will create a scrollable resultset and move through the `ResultSet` object, reading the data from it. Enter and save the `JDBCClient3.java` source for the class:

```java
package Ch06;

import java.sql.*;

public class JDBCClient3 {
  static Connection conn = null;
  static Statement stmt = null;
  static ResultSet rset = null;

  static String sqlInsert00 = "insert into COUNTRIES " +
    "(COUNTRY, COUNTRY_ISO_CODE, REGION) " +
    "values ('Kyrgyzstan', 'KG', 'Asia')";
  static String sqlInsert01 = "insert into COUNTRIES " +
    "(COUNTRY, COUNTRY_ISO_CODE, REGION) " +
    "values ('Great Britain', 'GB', 'Europe')";
  static String sqlInsert02 = "insert into COUNTRIES " +
    "(COUNTRY, COUNTRY_ISO_CODE, REGION) " +
    "values ('United States', 'US', 'North America')";
  static String sqlInsert03 = "insert into COUNTRIES " +
    "(COUNTRY, COUNTRY_ISO_CODE, REGION) " +
    "values ('Canada', 'CA', 'North America')";
  static String sqlInsert04 = "insert into COUNTRIES " +
    "(COUNTRY, COUNTRY_ISO_CODE, REGION) " +
    "values ('France', 'FR', 'Europe')";
  static String sqlQuery = "select * from COUNTRIES";

  public static void main(String[] args) {
    try {
      String url = "jdbc:cloudscape:rmi://localhost:1099/CloudscapeDB";
      conn = JDBCManagerV2.getConnection(url);
      stmt = conn.createStatement(
        ResultSet.TYPE_SCROLL_INSENSITIVE, ResultSet.CONCUR_READ_ONLY);

      doBatch();
      doQuery();
    } catch (SQLException e) {
      e.printStackTrace();
    } finally {
      JDBCManagerV2.close(rset);
      JDBCManagerV2.close(stmt);
      JDBCManagerV2.close(conn);
    }
  }
```

```
public static void doBatch() throws SQLException {
  stmt.addBatch(sqlInsert00);
  stmt.addBatch(sqlInsert01);
  stmt.addBatch(sqlInsert02);
  stmt.addBatch(sqlInsert03);
  stmt.addBatch(sqlInsert04);
  int[] results = stmt.executeBatch();
}
```

```
public static void doQuery() throws SQLException {
  rset = stmt.executeQuery(sqlQuery);
  System.out.println("rset.next()=" + rset.next());
  System.out.println(
    "Should be on first row: isFirst()=" + rset.isFirst());
  // Now move forward two rows
  rset.next();   // Row 2
  rset.next();   // Row 3
  System.out.println("row num should be 3, getRow()=" + rset.getRow());
  rset.next();   // Row 4
  System.out.print("Row 4 - ");
  System.out.print(rset.getString(1) + " - ");
  System.out.print(rset.getString(2) + " - ");
  System.out.println(rset.getString(3));
  rset.next(); //row 5
  System.out.println("Should be on last row: isLast()=" + rset.isLast());
  rset.previous();
  System.out.println(
    "Should not be on last row: isLast()=" + rset.isLast());
  rset.beforeFirst();
  System.out.println(
    "Should be before first row: isBeforeFirst()=" + rset.isBeforeFirst());
}
}
```

3. If it is not running, run the Cloudscape RMI server as shown in the previous example. As a reminder, to do this, open a command line window and run the `cloudscape` script located in the `/bin` directory of your J2EE installation:

> **`cloudscape -start`**

4. This class relies on the table created by the `JDBCClient2` class. If you did not run that class, you will need to do so before running this class.

5. After compiling the class files, make sure that the classpath contains `cloudclient.jar`, `RmiJdbc.jar`, and the current working directory up to the directory that contains the two files, `Ch06`. Now we can run the class and see the results:

> **`java -Djdbc.drivers=COM.cloudscape.core.RmiJdbcDriver Ch06.JDBCClient3`**
`rset.next()=true`

```
Should be on first row: isFirst()=true
row num should be 3, getRow()=3
Row 4 - Canada - CA - North America
Should be on last row: isLast()=true
Should not be on last row: isLast()=false
Should be before first row: isBeforeFirst()=true
```

```
Select Command Prompt                                                    _ □ ×

C:\8333>java -Djdbc.drivers=COM.cloudscape.core.RmiJdbcDriver Ch06.JDBCClient3
rset.next()=true
Should be on first row: isFirst()=true
row num should be 3, getRow()=3
Row 4 - Canada - CA - North America
Should be on last row: isLast()=true
Should not be on last row: isLast()=false
Should be before first row: isBeforeFirst()=true

C:\8333>_
```

How It Works

Most of the client class is the same as that we have used in the previous two examples. The client gets a connection from the JDBC manager, and creates a `Statement` object from the connection. The `Statement` object is created so that it is scrollable. We used the `createStatement(int,int)` method as shown here:

```
stmt = conn.createStatement(ResultSet.TYPE_SCROLL_INSENSITIVE,
                            ResultSet.CONCUR_READ_ONLY);
```

To ensure we used the correct arguments, we used the static variables defined in the `ResultSet` class to define the scroll type and updatability of the resultset.

You will need to consult your database and driver documentation to see if the driver supports scrollable resultsets. In our case, Cloudscape does support a scrollable resultset, but only if the resultset is not updateable, which is why the second argument to the `createStatement()` method above is `ResultSet.CONCUR_READ_ONLY`. We will see how to use updateable resultsets in the next section.

Then the `main()` method calls a `doBatch()` method to insert five rows of data into the table that was created by the `JDBCClient2` class. If you did not run the `JDBCClient2` class, this table will not be available to you and the code will not work. You can either enter and run `JDBCClient2`, or modify `JDBCClient3` to create the table itself.

The interesting part of the `JDBCClient3` class is in the `doQuery()` method. Here, I used various movement methods to jump around in the resultset. I also printed the column values for the fourth row of data. Here is a table showing what was printed out by the various lines of code:

Code	Output
`System.out.println("rset.next()=" +` `rset.next());`	`rset.next()=true`
`System.out.println("Should be on first row:` `isFirst()=" + rset.isFirst());`	`Should be on first` `row: isFirst()=true`
`// Now move forward two rows`	
`rset.next();   // Row 2`	
`rset.next();   // Row 3`	
`System.out.println("row num should be 3,` `getRow()=" + rset.getRow());`	`row num should be 3,` `getRow()=3`
`rset.next();   // Row 4`	

`System.out.print("Row 4 - ");`
 	
`System.out.print(rset.getString(1) + " - ");`
 	
`System.out.print(rset.getString(2) + " - ");`
 	
`System.out.println(rset.getString(3));`
	`Row 4 - Canada - CA -`
	`North America`

`rset.next(); //row 5`	
`System.out.println("Should be on last row:` `isLast()=" + rset.isLast());`	`Should be on last row:` `isLast()=true`
`rset.previous();`	
`System.out.println("Should not be on last` `row: isLast()=" + rset.isLast());`	`Should not be on last` `row: isLast()=false`
`rset.beforeFirst();`	

`System.out.println("Should be before first`
`row: isBeforeFirst()=" +`
`rset.isBeforeFirst());`
	`Should be before first`
	`row:`
	`isBeforeFirst()=true`

In the `finally` block, we called the new method of `JDBCManagerV2` to release the `ResultSet` object. We then released the `Statement` and `Connection` objects. They are closed in reverse order of their creation. As with the `Statement` objects, you should close the `ResultSet` as soon as your code is finished with it. One important point to remember is that you must not close the `Statement` or `Connection` objects until after you are finished with the `ResultSet` object, since closing the `Statement` or `Connection` objects will automatically close the `ResultSet` object. Just as with `Statements`, though, you shouldn't rely on closing the `Connection` to close the `ResultSet`. You should close resources as soon as you are finished with them.

> Always close the ResultSet before you close its corresponding Statement or
> Connection. Likewise, close the Statement before closing the Connection
> that created it.

Updateable ResultSets

The second parameter in the createStatement(int, int) and
createStatement(int, int, int) methods determines whether you can update the
database through the resultset. Prior to JDBC 2.0, resultsets could only be used to select data,
move forward through the data, and read the data in each column. To update the data, you
needed to execute another SQL command through a statement object.

JDBC 2.0 introduced the ability to update the data in the table directly through the resultset, so
as you move through the data, you can call methods that insert, update, or delete the data. Here
are some of the methods you would use:

Methods for inserting, updating, or deleting data	
void updateRow()	void cancelRowUpdates()
void moveToInsertRow()	void moveToCurrentRow()
void insertRow()	void deleteRow()
void updateBoolean(int, boolean)	void updateBoolean(String, boolean)
void updateByte(int, byte)	void updateByte(String, byte)
void updateDate(int, Date)	void updateDate(String, Date)
void updateDouble(int, double)	void updateDouble(String, double)
void updateFloat(int, float)	void updateFloat(String, float)
void updateInt(int, int)	void updateInt(String, int)
void updateLong(int, long)	void updateLong(String, long)
void updateNull(int)	void updateNull(String)
void updateString(int, String)	void updateString(String, String)

The table does not list all the updateXXX() methods available, but only the ones you are most
likely to use. You should consult the JavaDoc for the other update methods.

When you move through a resultset using the methods presented previously, you can update whichever row you are currently positioned at. You update the data in the current row with the updateXXX() methods. There is an updateXXX() method for every data type supported by JDBC. Each method comes in two overloaded versions. The first parameter of one version takes a String argument that gives the name of the column to be updated; the other version uses the column number of the column to be updated. The column number refers to the index of the column in the resultset, *not* the table. The column that is named first in the SELECT command is column 1, and so on.

> **Check your driver documentation for the requirements for updating a resultset. Some databases do not allow you to use SELECT * FROM for an updateable resultset. You may need to explicitly name each column in the SELECT command.**

The second parameter in each method is the new value for the column. After you have updated all the columns that you want to update, you call the updateRow() method to write the updated row to the table. The code snippet below shows how this could be accomplished:

```
// Assume the COUNTRIES table has bad data in it for Canada
// Assume COUNTRY is Canada and COUNTRY_ISO_CODE is CS
// Update row with good data
static String sqlQuery = "select COUNTRY, COUNTRY_ISO_CODE, REGION " +
                         "from COUNTRIES where " + "COUNTRY_ISO_CODE='CS'";
rset = stmt.executeQuery(sqlQuery);
rset.next();

rset.updateString(1, 'Canada');
rset.updateString(2, 'CA');
rset.updateRow();
```

Cloudscape, however, does not support updateable resultsets. The code snippet above, and the ones that follow, will not actually work with Cloudscape. In the example above, the first updateString() call will result in a SQLException with the message "Feature not implemented". As always, check your database and driver documentation to see if updateable resultsets are supported.

If, before you call updateRow(), you may decide that you don't want to update the row, you can call cancelRowUpdates().

You can also insert a new row of data through the resultset. This is accomplished by moving to a special row in the resultset; this row is known as the **insert row**. You move to the insert row by calling the following method:

```
rset.moveToInsertRow();
```

When you move to the insert row, the resultset remembers the position you were at; this remembered position is know as the **current row**. Then, you update each column with the appropriate value using the updateXXX() methods. When you are finished entering data for the new row, you call this method:

```
rset.insertRow();
```

After you have called insertRow(), the resultset is still positioned at the insert row. You can insert another row of data, or move back to the remembered position (the current row) in the resultset. You move back to the current row by calling moveToCurrentRow(). You also cancel an insert by calling moveToCurrentRow() before you call insertRow().

Finally, you can delete a row from the table and the result set by calling

```
rset.deleteRow();
```

Holdable ResultSets

When you execute another SQL command with a statement, any open resultsets are closed. Also, when commit() is called with a JDBC 2.0 or 1.0 driver, the resultset is closed. JDBC 3.0 adds a new ResultSet object feature called **holdability**, which refers to whether or not a resultset is closed when a new SQL command is executed by a statement or when commit() is called. JDBC 3.0 gives you the capability to keep the resultset open.

Two class constants were added to the ResultSet interface to provide parameters for the createStatement() method:

- ❑ ResultSet.HOLD_CURSORS_OVER_COMMIT – This specifies that the ResultSet object should *not* be closed when changes are committed.

- ❑ ResultSet.CLOSE_CURSORS_AT_COMMIT – The driver can close ResultSet object when changes are committed.

A new createStatement() method was added to the Connection class to support this feature:

```
createStatement(int resultSetType, int resultSetConcurrency, int
resultSetHoldability)
```

As of the time this chapter was written, Sun listed about a dozen drivers that support JDBC 3.0 Check your database documentation to see if it supports holdability functionality.

Summary

In this chapter we've looked at some of the ways you can communicate with databases. After finishing this chapter you should know:

❑ How to load a driver and how to get connections from the DriverManager. Loading driver classes can be done by calling `Class.forName(String)` with the fully qualified class name of the driver, or by setting the `jdbc.drivers` System property.

❑ `Statement` objects are used to send SQL commands to the database. `Statement` objects are created by `Connection` objects. SQL commands are sent using either `executeUpdate(String)` or `executeQuery(String)`.

❑ ResultSets are used to read the data returned by an SQL query. ResultSets can be scrollable or updateable. You move through a ResultSet using methods such as `next()`, `previous()`, `first()`, or `last()`. You read results using methods such as `getString(int)` or `getDouble(String)`.

This chapter has been mainly an introduction to the basics of JDBC. If you are brand new to JDBC programming, this chapter provided you enough information to start doing some JDBC programming. However, this book is about J2EE applications. As a J2EE developer, you are going to quickly encounter some more advanced situations. In the next chapter we will look at some of the more advanced topics that you will need to know as a J2EE developer.

Exercises

1. In the beginning of the chapter, the driver manager's `setLogWriter()` method was presented. Modify one of the examples from this chapter to use a log writer that writes to a file, and then run the class. After the class finishes executing, examine the log to see what was logged.

2. In the *Statements* section, the example inserted, updated, and deleted a row in the CloudscapeDB COUNTRIES table. Modify the code so that you can verify that each operation actually did occur.

3. If your driver supports updatable resultsets, write a class that uses a resultset to update a table.

CHAPTER 7

Prepared Statements	**298**
Callable Statements	**306**
Using Placeholders	**308**
Data Sources and Connection Pools	**310**
Transactions	**320**
Locking and Isolation	**334**
Summary	**349**
Exercises	**350**

Advanced Topics in JDBC

In the previous chapter, we looked at some basic features of JDBC: how to get a connection, how to query and update a database using `Statement` objects, and how to read the results of a query using a `ResultSet` object. Once you've gained an understanding of these fundamentals, you'll be able to write simple JDBC programs with no problem.

However, in the fast-paced world of web applications, you will soon find that you need more skills than those presented in the previous chapter. In this chapter, we will cover some advanced JDBC topics that you will find invaluable as a J2EE developer, and we will see how to use JDBC in a J2EE environment. As in the previous chapter, we will look at some problems you might encounter in a J2EE application and how to avoid them with well-designed JDBC code.

In this chapter you will learn:

- ❏ How to use `PreparedStatement` objects to make your JDBC more efficient and to insert non-primitive data types into a database.

- ❏ What sprocs are, why they are useful, and how you can call them with JDBC code.

- ❏ How to get a database connection in a J2EE environment; as this implies, it doesn't involve loading a driver or using a `DriverManager` to get a connection.

- ❏ How to ensure that your JDBC code takes the database from one valid and consistent state to another so that the database does not contain corrupted code.

- ❏ How to deal with the problem of multiple users trying to change data in the database at the same time.

Prepared Statements

One of the projects I recently worked on involved three different teams scattered across the country. Each team was responsible for a system, and the three systems were supposed to work together to solve the user's problem. In addition to developing one of the systems, the team I was on was responsible for integrating the whole mess together. As you'll see, the project provides an excellent example of the platform independence notion of Java and JDBC, but it also points out that there are differences between databases.

One of the teams was using MySql as its database for development, but the final system was using Sybase as the production database. As soon as I tried integrating their code, the method call I made threw an exception. What made it even more frustrating is that the error message did not seem to have any relation to what the problem was. Cloudscape reacts similarly to the problem I encountered. Let's run Cloudcsape's **isql tool** and look at it. Navigate to the /bin directory of your J2EE installation and run the following command at the prompt:

```
> cloudscape -isql
```

After the tool starts up, enter the following SQL command at the prompt and your command window will look something like the following:

```
ij> update countries set country="Canada";
ERROR 42X04: Column 'Canada' is not in any table in the FROM list or it
appears within a join specification and is outside the scope of the join
specification or it appears in a HAVING clause and is not in the GROUP BY
list. If this is a CREATE or ALTER TABLE statement then 'Canada' is not a
column in the target table
```

Okay, the error message is telling me that Canada is not a column in the table. I know that already, I created the table so I know what the column names are. The SQL appears to be correct. It certainly follows the syntax for an UPDATE command. It has:

- update – The command itself
- countries – The table name
- set – Part of the syntax for an update command
- country – Correct column name
- "Canada" – The new String value for the column

Look back at the JDBCClient3 class and see how we inserted the string data into the table. The SQL command used single quotes, ', to delimit string data. Most databases only accept single quotes to delimit strings – MySql accepts double quotes.

> The problem is that JDBC is platform-independent, but the SQL you use *may not* be platform-independent.

Another place this occurs is when dealing with data that includes single quotes as part of the data. This question gets asked a lot on JDBC discussion forums. Every once in a while, someone new to SQL and databases asks, "How do I insert a name such as 'O'Grady' into my database, since the apostrophe in the name acts as a delimiter?" The common answer to that question is change the single quote in the name to two single quotes. Thus O'Grady becomes O''Grady (notice that it's not a double quote, it's two single quotes in a row). With MySql, you can escape the single quotes so O'Grady becomes O\'Grady. (Unfortunately, escaping the apostrophe does not work with Sybase, so this was another problem we dealt with on my project.) The other part of the common answer is to write a little method that searches for single quotes in the strings and changes them to whatever works for the database in question.

There is a better answer though. Rather than worrying about how to delimit strings, or how to change single quotes into double quotes, JDBC provides a class that can do all this work for you. That class is the `PreparedStatement` class.

There is one other often-mentioned reason for using a `PreparedStatement` object. Most databases keep previously executed SQL in a cache. If you send a SQL command that matches one in the cache, the database reuses the SQL from the cache because it has already been compiled and optimized. This improves performance. To reuse a command, the SQL command you send must match one in the cache exactly. Suppose you send these two commands to a database:

```
insert into COUNTRIES values ('Kyrgyzstan', 'KG', 'Europe')
insert into COUNTRIES values ('Great Britain', 'GB', 'Europe')
```

You can easily see that these two SQL commands are essentially the same except for the literal values. For the database, however, these two SQL commands are entirely different. It cannot reuse the first SQL command when you send the second SQL command.

Suppose, however, you could pass the database an SQL command that had variables in it. Then the database could reuse the same SQL command any time you passed it new values for the variables. This is what the prepared statement does.

Creating a Prepared Statement

Creating a `PreparedStatement` object is similar to creating a `Statement` object. One difference is that with a prepared statement, you need to tell the database what SQL you intend to execute. You pass the SQL in the creation method, rather than in the execute method. The methods to create a `PreparedStatement` object are as follows:

Method	Description
`prepareStatement(String sql)`	Creates a prepared statement for the given SQL. If the prepared statement returns a resultset, the resultset has a type forward-only, is not updateable, and is not holdable.

`prepareStatement(`
   `String sql, int resultSetType,`
   `int resultSetConcurrency)`
	Create a prepared statement for the given SQL. If the prepared statement returns a resultset, the resultset has the given resultset type and concurrency, and is not holdable.

`prepareStatement(`
   `String sql, int resultSetType,`
   `int resultSetConcurrency,`
   `int resultSetHoldability)`
	JDBC 3.0: Create a prepared statement for the given SQL. If the prepared statement returns a resultset, the resultset has the given resultset type, concurrency, and holdability.

In the table above, `resultSetType` refers to whether a resultset is scrollable. `resultSetConcurrency` is the ability to update a resultset. `resultSetHoldability` refers to whether a resultset is closed when changes are committed. Refer to the Statement and ResultSet sections in the previous chapter for more information on these concepts.

The first argument in each method is a SQL string. The SQL string can have **placeholders** (variables) that represent data that will be set at a later time. The placeholder is represented by the question mark symbol (?). Let's take the SQL command presented above and change it so that it could be used as part of a prepared statement:

```
insert into COUNTRIES values (?, ?, ?)
```

Placeholders are referred to by their index in the SQL command. Placeholders are consecutively indexed starting with index 1 at the beginning of the SQL string. When the SQL in the prepared statement is sent to the database, the database compiles the SQL. Before you execute a prepared statement, you must set the placeholders with data. The driver sends the data to the database when the prepared statement is executed. Then, the database sets the variables with the data, and executes the SQL.

Using a Prepared Statement

After creating the `PreparedStatement` object, but before the SQL command can be executed, the placeholders in the command must be set. The `PreparedStatement` interface defines various methods for doing this. You can also use the `PreparedStatement` object for setting null values in a table. The other advantage of using a prepared statement is that the values you set do not need to be reset every time you want to execute the SQL command; that is, the values you set are persistent. Finally, you can perform batch updating with a prepared statement.

Setting Placeholders

The methods for setting placeholders take the form of `setXXX()` where XXX is a Java type name. Here is the method for setting a `String`:

```
void setString(int parameterIndex, String x)
```

There are other `setXXX()` methods available, one for each Java primitive, and methods for many object types such as `Date`, or `BigDecimal`. You should consult the JavaDoc for information on all the available methods.

The first argument in the `setXXX()` method will be the index of the placeholder in the SQL command. Each placeholder is referenced by its position in the SQL string. Starting from the beginning of the string, the first placeholder is at index 1, the second at 2, and so on.

The second argument is the data value that replaces the placeholder. So, using the same SQL `INSERT` from above, here's how the data values would be set:

```
String sdl = "insert into COUNTRIES values (?, ?, ?)"
// Placeholder index:                        1  2  3
PreparedStatement ps = conn.prepareStatement(sql);
ps.setString(1, "Canada");
ps.setString(2, "CA");
ps.setString(3, "North America");
ps.executeUpdate();
```

> If you do not set all the parameters before executing the SQL, the driver will throw a **SQLException**.

When the values have all been set, you execute the SQL command by calling the `executeUpdate()` method as shown above.

> If you call any of the **executeQuery(String)**, **executeUpdate(String)**, or **execute(String)** methods, the driver will throw a **SQLException**. You must call the 'no parameter' versions of those methods with a prepared statement.

301

Setting Null Values

You might think that you can insert a NULL into a database table by not setting the placeholder that corresponds to the column that will have the null value. As the note above states, however, this will cause the driver to throw a SQLException. Null values are inserted into the database by using one of two methods named setNull():

```
void setNull(int parameterIndex, int sqlType)
void setNull(int parameterIndex, int sqlType, String typeName)
```

As with the other setXXX() methods, the first parameter is the index of the placeholder. The second parameter is defined in the Java class java.sql.Types. The java.sql.Types class contains int constants that correspond to every JDBC type. Thus if you want to set a String column to null, you would pass java.sql.Types.STRING; using java.sql.Types.DATE would set a Date to null. You would pass the appropriate constant for the column you are setting to null.

The typeName parameter in the second method above must be the *fully qualified* type name of the type being set to null. This method can be used for any type, but is provided primarily for user-named types and REF type parameters. When a database supports user-defined types, you can create your own type, like creating a class, and create a column of that type. In your Java code, you create a class that corresponds to that type. In the method, you would pass java.sql.Types.OBJECT as the sqlType parameter, and the fully qualified class name of the class as the typeName parameter.

Showing how to create and map Java classes to database types is beyond the scope of this chapter. You can find more information on mapping in section 3.6 of the advanced JDBC Tutorial at http://developer.java.sun.com/developer/Books/JDBCTutorial/index.html.

Reusing a Prepared Statement

Once a placeholder has been set with data, that data remains set for that placeholder until the code explicitly changes the value for the placeholder. In other words, you are not required to set every placeholder every time you want to execute some SQL using the same prepared statement. If you set the placeholder at some point in the code, and that value is reused in multiple rows, you only need to set the placeholder the first time. All the placeholders can be cleared by calling the PreparedStatement class' clearParameters() method. The value of a placeholder is changed by calling one of the setXXX() methods again with the appropriate index like this:

```
ps.setString(1, "United States");
ps.setString(2, "US");
ps.executeUpdate();
```

The third placeholder was previously set with the value North America, and since it was not changed, that value is reused when the command is executed.

Batch Updates

Just as with a statement, you can use a prepared statement to perform batch updating. The difference is that with the prepared statement, you set each placeholder with the setXXX() methods as shown above. After you have set the placeholders, you call addBatch(). This adds the data values to the batch. After you have added all the rows you want, you call executeBatch(). This sends all the data values to the database for execution with the already stored SQL command.

Try It Out   **Using Prepared Statements**

In this example, we will modify the JDBCClient3 class that we used in the previous chapter to use a PreparedStatement object instead of a Statement object.

In order to compile this class, you need to have the JDBCManagerV2 class from the previous chapter. Simply copy and paste this class into the Ch07 folder, then make sure you change the package to Ch07 before you attempt to recompile.

1. The JDBCClient3 class was presented in the previous chapter. Make the modifications to the code as shown below:

```java
package Ch07;

import java.sql.*;

public class JDBCClient4 {
    static Connection conn = null;
    static PreparedStatement stmt = null;
    static ResultSet rset = null;

    static String sqlInsert = "insert into COUNTRIES " +
        "(COUNTRY, COUNTRY_ISO_CODE, REGION) " +
        "values (?, ?, ?)";

    static String sqlQuery = "select * from COUNTRIES";

    public static void main(String[] args) {
        try {
            String url = "jdbc:cloudscape:rmi://localhost:1099/CloudscapeDB";
            conn = JDBCManagerV2.getConnection(url);
            doBatch();
            doQuery();
        } catch (SQLException e) {
            e.printStackTrace();
        } finally {
            JDBCManagerV2.close(rset);
            JDBCManagerV2.close(stmt);
            JDBCManagerV2.close(conn);
```

```
      }
    }

  public static void doBatch() throws SQLException {
    stmt = conn.prepareStatement(sqlInsert);

    stmt.setString(1, "Kyrgyzstan");
    stmt.setString(2, "KG");
    stmt.setString(3, "Asia");
    stmt.addBatch();

    stmt.setString(1,"Great Britain");
    stmt.setString(2,"GB");
    stmt.setString(3,"Europe");
    stmt.addBatch();

    stmt.setString(1,"France");
    stmt.setString(2,"FR");
    stmt.addBatch();

    stmt.setString(1,"United States");
    stmt.setString(2,"US");
    stmt.setString(3, "North America");
    stmt.addBatch();

    stmt.setString(1,"Canada");
    stmt.setString(2,"CA");
    stmt.addBatch();

    int[] results = stmt.executeBatch();
    System.out.println("Results of inserts (value should be 1 for each):");
    for (int i = 0; i < results.length; i++) {
      System.out.println("results[" + i + "]=" + results[i]);
    }
  }

  public static void doQuery() throws SQLException {
    rset = stmt.executeQuery(sqlQuery);
    rset = stmt.executeQuery(sqlQuery);
    System.out.println("Checking the table:");
    int rownum = 1;
    while (rset.next()) {
      System.out.print("row " + rownum++ + " is ");
      System.out.print(rset.getString(1) + ", ");
      System.out.print(rset.getString(2) + ", ");
      System.out.println(rset.getString(3));
    }
  }
}
}
```

2. Compile the class using the usual command:

> `javac *.java`

and if the Cloudscape RMI Server is not running, start it from the /bin directory of your J2EE installation:

```
> cloudscape -start
```

3. If the COUNTRIES table has data in it from JDBCClient2, delete those rows through the Cloudscape isql tool. If the table does not exist at all, you will need to create it. Check the JDBCClient2 class for the SQL to create the table but here is the command to delete the rows in question:

```
> cloudscape -isql
ij> delete from countries;
5 rows inserted/updated/deleted
ij> exit;
```

4. As usual, make sure that the right classpath has been set. You need to include RmiJdbc.jar, cloudclient.jar, and the current working directory. Then, you can run the program and you should see something like the following:

```
> java -Djdbc.drivers=COM.cloudscape.core.RmiJdbcDriver Ch07.JDBCClient4
Results of inserts (value should be 1 for each):
results[0]=1
results[1]=1
results[2]=1
results[3]=1
results[4]=1
Checking the table:
row 1 is Kyrgyzstan, KG, Asia
row 2 is Great Britain, GB, Europe
row 3 is France, FR, Europe
row 4 is United States, US, North America
row 5 is Canada, CA, North America
```

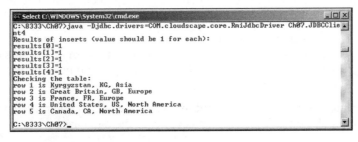

How It Works

Instead of five separate SQL commands to insert the rows of the COUNTRIES table, this class uses a single SQL INSERT command with placeholders for data. In the doBatch() method, five rows of data are inserted by using the PreparedStatement and batch updating. Each placeholder in the SQL command is set with the value for the row. After each value has been set, the addBatch() method is called. After all five rows of data have been added to the batch, the SQL is executed with a call to executeBatch(). Notice that we only needed to set the value for the region column three times.

Callable Statements

In many enterprise applications, the business logic for the application will be encapsulated in **sprocs** (which is short for **s**tored **proc**edures) inside the database. Stored procedures are just like methods in your Java code. They have names, they can have parameter lists, they have a body (containing SQL and procedural commands) that performs some work, and they can return values.

> *Unfortunately, Cloudscape does not support sprocs. Thus, this section of the chapter will not have an example showing how to use a* CallableStatement *object.*

In this section, the term *stored procedure* is used generically to refer to both procedures and functions. The main difference between the two is that a function returns a value and a procedure does not return a value. If your database supports storing procedural and SQL statements in the database for execution, but uses a different term, you should consider 'stored procedure' to be a synonym for the term used by your database.

There are many reasons why we would use stored procedures. Some of the services provided by stored procedures are encapsulation and reuse of functionality, control of transactions, and standardization of business rules:

❑ A sproc can encapsulate a common set of SQL commands. A client can access this functionality without needing to make many different JDBC calls.

❑ You can reuse sprocs that are already developed, rather than recreating their functionality from scratch in JDBC.

❑ The sproc makes transaction control easier. We look at transactions and transaction control in greater detail later in this chapter.

❑ Providing a given functionality in a sproc ensures that every part of the application that uses the functionality does so in the same way. If requirements change, only the procedure may need to be changed, and everyone who uses the procedure automatically gets the change.

❑ By having a procedure in a database, the code exists in one place only, yet is accessible to any client, Java or not, that can connect to the database.

Even though they provide useful features, not all databases implement stored procedures – MySQL is one of those. Other databases may provide similar functionality in a different manner. Cloudscape, for example, doesn't support storing SQL statements, but does support storing and executing Java classes.

JDBC code can call stored procedures using a CallableStatement object. A CallableStatement object is created in much the same way as the PreparedStatement object, by calling a method of the Connection object. The table below lists all the Connection interface methods for creating a CallableStatement object:

Method	Description
`prepareCall(String sql)`	Creates a `CallableStatement` object for the given SQL. If the `CallableStatement` returns a `ResultSet` object, the `ResultSet` has a type of forward-only, is not **updateable**, and is not **holdable**.

`prepareCall(`
   `String sql,`
   `int resultSetType,`
   `int resultSetConcurrency)`
	Create a `CallableStatement` object for the given SQL. If the `CallableStatement` returns a `ResultSet`, the `ResultSet` has the given `ResultSet` type and concurrency, and is not holdable.

`prepareCall(`
   `String sql, int resultSetType,`
   `int resultSetConcurrency,`
   `int resultSetHoldability)`
	JDBC 3.0: Create a `CallableStatement` object for the given SQL. If the `CallableStatement` returns a `ResultSet`, the `ResultSet` has the given `ResultSet` type, concurrency, and holdability.

See the "Statement" section in the previous chapter for information on scrolling, updating, and holding resultsets.

The first argument in each `prepareCall()` method is a SQL string. The SQL string for calling a stored procedure can take one of several forms. Common between all the forms is the SQL keyword `call` that appears before the procedure name, and the curly braces that surround the SQL. This signals the driver that the SQL is not an ordinary SQL statement and that the SQL must be converted into the correct form for calling a procedure in the target database. The most basic form is the SQL for calling a stored procedure that takes no parameters. The SQL string looks like this:

```
{ call procedure_name }
```

For example, suppose the database had a stored procedure named `adjust_prices`, which took no parameters and returned no value. The code to create a `CallableStatement` object for this stored procedure would look like:

```
String sql = "{ call adjust_prices }";
CallableStatement cs = connection.prepareCall(sql);
```

When a procedure or function takes parameters, the SQL will look something like this:

```
String sql = "{ call set_price(?, ?) }";
CallableStatement cs = connection.prepareCall(sql);
```

The `set_price` procedure takes two parameters and returns no value. Placeholders mark each parameter in the procedure call. We have already looked at placeholders in detail in the *Prepared Statements* section of this chapter.

Finally, the SQL for calling a stored function would look like this:

```
String sql = "{ ? = call get_price(?) }";
CallableStatement cs = connection.prepareCall(sql);
```

The return value of the function is marked by a placeholder, as is the parameter sent to the function.

Using Placeholders

Like the `PreparedStatement` object, the placeholders are numbered consecutively, starting with number 1 for the placeholder that appears in the left-most position in the string. Moving from left to right, each placeholder is given the next number in sequence.

If a placeholder is used to pass an argument to a stored procedure, this parameter is known as an `IN` parameter. Its value must be set before the statement can be executed. If you fail to set one of the placeholders, the driver will throw a `SQLException` when you attempt to execute the SQL. The `CallableStatement` interface inherits the `setXXX()` methods of the `PreparedStatement` interface for doing this.

A stored procedure can also set an input parameter to a new value, and that value is passed back to the caller through the parameter list. For example, this SQL command:

```
call set_price(?, ?)
```

has two parameters in the parameter list. If this were a Java method call, the method could set the value of either parameter inside the method, and that value is not visible to the caller. With a SQL stored procedure, the parameters can be set, and the new values can be visible to the caller. If the placeholder is used to pass data to the sproc, and the sproc passes data back through the parameter, this is an `INOUT` parameter. A placeholder that is only used to pass data back, or that is a return value, is an `OUT` parameter.

If any of the parameters in the SQL command are `INOUT` or `OUT` parameters, the JDBC type of the placeholder must be registered before the call can be executed. If you do not register a placeholder that returns a value, you will get a `SQLException`. This is done with the following methods:

```
void registerOutParameter(int parameterIndex, int jdbcType)

void registerOutParameter(int parameterIndex, int jdbcType, int scale)
```

Unlike the `setXXX()` methods, the `registerOutParameter()` method only has two forms. The first parameter in the method is the position of the placeholder in the SQL string. The second parameter is one of the constants defined in the `java.sql.Types` class. The `Types` class defines a constant for each generic JDBC type.

So, for example, if you were calling a stored procedure that passed a value through the second parameter in a parameter list, and the SQL type returned was a varchar (essentially a string), you would register the parameter like this:

```
cs.registerOutParameter(2, java.sql.Types.STRING);
```

If the return value of a function was a double, you could use this:

```
cs.registerOutParameter(1, java.sql.Types.DOUBLE);
```

For the complete list of the available `java.sql.Types` constants, consult the API Java documentation.

When registering a parameter that is one of the numeric types such as `float`, `double`, `numeric`, or `decimal`, you could also use the second form of the `registerOutParameter()` method. This method takes a third parameter that defines the scale of the returned value. For example, to register a return type that returned a number with two digits to the right of the decimal point, you could use:

```
cs.registerOutParameter(1, java.sql.Types.DOUBLE, 2);
```

Note that if any of the placeholders is an `INOUT` parameter, the JDBC code must call both a `setXXX()` method and a `registerOutParameter()` method prior to executing the callable statement. If you fail to set the value or register the parameter, the driver will throw a `SQLException`.

As with the `PreparedStatement` object, once a placeholder has been set with data, that placeholder remains set until the code explicitly changes the placeholder. All the placeholders can be cleared by calling the method `clearParameters()`. The value of a placeholder is changed by calling one of the `setXXX()` or `registerOutParameter()` methods, again with the appropriate index.

After the data values are set, the code calls one of the execute methods, `executeUpdate()`, `executeQuery()`, or `execute()`, to tell the database to execute the stored procedure.

> If you call any of the **executeQuery(String)**, **executeUpdate(String)**, or **execute(String)** methods, the driver will throw a **SQLException**. You must call the no parameter versions of those methods with a **CallableStatement**.

After executing the sproc, the return values of any placeholders are retrieved with getXXX() methods, similar to those used to retrieve the column values from a row in a resultset. The getXXX() methods only have one form, one that takes an int parameter. The parameter int is the index of the placeholder in the callable statement.

Data Sources and Connection Pools

Data sources were introduced as part of JDBC 2.0 and are currently the preferred method for obtaining database connections. The DataSource interface provides a more flexible architecture than using DriverManager for creating and using database connections. As you will see, by using a DataSource object to obtain a connection, you can access different databases without a single change in your client code. The data source hides the connection details so that you, as the client programmer, never need to worry about the connection URL, host, port, and so on.

Connection pools provide a *pool* of precreated database connections. This avoids the time-consuming activity of creating a new connection to a database. On the client side, there is little to no difference in how the connection is used. The difference lies in how connections are created, handed out, and returned to the pool.

Data Source Overview

A data source is usually obtained by performing a lookup in a **context**. A very simple definition of a context is that it is just a means to associate a *name* with a *resource*. One implementation of a context is a **directory**. There are numerous implementations of directory services and protocols. There is Active Directory, X.500, Lightweight Directory Access Protocol (LDAP), and your computer's directory (which associates a name with a file resource).

On the server side of the connection, some code will create a DataSource instance, and then **bind** that instance in the directory. Binding is the action that tells a directory that a particular name is associated with a particular resource. For example, when you created one of the examples in this chapter you caused a collection of bytes to be written to some media such as the hard drive; at the same time, you told the operating system to associate (or bind) that collection of bytes with some name. Thus, anyone that has access to the hard drive can get the collection of bytes by giving the correct name to the operating system. Likewise, a client can get a reference to a data source by giving the correct name to the directory server.

Just as JDBC provides a vendor-neutral interface to numerous databases, Java has provided a vendor-neutral interface to directory services: the **Java Naming and Directory Interface (JNDI)**. This API provides a common set of functions for accessing directories. Your code uses the JNDI API to communicate with a directory; the details of talking to a particular directory are provided by directory specific libraries, in a similar fashion to JDBC drivers.

Using a DataSource Object

A DataSource object is similar to the DriverManager interface in that it provides methods for obtaining a connection to a database. In fact, the basic method for obtaining a connection has the same name: getConnection(). Before any client code can get a connection from a data source, however, a server must create a DataSource object and bind it to a directory. The exact steps will be different for every directory and database. In general, the data source will be created with parameters (the server, port, database name, and so on) for connecting to the database, and then the data source will be bound to a directory. In the next *Try It Out* section, we will see one way to create and bind a data source resource.

Using a data source to get a connection, the JDBC client code doesn't need to know anything about the database. The client does not need to know the server, the port, the database name, or any other connection parameters. It simply performs a directory lookup and obtains a connection from the data source it gets from the directory. Getting a DataSource object involves two steps. Within a J2EE server, you create an InitialContext object, and then call its lookup() method. This is shown in the code snippet below:

```
InitialContext context = new InitialContext();
DataSource dataSource =
    (DataSource) context.lookup("java:comp/env/jdbc/CloudscapeDB");
```

The string passed to the lookup() method is the name which maps to a particular DataSource. Using a data source, a database administrator could change anything about the database such as the connection URL, username, password, and so on. By simply changing and rebinding the data source, the change would be completely transparent to the JDBC client code. As soon as the client code performs a lookup, it will automatically get the connection. The client will not know that anything about the connection has changed, because it only knows the lookup name, which does not change.

Once the client has the connection object, it is used in the same manner as connections that are obtained directly through a driver manager. The data source can even return a connection from a connection pool, and from the client's perspective, the code does not need to change at all.

Connection Pool Overview

In a distributed J2EE application, where different servers run on different machines, creating a network connection to a database is potentially a time-consuming operation. To alleviate this, many J2EE applications use **connection pools**. A connection pool is a collection of already-created connections to a database. When a client needs a connection, it gets one from the pool, performs the work it needs to do, then returns the connection to the pool.

In a J2EE environment, pooled connections are usually obtained using a data source, and the data source is provided through an application server. For example, both the J2EE server and Tomcat provide connection pooling for JSPs and Servlets. Every pool implementation will be different in how the pool is created and how you get access to the pool. What is important for you, as a developer, is not how to set up the pool, but how to use the connection you get.

Interestingly, the way you use a pooled connection is exactly the same way you would use a normal connection. After obtaining a pooled connection, you can set its autocommit mode the same as with a normal connection. You can call getStatement(), prepareStatement(), and prepareCall(). You can even call its close() method. The difference is that when you call close() on a connection from a connection pool, the connection is returned to the pool without being closed.

There are several connection pool libraries that you can use with your JDBC code (For example, http://www.bitmechanic.com/projects/jdbcpool/). However, in a J2EE environment, you will use a DataSource to get a connection from a connection pool. Both the J2EE server and Tomcat server have DataSources through which you can get a pooled connection object. In this next example, we will use a DataSource to get a connection from a connection pool. In the case of J2EE, the data source is already configured. For Tomcat, we will have to configure a DataSource.

Try It Out   Using Data Sources with J2EE

1. Since this example will run inside the J2EE server, the client will be a JSP. Here's the JSP that will query the Countries table that we created in previous examples. The JSP will perform a lookup of a resource using a resource name. The name that the JSP uses is jdbc/Countries. Save this file as PoolExample.jsp. Since we will use the J2EE deploytool, you can save it anywhere in the file system (we've included it in the Ch07 folder in the code download):

```
<html>
  <head>
    <title>Chapter 7 JSP Pool Example</title>
    <%@ page import="java.sql.*, javax.sql.*, java.io.*, javax.naming.*" %>
  </head>

  <body>
    <h1>Chapter 7 JSP Pool Example</h1>

    <%
      InitialContext context = new InitialContext();
      DataSource dataSource =
        (DataSource) context.lookup("java:comp/env/jdbc/Countries");
      Connection conn = dataSource.getConnection();
      Statement stmt = conn.createStatement();
      ResultSet rset = stmt.executeQuery("select * from COUNTRIES");
      if (rset.next()) {
```

```
    %>
      <table width="100%" border="1">
      <tr align="left">
        <th>Country</th><th>iso code</th><th>region</th>
      </tr>
    <%
      do {
    %>
      <tr><td><%= rset.getString(1) %></td>
      <td><%= rset.getString(2) %></td>
      <td><%= rset.getString(3) %></td></tr>
    <%
      } while (rset.next());
    %>
      </table>
    <%
      } else {
    %>
    No results from query
    <%
      }
      rset.close();
      stmt.close();
      conn.close();
      context.close();
    %>

  </body>
</html>
```

2. Since numerous JSPs have been deployed in previous chapters, detailed steps for using the deploytool are not shown here. However, there are two specific steps you need to take to ensure the `DataSource` is available to the JSP. These will be shown in the following steps. Refer back to Chapter 2 if you need to learn how to deploy a JSP. Start by creating the Application EAR (which we called `PoolExample`), and use the New Web Application WAR wizard to add `PoolExample.jsp` to it.

3. You must set up a Resource Reference for the web component. This is done in the **Resource Refs** tab of the web application. After selecting the tab as shown below, click the **Add** button to add a Resource Reference. The name of the resource must match the name used in the JSP, and that is "`jdbc/Countries`." Make sure that the case of the entered text is as shown here. Click in the type field and select javax.sql.DataSource. You can use the default entries for Authentication and Sharable.

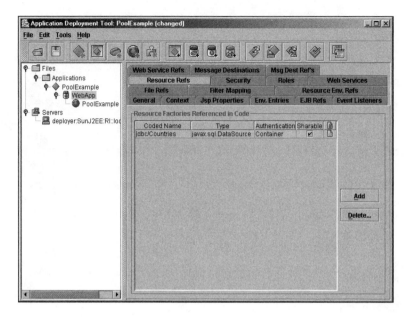

4. Next, you will need to change the application deployment descriptor to map the Resource Ref Coded Name to the JNDI Name. The application deployment descriptor is created by selecting File | Deployment Settings | Create New File from the menu and clicking OK.

5. Before closing and saving the Deployment Descriptor, select the application deployment descriptor under the WebApp in the left pane. Then select the Resource Reference in the Resource Refs tab in the right pane. This causes fields to appear in the lower end of the tab. Enter jdbc/Cloudscape as the JNDI Name, again, watching out for case sensitivity! Save the application deployment descriptor by selecting File | Deployment Settings | Close from the menu.

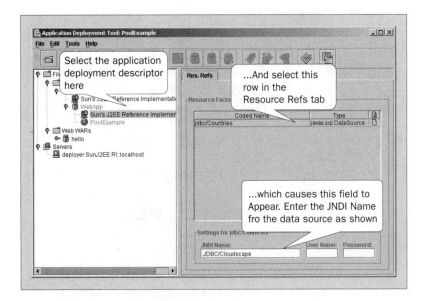

6. Set the **Web Context** for the application to have a contect root of pe, as shown below:

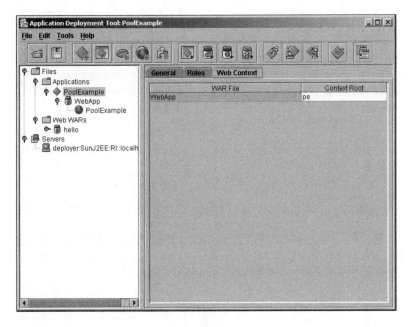

7. Save and deploy the application to the J2EE server. Access the application by using the correct URL for your deployment. Since we set the application context to be pe, the URL you should use is http://localhost:8000/pe/PoolExample.jsp. You should see the following output in your browser:

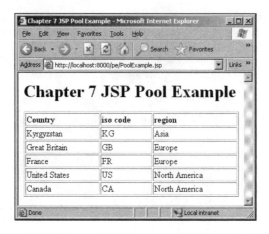

How It Works

The J2EE server comes pre-configured with a number of data sources for the Cloudscape database. You can find the complete list of DataSources by running the server and entering the address http://localhost:8000/j2ee-admin. The username and password for this admin tool are both j2ee.

In the JSP, we wanted to access the CloudscapeDB database. The reason we've been using this database throughout this chapter and the previous chapter is that it is the default example database for the J2EE server. Thus the J2EE server has a DataSource already configured for this database. The JNDI name for this DataSource is `jdbc/Cloudscape`. This DataSource is preconfigured with the correct driver URL and other parameters needed to connect to the database. While not required, a common practice is to prefix the resource name with a short word that describes the resource: for database resources we use "jdbc". In the EJB chapters later in the book, we will use "ejb" for EJB resources.

In the JSP code, we created an instance of `InitialContext`, and then used this context to perform a lookup:

```
DataSource dataSource =
    (DataSource) context.lookup("java:comp/env/jdbc/Countries");
```

Notice that in this example, we actually had to prepend some additional information to the lookup name. The prefix `java:comp/env` is used when you are performing a lookup of resources provided by the server that your component is running in.

Then, to get this example to work, we had to ensure the deployment descriptors for the web component and the application were configured to map the lookup name to the JNDI name. First, in the deployment descriptor for the web application, we identified that the resource for the name `jdbc/Countries` would be an instance of `javax.sql.DataSource`. In the application deployment descriptor, we mapped the name `jdbc/Countries` to the JNDI name `jdbc/Cloudscape`. This ensured that when the code performed the lookup, the server would locate the correct `DataSource` object and return it to the JSP.

After that, the JSP was able to use the connection object, just like any other client in the JDBC examples used a connection obtained from a Driver Manager.

Now let's look at this same JSP running in Tomcat standalone.

Try It Out   Using Data Sources with Tomcat

1. We can use the same JSP from above with the Tomcat standalone server, but it takes a little more work. First, copy the cloudscape `cloudclient.jar` and `RmiJdbc.jar` file from the `%J2EE_HOME%\lib\cloudscape` directory to `%CATALINA_HOME%/common/lib`.

2. Next, we need to configure Tomcat to talk to the Cloudscape database. Edit the `%CATALINA_HOME%/conf/server.xml` file. You are looking for the end of the `</Host>` tag. Insert the `<DefaultContext>` element shown below; it should be inserted immediately before the `</Host>` tag:

```
<!-- Example Server Configuration File -->
<!-- Note that component elements are nested corresponding to their
     parent-child relationships with each other -->

  ...lots of lines from the server.xml file not shown...

       <!-- Define the default virtual host -->
       <Host name="localhost" debug="0" appBase="webapps"
        unpackWARs="true" autoDeploy="true">

  ...more lines from the server.xml file not shown...

          <DefaultContext>
            <Resource name="jdbc/Countries" auth="Container"
                      type="javax.sql.DataSource" />
            <ResourceParams name="jdbc/Countries">
              <parameter>
                <name>driverClassName</name>
                <value>COM.cloudscape.core.RmiJdbcDriver</value>
              </parameter>
              <parameter>
                <name>url</name>
            <value>jdbc:cloudscape:rmi://localhost:1099/CloudscapeDB</value>
              </parameter>
            </ResourceParams>
          </DefaultContext>

       </Host>

   </Engine>
```

```
    </Service>

    ...more lines from the server.xml file not shown...

</Server>
```

The `<DefaultContext>` section shown above configures Tomcat to create a `javax.sql.DataSource` object and bind it to the name `jdbc/Countries`. Notice that both the `Resource` and `ResourceParams` elements use the same value for the name attribute. The `DataSource` is created to talk to the database at the URL given by the `url` parameter, using the driver given by the `driverClassName` parameter.

3. Next create a web application directory in the Tomcat `/webapps` directory. Name this directory `/pe`, and copy the `PoolExample.jsp` file into this directory. Create this `web.xml` file and place it into the `webapps/pe/WEB-INF` directory:

```xml
<?xml version="1.0"?>
<web-app>
  <display-name>WebApp</display-name>
  <servlet>
    <servlet-name>PoolExample</servlet-name>
    <jsp-file>/PoolExample.jsp</jsp-file>
  </servlet>
  <resource-ref>
    <res-ref-name>jdbc/Countries</res-ref-name>
    <res-type>javax.sql.DataSource</res-type>
  </resource-ref>
</web-app>
```

4. Start Tomcat, open a browser, and navigate to this URL http://localhost:8080/pe/PoolExample.jsp. If everything is correct and running OK, you should see the same display as in Step 5 of the previous *Try It Out* example.

How It Works

The `server.xml` and `web.xml` files identify the database and connection parameters to Tomcat. In the `server.xml`, we told Tomcat what name (`Countries`) to use for the resource and which parameters to use to create the `DataSource`. The `<Resource>` element contains a `<ResourceParams>` element that contains parameters for the data source. The following parameters are recognized:

Parameter	Description
driverClassName	The full name of the driver class
maxActive	The maximum number of active connections in pool
maxIdle	The maximum number of idle connections in pool
maxWait	The maximum wait for a connection in milliseconds, throws an exception if exceeded
user	The database username
password	The database password
url	The URL for the database
validationQuery	A query that can be sent to the database to ensure a valid active connection

When Tomcat starts up, it reads the `server.xml` file, and creates a data source based on the parameters in the `ResourceParams` list. It then makes it available to clients using a JNDI interface.

Note that Tomcat does not really use a directory to store the resource. It just uses JNDI semantics to make the resource available to clients. As clients, though, we really don't care how Tomcat stores the resource, as long as it fulfills the contract of the JNDI interface.

In `web.xml`, we told the web application the name and the type of the resource we would be using. The JSP then obtained the data source reference and used it to talk to the database. This code was the same code as used in the previous example. Here is the relevant part of the code:

```
InitialContext context = new InitialContext();
DataSource dataSource =
  (DataSource) context.lookup("java:comp/env/CloudscapeDB");
Connection conn = dataSource.getConnection();
Statement stmt = conn.createStatement();
ResultSet rset = stmt.executeQuery("select * from COUNTRIES");
```

As shown previously in this section, the code creates an instance of `InitialContext`. This context object represents the directory of names and resources. Using the context, we then look up a resource that we want to use. To get the correct resource, we create a URL by appending the name of the resource, `CloudscapeDB`, to the string `jdbc:/comp/env`. This string is used within the application server to identify resource names.

Then, just as we have done so many times previously, we call the `getConnection()` method. Unlike with the `DriverManager` class, we do not need to pass the URL to the `getConnection()` method of the data source. The URL and other parameters have already been set in the data source. If we wanted to change the database for the J2EE application, there would not need to be any code changes involved in the client code. We just change the `server.xml` and `web.xml` files, restart Tomcat, and every client gets the new connection the next time they use the data source. The rest of the JDBC is just like we have seen in the other examples in this chapter.

Notice also, that the client has no idea that they are dealing with a pooled connection. The client continues to access the database using the same `Connection` interface that we used when we created the connection directly. This means that even the `close()` method is the same from the client's point of view. However, when you close a pooled connection, rather than closing the physical connection to the database, the connection is returned to the pool.

Earlier, I stated that what's important about pooled connections is not how they are *created* (because that will differ between implementations) but how they are *used*. Now, you should see that from the client's point of view, there is no difference between how you use pooled connections and non-pooled connections. In fact, you could take the `JDBCManager` class developed in this chapter, and modify it to use `Context` and `DataSource` for getting connections. This new `JDBCManager` class could then be used from inside JSPs and servlets, and the JSP or servlet would then never need to know whether the connection came from a driver manager or a data source.

Transactions

So far in this chapter, every SQL command that we sent to the database was immediately executed and the change was made permanent in the database. In database terms, when the change is made permanent, we say that we **commit** the change, or that the change was **committed**. In an earlier example, we inserted a row into a table named COUNTRIES in the CloudscapeDB database, and as soon as the SQL was sent to the database, the change was committed. If we had done a query on the table, the new data would be returned by the query. Suppose we were inserting 50 rows into that table, and halfway through the 50 inserts, our workstation suffered a power failure. Rather than having a total failure, with no changes made to the database, the half of the rows that had been sent to the table before the power failure would be in the table. Only half of the work would have been incomplete. In this case, that's probably okay; the fact that we're able to insert Kyrgyzstan, but not Zambia does not make the table invalid.

However, sometimes, a partial success would be bad and would make the table invalid. If you were working on an Internet stock trading application, and the "sell stock" process failed halfway through, the software may have deposited the funds, but not moved the stock, or vice versa. In either case, the database is in an invalid state: the client's account has both the proceeds and the stock, or neither the proceeds nor the stock. In this case, we want all the changes to be made to a database, or none of the changes to be made.

This is the main purpose of **transactions** in the database – they take the database from one consistent state to the next. That is their job. When you commit work in the database, you are assured that all of your changes have been saved; if you rollback the work, none of the changes are saved.

In some SQL dialects, the code must explicitly tell the database that a transaction is beginning before it executes SQL commands. In SQL Server, for example, the BEGIN TRAN command starts a transaction. JDBC does not require you to explicitly begin a transaction (and thus, does not provide any class or methods for you, the application programmer, to perform this action). The JDBC driver you are using will start a transaction for you automatically. The transaction can be ended automatically, or manually.

Whether the transaction is committed automatically or manually is determined by the **autocommit** status of the connection. For JDBC, the default autocommit status is true. That is, transactions are automatically committed by the connection. The point at which the transaction ends depends on what type of statement is being executed, as shown in the table below:

Statement type	Transaction committed when...
SQL INSERT, UPDATE, or DELETE	The statement has finished executing, from the client's view, as soon as executeUpdate(), or execute() returns
SQL SELECT	All the rows in the ResultSet object have been retrieved, or a Statement object is used to execute a new SQL command on the same connection

With autocommit enabled, the driver ends the transaction by automatically calling the commit method. Even with a SQL query, which has no changes to be saved, there is still a transaction. The driver still has to signal the database that the transaction has ended.

When the autocommit status is false, then it is the responsibility of the client to explicitly end transactions. The Connection class provides several methods to handle transactions:

Method	Description
void setAutoCommit(boolean)	Sets the autocommit mode to true (commit transaction automatically, the default setting) or false (require explicit transaction commit)
void commit()	Commits the current transaction. All changes made since the last commit or rollback are made permanent. Any database locks are released.

Table continued on following page

Method	Description
`void close()`	Not explicitly part of transaction management. However, closing the `Connection` may cause a transaction to be committed. The exact behavior is database dependent; the JDBC specification does not require a particular behavior.
`void rollback()`	Returns the database to the state that existed at the start of the current transaction.
`Savepoint setSavepoint()`	JDBC 3.0: Creates an unnamed `Savepoint` in the current transaction and returns that `Savepoint` object.
`Savepoint setSavepoint(String)`	JDBC 3.0: Creates a named `Savepoint` in the current transaction and returns that `Savepoint` object.
`void releaseSavepoint(Savepoint)`	JDBC 3.0: Removes the given `Savepoint` from the current transaction.
`void rollback(Savepoint)`	JDBC 3.0: Undoes all the changes that were performed after the given `Savepoint` was created.

We'll look at some of these methods in more detail in the next section and in the *Try It Out* that follows.

Connection Methods for Transaction Control

When your code gets a connection from the driver manager, a data source, or a connection pool, JDBC requires that the connection be in autocommit mode (autocommit enabled). When autocommit is enabled, each SQL command is treated as a transaction and the transaction is committed when the statement is complete as shown in the table above.

Having the driver in autocommit mode may be acceptable when you are learning JDBC or when you are using a single-user database. However, the fact that the JDBC (and ODBC) API defaults to autocommit enabled is problematic for any type of real-world application. Real-world database applications are almost always multi-user applications or applications that touch more than a single table to complete a given task. Thus, for almost any type of real-world application, the next method call after obtaining a connection should be a call to `setAutoCommit(boolean)` as shown here:

```
Connection conn = DriverManager.getConnection(strUrl);
conn.setAutoCommit (false);    // Autocommit disabled
```

Now, all the control of the transaction resides with the client, which is where it belongs. The developer can code the transaction so that it includes all the queries, inserts, updates, and deletes to take the database from one consistent state to another, and commit only after all the statements have succeeded (or rollback if there are problems).

When the `autocommit` mode is set to `false`, transaction management must now be performed explicitly by the code. SQL commands sent to the database will still be executed, but the transaction is not committed when the statement is complete. The transaction will be committed when the code calls the `commit()` method of the `Connection` object. Alternatively, the transaction could be rolled back if the code calls the `rollback()` method. Here is an example of code that shows how we might do this:

```
try {
  stmt = conn.createStatement();
  stmt.executeUpdate("delete from COUNTRIES");
  conn.commit();
} catch (Exception e) {
  JDBCManager.rollback(conn);
} finally {
  JDBCManager.close(stmt);
}
```

In addition to `commit()` or `rollback()`, you might be able to control transactions with a feature known as a **savepoint**. Savepoints have been available in databases for some time, but they are a new feature for JDBC. They are part of the JDBC 3.0 specification, so are not widely supported by drivers yet. Check your driver documentation to see if savepoints are supported.

Let's look at an example that shows how savepoints might be used. Suppose we have a transaction that manipulates data in two tables, A and B. If the changes to table A succeed, the database will be left in a consistent state and the transaction could be committed at that point; however, for business reasons, the changes to table B are required to be part of the transaction. However, if the SQL for table A succeeds but some or all of the SQL for table B fails, the database will be in an inconsistent state; if the transaction were committed, the database would contain bad data.

Here is what this scenario might look like:

Time	Transaction without savepoint
T0	Transaction begins
T1	SQL insert, update, or delete data into table A, SQL succeeds
T2	SQL insert, update, or delete data into table B, some SQL succeeds and some fails
T3	Client must ROLLBACK, all changes are lost

Without savepoints, all the changes in the transaction must be rolled back because there is no way to perform a partial rollback. Also, there is no easy way to know which parts of table B need to be fixed, so there is no way to recover from the failure and commit the changes to table A.

Now, let's try the same example, but with savepoints:

Time	Transaction with savepoint
T0	Transaction begins
T1	SQL insert, update, or delete data into table A, SQL succeeds
T2	Savepoint s1 created
T3	SQL insert, update, or delete data into table B, SQL fails
T4	Client calls rollback to savepoint s1
T5	Client performs additional SQL
T6	Client commits transaction

With save points, the client is able to perform a partial rollback of data, perform some additional work, if needed, to put the database into a consistent state, and then commit the transaction. Thus, some of the work performed in a transaction is not lost. Below is an example of what this might look like in code. In the snippet below, insertIntoTable1() and insertIntoTable2() are methods that perform some database actions. If there is a problem, the methods will throw a SQLException. Based on whether or not an exception is thrown, and whether or not the savepoint is set, the code commits all the data, performs a partial rollback and commit, or does a complete rollback:

```
Savepoint sp1 = null;
try {
  insertIntoTable1();
  sp1 = conn.setSavepoint();

  insertIntoTable2();

  // No exceptions, so commit the changes
  conn.commit();
} catch (SQLException e) {
  // This exception means either insertIntoTable1()
  // or insertIntoTable2() failed
  try {
    // If Savepoint is NOT null, then insertIntoTable1() was good
    // but insertIntoTable2() failed, do partial rollback, then commit
    if (sp1 != null) {
```

```
        conn.rollback(recordSavepoint);
        conn.commit();
      } else {
        // insertIntoTable1() failed, do complete rollback
        connection.rollback();
      }
    } catch (SQLException e2) {
      e2.printStackTrace();
    }
  }
```

Here are some additional points that you need to be aware of when using savepoints:

❑ Calling `commit()` or `rollback()` invalidates all savepoints created since the transaction started

❑ Calling `releaseSavepoint(Savepoint)` invalidates the given savepoint

❑ Calling `rollback(Savepoint)` invalidates any savepoints that had been created after the given savepoint

Transactions and Stored Procedures

I mentioned previously that transaction control belongs in the hands of the developer. The system requirements should provide information on the business rules for the application and the developer can use those requirements to make the best decision on what sequence of SQL constitutes the transactions for the system, and when those transactions should be committed. Another way to provide this control is to put all the statements that constitute a transaction into a stored procedure.

Stored procedures are perhaps the easiest and most accessible method to ensure correct transactions. If you follow a programming paradigm that says "a stored procedure call is a transaction", you'll have an easier time controlling your transactions and building new ones. You would code stored procedures that received all of the necessary inputs to perform its work. It would take the database from one consistent state to the next. When you invoke this procedure, you would wrap the procedure call in transaction control statements:

```
// Disable autocommit
connection.setAutoCommit(false);

String sql = "{ call MyProcedure }";
CallableStatement cs = connection.prepareCall(sql);

// Call procedure
cs.executeUpdate();
connection.commit();
```

Now, if `MyProcedure` completes successfully, we will commit all of the work it did. If it fails we'll roll back the work (although that is not shown in the snippet above). The reason we would not put the commit directly into `MyProcedure` itself is because at some later date we might need to combine two or three procedures into one transaction. By leaving transaction control to the client (which is where the choice belongs) we can assemble larger transactions as a collection of stored procedures.

Try It Out   **Using Transaction Control**

Let's modify the `JDBCManager` class one final time in this chapter. This will be the last version of `JDBCManager`. With this change, we'll give the class the ability to give the client a connection that is configured to return a connection with autocommit already enabled or disabled, depending upon the user's preference.

1. First, make the following changes to the code:

```
package Ch07;

import java.sql.*;
import java.util.*;
```

```
public class JDBCManager {
  private JDBCManager() {}

    //Returns a connection with autocommit true
  public static Connection getConnection(String url)
    throws SQLException
  {
    return getConnection(url, true);
  }

    //Returns a connection with autocommit set by the autocommit parameter
  public static Connection getConnection(String url, boolean autocommit)
    throws SQLException
  {
    Connection connection = DriverManager.getConnection(url);
    connection.setAutoCommit(autocommit);
    return connection;
  }

    //Returns a connection with autocommit true
  public static Connection getConnection(
    String url, String user, String password)
      throws SQLException
  {
    return getConnection(url, user, password, true);
  }
```

```java
  //Returns a connection with autocommit set by the autocommit parameter
  public static Connection getConnection(
    String url, String user, String password, boolean autocommit)
      throws SQLException
  {
    Connection connection =
      DriverManager.getConnection(url, user, password);
    connection.setAutoCommit(autocommit);
    return connection;
  }

  //Returns a connection with autocommit true
  public static Connection getConnection(String url, Properties props)
    throws SQLException
  {
    return getConnection(url, props, true);
  }

  //Returns a connection with autocommit set by the autocommit parameter
  public static Connection getConnection(
    String url, Properties props, boolean autocommit)
      throws SQLException
  {
    Connection connection = DriverManager.getConnection(url, props);
    connection.setAutoCommit(autocommit);
    return connection;
  }

  public static void rollback(Connection conn) {
    try {
      conn.rollback();
    } catch (Exception e) {
      e.printStackTrace();
    }
  }

// close(Connection conn) not shown
// close(Statement stmt) not shown
// close(ResultSet rset) not shown

}
```

2. Now create the following client class:

```java
package Ch07;

import java.sql.*;
import java.io.*;

public class JDBCClient5 {
  static Connection conn = null;
```

```java
static PreparedStatement pstmt = null;
static ResultSet rset = null;

static String sqlInsert = "insert into COUNTRIES " +
  "(COUNTRY, COUNTRY_ISO_CODE, REGION) " +
  "values (?, ?, ?)";

static String sqlQuery = "select * from COUNTRIES";

public static void main(String[] args) {
  try {
    String url = "jdbc:cloudscape:rmi://localhost:1099/CloudscapeDB";
    conn = JDBCManagerV3.getConnection(url, false);
    pstmt = conn.prepareStatement(sqlInsert);

    // Transaction begins here
    cleanupTable();
    doEUBatch();
    doNABatch();
    System.out.println("\nChecking the table before " +
      "commit or rollback:");
    doQuery();

    // Pretend we need to rollback
    JDBCManagerV3.rollback(conn);
    System.out.println("\nChecking the table after rollback:");
    doQuery();
    JDBCManagerV3.close(pstmt);

    pstmt = conn.prepareStatement(sqlInsert);
    doEUBatch();
    doNABatch();
    conn.commit();
    System.out.println("\nChecking the table after commit:");
    doQuery();
  } catch (SQLException e) {

    // An exception means something failed, so do rollback
    JDBCManagerV3.rollback(conn);
    e.printStackTrace();
  } finally {
    JDBCManagerV3.close(rset);
    JDBCManagerV3.close(pstmt);
    JDBCManagerV3.close(conn);
  }
}

public static void cleanupTable() {
  // If there is data in the COUNTRIES table from previous examples
  // then delete this old data
  Statement stmt = null;
```

```
    try {
      stmt = conn.createStatement();
      stmt.executeUpdate("delete from COUNTRIES");
      conn.commit();
      System.out.println("Database has been cleaned");
    } catch (Exception e) {
      JDBCManagerV3.rollback(conn);
    } finally {
      JDBCManagerV3.close(stmt);
    }
  }

  public static void doEUBatch() throws SQLException {
    pstmt.setString(1, "Kyrgyzstan");
    pstmt.setString(2, "KG");
    pstmt.setString(3, "Asia");
    pstmt.addBatch();

    pstmt.setString(1,"Great Britain");
    pstmt.setString(2,"GB");
    pstmt.setString(3,"Europe");
    pstmt.addBatch();

    pstmt.setString(1,"France");
    pstmt.setString(2,"FR");
    pstmt.addBatch();

    pstmt.executeBatch();
  }

  public static void doNABatch() throws SQLException {
    pstmt.setString(1,"United States");
    pstmt.setString(2,"US");
    pstmt.setString(3, "North America");
    pstmt.addBatch();

    pstmt.setString(1,"Canada");
    pstmt.setString(2,"CA");
    pstmt.addBatch();

    pstmt.executeBatch();
  }

  public static void doQuery() throws SQLException {
    rset = pstmt.executeQuery(sqlQuery);
    int rownum = 1;
    if (rset.next()) {
      do {
        System.out.print("row " + rownum++ + " is ");
        System.out.print(rset.getString(1) + ", ");
        System.out.print(rset.getString(2) + ", ");
        System.out.println(rset.getString(3));
```

```
      } while (rset.next());
    } else {
      System.out.println("No results in table");
    }
  }
}
```

3. Compile the classes and run the Cloudscape RMI server:

```
> java *.java
> cloudscape -start
```

4. As usual, check that the classpath includes the RmiJdbc.jar and cloudclient.jar
files as well as the directory above the working directory. Then, you can run the program:

```
> set
classpath=c:\j2sdkee1.4\lib\cloudscape\RmiJdbc.jar;c:\j2sdkee1.4\lib\cloudsca
pe\cloudclient.jar;C:\8333

> java -Djdbc.drivers=COM.cloudscape.core.RmiJdbcDriver Ch07.JDBCClient5
Database has been cleaned

Checking the table before commit or rollback:
row 1 is Kyrgyzstan, KG, Asia
row 2 is Great Britain, GB, Europe
row 3 is France, FR, Europe
row 4 is United States, US, North America
row 5 is Canada, CA, North America

Checking the table after rollback:
No results in table

Checking the table after commit:
row 1 is Kyrgyzstan, KG, Asia
row 2 is Great Britain, GB, Europe
row 3 is France, FR, Europe
row 4 is United States, US, North America
row 5 is Canada, CA, North America
```

This class uses the COUNTRIES table that was created in earlier examples. If you did not run those earlier examples, you should refer back to the JDBCClient3 example for the SQL to create the table. This code also assumes there is data in the table, so it uses the cleanupTable() method to delete any existing rows in the table.

Then, the class calls two methods that insert data into the table. This shows that transactions within a single connection can span multiple methods; you don't need to confine a transaction to a single method in a class.

After both methods complete, the code queries the table. Since this occurs within the same transaction, the changes the code made are visible in a query. (Other transactions may or may not be able to see these changes before the commit. See the *Locking and Isolation* section later for more information.) Now, the code pretends there was some problem and calls rollback(). This ends the transaction, and since a rollback discards the changes, a subsequent query finds no rows in the table.

The code then inserts the data again, this time calling commit when all inserts are complete. Calling commit() ends the transaction, but since it saves all the changes, a subsequent query finds all five rows in the table.

Introduction to Distributed Transactions

Previously in this section, we've been looking at transactions involving a single connection to a single database. In your work with J2EE applications, you may be faced with a situation where you need to use **distributed transactions**.

Distributed transactions can include two or more databases:

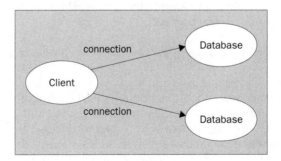

or transactions can span multiple connections to the same data source:

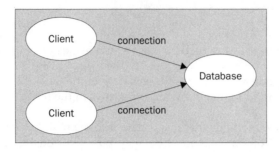

Just as for single connection transactions, all the changes made by each connection in the distributed transaction must be successful for the transaction to be committed.

From the client's point of view, coding a distributed transaction is almost the same as coding for a single connection transaction, so we will be able to look at distributed transactions from that perspective.

While you can use multiple data sources or connections within your JDBC application, the term "distributed transactions" usually applies to applications or classes that have distributed components. One place where you are likely to run into distributed applications is, of course, a J2EE application, where various components may execute on different servers. We've seen some of these components already – JSPs, servlets, and databases. In the following chapters, we'll look at other J2EE components such as Enterprise JavaBeans (EJBs). These components will most likely be running inside a container called an **application server**. You'll learn more about application servers in the EJB chapters. For now, we'll define an application server as an application that acts as a container for J2EE components and provides the infrastructure support to business logic components.

When separate components provide part of a transaction, no single component can determine when or how to commit or roll back changes. This then becomes the responsibility of the transaction manager. Since we're working in the Java world, that manager will be an implementation of the **Java Transaction API (JTA)**.

You can learn more about the JTA at http://java.sun.com/products/jta.

The application server will use a transaction manager to provide distributed transaction support to the components in a J2EE application. As part of providing transaction support, the application server will use special JDBC classes. Those classes will implement the XADataSource, XAConnection, and XAResource interfaces. The application server vendor or the database vendor will provide these classes. At least one of these classes might look vaguely familiar: the XAConnection. Its name is similar to Connection, but it's got that XA bit on the front. As its name suggests, the XAConnection interface represents connections. However, in this case, it represents a connection that can be used in a distributed transaction. Likewise, XADataSource and XAResource represent datasources and resources used in distributed transactions.

However, the client does not need to use or be aware of these classes. At the client level, the code will use the same interfaces that we have seen throughout this chapter: `Connection`, `Statement`, and `ResultSet`. Just like when the `JDBCClient1` or `JDBCClient2` classes got a `Connection` object, the reference was of type `java.sql.Connection`. Even though the underlying object may have been a `COM.cloudscape.core.JDBCDriver`, the client simply used a `Connection` object. Likewise, even though the underlying object may be an `XAConnection`, the client will still use a reference of type `Connection`. The client code used to talk to the database will not look very different from code we have seen previously in this chapter. For example, the code to get a connection might look like this:

```
Context context = new InitialContext();
DataSource dataSource = context.lookup("jdbc/oracle");
Connection connection = dataSource.getConnection();
```

If you look at the *Data Source and Connection Pools* section earlier in this chapter, you will see that the code used to get a "normal" data source is essentially the same that an application involved in a distributed transaction will use. Under the covers, the application server will likely use an `XAConnection` implementation to get the connection that is passed to the client, but in the client, the object will be referenced as a `Connection`. After getting the connection, the code would use one of the statement objects to send SQL to the data source. The difference between a nondistributed and a distributed transaction is in how the transaction is committed or rolled back.

Since the transaction is being controlled by a transaction manager outside the client, any class involved in a distributed transaction is prohibited from calling any of these methods:

❑ `commit()`

❑ `rollback()`

❑ `setSavepoint()`

❑ `setAutoCommit(true)`

Committing or rolling back a transaction is entirely under the control of the transaction manager. The client does not need to do anything special other than call the `close()` method of the `Connection` interface when it has completed its work. After all the components involved in the transaction have completed, the transaction manager will commit or roll back the transaction.

This commit (or rollback) is called a **two-phase commit**. It has two phases because the transaction manager must poll all the data sources before deciding to commit or roll back. As each data source is polled, it throws an exception if it cannot commit its changes. If no data source throws an exception in the polling phase, the transaction manager instructs the data sources to commit their changes. Suppose we have two clients involved in a distributed transaction. Here's an illustration of how the two-phase commit would proceed:

Time	
T0	Both clients have called `close()` to signal that they have completed their work.
T1	Transaction manager calls the `prepare()` method of `XAResource`. There is an `XAResource` for each data source.
T2	If neither `XAResource` throws an exception, then each is ready to commit.
T3	Transaction manager calls the `commit()` method of each `XAResource`. This message is passed to each data source, which then commits.

Note that the above would all occur outside the client code. It is entirely handled by the transaction manager. If no data sources throw an exception in the polling phase, the transaction manager tells all the data sources to commit their changes. If any data source throws an exception, all the data sources are notified to roll back the changes.

We've seen in this section how to deal with situations where you are updating more than a single table. These are situations where you might be making numerous changes to a database, and all the changes must succeed for the database to be in a consistent state at the end of the transaction.

Often, though, in a web application, your client application will only be one of many that are trying to perform a transaction simultaneously. In the few minutes it took me to write this paragraph, during the busy shopping season of December, Amazon.com just processed 1,324 transactions. That's 1,324 transactions potentially touching the same rows in the database. (Well, let's caveat that; more likely for the top ranked sellers, almost nil for the bottom ranked sellers.) Using transaction control will ensure that all of the changes in a transaction are committed or rolled back, but it says nothing about what happens when two or more transactions are dealing with the same data. To deal with that situation, we need to look at the topic of locking.

Locking and Isolation

In any application where you must be concerned with two or more clients interacting with the database (and that includes almost every J2EE application with a database) you need to be concerned with the problem of **concurrency**. That is, how do allow multiple users to interact with the database, and yet prevent their actions from interfering with each other.

Databases handle this problem through **isolation** and some type of concurrency control that usually involves **locking** the data in the database. However, different databases handle isolation and locking differently. You can tell the database what level of isolation to use, and thus have some control over isolation. Locking, however, is totally under the control of the database. There is no way for you, as a JDBC developer, to tell the database how to lock the data. The database chooses to lock or not, based on the SQL commands you are executing. For this reason, we will not discuss the locking behavior of any particular database.

> Locking is highly database-dependent. You *must* check the database documentation to determine how your database handles concurrency control and locking.

Isolation

Isolation refers to the degree to which actions taken in one transaction can be seen by other transactions. At the highest level of isolation, any actions taken in a transaction cannot be seen by any other transaction. This applies to both reads and writes. That is, if one transaction reads a row or rows of data, no other transaction is impacted by the first transaction. At the lowest level of isolation (as defined by the SQL specification) everything done in any transaction, whether committed or not, can be seen by any other transaction.

The ANSI/ISO SQL92 standard identifies three different types of interactions between transactions. From the lowest to the highest levels of isolation, these types are dirty reads, non-repeatable reads, and phantom reads:

❑   **Dirty reads** – Changes made in one transaction can be seen in other transactions, whether committed or not.

❑   **Non-repeatable reads** – Updates to existing rows made in one transaction are seen by other transactions as soon as they are committed. Thus, multiple queries that are the same may retrieve different data within a single transaction.

❑   **Phantom reads** – Inserts to tables made in one transaction are seen by other transactions as soon as they are committed.

The transaction level you select will depend on the business requirements of your application. The SQL specification identifies four isolation levels that indicate which interactions above are allowed or prevented. Those levels are read uncommitted, read committed, repeatable read, and serializable:

❑   **Read uncommitted** – lowest level, allows all interactions

❑   **Read committed** – prevents dirty reads

❑   **Repeatable read** – prevents nonrepeatable reads

❑   **Serializable** – Highest level, prevents all interactions

Most databases have a default level of read committed, and this will be sufficient for most applications. You can select a higher level with the method from the `Connection` interface:

```
void setTransactionIsolation(int level)
```

This method is called before a transaction begins. You pass one of four arguments to the method. The arguments are defined as constants in the `Connection` interface. They are

❏ TRANSACTION_READ_UNCOMMITTED

❏ TRANSACTION_READ_COMMITTED

❏ TRANSACTION_REPEATABLE_READ

❏ TRANSACTION_SERIALIZABLE

A database may not support all levels of isolation. For example, Cloudscape 4.0 does not support the read uncommitted level. Check your database documentation to see which levels are supported.

Locking

Even though you can't control how the database locks data, the SQL commands you execute and how you execute them can have a big impact on how separate concurrent transactions in a database interfere, or don't interfere, with each other.

Let's look at what might happen if two transactions attempt to modify the same data when the application is not properly designed for concurrency and isolation. Let's assume that we are working on an online reservation system for a small bed & breakfast style hotel. A guest can log on to the site, see which rooms are available, and make reservations for an available room:

Time	Transaction A	Transaction B
T0	Beth logs onto the web site and queries the application for available rooms. The system reads from the database and shows that the Pikes Peak Room is available.	Jennifer logs onto the web site and performs the same query. Again, the Pikes Peak room is shown as available.
T1		Jennifer makes a reservation for the Pikes Peak room. The application updates the database to show that the Pikes Peak room is reserved for Jennifer.
T2	Beth makes a reservation for the Pikes Peak room. The application updates the database, this time setting the data to show that the room is reserved for Beth.	

You can see that at T1, the database has been placed into a particular state. In this state, a table has been updated to show certain information. However, because transaction A was operating on the database based on its original view of the data, when it updates the same table, the updates from transaction B are overwritten or lost. This is known as a lost update.

Either transaction could have prevented this problem by the proper use of locking. If **pessimistic locking** had been used, then the first transaction to perform the original query would have locked that data, preventing the other transaction from modifying the data. If **optimistic locking** had been used, then the second transaction to attempt to update the table would have been prevented from doing so because it would have found that the table had changed since the original query. In the next two sections, we'll look at each type of locking in more detail.

Pessimistic Locking

Pessimistic locking is usually used when there is a high likelihood that other transactions might want to change the table between a query and an update. For example, in an online concert ticketing system, if the user selects a particular seat, there is an implicit promise that the user can buy that seat before any other user. The application should give that user the option of completing the purchase; only if the user declines to purchase the ticket should it be re-offered to anyone else. Thus, the application should somehow lock that data at the time the seat is selected. We call it pessimistic locking because we are pessimistic about the chances of no one wanting to buy the same tickets (or access the same data) between the times the user checks the availability of seats and purchases the tickets.

In SQL, you indicate that you intend to update some data using the FOR UPDATE clause of your SELECT statement. When you use FOR UPDATE with SELECT, it signals to the database that it should lock the data against other updates until your transaction is complete. Remember, however, that every database will do this differently.

In the next example, we'll see how Cloudscape performs this pessimistic locking.

Try It Out   Using Pessimistic Locking

We need two client classes for this example, one for each simulated transaction.

1. Create the PessimisticLockerA.java class using the code shown below. Notice that it uses the final version of the JDBCManager class from earlier in this chapter. You will need to create that class also, if you have not already done so. This class creates the table for this example, in addition to querying and updating the table:

```
package Ch07;

import java.sql.*;
import java.io.*;

public class PessimisticLockerA {
   static Connection conn;
   static Statement stmt;
```

```java
  static Statement stmtA;
  static PreparedStatement pstmt;
  static ResultSet rsetA;

  static String sqlCreate = "create table RESERVE " +
    "(ROOMID varchar(5), RES_DATE date, RES_FLAG boolean, " +
    "RES_NAME varchar(30))";
  static String sqlInsert = "insert into RESERVE values " +
    "(?, ?, ?, ?)";
  static String sqlUpdate = "update RESERVE set RES_FLAG=?, " +
    "RES_NAME=? WHERE ROOMID=? AND RES_DATE=?";
  static String sqlSelect = "select ROOMID, RES_DATE, " +
    "RES_FLAG, RES_NAME from RESERVE WHERE RES_FLAG=false FOR UPDATE";

  static String roomName;
  static java.sql.Date roomDate;

  public static void main(String[] args) {
    try {
      String url = "jdbc:cloudscape:rmi://localhost:1099/CloudscapeDB";
      conn = JDBCManagerV3.getConnection(url, false);
      System.out.println("conn autocommit is " + conn.getAutoCommit());
      setup();
      userAQuery();
      System.out.println("Sleeping for 15 seconds, " +
                         "run PessimisticLockerB");
      try {Thread.sleep(15000);} catch (Exception e) {}
        System.out.println("PessimisticLockerA is awake");
        userAUpdate();
      } catch (Exception e) {
        e.printStackTrace();
      } finally {
        JDBCManagerV3.close(conn);
    }
  }

  static void setup() throws SQLException {
    System.out.println("Creating RESERVE table");
    try {
      stmt = conn.createStatement();
      stmt.addBatch(sqlCreate);
      stmt.executeBatch();
      System.out.println("Inserting row of data");
      pstmt = conn.prepareStatement(sqlInsert);
      pstmt.setString(1, "PIKE");
      pstmt.setDate(2, new java.sql.Date(System.currentTimeMillis()));
      pstmt.setBoolean(3,false);
      pstmt.setNull(4, java.sql.Types.VARCHAR);
      pstmt.executeUpdate();
      conn.commit();
    } finally {
      JDBCManagerV3.close(pstmt);
```

```
      JDBCManagerV3.close(stmt);
    }
  }

  static void userAQuery() throws SQLException {
    System.out.println("User A is querying for rooms");
    stmtA = conn.createStatement();
    rsetA = stmtA.executeQuery(sqlSelect);
    if (rsetA.next()) {
      System.out.println("Query returned one row");
      roomName = rsetA.getString(1);
      roomDate = rsetA.getDate(2);
    }
    // Neither the statement nor resultset are closed here
    // We need them open for the userAUpdate() method
  }

  static void userAUpdate() throws SQLException {
    try {
      if (roomName != null && roomDate != null) {
        System.out.println("User A is attempting to reserve room");
        pstmt = conn.prepareStatement(sqlUpdate);
        pstmt.setBoolean(1, true);
        pstmt.setString(2, "User A");
        pstmt.setString(3,roomName);
        pstmt.setDate(4, roomDate);
        int result = pstmt.executeUpdate();
        if (result == 0) {
          System.out.println("Reservation did NOT succeed!");
          System.out.println("The user will have to try " +
                             "another room, or another date");
        } else {
          System.out.println("Calling commit for user A");
          conn.commit();
        }
      }
    } catch (SQLException e) {
      e.printStackTrace(DriverManager.getLogWriter());
      System.out.println(e.getErrorCode());
      System.out.println(e.getMessage());
    } finally {
      JDBCManagerV3.close(pstmt);
      JDBCManagerV3.close(rsetA);
      JDBCManagerV3.close(stmtA);
    }
  }
}
```

2. Now we create the `PessimisticLockerB` class. This class simply queries the table and attempts to update it:

```
package Ch07;

import java.sql.*;
import java.io.*;

public class PessimisticLockerB {
  static Connection conn;
  static Statement stmt;
  static Statement stmtB;
  static PreparedStatement pstmt;
  static ResultSet rsetB;

  static String sqlUpdate = "update RESERVE set RES_FLAG=?, " +
    "RES_NAME=? WHERE ROOMID=? AND RES_DATE=?";
  static String sqlSelect = "select ROOMID, RES_DATE, " +
    "RES_FLAG, RES_NAME from RESERVE WHERE RES_FLAG=false FOR UPDATE";

  static String roomName;
  static java.sql.Date roomDate;

  public static void main(String[] args) {
    try {
      String url = "jdbc:cloudscape:rmi://localhost:1099/CloudscapeDB";
      conn = JDBCManagerV3.getConnection(url, false);
      System.out.println("conn autocommit is " + conn.getAutoCommit());
      userBQueryAndUpdate();
    } catch (Exception e) {
      e.printStackTrace();
    } finally {
      JDBCManagerV3.close(conn);
    }
  }

  static void userBQueryAndUpdate() throws SQLException {
    System.out.println("User B is querying for rooms");
    try {
      stmtB = conn.createStatement();
      rsetB = stmtB.executeQuery(sqlSelect);
      if (rsetB.next()) {
        System.out.println("User B is reserving room");
        pstmt = conn.prepareStatement(sqlUpdate);
        pstmt.setBoolean(1, true);
        pstmt.setString(2, "User B");
        pstmt.setString(3,rsetB.getString(1));
        pstmt.setDate(4, rsetB.getDate(2));
        pstmt.executeUpdate();
        System.out.println("Calling commit for user B");
        conn.commit();
      } else {
        System.out.println("User B found no available rooms");
      }
    } catch (SQLException e) {
```

```
      e.printStackTrace();
      System.out.println(e.getErrorCode());
      System.out.println(e.getMessage());
    } finally {
      JDBCManagerV3.close(pstmt);
      JDBCManagerV3.close(rsetB);
      JDBCManagerV3.close(stmtB);
    }
  }
}
```

3. Compile the classes and start the Cloudscape RMI server if it isn't already running, using the usual commands at the prompt.

4. These two classes need to be run at the same time, so you will need to open two windows, one for each class. Open the windows and prepare the usual classpath for each class:

```
> set classpath=C:\j2sdkee1.4\lib\cloudscape\RmiJdbc.jar
> set classpath=%classpath%;C:\j2sdkee1.4\lib\cloudscape\cloudclient.jar
> set classpath=%classpath%;C:\8333
```

5. PessimisticLockerA needs to be run first, and then after it performs the query, PessimisticLockerB is run. I've inserted a sleep into the code for PessimisticLockerA so that you have time to run PessimisticLockerB. In each window, prepare the command line for running the class. In the first window enter the following:

```
> java -Djdbc.drivers=COM.cloudscape.core.RmiJdbcDriver
Ch07.PessimisticLockerA
```

And in the second window, enter this command:

```
> java -Djdbc.drivers=COM.cloudscape.core.RmiJdbcDriver
Ch07.PessimisticLockerB
```

Now execute the command for PessimisticLockerA. You will see this output:

```
conn autocommit is false
Creating RESERVE table
Inserting row of data
User A is querying for rooms
Query returned one row
Sleeping for 15 seconds, run PessimisticLockerB
```

When you see the message that PessimisticLockerA is sleeping, run PessimisticLockerB, and you will see this output:

```
conn autocommit is false
User B is querying for rooms
```

Then, `PessimisticLockerB` will appear to freeze while it waits for the query to return. Its query is blocked because the database has locked the table row as a result of user A's query. After 15 seconds have passed, the code for `PessimisticLockerA` wakes up and continues to execute. This is what you see:

```
PessimisticLockerA is awake
User A is attempting to reserve room
Calling commit for user A
```

After the code calls commit, Cloudscape release the lock on the row, and `PessimisticLockerB`'s query returns. Unfortunately for B, user A got the last room:

```
User B found no available rooms
```

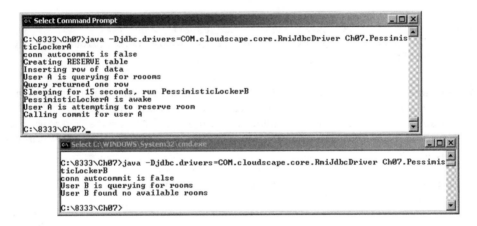

How It Works

This is probably the most complicated of the examples in this chapter, since it relies on the timing between the two client classes and the locking behavior of the database.

> Locking is very dependent on the database. This example may or may not work with other databases. Even if it does work with different databases, the behavior you see may be different. Consult the database documentation to understand how locking works so that you understand how the database deals with multiple users in the database and how to control their interactions

First, the code in `PessimisticLockerA` creates the `RESERVE` table that represents a room reservation system. The table has four columns, a room ID, a reservation date, a flag for whether the room is reserved, and the name of the person reserving the room. The code also inserts a single row of data into the table. Notice that because the table includes a date and a Boolean column, and a null value is inserted, it uses a prepared statement to insert the row. As we saw in the *Prepared Statement* section of this chapter, with some data types, such as date, it's easier to use a prepared statement; with other data values such as Boolean or null, using a prepared statement may be the only way to insert those values into the table with JDBC.

Each of the classes shown above queries the database to find a row of data. This query is performed with this SQL `SELECT` command:

```
SELECT ROOMID, RES_DATE, RES_FLAG, RES_NAME
  from RESERVE
 WHERE RES_FLAG=false FOR UPDATE
```

The `FOR UPDATE` clause tells the database that the transaction intends to update the table, and that the database should perform locking to ensure that no other transaction can modify the data until the first transaction is complete. However, notice that there is no way to tell the database how to lock the data. This is one of the features of a declarative language like SQL. You instruct the database to execute a command, such as select, insert, or lock, and the database determines how to execute the command. Cloudscape, for example, has row locks and table locks, but which lock it decides to use depends on several factors, and there is no way to tell which lock will be used.

Also, the code uses a connection with autocommit disabled. In Cloudscape, a `SELECT` command with the `FOR UPDATE` clause creates what Cloudscape calls an updatable cursor. (A cursor is a database term that is analogous to a resultset.) Cloudscape requires that autocommit be disabled for updateable cursors.

After user A queries the table, the code saves the value of the `ROOMID` and `RES_DATE` columns. Also, it does not close the statement or result set; this is because the code is simulating a real-world situation in which a client may keep those objects open while updating the data. The code then executes a Java `sleep()` method. This simulates the real-world behavior of some lag in time between when a user queries some data and submits new data for updating the database. It also provides a time gap in which the `PessimisticLockerB` class can be run.

Like user A, user B executes a query that looks for rooms in the database that have not yet been reserved. If user B finds such a row, user B attempts to reserve the room. However, user B's query is blocked, apparently because the database has locked the `RESERVE` table for update by user A.

After 15 seconds, the code for `PessimisticLockerA` wakes, and continues executing. The code performs an SQL `UPDATE` to reserve the room for user A, and then commits the transaction. At this point, user B's query unblocks. Unfortunately, because no rows now match the query, `rset.next()` returns false. User B finds no rooms available.

In this example, we allowed one transaction to get access to and update data from the database. With the proper use of pessimistic locking, the first user to access the data was the user that got to update the data. However, that came at a cost. With the particular way this example was structured, any other user was completely prevented from access the table at all. Suppose user A had walked away from their computer for 15 minutes, or even 15 hours. User B's application may have been frozen for that entire length of time. That's a heavy price to pay to ensure a good user experience (for user A, not B). It's very important to stress, though, that other situations or other databases may not have prevented B from querying the table. That's why it's so important for you to understand how your database handles this situation.

Optimistic Locking

Optimistic locking is usually used when there is a low likelihood that other transactions might want to change the table between a query and an update. In fact, unlike pessimistic locking, it really does not involve locking at all, but it still prevents the problem of lost updates. We call it optimistic because we are optimistic about the chances of no one wanting to access the same data (or reserve the same room) between the time the user queries the data and attempts to update the data.

To implement optimistic locking in your code, when your code performs a query, it keeps a local copy of all the data it retrieved. It then presents this data to the user for him to modify. Then when your code issues the update statement, it includes a WHERE clause in the SQL command which checks that the data in the table still matches the data originally retrieved. If it does not, that means some other user has modified the data between your query and your update. Your update command fails, but the other user's update is not lost. We can see how this works with the following example.

Try It Out   Using Optimistic Locking

1. Here is a client class that demonstrates how optimistic locking might be used. Enter and save this file as `OptimisticLocker.java`:

```
package Ch07;

import java.sql.*;
import java.io.*;

public class OptimisticLocker {
   static Connection conn;
   static Statement stmt;
   static PreparedStatement pstmt;
   static ResultSet rset;

   static String sqlCreate = "create table RESERVE " +
      "(ROOMID varchar(5), RES_DATE date, RES_FLAG boolean, " +
```

```
  "RES_NAME varchar(30))";
static String sqlInsert = "insert into RESERVE values " +
  "(?, ?, ?, ?)";
static String sqlUpdate = "update RESERVE set RES_FLAG=?, " +
  "RES_NAME=? WHERE ROOMID=? AND RES_DATE=? AND RES_FLAG=?";
static String sqlSelect = "select ROOMID, RES_DATE, " +
  "RES_FLAG, RES_NAME from RESERVE WHERE RES_FLAG=0";

static String roomName;
static java.sql.Date roomDate;
static boolean reserveStatus;

public static void main(String[] args) {
  try {
    String url = "jdbc:cloudscape:rmi://localhost:1099/CloudscapeDB";
    conn = JDBCManagerV3.getConnection(url);
    stmt = conn.createStatement();
    setup();
    userAQuery();
    userBQueryAndUpdate();
    userAUpdate();
  } catch (Exception e) {
    e.printStackTrace();
  } finally {
    JDBCManagerV3.close(rset);
    JDBCManagerV3.close(pstmt);
    JDBCManagerV3.close(stmt);
    JDBCManagerV3.close(conn);
  }
}

static void setup() throws SQLException {
  System.out.println("Creating RESERVE table");
  stmt.addBatch(sqlCreate);
  stmt.executeBatch();
  System.out.println("Inserting row of data");
  pstmt = conn.prepareStatement(sqlInsert);
  pstmt.setString(1, "PIKE");
  pstmt.setDate(2, new java.sql.Date(System.currentTimeMillis()));
  pstmt.setBoolean(3,false);
  pstmt.setNull(4, java.sql.Types.VARCHAR);
  pstmt.executeUpdate();
  JDBCManagerV3.close(pstmt);
}

static void userAQuery() throws SQLException {
  System.out.println("User A is querying for roooms");
  rset = stmt.executeQuery(sqlSelect);
  rset.next();
  roomName = rset.getString(1);
  roomDate = rset.getDate(2);
  reserveStatus = rset.getBoolean(3);
```

```
      JDBCManagerV3.close(rset);
  }

  static void userBQueryAndUpdate() throws SQLException {
    System.out.println("User B is querying for rooms");
    rset = stmt.executeQuery(sqlSelect);
    rset.next();
    System.out.println("User B is reserving room");
    pstmt = conn.prepareStatement(sqlUpdate);
    pstmt.setBoolean(1, true);
    pstmt.setString(2, "Jennifer");
    pstmt.setString(3,rset.getString(1));
    pstmt.setDate(4, rset.getDate(2));
    pstmt.setBoolean(5, rset.getBoolean(3));
    pstmt.executeUpdate();
    JDBCManagerV3.close(rset);
    JDBCManagerV3.close(pstmt);
  }

  static void userAUpdate() throws SQLException {
    System.out.println("User A is attempting to reserve room");
    pstmt = conn.prepareStatement(sqlUpdate);
    pstmt.setBoolean(1, true);
    pstmt.setString(2, "Beth");
    pstmt.setString(3,roomName);
    pstmt.setDate(4, roomDate);
    pstmt.setBoolean(5, reserveStatus);
    int result = pstmt.executeUpdate();
    if (result == 0) {
      System.out.println("Reservation did NOT succeed!");
      System.out.println("The user will have to try " +
                         "another room, or another date");
    }
    JDBCManagerV3.close(pstmt);
  }
}
```

2. Note that before this code can be run, you need to delete the reservations table we created in the previous example. At the command prompt, enter the following:

```
> cloudscape -isql
ij version 4.0 (c) 1997-2001 Informix Software, Inc.
WARNING 01J01: Database 'CloudscapeDB' not created, connection made to
existing database instead.
CONNECTION0* - jdbc:cloudscape:CloudscapeDB;create=true
* = current connection

ij> drop table RESERVE;
0 rows inserted/updated/deleted
ij> exit;
```

3. Compile the class using the usual compile command, make sure the Cloudscape RMI server is running, set the relevant classpath and then run the program using:

```
> java -Djdbc.drivers=COM.cloudscape.core.RmiJdbcDriver Ch07.OptimisticLocker
```

4. Here is the output from running the program on my system:

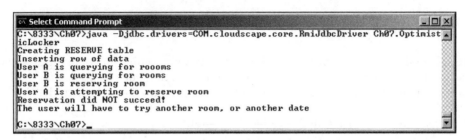

5. You can also verify that one reservation occurred and the other did not by running the Cloudscape `isql` tool. It runs from the same script file that runs the RMI server. Here's the output from my system:

```
> cloudscape -isql
ij version 4.0 (c) 1997-2001 Informix Software, Inc.
WARNING 01J01: Database 'CloudscapeDB' not created, connection made to
existing database instead.
CONNECTION0* -  jdbc:cloudscape:CloudscapeDB;create=true
* = current connection
ij> SELECT * from RESERVE;
ROOM&|RES_DATE   |RES_&|RES_NAME
--------------------------------------------------
PIKE |2002-12-20|true |Jennifer

1 row selected
```

You can see from the output of the SELECT command, that the table was updated with the reservation for user B, but not for user A.

How It Works

The four methods called by `main()`, demonstrate how optimistic locking works. The first method is the `setup()` method. This method creates the table and inserts a row of data into the table. The table simulates a room reservation system and it has four columns, one for a room ID, one for reservation date, one for a flag that indicates whether the room is reserved, and one for the name of the person who has the room reserved. The reservation name column is expected to be null when the room is not reserved. If you created the RESERVE table previously in the pessimistic locking example, you should drop that table using the `isql` tool:

```
> cloudscape -isql
ij version 4.0 (c) 1997-2001 Informix Software, Inc.
ij> drop table RESERVE;
```

The setup() method has to use a prepared statement to insert the row of data because of the special values used by the table. For instance, to set the reservation name column to null, the code has this line:

```
pstmt.setNull(4, java.sql.Types.VARCHAR);
```

As we saw in the *Prepared Statement* section of this chapter, with some data types, such as Date, it's easier to use a prepared statement; with other data values such as Boolean or null, using a prepared statement is the only way to insert those values into the table with JDBC.

Next, the userAQuery() method is called. This simulates a user querying for data from the table. To do the optimistic locking, this method also saves the values of the row it retrieved from the query. This can be done in this simple manner because I only inserted a single row into the table, and I knew that the query would return only a single row. In a real world application, the original query might return many rows, so you would want to wait until the user had selected a particular row before your code saves the data. At the completion of this method, the result set is no longer needed, so the code closes it.

The userBQueryAndUpdate() method simulates a second user querying and retrieving the same row as user A, and then updating that row. Since there is no lock on the data queried by user A, user B is not restricted from querying or updating the same data that user A is working with. This method also uses the prepared statement to update the data in the table. This time, however, the SQL command is an UPDATE command that uses optimistic locking. When the placeholders in the prepared statement are set with values, the SQL looks like this:

```
UPDATE RESERVE
   set RES_FLAG=true, RES_NAME='Jennifer'
  WHERE ROOMID='Pike' AND RES_DATE='2002-12-20' AND RES_FLAG=false
```

The SQL command that updates the two fields RES_FLAG and RES_NAME has a WHERE clause that checks that no one else has changed the row since user B queried the table. Since no one has, the WHERE clause matches the row, and the update proceeds.

Finally, user A attempts to reserve the room. The code in userAUpdate() uses the same UPDATE command with optimistic locking. When this SQL command is executed, the WHERE condition does not match any data in the table, because RES_FLAG is now true whereas it was false when user A first queried the table. Thus, there are no rows that can be updated and the update fails. The code checks for the return value, and when it sees that zero rows were updated, it logs the failure. If the SQL UPDATE command had only included the ROOM_ID and RES_DATE fields, the update would have proceeded and user B's update would have been lost.

Note that even though the example code executed step by step with no pauses, this does not need to be the case for lost updates to occur. All that need happen is for two or more users to query and attempt to change the same data in the same relative order as shown above: one user reads the data, a second user updates the data, the first user then attempts to update his view of the data which no longer matches what is in the database.

Notice also the differences between pessimistic locking and optimistic locking. With pessimistic locking, the first user to query the data gets to commit his changes. With optimistic locking, the first user to update the table gets to commit his changes. Pessimistic locking works better from the user's point of view; with optimistic locking, the user may expend significant effort to input all the changes he wants only to be told that the update failed when he tries to submit the data. On the other hand, pessimistic locking ties up a database resource, and depending on the database, can prevent other users from working with the database. Which method you choose will depend on the business rules of your application, and the type of locking supported by your database.

Summary

In this chapter we've looked at some advanced topics in JDBC, and how to use JDBC in a J2EE environment. If you are working in a real-world J2EE application, you will almost certainly find that you will be using at least some of the concepts in this chapter. Still, as mentioned in the overview of the first JDBC chapter of this book, there's so much more that wasn't covered. If you find yourself deeply into database programming, you should definitely explore some of the more advanced books that focus on the subject of databases and JDBC programming. If you're not heavily into JDBC, then hopefully this chapter has given you enough to keep you from becoming overwhelmed.

After finishing this chapter you should have learned:

- ❑ That connections in a J2EE environment are obtained from a `DataSource`. Data sources hide the connection details away from the client, making it easier to change databases. From the client's point of view, it doesn't matter where the connection comes from.

- ❑ `PreparedStatement` objects are used to send SQL commands to the database. `PreparedStatement` objects are useful when you are sending many SQL commands to the database, and only the data values are changing. Because the database caches the SQL, `PreparedStatements` can be more efficient that `Statement` objects. `PreparedStatements` are also useful when you need to insert non-primitive data into a table. `PreparedStatements` make it easy to insert Dates, Nulls, Strings, and so on, because the driver formats the data for you.

- ❑ `CallableStatement` objects are used to call stored procedures, aka sprocs, in a database. Stored procedures have many advantages, so if your system contains sprocs, you should consider using them rather than recreating their behavior in JDBC.

❏ Connection pools provide a way to avoid the time-consuming creation of new connections. Although you can use connection pools with or without data sources, in a J2EE environment, you will get pooled connections from a `DataSource`. Pooled connections are used just like non-pooled connections.

❏ Transactions are used to ensure that databases move from one consistent state to another. Properly using transactions can ensure that all the changes your code makes all succeed, or are all rolled back.

❏ A J2EE application needs to deal with problems of isolation and locking. Setting the proper isolation level can prevent one transaction from seeing changes made to the database by other transactions. Preventing two users from changing the same data such that one update is lost is usually done through pessimistic or optimistic locking.

Exercises

1. If your database does support stored procedures, find an existing stored procedure, or create one of your own, and write JDBC code that calls the stored procedures.

2. While not supporting stored procedures, Cloudscape does allow you to write Java code that works from the database. They call this a database-side JDBC method. Using the Cloudscape Developer's Guide, available at http://www-3.ibm.com/software/data/cloudscape/pubs/collateral.html, as a reference, write a database-side JDBC method and call it from Java code running outside the database.

3. Rewrite the `JDBCManager` class to use the Tomcat data source for getting connections. Rewrite the JSP presented in this chapter to use this new `JDBCManager` class.

CHAPTER 8

Understanding EJBs   353

A Closer Look at Session Beans   358

Summary   385

Exercises   386

EJB Fundamentals

So far we've discussed the user interface, business logic, and database connection aspects of developing J2EE applications. The primary mechanism discussed to this point for expressing business logic has been JavaBeans accessed from JSP and servlet code. J2EE has a powerful facility dedicated to expressing the business logic of an application, and for accessing a database using a JavaBeans-like concept. That facility is **Enterprise JavaBeans**, also know as **EJBs** for short.

In this chapter, we'll begin exploring the world of EJBs, which is a very important capability of the J2EE platform. EJBs provide infrastructure for developing and deploying mission-critical, enterprise applications.

Throughout the chapter, you will learn:

❑   The benefits of using EJBs

❑   The three kinds of EJBs; session, entity, and message-driven beans

❑   What is an EJB container

❑   How to develop session beans

❑   How to use **Java Naming and Directory Interface (JNDI)** to locate EJBs

❑   Differences between stateful and stateless session beans

Understanding EJBs

Application architectures often consist of several **tiers** that each have their own responsibilities. One such architecture that consists of three tiers is illustrated in the Unified Modeling Language (UML) diagram below:

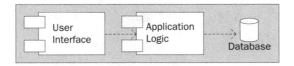

*The two elements on the left-hand side of the diagram are called **components** in the Unified Modeling Language (UML) notation. Components represent software modules. An overview of the UML is given in as part of the download bundle with this book, available on the Wrox web site.*

Multi-tiered, or **layered**, architectures have many advantages, not the least of which is the ability to change any one of the layers *without* affecting all of them. In the illustration above, if the *Database* layer is changed, only the *Application Logic* layer is affected. The *Application Logic* layer shields the *User Interface* layer from changes to the *Database* layer. This facilitates ongoing maintenance of the application, and increases its ability to incorporate new technologies in its layers. EJBs provide an application logic layer and a JavaBeans-like abstraction of the database layer. The application logic layer is also known as the middle tier.

> **JavaBeans and *Enterprise* JavaBeans are two different things, but because of their similarities (and for marketing reasons) they share a common name. JavaBeans are components built in Java that can be used on any tier in an application. They often thought of in relationship to servlets, and as GUI components. Enterprise JavaBeans are special, server-based components used for building the business logic and data access functionality of an application.**

Why Use EJBs?

Not too long ago, when system developers wanted to create an enterprise application, they would often start by "rolling their own" (or purchasing a proprietary) application server to support the functionality of the application logic layer. Some of the features of an application server include:

- ❑ **Client communication** – The client, which is often a user interface, must be able to call the methods of objects on the application server via agreed-upon protocols.

- ❑ **Session state management** – You'll recall our discussions on this topic in the context of JSP and servlet development back in Chapter 5.

- ❑ **Transaction management** – Some operations, for example when updating data, must occur as a unit of work. If one update fails, they all should fail. Recall that transactions were discussed in Chapter 7.

- ❑ **Database connection management** – An application server must connect to a database, often using **pools** of database connections for optimizing resources.

- ❏ **User authentication and role-based authorization** – Users of an application must often log in for security purposes. The functionality of an application to which a user is allowed access is often based upon the role associated with their user ID.

- ❏ **Asynchronous Messaging** – Applications often need to communicate with other systems in an **asynchronous manner**, that is, without waiting on the other system to respond. This requires an underlying messaging system that provides guaranteed delivery of these asynchronous messages.

- ❏ **Application server administration** – Application servers must be **administered**. For example, they need to be monitored and tuned.

The Enterprise JavaBeans specification defines a common architecture, which has prompted several vendors to build application servers that comply with this specification. Now we can get off-the-shelf application servers that comply with a common standard, benefiting from the competition (in areas such as price, features, and performance) among those vendors. Some of the more common commercial Enterprise JavaBeans application servers are: WebLogic (BEA), Sun ONE (Sun), and WebSphere (IBM).

There are also some very good open-source entries in this market such as JBoss and JOnAS. As you know, Sun provides a freeware Reference Implementation (J2EE SDK) of the J2EE 1.4 and EJB 2.1 specifications that may be used to develop as well as to test an application for compliance with those specifications. The Reference Implementation may not, however, be used to deploy production systems.

> *The Sun Reference Implementation was used to develop all of the examples and exercises contained in this book.*

These application servers, in conjunction with the capabilities defined in the EJB specification, support all of the features listed above and many more. Since they all support the EJB specification, we can develop full-featured enterprise applications and still avoid application server, operating system, and hardware platform vendor lock-in.

Yes, things sure have improved! We now have a standard, specification-based way to develop and deploy enterprise-class systems. We are approaching the Java dream of developing an application that can run on any vendor platform as-is. This is in contrast to the vendor-specific way we used to develop where each server had its own way of doing things, and where the developer was locked into the chosen platform once the first line of code was written!

For more information on the EJB specification, see the associated web site listed in the *Resources* section of this chapter.

The Three Kinds of EJBs

As we mentioned briefly at the start of this chapter, there are actually three kinds of EJBs:

❑ Session beans

❑ Entity beans

❑ Message-driven beans

When referring to them in the general sense in this book, we'll use the term **EJBs**, **enterprise beans**, or simply **beans**. Here is a brief introduction to each type of bean. The balance of this chapter will then focus on **session beans**.

Session Beans

One way to think about the application logic layer (middle tier) in the example architecture described above is as a set of objects that, together, implement the business logic of an application. Session beans are the construct in EJBs designed for this purpose. In the diagram below, we see that that there may be multiple session beans in an application and each handles a subset of the application's business logic. A session bean tends to be responsible for a group of related functionality. For example, an application for an educational institution might have a session bean whose methods contain logic for handling student records. Another session bean might contain logic that maintains the lists of courses and programs available at that institution.

There are two types of session bean, which are defined by their use in a client interaction:

❑ **Stateless** – these beans do not declare any instance (class-level) variables so that the methods contained within can only act upon any local parameters. There is no way to maintain state across method calls.

❑ **Stateful** – these beans can hold client state across method invocations. This is possible with the use of instance variables declared in the class definition. The client will then set the values for these variables and then use these values in other method calls.

Stateless session beans provide excellent scaleability because the EJB container does not have to keep track of their state across method calls. However, storing the state of an EJB is a very resource-intensive process. There may be more work involved for the server to share stateful session beans than stateless beans. So the use of stateful beans in your application may not make it as easily scaleable as using stateless beans.

All EJBs, session beans included, operate within the context of an **EJB Server**, shown in the diagram below. An **EJB Server** contains constructs known as **EJB containers** that are responsible for providing an operating environment for managing and providing services to the EJBs that are running within it.

In a typical scenario, the user interface (UI) of an application calls the methods of the session beans as it requires the functionality that they provide. Session beans can call other session beans and entity beans. The diagram below illustrates typical interactions between the user interface, session beans, entity beans, and the database:

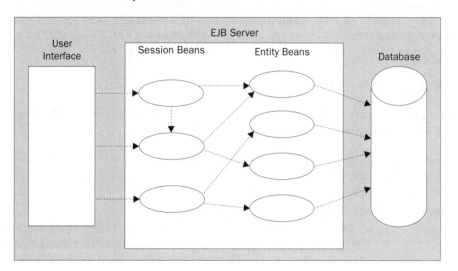

Entity Beans

Before object orientation became popular, programs were usually written in procedural languages and often employed relational databases to hold the data. Because of the strengths and maturity of relational database technology, it is now often advantageous to develop object-oriented applications that use relational databases. The problem with this approach is that there is an inherent difference between object-oriented and relational database technologies, making it less than natural for them to coexist in one application. The use of entity beans is one way to get the best of both of these worlds, because:

❏ Entity beans are objects, and they can be designed using object-oriented principles and utilized in applications as objects.

❏ The data in these entity bean objects are usually persisted in relational databases. All of the benefits of relational technologies, including maturity of products, speed, reliability, ability to recover, and ease of querying, can be leveraged.

In a typical EJB scenario, when a session bean needs to access data it calls the methods of an entity bean. Entity beans represent the persistent data in an EJB application. For example, an application for an educational institution might have an entity bean named Student that has one instance for every student that is enrolled in an institution. Entity beans, often "backed" by a relational database, read and write to tables in the database. Because of this, they provide an object-oriented abstraction to a relational database. Entity beans will be covered in detail in the next chapter.

Message-Driven Beans

When an EJB-based application needs to receive asynchronous messages from other systems, it can leverage the power and convenience of **message-driven beans**. Asynchronous messages between systems can be analogous to the events that are fired from a UI component to an event handler in the same JVM. One example application that could use message-driven beans is in the business to business (B2B) domain: a wholesaler could have an EJB application that uses message-driven beans to listen for purchase orders issued electronically from retailers.

Decisions, Decisions

So, how do you decide whether a given enterprise bean should be a session bean, entity bean, or a message-driven-bean? A set of rules to remember here:

❑ Session beans are great at implementing business logic, processes, and workflow. For example, a `StockTrader` bean with `buy()` and `sell()` methods, among others, would be a good fit for a session bean.

❑ Entity beans are the persistent data objects in an EJB application. In a stock trading application, a `Stock` bean with `setPrice()` and `getPrice()` methods would be an appropriate use of an entity bean. The `buy()` method of the previously mentioned `StockTrader` session bean would interact with instances of the `Stock` entity bean by calling their `getPrice()` methods for example.

❑ Message-driven beans are used for the special purpose of receiving asynchronous messages from other systems, like the fictitious wholesaler application mentioned above that listens for purchase orders.

By the way, as seen in the diagram above, it is a good practice to call only session beans directly from the client, and to let the session beans call the entity beans. Here are some reasons for this:

❑ This practice doesn't circumvent the business logic contained in the session beans. Calling entity beans directly tends to push the business logic into the UI logic, which is usually a bad thing.

❑ The UI doesn't have to be as dependent upon changes to the entity beans. The UI is shielded from these changes by the session beans.

❑ In order for a client to interact with a bean on the EJB server, there must be a remote reference to the bean, which takes resources. There tends to be far more (orders of magnitude) entity bean instances in an application than session bean instances. Restricting client access to session beans conserves server and network resources considerably.

A Closer Look at Session Beans

Now that we've covered some basics concerning the three types of EJBs, we'll use the rest of this chapter to take a closer look at the first type mentioned – session beans.

The Anatomy of a Session Bean

To develop a session bean, you actually need to create two Java interfaces and a Java class. These interfaces and the class are called the **home interface**, **bean interface**, and **bean class**, respectively. These are illustrated in the following diagram:

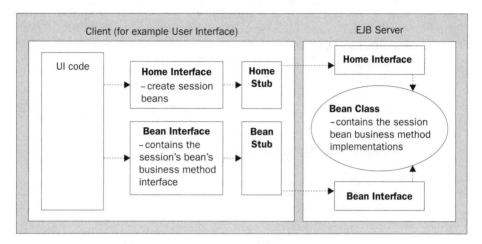

It is worth noting that developing entity beans also requires that you create a home interface, a bean interface, and a bean class. We'll make some entity beans in the next chapter.

The Home Interface

In order for the client of a session bean to get a reference to that bean's interface, it must use the bean's home interface. Incidentally, the home interface for an EJB extends the `EJBHome` interface of the `javax.ejb` package; the package that EJB-related classes reside in.

As a naming convention for this book, we'll append the word `Home` to the name of a bean to indicate that it is a home interface. For example, a session bean with the name StockTrader would have a home interface named `StockTraderHome`.

The Bean Interface

Session beans have an interface that exposes their business methods to clients. This bean interface extends the `EJBObject` interface of the `javax.ejb` package.

As a naming convention for this book, we'll use the name of a bean as the name of its bean interface. For example, a session bean with the name StockTrader would have a bean interface named `StockTrader`.

The Bean Class

The implementation of the business logic of a session bean is located in its bean class. The bean class of a session bean extends the `SessionBean` interface of the `javax.ejb` package.

As a naming convention for this book, we'll append the word Bean to the name of a bean to indicate that it is a bean class. For example, a session bean with the name StockTrader would have a bean class named `StockTraderBean`.

The Home and Bean Stubs

Also in the previous diagram are the **home stub** and the **bean stub** classes. These stubs are the mechanism by which the UI code on the client can invoke methods of the EJBs that are located on the server. The stubs invoke their respective interfaces on the server side via Java Remote Method Invocation (RMI). RMI is a protocol, included in J2SE 1.4, for invoking the Java methods of a class that exists on another JVM, perhaps on a different machine.

These stubs are created for you by the Deployment Tool that has been used in this book to build and deploy JSPs and servlets. We will use it to build and deploy EJBs as well.

Here is a UML class diagram that depicts the classes, interfaces, and relationships described above:

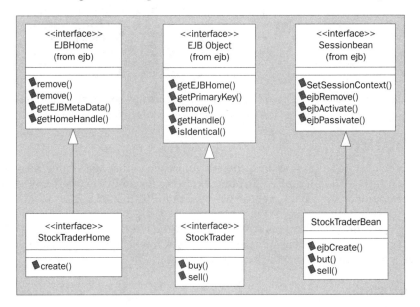

Developing Session Beans

Well, it is now time to put all this theory into practice. In this section, we're going to develop our first session bean in an example that's on par with the traditional "Hello World!" example program.

First, we'll walk through the bean creation code in a good bit of detail, reinforcing concepts we just learned, and covering new ones. Then, we'll explain how to compile the example. For this, we'll use the Java compiler that comes with the Java 2 SDK Standard Edition 1.4 (J2SE SDK 1.4). Then, we'll show you how deploy the example. For this we'll use the Deployment Tool. Finally, we'll run the application.

At the time of this writing, the beta version of J2EE SDK 1.4 is available. Please be advised that minor changes could occur in the API and tools between the beta and final releases.

Try It Out   **Creating a Session Bean**

Since this is the first EJB example, and we haven't learned to build and deploy EJBs yet, we're going to walk through the code now and then run it later. There are four Java source files for this example:

- ❑   SimpleSessionHome.java
- ❑   SimpleSession.java
- ❑   SimpleSessionBean.java
- ❑   SimpleSessionClient.java

1. The first source file contains the code for the home interface, and should be named SimpleSessionHome.java. The code that this file contains should be as follows:

```
package beans;
import java.rmi.RemoteException;
import javax.ejb.EJBHome;
import javax.ejb.CreateException;

public interface SimpleSessionHome extends EJBHome {
  // The create() method for the SimpleSession bean
  public SimpleSession create()
    throws CreateException, RemoteException;
}
```

2. This is the code for the bean interface, SimpleSession.java:

```
package beans;

import java.rmi.RemoteException;
import javax.ejb.EJBObject;

public interface SimpleSession extends EJBObject {
  // The public business method on the SimpleSession bean
  public String getEchoString(String clientString)
    throws RemoteException;
}
```

3. Next is the code for the bean class, SimpleSessionBean.java:

```
package beans;

import javax.ejb.SessionBean;
import javax.ejb.SessionContext;
```

```
public class SimpleSessionBean implements SessionBean {
  // The public business method. This must be coded in the
  // remote interface also.
  public String getEchoString(String clientString) {
    return clientString + " - from session bean";
  }

  // Standard ejb methods
  public void ejbActivate() {}
  public void ejbPassivate() {}
  public void ejbRemove() {}
  public void ejbCreate() {}
  public void setSessionContext(SessionContext context) { }
}
```

4. And this is the client code to test our session bean, `SimpleSessionClient.java`:

```
package client;

import beans.SimpleSession;
import beans.SimpleSessionHome;
import javax.naming.InitialContext;
import javax.rmi.PortableRemoteObject;

public class SimpleSessionClient {
  public static void main(String[] args) {
    try {
      // Get a naming context
      InitialContext jndiContext = new InitialContext();

      // Get a reference to the SimpleSession JNDI entry
      Object ref = jndiContext.lookup("ejb/beans.SimpleSession");

      // Get a reference from this to the Bean's Home interface
      SimpleSessionHome home = (SimpleSessionHome)
      PortableRemoteObject.narrow(ref, SimpleSessionHome.class);

      // Create a SimpleSession object from the Home interface
      SimpleSession simpleSession = home.create();

      // Loop through the words
      for (int i = 0; i < args.length; i++) {
        String returnedString = simpleSession.getEchoString(args[i]);
        System.out.println("sent string: " + args[i] +
                          ", received string: " + returnedString);
      }
    } catch(Exception e) {
      e.printStackTrace();
    }
  }
}
```

These files should be organized in the following subdirectory structure:

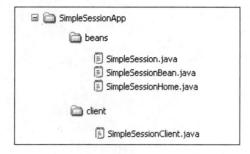

5.   Open a Command Prompt in the `SimpleSessionApp` directory.

6.   Now compile the classes ensuring that the `classpath` is set to contain the `j2ee.jar` library. At the command line type:

```
> set classpath=.;C:\j2sdkee1.4\lib\j2ee.jar
```

7.   Within the `SimpleSessionApp` directory that the `client` and `beans` directories are located, execute the following commands from the command prompt:

```
> javac -d . client/*.java
> javac -d . beans/*.java
```

The `-d` option tells the Java compiler to place the class files in subdirectories matching their package structure, subordinate to the given directory. In this case, the given directory is the current directory, signified by the period. As a result, the Java class files should end up in the same directories as the source files.

8.   Now we need to start the J2EE Server. This is very simple, just type `j2ee` at the command prompt.

9.   Once the J2EE Server is up and running we need to start the Deployment Tool. You can either start the tool from the command prompt by typing `deploytool`, or from the **Start** menu under the **Java 2 SDK, Enterprise Edition** program folder.

This will display a window that looks something like this:

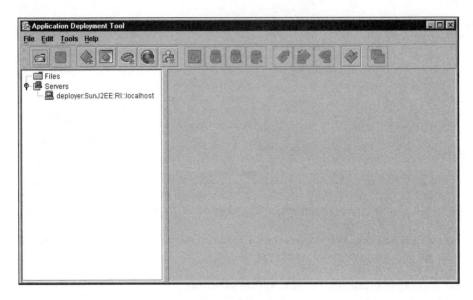

The first thing that we need the Deployment Tool to do is create the J2EE application, which will be bundled together in an **enterprise application resource** (**EAR**) file. EAR files are JAR files that contain all of the components of a J2EE application, including other JAR files and application deployment information. These other JAR files could contain:

❏ Enterprise beans and their deployment information

❏ Web application components and deployment information (recall our earlier discussion about WAR files in Chapter 7)

❏ Application client components and deployment information.

10. To create the application EAR file, from the File menu choose New I Application EAR.

11. A dialog box will be displayed, prompting you to enter the name of the EAR file, and the application name that you want displayed. Let's name the EAR file SimpleSessionApp.ear, and the application display name SimpleSessionApp:

Click OK to accept the changes to this dialog.

12. Now we'll create the JAR file in which the session bean classes and resources will be packaged. To do this, choose File | New | Enterprise JavaBean JAR menu item.

13. This will start the Enterprise Bean Wizard. The first page of this wizard is informational only, and on the second page (shown below) you will be asked to choose where you want the bean JAR to be placed. We're going to put it in our newly created `SimpleSessionApp.ear`. Also on this page is a place to enter the name for the bean JAR, we will call it SimpleSessionJar. Finally, click the Edit button on the page to pick the bean class files that you want to put in the bean JAR.

14. In the Available Files panel of the dialog box shown below, navigate to the `beans` directory of this `SimpleSessionApp` example. Choose the bean interface, the bean class, and the home interface, and click the Add button. Those bean classes will appear in the Contents of <EJB Bundle> panel as seen below:

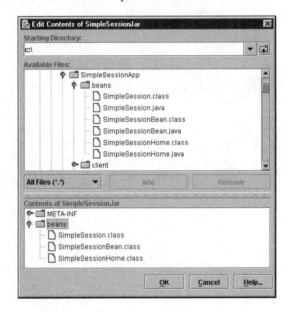

15. Click OK on the dialog box and then click the Next button.

The bean in the `SimpleSessionApp` example is a session bean, and we're going to make it a stateless session bean, so click that option. To remind you, stateless means it is not capable of storing any information within itself. We'll go into more detail about stateless session beans soon, but for now, make sure that Session and Stateless are the options selected.

16. You will then have three drop-down lists in which to make choices:

❏ From the Enterprise Bean Class drop-down, choose beans.SimpleSessionBean

❏ From the Remote Home Interface drop-down, choose beans.SimpleSessionHome

❏ From the Remote Interface drop-down, choose beans.SimpleSession

The Enterprise Bean Display Name is the name for the bean that you'd like to appear in EJB tools. The convention that we'll use is the name of the bean interface concatenated with Ejb, so enter SimpleSessionEjb into this field. When you're done with all this, your window should look like this:

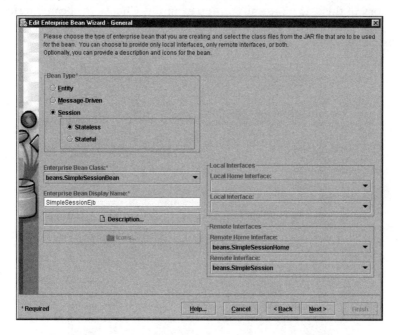

17. Click Next and the resulting dialog lets you choose the features that you want the bean to have. For example, you can indicate that you want the bean to be exposed as a **web service**; a concept that we'll cover in detail in Chapter 12 and Chapter 13. For this example, none of those features are necessary, so just click Next.

18. The last page of the Enterprise Bean Wizard shows the deployment descriptor that will be generated by the Deployment Tool, based upon the choices that you've made in the wizard. After you've looked it over, click the Finish button to leave the wizard:

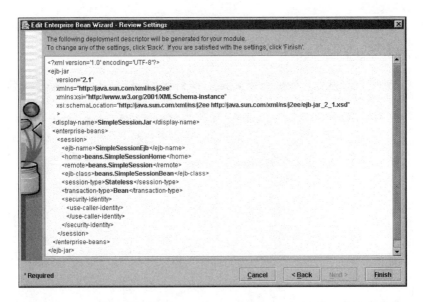

We now have the beans configured the way we want them, so we can deploy them.

To deploy the application on the J2EE server that comes with the J2EE SDK 1.4, in addition to the EJB deployment descriptor you just saw above, we need to create a deployment descriptor for that server. This is called a *platform-specific* deployment descriptor. To create this, complete the following steps:

19. Make sure that the SimpleSessionApp is selected in the left-hand panel. Then, choose File | Deployment Settings | Create New File... menu item.

20. A dialog box will be displayed, prompting you to enter the location that you want the platform-specific deployment descriptor to be placed. We'll take all of the defaults in this dialog box:

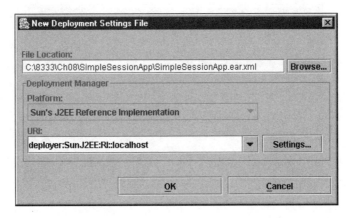

21. Now select the second node in the tree in the panel on the left that is labeled Sun's J2EE Reference Implementation. It should appear just below the SimpleSessionJar node.

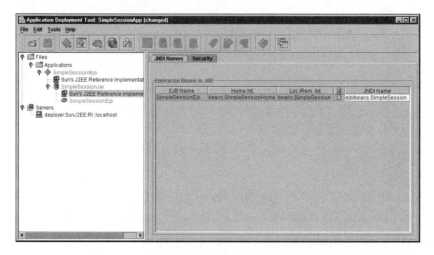

Remember the discussion we had about JNDI and how it helped the client get a reference to the home interface of the session bean. The screen shown above is where we can associate a JNDI name with a bean's home interface.

22. In the JNDI Name column of the table, type the same JNDI name that the client application uses in the `lookup()` method to obtain the bean's home reference. In this case, it is `ejb/beans.SimpleSession`.

23. To save the platform-specific deployment descriptor that we just created, choose the Deployment Settings menu item from the File menu, and then the Close File menu item. You should be prompted to save the deployment descriptor, so click the Save button:

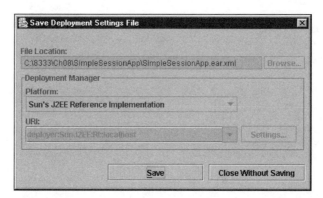

24. It is very important to save the whole application before performing the next step, so select Save All from the File menu.

There is one more thing to do before deploying the application: run the Verifier Tool to check whether we've configured the beans according to the EJB specifications.

25. Select the SimpleSessionApp node from the tree on the left panel and choose Verifier from the Tools menu.

26. To run the verification tests against the application, choose one of the Display options and click the OK button. We usually choose Failures Only option as shown below so that only the failed tests show up. The Results and the Details panels show the results of the tests and details of any problems encountered, respectively. If there are any problems encountered, then read the Details and go to the Deployment Tool page in which that detail is configured.

27. If there were no failed tests, then go ahead and deploy the application by selecting the SimpleSessionApp node in the tree in the left panel and selecting the Tools | Deploy menu item.

28. As a result, you should be prompted for the platform-specific deployment descriptor. As shown in the dialog box below, the default is the deployment descriptor that you just created, so just click the OK button:

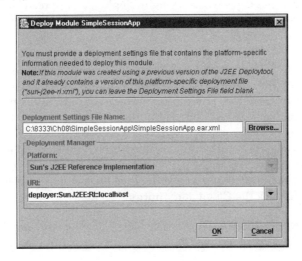

29. The following dialog will appear, and with any luck your bean should successfully deploy and start up, ready for clients to invoke its methods. Click the Close button when it becomes enabled:

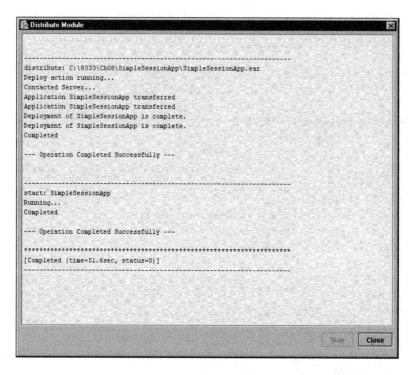

If there were any error messages when trying to deploy, please read the section called *Troubleshooting the Deploy*.

Creating the Client JAR

We now need to create a client JAR file that contains the stubs that we discussed earlier. Recall that these stubs live on the client and implement the home interface and bean interface. The client can call the methods defined by those interfaces, and the stubs propagate the method invocations to the home interface and bean interface on the server.

1. To create the client JAR, select the deployer:SunJ2EE:RI:localhost node in the **Servers** tree in the left panel. The right panel will display all of the deployed objects, including the SimpleSessionApp that you just deployed.Select the SimpleSessionApp entry in the panel, and click the **Client Jar...** button.

> *Note: As a good housekeeping measure, when you no longer need an application deployed you should visit this page, select the **Deployed Object**, and click **Undeploy**.*

2. You should be prompted for the name and location that you want the client JAR file to have. Choose the same directory that the bean and client directories are rooted in, which should also be the same directory that the platform-specific deployment descriptor was placed in. For this example, specify the name of file as SimpleSessionStubs.jar.

3. After clicking the **OK** button and encountering a confirmation dialog, we'll finally be ready to run the application.

Running the Application

The directory structure should now have the following files:

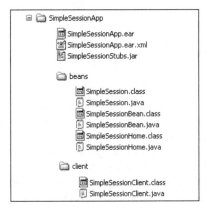

To run the example client, set the CLASSPATH to:

❑ The current directory (this example has used SimpleSessionApp)

❑ The j2ee.jar file that is in the lib directory of the Java 2 SDK, Enterprise Edition 1.4 (J2EE SDK 1.4) installation

❑ The SimpleSessionStubs.jar file of the current directory

Note that it is important to use the same filename for the client JAR in the CLASSPATH as you named it when creating it. In future examples, if you ever get a ClassCastException when first running the client, check to make sure that you used the same name in both places.

1. On a default J2EE SDK 1.4 Windows installation, ensure the CLASSPATH is set correctly by using the following command:

```
> set classpath=.;C:\j2sdkee1.4\lib\j2ee.jar;SimpleSessionStubs.jar
```

2. With SimpleSessionApp as the current directory, execute the following command from the command prompt:

```
> java client.SimpleSessionClient now is the time
```

3. When you run the SimpleSessionClient client program, it will produce the following output:

```
sent string: now, received string: now - from session bean
sent string: is, received string: is - from session bean
sent string: the, received string: the - from session bean
sent string: time, received string: time - from session bean
```

Not much output for all that work!

How It Works

We have four Java source files to walk through here. We'll start with the client and work our way back up to the session bean interfaces and class.

Using JNDI to Phone Home

The `main()` method of the `SimpleSessionClient` class kicks things off by using the Java Naming and Directory Interface (JNDI) to help us get a reference to the home interface of the session bean. JNDI provides a common interface to directories. The directory that we're dealing with here is internal to the EJB server and holds the reference to the home interface of our session bean. That reference is accessed using the JNDI name `ejb/beans.SimpleSession` which is the name we'll give it when we configure it using the Deployment Tool. The "/" and "." characters are used here as separators in the JNDI name.

```
InitialContext jndiContext = new InitialContext();

Object ref    = jndiContext.lookup("ejb/beans.SimpleSession");
```

After we get the reference, the following statement casts the reference to type `SimpleSessionHome`:

```
SimpleSessionHome home = (SimpleSessionHome)
PortableRemoteObject.narrow(ref, SimpleSessionHome.class);
```

Creating and Using the Session Bean Instance

A reference to the home interface of the session bean now exists on the *client*. We use that client-held home interface to create an instance of that bean on the *server* so that its methods may be invoked. The `create()` method creates an object that implements the bean interface on the client and returns it. In this example, that reference is stored in the variable named `simpleSession`:

```
SimpleSession simpleSession = home.create();
```

The client code for this example, which is shown below, demonstrates that we can pass an argument to a method of a session bean that exists on the server, operate on the argument in the method, and return a different value to the client. More specifically, the code loops through the arguments that were passed to the client's `main()` method via the command line, and passes them one at a time to the `getEchoString()` method of the session bean class. This is accomplished by calling the `getEchoString()` method of the bean interface that exists on the client:

```
for (int i = 0; i < args.length; i++) {
  String returnedString = simpleSession.getEchoString(args[i]);
  System.out.println("sent string: " + args[i] +
                     ", received string: " + returnedString);
}
```

Note that invoking the getEchoString() method of the bean interface on the client invokes the getEchoString() method of the session bean class on the server. This is possible due to the **stub classes** described above. These stub classes are also the reason that invoking the create() method of the bean's home interface on the client was able to cause the session bean to be created on the server. When the create() method of the home interface was called using the following line of code:

```
SimpleSession simpleSession = home.create();
```

it called the home stub class that was generated by the Deployment Tool. This home stub class implements the home interface that is defined in the SimpleSessionHome.java code listing, which we'll turn our attention to now. This interface extends the EJBHome interface located in the javax.ejb package:

```
public interface SimpleSessionHome extends EJBHome {
```

The EJBHome interface defines three methods:

❑   getEJBMetaData()

❑   getHomeHandle()

❑   remove()

SimpleSessionHome defines an additional method:

```
public SimpleSession create()
  throws CreateException, RemoteException;
```

The create() method is analogous to a constructor in a normal Java class. This particular create() method takes no arguments, but it is valid to define this method with parameters when it is desirable to pass in values at bean creation time. Like constructors, the create() method may be overloaded. When the bean is created in the EJB server, the ejbCreate() method of the bean class (SimpleSessionBean.java) will be called by the EJB container:

```
public void ejbCreate() {}
```

In this example, the ejbCreate() method is empty, so no additional initialization will take place apart from what the EJB container will perform. Note that if we had defined a create() method with parameters in the home interface, an ejbCreate() with matching parameters would be required in the bean class.

Since `SimpleSessionBean` implements the `SessionBean` interface of the `javax.ejb` package, it is necessary to implement the other session bean lifecycle methods defined by that interface as well. The EJB container is responsible for calling these methods at various points in the session bean's life cycle. In this case, they are implemented with empty methods:

```
public void ejbActivate() {}
public void ejbPassivate() {}
public void ejbRemove() {}
public void setSessionContext(SessionContext context) { }
```

The one and only business method in this particular session bean takes the argument passed in, appends a string of characters to it, and returns the result:

```
public String getEchoString(String clientString) {
  return clientString + " - from session bean";
}
```

This method is also defined in the bean interface specified in the `SimpleSession.java` code listing:

```
public String getEchoString(String clientString)
    throws RemoteException;
}
```

Note that the `getEchoString()` method defined in the bean interface declares that it throws a `RemoteException`, but the same method in the `SimpleSessionBean` class does need to declare that it throws that exception. This is because the business methods of the bean class are called by the EJB container, and not via RMI.

It may be helpful to refer again to the UML class diagram that depicts these classes, interfaces, and relationships. Now that we've looked at the session bean's Java source code, let's look at another source file that is necessary for session beans, the **deployment descriptor**.

About Bean Jars and Deployment Descriptors

A **bean jar** is a JAR file that is used by an EJB server, and which contains the class files for the EJBs and other resources. A **deployment descriptor** is an XML file that tells the EJB server how to deploy the beans that are in the **bean jar** file by defining their characteristics. Example characteristics include bean names, home interface names, transaction types, and bean method security access. Characteristics can be changed by editing the deployment descriptor without having to recompile the beans, which makes EJBs very flexible and maintainable. The deployment descriptor for this example was generated by the J2EE SDK 1.4 Deployment Tool, but it is possible to create and maintain it manually via a text or XML editor, and with other EJB server vendors' tools. The filename of the deployment descriptor is `ejb-jar.xml`, which is the EJB deployment descriptor that is portable across EJB server implementations. This XML file gets packaged and placed into the bean jar file by the Deployment Tool. The deployment descriptor for the `SimpleSession` example is shown below:

There are platform-specific deployment descriptors as well, which you could see by cracking open jar files that are created by various EJB tools.

```xml
<?xml version='1.0' encoding='UTF-8'?>
<ejb-jar
    version="2.1"
    xmlns="http://java.sun.com/xml/ns/j2ee"
    xmlns:xsi="http://www.w3.org/2001/XMLSchema-instance"
    xsi:schemaLocation="http://java.sun.com/xml/ns/j2ee
                        http://java.sun.com/xml/ns/j2ee/ejb-jar_2_1.xsd"
    >
  <display-name>SimpleSessionJar</display-name>
  <enterprise-beans>
    <session>
      <ejb-name>SimpleSessionEjb</ejb-name>
      <home>beans.SimpleSessionHome</home>
      <remote>beans.SimpleSession</remote>
      <ejb-class>beans.SimpleSessionBean</ejb-class>
      <session-type>Stateless</session-type>
      <transaction-type>Bean</transaction-type>
      <security-identity>
        <use-caller-identity>
        </use-caller-identity>
      </security-identity>
    </session>
  </enterprise-beans>
</ejb-jar>
```

Since the `ejb-jar.xml` file is portable across EJB server implementations, we will examine it in conjunction with the EJB code examples to learn about configuring enterprise bean characteristics. Let's look at a few characteristics in this example.

A bean jar's `display-name` is the name that would appear in a given vendor's EJB tools, for example an EJB server administration tool:

```xml
<display-name>SimpleSessionJar</display-name>
```

A bean's `ejb-name` is a unique name for that bean within the `ejb-jar.xml` file:

```xml
<ejb-name>SimpleSessionEjb</ejb-name>
```

The class names of the home interface, bean interface, and bean class are specified as well:

```xml
<home>beans.SimpleSessionHome</home>
<remote>beans.SimpleSession</remote>
<ejb-class>beans.SimpleSessionBean</ejb-class>
```

We mentioned briefly that a bean interface can be a *remote* interface or a *local* interface. This will be covered in detail in the next chapter, but for now, note that the `<remote>` element indicates that the bean interface is a remote interface. This indicates that the bean's methods can be called from outside the JVM that it resides in.

Another bean characteristic in the `ejb-jar.xml` file is the `session-type`. In this example, the `SimpleSessionBean` is `Stateless`, which means that it can't be relied upon to remember anything after each method invocation. Anyway, we'll have more to say about **stateless** (and **stateful**) session beans later in this chapter.

Troubleshooting the Deploy

We know that it's hard to believe, but occasionally your application may not deploy successfully on the first try. This is exacerbated by the fact that we're using a reference implementation deployment tool, and a beta version (as of this writing) at that. So if you get an exception in the Distribute Module dialog after attempting deployment, there are a few things you can do to rectify the situation:

❑   Obviously, go back and verify that all the instructions were followed, and run the Verifier Tool.

❑   If you are still getting exceptions when deploying, then try the following steps until you get a successful deploy. Again, we were using a beta version of the Deployment Tool, so perhaps some of this won't be necessary for you:

1.   Select the applications in the tree on the left, and select Close from the File menu. Exit the Deployment tool. Stop the J2EE application (closing the J2EE window will usually accomplish this). Start the J2EE application again. Start the Deployment Tool. Open your application again by selecting the Open from the File menu and finding your application EAR file. Try to deploy again.

2.   If it still doesn't deploy, then repeat the above step, rebooting your machine after stopping the J2EE application.

3.   If it still doesn't deploy, then uninstall the J2EE SDK (backing up anything that you care about in J2EE SDK directory structure) and reinstall. This may seem like a drastic measure but since we are working with a beta version it may be required.

4.   If the application still won't deploy, then it seems reasonable that a bean configuration detail has been missed or incorrectly performed.

When the bean is successfully deployed, we'll get the client ready to access it.

What Did We Learn from This?

In this `SimpleSessionApp` example, we learned how to develop a session bean, including how to deploy and start it in a J2EE application server. We also learned how to develop a client application that uses session beans. As we briefly mentioned in the deployment descriptor discussion, the `SimpleSessionBean` was deployed as a stateless session bean, which means that it can't be counted on to retain data between method invocations. The next section will introduce the idea of a **stateful** session bean, and compare these two types.

Stateful vs. Stateless Session Beans

As mentioned previously, session beans are great choice for implementing business logic, processes, and workflow. When you choose to use a session bean to implement that logic, you have yet another choice to make: whether to make that session bean **stateful** or **stateless**.

Choosing Between Stateful and Stateless

Consider a fictitious stock trading application where the client uses the `buy()` and `getTotalPrice()` methods of a `StockTrader` session bean. If the user has several different stocks to buy and wants to see the running total price on the tentative purchases, then that state needs to be stored somewhere. One place to store that kind of transient information is in the instance variables of the session bean itself. This requires that the session bean be defined as stateful, as we learned previously, in the `ejb-jar.xml` (EJB deployment descriptor) file.

There are advantages for choosing that a session bean be stateful, and some for it being stateless. Some advantages of being stateful are:

❑   Transient information, such as that described in the stock trading scenario, can be stored easily in the instance variables of the session bean, as opposed to defining and using entity beans (or JDBC) to store it in a database.

❑   Since this transient information is stored in the session bean, the client doesn't have to store it and potentially waste bandwidth by sending the session bean the same information repeatedly with each call to a session bean method. This bandwidth issue is a big deal when the client is installed on a user's machine that invokes the session bean methods over a phone modem, for example. Bandwidth is also an issue when the data is very large or needs to be sent many times repeatedly.

The main disadvantage of being stateful is:

❑   Stateful session beans don't scale up as well on an EJB server, because they require more system resources than stateless session beans do. A couple of reasons for this are that:

   ❑   Stateful session beans require memory to store the state.

❑   Stateful session beans can be swapped in and out of memory (activated and passivated) as the EJB container deems necessary to manage server resources. The state gets stored in a more permanent form whenever a session bean is passivated, and that state is loaded back in when the bean is activated.

By the way, you may recall that the SessionBean interface defines several session bean lifecycle methods, including ejbActivate() and ejbPassivate(). A stateful session bean class can implement these methods to cause special processing to occur when it is activated or passivated.

Let's look at an example of using stateful session beans in the context of a device that stores state – a calculator.

Try It Out   Creating a Stateful Session Bean

This example mimics some very simple operations on a calculator: adding, subtracting, and keeping a running total. Not very impressive by today's standards, but you would have paid good money for a calculator with those functions in the early 1970s! That "keeping a running total" part is what we'll be demonstrating with the help of a stateful session bean. A screenshot of the GUI client follows the instructions to build and run the example.

There are four Java source files in this example:

❑   Calculator.java (in the beans package)

❑   CalculatorBean.java (in the beans package)

❑   CalculatorHome.java (in the beans package)

❑   CalculatorClient.java (in the client package)

Listed below are the bean-related classes only. The source code for CalculatorClient.java, as well as the source code for all the examples in this book, may be downloaded from the Wrox web site.

1.   Add the following code files to a new application directory called SimpleCalculatorApp. Within the directory add beans and client subdirectories. Copy the code for CalculatorClient.java into the client directory.

Here is the code for the home interface, CalculatorHome.java:

```
package beans;

import java.rmi.RemoteException;
import javax.ejb.EJBHome;
import javax.ejb.CreateException;
```

```
public interface CalculatorHome extends EJBHome {
  // The create method for the Calculator bean.
  public Calculator create()
    throws CreateException, RemoteException;
}
```

As in the previous example, we supply a no-argument `create()` method.

This is the code for the bean interface, `Calculator.java`:

```
package beans;

import java.rmi.RemoteException;
import javax.ejb.EJBObject;

public interface Calculator extends EJBObject {
  // The public business methods on the Calculator bean
  public void clearIt() throws RemoteException;
  public void calculate(String operation, int value)
    throws RemoteException;
  public int getValue() throws RemoteException;
}
```

It defines the three business methods of the calculator.

The code for the bean class, `CalculatorBean.java`:

```
package beans;

import java.rmi.RemoteException;
import javax.ejb.SessionBean;
import javax.ejb.SessionContext;

public class CalculatorBean implements SessionBean {
  // Holds the calculator value
  private int _value = 0;

  // The public business methods. These must be coded in the
  // remote interface also.

  // Clear the calculator
  public void clearIt() {
    _value = 0;
  }

  // Add or subtract
  public void calculate(String operation, int value)
    throws RemoteException {
    // If "+", add it
```

379

```
    if (operation.equals("+")) {
      _value = _value + value;
      return;
    }

    // If "-", subtract it
    if (operation.equals("-")) {
      _value = _value - value;
      return;
    }

    // If not "+" or "-", it is not a valid operation
    throw new RemoteException("Invalid Operation");
  }

  // Return the value
  public int getValue() throws RemoteException {
    return _value;
  }

  // Standard ejb methods
  public void ejbActivate() {}
  public void ejbPassivate() {}
  public void ejbRemove() {}
  public void ejbCreate() {}
  public void setSessionContext(SessionContext context) { }
}
```

2. Now compile the java files following the same instructions as in the previous example. At the command line type:

```
> set classpath=.;C:\j2sdkee1.4\lib\j2ee.jar
```

3. Within the `SimpleCalculatorApp` directory that the `client` and `beans` directories are located, execute the following commands from the command prompt:

```
> javac -d . client/*.java
> javac -d . beans/*.java
```

4. Now start the J2EE Server and then the Deployment Tool.

5. Create a new EAR file for the application, from the File menu choose New I Application EAR.

6. In the New Application dialog box, name the Application File Name `SimpleCalculatorApp.ear`. As before, this file should be located in the base directory of the example. In the same New Application dialog box, make the Application Display Name SimpleCalculatorApp.

7. Now create the JAR file for the session bean classes and resources. Choose the File | New | Enterprise JavaBean JAR menu item.

8. In the EJB JAR page of the Edit Enterprise Bean Wizard, make the JAR Display Name SimpleCalculatorJar. We will create the JAR in the `SimpleCalculatorApp.ear`.

9. Press the Edit button in the Contents section of the page. In the Available Files dialog that appears, navigate to the `beans` directory and choose the three Calculator bean-related classes.

10. Once these have been added, click Next.

11. In the General page of the wizard, it is very important that you choose session and stateful as the bean type, as this example demonstrates the use of stateful session beans.

12. You will then have three drop-down lists in which to make choices:

❑ From the Enterprise Bean Class drop-down, choose beans.CalculatorBean

❑ From the Remote Home Interface drop-down, choose beans.CalculatorHome

❑ From the Remote Interface drop-down, choose beans.Calculator

13. Enter SimpleCalculatorEjb as the Enterprise Bean Display Name, and then click Next.

14. Again leave the Configuration Options page at its default settings and click Next.

15. Check the deployment descriptor to see if all the settings are correct and click Finish.

We now have the beans configured; we now need to create the platform-specific deployment descriptor.

1. Make sure that the SimpleCalculatorApp is selected in the left-hand panel. Then, choose File | Deployment Settings | Create New File... menu item. Accept all the defaults in the dialog.

2. Again select the second node in the tree in the left-hand panel below the SimpleCalculatorJar node and enter `ejb/beans.SimpleCalculator` in the JNDI Name column of the table that is in the JNDI Names tab.

3. To save the platform-specific deployment descriptor that we just created, choose the Deployment Settings menu item from the File menu, and then the Close File menu item. You should be prompted to save the deployment descriptor, so click the Save button.

4. Again run the Verifier tool to check your application remembering to save the application before verifying.

5. We can now deploy the application by selecting the SimpleCalculatorApp node in the tree in the left panel and selecting the Tools | Deploy menu item. Again you will be prompted for the platform-specific deployment descriptor. The default is the deployment descriptor that you just created, so just click the OK button.

Creating the Client JAR

1. In the Deployed Objects screen select and click the Client Jar... button, be sure to select the SimpleCalculatorApp entry before clicking the button.

2. In the dialog box, name the client JAR file SimpleCalculatorStubs.jar. While you're on this screen, go ahead and undeploy the previous example if still deployed, by clicking the Undeploy button.

After doing all of the above steps, we can now get on with running the application.

Running the Application

1. On a default J2EE SDK 1.4 Windows installation, the CLASSPATH would be set correctly by using the following command:

```
> set classpath=.;c:\j2sdkee1.4\lib\j2ee.jar;SimpleCalculatorStubs.jar
```

2. With SimpleCalculatorApp as the current directory, execute the following command from the operating system prompt:

```
> java client.CalculatorClient
```

The graphical user interface (GUI) of the client should appear like this when run:

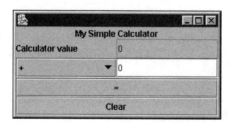

To operate the calculator, type a number into the text box, select an operation (+ or -) from the drop-down, and click the = button. The running total will be displayed beside the Calculator value label.

How It Works

To understand how this example works, we'll walk through some of the GUI client code contained in the `CalculatorClient.java` source file, and then we'll take a closer look at some of the EJB code shown above. By the way, in the code examples you'll notice that some of the `import` statements are wildcards and some explicitly name the class or interface. For instructional purposes, we've chosen to be explicit on the imports that are relevant to J2EE, the subject of this book. We've chosen to be more frugal with lines of code by using wildcards the more familiar ones that are relevant to J2SE.

The client is a standard Java Swing application, complete with GUI components and event handler methods. The client needs to call methods of the stateful session bean, so as in the previous example it gets a reference to the bean's home interface and creates the session bean on the server. The code that performs this is in the `getCalculator()` method of the `CalculatorClient` class, which is called from the constructor:

```
    private Calculator getCalculator() {
      Calculator calculator = null;
      try {
        // Get a naming context
        InitialContext jndiContext = new InitialContext();

        // Get a reference to the Calculator JNDI entry
        Object ref  = jndiContext.lookup("ejb/beans.SimpleCalculator");

        // Get a reference from this to the Bean's Home interface
        CalculatorHome home = (CalculatorHome)
          PortableRemoteObject.narrow(ref, CalculatorHome.class);

        // Create a Calculator object from the Home interface
        calculator = home.create();
      } catch(Exception e) {
        e.printStackTrace();
      }
      return calculator;
    }
```

When the = button is clicked, two things are passed to the `calculate()` method of the calculator session bean: the operator (either + or -), and the value to be added or subtracted from the running total:

```
        _calculator.calculate(oper, operVal);
```

Since it is a stateful session bean, it is able to store the running total in an instance variable. The client then calls the `getValue()` method of the calculator session bean to retrieve the running total and subsequently display it:

```
        _topNumber.setText("" + _calculator.getValue());
```

When the user presses the Clear button, the `clearIt()` method of the calculator session bean is called, which sets the running total to 0.

And Now the Bean Code

The implementations of the three calculator business methods of the `CalculatorBean` class are shown below. They manipulate the instance variable named `_value`, which holds the running total between invocations of any of these calculator session bean methods.

```
// Clear the calculator
public void clearIt() {
  _value = 0;
}

// Add or subtract
public void calculate(String operation, int value)
   throws RemoteException {
   // If "+", add it
   if (operation.equals("+")) {
     _value = _value + value;
     return;
   }

   // If "-", subtract it
   if (operation.equals("-")) {
     _value = _value - value;
     return;
   }

   // If not "+" or "-", it is not a valid operation
   throw new RemoteException("Invalid Operation");
}

// Return the value
public int getValue() throws RemoteException {
   return _value;
}
```

There are a couple of more points to take away from this example:

❑   There is no indication in any of the session bean code that it is stateful – that is controlled by the `ejb-jar.xml` file (deployment descriptor). An excerpt of the `ejb-jar.xml` file for the calculator stateful session bean appears below.

❑   A session bean that holds values in instance variables should never be configured as stateless, because the values of the instance variables are not predictable. This is because the EJB container has complete control over managing stateless (and stateful) session beans, including initializing the values of instance variables as the bean is shared among various clients. This is a common trap because sometimes the values are retained, giving a false indication that everything is OK, and then one day you can't figure out why the program isn't working correctly. From personal experience, that's a fun one to diagnose!

Indicating Stateful in the Deployment Descriptor

Here is an excerpt of the `ejb-jar.xml` file for the calculator example. Note that the `session-type` is `Stateful`:

```
   ...
<display-name>SimpleCalculatorJar</display-name>
<enterprise-beans>
  <session>
    <ejb-name>CalculatorEjb</ejb-name>
    <home>beans.CalculatorHome</home>
    <remote>beans.Calculator</remote>
    <ejb-class>beans.CalculatorBean</ejb-class>
    <session-type>Stateful</session-type>
    <transaction-type>Bean</transaction-type>
    <security-identity>
      <use-caller-identity>
      </use-caller-identity>
    </security-identity>
  </session>
</enterprise-beans>
</ejb-jar>
```

Summary

In this chapter, we learned what Enterprise JavaBeans are, and built a case for using them. We touched on the three types of EJBs: session beans, entity beans, and message-driven beans. Then we covered when to use each type.

The balance of this chapter was then devoted to session beans, and we started that discussion by explaining that session beans are made up of three parts; the home interface, the bean interface, and the bean class. During the session bean discussions we experienced the following concepts in the context of code examples:

- ❑ Java Naming and Directory Interface (JNDI)
- ❑ Creating session beans
- ❑ Application EAR, bean JAR, and client JAR files
- ❑ Deployment descriptors
- ❑ Compiling, configuring, and deploying session beans
- ❑ Using the J2EE SDK Deployment Tool to configure EJBs
- ❑ Stateless and stateful session beans

Now that we've explored session beans, in the next chapter we'll turn our attention to another type of enterprise bean – the entity bean.

Exercises

1. Write a stateless session bean that takes a word and returns it spelled backwards.

2. Write a stateful session bean that takes one word at a time and appends it to the previous words received to make a sentence. Return the entire sentence each time a word is added.

3. Modify the previous exercise, adding a stateless session bean with a method that counts the number of letters in a word. Call this method from the builder bean to count the number of letters in each word. Show this number in the returned string.

CHAPTER 9

A Closer Look at Entity Beans   389

Developing CMP Entity Beans   395

Developing BMP Entity Beans   415

Summary   444

Exercises   445

EJB Entity Beans

The previous chapter gave us an introduction to enterprise beans, including an overview of the different types of enterprise beans. These types are session beans, entity beans, and message-driven beans. We previously looked at session bean development in a good level of detail.

In this chapter and the following one, we'll focus on developing the second type of enterprise beans, **entity beans**, which are the persistent data objects in an EJB application.

In this chapter you will learn:

- ❑ More about what an entity bean is
- ❑ Similarities and differences between entity bean and session beans
- ❑ How to develop entity beans
- ❑ Finding an entity bean via its primary key
- ❑ Local vs. remote interfaces
- ❑ Container-managed persistence
- ❑ Finding entity beans with the EJB Query Language

A Closer Look at Entity Beans

As mentioned in the previous chapter, entity beans can provide an object-oriented abstraction of a relational database. They are essentially JavaBeans that are backed by a persistent data store. Entity beans work well with session beans in providing the server-side functionality of the application. The following diagram from Chapter 8 depicts how session and entity beans work together for this purpose:

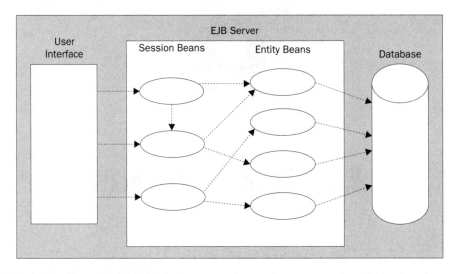

Session beans generally implement the business logic, processes, and workflow of an application, and entity beans are the persistent data objects. For example, the first example in this chapter is an application that manipulates stocks. We will create a session bean named StockList that implements the processes that a stockbroker might use for manipulating stocks. We will also create an entity bean named Stock whose instances represent individual stocks.

For the reasons discussed in the previous chapter, it is a good practice for the client to call session beans methods, and for session beans to manipulate the entity beans. These reasons are:

❑ Calling entity bean methods directly circumvents the business logic contained in session beans, and tends to push the business logic into the UI code.

❑ Session beans can protect the UI from changes to the entity beans.

❑ Restricting client access to session beans conserves server and network resources.

The Anatomy of an Entity Bean

Since entity beans are *enterprise* beans, they have some anatomy in common with their session bean siblings. Some of these commonalities are the entity bean's home interface, bean interface, and bean class. The following diagram illustrates these:

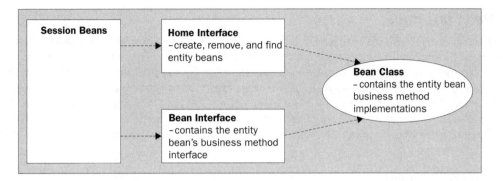

Session beans use an entity bean's home and bean interfaces to create, find, remove, and use entity beans. Strictly speaking, other clients such as user interfaces and external systems could use these interfaces as well, although as we stated previously, this is not usually the best practice.

The Home Interface

The home interface of an entity bean is used to create a new entity bean, remove one, or find an existing one. Because entity beans are backed by an underlying database, these methods cause the database to be queried and/or updated. This will be covered in the upcoming *Container-Managed Persistence* section.

- ❑ Calling a `create()` method creates a new entity bean instance. As with session beans, `create()` methods in EJBs are analogous to constructors in regular classes, and can be overloaded.

- ❑ Calling a `remove()` method of the home interface deletes the specified entity bean.

- ❑ Calling a **find** method of the home interface finds the appropriate entity bean instances and returns them. Entity beans have at least one such find method, named `findByPrimaryKey()`, and more find methods can be defined by the developer.

As with session beans, the home interface for an entity bean extends the `EJBHome` interface of the `javax.ejb` package. As a naming convention, we'll append the word `Home` to the name of an entity bean to indicate its home interface. For example, an entity bean with the name `Stock` would have a home interface named `StockHome`.

The Local Home Interface

When two beans are in the same EJB container, a leaner variation of the home interface theme may be used, called the **local home interface**. Local home interfaces have less overhead because they don't require the use of Java RMI and stubs to communicate, since the beans exist within the same JVM. By the way, when a home interface isn't a local one, it is sometimes referred to as a **remote home interface**. The home interfaces that we developed in the previous chapter were remote home interfaces, characterized by the fact that they utilize Java RMI and stubs.

The Bean Interface

The bean interface for an entity bean is analogous to the bean interface for a session bean. They both are interfaces that expose a bean's methods. In the case of entity beans, however, the exposed methods are primarily setters and getters for the fields of the entity bean, but they often contain business logic as well. In this way, entity beans are very much like traditional JavaBeans. Like session beans, the **bean interface** extends the EJBObject interface of the javax.ejb package. As a naming convention, we'll use the name of an entity bean as the name of its bean interface. For example, an entity bean with the name Stock would have a bean interface named Stock.

The Local Bean Interface

Similar to the local home interface introduced earlier, there is a variation of the bean interface called the **local bean interface**, or more commonly, the **local interface**. By the way, when a bean interface isn't a local one, it is sometimes referred to as a **remote bean interface**, or more commonly, a **remote interface**. The interfaces that we developed in the previous chapter were remote interfaces, characterized by the fact that they utilize Java RMI and stubs. Local interfaces and local home interfaces can be used with both session and entity beans. We'll discuss local interfaces and local home interfaces in more detail a little later in the chapter.

The Bean Class

The bean class of an entity bean contains:

- ❑ The getter and setter methods specified in the bean interface. For example, a StockBean class might have a field named tickerSymbol, with a getter method named getTickerSymbol() and a setter method named setTickerSymbol(). We sometimes call entity bean fields **virtual fields** because it is not required that there is actually a field in the entity bean named tickerSymbol. The getter and setter method names just imply the name of a field, similar to JavaBean properties.

- ❑ Methods specified in the bean interface that contain business logic. These methods typically access and manipulate the fields of the entity bean. For example, if we had an entity bean named StockTransactionBean with a price field and a quantity field, a method named getTransactionAmount() could be created to multiply the two fields and return the amount of the transaction.

- ❑ Life-cycle methods that are called by the EJB container. For example, as with session beans, the ejbCreate() method is called by the container when the create() method of the home interface is called. These are analogous to constructors in normal Java classes, and can be overridden to pass in initialization values.

The bean class of an entity bean extends the EntityBean interface of the javax.ejb package. As with session beans, we'll append the word Bean to the name of a bean to indicate that it is a bean class. For example, an entity bean with the name Stock would have a bean class named StockBean.

Here is a UML class diagram that depicts some of the classes, interfaces, and relationships described above. It will also serve as the class diagram of the first *Try It Out* example a little later in this chapter:

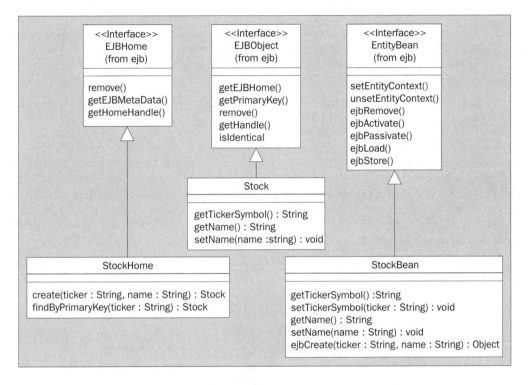

Other Features of Entity Beans

We've been discussing the features of entity beans that have some commonality with session bean features. Now let's turn our attention to some features that are *unique* to entity beans.

Container-Managed Persistence

Entity beans are backed by some type of persistent data store, often a relational database. There is a feature of entity beans that makes this persistence automatic, which is called **container-managed persistence** (**CMP**). Recall from the previous chapter that an EJB **container** is a facility within an EJB server that manages, and provides services to, the EJBs running within it. With CMP, an entity bean is mapped to a database table that is dedicated to the purpose of storing instances of that entity bean. For example, an entity bean named Stock might have a table named stock, stock_table, or perhaps StockBeanTable dedicated to it. Each record in the table would represent an instance of the entity bean. So, using a table named StockBeanTable and looking back at the home interface methods:

- ❑ Calling a `create()` method of the home interface of the `Stock` bean not only creates the entity bean – it also creates a row in the `StockBeanTable` table to persist it. Note that the EJB container manages this process for you, including choosing at what point in time to create the new row.

- ❑ Calling a `find()` method of the home interface finds the appropriate row(s) in the `StockBeanTable` table and returns an entity bean from each of those rows. The fields of the entity beans are loaded from the columns in the corresponding row of the `StockBeanTable` table.

- ❑ Calling a `remove()` method of the home interface deletes the entity bean, and deletes the associated row from the `StockBeanTable` table. Again, it is up to the EJB container to choose when the row gets deleted.

Also, calling the getter and setter methods corresponding to the fields of the entity bean cause the fields of the database table to be read from, and written to, respectively. These fields are often called **CMP fields**, as they are managed by the container. In the class diagram above, the `Stock` entity bean has two CMP fields: `tickerSymbol` and `name` as indicated by its getters and setters. When using CMP, the schema of the database directly reflects the design of the entity beans, as shown below:

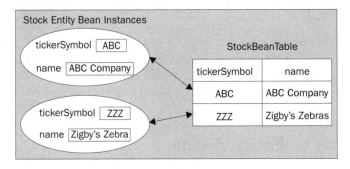

The alternative to container-managed persistence is **bean-managed persistence (BMP)**, in which you get to write all that persistence logic yourself. This should be considered in situations where:

- ❑ A database already exists in a legacy system, and you are building an EJB-based application on top of that database. If the design of the entity beans do not match the existing database schema, then a BMP would be required.

- ❑ There is no database, but rather, the entity beans are "wrapper" for an external system.

- ❑ The EJB server doesn't support CMP with the database that you are using.

Because of their simplicity, we prefer to use CMP whenever possible. Note that most of the entity bean discussions and examples in this book are of the CMP variety, and are in accordance with the EJB 2.1 specification. There is one BMP example coming up, however, to give you an idea of how to develop this type of entity bean. Now let's look at another enterprise bean feature that is unique to entity beans; **primary keys**.

Primary Keys

A requirement of an entity bean is that one or more of its CMP fields must make it unique. This field (or combination of fields) is known as the **primary key**, which is useful in finding a particular entity bean. A primary key may be any serializable object, such as a `String` or an `Integer`. Primary keys also enable another nice feature of entity beans: the ability of the EJB container to manage the relationships between entity beans. This feature is called **container-managed relationships**, or **CMR**.

Container-Managed Relationships

Like a relational database, entity beans have an **abstract schema**, this defines the CMP fields of each entity bean and the container-managed relationships between entity beans. For each relationship, there are corresponding methods in the related entity beans that refer to each other. Container-managed relationships will be covered in more detail in the next chapter.

EJB Query Language

There is a feature of entity beans called the EJB Query Language (EJB-QL) that enables SQL-like queries to be run against entity beans. These queries are encapsulated in entity bean methods so that developers that use an entity bean can call methods instead of constructing SQL queries.

We'll work through code that demonstrates the entity bean features described above in the *Try It Out* examples, so let's get busy!

Developing CMP Entity Beans

As mentioned above, entity beans can have their data persistence managed by the EJB container through the use of a database. Consequently, designing the entity beans in an application can be very much like designing the tables in a relational database, keeping in mind that entity beans are objects and therefore can have business methods as well as data.

During analysis, the entities, which are often "nouns", in a problem domain are analyzed as candidates for being represented as entity beans. For example, an application that helps students manage their education might have entity beans such as `Student`, `Institution`, `Counselor`, `Course`, and `Program`.

Another logical step is to discover what persistent fields each entity bean should have. For example, the `Course` entity bean could have CMP fields such as name of the course, and the course abstract.

Let's now work through an example to get some experience with entity beans that have container-managed persistent fields.

Try It Out   Creating an Entity Bean that uses CMP

This example application demonstrates the container-managed persistence feature of entity beans. It is a very simple application in which the user can create, find, update, and delete stocks. This application uses two enterprise beans:

❑   An entity bean named Stock that holds information about stocks. There is one instance of this entity bean per stock.

❑   A session bean named StockList that uses the Stock beans and provides business methods to the UI that enables it to maintain the Stock beans.

A screenshot of the GUI client, and a description of its behavior, follows the instructions to build and run the example. Let's go ahead and build the application so that you can use it yourself.

The source files involved in this example used to define the Stock entity bean are contained in the beans subfolder:

❑   Stock.java

❑   StockBean.java

❑   StockHome.java

The source files that define the StockList session bean are also contained in the beans subfolder:

❑   StockList.java

❑   StockListBean.java

❑   StockListHome.java

The source file that defines the user interface client lives in the client subfolder:

❑   StockClient.java

1.   Add the following code files to their respective subfolders in the StockListApp application directory.

First is Stock.java:

```
package beans;

import java.rmi.RemoteException;
import javax.ejb.EJBObject;

public interface Stock extends EJBObject {
    // The public business methods on the Stock bean
    // These include the accessor methods from the bean
```

```
  // Get the ticker. Do not allow ticker to be set through the
  // interface because it is the primary key.
  public String getTickerSymbol() throws RemoteException;

  // Get and set the name
  public String getName() throws RemoteException;
  public void setName(String name) throws RemoteException;
}
```

Next is `StockBean.java`:

```java
package beans;

import javax.ejb.CreateException;
import javax.ejb.EntityBean;
import javax.ejb.EntityContext;

public abstract class StockBean implements EntityBean {

  // Keeps the reference to the context
  private EntityContext _context;

  // The abstract access methods for persistent fields
  public abstract String getTickerSymbol();
  public abstract void setTickerSymbol(String ticker);

  public abstract String getName();
  public abstract void setName(String name);

  // Standard entity bean methods
  public Object ejbCreate(String ticker, String name)
    throws CreateException {

    setTickerSymbol(ticker);
    setName(name);
    return null;
  }

  public void ejbPostCreate(String ticker, String name)
    throws CreateException { }

  public void setEntityContext(EntityContext ctx) {
    _context = ctx;
  }

  public void unsetEntityContext() {
    _context = null;
  }

  public void ejbRemove() { }
```

```
   public void ejbLoad() { }
   public void ejbStore() { }
   public void ejbPassivate() { }
   public void ejbActivate() { }
}
```

Then `StockHome.java`:

```
package beans;

import java.rmi.RemoteException;
import javax.ejb.CreateException;
import javax.ejb.EJBHome;
import javax.ejb.FinderException;

public interface StockHome extends EJBHome {
  // The create method for the Stock bean
  public Stock create(String ticker, String name)
    throws CreateException, RemoteException;

  // The find by primary key method for the Stock bean
  public Stock findByPrimaryKey(String ticker)
    throws FinderException, RemoteException;
}
```

Then `StockList.java`:

```
package beans;

import java.rmi.RemoteException;
import javax.ejb.CreateException;
import javax.ejb.EJBObject;
import javax.ejb.FinderException;

public interface StockList extends EJBObject {
   // The public business methods on the StockList bean
   public String getStock(String ticker)
     throws FinderException, RemoteException;
   public void addStock(String ticker, String name)
     throws CreateException, RemoteException;
   public void updateStock(String ticker, String name)
     throws FinderException, RemoteException;
   public void deleteStock(String ticker)
     throws FinderException, RemoteException;
}
```

Next is `StockListBean.java`:

```
package beans;

import javax.ejb.CreateException;
import javax.ejb.FinderException;
import javax.ejb.SessionBean;
import javax.ejb.SessionContext;
import javax.naming.InitialContext;
```

```
import javax.naming.NamingException;
import javax.rmi.PortableRemoteObject;

public class StockListBean implements SessionBean {

  // The public business methods. These must be coded in the
  // remote interface also.

  public String getStock(String ticker) throws FinderException {
    try {
      StockHome stockHome = getStockHome();
      Stock stock = stockHome.findByPrimaryKey(ticker);
      return stock.getName();
    } catch (FinderException fe) {
      throw fe;
    } catch (Exception ex) {
      throw new RuntimeException(ex.getMessage());
    }
  }

  public void addStock(String ticker, String name) throws CreateException {
    try {
      StockHome stockHome = getStockHome();
      stockHome.create(ticker, name);
    } catch (CreateException ce) {
      throw ce;
    } catch (Exception ex) {
      throw new RuntimeException(ex.getMessage());
    }
  }

  public void updateStock(String ticker, String name)
   throws FinderException {
    try {
      StockHome stockHome = getStockHome();
      Stock stock = stockHome.findByPrimaryKey(ticker);
      stock.setName(name);
    } catch (FinderException fe) {
      throw fe;
    } catch (Exception ex) {
      throw new RuntimeException(ex.getMessage());
    }
  }

  public void deleteStock(String ticker) throws FinderException {
    try {
      StockHome stockHome = getStockHome();
      Stock stock = stockHome.findByPrimaryKey(ticker);
      stock.remove();
    } catch (FinderException fe) {
      throw fe;
    } catch (Exception ex) {
```

```
      throw new RuntimeException(ex.getMessage());
    }
  }

  private StockHome getStockHome() throws NamingException {
    // Get the initial context
    InitialContext initial = new InitialContext();

    // Get the object reference
    Object objref = initial.lookup("ejb/beans.Stock");
    StockHome home = (StockHome)
      PortableRemoteObject.narrow(objref, StockHome.class);
    return home;
  }

  // Standard ejb methods
  public void ejbActivate() {}
  public void ejbPassivate() {}
  public void ejbRemove() {}
  public void ejbCreate() {}
  public void setSessionContext(SessionContext context) {}
}
```

And finally `StockListHome.java`:

```
package beans;

import java.rmi.RemoteException;
import javax.ejb.CreateException;
import javax.ejb.EJBHome;

public interface StockListHome extends EJBHome {
  // The create method for the Stock List bean.
  public StockList create() throws CreateException, RemoteException;
}
```

We're not going to show the complete client code here due to it's size since it is available in the code download from the Wrox web site. However, the code contained in the file will be discussed later.

2. Now compile the source code for the application:

❑ As pointed out in the previous example, on a default J2EE SDK 1.4 Windows installation the `classpath` would be set correctly by using the following command:

> **set classpath=.;C:\j2sdkee1.4\lib\j2ee.jar**

❑ Within the directory that the `client` and `beans` directories are located, execute the following commands from the command prompt:

```
> javac -d . client/*.java
> javac -d . beans/*.java
```

3. We now need to start the J2EE Server, the Deployment Tool, and the Cloudscape database server. Using the same command prompt used for the compiling of the java files enter `j2ee`. Once the J2EE server has started start the deployment tool by typing `deploytool`.

Cloudscape is a lightweight database server that comes with the J2EE SDK 1.4, and will serve as the database in which our entity beans will be persisted. To start it up, type the following command from your operating system prompt:

```
> cloudscape -start
```

4. Once these are all running we can then create the application EAR file by choosing New | Application EAR from the File menu. Set the Application File Name to StockListApp.ear in the application directory, and the Application Display Name to StockListApp.

5. We can now create the bean JAR. Start the Edit Enterprise Bean Wizard by choosing the File | New | Enterprise JavaBean JAR menu item.

❑ Set the JAR Display Name to StockListJar. You will see the class files for the `Stock` entity bean, but you only need to choose the three EJB class files for the `StockList` session bean. For your convenience you can use the drop-down list in the dialog shown below to show only the files with the `.class` extension:

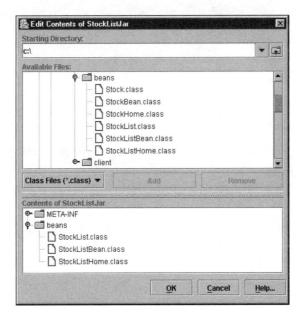

6. After clicking Next, in the General dialog make the session bean Stateless, choose the class and interfaces in the drop-downs for the session bean, and set the Enterprise Bean Display Name to StockListEjb. Click Next.

7. Don't choose any of the options on the Configuration Options page.

8. Now we're going to create another bean JAR, this time for the Stock entity bean. You'll start this process the same way that you created the bean JAR for the session bean: by choosing the New menu item from the File menu, and then choosing Enterprise JavaBean JAR. When the following page appears:

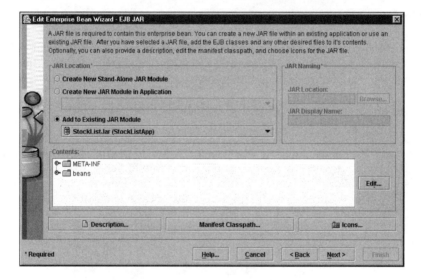

We will need to do the following:

❑ Choose the Add to Existing JAR Module option if it isn't already selected. This is because we're going to put our entity bean in the same bean JAR file as the session bean.

❑ Verify that the application shown in the drop-down is StockListApp.

❑ Then click the Edit button to select only the three Stock entity bean .class files (Stock.class, StockBean.class, and StockHome.class) to be put into this JAR. In the dialog box (not shown), don't forget to click the Add button before clicking OK.

9. When you click the Next button, select the Entity Bean Type, and choose the class and interface names from the three drop-downs as shown. Also, set the Enterprise Bean Display Name to StockEjb:

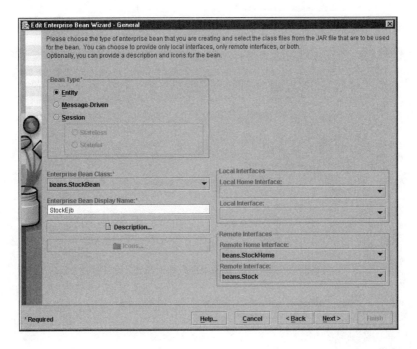

10. It is recommended for many of the methods of container-managed entity beans to run in the auspices of a transaction, so please choose the Transaction Management option from the Configuration Options page.

11. The next page in this wizard is the Entity Settings page:

❑ Our entity bean is going to use Container-Managed Persistence 2.0, so select that option. Version 1.1, by the way, didn't support **container-managed relationships**, a feature that we'll be discussing a little later.

❑ The Deployment Tool used reflection to discover the getter/setter methods so that it could offer the Fields To Be Persisted choices shown. We'll choose both fields to be CMP fields because we want both of them to be persisted.

❑ We're going to use the tickerSymbol field as the primary key for the Stock bean since ticker symbols are unique, so select it in the Primary Key Field Name drop-down. The setter and getter methods for this field accept and return a String, so select java.lang.String in the Primary Key Class drop-down.

❑ You'll recall from our earlier discussion that the CMP fields of entity beans define an **abstract schema**, which is sometimes referred to as an **abstract persistence schema**. The Deployment Tool creates tables in a database, for persistence purposes, that matches the schema defined by our entity beans and fields. Let's make Stock the Abstract Schema Name for this entity bean. We'll be able to use that name in EJB-QL queries later in the chapter.

The page should now look like below:

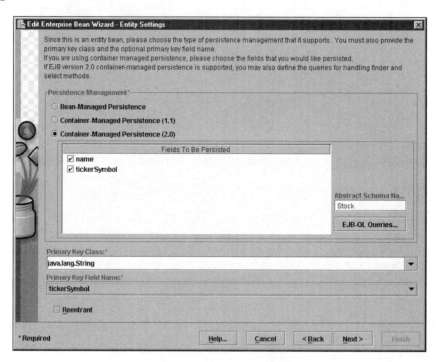

12. The Transaction Management page should appear next:

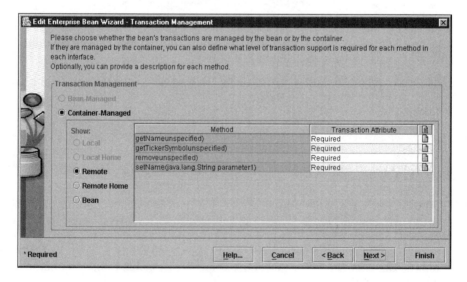

❑   **Container-Managed** should be selected, and we'll specify that transactions are required for all of this entity bean's methods. To do this, select **Remote**, and then **Remote Home**, verifying that the **Transaction Attribute** of each method is set to **Required**.

*In the beta version of the J2EE SDK 1.4 Deployment Tool used as of this writing, we' found it necessary to manually select the **Required Transaction Attribute** for the* `create()` *method in the **Remote Home** option. Failing to do so resulted in problems when trying to deploy the application. When running the Verifier, this problem is characterized by failing the following test:*

```
tests.ejb.entity.TransactionDemarkationHomeInterface
```

This is a known issue in the J2EE SDK Deployment Tool, and is, hopefully, fixed in the final release.

13. Now we create the platform-specific deployment descriptor, making sure that **StockListApp** is selected in the left pane. Choose the **Deployment Settings** menu item from the **File** menu, and then choose the **Create New File** menu item. After the file has been created, select the **Sun's J2EE Reference Implementation** entry that is subordinate to the **StockListJar** entry in the tree in the left pane.

The next page that should appear is where we can take care of the platform-specific business of deploying the entity bean:

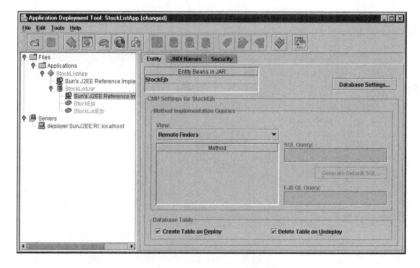

14. In the Entity tab, we're going to take care of database-related issues:

❑   Select the **StockEjb** entry in the **Entity Beans in JAR** panel, which is in the Entity tab.

❑   We can choose for the Deployment Tool to create the table that provides the persistence for this entity bean when you deploy the application. To make this choice, verify that the **Create Table on Deploy** checkbox is checked.

405

❑ Let's also choose that the table that persists the entity bean be deleted when that entity bean is undeployed. To do this, make sure that the **Delete Table on Undeploy** checkbox is checked. You would almost never want to check this option in a "live" application, because it would delete your data when undeployed.

15. Click the **Database Settings** button, will produce the following dialog box:

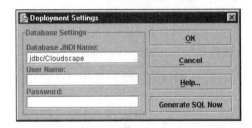

In this dialog box, we'll tell the Deployment Tool which database server to use, and we'll let it generate the SQL required for each of the CMP methods to interact with the table. To accomplish both of these things, you will need to:

❑ Enter jdbc/Cloudscape as the **Database JNDI Name**

❑ Click the **Generate SQL Now** button

16. After closing this dialog, click on the **JNDI Names** tab and you will see something like the following:

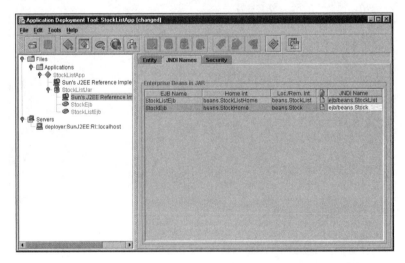

In this dialog:

❑ Give the Stock entity bean the **JNDI Name** ejb/beans.Stock.

❑ Give the StockList session bean the **JNDI Name** ejb/beans.StockList

17. Close and save the deployment settings file.

18. Now save the application. You can do this by selecting StockListApp in the tree on the left and then selecting the Save menu item from the File menu. Failing to do so has been known to result in problems when trying to deploy the application!

Before deploying the application, let's get in the habit of making sure that no other applications are deployed.

The main reason for doing this is that some of these examples use the same JNDI name for a session bean, and we want the correct session bean reference to be found. Also, we want this reference implementation of the J2EE server to be stable as long as possible. To verify that no other applications are deployed, select deployer:SunJ2EE:RI::localhost in the tree in the left panel, and click the Undeploy button for any applications that are listed in the table.

19. Select the StockListApp node from the tree on the left panel and choose Verifier from the Tools menu. Choose Failures Only from the button list and run the Verifier.

20. If there are no error then we can deploy the application. Select the StockListApp node in the tree in the left panel and selecting the Tools | Deploy menu item.

21. Once the application is deployed we can then create the client stubs JAR.

Select deployer:SunJ2EE:RI::localhost again, selecting the deployed StockListApp application, and clicking the Client Jar button. Let's go with the name StockListStubs.jar for this.

22. To run the client, set the classpath to use the client JAR, from the command prompt enter the following:

```
> set classpath=.;c:\j2sdkee1.4\lib\j2ee.jar;StockListStubs.jar
```

You can enter the following command to run the client that uses the beans we've built:

```
> java client.StockClient
```

Here is a screenshot of the Stock List application user interface that was taken while the user was adding an entry for Sun Microsystems stock:

After at least one stock name has been added, the user can enter a symbol and click the **Get** button, which causes the desired entity bean to be found and its name displayed. Changing the **Name** text field and clicking the **Update** button causes the CMP name field of the entity bean to be updated. Clicking the **Delete** button results in the entity bean being deleted.

Now that we've built, deployed, and run the application, let's see how it works.

How It Works

We're going to examine the code for this example from the inside out, beginning with the entity bean. A diagram of these entity bean classes is contained in the section titled *The Bean Class*, which we passed through earlier in the chapter. Let's first look at the entity bean home interface, StockHome.java:

```
. . .
public interface StockHome extends EJBHome {
   // The create method for the Stock bean
   public Stock create(String ticker, String name)
     throws CreateException, RemoteException;

   // The find by primary key method for the Stock bean
   public Stock findByPrimaryKey(String ticker)
     throws FinderException, RemoteException;
}
```

There are two methods defined in the Stock entity bean's home interface.

❑ The create() method acts like a constructor in that it creates a new instance of the Stock entity bean, allowing initialization arguments to be passed in. As we'll see in the bean class code, these arguments will be tucked away into CMP fields of the new entity bean instance. Note that if the entity bean couldn't be created, a CreateException will be thrown. This exception will be thrown, for example, when an entity bean with the given primary key (in this case the ticker argument) already exists.

❑ The findByPrimaryKey() method locates and returns the entity bean with the specified primary key. In the case of the Stock entity bean, the primary key is the ticker symbol. One very nice feature of the findByPrimaryKey() method is that all you have to do is declare the method in the home interface. The deployment tool generates the code to implement it. Note that if the desired entity bean doesn't exist, a FinderException will be thrown.

Now let's look at the entity bean interface, Stock.java:

```
. . .
public interface Stock extends EJBObject {
   // The public business methods on the Stock bean
   // These include the accessor methods from the bean
```

```
    // Get the ticker. Do not allow ticker to be set through the
    // interface because it is the primary key.
    public String getTickerSymbol() throws RemoteException;

    // Get and set the name
    public String getName() throws RemoteException;
    public void setName(String name) throws RemoteException;
}
```

There are setter and getter methods for the name CMP field, but only a getter method for the tickerSymbol field. This is because we don't want the primary key to be altered after the entity bean instance has been created, so we make the setTickerSymbol() method unavailable in the bean interface. The methods of a remote interface must declare that they throw RemoteException, but the same methods in the bean class, as we see below, are not required to throw that exception.

Next we'll look at the entity bean class, StockBean.java:

```
    ...
    public abstract class StockBean implements EntityBean {

        // Keeps the reference to the context
        private EntityContext _context;

        // The abstract access methods for persistent fields
        public abstract String getTickerSymbol();
        public abstract void setTickerSymbol(String ticker);

        public abstract String getName();
        public abstract void setName(String name);
```

Why are the two pairs of setter and getter methods for the CMP fields declared abstract? The answer is that the implementation code is created by the deployment tool, because that behavior is specific to the EJB server and database server implementation.

```
        // Standard entity bean methods
        public Object ejbCreate(String ticker, String name)
          throws CreateException {

          setTickerSymbol(ticker);
          setName(name);
          return null;
        }
```

The constructor-like ejbCreate() method takes the arguments passed in and initializes the CMP fields with those values. There are a few things worth pointing out here:

❑   This is where `tickerSymbol`, the primary key field, gets initialized.

❑   The value of the `tickerSymbol` field is set via the `setTickerSymbol()` method of this bean class. This is the same method that we removed from the bean interface earlier to prevent clients from changing the primary key value.

❑   It is standard for the `ejbCreate()` method to return a `null` value.

```
public void ejbPostCreate(String ticker, String name)
  throws CreateException { }
```

The `ejbPostCreate()` method gives you a chance to do extra initialization after the CMP fields are initialized, but before the entity bean is used by other beans. For example, manipulating container-managed relationship fields is not allowed in an `ejbCreate()` method, but is allowed in an `ejbPostCreate()` method. Container-managed relationships will be covered in the next chapter.

```
public void setEntityContext(EntityContext ctx) {
  _context = ctx;
}

public void unsetEntityContext() {
  _context = null;
}

public void ejbRemove() { }
public void ejbLoad() { }
public void ejbStore() { }
public void ejbPassivate() { }
public void ejbActivate() { }
}
```

The rest of the methods are called by the EJB container during key points in the entity bean's life cycle. For example:

❑   The `setEntityContext()` is called by the EJB container after the entity bean instance is created. The `EntityContext` passed in is the environment in which the entity bean is running. This is analogous to the relationship of an `Applet` and the `AppletContext` in which is running, for example.

❑   The `ejbRemove()` method is called by the EJB container after the `remove()` method of the home interface or bean interface is called, and just before the entity bean is deleted. Implementing this method gives you the opportunity to do extra cleanup if desired.

The Session Bean

Let's turn our attention to the `StockList` session bean, which uses our entity bean. The session bean home interface, `StockListHome.java`, should be quite obvious with the single `create()` method.

410

Now the session bean interface, `StockList.java`:

```
...
public interface StockList extends EJBObject {
   // The public business methods on the StockList bean
   public String getStock(String ticker)
     throws FinderException, RemoteException;
   public void addStock(String ticker, String name)
     throws CreateException, RemoteException;
   public void updateStock(String ticker, String name)
     throws FinderException, RemoteException;
   public void deleteStock(String ticker)
     throws FinderException, RemoteException;
}
```

The four methods in that interface will be used by the client to carry out the **Get**, **Add**, **Update**, and **Delete** stock operations shown in the GUI client. Notice that they throw either the `FinderException` or the `CreateException` located in the `javax.ejb` package. These exceptions are the mechanism in which we will tell the client that an EJB operation failed. For example, when calling the `updateStock()` method, if the supplied `ticker` didn't exist, it would throw the `FinderException`.

And now, on to the session bean class, `StockListBean.java`. To support the functionality we have built into the GUI client, the following methods of the session bean are employed, respectively:

- ❑ `getStock()`
- ❑ `addStock()`
- ❑ `updateStock()`
- ❑ `deleteStock()`

Each of these methods calls the `getStockHome()` method of the session bean to get a home interface reference to the `Stock` entity bean. The code in that method is the same as we've used in past examples to get a home interface reference to a session bean from our clients. Why do each of these methods call `getStockHome()`, as opposed to calling it once and putting it in an instance variable? The reason is that we specified when using the deployment tool that the session bean should be stateless. Therefore it cannot be trusted to retain the home interface reference.

```
public String getStock(String ticker) throws FinderException {
   try {
     StockHome stockHome = getStockHome();
     Stock stock = stockHome.findByPrimaryKey(ticker);
     return stock.getName();
   ...
}
```

After the `getStock()` method gets a `Stock` entity bean home interface reference, it calls the `findByPrimaryKey()` method of the home interface, passing in the desired ticker symbol. If successfully found, it asks the `Stock` entity bean for the value held in its CMP name field, and returns the value:

- ❑ The `addStock()` method gets the `Stock` entity bean's home interface reference and calls its `create()` method.

- ❑ The `updateStock()` method uses the `findByPrimaryKey()` method to get the desired `Stock` entity bean reference, and uses a CMP method to update the name field.

- ❑ The `deleteStock()` method uses the `findByPrimaryKey()` method to get the desired `Stock` entity bean reference. It then calls the `remove()` method that the `Stock` interface inherited from the `EJBObject` interface. It is worth pointing out that the `remove()` method exists in both the home interface and bean interface. It is also worth noting that, as with some other methods noted previously, the code for the `remove()` method is generated for you.

The source code for `StockClient.java`, as well as the source code for all the examples in this book, may be downloaded from the Wrox web site. The `StockClient` class gets a reference to a session bean as shown below:

```java
private StockList getStockList() {
  StockList stockList = null;
  try {
    // Get a naming context
    InitialContext jndiContext = new InitialContext();

    // Get a reference to the StockList JNDI entry
    Object ref = jndiContext.lookup("ejb/beans.StockList");

    // Get a reference from this to the Bean's Home interface
    StockListHome home = (StockListHome)
      PortableRemoteObject.narrow(ref, StockListHome.class);

    // Create a StockList object from the Home interface
    stockList = home.create();
  } catch(Exception e) {
    e.printStackTrace();
  }

  return stockList;
}
```

It also calls the session bean's methods as needed by the user interface. The methods that call the session bean's methods catch either the `FinderException` or `CreateException` thrown from the enterprise beans in order to alert the user to these conditions. This is seen, for example, in the `addStock()` method below:

```
private void addStock() {
  // Get the ticker
  String ticker = _ticker.getText();
  if (ticker == null || ticker.length() == 0) {
    JOptionPane.showMessageDialog(this, "Ticker is required");
    return;
  }

  // Get the name
  String name = _name.getText();
  if (name == null || name.length() == 0) {
    JOptionPane.showMessageDialog(this, "Name is required");
    return;
  }

  // Add the stock
  try {
    _stockList.addStock(ticker, name);
    JOptionPane.showMessageDialog(this, "Stock added!");
  } catch (CreateException fe) {
    JOptionPane.showMessageDialog(this, "Already found!");
  } catch (Exception e) {
    e.printStackTrace();
  }
}
```

The Deployment Descriptor

Here is an excerpt of the `ejb-jar.xml` file that holds the deployment descriptor for both the `StockList` and `Stock` beans. This excerpt reflects some choices that we made in the deployment tool:

```
...
<display-name>StockListJar</display-name>
<enterprise-beans>
  <session>
    <ejb-name>StockListEjb</ejb-name>
    <home>beans.StockListHome</home>
    <remote>beans.StockList</remote>
    <ejb-class>beans.StockListBean</ejb-class>
    <session-type>Stateless</session-type>
    <transaction-type>Bean</transaction-type>
    <security-identity>
      ...
    </security-identity>
  </session>
  <entity>
    <ejb-name>StockEjb</ejb-name>
    <home>beans.StockHome</home>
    <remote>beans.Stock</remote>
    <ejb-class>beans.StockBean</ejb-class>
```

413

```
      <persistence-type>Container</persistence-type>
      <prim-key-class>java.lang.String</prim-key-class>
      <reentrant>false</reentrant>
      <cmp-version>2.x</cmp-version>
      <abstract-schema-name>Stocks</abstract-schema-name>
      <cmp-field>
        <description>no description</description>
        <field-name>name</field-name>
      </cmp-field>
      <cmp-field>
        <description>no description</description>
        <field-name>tickerSymbol</field-name>
      </cmp-field>
      <primkey-field>tickerSymbol</primkey-field>
      <security-identity>
        ...
      </security-identity>
    </entity>
  </enterprise-beans>
  <assembly-descriptor>
    ...
    <container-transaction>
      <method>
        <ejb-name>StockEjb</ejb-name>
        <method-intf>Remote</method-intf>
        <method-name>getTickerSymbol</method-name>
      </method>
      <trans-attribute>Required</trans-attribute>
    </container-transaction>
    ...
  </assembly-descriptor>
</ejb-jar>
```

You'll notice that both the session and entity beans are defined in the <session> and <entity> elements, respectively.

Also, the following snippet specifies that the Stock bean will use container-managed persistence:

```
      <persistence-type>Container</persistence-type>
```

And this snippet specifies that one of the CMP fields will be tickerSymbol:

```
      <cmp-field>
        <description>no description</description>
        <field-name>tickerSymbol</field-name>
      </cmp-field>
```

The following snippet specifies that the primary key is a String, and that the tickerSymbol field is the primary key:

```
<prim-key-class>java.lang.String</prim-key-class>
...
<primkey-field>tickerSymbol</primkey-field>
```

In this section, we learned about, and walked through an example of, an entity bean that uses container-managed persistence. In the next section, we'll learn how to develop entity beans that don't rely on the EJB container to provide persistence.

Developing BMP Entity Beans

In the event that container-managed persistence is not an option, perhaps for one of the reasons mentioned previously, entity beans must supply their own persistence mechanism. Such entity beans use a technique that is appropriately named **bean-managed persistence** (**BMP**).

The following example demonstrates this technique by converting the Stock entity bean in the previous example from a CMP entity bean to a BMP entity bean. Let's see how this works:

Try It Out   Creating an Entity Bean that uses BMP

This example application demonstrates how to develop an entity bean that uses bean-managed persistence. Everything, including the GUI client behavior, is the same as the previous example. In fact, only one Java source file changed: StockBean.java. This file contains the source for the bean implementation class, and may be downloaded from the Wrox web site. We won't show it here due to its size.

Building and Deploying the BMP Example

The process to build and run this example is almost the same as the previous example, and all of the Java source filenames are the same. Follow the steps from the previously example for compiling, configuring, and deploying the application (with the suggested differences noted below).

1. Create a new application directory called StockListBMPApp with beans and client subfolders. Copy the code files into their respective directories.

2. After compiling the files start the J2EE Server, Deployment Tool, and Cloudscape.

3. Create a new application EAR file, the application name we will use in this example is: StockListBmpApp.

4. Create and populate the bean JAR using StockListBmpJar as the JAR Display Name. The steps for the creation of the session bean will stay the same as in the previous example.

5. While configuring the `Stock` entity bean in the **Edit Enterprise Bean Wizard**, when you get to the **Configuration Options** page, select **Resource References** in addition to Transaction Management:

6. In the **Entity Settings** page of the wizard, select **Bean-Managed Persistence**, the **Abstract Schema Name** should automatically fill in as `StockEjb`. Change the **Primary Key Class** to `String`:

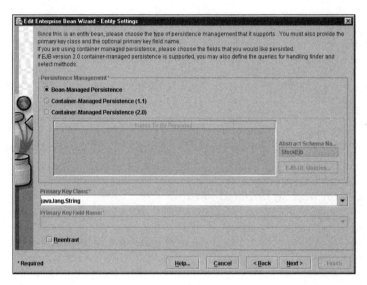

7. In the **Resource References** page enter a **Coded Name** of jdbc/StockDB. This allows the JNDI name, java:comp/env/jdbc/StockDB, to be used in the `StockBean` class to obtain a reference to the underlying data source. This is shown in the `StockBean.java` listing earlier, in the following statement:

```
DataSource ds = (DataSource) ctx.lookup("java:comp/env/jdbc/StockDB");
```

The concept of **Coded Name** will be covered later in this chapter. You should see a screen like the following:

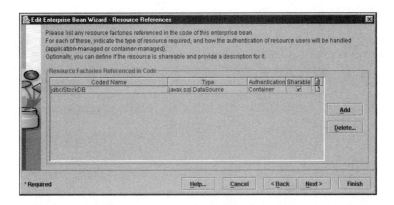

8. Create the platform-specific deployment descriptor. Set the JNDI Names to the same as the previous example. While you are configuring the platform-specific deployment settings, click the **Res. Refs** tab and select the **StockEjb** entry in the **Enterprise Beans in Jar** panel as shown below:

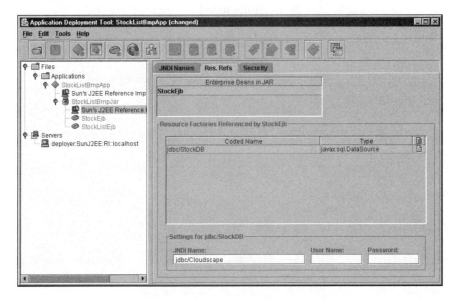

Then, select the jdbc/StockDB row in the **Resource Factories Referenced by StockEjb** panel. A text field should become available at the bottom of the page in which you can enter the **JNDI Name** of the database. Enter jdbc/Cloudscape in this text field and continue on with the process.

9. Save the deployment descriptor and then the whole application. Now we can run the application through the verifier.

10. If there aren't any errors we can finally deploy the application. Because the `Stock` bean uses bean-managed persistence, before we can actually deploy the application we have to create a table for use as its underlying data store. To do this, create a file (we named ours `stock.sql`) that contains SQL statements for creating a `stock` table, as shown below:

```
drop table stock;

create table stock
(tickerSymbol varchar(10) constraint pk_stock primary key,
name varchar(50));

exit;
```

11. To create the table, enter the following command from the command prompt, with the `stock.sql` file you just created in the directory:

```
> cloudscape -isql < stock.sql
```

Now you can deploy the beans in the usual manner.

12. Once the application is deployed create the client stubs JAR file, call it StockListBmpStubs.jar.

13. To run the client, set the classpath to use the client JAR, from the command prompt enter the following:

```
> set classpath=.;c:\j2sdkee1.4\lib\j2ee.jar;StockListBmpStubs.jar
```

You can enter the following command to run the client that uses the beans we've built:

```
> java client.StockClient
```

The application will look the same as the CMP version.

How It Works

Looking at the code for this BMP entity bean we begin to appreciate what the EJB container does for us when using container-managed persistence. In this example, as with CMP, a table in the database is dedicated to our BMP entity bean. Each row represents a bean instance. Here's a list of things that the entity bean is responsible for when managing its own persistence:

❑   The BMP entity bean must supply implementations for the persisted field's getter and setter methods. In our example, this consists of using instance variables to hold these values as seen in the `getTickerSymbol()`, `getName()`, and `setName()` methods, shown below:

```
public String getTickerSymbol() {
  return tickerSymbol;
}

public String getName() {
  return name;
}

public void setName(String name) {
  this.name = name;
}
```

❑ The implementation of the `findByPrimaryKey()` method declared in the home interface *must* be supplied. This is seen in the `ejbFindByPrimaryKey()` method below. Notice that JDBC is used to enable this find method:

```
public String ejbFindByPrimaryKey(String primaryKey)
  throws FinderException {

  boolean result;

  try {
    String stmt =
      "select tickerSymbol " + "from stock where tickerSymbol = ? ";
    PreparedStatement pstmt = connection.prepareStatement(stmt);
    pstmt.setString(1, primaryKey);

    ResultSet rs = pstmt.executeQuery();
    result = rs.next();
    pstmt.close();
  }
  catch (SQLException ex) {
    throw new EJBException("ejbFindByPrimaryKey: " + ex.getMessage());
  }

  if (result) {
    return primaryKey;
  } else {
    throw new ObjectNotFoundException
      ("Ticker " + primaryKey + " not found.");
  }
}
```

❑ The `ejbCreate()` method, rather than simply tucking away arguments into instance variables, uses JDBC to insert the corresponding row into the table. This method is shown below:

```
public String ejbCreate(String tickerSymbol, String name)
  throws CreateException {
```

```
  try {
    String findstmt =
      "select tickerSymbol " +
      "from stock where tickerSymbol = ? ";
    PreparedStatement pfindstmt =
      connection.prepareStatement(findstmt);
    pfindstmt.setString(1, tickerSymbol);

    ResultSet rs = pfindstmt.executeQuery();
    boolean findresult = rs.next();
    if (findresult) {
      throw new CreateException("Ticker already exists!");
    }

    String stmt = "insert into stock values ( ? , ? )";
    PreparedStatement pstmt = connection.prepareStatement(stmt);

    pstmt.setString(1, tickerSymbol);
    pstmt.setString(2, name);

    pstmt.executeUpdate();
    pstmt.close();
  } catch (SQLException ex) {
    ex.printStackTrace();
    throw new EJBException("ejbCreate: " + ex.getMessage());
  }

  this.tickerSymbol = tickerSymbol;
  this.name = name;

  return tickerSymbol;
}
```

❑   The `ejbRemove()` method, shown below, is responsible for deleting the row that represents the entity bean's instance from the table:

```
public void ejbRemove() {
  try {
    String stmt = "delete from stock where tickerSymbol = ? ";
    PreparedStatement pstmt = connection.prepareStatement(stmt);

    pstmt.setString(1, tickerSymbol);
    pstmt.executeUpdate();
    pstmt.close();
  } catch (SQLException ex) {
    throw new EJBException("ejbRemove: " + ex.getMessage());
  }
}
```

❑ In a bean's lifecycle, the values of its fields are often changed by the application. As a result of this, the EJB container calls the `ejbLoad()` and `ejbStore()` methods, shown below, when it deems appropriate to keep the state of the entity bean in sync with the underlying data store. The BMP entity bean performs SQL SELECT and UPDATE statements via JDBC to implement these methods:

```
public void ejbLoad() {
  try {
    String stmt = "select name from stock where tickerSymbol = ? ";
    PreparedStatement pstmt = connection.prepareStatement(stmt);

    pstmt.setString(1, tickerSymbol);
    ResultSet rs = pstmt.executeQuery();

    if (rs.next()) {
      this.name = rs.getString(1);
      pstmt.close();
    } else {
      pstmt.close();
      throw new NoSuchEntityException("Ticker: " +
        tickerSymbol + " not in database.");
    }
  } catch (SQLException ex) {
    throw new EJBException("ejbLoad: " + ex.getMessage());
  }
}

public void ejbStore() {
  try {
    String stmt =
        "update stock set name = ? " +
        "where tickerSymbol = ?";
    PreparedStatement pstmt = connection.prepareStatement(stmt);

    pstmt.setString(1, name);
    pstmt.setString(2, tickerSymbol);
    int rowCount = pstmt.executeUpdate();
    pstmt.close();

    if (rowCount == 0) {
      throw new EJBException("Store for " +
        tickerSymbol + " failed.");
    }
  } catch (SQLException ex) {
    throw new EJBException("ejbStore: " + ex.getMessage());
  }
}
```

❑ The `setEntityContext()` method is called by the EJB container after an entity bean is created. Since this entity bean uses JDBC to manage its persistence, we take this opportunity to get a JDBC connection. This connection is obtained within the private `getDatabaseConnection()` method in the listing above. We close the JDBC connection when the `unsetEntityContext()` method is called by the container. These methods are shown below:

```
   public void setEntityContext(EntityContext ctx) {
     context = ctx;

     try {
       getDatabaseConnection();
     } catch (Exception ex) {
       throw new EJBException("Unable to connect to database. " +
         ex.getMessage());
     }
   }

   public void unsetEntityContext() {
     context = null;
     try {
       connection.close();
     } catch (SQLException ex) {
       throw new EJBException("unsetEntityContext: " + ex.getMessage());
     }
   }

   private void getDatabaseConnection()
     throws NamingException, SQLException {

     InitialContext ctx = new InitialContext();
     DataSource ds =
       (DataSource) ctx.lookup("java:comp/env/jdbc/StockDB");
     connection =  ds.getConnection();
   }
 }
```

In this section we learned about, and walked through an example of, an entity bean that uses bean-managed persistence. In the next section, we'll learn about the concept of **local interfaces** and will retrofit the container-managed persistence example from earlier in this chapter.

EJB Local Interfaces

Local interfaces are a relatively new feature of EJBs, and were created primarily to increase performance among enterprise beans that exist in the same EJB container. Consider a case in which an application has several beans, where each bean instance holds references to several others. Calling each other's home and bean interface methods, since they utilize stubs and Java RMI, can be resource-intensive and have less than optimal speed. Local interfaces address these issues. For example, a session bean that calls the methods of an entity bean that has local interfaces exists within the same JVM as the session bean. Local interfaces, therefore, can be much faster and use less resources because they use Java memory references rather than Java RMI to pass data.

Remote interfaces must still be used when the caller of a bean is outside of the EJB server that the bean is running in. Because of this, we use the guidelines listed below to decide whether an enterprise bean should have local or remote interfaces:

❑ When a session bean's methods are invoked from a client that is external to the EJB server, that session bean should have remote interfaces.

❑ When a session bean's methods are only invoked from another bean from within the same EJB server, that bean should have local interfaces.

❑ Entity beans should have local interfaces.

Understanding EJB Local Interfaces

Up to now, the home interface of each of our enterprise beans has been a *remote* home interface. The bean interface of each of the enterprise beans has been a *remote* bean interface, more commonly known as a remote interface. There is a counterpart to each of these interfaces that is lighter weight, and potentially faster:

❑ The counterpart of the remote home interface is known as the **local home interface**. Instead of extending the EJBHome interface, a local home interface extends the EJBLocalHome interface.

❑ The counterpart of the remote interface is known as the **local interface**. Instead of extending the EJBObject interface, a **local interface** extends the EJBLocalObject interface.

The local home interface and the local interface are used in much the same way as their remote counterparts, and they are available to session beans as well as entity beans. The class diagram shown below depicts these interfaces in the context of the next example:

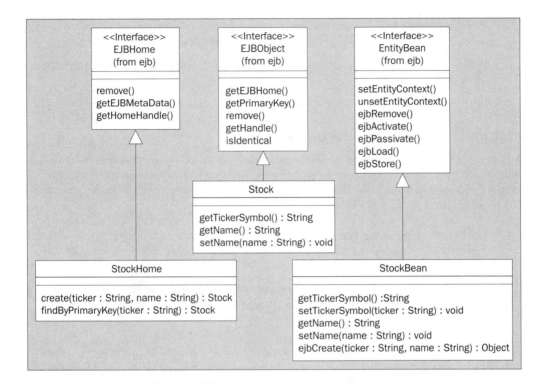

Create an Entity Bean that has Local References

In this example, we're going to change the Stock entity bean into one that has a local home interface and a local interface. For brevity when speaking about this, we say that this bean has **local interfaces**.

We'll leave the StockList session bean alone, letting it continue to have remote references. This is because the StockList bean needs to be accessed from a client that is external to the EJB container in which the bean resides.

We'll also leave the StockClient unscathed so that the application will have the same behavior as the previous example.

Building and Running the Example

The only source files that changed from the previous example are Stock.java, StockHome.java, and StockListBean.java. The rest of the files have not been changed, and all are mentioned below.

The following source files define the Stock entity bean, and are contained in the beans package:

- ❏ `LocalStock.java` (was `Stock.java`, but now changed to being a local interface)
- ❏ `StockBean.java`
- ❏ `LocalStockHome.java` (was `StockHome.java`, but now changed to being a local home interface)

Note that we called the entity bean by the name `Stock`, even though the bean interface is now named `LocalStock`. This is because we're referring to the bean's abstract schema name, for which we'll continue to use the name `Stock`. Recall that we assign that name in the Deployment Tool.

These source files define the `StockList` session bean, also contained in the `beans` package:

- ❏ `StockList.java`
- ❏ `StockListBean.java` (changed to using the `Stock` bean's local home interface)
- ❏ `StockListHome.java`

The final source file defines the user interface client, and is contained in the `client` package:

- ❏ `StockClient.java`

1. Create a new application directory called `StockListLocalApp` with `beans` and `client` subfolders. Into these folders put the correct code files.

2. Compile these source files, and start the J2EE server, the Deployment Tool, and Cloudscape.

3. Create a new application EAR, calling it **StockListLocalApp**.

4. Add the bean JAR, call it **StockListJar**.

5. Add the session bean information as before. Only including the `StockList`, `StockListBean`, and `StockListHome` class files.

6. Continue on with the process, choosing **Stateless** when given the option, until you get to the **Configuration Options** page of the **Edit Enterprise Bean Wizard** (during the first pass, when you are creating the bean JAR for the session bean).

Select the **Enterprise Bean References** option, because we'll use that mechanism to get a reference to the local interfaces of the entity bean.

7. Clicking the **Next** button should cause the **Enterprise Bean References** page to be displayed. Click the **Add...** button on that page to produce the following dialog:

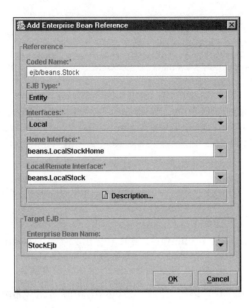

Fill in the dialog with the information about the `Stock` bean's local interfaces as shown in the screenshot. The only information in this dialog that we haven't covered yet is the **Coded Name:** field, which will be explained when we walk through the code.

8. Clicking the **OK** button will fill in a row of the table on the underlying page with the values that you entered:

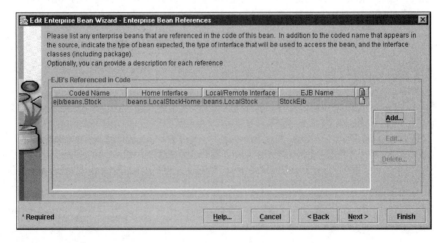

This information provides the linkage, internal to the EJB container, between the `StockList` session bean and the `Stock` entity bean that it accesses. This means that the `StockList` session bean doesn't have to use an external JNDI mechanism to get a reference to the home interface of the `Stock` entity bean, which means that performance is increased.

9. When you create the JAR for the entity bean ensure you choose only the class files of the `Stock` bean, as shown below:

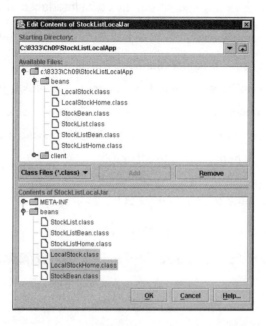

10. Click OK and then Next. You then get to the General page in the Edit Enterprise Bean Wizard:

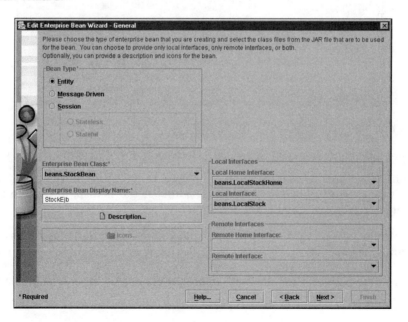

Make the same choices that you did in the previous example, but instead of using the **Remote Interfaces** drop-downs, choose the `beans.LocalStockHome` and `beans.LocalStock` interfaces from the **Local Interfaces** drop-downs.

11. Leave the Configurations Options page as default. Set the Entity settings page so:

❑ Our entity bean uses **Container-Managed Persistence 2.0**.

❑ In the **Fields To Be Persisted** window, choose both fields to be CMP fields.

❑ Use the **tickerSymbol** field as the primary key for the `Stock`.

❑ `java.lang.String` is selected in the **Primary Key Class** drop-down.

❑ Set the **Abstract Schema Name** to Stock.

12. When creating the platform-specific deployment descriptor remember to add the database settings and to generate the SQL.

13. On the **JNDI Names** tab in the **StockListJar** settings page:

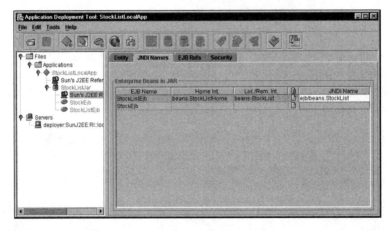

On this page, you need to do the following:

❑ Enter **ejb/beans.StockList** in the **JNDI Name** column of the `StockList` session bean.

❑ Unlike the previous example, you don't need to enter a **JNDI Name** for the `Stock` entity bean, because we're going to use a linkage mechanism internal to the EJB container, as we discussed previously.

14. Continue on to the end of the process that you followed in the previous example, saving the application, verifying it, deploying it, and making the client stubs JAR.

15. To run the client, set the classpath to use the client JAR: from the command prompt enter the following:

```
> set classpath=.;c:\j2sdkee1.4\lib\j2ee.jar;StockListLocalStubs.jar
```

You can enter the following command to run the client that uses the beans we've built:

```
> java client.StockClient
```

For good housekeeping, make sure that you undeployed anything that was previously deployed.

How It Works

Only three source files and a deployment descriptor were altered in the making of this local interfaces example. Within those files, there were very few changes required to turn the previous example into a local interfaces example. We'll walk through them one at a time, beginning with `LocalStockHome.java`.

Making the Home Interface Local

Here are the modifications that we needed to make to the `LocalStockHome` file:

```java
package beans;

import javax.ejb.CreateException;
import javax.ejb.EJBLocalHome;
import javax.ejb.FinderException;

public interface LocalStockHome extends EJBLocalHome {
  // The create method for the Stock bean
  public LocalStock create(String ticker, String name)
    throws CreateException;

  // The find by primary key method for the Stock bean
  public LocalStock findByPrimaryKey(String ticker)
    throws FinderException;
}
```

There are a couple of things (other than the interface name) that changed in the home interface to make it local:

❑   The interface now extends `EJBLocalHome` instead of `EJBHome`.

❑   The methods of the interface don't declare that they throw `RemoteException`, because they are not accessed remotely.

429

Making the Bean Interface Local

Let's check out the changes to `LocalStock.java`:

```
package beans;

import javax.ejb.EJBLocalObject;

public interface LocalStock extends EJBLocalObject {
    // The public business methods on the Stock bean
    // These include the accessor methods from the bean

    // Get the ticker. Do not allow ticker to be set through the
    // interface because it is the primary key.
    public String getTickerSymbol();

    // Get and set the name
    public String getName();
    public void setName(String name);
}
```

As with the home interface, there are a couple of things that changed in the remote interface to make it local:

❑   The interface now extends `EJBLocalObject` instead of `EJBObject`.

❑   The methods of the interface don't declare that they throw `RemoteException`, because they are not accessed remotely.

Using Local Home Interfaces vs. Remote Home Interfaces

To see how to access a local home interface, let's look at the new `StockListBean.java`:

```
...
public class StockListBean implements SessionBean {

    // The public business methods, these must also be coded in the
    // remote interface.

    public String getStock(String ticker) throws FinderException {
        try {
            LocalStockHome stockHome = getStockHome();
            LocalStock stock = stockHome.findByPrimaryKey(ticker);
            return stock.getName();
        } catch (FinderException fe) {
            throw fe;
        } catch (Exception ex) {
            throw new RuntimeException(ex.getMessage());
        }
    }
}
```

```java
  public void addStock(String ticker, String name) throws CreateException {
    try {
      LocalStockHome stockHome = getStockHome();
      stockHome.create(ticker, name);
    } catch (CreateException ce) {
      throw ce;
    } catch (Exception ex) {
      throw new RuntimeException(ex.getMessage());
    }
  }

  public void updateStock(String ticker, String name)
    throws FinderException {
    try {
      LocalStockHome stockHome = getStockHome();
      LocalStock stock = stockHome.findByPrimaryKey(ticker);
      stock.setName(name);
    } catch (FinderException fe) {
      throw fe;
    } catch (Exception ex) {
      throw new RuntimeException(ex.getMessage());
    }
  }

  public void deleteStock(String ticker) throws FinderException {
    try {
      LocalStockHome stockHome = getStockHome();
      LocalStock stock = stockHome.findByPrimaryKey(ticker);
      stock.remove();
    } catch (FinderException fe) {
      throw fe;
    } catch (Exception ex) {
      throw new RuntimeException(ex.getMessage());
    }
  }

  private LocalStockHome getStockHome() throws NamingException {
    // Get the initial context
    InitialContext initial = new InitialContext();

    // Get the object reference
    Object objref = initial.lookup("java:comp/env/ejb/beans.Stock");
    LocalStockHome home = (LocalStockHome) objref;
    return home;
  }

  // Standard ejb methods
  public void ejbActivate() {}
  public void ejbPassivate() {}
  public void ejbRemove() {}
  public void ejbCreate() {}
  public void setSessionContext(SessionContext context) { }
}
```

Recall that when using the Deployment Tool to configure the `StockList` session bean, we selected the **Enterprise Bean References** option that allowed you to enter information about the local interfaces of the `Stock` entity bean. One of the entry fields is called **Coded Name**, which holds a shorthand name for the name that the `StockList` session bean will use to lookup the local home interface. This **Coded Name**, when appended to `java:comp/env/`, produces a JNDI name that can reference another bean in the same EJB container. Here is the code that uses this JNDI name:

```
Object objref = initial.lookup("java:comp/env/ejb/beans.Stock");
LocalStockHome home = (LocalStockHome) objref;
```

Since the JNDI lookup is internal to the EJB container, it is very efficient for a bean to use. Also, notice that the cast is to a different class (`LocalStockHome`), and it is more straightforward than in the previous remote interface example where the complexities of Java RMI had to be dealt with, as shown below:

```
Object objref = initial.lookup("ejb/beans.Stock");
StockHome home = (StockHome)
    PortableRemoteObject.narrow(objref, StockHome.class);
```

Another thing worth noting in this class is that the methods of the local home interface return local bean references. This is demonstrated by the `findByPrimaryKey()` method invocation shown below. By the same token, the methods of a remote home interface return remote bean references.

```
LocalStockHome stockHome = getStockHome();
LocalStock stock = stockHome.findByPrimaryKey(ticker);
```

The Deployment Descriptor

Here is an excerpt from the deployment descriptor. The differences between this deployment descriptor and the one for the previous example are due to fact that the `Stock` entity bean now has local interfaces:

```
...
<display-name>StockListJar</display-name>
<enterprise-beans>
  <session>
    <ejb-name>StockListEjb</ejb-name>
    <home>beans.StockListHome</home>
    <remote>beans.StockList</remote>
    <ejb-class>beans.StockListBean</ejb-class>
    <session-type>Stateless</session-type>
    <transaction-type>Bean</transaction-type>
    <ejb-local-ref>
      <ejb-ref-name>ejb/beans.Stock</ejb-ref-name>
      <ejb-ref-type>Entity</ejb-ref-type>
      <local-home>beans.LocalStockHome</local-home>
```

```
      <local>beans.LocalStock</local>
      <ejb-link>StockEjb</ejb-link>
    </ejb-local-ref>
    ...
  </session>
  <entity>
    <ejb-name>StockEjb</ejb-name>
    <local-home>beans.LocalStockHome</local-home>
    <local>beans.LocalStock</local>
    <ejb-class>beans.StockBean</ejb-class>
    <persistence-type>Container</persistence-type>
    ...
  </entity>
</enterprise-beans>
<assembly-descriptor>
  ...
</assembly-descriptor>
</ejb-jar>
```

Notice the XML elements used to specify the local interfaces:

```
<local-home>beans.LocalStockHome</local-home>
<local>beans.LocalStock</local>
```

The remote interfaces version was:

```
<home>beans.StockHome</home>
<remote>beans.Stock</remote>
```

Also, the StockList session bean uses a different mechanism to get a reference to the Stock bean's home interface since it is now a local home interface. As noted previously, this mechanism is still JNDI, but it is *internal* to the EJB container, which, as we've said before, makes the whole process much more efficient. The following lines in the deployment descriptor make the local interfaces of the Stock entity bean available to the StockList session bean. It does this by linking the JNDI name java:comp/env/ejb/beans.Stock with the local interfaces of the Stock entity bean:

```
<ejb-local-ref>
  <ejb-ref-name>ejb/beans.Stock</ejb-ref-name>
  <ejb-ref-type>Entity</ejb-ref-type>
  <local-home>beans.LocalStockHome</local-home>
  <local>beans.LocalStock</local>
  <ejb-link>StockEjb</ejb-link>
</ejb-local-ref>
```

In this section, we discussed how to develop entity beans that have local interfaces, but the same concepts apply to session beans as well. We converted the previous container-managed persistence example that used remote interfaces into one that uses local interfaces.

433

In the next section, we'll explore a very powerful capability of Enterprise JavaBeans: the ability to use **SQL queries** on entity beans.

The EJB Query Language

Entity beans provide an object-oriented abstraction to an underlying database, complete with the ability to create business methods that operate on the data contained in the entity beans. One problem with this is that the abstract schema can become quite complex, making it very tedious and slow to do query-like operations that span multiple entity beans using Java code. EJB-QL lets you embed queries with SQL-like syntax into entity beans that can be accessed via methods of the entity beans. The results of EJB-QL queries are often entity bean references, which can be directly operated upon, so you get the combined advantages of object-orientation and SQL.

If you need a quick start guide to EJB QL then please see Appendix B.

EJB-QL Find vs. Select Methods

There are two ways to implement EJB-QL in entity beans:

❑ **EJB-QL find methods** in the entity bean's home interface

❑ **EJB-QL select methods** in the entity bean class

Find methods are a natural extension of the concept of having the `findByPrimaryKey()` method in the home interface. As you recall, this method comes for free with entity beans – it's generated for you. You may want other methods in the home interface that find certain entity bean instances. Consider a fictional astronomy application that has an entity bean named `Planet`. A find method could be declared in the home interface and implemented via EJB-QL that returns only the planets with a given number of moons. This find method could have the following signature:

```
public Collection findByNumMoons(int moons) throws FinderException;
```

If that method were called with an argument having the value of 0, it would return a `Collection` containing two `Planet` entity bean references, representing Mercury and Venus, the two planets with no moons. The EJB-QL behind it could be something like this:

```
SELECT OBJECT(p)
  FROM Planet p
  WHERE p.numMoons = ?1
```

This query will:

❑ Take the argument passed into the method (in this case 0), which is represented by the `?1` portion of the query. This is just like the concept of SQL parameters.

❑ Find all of the entity bean instances with the abstract schema name of `Planet` whose `numMoons` field contains the value of 0. This is indicated by the `WHERE p.numMoons = ?1` portion of the code snippet.

❑ Return a collection of references to `Planet` entity bean interfaces.

The `SELECT OBJECT` portion of the above snippet indicates that the result will be an entity bean reference or collection of references. The `(p)` indicates that the type of entity bean reference returned will be one with an abstract schema name of `Planet`. That association was indicated by the `Planet p` portion.

The EJB-QL query is placed in the deployment descriptor, as the next example we see will demonstrate.

Find methods can also return a single entity bean reference, rather than a `Collection`. In this case, the entity bean's interface would be declared as the return type of the find method, and the EJB-QL query would be designed to return only one entity bean. For example, a find method in our fictional astronomy application that gets a planet by its diameter could have the following signature:

```
public Planet findByDiameter(int diameter) throws FinderException;
```

Select methods use EJB-QL as well, but are not declared in the home interface. Rather, they are declared in the entity bean class, and only available to other methods of the bean class. We'll discuss, and create, an example using select methods in the context of container-managed relationships in the next chapter.

Let's put these concepts into practice by working through an example of developing find methods.

Try It Out   Create Entity Beans that use EJB-QL Find

This example will highlight the development of EJB-QL find methods by adding two such methods to the `Stock` entity bean. To demonstrate the functionality supplied by the find methods, the `StockList` bean and `StockClient` application will be changed quite a bit. Here is a screenshot of the user interface that we will be using for this modified application:

When the client starts up, the scrolling panel is populated with radio buttons that represent all of the stock entity beans. If you select one of the stocks and click the **Get** button, a message dialog appears with the ticker symbol and name of the stock. When the **3 Letter Tickers Only** checkbox is selected, only the stocks with three-letter ticker symbols appear in the scrolling panel.

Building and Running the Example

The names of the source files are the same as the previous example, and the process of building, configuring, deploying, and running the example is nearly the same as well.

1. Create a new application directory called `StockListEJBQLApp` and create the `beans` and `client` subfolders within it.

2. Copy the code files from the download into their respective folders and then compile them.

3. Start the J2EE server, Cloudscape, and the Deployment tool.

4. Create a new application EAR calling it **StockListApp** and add an EJB jar, calling it **StockListJar**.

5. The creation of the session bean is the same as for the last example.

When creating the entity bean there are a couple of additional steps involved, as if there weren't enough already! They are as follows:

❏   Entering the EJB-QL queries for the find methods

❏   Loading the database with CMP field data for the `Stock` entity beans

Entering the EJB-QL Queries for the Find Methods

The first additional step will occur when you are configuring the `Stock` entity bean and get to the **Entity Settings** page of the **Edit Enterprise Bean Wizard** shown below:

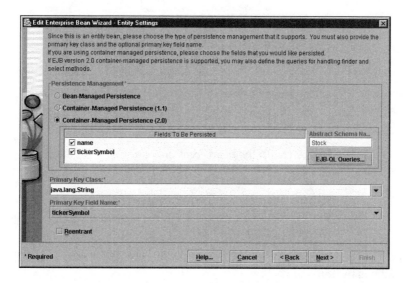

1. After filling in the information shown above, click the **EJB-QL Queries** button to enter the queries for the two find methods. The dialog box shown below will appear, preloaded with the find methods that it found while reflecting upon the local home interface of the `Stock` bean:

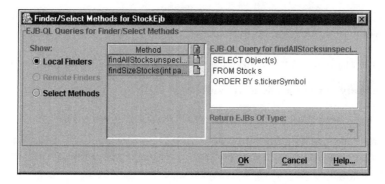

2. Select the findAllStocks entry in the Method panel, and enter the query shown below in the EJB-QL Query textbox:

```
SELECT Object(s)
FROM Stock s
ORDER BY s.tickerSymbol
```

This query will select all of the `Stock` entity beans, and return them in `tickerSymbol` order. Now select the findSizeStocks entry and enter the following query:

```
SELECT Object(s)
FROM Stock s
WHERE LENGTH(s.tickerSymbol) = ?1
ORDER BY s.tickerSymbol
```

This query will select and return only the `Stock` entity beans whose
`tickersSymbols` are the same length as the argument passed to the
`findSizeStocks()` method.

3. Once you have finished with the bean creation, continue with the deployment
   descriptor.

4. Remember to click the **Database Settings** button when you are creating the descriptor.
   Clicking the **Generate SQL Now** button from the dialog that pops up, takes your EJB-
   QL queries and makes SQL out of them.

You can view the generated SQL queries from the same page in which you clicked the
Database Settings button.

5. On the **JNDI Names** tab in the **StockListJar** settings page, enter **ejb/beans.StockList** in
   the **JNDI Name** column of the `StockList` session bean.

6. Save the deployment descriptor and the save the complete application.

7. You can now test the application using the Verifier tool; if it passes without any errors
   then you can deploy the application.

8. Once the application is deployed you can the create the client stubs JAR file.

Before you are ready to run the client we will load the database with some `Stock` entity bean data:

Loading the Database with CMP Field Data for the Stock Entity Beans

To load the database, create a file with some SQL `INSERT` statements in it that contain sample
`Stock` entity bean data. Here are the contents of a sample file, named `inserts.sql`, which
contains test data:

```
INSERT into "StockBeanTable" values ('ABC Company', 'ABC');
INSERT into "StockBeanTable" values ('Zigby Zebras', 'ZZZ');
INSERT into "StockBeanTable" values ('Internet Corp of Slobovia', 'ICS');
INSERT into "StockBeanTable" values ('Digby Door Company', 'DDC');
INSERT into "StockBeanTable" values ('Zapalopalorinski Ltd.', 'ZAP');
INSERT into "StockBeanTable" values ('Jimco', 'JIM');
INSERT into "StockBeanTable" values ('Stocks R Us', 'SRU');
INSERT into "StockBeanTable" values ('Shelves and Radios Inc', 'SRI');
INSERT into "StockBeanTable" values ('Foo Bar Company', 'FBC');
INSERT into "StockBeanTable" values ('Ding Dong Bell Company', 'DDBC');
INSERT into "StockBeanTable" values ('Upn Down Elevator Company', 'UDE');
exit;
```

The SQL to create the `StockBeanTable` *table referenced in the* `INSERT` *statements above was generated by the Deployment Tool when you clicked the* **Generate SQL Now** *button in the dialog shown above. The* `StockBeanTable` *table was created via that SQL when you deployed the application.*

1. To start the process of loading the data, enter the following command from the operating system prompt, with the `inserts.sql` file you just created in the current directory:

```
> cloudscape -isql < inserts.sql
```

Now you can run the client, which will show these EJB-QL find methods in action. When you've done that, let's walk through the code for this example.

How It Works

The following four Java source files changed from the last example:

- ❏   LocalStockHome.java
- ❏   StockList.java
- ❏   StockListBean.java
- ❏   StockClient.java

The `Stock` entity bean's local interface and bean class didn't change, and the `StockList` session bean's home interface didn't change.

First, here is the `Stock` entity bean local home interface, `LocalStockHome.java`:

```java
...
// General imports
import java.util.*;

public interface LocalStockHome extends EJBLocalHome {
  // The create method for the Stock bean
  public LocalStock create(String ticker, String name)
    throws CreateException;

  // The find by primary key method for the Stock bean
  public LocalStock findByPrimaryKey(String ticker)
    throws FinderException;

  // The find all method for the Stock bean
  public Collection findAllStocks() throws FinderException;

  // The find by size method for the Stock bean
  public Collection findSizeStocks(int siz) throws FinderException;
}
```

439

You'll notice that all of our find methods are declared here. The `findByPrimaryKey()` method is required and the implementation is generated for you. The other two find methods have EJB-QL behind them, which as we'll soon see are located in the deployment descriptor. Both of them return a `Collection` of local interface references to `Stock` entity beans. The `findAllStocks()` method returns all of the `Stock` references. The `findSizeStocks()` method returns only those `Stock` entity bean references in which the `tickerSymbol` length is the same as the value passed in to the method. As you can see, EJB-QL is a very powerful feature that provides a lot of functionality with very little code!

Here is the `StockList` session bean's remote interface, `StockList.java`:

```
...
// General imports
import java.util.*;

public interface StockList extends EJBObject {
  // The public business methods on the Stock List bean
  public String[] getSizeStocks(int siz)
    throws FinderException, RemoteException;
  public String[] getAllStocks()
    throws FinderException, RemoteException;
  public String getStock(String ticker)
    throws FinderException, RemoteException;
}
```

As expected, this interface declares the methods that will be called by the client application. Here is the bean class for the `StockList` session bean, `StockListBean.java`:

```
package beans;

import javax.ejb.FinderException;
import javax.ejb.SessionBean;
import javax.ejb.SessionContext;
import javax.naming.InitialContext;
import javax.naming.NamingException;

// General imports
import java.util.*;

public class StockListBean implements SessionBean {

  // The public business methods. These must also be coded in the
  // remote interface.
  public String getStock(String ticker) throws FinderException {
    try {
      LocalStockHome stockHome = getStockHome();
      LocalStock stock = stockHome.findByPrimaryKey(ticker);
      return stock.getName();
    } catch (FinderException fe) {
```

```
      throw fe;
    } catch (Exception ex) {
      throw new RuntimeException(ex.getMessage());
    }
}

  public String[] getAllStocks() throws FinderException {
    try {
      LocalStockHome stockHome = getStockHome();
      Collection stockColl = stockHome.findAllStocks();
      String[] stocks = new String[stockColl.size()];
      int j = 0;
      Iterator i = stockColl.iterator();
      while (i.hasNext()) {
        LocalStock stock = (LocalStock) i.next();
        stocks[j++] = stock.getTickerSymbol();
      }
      return stocks;
    } catch (FinderException fe) {
      throw fe;
    } catch (Exception ex) {
      throw new RuntimeException(ex.getMessage());
    }
}

  public String[] getSizeStocks(int siz) throws FinderException {
    try {
      LocalStockHome stockHome = getStockHome();
      Collection stockColl = stockHome.findSizeStocks(siz);
      String[] stocks = new String[stockColl.size()];
      int j = 0;
      Iterator i = stockColl.iterator();
      while (i.hasNext()) {
        LocalStock stock = (LocalStock) i.next();
        stocks[j++] = stock.getTickerSymbol();
      }
      return stocks;
    } catch (FinderException fe) {
      throw fe;
    } catch (Exception ex) {
      throw new RuntimeException(ex.getMessage());
    }
}

  private LocalStockHome getStockHome() throws NamingException {
    // Get the initial context
    InitialContext initial = new InitialContext();

    // Get the object reference
    Object objref = initial.lookup("java:comp/env/ejb/beans.Stock");
    LocalStockHome home = (LocalStockHome) objref;
    return home;
```

```
   }

   // Standard EJB methods
   public void ejbActivate() { }
   public void ejbPassivate() { }
   public void ejbRemove() { }
   public void ejbCreate() { }
   public void setSessionContext(SessionContext context) { }
}
```

The getStock() method is the same as in the previous example.

The getAllStocks() method calls the newly created findAllStocks() method of the Stock entity bean's local home interface. The findAllStocks() method, you'll recall, returns a collection of local interface references to Stock entity beans. The getAllStocks() method then iterates over these references and returns an array of Strings containing all of the ticker symbols.

The getSizeStocks() method calls the findSizeStocks() method of the Stock bean's local home interface, passing in the same value for desired tickerSymbol length that it received. The getSizeStocks() method then iterates over these references and returns an array of Strings containing only the ticker symbols with the desired length.

Notice that the getSizeStocks() and getAllStocks() methods return an array of Strings rather than a Collection of Stock entity bean references. There are a couple of reasons for this:

❑   Local interfaces can't be referenced from outside of the EJB container.

❑   Even if we were using remote interfaces, referencing entity beans from a user interface rather than through a session bean is usually not the best architecture. Recall that reasons for this were discussed earlier.

There are challenges to be overcome when not allowing entity bean references to be accessed from the client. These challenges will be dealt with in the next chapter when we discuss the "Value Object" architectural pattern.

Turning our attention to the client, the source code for StockClient.java may be downloaded from the Wrox web site. In the StockClient class, when deselecting the checkbox, the getAllStocks() method of the StockList session bean is called to provide the ticker symbols of all the Stock entity beans. When selecting the checkbox, the getSizeStocks() of the session bean is called, passing in a value of 3, which returns a subset of the Stock entity beans' ticker symbols. This is shown in the stateChanged() method below:

```
public void stateChanged(ChangeEvent ce) {
  try {
    if (_threeOnly.isSelected()) {
      String[] stocks = _stockList.getSizeStocks(3);
```

```
          populateStockPanel(stocks);
       } else {
          String[] stocks = _stockList.getAllStocks();
          populateStockPanel(stocks);
       }
    } catch (Exception e) {
       e.printStackTrace();
    }
```

Here is an excerpt from the deployment descriptor that shows the EJB-QL queries that we entered:

```
   ...
   <display-name>StockListJar</display-name>
   <enterprise-beans>
     <entity>
        <ejb-name>StockEjb</ejb-name>
          ...
        <query>
          <query-method>
            <method-name>findAllStocks</method-name>
            <method-params>
            </method-params>
          </query-method>
          <result-type-mapping>Local</result-type-mapping>
          <ejb-ql>SELECT Object(s)<BR>
FROM Stock s <BR>
ORDER BY s.tickerSymbol</ejb-ql>
        </query>
        <query>
          <query-method>
            <method-name>findSizeStocks</method-name>
            <method-params>
               <method-param>int</method-param>
            </method-params>
          </query-method>
          <result-type-mapping>Local</result-type-mapping>
          <ejb-ql>SELECT Object(s) <BR>
FROM Stock s <BR>
WHERE LENGTH(s.tickerSymbol) = ?1<BR>
ORDER BY s.tickerSymbol</ejb-ql>
        </query>
     </entity>
     <session>
        ...
     </session>
   </enterprise-beans>
   <assembly-descriptor>
      ...
   </assembly-descriptor>
</ejb-jar>
```

As shown above, there is a `<query>` element subordinate to the `<entity>` element that defines the find methods, their parameters, and the EJB-QL query that gets executed. By the way, if you are interested in the details of any element of the deployment descriptor, or have a bad case of insomnia, the element definitions are located at http://java.sun.com/xml/ns/j2ee/ejb-jar_2_1.xsd. This URL is also at the top of every `ejb-jar.xml` file that complies with the EJB 2.1 specification.

Summary

This chapter was completely devoted to entity beans, which are the persistent data objects in an EJB application. We found out that entity beans share a common anatomy with session beans, but that there are some basic differences between them. Entity beans also have several features that session beans don't have, such as:

❑ Container-managed persistence (CMP)

❑ Primary keys

❑ Their very own query language: EJB-QL

❑ Container-managed relationships (CMR)

We saw that by using CMP, an entity bean type is mapped to its own database table, and the data for each individual entity bean is stored in a row of that table. The EJB container handles all of the database persistence functionality for you. This saves a huge amount of time when developing applications, thereby increasing a developer's productivity.

We learned that each entity bean has a primary key that uniquely identifies it. Every entity bean's home interface has a method named `findByPrimaryKey()` that uses this primary key to return the corresponding entity bean. We touched on the fact that primary keys enable container-managed relationships; a concept that will be covered in the next chapter.

We also examined local interfaces and compared them with the remote interfaces that we'd been using up to that point. As a result of their speed and resource usage advantages, we switched to using local interfaces for entity beans. We continued using remote interfaces for the session beans, however, because they needed to be accessed from a client outside of the EJB container. In an application with more than one session bean, the ones that aren't called from the outside (presumably called by other session beans) can be local as well. Using local interfaces when applicable can boost the performance of an application.

We discussed the EJB query language, which provides the ability to create SQL-like queries that operate upon entity beans. These queries are encapsulated in entity bean methods so that their functionality is available via a method call. We demonstrated the use of one variety of EJB-QL: find methods. On this note, there is an EJB-QL chapter in the EJB Specification that provides a complete reference for the EJB Query Language. To view it, download the Enterprise JavaBeans Specification, version 2.1 from http://java.sun.com/products/ejb/docs.html#specs.

In the next chapter, we'll demonstrate how to create relationships among entity beans using container-managed relationships. In that context, we'll cover how to implement EJB-QL select methods. We'll also cover more EJB topics such as using JDBC with session beans, message-driven beans, EJB Timers, and implementing design patterns in EJB applications.

Exercises

1. Referring to the class diagram in the next chapter of the fictitious "Audio CD Collection" application, implement an entity bean with remote references for `CompactDiscTitle`. Attributes should be: `name` (String, and it will be the primary key) and `price` (double). Write a stateless session bean that allows you to get, add, update, and remove a CD title. Write a client application to test the beans.

2. Modify the previous exercise to use local references for the `CompactDiscTitle` entity bean.

3. Modify the previous exercise implementing a finder that returns all CD titles in ascending order by name, and a finder that returns all CD titles within a certain price range in ascending order by name. Write a simple client application to test the new methods.

4. Modify the stock list example in this chapter to return a list of stock tickers that start with a string entered by the user. Order the list ascending by ticker symbol.

CHAPTER 10

Container-Managed Relationships   **447**

Using JDBC with Enterprise JavaBeans   **478**

Summary   **485**

Exercises   **485**

More EJB Topics

The previous chapter explored EJB **entity beans**, which are the persistent data objects in an EJB application. In this chapter, we will continue to deal with entity beans, and cover some more EJB-related topics.

In this chapter you will learn how to develop:

❑ Entity beans that have **container-managed relationships**

❑ EJB-QL **select methods**

❑ Sessions beans that leverage JDBC to augment EJB-QL

We'll kick things off by demonstrating how to create relationships among entity beans. In that context, we'll cover how to implement EJB-QL **select methods**.

Container-Managed Relationships

As mentioned in the previous chapter, entity beans have an **abstract schema** that defines the **container-managed relationships** (**CMR**) between entity beans. For example, consider a fictitious application that manages a personal CD collection (audio compact discs, not certificates of deposit). We'll call it the "Audio CD Collection" application. In the music CD domain, a few candidates for entity beans jump to mind:

❑ `CompactDiscTitle`

❑ `SongTrack`

❑ `MusicalGenre`

❑ `Artist`

❑ `RecordLabel`

These entity beans have relationships with each other. For example, a `CompactDiscTitle` is published by one `RecordLabel`, and a `RecordLabel` has many `CompactDiscTitles`. Therefore, in our abstract schema there is a **one-to-many relationship** between `RecordLabel` and `CompactDiscTitle` entity bean instances. To be able to *navigate* these relationships from one entity bean to another, the following methods would be useful:

- ❑ A method of the `CompactDiscTitle` entity bean that would return the `RecordLabel` entity bean instance for a given `CompactDiscTitle`. A logical name for this would be `getRecordLabel()`.

- ❑ Conversely, a method of the `RecordLabel` entity bean would return all of the `CompactDiscTitle` entity bean instances published by a given `RecordLabel`. A good name for this would be `getCompactDiscTitles()`.

The term "navigate" is used to describe the process of obtaining, from a given entity bean, a reference to a related entity bean (or collection of entity beans).

The **primary key** of each entity bean helps establish these relationships with the other entity bean. The crude beginning of an "Audio CD Collection" class diagram illustrates the entity bean concepts presented so far:

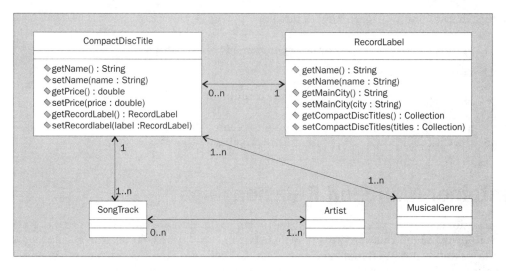

The CMP methods of the `RecordLabel` entity bean are `getName()`, `setName()`, `getMainCity()`, and `setMainCity()`. The `name` field is the name of the record company, and the `mainCity` field is where that record company is headquartered.

The CMR methods of the `RecordLabel` entity bean are `getCompactDiscTitles()` and `setCompactDiscTitles()`. CMR methods that interact with the "many" side of a relationship can use a `java.util.Collection` object to hold the bean interface references. For example, the `getCompactDiscTitles()` method returns a `Collection` of `CompactDiscTitle` bean interface references.

The primary key of the `RecordLabel` entity bean could be the `name` field, if that field was going to be unique among the `RecordLabel` entity bean instances.

Note the multiplicity notation on the relationships in the diagram, for example, a `RecordLabel` can have 0 or more (0...n in the diagram) `CompactDiscTitles`. A `CompactDiscTitle` can have only 1 `RecordLabel`.

The entity bean relationship multiplicity possibilities are:

❑ One-to-one

❑ One-to-many (which is also many to one depending on your perspective)

❑ Many-to-many

Each of these multiplicities can be **bi-directional** or **unidirectional**. The container-managed relationship between the `CompactDiscTitle` and `RecordLabel` entity beans in the diagram above is bi-directional. This is because there is a CMR getter method in both entity beans that accesses the entity bean(s) on the other side of the relationship. In a unidirectional relationship, only one of the entity beans would have a CMR getter method to access the other entity bean.

Also, with a many-to-many relationship, an additional database table exists behind the scenes that contains the primary keys from both of the entity beans in the relationship.

Now that we've discussed container-managed relationships, it's time to introduce a form of EJB-QL that can really exploit them: **EJB-QL select methods**.

Creating an EJB-QL Select Method

EJB-QL select methods are similar to finder methods in that they both are enabled by EJB-QL, but are different in a few ways, including:

❑ Finder methods are declared in an entity bean's home interface, but select methods are declared in its bean class.

❑ Finder methods are visible to other beans, but select methods are only accessible by methods of the same entity bean.

❑ Finder methods can return an entity bean reference or collection of references. In addition to these, select methods can return CMP field values and collections of these values.

❑ Finder methods have the form `findXxx()` but select methods use the naming convention `ejbSelectXxx()`.

For example, in the Audio CD Collection application above, let's say we want to know the names of the compact disc titles on record labels that have headquarters in a given city. To accomplish this we could declare the following select method in the `CompactDiscTitle` bean class:

```
public abstract Collection ejbSelectByRecordLabelCity(String city)
throws FinderException;
```

If this method were called with an argument having the value of `Detroit`, a `Collection` of `Strings` would be returned that contains titles such as "Songs in the Key of Life" and "Cloud Nine", by Stevie Wonder, and The Temptations, respectively. The EJB-QL that provides the functionality for this method would be something on this order:

```
SELECT c.name
  FROM CompactDiscTitle c
 WHERE c.recordLabel.mainCity = ?1
```

This query will:

❑   Take the argument passed into the method (in this case `Detroit`), which is represented by the `?1` portion of the query.

❑   Find all of the entity bean instances of `RecordLabel` whose `mainCity` field contains the value of `Detroit`. This is indicated by the `WHERE c.recordLabel.mainCity = ?1` clause. The reason why `c.recordLabel.mainCity` represents the `mainCity` field of the `RecordLabel` entity bean is because:

  ❑   c represents the `CompactDiscTitle` entity bean, because of the `FROM` clause.

  ❑   `c.recordLabel` represents the `RecordLabel` entity bean instance that is related to the `CompactDiscTitle` entity bean. It is like calling the `getRecordLabel()` method on the `CompactDiscTitle` bean.

There is a caveat with using the dot operator to navigate between entity beans like we did just now; you can't navigate to the "many" side of a relationship using it. You can use operators like IN and MEMBER OF for that kind of functionality. IN is a standard SQL operator, and we'll see an example of using MEMBER OF in the upcoming example. Notice that we used the dot notation to navigate through the "one" side of the relationship.

❑   Return a collection of `Strings` containing the name field of the related `CompactDiscTitle` entity beans.

For more information on EJB-QL, take a look at Appendix B at the back of this book.

Now, let's work through an example that demonstrates both container-managed relationships and EJB-QL select methods.

Try It Out   Create Entity Beans that use CMR and EJB-QL Select

In this example, we're going to expand the `StockList` example from the previous chapter by adding an entity bean named `Analyst`. Each instance of the `Analyst` bean represents a stock analyst who assigns ratings to stocks. The `Analyst` entity bean and the `Stock` entity bean have a container-managed relationship that represents the stocks that a given analyst has rated.

Here is a screenshot of the Stock List application after Nancy the analyst rated the stock for Slobovia's largest Internet company:

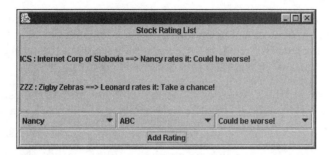

Shown below is a class diagram that depicts the enterprise beans involved in this application:

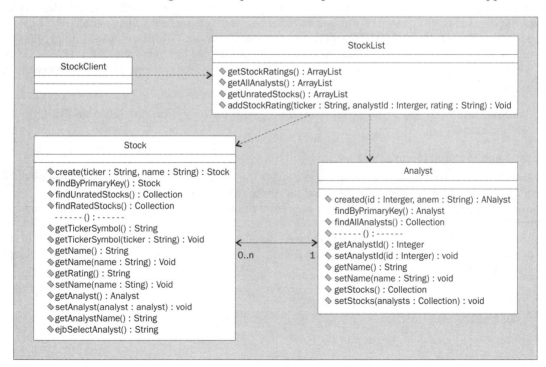

Note that the `Stock` and `Analyst` entity beans in the diagram represent all of their respective entity bean classes. To represent this, both of these classes have a dashed line that separates the home interface methods from the bean class methods.

Studying the diagram a bit more detail, we see that the `StockClient` GUI uses methods of the `StockList` session bean to access and manipulate the `Stock` and `Analyst` entity beans. For example:

- To populate the drop-down listbox that contains the analyst's names, it calls the `getAllAnalysts()` method of the session bean.

- When the user clicks the **Add Rating** button, the `addStockRating()` method of the session bean will be called upon to create a relationship between the analyst and the stock being rated. That method will also set the value of the rating (for example, **Could be worse!** and **Take a chance!**) into the `rating` field of the `Stock` bean.

Turning our attention to the `Stock` bean, notice that in addition to the usual `create()` and `findByPrimaryKey()` methods, the `Stock` bean's home interface has a couple of EJB-QL finder methods.

As we'll examine shortly, the `Stock` bean also has an EJB-QL select method named `ejbSelectAnalyst()`. EJB-QL select methods can only be called from methods inside the same bean. We'll see, however, that the public `getAnalystName()` method offers the services of the `ejbSelectAnalyst()` method to other beans by calling it on their behalf. The `Stock` bean also has a couple of CMR methods, named `getAnalyst()` and `setAnalyst()`, that maintain its relationship to the `Analyst` bean. To round out the overview of the `Stock` bean, we'll also point out that it has three CMP fields (`tickerSymbol`, `name`, `rating`) represented by six CMP methods.

The `Analyst` bean has a similar set of methods, with the exception that it has no EJB-QL select method.

Building and Running the Example

Now we need to compile, configure, and deploy the application as we did in the previous chapter. The steps are basically the same but there will be some additional instructions intermingled, that pertain to container-managed relationships and EJB-QL select methods.

The names of the source files are the same as the last example of the previous chapter, with the addition of the three files that define the `Analyst` bean. These files are in the `beans` package, and are as follows:

- `LocalAnalyst.java`
- `AnalystBean.java`
- `LocalAnalystHome.java`

The Java source filenames carried over from the example in the previous chapter are:

- ❏ LocalStock.java
- ❏ StockBean.java
- ❏ LocalStockHome.java
- ❏ StockList.java
- ❏ StockListBean.java
- ❏ StockListHome.java
- ❏ StockClient.java (found in the client subdirectory)

Also, one Java program has been added to initially populate the entity beans. It is in the client package, and its name is: StockListAdder.java. All the code files for this example are available in the code download.

1. Open a command prompt in the application directory, StockListCmrApp, and set the classpath. As pointed out previously, on a default J2EE SDK 1.4 Windows installation the classpath would be set correctly by using the following command:

```
> set classpath=.;C:\j2sdkee1.4\lib\j2ee.jar
```

2. Within the StockListCmrApp directory execute the following commands from the command prompt:

```
> javac -d . client/*.java
> javac -d . beans/*.java
```

3. Start the J2EE server, Cloudscape database server, and the Deployment Tool, this can be done by typing the following commands from your operating system prompt:

```
> j2ee
> cloudscape -start
> deploytool
```

4. Create the application EAR file by choosing New | Application EAR from the File menu. Set the Application File Name to StockListCmrApp.ear and the Application display name to StockListCmrApp.

5. Start the Edit Enterprise Bean Wizard by choosing the File | New | Enterprise JavaBean JAR menu item.

6. Follow the normal process for creating the bean JAR for the StockList session bean, setting the JAR Display Name to StockListCmrJar. Because the entity beans have local interfaces, remember to select the Enterprise Bean References option from the Configuration Options page.

7. You'll need to invoke the Add Enterprise Bean References dialog from the Enterprise Bean References page an additional time for the `Analyst` bean. Shown below are the dialogs for both the `Stock` bean and the `Analyst` bean:

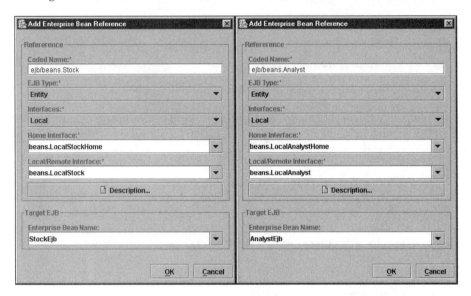

8. You'll also need to run through the Edit Enterprise Bean Wizard once for each entity bean. Remember to select the Transaction Management option on the Configuration Options page each time. Shown below is the Entity Settings page of this wizard for the `Stock` bean:

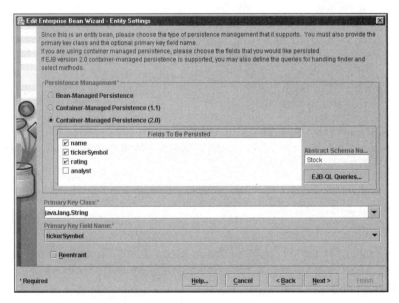

❏ Notice that only the three CMP fields are checked. The `analyst` field is used for a container-managed relationship (CMR), so we'll leave it unchecked. As with the `Stock` bean in the previous example, the **Primary Key Field Name** is tickerSymbol, the **Primary Key Class** is `java.lang.String`, and we've chosen an **Abstract Schema Name** of **Stock**.

9. Click on the **EJB-QL Queries** button and we'll enter the queries for the finder methods and select method mentioned previously:

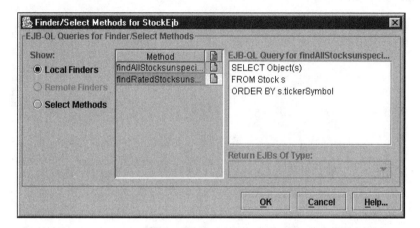

❏ In the dialog box shown, select the **findAllStocks** entry in the **Method** panel, and enter the query shown in the EJB-QL Query textbox:

```
SELECT DISTINCT OBJECT(s)
FROM Stock s
ORDER BY s.tickerSymbol
```

This query will select all of the `Stock` entity beans, and return them in `tickerSymbol` order.

❏ Now select the **findRatedStocks** entry and enter the following query for it:

```
SELECT DISTINCT OBJECT(s)
FROM Analyst a, Stock s
WHERE s MEMBER OF a.stocks
ORDER BY s.tickerSymbol
```

This query selects and returns only the `Stock` entity beans that have been rated. The ones that have been rated are a `MEMBER OF` the collection of `Stock` beans that would be returned by calling the `getStocks()` method of each of the `Analyst` beans. The `DISTINCT` keyword ensures that an entity bean isn't returned twice.

❏ Now choose the **Select Methods** option, and choose the **ejbSelectAnalyst** entry. We'll enter the query for our EJB-QL select method, as shown below:

455

```
SELECT s.analyst.name
FROM Stock s
WHERE s.tickerSymbol = ?1
```

This query selects and returns the name of the Analyst that rated the Stock whose tickerSymbol was passed into the ejbSelectAnalyst() method.

❑ Since the Analyst entity bean has a local interface, choose **Local** in the **Return EJBs of Type** drop-down list:

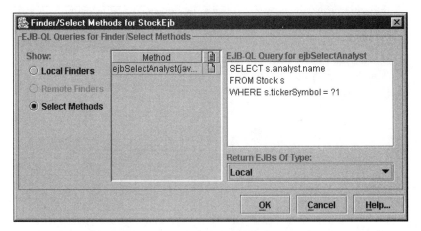

*In the beta version of the J2EE SDK 1.4 Deployment Tool used as of this writing, the **Transaction Management** page of this wizard, shown below, had an issue. We found it necessary to manually select the **Required Transaction Attribute** for the create() method in the **Local Home** option even though it appears automatically filled in. Failing to do so resulted in problems when trying to deploy the application. This is a known issue in the J2EE SDK Deployment Tool, and is hopefully fixed in the final release.*

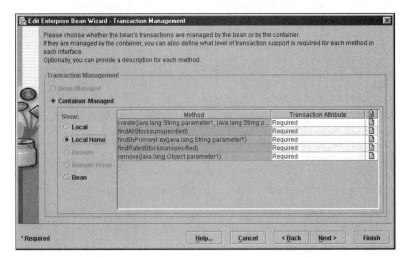

10. Shown below is the General page of the Edit Enterprise Bean Wizard when configuring the `Analyst` entity bean, create the `Analyst` entity bean using these settings:

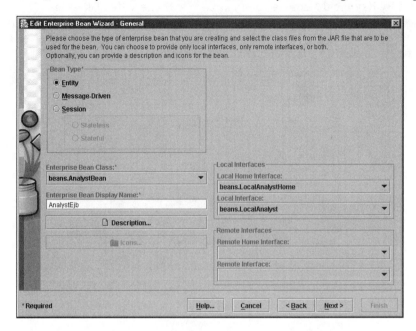

11. The Entity Settings page of this wizard when configuring the `Analyst` bean is shown below:

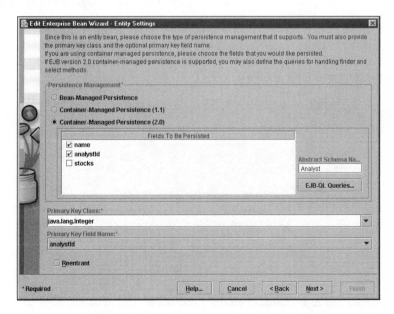

❏ Only the two CMP fields are checked, `name` and `analystId`. The `stocks` field is used for a container-managed relationship (CMR), so we'll leave it unchecked. The **Primary Key Field Name** is `analystId`, the **Primary Key Class** is `java.lang.Integer`, and we've chosen an **Abstract Schema Name** of Analyst. Note that `java.lang.Integer` wasn't one of the choices in the **Primary Key Class** drop-down list, so you will have to type it in.

12. Click on the **EJB-QL Queries** button and we'll enter the query for the `Analyst` bean's EJB-QL finder method.

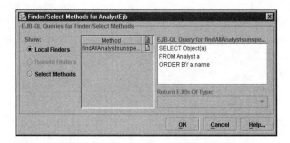

❏ In the dialog box shown above, select the **findAllAnalysts** entry in the **Method** panel, and enter the query shown in the **EJB-QL Query** textbox, repeated below:

```
SELECT Object(a)
FROM Analyst a
ORDER BY a.name
```

This query will return all of the `Analyst` entity beans, and return them in `name` order.

13. After configuring each of the entity beans in the **Edit Enterprise Bean Wizard**, we need to define the container-managed relationship between them. To do this, select the EJB JAR (we used the name **StockListCmrJar**) from the tree in the left-hand panel and click the **Relationships** tab as shown below:

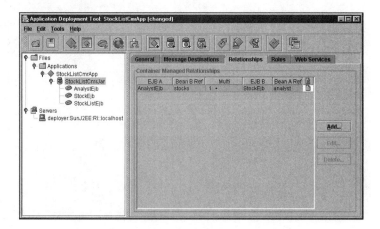

14. Click the **Add...** button on the page shown above will enable you to define a relationship between the `Analyst` and the `Stock` entity beans in the dialog shown below. To do this, choose the options outlined here:

❑ As seen previously in the UML diagram for this example, there is a one-to-many relationship between these entity beans.

❑ On the "one" side (**Enterprise Bean A**) of the relationship is the `Analyst` bean, whose **Enterprise Bean Name** is **AnalystEjb**.

❑ To specify that `getStocks()` and `setStocks()` are to be the CMR methods that manage the relationship with the `Stock` bean, we'll choose **stocks** from the **Field Referencing Bean B** drop-down list.

❑ As we'll see from the `AnalystBean.java` source code in a moment, the `getStocks()` method returns a `java.util.Collection` (of `LocalStock` bean references). The `setStocks()` method takes a `java.util.Collection` (of `LocalStock` bean references) as its argument. Therefore, we'll choose a **Field Type** of `java.util.Collection`.

❑ On the "many" side (**Enterprise Bean B**) of the relationship is the `Stock` bean, whose **Enterprise Bean Name** is **StockEjb**.

❑ To specify that `getAnalyst()` and `setAnalyst()` are to be the CMR methods that manage the relationship with the `Analyst` bean, well choose **analyst** from the **Field Referencing Bean A** drop-down list.

❑ Since the other side of this relationship has a multiplicity of "one", the `getAnalyst()` and `setAnalyst()` methods return and take a `LocalAnalyst` bean reference, as opposed to a `Collection` of them. We'll see this in the `StockBean.java` source code. Therefore, we're not given a choice of **Field Type**.

❑ We can specify that whenever an `Analyst` bean is deleted, the `Stock` beans that are related to it should be automatically deleted. This is called **cascading delete**, and can be specified by choosing the **Delete When Bean X is Deleted** option. We don't need that functionality in this example because we don't delete any `Analyst` beans. You'll want to think through the ramifications before choosing that option.

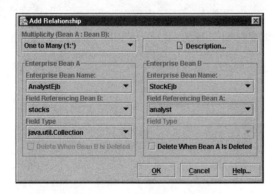

We noticed an occasional issue in the beta version of the Deployment Tool with getting the container-managed relationship information to be saved successfully in the EAR file. Running the Verifier (Tools | Verifier menu item) will point out when this information didn't stick.

Now we begin the usual process for creating the platform-specific deployment descriptor, making sure that StockListCmrApp is selected in the left pane. As a refresher, to do that, you need to choose the Deployment Settings menu item from the File menu, and then choose the Create New File menu item. After the file has been created, select the Sun's J2EE Reference Implementation entry that is subordinate to the StockListCmrJar entry in the tree in the left pane, as shown in the following screenshot.

15. Remember to click the Entity tab, and click on the Database Settings button for each of the Entity Beans in JAR entries. Recall that you'll supply a Database JNDI Name of jdbc/Cloudscape and click the Generate SQL Now button from the dialog that appears.

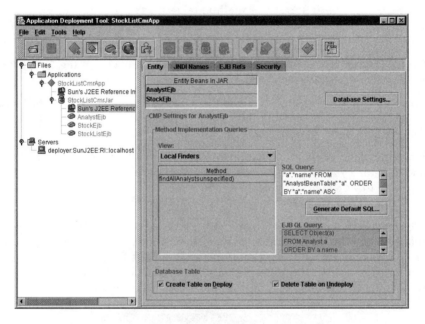

16. When you get to the JNDI Names tab in the platform-specific deployment settings page shown below, remember to enter ejb/beans.StockList in the JNDI Name column of the StockListEjb session bean:

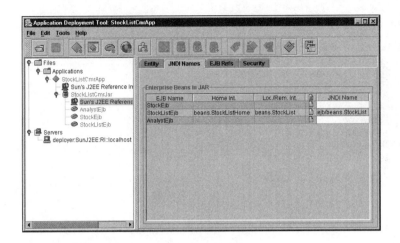

17. Close and save the deployment settings file. Then, *be sure to save* the application. You can do this by selecting StockListCmrApp in the tree on the left and then selecting the Save menu item from the File menu.

18. Now run the Verifier Tool. Select the StockListCmrApp node from the tree on the left panel and choose Verifier from the Tools menu. If everything passes then proceed with deploying the application.

For good housekeeping, make sure that you undeployed anything that was previously deployed. By the way, if you have trouble undeploying an application, please refer to the *Troubleshooting the Deploy* section of Chapter 8, and follow the instructions in the first three numbered steps, substituting "undeploy" for "deploy" in the instructions:

19. Select the StockListCmrApp node in the tree in the left panel and selecting the Tools | Deploy menu item.

20. Create the client stubs JAR as usual by selecting deployer:SunJ2EE:RI::localhost again, selecting the deployed StockListCmrApp application, and clicking the Client Jar button. Let's go with the name StockListCmrStubs.jar for this.

Before proceeding to the *Running the client application* step, we're going to populate the entity beans.

Loading the Database with CMP Field Data for both Entity Beans

We're going to use a Java program this time to load the database, rather than using INSERT statements as in the last chapter. This program will use methods of the StockList session bean to create some Analyst and Stock entity beans. It will also use the StockList session bean to create a stock rating by associating a Stock entity bean with an Analyst entity bean and setting the rating field of the Stock entity bean. Here is the source code for this program that loads the database, StockListAdder.java:

```
package client;

import beans.StockList;
import beans.StockListHome;
import javax.naming.InitialContext;
import javax.rmi.PortableRemoteObject;

// General imports
import java.awt.*;
import java.awt.event.*;
import javax.swing.*;
import javax.swing.event.*;

public class StockListAdder {

   public static void main(String[] args) {
      try {
         InitialContext jndiContext = new InitialContext();

         // Get a reference to the StockList JNDI entry
         Object ref = jndiContext.lookup("ejb/beans.StockList");

         // Get a reference from this to the Bean's Home interface
         StockListHome home = (StockListHome)
           PortableRemoteObject.narrow(ref, StockListHome.class);

         // Create a StockList object from the Home interface
         StockList stockList = home.create();

         // Add analysts
         System.out.println("adding analysts");
         stockList.addAnalyst(new Integer(1), "Fred");
         stockList.addAnalyst(new Integer(2), "Leonard");
         stockList.addAnalyst(new Integer(3), "Sarah");
         stockList.addAnalyst(new Integer(4), "Nancy");
         System.out.println("analysts added");
      } catch (Exception e) {
         System.out.println("exception adding analysts");
         e.printStackTrace();
      }

      try {
         InitialContext jndiContext = new InitialContext();

         // Get a reference to the StockList JNDI entry
         Object ref = jndiContext.lookup("ejb/beans.StockList");

         // Get a reference from this to the Bean's Home interface
         StockListHome home = (StockListHome)
           PortableRemoteObject.narrow(ref, StockListHome.class);

         // Create a StockList object from the Home interface
         StockList stockList = home.create();

         // Add stocks
         System.out.println("adding stocks");
         stockList.addStock("ABC", "ABC Company");
```

```
                stockList.addStock("ZZZ",  "Zigby Zebras");
                stockList.addStock("ICS",  "Internet Corp of Slobovia");
                stockList.addStock("DDC",  "Digby Door Company");
                stockList.addStock("ZAP",  "Zapalopalorinski Ltd.");
                stockList.addStock("JIM",  "Jimco");
                stockList.addStock("SRU",  "Stocks R Us");
                stockList.addStock("SRI",  "Shelves and Radios Inc");
                stockList.addStock("FBC",  "Foo Bar Company");
                stockList.addStock("DDBC", "Ding Dong Bell Company");
                stockList.addStock("UDE",  "Upn Down Elevator Company");
                System.out.println("stocks added");
            } catch (Exception e) {
                System.out.println("exception adding stocks");
                e.printStackTrace();
            }

            try {
                InitialContext jndiContext = new InitialContext();

                // Get a reference to the StockList JNDI entry
                Object ref  = jndiContext.lookup("ejb/beans.StockList");

                // Get a reference from this to the Bean's Home interface
                StockListHome home = (StockListHome)
                    PortableRemoteObject.narrow(ref, StockListHome.class);

                // Create a StockList object from the Home interface
                StockList stockList = home.create();

                // Add ratings
                System.out.println("adding ratings");
                stockList.addStockRating("ZZZ", new Integer(2),
                    "Take a chance!");
                System.out.println("ratings added");
            } catch (Exception e) {
                System.out.println("exception adding stocks");
                e.printStackTrace();
            }
        }
    }
```

This class should already be compiled from when you compiled the client package.

1. To run `StockListAdder`, as well as `StockClient`, this would be the appropriate `classpath` for a default J2EE SDK 1.4 Windows installation:

> **set CLASSPATH=.;C:\j2sdkee1.4\lib\j2ee.jar;StockListCmrStubs.jar**

2. Run the application listed above to populate the beans by entering the following on the command line:

> **java client.StockListAdder**

When this command is run you will get the following output displayed in the command prompt:

```
adding analysts
analysts added
adding stocks
stocks added
adding ratings
ratings added
```

3. Now that the database is populated we run the client that uses the beans we've built, using the following command:

```
> java client.StockClient
```

Congratulations! A screenshot of what the GUI client should look like is at the beginning of this example. Here it is again:

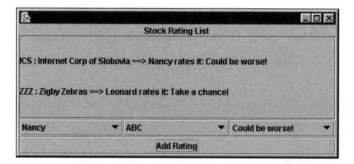

How It Works

In addition to the StockListAdder.java listing above, the source code for this example is listed below in ten Java source files:

For the Analyst entity bean:

- ❑ LocalAnalyst.java
- ❑ AnalystBean.java
- ❑ LocalAnalystHome.java

For the Stock entity bean:

- ❑ LocalStock.java
- ❑ StockBean.java
- ❑ LocalStockHome.java

For the `StockList` session bean:

- ❑   `StockList.java`

- ❑   `StockListBean.java`

- ❑   `StockListHome.java`

And for the clients:

- ❑   `StockClient.java`

Let's look at these and note some of the highlights after each listing, especially as they pertain to container-managed persistence and EJB-QL select methods.

Here is the Java source code for the implementation of the `Analyst` entity bean, `AnalystBean.java`:

```java
package beans;

import javax.ejb.CreateException;
import javax.ejb.EJBException;
import javax.ejb.EntityBean;
import javax.ejb.EntityContext;

import java.util.*;

public abstract class AnalystBean implements EntityBean {

    // Keeps the reference to the context
    private EntityContext _context;

    // The abstract access methods for persistent fields
    public abstract Integer getAnalystId();
    public abstract void setAnalystId(Integer id);

    public abstract String getName();
    public abstract void setName(String name);

    // The abstract access methods for CMR fields
    public abstract Collection getStocks();
    public abstract void setStocks(Collection stocks);

    // Business methods
    public void assignStock(LocalStock stock) {
        try {
            Collection stocks = getStocks();
            stocks.add(stock);
        } catch (EJBException ex) {
            ex.printStackTrace();
```

```
      throw ex;
    }
  }

// Standard entity bean methods
public Object ejbCreate(Integer id, String name) throws CreateException {

  setAnalystId(id);
  setName(name);
  return null;
}

public void ejbPostCreate(Integer id, String name)
  throws CreateException { }

public void setEntityContext(EntityContext ctx) {
  _context = ctx;
}

public void unsetEntityContext() {
  _context = null;
}

public void ejbRemove() { }
public void ejbLoad() { }
public void ejbStore() { }
public void ejbPassivate() { }
public void ejbActivate() { }
}
```

The stocks CMR field is defined by the getStocks() and setStocks() methods listed above. As noted while building this example, these methods return and take a Collection of LocalStock bean references, respectively. They are declared abstract for the same reason that CMP methods are; the implementation code is created by the deployment tool because that behavior is specific to the EJB server and database server implementations. The java.util.* import is there because the Collection interface is in that package.

We've created a convenience method named assignStock() that adds a LocalStock reference to the "many" side of the relationship by performing the following steps:

❑   Use the getStocks() method to retrieve the Collection of related LocalStock references.

❑   Add the LocalStock reference argument to the Collection.

Since we've defined this relationship as bi-directional, the EJB container manages the other side of this relationship by using the setAnalyst() method of the Stock bean. Recall that we defined the relationship as bi-directional by declaring a CMR method in both entity beans that reference each other, and by specifying the relationship in the **Add Relationship** dialog of the **Deployment Tool**.

This `assignStock()` method is called by the `StockList` session bean when assigning a `Stock` entity bean to an `Analyst` entity bean.

Here is the Java source code for the local interface of the `Analyst` entity bean, `LocalAnalyst.java`:

```java
package beans;

import javax.ejb.EJBLocalObject;
import java.util.*;

public interface LocalAnalyst extends EJBLocalObject  {
    // The public business methods on the Analyst bean
    // These include the accessor methods from the bean

    // Add stock assignment
    public void assignStock(LocalStock stock);

    // Get the ID, no setter because primary key
    public Integer getAnalystId();

    // Get and set the name
    public String getName();
    public void setName(String name);

    // The public CMR methods on the Analyst bean
    // These include the CMR methods from the bean
    // No setters exposed to the local interface
    public abstract Collection getStocks();
}
```

In the local interface, listed above, we're exposing the `getStocks()` method to other classes, but notice that the `setStocks()` method is not declared. This protects the entity bean from having this relationship corrupted by other classes. This is a good time to point out that, although CMR methods are useful to the developer, they are mainly used by the EJB container to manage the entity bean relationships (hence the name).

Here is the Java source code for the local home interface of the `Analyst` entity bean, `LocalAnalystHome.java`:

```java
package beans;

import javax.ejb.CreateException;
import javax.ejb.EJBLocalHome;
import javax.ejb.FinderException;

// General imports
import java.util.*;
```

```
public interface LocalAnalystHome extends EJBLocalHome {
  // The create method for the Analyst bean
  public LocalAnalyst create(Integer id, String name)
    throws CreateException;

  // The find by primary key method for the Analyst bean
  public LocalAnalyst findByPrimaryKey(Integer id)
    throws FinderException;

  // The find all method for the Analyst bean
  public Collection findAllAnalysts()
    throws FinderException;
}
```

There are no new concepts to discuss in the LocalAnalystHome interface listed above. Recall, however, that EJB-QL finder methods such as the findAllAnalysts() method are declared in the home interface, and that EJB-QL select methods are declared in the bean implementation class. We'll see one these select methods in the next listing.

Here is the Java source code for the implementation of the Stock entity bean, StockBean.java:

```
package beans;

import javax.ejb.CreateException;
import javax.ejb.EntityBean;
import javax.ejb.EntityContext;
import javax.ejb.FinderException;

public abstract class StockBean implements EntityBean {

  // Keeps the reference to the context
  private EntityContext _context;

  // The abstract access methods for persistent fields
  public abstract String getTickerSymbol();
  public abstract void setTickerSymbol(String ticker);

  public abstract String getName();
  public abstract void setName(String name);

  public abstract String getRating();
  public abstract void setRating(String rating);

  // The abstract access methods for CMR fields
  public abstract LocalAnalyst getAnalyst();
  public abstract void setAnalyst(LocalAnalyst analyst);

  // The abstract ejbSelect methods
  public abstract String ejbSelectAnalyst(String ticker)
    throws FinderException;
```

```
    // Business methods
    public String getAnalystName() throws FinderException {
      return ejbSelectAnalyst(getTickerSymbol());
    }

    // Standard entity bean methods
    public Object ejbCreate(String ticker, String name)
      throws CreateException {

      setTickerSymbol(ticker);
      setName(name);
      return null;
    }

    public void ejbPostCreate(String ticker, String name)
      throws CreateException { }

    public void setEntityContext(EntityContext ctx) {
      _context = ctx;
    }

    public void unsetEntityContext() {
      _context = null;
    }

    public void ejbRemove() { }
    public void ejbLoad() { }
    public void ejbStore() { }
    public void ejbPassivate() { }
    public void ejbActivate() { }
}
```

The `analyst` CMR field is defined by the `getAnalyst()` and `setAnalyst()` methods listed above. As you might have noted while building this example, these methods return and take a `LocalAnalyst` bean reference, respectively. Recall that the relationship we defined in the Deployment Tool dictates that a stock can *only* be rated by *one* analyst, but an analyst can rate *many* stocks. Note that because their implementation code is generated by the deployment tool, the `getAnalyst()` and `setAnalyst()` methods are declared `abstract`.

We can also see the EJB-QL select method named `ejbSelectAnalyst()` in the listing above. It is declared as `abstract` because its implementation is generated for you. Note that, like EJB-QL finder methods, EJB-QL select methods throw a `javax.ejb.FinderException`.

EJB-QL select methods may not be directly called by methods outside of the bean in which they are located. To offer the services of the `ejbSelectAnalyst()` method to the `StockList` session bean, we created the `getAnalystName()` method. This method calls the EJB-QL select method, which returns the analyst's name.

Here is the Java source code for the local interface of the Stock entity bean, `LocalStock.java`:

```
package beans;

import javax.ejb.EJBLocalObject;
import javax.ejb.FinderException;

public interface LocalStock extends EJBLocalObject {
    // The public business methods on the Stock bean
    // These include the accessor methods from the bean

    // Find rated stock analyst name
    public String getAnalystName() throws FinderException;

    // Get the ticker, no setter because primary key
    public String getTickerSymbol();

    // Get and set the name
    public String getName();
    public void setName(String name);

    // Get and set the rating
    public String getRating();
    public void setRating(String rating);

    // The public cmr methods on the Stock bean
    // These include the cmr methods from the bean
    // No setters exposed to the local interface
    public LocalAnalyst getAnalyst();
}
```

In the local interface listed above, note that we're exposing the `getAnalyst()` CMR method to other classes, but that the `setAnalyst()` method is not declared.

Here is the Java source code for the local home interface of the `Stock` entity bean, `LocalStockHome.java`:

```
package beans;

import javax.ejb.CreateException;
import javax.ejb.EJBLocalHome;
import javax.ejb.FinderException;

// General imports
import java.util.*;

public interface LocalStockHome extends EJBLocalHome {
    // The create method for the Stock bean
    public LocalStock create(String ticker, String name)
      throws CreateException;

    // The find by primary key method for the Stock bean
```

```
public LocalStock findByPrimaryKey(String ticker)
  throws FinderException;

// The find all stocks method for the Stock bean
public Collection findAllStocks() throws FinderException;

// Find rated stocks
public Collection findRatedStocks() throws FinderException;
}
```

The EJB-QL finder methods are declared in the `LocalStockHome` interface listed above. Recall that EJB-QL select methods, however, are not declared in the home interface.

Here is the Java source code for the remote interface of the `StockList` session bean, `StockList.java`:

```
package beans;

import java.rmi.RemoteException;
import javax.ejb.EJBObject;

// General imports
import java.util.*;

public interface StockList extends EJBObject {
  // The public business methods on the Stock List bean
  public ArrayList getStockRatings() throws RemoteException;
  public ArrayList getAllAnalysts() throws RemoteException;
  public ArrayList getUnratedStocks() throws RemoteException;
  public void addStockRating(String ticker,
                             Integer analystId,
                             String rating) throws RemoteException;
  public void addAnalyst(Integer id, String name) throws RemoteException;
  public void addStock(String ticker, String name) throws RemoteException;
}
```

The first four of these methods are used by the `StockClient` class, which provides the client UI. The last three methods are used by the `StockListAdder` class, which populates the entity beans initially. We'll discuss the implementation of these methods after the next code listing.

Let's examine some of the methods in the Java source code for the implementation of the `StockList` session bean, `StockListBean.java`:

```
package beans;

import javax.ejb.EJBException;
import javax.ejb.SessionBean;
import javax.ejb.SessionContext;
import javax.naming.InitialContext;
```

471

```
// General imports
import java.util.*;

public class StockListBean implements SessionBean {

   // The public business methods. These must also be coded in the
   // remote interface.

   public ArrayList getStockRatings() {
      try {
         // Get the initial context
         InitialContext initial = new InitialContext();
         // Get the object reference
         LocalStockHome home = (LocalStockHome)
            initial.lookup("java:comp/env/ejb/beans.Stock");

         // Get the stocks
         ArrayList stkList = new ArrayList();
         Collection stocks = home.findRatedStocks();
         Iterator i = stocks.iterator();
         while (i.hasNext()) {
            LocalStock stock = (LocalStock) i.next();
            String[] stockData = new String[4];
            stockData[0] = stock.getTickerSymbol();
            stockData[1] = stock.getName();
            stockData[2] = stock.getAnalystName();
            stockData[3] = stock.getRating();
            stkList.add(stockData);
         }
         return stkList;
      } catch (Exception e) {
         throw new EJBException(e.getMessage());
      }
   }
}
```

The getStockRatings() method, shown above, calls the findRatedStocks() method of the Stock entity bean's home interface to get references to the Stock beans that have been rated. This getStockRatings() method, then returns an ArrayList of String arrays. Each String array has four elements that contain the stock's ticker symbol, the stock's name, the name of the analyst that rated it, and the rating. The client UI uses this method each time it needs to display a current list of the stocks that have been rated. In the *Using Design Patterns in EJB Applications* section of the next chapter, we'll move away from using String arrays to pass data between clients and session beans in favor of using classes that are modeled after the Stock and Analyst entity beans. Note that in all of these methods, we're throwing an EJBException. This practice, and the topic of exception handling within EJBs in general, will be discussed in the context of the next example.

```
public ArrayList getAllAnalysts() {
  try {
    // Get the initial context
    InitialContext initial = new InitialContext();

    // Get the object reference
    LocalAnalystHome home = (LocalAnalystHome)
      initial.lookup("java:comp/env/ejb/beans.Analyst");

    // Get the analysts
    ArrayList analystList = new ArrayList();
    Collection analysts = home.findAllAnalysts();
    Iterator i = analysts.iterator();
    while (i.hasNext()) {
      LocalAnalyst analyst = (LocalAnalyst) i.next();
      Object[] analystData = new Object[2];
      analystData[0] = analyst.getAnalystId();
      analystData[1] = analyst.getName();
      analystList.add(analystData);
    }
    return analystList;
  } catch (Exception e) {
    throw new EJBException(e.getMessage());
  }
}
```

The `getAllAnalysts()` method, shown above, calls the `findAllAnalysts()` method of the `Analyst` entity bean's home interface to get references to all of the `Analyst` beans. It returns the data contained in the `Analyst` beans via an `ArrayList` of `String` arrays. The client UI uses this method when it needs to populate the drop-down list that contains the names of the analysts.

```
public ArrayList getUnratedStocks() {
  try {
    // Get the initial context
    InitialContext initial = new InitialContext();

    // Get the object reference
    LocalStockHome home = (LocalStockHome)
      initial.lookup("java:comp/env/ejb/beans.Stock");

    // Get the rated stocks
    Collection stocks = home.findRatedStocks();
    LocalStock[] ratedStocks = new LocalStock[stocks.size()];
    Iterator i = stocks.iterator();
    int ctr = 0;
    while (i.hasNext()) {
      LocalStock stock = (LocalStock) i.next();
      ratedStocks[ctr++] = stock;
    }
```

```
      // Get all stocks
      Collection allStocks = home.findAllStocks();
      ArrayList stkList = new ArrayList();

      // Eliminate the rated stocks
      Iterator j = allStocks.iterator();
      while (j.hasNext()) {
        LocalStock stock = (LocalStock) j.next();
        boolean rated = false;
        for (int k = 0; k < ratedStocks.length; k++) {
          String ratedTicker = ratedStocks[k].getTickerSymbol();
          if (stock.getTickerSymbol().equals(ratedTicker)) {
            rated = true;
            break;
          }
        }
        if (!rated) {
          stkList.add(stock.getTickerSymbol());
        }
      }
      return stkList;
    } catch (Exception e) {
      throw new EJBException(e.getMessage());
    }
  }
```

The getUnratedStocks() method, shown above, calls the findRatedStocks() and findAllStocks() methods of the Stock entity bean's home interface. It uses the collections returned from these methods to identify the stocks that haven't been rated, and it returns an ArrayList of Strings containing ticker symbols. The client UI uses this method when it needs to populate the drop-down list that contains the ticker symbols for stocks that haven't been rated. A good exercise for you at this point would be to create an EJB-QL finder method in the Stock bean named findUnratedStocks() that returns only the stocks that haven't been rated. Having this method available would simplify this getUnratedStocks() method considerably:

```
  public void addStockRating(String ticker, Integer analystId,
    String rating) {
    try {
      // Get the initial context
      InitialContext initial = new InitialContext();
      // Get the home references
      LocalStockHome stockHome = (LocalStockHome)
        initial.lookup("java:comp/env/ejb/beans.Stock");
      LocalAnalystHome analystHome = (LocalAnalystHome)
        initial.lookup("java:comp/env/ejb/beans.Analyst");
      LocalStock stock = stockHome.findByPrimaryKey(ticker);

      // Get the local references
      LocalAnalyst analyst =
        analystHome.findByPrimaryKey(analystId);
```

```
            analyst.assignStock(stock);
            stock.setRating(rating);
        } catch (Exception e) {
            e.printStackTrace();
            throw new EJBException(e.getMessage());
        }
    }
```

The addStockRating() method, shown above, takes two arguments; the ticker symbol of the stock being rated, and the ID number of the analyst rating the stock. These are the primary keys of the Stock and Analyst entity beans, respectively. This method uses these arguments to get references to a Stock bean and an Analyst bean. It then calls the assignStock() method of the Analyst bean that we examined earlier, passing in the reference of the Stock bean being rated. The client UI uses this method when the user clicks the **Add Rating** button. The StockListAdder class uses this addStockRating() method as well to set up an initial stock rating:

```
    public void addAnalyst(Integer id, String name) {
        try {
            InitialContext initial = new InitialContext();

            // Get the object reference
            LocalAnalystHome analystHome = (LocalAnalystHome)
                initial.lookup("java:comp/env/ejb/beans.Analyst");
            analystHome.create(id, name);
        } catch (Exception e) {
            e.printStackTrace();
            throw new EJBException(e.getMessage());
        }
    }

    public void addStock(String ticker, String name) {
        try {
            InitialContext initial = new InitialContext();

            // Get the object reference
            LocalStockHome stockHome = (LocalStockHome)
                initial.lookup("java:comp/env/ejb/beans.Stock");
            stockHome.create(ticker, name);
        } catch (Exception e) {
            e.printStackTrace();
            throw new EJBException(e.getMessage());
        }
    }
```

The addAnalyst() and addStock() methods, shown above, take as arguments the values required for creating Analyst and Stock beans, respectively, after which they call the create() method of the proper home interface. The StockListAdder class uses these methods to create entity beans, and the client UI (the StockClient class) does not use them at all.

Shown below is the rest of the `StockListBean.java` listing; a standard refrain for our session bean implementation classes:

```
   // Standard ejb methods
   public void ejbActivate() { }
   public void ejbPassivate() { }
   public void ejbRemove() { }
   public void ejbCreate() { }
   public void setSessionContext(SessionContext context) { }
}
```

Here is the Java source code for the home interface of the `StockList` session bean, `StockListHome.java`:

```
package beans;

import java.rmi.RemoteException;
import javax.ejb.CreateException;
import javax.ejb.EJBHome;

public interface StockListHome extends EJBHome {
   // The create method for the StockList bean
   public StockList create() throws CreateException, RemoteException;
}
```

As you can see the code is pretty simple.

Last but not least the Java source code for the GUI client, `StockClient.java`, may be downloaded from the Wrox web site. It's not listed here because there isn't much code in there relevant to the EJB concepts we've been discussing. You might take a moment, however, to peruse that code, especially in areas where `StockList` session bean methods are being utilized. Doing so will help prepare you for the example in the *Using Design Patterns in EJB Applications* section of the next chapter, because it builds on this example.

Here is a relevant excerpt from the deployment descriptor:

```
   ...
   <display-name>StockListCmrJar</display-name>
   <enterprise-beans>
     ...
     <entity>
       <ejb-name>AnalystEjb</ejb-name>
       ...
     </entity>
     <entity>
       <ejb-name>StockEjb</ejb-name>
       ...
       <query>
```

```
      <query-method>
        <method-name>findAllStocks</method-name>
        ...
      </query-method>
      <result-type-mapping>Local</result-type-mapping>
      <ejb-ql>SELECT DISTINCT OBJECT(s)<BR>
                FROM Stock s<BR>
                ORDER BY s.tickerSymbol</ejb-ql>
    </query>
    <query>
      <query-method>
        <method-name>ejbSelectAnalyst</method-name>
        <method-params>
          <method-param>java.lang.String</method-param>
        </method-params>
      </query-method>
      <result-type-mapping>Local</result-type-mapping>
      <ejb-ql>SELECT s.analyst.name<BR>
                FROM Stock s<BR>
                WHERE s.tickerSymbol = ?1</ejb-ql>
    </query>
    <query>
      <query-method>
        <method-name>findRatedStocks</method-name>
        ...
      </query-method>
      <result-type-mapping>Local</result-type-mapping>
      <ejb-ql>SELECT DISTINCT OBJECT(s)<BR>
                FROM Analyst a, Stock s<BR>
                WHERE s MEMBER OF a.stocks<BR>
                ORDER BY s.tickerSymbol</ejb-ql>
    </query>
  </entity>
</enterprise-beans>
<relationships>
  <ejb-relation>
    <ejb-relationship-role>
      <ejb-relationship-role-name>AnalystEjb
      </ejb-relationship-role-name>
      <multiplicity>One</multiplicity>
      <relationship-role-source>
        <ejb-name>AnalystEjb</ejb-name>
      </relationship-role-source>
      <cmr-field>
        <cmr-field-name>stocks</cmr-field-name>
        <cmr-field-type>java.util.Collection</cmr-field-type>
      </cmr-field>
    </ejb-relationship-role>
    <ejb-relationship-role>
      <ejb-relationship-role-name>StockEjb</ejb-relationship-role-name>
      <multiplicity>Many</multiplicity>
      <relationship-role-source>
```

```
              <ejb-name>StockEjb</ejb-name>
          </relationship-role-source>
          <cmr-field>
            <cmr-field-name>analyst</cmr-field-name>
          </cmr-field>
        </ejb-relationship-role>
      </ejb-relation>
    </relationships>
    ...
  </ejb-jar>
```

In the listing above, the `<query>` element in the `<entity>` element for `StockEjb` holds the EJB-QL for the `ejbSelectAnalyst()` select method. Also shown are the descriptors for the container-managed relationships that we defined earlier using the **Add Relationship** dialog of the Deployment Tool.

In this section we've discussed, and walked through an example of, container-managed relationships and EJB-QL select methods. In the next section, we'll use JDBC in the context of an EJB application.

Using JDBC with Enterprise JavaBeans

EJB-QL is an exciting technology that greatly enhances the functionality of Enterprise JavaBeans. There are times, however, that you may want to use JDBC instead of EJB-QL:

❑   For example, EJB-QL is still a developing part of the specification. The EJB 2.1 specification added new keywords, which supports more complex queries. SQL is a much more developed specification, however, and functionality accompanies that maturity. In addition, SQL can be more straightforward than EJB-QL. When you need functionality not yet supported by the EJB-QL specification, or want a more understandable query, you might want to consider using JDBC.

❑   You may also want to use JDBC for performance reasons. Often, a JDBC query written especially for performance will execute faster than a similar EJB-QL query. When you encounter a poorly performing EJB-QL query, you might consider implementing the query in JDBC, along with the appropriate database tuning.

Let's look at an example of using JDBC within a session bean as an alternative to using EJB-QL.

Try It Out   **Using JDBC from within a Session Bean**

This example alters the previous example slightly to demonstrate the use of JDBC within the `StockList` session bean. To accomplish this, we're going to modify the `getAllAnalysts()` method of the `StockListBean` class that we walked through a bit ago. This modification will entail removing the call to the `findAllAnalysts()` method of the `Analyst` bean's home interface, and executing a JDBC query instead.

Building and Running the Example

The process to build and run this example is the same as the previous example, including all of the Java source filenames. The differences are:

1. Create a new application directory called `StockListJdbcApp`, and within it create the `beans` and `client` subfolders.

2. When creating the application EAR file and the bean JAR use the names StockListJdbcApp.ear and StockListJdbcJar. When creating the client stubs JAR file use StockListJdbcStubs.jar for the filename.

There also are two additional pages of the Deployment Tool involved because of the fact that we're going to connect to the underlying database from a session bean.

1. After defining the relationship between the `Analyst` and `Stock` beans, choose StockListEjb from the tree in the left-hand panel and select the **Resource Refs** tab. In that tab, enter a **Coded Name** of jdbc/StockDB as shown in the following screenshot:

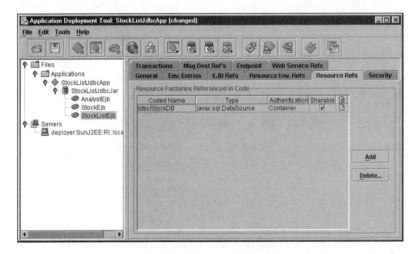

2. While you are configuring the platform-specific deployment settings, visit the **Res. Refs** tab and select the **StockListEjb** entry in the **Enterprise Beans in Jar** panel as shown below:

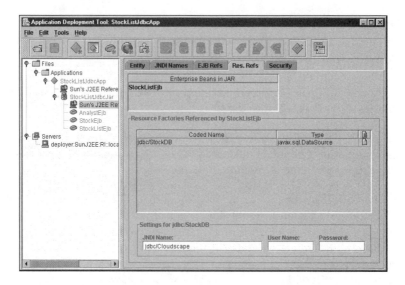

Then select the jdbc/StockDB row in the **Resource Factories Referenced by StockListEjb** panel. A text field should become available at the bottom of the page in which you can enter the **JNDI Name** of the database. Enter jdbc/Cloudscape in this text field and continue on with the process.

3. When you run the client, you'll see that it has the same GUI as the previous example, shown again below for your convenience:

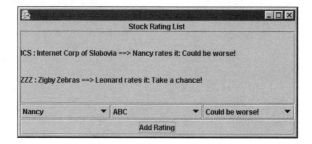

How It Works

Only one Java source file changed from the previous example. This file contains the implementation of the `StockList` session bean, `StockListBean.java`:

```
package beans;

import java.sql.Connection;
import java.sql.ResultSet;
import java.sql.SQLException;
import java.sql.Statement;
```

```
import javax.ejb.EJBException;
import javax.ejb.SessionBean;
import javax.ejb.SessionContext;
import javax.naming.InitialContext;
import javax.naming.NamingException;
import javax.sql.DataSource;

// General imports
import java.util.*;

public class StockListBean implements SessionBean {

    // The public business methods. These must be coded in the
    // remote interface also.

    public ArrayList getStockRatings() {
        try {
            // Get the initial context
            InitialContext initial = new InitialContext();

            // Get the object reference
            LocalStockHome home = (LocalStockHome)
                initial.lookup("java:comp/env/ejb/beans.Stock");

            // Get the stocks
            ArrayList stkList = new ArrayList();
            Collection stocks = home.findRatedStocks();
            Iterator i = stocks.iterator();
            while (i.hasNext()) {
                LocalStock stock = (LocalStock) i.next();
                String[] stockData = new String[4];
                stockData[0] = stock.getTickerSymbol();
                stockData[1] = stock.getName();
                stockData[2] = stock.getAnalystName();
                stockData[3] = stock.getRating();
                stkList.add(stockData);
            }

            return stkList;
        } catch (Exception e) {
            throw new EJBException(e.getMessage());
        }
    }

    public ArrayList getAllAnalysts() {
        try {
            // Make the SQL statements
            StringBuffer sql = new StringBuffer();
            sql.append("SELECT \"analystId\", \"name\" ");
            sql.append("FROM \"AnalystBeanTable\" ");
            sql.append("ORDER BY \"name\"");
```

```
      // Get the DB connection, statement, and resultset
      Connection conn = makeConnection();
      Statement stmt = conn.createStatement();
      ResultSet results = stmt.executeQuery(sql.toString());

      // Get the analysts
      ArrayList analystList = new ArrayList();
      while (results.next()) {
        Object[] analystData = new Object[2];
        analystData[0] = new Integer(results.getInt(1));
        analystData[1] = results.getString(2);
        analystList.add(analystData);
      }

      results.close();
      stmt.close();
      conn.close();

      return analystList;
    }
    catch (Exception e) {
      throw new EJBException(e.getMessage());
    }
  }

  public ArrayList getUnratedStocks() {
    try {
      // Get the initial context
      InitialContext initial = new InitialContext();

      // Get the object reference
      LocalStockHome home = (LocalStockHome)
        initial.lookup("java:comp/env/ejb/beans.Stock");

      // Get the rated stocks
      Collection stocks = home.findRatedStocks();
      LocalStock[] ratedStocks = new LocalStock[stocks.size()];
      Iterator i = stocks.iterator();
      int ctr = 0;
      while (i.hasNext()) {
        LocalStock stock = (LocalStock) i.next();
        ratedStocks[ctr++] = stock;
      }

      // Get all stocks
      Collection allStocks = home.findAllStocks();
      ArrayList stkList = new ArrayList();

      // Eliminate the rated stocks
      Iterator j = allStocks.iterator();
      while (j.hasNext()) {
        LocalStock stock = (LocalStock) j.next();
```

```
      boolean rated = false;
      for (int k = 0; k < ratedStocks.length; k++) {
        String ratedTicker = ratedStocks[k].getTickerSymbol();
        if (stock.getTickerSymbol().equals(ratedTicker)) {
          rated = true;
          break;
        }
      }
      if (!rated) {
        stkList.add(stock.getTickerSymbol());
      }
    }
    return stkList;
  } catch (Exception e) {
    throw new EJBException(e.getMessage());
  }
}

public void addStockRating(String ticker,
                           Integer analystId,
                           String rating) {
  try {
    // Get the initial context
    InitialContext initial = new InitialContext();

    // Get the home references
    LocalStockHome stockHome = (LocalStockHome)
      initial.lookup("java:comp/env/ejb/beans.Stock");
    LocalAnalystHome analystHome = (LocalAnalystHome)
      initial.lookup("java:comp/env/ejb/beans.Analyst");
    LocalStock stock = stockHome.findByPrimaryKey(ticker);

    // Get the local references
    LocalAnalyst analyst = analystHome.findByPrimaryKey(analystId);
    analyst.assignStock(stock);
    stock.setRating(rating);
  } catch (Exception e) {
    e.printStackTrace();
    throw new EJBException(e.getMessage());
  }
}

public void addAnalyst(Integer id, String name) {
  try {
    InitialContext initial = new InitialContext();
    // Get the object reference
    LocalAnalystHome analystHome = (LocalAnalystHome)
      initial.lookup("java:comp/env/ejb/beans.Analyst");
    analystHome.create(id, name);
  } catch (Exception e) {
    e.printStackTrace();
    throw new EJBException(e.getMessage());
```

483

```
      }
    }

    public void addStock(String ticker, String name) {
      try {
        InitialContext initial = new InitialContext();

        // Get the object reference
        LocalStockHome stockHome = (LocalStockHome)
          initial.lookup("java:comp/env/ejb/beans.Stock");
        stockHome.create(ticker, name);
      } catch (Exception e) {
        e.printStackTrace();
        throw new EJBException(e.getMessage());
      }
    }

    private Connection makeConnection()
      throws NamingException, SQLException {

      InitialContext ic = new InitialContext();
      DataSource ds = (DataSource) ic.lookup("java:comp/env/jdbc/StockDB");
      return ds.getConnection();
    }

    // Standard ejb methods
    public void ejbActivate() { }
    public void ejbPassivate() { }
    public void ejbRemove() { }
    public void ejbCreate() { }
    public void setSessionContext(SessionContext context) { }
  }
```

As shown in the listing above, the getAllAnalysts() method executes a JDBC query to get the data from the all of the Analyst beans. This is in contrast to invoking the findAllAnalysts() method of the home interface of the Analyst bean as the previous example did. Note that in the makeConnection() method we're using the resource reference (jdbc/StockDB) that we specified in the Deployment Tool to get a reference to the data source.

Notice that most of these methods catch an Exception and throw an EJBException (located in the javax.ejb package) with the message from the original exception being passed into its constructor. EJB methods of a production application should be more discriminating in their exception handling. There are three main exception-handling scenarios that should be dealt with:

❑   When a checked exception can occur that is defined by the application (as opposed to those defined in the standard Java libraries), a good approach is to declare that the EJB method throws that exception. This allows that exception to be thrown to the caller to communicate the exception condition.

❑ When a checked exception can occur that is defined by standard Java libraries, the preferred approach is to wrap that exception, or the message contained within it, in an EJBException. An example of a checked Java library exception is the SQLException that could occur as a result of the executeQuery() method in the getAllAnalysts() method shown above.

❑ Unchecked exceptions (java.lang.RuntimeException and its subclasses) should typically not be caught, but rather allowed to be handled by the EJB container.

Summary

In this chapter, we continued the discussion of entity beans from the previous chapter, covering concepts such as **container-managed relationships,** EJB-QL **select methods**, and using JDBC to augment EJB-QL.

❑ Container-managed relationships are a huge convenience to the developer, because the work in maintaining the relationships is performed by the EJB container. These relationships can be one to one, one to many, and many to many. In addition, each kind of relationship can be unidirectional or bi-directional.

❑ EJB-QL select methods are similar to EJB-QL finder methods in that they provide for using a SQL-like language to query entity beans. We pointed out some major differences, however, in the areas of: where they are declared, visibility, what they can return, and naming convention.

❑ EJB-QL is a very powerful feature of EJBs, but there are times when it is advantageous to use JDBC as well. The most compelling reason for using it is *performance*, especially when querying many rows across several entity beans.

In the next chapter we'll cover more EJB topics such as implementing design patterns in EJB applications, developing message-driven beans, and using the new EJB Timer Service. We're also going to modify a JSP example from Chapter 5 to use the EJBs that we've been developing for the StockList examples.

Exercises

1. Using the class diagram in this chapter of the fictitious "Audio CD Collection" application, implement the CompactDiscTitle and RecordLabel entity beans using local references, including the container-managed relationship. Implement a stateless session bean that allows you to add record labels and CD titles. Write a simple client application to test your beans.

2. Modify the previous exercise, adding a method to the session bean that uses JDBC to find all CD titles ordered by name. Change the client application to execute this method.

CHAPTER 11

Using Design Patterns in EJB Applications   **487**

Using JSP and Servlets with EJBs   **507**

Developing Message-Driven Beans   **514**

Summary   **528**

Resources   **528**

Exercises   **529**

Design Patterns and Message-Driven Beans

The previous chapter introduced EJB container-managed relationships, and the use of JDBC in session beans. In this chapter, we will move on to some more advanced topics and another type of bean. You will learn about:

❑   What **design patterns** are, and how they can be applied in EJB applications.

❑   How to combine JSP and EJB technologies in one application. To demonstrate this, we'll fuse together the StockList example from the servlets chapter, Chapter 5, with an EJB-based version of the StockList application.

❑   Message-driven beans and the underlying Java Message Service (JMS) API.

❑   How to use the EJB Timer Service.

We'll start off by introducing the subject of design patterns, and how they can facilitate the development and maintenance of EJB applications.

Using Design Patterns in EJB Applications

When object-oriented software design is compared to designing a house, we know that software objects are analogous to some of the construction materials, or components, used to build the house. These materials or components range in size and complexity, some examples being a simple nail, a light switch, or a gas furnace.

Continuing this analogy, software **design patterns** are analogous to some of the concepts and styles used in house building. For example, when designing a house, an architect may specify that it have a gable roof, as opposed to, say, a hip roof or a gambrel (barn-style) roof. These well known roofing styles, or patterns, can be used to facilitate the task of designing and building a house – the architect doesn't have to invent a roofing style each time he or she designs a house, and the builder is familiar with implementing the design pattern of a gable roof. Not so coincidentally perhaps, roof trusses themselves are often built using a template, or pattern.

The concept of software design patterns became well known as a result of a book published in 1994 named *Design Patterns, Elements of Reusable Object-Oriented Software*. It was written by Erich Gamma, Richard Helm, Ralph Johnson, and John Vlissides (the "Gang of Four"), and it has a good starter set of software design patterns. Other works have been created since then that offer additional design patterns for the general object-oriented software domain, a well as for specific domains such as J2EE applications. One such work is Sun Microsystems' Java BluePrints Patterns Catalog, which can be viewed from the following link http://java.sun.com/blueprints/patterns/catalog.html.

Software design patterns describe solutions to specific software design problems, such as:

❑ Designing an application in such a way that the client UI doesn't have to worry about the architecture or location of the application logic layer of an application. We'll demonstrate shortly how a couple of common patterns, specifically the **façade** and **value object** design patterns, can be employed to address this design problem.

❑ Providing the ability to create an instance of a class that is vendor- or product-specific, in a generic way. We'll look at a very simple case of a pattern that enables this, known as the **factory pattern**.

❑ Designing a method in such a way that it will create and return the same instance of a class to any method that calls it. We'll see how the **singleton** design pattern can be used to enable this.

We'll build upon the now familiar `StockList` example to demonstrate the design patterns mentioned above.

Try It Out   Implementing Design Patterns

This example introduces the **façade**, **value object**, and **singleton** patterns to the previous `StockList` example. These design patterns will be explained in the context of this example.

Shown below is a class diagram for this example. The dashed lines indicate dependencies between classes in the direction of the arrow. For example, methods of the `StockClient` class hold references to `StockVo` instances. As the class name reveals, we'll implement the façade pattern with the help of the `StockListFacade` class. The singleton pattern will be employed in that class as well. The `StockVo` and `AnalystVo` classes will be used to implement the value object pattern:

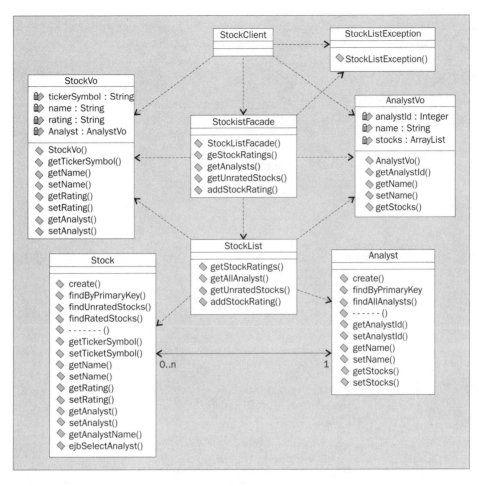

In this example, there are four new Java source files, as seen in the class diagram above. These are:

❑ StockListFacade.java

❑ StockListException.java

❑ AnalystVo.java

❑ StockVo.java

In addition, four Java source files from the CMR example were modified:

❑ StockList.java

❑ StockListBean.java

❑ StockClient.java

❑ StockListAdder.java

1. Firstly, you will need to type in the code for the `StockListFacade.java` source file, in which you can see an implementation of the façade pattern:

```
package facade;

import beans.StockList;
import beans.StockListHome;
import vo.AnalystVo;
import vo.StockVo;
import javax.naming.InitialContext;
import javax.rmi.PortableRemoteObject;

// General imports
import java.util.*;

public class StockListFacade {
  // Reference to singleton facade
  private static StockListFacade stockListFacade;

  // The reference to the stock list bean
  private StockList stockList;

  // private constructor - makes connection to session bean
  private StockListFacade() throws StockListException {
    try {
      // Get a naming context
      InitialContext jndiContext = new InitialContext();

      // Get a reference to the StockList JNDI entry
      Object ref  = jndiContext.lookup("ejb/beans.StockList");

      // Get a reference from this to the Bean's Home interface
      StockListHome home = (StockListHome)
        PortableRemoteObject.narrow(ref, StockListHome.class);

      // Create a StockList object from the Home interface
      stockList = home.create();
    } catch(Exception e) {
      throw new StockListException(e.getMessage());
    }
  }

  // The business methods. No exposure to actual implementation
  // on the server and the communication method between client and
  // server is hidden to the client.

  public ArrayList getStockRatings() throws StockListException {
    try {
      ArrayList ratings = stockList.getStockRatings();
      return ratings;
    }
    catch (Exception re) {
```

```
      throw new StockListException(re.getMessage());
    }
  }

  public ArrayList getAllAnalysts() throws StockListException {
    try {
      ArrayList analysts = stockList.getAllAnalysts();
      return analysts;
    }
    catch (Exception re) {
      throw new StockListException(re.getMessage());
    }
  }

  public ArrayList getUnratedStocks() throws StockListException {
    try {
      ArrayList stocks = stockList.getUnratedStocks();
      return stocks;
    }
    catch (Exception re) {
      throw new StockListException(re.getMessage());
    }
  }

  public void addStockRating(StockVo stock)
    throws StockListException {
    try {
      stockList.addStockRating(stock);
    }
    catch (Exception re) {
      throw new StockListException(re.getMessage());
    }
  }

  public void addAnalyst(AnalystVo analyst)
    throws StockListException {
    try {
      stockList.addAnalyst(analyst);
    }
    catch (Exception re) {
      throw new StockListException(re.getMessage());
    }
  }

  public void addStock(StockVo stock) throws StockListException {
    try {
      stockList.addStock(stock);
    }
    catch (Exception re) {
      throw new StockListException(re.getMessage());
    }
  }
```

```
  public static StockListFacade getFacade()
    throws StockListException {
    if (stockListFacade == null) {
      stockListFacade = new StockListFacade();
    }

    return stockListFacade;
  }
}
```

2. Next up, enter the code for `StockListException.java`:

```
package facade;

public class StockListException extends Exception {

  public StockListException(String msg) {
    super(msg);
  }
}
```

3. And now `AnalystVo.java`:

```
package vo;

import java.io.Serializable;
import java.util.*;

public class AnalystVo implements Serializable {

  // Holds references to the attribute data
  private Integer analystId;
  private String name;

  // Holds references to the relationships
  private ArrayList stocks;

  public AnalystVo(Integer analystId, String name) {
    this.analystId = analystId;
    this.name = name;
    stocks = new ArrayList();
  }

  // Get analyst ID. No setter because primary key
  public Integer getAnalystId() {
    return analystId;
  }
```

```
    // Get, set name
    public String getName() {
      return name;
    }

    public void setName(String name) {
      this.name = name;
    }

    // Get stocks
    public ArrayList getStocks() {
      return stocks;
    }
}
```

4. And finally, enter `StockVo.java`:

```
package vo;

import java.io.Serializable;
import java.util.*;

public class StockVo implements Serializable {

  // Holds references to the attribute data
  private String tickerSymbol;
  private String name;
  private String rating;

  // Holds references to the relationships
  private AnalystVo analyst;

  public StockVo(String tickerSymbol, String name, String rating) {
    this.tickerSymbol = tickerSymbol;
    this.name = name;
    this.rating = rating;
    analyst = null;
  }

  // Get ticker symbol. No setter because primary key
  public String getTickerSymbol() {
    return tickerSymbol;
  }

  // Get, set name
  public String getName() {
    return name;
  }

  public void setName(String name) {
    this.name = name;
  }
```

```
  // Get, set rating
  public String getRating() {
    return rating;
  }

  public void setRating(String rating) {
    this.rating = rating;
  }

  // Get, set analyst
  public AnalystVo getAnalyst() {
    return analyst;
  }

  public void setAnalyst(AnalystVo analyst) {
    this.analyst = analyst;
  }
}
```

5. Next, we need to modify the source code for the `StockList` session bean to see how it uses value objects. Here is the `StockList` session bean's remote interface, `StockList.java`:

```java
package beans;

import vo.AnalystVo;
import vo.StockVo;
import java.rmi.RemoteException;
import javax.ejb.EJBObject;

// General imports
import java.util.*;

public interface StockList extends EJBObject {
  // The public business methods on the Stock List bean
  public ArrayList getStockRatings() throws RemoteException;
  public ArrayList getAllAnalysts() throws RemoteException;
  public ArrayList getUnratedStocks() throws RemoteException;
  public void addStockRating(StockVo stockVo) throws RemoteException;
  public void addAnalyst(AnalystVo analystVo) throws RemoteException;
  public void addStock(StockVo stockVo) throws RemoteException;
}
```

6. Every method in the interface shown above either takes value objects as an argument, or returns value objects (actually in these cases, an `ArrayList` of them). So let's see how they are used by the new, value object-enabled version of the session bean's implementation class, `StockListBean.java`:

```
package beans;

import vo.AnalystVo;
import vo.StockVo;
import javax.ejb.EJBException;
import javax.ejb.SessionBean;
import javax.ejb.SessionContext;
import javax.naming.InitialContext;

// General imports
import java.util.*;

public class StockListBean implements SessionBean {

  // The public business methods. These must be coded in the
  // remote interface also.

  public ArrayList getStockRatings() {
    try {
      // Get the initial context
      InitialContext initial = new InitialContext();
      // Get the object reference
      LocalStockHome home = (LocalStockHome)
        initial.lookup("java:comp/env/ejb/beans.Stock");

      // Get the stocks
      ArrayList stkList = new ArrayList();
      Collection stocks = home.findRatedStocks();
      Iterator i = stocks.iterator();
      while (i.hasNext()) {
        LocalStock stock = (LocalStock) i.next();
        StockVo stockVo = new StockVo(stock.getTickerSymbol(),
          stock.getName(), stock.getRating());
        LocalAnalyst analyst = stock.getAnalyst();
        AnalystVo analystVo = new AnalystVo(analyst.getAnalystId(),
          analyst.getName());
        stockVo.setAnalyst(analystVo);
        stkList.add(stockVo);
      }
      return stkList;
    }
    catch (Exception e) {
      throw new EJBException(e.getMessage());
    }
  }
}
```

In the `getStockRatings()` method shown above:

❑ A call is made to the `findRatedStocks()` method of the `Stock` entity bean's home
   interface, which returns a `Collection` of `Stock` entity bean references.

❑ We iterate over that `Collection` and create a `StockVo` instance from the fields of each entity bean, populating an `ArrayList` with the `StockVo` references:

   ❑ Since the client UI is going to display information from the related `Analyst` entity bean, we use the `getAnalyst()` CMR method of each `Stock` bean to get a reference to the `Analyst` bean. An `AnalystVo` instance is then created from the fields of the `Analyst` bean, which is then associated with the `StockVo` instance via its `setAnalyst()` method.

❑ The `ArrayList` that contains `StockVo` references, each of which holds an `AnalystVo` reference, is serialized and streamed back to the caller. Recall that the caller in this case is the `StockListFacade` class.

If you decide to implement the idea of having methods in your value objects that mimic CMR methods, care should be taken not to carry the idea too far. You probably don't want to stream a graph of value objects back to the client in one method invocation that contains the data from all of the entity beans in the application, for example.

7. The other methods that return an `ArrayList`, shown below, are similar in nature to the `getStockRatings()` method:

```java
public ArrayList getAllAnalysts() {
  try {
    // Get the initial context
    InitialContext initial = new InitialContext();
    // Get the object reference
    LocalAnalystHome home = (LocalAnalystHome)
      initial.lookup("java:comp/env/ejb/beans.Analyst");

    // Get the analysts
    ArrayList analystList = new ArrayList();
    Collection analysts = home.findAllAnalysts();
    Iterator i = analysts.iterator();
    while (i.hasNext()) {
      LocalAnalyst analyst = (LocalAnalyst) i.next();
      AnalystVo analystVo = new AnalystVo(analyst.getAnalystId(),
        analyst.getName());
      analystList.add(analystVo);
    }
    return analystList;
  }
  catch (Exception e) {
    throw new EJBException(e.getMessage());
  }
}

public ArrayList getUnratedStocks() {
  try {
    // Get the initial context
    InitialContext initial = new InitialContext();
```

```
      // Get the object reference
      LocalStockHome home = (LocalStockHome)
        initial.lookup("java:comp/env/ejb/beans.Stock");

      // Get the rated stocks
      Collection stocks = home.findRatedStocks();
      LocalStock[] ratedStocks = new LocalStock[stocks.size()];
      Iterator i = stocks.iterator();
      int ctr = 0;
      while (i.hasNext()) {
        LocalStock stock = (LocalStock) i.next();
        ratedStocks[ctr++] = stock;
      }

      // Get all stocks
      Collection allStocks = home.findAllStocks();
      ArrayList stkList = new ArrayList();

      // Eliminate the rated stocks
      Iterator j = allStocks.iterator();
      while (j.hasNext()) {
        LocalStock stock = (LocalStock) j.next();
        boolean rated = false;
        for (int k = 0; k < ratedStocks.length; k++) {
          String ratedTicker = ratedStocks[k].getTickerSymbol();
          if (stock.getTickerSymbol().equals(ratedTicker)) {
            rated = true;
            break;
          }
        }
        if (!rated) {
          StockVo stockVo = new StockVo(stock.getTickerSymbol(),
            stock.getName(), null);
          stkList.add(stockVo);
        }
      }
      return stkList;
    }
    catch (Exception e) {
      throw new EJBException(e.getMessage());
    }
  }
```

The addStockRating() method, shown below, passes the primary key fields contained in the AnalystVo and StockVo value objects to findByPrimaryKey() methods. This is for the purpose of obtaining references to the entity beans from which these value objects were originally created:

```
public void addStockRating(StockVo stockVo) {
  try {
    // Get the initial context
```

```
      InitialContext initial = new InitialContext();
      // Get the home references
      LocalStockHome stockHome = (LocalStockHome)
        initial.lookup("java:comp/env/ejb/beans.Stock");
      LocalAnalystHome analystHome = (LocalAnalystHome)
        initial.lookup("java:comp/env/ejb/beans.Analyst");
      LocalStock stock =
        stockHome.findByPrimaryKey(stockVo.getTickerSymbol());
      // Get the local refs
      LocalAnalyst analyst = analystHome.findByPrimaryKey(
        stockVo.getAnalyst().getAnalystId());
      analyst.assignStock(stock);
      stock.setRating(stockVo.getRating());
    }
    catch (Exception e) {
      e.printStackTrace();
      throw new EJBException(e.getMessage());
    }
  }
```

8. Turning our attention to the addAnalyst() method, shown below, we see that it takes an AnalystVo instance as its argument, which it uses to create an Analyst entity bean. The addStock() method is very similar in nature to the addAnalyst() method:

```
public void addAnalyst(AnalystVo analystVo) {
  try {
    InitialContext initial = new InitialContext();
    // Get the object reference
    LocalAnalystHome analystHome = (LocalAnalystHome)
      initial.lookup("java:comp/env/ejb/beans.Analyst");
    analystHome.create(analystVo.getAnalystId(),
      analystVo.getName());
  }
  catch (Exception e) {
    e.printStackTrace();
    throw new EJBException(e.getMessage());
  }
}
```

```
public void addStock(StockVo stockVo) {
  try {
    InitialContext initial = new InitialContext();
    // Get the object reference
    LocalStockHome stockHome = (LocalStockHome)
      initial.lookup("java:comp/env/ejb/beans.Stock");
    stockHome.create(stockVo.getTickerSymbol(),
      stockVo.getName());
  }
  catch (Exception e) {
    e.printStackTrace();
```

```
        throw new EJBException(e.getMessage());
    }
}

// Standard ejb methods
public void ejbActivate() { }
public void ejbPassivate() { }
public void ejbRemove() { }
public void ejbCreate() { }
public void setSessionContext(SessionContext context) { }
}
```

Notice that the logic that creates an entity bean from a value object, and vice-versa, is contained in these session bean methods. Another appropriate place to put this logic would be in helper methods, perhaps located in a parent class of the entity beans' implementation classes. In that scenario, the session bean could call a hypothetical `getValueObject()` method of the entity bean, which would return a value object populated with the data in that bean.

9. Next, we will take a brief look at the client classes, beginning with the `StockListAdder` class, which initially loads the data into the entity beans via these value objects. Here's the source code listing for `StockListAdder.java`:

```
package client;

import facade.StockListFacade;
import vo.AnalystVo;
import vo.StockVo;

public class StockListAdder {

    public static void main(String[] args) {
        try {
            StockListFacade facade = StockListFacade.getFacade();

            // Add analysts
            System.out.println("adding analysts");

            facade.addAnalyst(new AnalystVo(new Integer(1), "Fred"));
            facade.addAnalyst(new AnalystVo(new Integer(2), "Leonard"));
            facade.addAnalyst(new AnalystVo(new Integer(3), "Sarah"));
            facade.addAnalyst(new AnalystVo(new Integer(4), "Nancy"));
            System.out.println("analysts added");
        }
        catch (Exception e) {
            System.out.println("exception adding analysts");
            e.printStackTrace();
        }

        try {
            StockListFacade facade = StockListFacade.getFacade();
```

```
        // Add stocks
        System.out.println("adding stocks");
        facade.addStock(new StockVo("ABC", "ABC Company", null));
        facade.addStock(new StockVo("ZZZ", "Zigby Zebras", null));
        facade.addStock(new StockVo("ICS",
                              "Internet Corp of Slobovia", null));
        facade.addStock(new StockVo("DDC", "Digby Door Company", null));
        facade.addStock(new StockVo("ZAP", "Zapalopalorinski Ltd.", null));
        facade.addStock(new StockVo("JIM", "Jimco", null));
        facade.addStock(new StockVo("SRU", "Stocks R Us", null));
        facade.addStock(new StockVo("SRI",
                              "Shelves and Radios Inc", null));
        facade.addStock(new StockVo("FBC", "Foo Bar Company", null));
        facade.addStock(new StockVo("DDBC",
                              "Ding Dong Bell Company", null));
        facade.addStock(new StockVo("UDE",
                              "Upn Down Elevator Company", null));
        System.out.println("stocks added");
    }
    catch (Exception e) {
      System.out.println("exception adding stocks");
      e.printStackTrace();
    }

    try {
        StockListFacade facade = StockListFacade.getFacade();

        // Add ratings
        System.out.println("adding ratings");
        StockVo stockVo = new StockVo("ZZZ", null, "Take a chance!");
        stockVo.setAnalyst(new AnalystVo(new Integer(2), null));
        facade.addStockRating(stockVo);
        System.out.println("ratings added");
    }
    catch (Exception e) {
      System.out.println("exception adding stocks");
      e.printStackTrace();
    }
  }
}
```

To create and populate an `Analyst` entity bean, for example, the desired data is passed into the constructor of the `AnalystVo` value object. The new `AnalystVo` object is then passed into the `addAnalyst()` method of the `StockListFacade` class that we walked through previously. This is all performed in one method, as seen below:

```
facade.addAnalyst(new AnalystVo(new Integer(1), "Fred"));
```

The way that this client method got a reference to the `StockListFacade` instance is in the statement shown here, which was previously shown after discussing the singleton and factory design patterns:

```
                   StockListFacade facade = StockListFacade.getFacade();
```

10. And finally, here is the Java source code for our new "value object-ized" version of the GUI client, `StockClient.java`:

```java
package client;

import facade.StockListFacade;
import vo.AnalystVo;
import vo.StockVo;

import java.util.*;

// Other general imports
import java.awt.*;
import java.awt.event.*;
import javax.swing.*;

public class StockClient extends JFrame
    implements ActionListener {
    private Integer[] _analystIds;
    private JButton _get = new JButton("Add Rating");
    private JPanel _stockPanel = new JPanel();
    private JComboBox _analysts = new JComboBox();
    private JComboBox _tickers = new JComboBox();
    private JComboBox _ratings = new JComboBox();

    public StockClient() {
        // Add the title
        JLabel title = new JLabel("Stock Rating List");
        title.setHorizontalAlignment(JLabel.CENTER);
        getContentPane().add(title, BorderLayout.NORTH);

        JPanel activityPanel = new JPanel(new BorderLayout());
        try {
            // Add the stock list
            buildStockList();
            JScrollPane scroller = new JScrollPane(_stockPanel);
            activityPanel.add(scroller, BorderLayout.CENTER);

            // Add the rating panel
            JPanel ratingPanel = new JPanel(new GridLayout(1, 3));
            // Add the analysts
            populateAnalysts();
            ratingPanel.add(_analysts);
            // Add the unrated stocks
            populateTickers();
            ratingPanel.add(_tickers);
            // Add the ratings to pick from
            _ratings.addItem("Run away! Run away!");
            _ratings.addItem("Could be worse!");
```

```
      _ratings.addItem("A bit of OK!");
      _ratings.addItem("Take a chance!");
      _ratings.addItem("Smashing!");
      ratingPanel.add(_ratings);
      activityPanel.add(ratingPanel, BorderLayout.SOUTH);

      getContentPane().add(activityPanel, BorderLayout.CENTER);
    }
    catch (Exception e) {
      e.printStackTrace();
    }

    // Add the buttons panel
    JPanel buttons = new JPanel(new GridLayout(1, 1));
    _get.addActionListener(this);
    buttons.add(_get);
    getContentPane().add(buttons, BorderLayout.SOUTH);

    addWindowListener(new WindowAdapter() {
      public void windowClosing(WindowEvent e) {
        System.exit(0);
      }
    });

    setSize(480, 250);
    setVisible(true);
  }

  private void buildStockList() throws Exception {
    ArrayList stoks = StockListFacade.getFacade().getStockRatings();
    _stockPanel.removeAll();
    _stockPanel.setLayout(new GridLayout(stoks.size(), 1));
    for (int i = 0; i < stoks.size(); i++) {
      StockVo stokInfo = (StockVo) stoks.get(i);
      Box stokLine = Box.createHorizontalBox();
      String stokDesc = stokInfo.getTickerSymbol() + " : " +
        stokInfo.getName() + " ==> " +
        stokInfo.getAnalyst().getName() + " rates it: " +
        stokInfo.getRating();
      stokLine.add(new JLabel(stokDesc));
      _stockPanel.add(stokLine);
    }
    _stockPanel.invalidate();
    _stockPanel.validate();
  }

  private void populateAnalysts() throws Exception {
    ArrayList anlysts = StockListFacade.getFacade().getAllAnalysts();
    _analystIds = new Integer[anlysts.size()];
    for (int i = 0; i < anlysts.size(); i++) {
      AnalystVo analystData = (AnalystVo) anlysts.get(i);
```

```
      _analystIds[i] = analystData.getAnalystId();
      _analysts.addItem(analystData.getName());
   }
}

private void populateTickers() throws Exception {
  _tickers.removeAllItems();
  ArrayList tkrs = StockListFacade.getFacade().getUnratedStocks();
  for (int i = 0; i < tkrs.size(); i++) {
    StockVo stockVo = (StockVo) tkrs.get(i);
    _tickers.addItem(stockVo.getTickerSymbol());
  }
  _tickers.invalidate();
  _tickers.validate();
}

public void actionPerformed(ActionEvent ae) {
  // Get was clicked
  if (ae.getSource() == _get) {
    try {
      int anlystNo = _analysts.getSelectedIndex();
      if (anlystNo < 0) {
        JOptionPane.showMessageDialog(this, "No analyst selected!");
        return;
      }
      Integer aId = _analystIds[anlystNo];
      if (_tickers.getSelectedIndex() < 0) {
        JOptionPane.showMessageDialog(this, "No ticker selected!");
        return;
      }
      String tkr = (String) _tickers.getSelectedItem();
      if (_ratings.getSelectedIndex() < 0) {
        JOptionPane.showMessageDialog(this, "No rating selected!");
        return;
      }
      String rtg = (String) _ratings.getSelectedItem();
      StockVo stockVo = new StockVo(tkr, null, rtg);
      stockVo.setAnalyst(new AnalystVo(aId, null));
      StockListFacade.getFacade().addStockRating(stockVo);
      buildStockList();
      populateTickers();
    }
    catch (Exception e) {
      e.printStackTrace();
    }
  }
}

public static void main(String[] args) {
  StockClient stockClient = new StockClient();
}
}
```

As you can see from the last two source code listings shown above, the clients in an application that use these design patterns can be well shielded from the realities of the application logic tier. The client's view of the rest of the application is the abstraction provided by the façades and value objects.

Now we can build and run the example. We used StockListPatternsApp.ear for the EAR filename, StockListPatternsJar for the EJB JAR name, and StockListPatternsStubs.jar for the client JAR (stubs) filename. The build process is identical to the one that we used for the first example in the previous chapter (the CMR example), with a couple of tweaks:

1. In addition to the usual packages, `beans` and `client`, you'll need to compile the classes in the `vo` and `facade` packages. These additional classes may be compiled by using the following commands:

```
> javac -d . vo/*.java

> javac -d . facade/*.java
```

The classes in these packages pertain to the value object and façade pattern, respectively.

2. The other tweak to the process is to put the classes located in the `vo` package into the EJB JAR, as shown below, when you are configuring the `StockList` session bean. We do this because the `StockList` bean is dependent upon those classes as illustrated in the class diagram above:

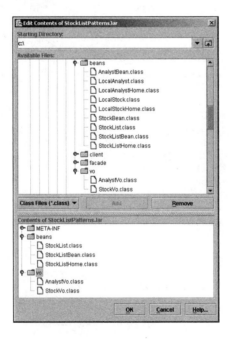

And that's it. The appearance and behavior of the client UI is the same as in both of the examples in the previous chapter.

How It Works

Now that you've seen the design patterns in action, let's take a look at how they work. The first piece of code uses the façade pattern.

The **façade pattern** hides the server side of an application from the client with a thin veneer, or façade. As seen in the class diagram above, the StockClient class is no longer directly dependent upon the StockList session bean, but instead only "knows about" the StockListFacade class. The client calls methods of the façade class as if it were the application logic layer, and the façade class invokes methods of the application logic layer (the StockList session bean in this case) as needed. This approach has several advantages, including:

❑ The location of the application logic layer of the application is hidden behind the façade, so if its location changes, only the façade has to know about it.

❑ The client is insulated from changes to the application logic layer by the façade. This tends to reduce maintenance by localizing the necessary changes to façade classes, rather than scattered all over the UI.

❑ Data can be cached in the façade. This is especially helpful in terms of optimization when the client and application logic layers are separated by a network. In this way, the façade can maintain state for the UI.

❑ During development, the façade methods can first be developed as stubs, mimicking the eventual functionality of the application tier methods. This facilitates simultaneous development of these tiers.

A disadvantage of using facades is that by introducing a façade layer between the client and the application logic, data is passed from the client to the façade and then from the façade to the application logic. Therefore the data is passed one more time than necessary, but in our opinion, the advantages far outweigh this disadvantage.

When the constructor for the StockListFacade class is called, it does the same thing that our client UIs have done in the past: get a reference to a session bean. It stores that reference in an instance variable so that methods of the façade, when invoked by the client, can use the reference to call methods of the session bean. Of course, larger applications would typically contain multiple façades and session beans.

Notice that each of the methods of the StockListFacade class throws a StockListException. The methods that call methods of the StockList session bean catch an exception and throw the StockListException, with the message of the original exception passed into the constructor. Techniques such as this allow the façade to further insulate the client from the implementation details of the application logic tier, never having to know about a RemoteException, for example.

The `StockListFacade` class employs another design pattern as well – the **singleton pattern**. Take a look at the `getFacade()` method and you'll see that it is responsible for creating and returning and instance of a class. Notice, however, that if an instance already exists it returns that instance. This is called the *singleton* pattern because only a *single* instance of the returned class exists. This is useful in cases such as this façade example because multiple client UI classes may need a reference to a `StockClientFacade` instance, but there is no need for more than one to exist. In fact, we wouldn't want more than one because each one would have a remote reference to the session bean, which consumes resources.

Note that in the case where the client is a servlet or JSP, if we wanted the façade to hold some state without having it shared by all the clients, we would use a modified singleton pattern in conjunction with an `HttpSession` object. The `getFacade()` method would return the `StockClientFacade` instance for a *given session*, creating one if it doesn't exist.

In addition to implementing the singleton pattern, the `getFacade()` method implements a simple version of another design pattern known as the **factory pattern**. This pattern is characterized by a method, typically `static`, that creates and returns an instance of a class. The method that creates the instance is called a **factory method**, and it returns an object that is guaranteed to be of some type. This type is often either an interface that the object implements, or an abstract class that the object's class is a subclass of. This is preferable to directly using a constructor in some cases, because the returned class can be vendor-specific but created in a generic way.

As you have seen in the `StockClient.java` listing, the clients of this particular façade class call `StockListFacade.getFacade()` to obtain an instance of the `StockListFacade` class.

The Value Object Pattern

For reasons mentioned in Chapter 8, it is usually not good practice to allow clients to have remote references to entity beans. These reasons can be summarized as follows:

❑ Calling entity bean methods directly circumvents the business logic contained in session beans, and tends to push the business logic into the UI code.

❑ Session beans can protect the UI from changes to the entity beans.

❑ Restricting client access to session beans conserves server and network resources.

However, as we saw in the CMR example, awkward mechanisms were employed in their absence. For example, `ArrayLists` of arrays of `Strings` were used to pass entity bean data between the client and the application logic tier. The **value object pattern** addresses this problem by providing classes that are modeled after the entity beans. These classes are mainly used to carry entity bean data between tiers. There are two value object classes in this example: the `AnalystVo` class represents the `Analyst` entity bean, and the `StockVo` class represents the `Stock` entity bean. To keep them separate from other classes, we've put them in their own package, named `vo`.

The `AnalystVo` value object class contains an instance variable for each of the CMP fields of the `Analyst` entity bean. Its constructor takes all of these fields as arguments (although some value object implementations we've seen have only a no-argument constructor, and some have both forms of constructors). The `AnalystVo` value object also contains a getter and setter method for each of the non-primary key fields. It has only a getter for the primary key field because that field won't be changed.

Although not typical of value object pattern implementations, our value object also models container-managed relationships. To do this, it contains an instance variable that is capable of referencing an `ArrayList` of `StockVo` instances.

Since value objects are designed to carry data between tiers, they must implement the `Serializable` interface of the `java.io` package.

While we're looking at value objects, let's briefly describe the value object that represents the `Stock` entity bean, `StockVo.java`. All of the things that were said about the `AnalystVo` class apply to this `StockVo` class as well. Due to the nature of the CMR relationship in the `Stock` entity bean, the analogous methods in this value object return and take a single instance.

If you take another look at the `StockListFacade` class listing, you'll notice that these value object classes are passed into and returned by these methods, either as individual objects or inside of `ArrayList` objects. The classes in this example that manipulate them most, however, are the ones associated with the `StockList` session bean, and the client classes.

Using JSP and Servlets with EJBs

All of the EJB examples shown up until this point have had clients that were one of the following types:

- ❏   Simple command-line Java application
- ❏   Java Swing application

To tie things together a bit, now we're going to demonstrate an example EJB application whose client UI consists of JSPs and servlets. To facilitate this, we'll use the patterns discussed in the previous section. In fact, all the code in this example is exactly the same as in the previous example, with one exception: instead of using the `StockClient` class as the client UI, we'll use a modified version of the JSP and servlets-based **StockList** example from Chapter 5.

Since the EJB portion of the application is identical to the previous example, you can use the same process to build and configure it. Refer back to the first example of Chapter 3 for instructions on configuring the JSP part of this application in the Deployment Tool.

None of the source code changed for the session and entity beans, façades, and value objects. The only source code that did change was JSP and servlet code. Those changes were for the purpose of adapting the UI portion of the previous JSP and servlets-based `StockList` application to using our façades and value objects. The modified source files are:

❑ `StockListServlet.java`

❑ `RatingsForm.jsp`

❑ `AddRating.java`

❑ `AnalystForm.jsp`

The `StockList` application was first presented in Chapter 5. It has been rewritten here to use the façade and value objects. The general flow will be reviewed here, however, for the purpose of pointing out the use of façades and value objects.

The entry point into the StockList web application was this HTML page, `index.html`:

```
<!DOCTYPE HTML PUBLIC "-//W3C//DTD HTML 4.01 Transitional//EN">
<html>
  <head>
    <title>Stocks and Analysts</title>
  </head>

  <body>
    <h1>Stocks and Analysts</h1>
    <p>
      <a href="/stock/StockList/AnalystForm">See all Analysts</a>
    <p>
      <a href="/stock/StockList/RatingsForm">See all Ratings</a>
    <hr>
  </body>
</html>
```

When one of the links is clicked, `index.html` submits a request to a servlet called `StockList`, which is in the following `StockListServlet.java` listing:

```
import java.io.*;
import java.util.*;
import facade.*;

public class StockListServlet extends HttpServlet {
```

```java
public void doPost(HttpServletRequest request,
                   HttpServletResponse response)
{
  doGet(request, response);
}

public void doGet(HttpServletRequest request,
                  HttpServletResponse response)
{
  try {
    ArrayList data = null;
    RequestDispatcher dispatcher;
    ServletContext context = getServletContext();
    StockListFacade facade = StockListFacade.getFacade();
    String name = request.getPathInfo();
    name = name.substring(1);  //strip the leading forward slash
    if ("AnalystForm".equals(name)) {
      data = facade.getAllAnalysts();
      request.setAttribute("data", data);
    } else if ("RatingsForm".equals(name)) {
      data = facade.getStockRatings();
      request.setAttribute("data", data);
      request.setAttribute("analysts", facade.getAllAnalysts());
      request.setAttribute("unrated", facade.getUnratedStocks());
    } else if ("AddRating".equals(name)) {
      //nothing to do here, just forward request
    } else {
      name = "Error";
    }

    dispatcher = context.getNamedDispatcher(name);
    if (dispatcher == null) {
      dispatcher = context.getNamedDispatcher("Error");
    }
    dispatcher.forward(request, response);
  } catch (Exception e) {
    e.printStackTrace();
  }
}
```

Here is the `RatingsForm.jsp` source code:

```html
<!DOCTYPE HTML PUBLIC "-//W3C//DTD HTML 4.01 Transitional//EN">
<html>
  <head>
    <title>Stock Ratings</title>
  </head>

  <body>
    <h1>Stock Ratings</h1>
```

```jsp
<%@ page import="java.util.*, vo.*" %>
<%
    ArrayList stocks = (ArrayList) request.getAttribute("data");
    if (stocks != null && stocks.size() > 0) {
%>
    <form action="/stock/StockList/AddRating" method="post">
    <table border="1">
      <tr>
        <th>Ticker</th>
        <th>Analyst</th>
        <th>Rating</th>
      </tr>
<%
    for (int i = 0; i < stocks.size(); i++) {
        StockVo stockInfo = (StockVo) stocks.get(i);
        String ticker = stockInfo.getTickerSymbol();
        String analyst = stockInfo.getAnalyst().getName();
        String rating = stockInfo.getRating();
%>
    <tr>
      <td><%= ticker %></td>
      <td><%= analyst %></td>
      <td><%= rating %></td>
    </tr>
<%
    }
%>
    </table>
    <table>
      <tr>
      <td>
        <select name="analysts">
<%
        ArrayList analysts =
                (ArrayList) request.getAttribute("analysts");
        for (int i = 0; i < analysts.size(); i++) {
          AnalystVo analyst = (AnalystVo) analysts.get(i);
%>
          <option value="<%= analyst.getAnalystId() %>">
              <%= analyst.getName() %>
<%
        }
%>
        </select>
      </td>
      <td>
        <select name="stocks">
<%
        ArrayList unratedStocks =
            (ArrayList) request.getAttribute("unrated");
        for (int i = 0; i < unratedStocks.size(); i++) {
          StockVo stock = (StockVo) unratedStocks.get(i);
```

```
%>
            <option value="<%= stock.getTickerSymbol() %>">
                <%= stock.getTickerSymbol() %>
<%
        }
%>
            </select>
        </td>
        <td>
          <select name="ratings">
            <option value="Run away! Run away!">Run away! Run away!
            <option value="Could be worse!">Could be worse!
            <option value="A bit of OK!">A bit of OK!
            <option value="Take a chance!">Take a chance!
            <option value="Smashing!">Smashing!
          </select>
        </td>
        </tr>
        <tr>
        <td>
          <input type="submit" value="Submit Rating">
        </td>
        </tr>
      </table>
      </form>
<%
      } else {
%>
      No stock information found
<%
      }
%>
      <hr>
    </body>
</html>
```

Here is the `AddRating.java` source code:

```java
package web;

import javax.servlet.*;
import javax.servlet.http.*;
import facade.*;
import vo.*;

public class AddRating extends HttpServlet {
  public void doPost(HttpServletRequest request,
                     HttpServletResponse response)
  {
    try {
      String analyst = request.getParameter("analysts");
```

```
        Integer id = new Integer(analyst);
        String ticker = request.getParameter("stocks");
        String rating = request.getParameter("ratings");

        StockVo stockVo = new StockVo(ticker, null, rating);
        stockVo.setAnalyst(new AnalystVo(id, null));
        StockListFacade facade = StockListFacade.getFacade();
        facade.addStockRating(stockVo);

        request.setAttribute("data", facade.getStockRatings());
        request.setAttribute("analysts", facade.getAllAnalysts());
        request.setAttribute("unrated", facade.getUnratedStocks());

        ServletContext context = getServletContext();
        RequestDispatcher dispatcher =
            context.getNamedDispatcher("RatingsForm");
        dispatcher.forward(request, response);
    } catch (Exception e) {
    }
  }
}
```

Like the `StockList` servlet, the `AddRating` servlet shown above uses the methods of the `StockListFacade` class to access the services of the `StockList` session bean.

The other option available from the main page is the **Analyst Management Form**, whose UI logic is in the `AnalystForm.jsp` file, shown below:

```
<!DOCTYPE HTML PUBLIC "-//W3C//DTD HTML 4.01 Transitional//EN">
<html>
  <head>
    <title>Analyst Management</title>
  </head>

<body>
  <%@ page import="java.util.*,vo.*" %>
  <h1>Analyst Management Form</h1>
  <form action="/stock/servlet/ProcessAnalyst" method="POST">
    <table>

  <%
  ArrayList anlysts = (ArrayList) request.getAttribute("data");
  if (anlysts == null) {
  %>
        <h2> Attribute is null </h2>
      <%
      } else {
        for (int i = 0; i < anlysts.size(); i++) {
      AnalystVo analystData = (AnalystVo) anlysts.get(i);
      //String name = analystData.getName();
```

```
%>
  <tr>
    <td>
      <input type="checkbox" name="checkbox"
                value="<%= analystData.getName() %>"
    </td>
    <td>
        <%= analystData.getName() %>
    </td>
  </tr>
<%
      }
    }
    %>
  </table>
  <input type="submit" value="Delete Selected" name="delete">
  <p>
  <input type="text" size="40" name="addname">
  <input type="submit" value="Add New Analyst" name="add">
  </form>

  <hr>
  </body>
</html>
```

Again, note the use of the `AnalystVo` value object.

And that's all the code over and done with. Next is to deploy the application, using pretty much the same procedure as previously. After deploying the application, remember to populate the entity beans by running the `StockListAdder` application as before. You can run this application by pointing your browser to the following URL:

http://localhost:8000/stock/index.html

Here is a screenshot of this web application after Fred the Analyst rated the stock for the world's smallest tricycle infomercial company, Zapalopalorinski Ltd.:

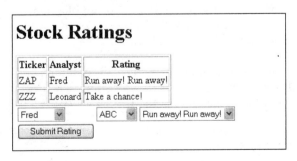

How it Works

The `StockList` servlet uses the static `StockListFacade.getFacade()` method to get the singleton `StockListFacade` instance, as seen above. It uses that façade reference to get the data, and then forwards to a JSP for display. The request is forwarded based on the extra path information passed with the request. If `getPathInfo()` returns "/AnalystForm", the request is forwarded to `AnalystForm.jsp`. If `getpathInfo()` returns "/RatingsForm", the request is forwarded to `RatingsForm.jsp`. If `getpathInfo()` returns "/AddRating" the request is forwarded to the `AddRating` servlet.

The `RatingsForm` JSP creates a form that POSTs a request to the `StockList` servlet. This request is forwarded to the `AddRating` servlet. Take a moment to examine the use of value objects in the `RatingsForm` JSP shown above. After adding the rating, the `AddRating` servlet forwards to the `RatingsForm` JSP to display the new data.

This example again illustrates some of the advantages of using the façade and value object patterns in your web application. JSPs are primarily designed to provide a data visualization layer for a web application. Servlets are primarily designed to receive and respond to requests. By encapsulating the data access details in the façade and value objects, the JSPs and servlets don't need to worry about which EJB to access or how to access the EJBs. The JSPs and servlets don't even need to know that the data came from an EJB. The data could come directly from a database, or a flat file, or over the network.

Before we leave this chapter, let's take a look at two more EJB concepts: **message-driven beans**, and **EJB timers**.

Developing Message-Driven Beans

As discussed in Chapter 8, in addition to session beans and entity beans, there is a type of EJB known as **message-driven beans**. Message-driven beans exist for the purpose of receiving and processing **asynchronous messages**. These messages could be from external systems, or from components of the same application. The reason that they are called *asynchronous* is that they can arrive at any time, as opposed to being a direct result of a remote method invocation for example. Similar to the way that UI event handling works, message-driven beans "listen" for asynchronous messages that have been sent to it.

Message-driven beans are enabled not only by the EJB container, but by a facility in J2EE known as the **Java Message Service** API, or JMS for short. The diagram below shows the context in which the next example will operate, and will serve as a basis for our discussion of the JMS API:

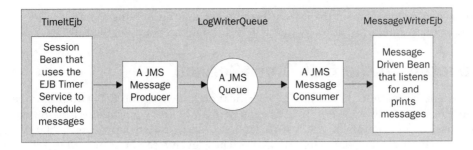

Introduction to the Java Message Service API

The JMS API is a Java API, located in the `javax.jms` package, which provides an interface for applications that require the services of a messaging system. A messaging system enables messages containing text, objects, and other message types to be sent and received *asynchronously*. This is in contrast with the remote procedure call (RPC) model that we've been using so far for EJBs, where interactions between components occur *synchronously*.

An implementation of a messaging system that complies with the JMS API is called a **JMS provider**. The J2EE SDK 1.4 has a JMS provider that we'll be using to enable the example in this section, and several vendors have commercial implementations available for use in enabling messaging in enterprise applications.

In the diagram above, the `TimeIt` session bean on the left sends asynchronous messages to the `MessageWriter` message-driven bean on the right. Both of these beans have been created for this example (they aren't Java library classes). These `TimeIt` and `MessageWriter` beans are known as **JMS clients** because they are *clients* of the underlying messaging system.

Messaging systems enable asynchronous communication by providing a **destination** for messages to be held until they can be delivered to the recipient. The circle in the middle, `LogWriterQueue`, is the destination that holds messages from the `TimeIt` session bean, which are bound for the `MessageWriter` message-driven bean. There are two types of destinations in JMS:

- ❑ A **queue** is used to hold messages that are sent from one JMS client to be delivered to another. This model of messaging is known as **point-to-point**.

- ❑ A **topic** is used to hold messages that are sent from potentially many JMS clients to be delivered to, potentially multiple, JMS clients. This model of messaging is known as **publish/subscribe**.

The example we will look at later in this section uses a queue type destination, which is reflected in the diagram. Also in the diagram above are boxes for a JMS **message producer** and a JMS **message consumer**. These represent classes in a JMS provider that work on behalf of the JMS clients to send and receive messages. As we'll see later, you don't have to create a JMS message consumer when working with message-driven beans, because the EJB container does that on the message-driven bean's behalf.

515

We'll have more to say about the JMS API when walking through the example code, so let's turn our attention to another technology that will be used in the example, the EJB Timer Service.

Introduction to the EJB Timer Service

There is a new capability in the EJB 2.1 specification known as the **EJB Timer Service**. Its purpose in life is to provide enterprise beans with a way to be notified of time-based events. This is useful, for example, if you want a session bean to initiate a process at 2:00 every morning to gather data from external system. These events can be triggered as follows:

❑   At a particular time. Perhaps you could have your EJB notified on July 28, 2061 at midnight that it should do something special (to celebrate the next date that Halley's Comet will be closest to the Sun).

❑   After a given elapsed time.

❑   On a recurring basis, after a given time interval.

These timer services are provided by the EJB container, and are defined by four interfaces located in the `javax.ejb` package:

❑   An EJB implements the `TimedObject` interface when it wishes to be notified of time-based events. The `TimedObject` interface contains one method, `ejbTimeout()`, whic is called when a timer "expires".

❑   The `TimerService` interface provides access to the EJB Timer Service to an enterprise bean. It contains methods that create `Timer` objects, and that retrieve the `Timer` objects that have been created.

❑   Objects that implement the `Timer` interface implement the time-based logic described above (expiring at a specific time, elapsed time, or interval). Methods of the `Timer` interface allow you to get information about a `Timer` object, and to cancel the `Timer` as well.

❑   A `TimerHandle` can be used to retrieve a `Timer` object. Our example doesn't use that interface.

Let's go ahead and look at an example that demonstrates the technologies (message-driven beans, the JMS API, and the EJB Timer Service) mentioned above.

Try It Out	Using an EJB Timer to Invoke a Message-Driven Bean

The diagram from earlier in this section depicts the behavior of this *Try It Out* example, which is as follows:

❑   The `TimeIt` session bean uses the EJB Timer Service to be notified every 10 seconds.

- Each time the `TimeIt` bean is notified, it uses the JMS API to create a JMS message producer.

- The `TimeIt` bean uses the JMS message producer to create and send a message that it wants delivered to the `MessageWriter` message-driven bean. In our example, this message is a text message that contains the date and time that the message was sent.

- The JMS message producer sends the message to the `LogWriterQueue`, which is an arbitrarily-named JMS queue created for this example.

- A JMS message consumer, which is created and managed by the EJB container, receives the text message.

- The EJB container calls the `onMessage()` method of the `MessageWriter` message-driven bean, passing the text message into the method.

The `MessageWriter` bean creates a `String`, concatenates the text message received, and sends it to `System.out`. Note the `System.out` is managed by the J2EE Server (`j2ee`), so we'll start it up in a special way to see the output.

To build the example, we have the following new `.java` files:

- `TimeItHome.java` in the `timer` package
- `TimeIt.java` in the `timer` package
- `TimeItBean.java` in the `timer` package
- `TimeItTester.java` in the `timer` package
- `MessageWriterBean.java` in the `msg` package

We'll implement the code involved in this example according to the flow of the message being sent.

Firstly, here is the home interface of the `TimeIt` session bean, `TimeItHome.java`:

```
package timer;

import java.rmi.RemoteException;
import javax.ejb.EJBHome;
import javax.ejb.CreateException;

public interface TimeItHome extends EJBHome {
  // The create method for the timer bean.
  public TimeIt create()
    throws CreateException, RemoteException;
}
```

And here is the remote interface of the `TimeIt` session bean, `TimeIt.java`:

```
package timer;

import java.rmi.RemoteException;
import javax.ejb.EJBObject;

public interface TimeIt extends EJBObject {
  // The public business method on the timer bean
  public void startTimer() throws RemoteException;
}
```

The remote interface only has one business method, named `startTimer()`. This method will be invoked by the `TimeItTester` client application, seen in the `TimeItTester.java` listing shown below, just to get things started up:

```
package timer;

import javax.naming.InitialContext;
import javax.rmi.PortableRemoteObject;

public class TimeItTester {
  public static void main(String[] args) {
    try {
      // Get a naming context
      InitialContext jndiContext = new InitialContext();

      // Get a reference to the SimpleSession JNDI entry
      Object ref = jndiContext.lookup("ejb/timer.TimeIt");

      // Get a reference from this to the Bean's Home interface
      TimeItHome home = (TimeItHome)
       PortableRemoteObject.narrow(ref, TimeItHome.class);

      // Create a SimpleSession object from the Home interface
      TimeIt timeIt = home.create();

      timeIt.startTimer();

    } catch(Exception e) {
      e.printStackTrace();
    }
  }
}
```

Now we'll get to code that is the heart of the example – using the EJB Timer Service. Here is the implementation of the `TimeIt` session bean, contained in `TimeItBean.java`:

```
package timer;

import javax.ejb.SessionBean;
import javax.ejb.SessionContext;
```

```
import javax.ejb.TimedObject;
import javax.ejb.Timer;
import javax.ejb.TimerService;
import javax.jms.Queue;
import javax.jms.QueueConnection;
import javax.jms.QueueConnectionFactory;
import javax.jms.QueueSender;
import javax.jms.QueueSession;
import javax.jms.Session;
import javax.jms.TextMessage;
import javax.naming.InitialContext;

// General imports
import java.text.*;
import java.util.*;

public class TimeItBean
   implements SessionBean, TimedObject {
   // Save a reference to the context
   private SessionContext ctx;

   // public business method to start the timer
   public void startTimer() {
      TimerService timerService = ctx.getTimerService();
      // After initial five seconds, then every ten seconds
      Timer timer = timerService.createTimer(5000, 10000, "timer");
   }

   // timer ejb method - timer expires - send message to queue
   public void ejbTimeout(Timer timer) {
      QueueConnection queueConnection = null;
      try {
         InitialContext jndiContext = new InitialContext();
         // Look up the connection factory
         QueueConnectionFactory queueConnectionFactory =
            (QueueConnectionFactory) jndiContext.lookup
            ("jms/QueueConnectionFactory");
         // Look up the queue (destination)
         Queue queue = (Queue) jndiContext.lookup("jms/LogWriterQueue");
         // Get a connection from the factory
         queueConnection = queueConnectionFactory.createQueueConnection();
         // Create a session
         QueueSession queueSession = queueConnection.createQueueSession(false,
            Session.AUTO_ACKNOWLEDGE);
         // create a sender for the session to the queue
         QueueSender queueSender = queueSession.createSender(queue);
         // Create a text message
         TextMessage message = queueSession.createTextMessage();
         // Create the message - a string to print on the other side
         SimpleDateFormat sdf =
            new SimpleDateFormat("yyyy.MM.dd 'at' HH:mm:ss.SSS");
```

```
      // Set the text of the message
      message.setText("log entry, the time is: " + sdf.format(new Date()));
      // Send the message
      queueSender.send(message);

    }
    catch (Exception e) {
      System.out.println("Exception in message: " + e.toString());
      e.printStackTrace();
    }
    finally {
      if (queueConnection != null) {
        try {
          queueConnection.close();
        }
        catch (Exception e) {}
      }
    }
  }

  // Standard ejb methods

  public void setSessionContext(SessionContext context) {
    ctx = context;
  }

  public void ejbCreate() {}
  public void ejbRemove() {}
  public void ejbActivate() {}
  public void ejbPassivate() {}
}
```

Here is the listing for our message-driven bean, `MessageWriterBean.java`. There aren't any home or bean interface listings to show because message-driven beans do not use them:

```
package msg;

import javax.ejb.MessageDrivenBean;
import javax.ejb.MessageDrivenContext;
import javax.jms.JMSException;
import javax.jms.Message;
import javax.jms.MessageListener;
import javax.jms.TextMessage;

public class MessageWriterBean
  implements MessageDrivenBean, MessageListener {

  // Abstract method from message listener. Here is where the
  // work is done.
  public void onMessage(Message message) {
    TextMessage msg = null;
```

```
    try {
      if (message instanceof TextMessage) {
        msg = (TextMessage) message;
        System.out.println("Got message: " + msg.getText());
      }
      else {
        System.out.println("Got message of type: "
          + message.getClass().getName() + " ==> ignored!");
      }
    }
    catch (Throwable te) {
      te.printStackTrace();
    }
  }

  // Standard ejb methods
  public void ejbCreate() { }
  public void ejbRemove() { }
  public void setMessageDrivenContext(MessageDrivenContext mdContext) { }
}
```

That's all the code you need to type in out of the way. It's time to build and run the example.

You can use the following commands to compile these files:

> **javac -d . timer/*.java**

> **javac -d . msg/*.java**

When you start the J2EE server, use the `-verbose` option:

> **j2ee -verbose**

This will cause the messages from the J2EE server to appear on the console, including the output from our `MessageWriter` message-driven bean.

You'll use the Deployment Tool to configure and deploy the beans. Since neither entity beans nor JDBC are used in this example, you won't have to start up the Cloudscape database server. We used TimerMessageApp.ear for the EAR filename, TimerMessageJar for the EJB JAR name, and TimerMessageStubs.jar for the client JAR (stubs) filename.

You'll go through the **Edit Enterprise Beans Wizard** twice: once for the `TimeIt` stateless session bean, and once for the `MessageWriter` message-driven bean.

Using this wizard for the `TimeIt` session bean will be the same as usual for a session bean. Please note that even though we put the `TimeItTester` client code in the same package as the beans, you shouldn't put the `TimeItTester.class` file in the bean JAR. Also, you won't have to choose any options from the **Configuration Options** page of this wizard.

521

When using the Edit Enterprise Beans Wizard for the `MessageWriter` message-driven bean, take note of the instructions that follow.

Since message-driven beans don't have home and bean interfaces, you'll only need to add the `MessageWriterBean.class` file to the bean JAR:

You'll choose Message-Driven Bean as the Bean Type, and `msg.MessageWriterBean` as the Enterprise Bean Class:

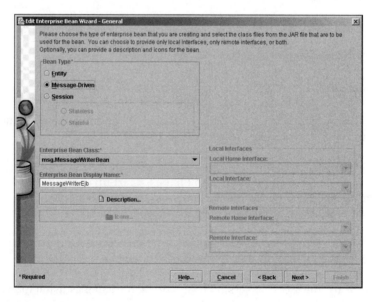

You won't have to choose any options from the Configuration Options page of this wizard, and as a result, we haven't shown this.

In the **Message-Driven Bean Settings** page below, choose `javax.jms.MessageListener` in the **Message Listener Interface** drop-down list. This is the interface that specifies the `onMessage()` method:

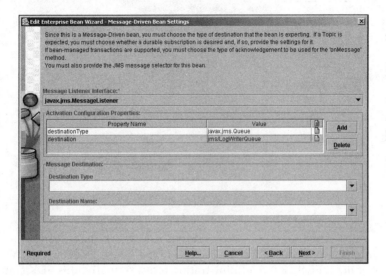

Also, use the **Add** button, shown above, to add each of two **Activation Configuration Properties**:

❑ The **destinationType** property, which as explained previously is `javax.jms.Queue`

❑ The **destination** property, which is **jms/LogWriterQueue**

The message-driven bean will listen for messages arriving at the destination specified in these properties.

After finishing the **Edit Enterprise Beans Wizard**, while you are configuring the platform-specific deployment settings, assign the JNDI name **ejb/timer.TimeIt** to the `TimeIt` session bean, as shown below:

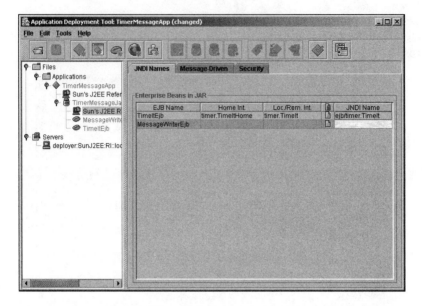

Before deploying the application, we need to create the `LogWriterQueue`. We're going to do this using one of the J2EE SDK 1.4 administration tools. Actually, this SDK comes with two administration tools:

❑   One has a web browser-based interface.

❑   The other tool, known as `j2eeadmin`, is command line-based.

To create the `LogWriterQueue`, we'll use the command line J2EE Administration Tool with the following command:

```
> j2eeadmin -addJmsDestination jms/LogWriterQueue queue
```

Now you can deploy the application, create the client stubs, and run the `timer.TimeItTester` client to test it out. After five seconds, and every ten seconds thereafter, a message sent from the `TimeIt` session bean to the `MessageWriter` message-driven bean should appear in the console in which you start the server using with the `-verbose` switch. Here is some sample output:

```
Got message: log entry, the time is: 2003.03.15 at 17:29:37.124
Got message: log entry, the time is: 2003.03.15 at 17:29:44.524
Got message: log entry, the time is: 2003.03.15 at 17:29:51.715
Got message: log entry, the time is: 2003.03.15 at 17:30:00.000
Got message: log entry, the time is: 2003.03.15 at 17:30:07.177
```

As a good housekeeping tip, to remove the `LogWriterQueue` queue you can enter the following command:

```
> j2eeadmin -removeJmsDestination jms/LogWriterQueue
```

How It Works

Let's first look at how the EJB Timer Service is implemented in the `TimeItBean` class.

The `setSessionContext()` method of the session bean, shown below, is called by the EJB container after the session bean is created. The container passes in a `SessionContext` object, which represents the EJB container context in which the session bean is running. This is analogous to a servlet having access to its `ServletContext` object, which was discussed in Chapter 5.

```
public void setSessionContext(SessionContext context) {
  ctx = context;
}
```

The reason that we suddenly care about the `SessionContext` of session beans is that we'll use it, as seen in the `startTimer()` below, to get access to the EJB Timer Service. Recall that the `startTimer()` method is the one and only business method of this `TimeIt` session bean.

We'll use the `TimerService` object to create a `Timer` object that is supposed to expire, trigger, fire, go off, however you want to say it, in 5 seconds, and every 10 seconds thereafter. Note that because EJB Timer Service is mainly for larger time intervals (hours, days, and so on), you shouldn't count on the kind of precision those milliseconds would seem to indicate. This is borne out by the sample output above, which shows that our ten-second timer triggered closer to every seven seconds. So, a timer will expire precisely when it is supposed to, give or take a few thousand milliseconds:

```
public void startTimer() {
  TimerService timerService = ctx.getTimerService();
  // After initial five seconds, then every ten seconds
  Timer timer = timerService.createTimer(5000, 10000, "timer");
}
```

You might want to take a few moments at this point to examine the J2EE SDK 1.4 Java API documentation for the overloaded `createTimer()` method of the `TimerService` class. These will familiarize you with how to create `Timer` objects with the different types of time-based logic (expiring at a specific time, elapsed time, or interval) described above. By the way, one of the exercises at the end of this chapter specifies creating the different types of timers.

Whenever a timer fires, the `ejbTimeout()` method of the enterprise bean gets invoked. In our example, this method uses the JMS API to send an asynchronous message to a message-driven bean, so let's now turn our attention to that subject.

Next, we focus on how we use the Java Message Service API by reviewing the code we just saw in the `MessageWriterBean` class.

According to the diagram and description of this example's behavior given above, one thing that our ejbTimeout() method needs to do is to create a JMS message producer that can send messages to the LogWriterQueue. In order to do that, it will need a couple of **administered objects**, which are resources that are typically administered by JMS provider-specific administration tools. These administered objects are:

❑ A **connection factory**, which is used to create a connection to the JMS provider, discussed previously. As its name implies, a connection factory uses the factory design pattern that we covered earlier in this chapter.

❑ A **destination**, which in this case is a javax.jms.Queue that we're calling LogWriterQueue.

To begin the process of creating a JMS message producer, in the ejbTimeout() method we use JNDI to look up a connection factory as shown below. The connection factory that we're using here is a QueueConnectionFactory, because we'll be sending messages to a Queue:

```
InitialContext jndiContext = new InitialContext();
// Look up the connection factory
QueueConnectionFactory queueConnectionFactory =
  (QueueConnectionFactory) jndiContext.lookup
  ("jms/QueueConnectionFactory");
```

As seen below, we also use JNDI to look up the LogWriterQueue destination, which is an administered object. Recall that we used the j2eeadmin tool to create the LogWriterQueue destination:

```
// Look up the queue (destination)
Queue queue = (Queue) jndiContext.lookup("jms/LogWriterQueue");
```

Shown below, the QueueConnectionFactory is used to create a QueueConnection object, which is used to create a QueueSession object. For more information on these classes of the javax.jms package, consult the J2EE API documentation:

```
// Get a connection from the factory
queueConnection = queueConnectionFactory.createQueueConnection();
// Create a session
QueueSession queueSession = queueConnection.createQueueSession(false,
  Session.AUTO_ACKNOWLEDGE);
```

The createSender() method of the QueueSession object is passed a reference to our LogWriterQueue, and it creates a QueueSender object that can send messages to that destination, as shown below. The QueueSender, being a subinterface of MessageProducer, is represented by the JMS message producer in the example's diagram earlier:

```
// create a sender for the session to the queue
QueueSender queueSender = queueSession.createSender(queue);
```

As seen below, a `TextMessage` object is created by calling the `createTextMessage()` method of the `QueueSession` object. This particular message type is a `TextMessage`, but you can look at `javax.jms.Message` (its superinterface) in the J2EE API documentation to see a description of the other four message types available in JMS.

The `String` to be sent is built, placed into the `TextMessage` object, and sent to the destination (our `LogWriterQueue`), as shown below:

```
// Create the message - a string to print on the other side
SimpleDateFormat sdf =
  new SimpleDateFormat("yyyy.MM.dd 'at' HH:mm:ss.SSS");
// Set the text of the message
message.setText("log entry, the time is: " + sdf.format(new Date()));
// Send the message
queueSender.send(message);
```

We're not going to send any more messages until the next time the `ejbTimeout()` method is called, so we'll close the `QueueConnection`, which closes the `QueueSession` and `QueueSender` that were created earlier. This all happens in the code located in the `finally` block of the example:

```
finally {
  if (queueConnection != null) {
    try {
      queueConnection.close();
    }
    catch (Exception e) {}
  }
}
```

Now it's up to the JMS provider to deliver the message to the `LogWriterQueue`, and on to our `MessageWriterBean`, which is a message-driven bean.

Finally, we take a quick look at the code used for our message-driven bean, in `MessageWriterBean.java`. There aren't any home or bean interface listings to show because message-driven beans do not use them.

As seen in the listing for the `MessageWriterBean` class, message-driven beans must implement a couple of interfaces:

❑ `MessageDrivenBean` – Contains message-driven bean lifecycle methods.

❑ `MessageListener` – Contains the `onMessage()` method. This is the method that is called when a message arrives for a message-driven bean.

The `onMessage()` method of this example is expecting a `TextMessage`, and will use the `getText()` method to obtain the `String` that was sent. Then, regardless of the message type received, we print something to `System.out`.

Summary

In this chapter, we continued the discussion of EJBs from the previous chapter, covering the following concepts:

- ❑ Software design patterns
- ❑ Utilizing JSPs and servlets with EJBs in an application
- ❑ Message-driven beans
- ❑ The Java Message Service (JMS) API
- ❑ EJB Timer Service

Design patterns describe solutions to specific design problems, and improve developer productivity by leveraging these solutions. They are analogous to patterns such roof styles when designing a house. There are many design patterns in use today, and new ones are continually being identified and documented by developers. The four that we discussed were façade, value object, factory, and singleton.

The design patterns example was fused with a JSP and servlets example from a previous chapter to show how JSPs, servlets, and EJBs could be used in the same application.

Message-driven beans are one of the three types of enterprise beans (session and entity are the other two). They are the mechanism to use when you want an EJB application to receive asynchronous messages via an underlying JMS provider (messaging system).

The new EJB Timer Service is useful when you have EJB application functionality that needs to be executed at defined times or time intervals. Keep in mind that EJB Timers were design for large time intervals, not sub-second precision, so you can't depend on the timing being too precise.

Resources

A catalog of J2EE Patterns may be found at:

- ❑ http://java.sun.com/blueprints/patterns/catalog.html

More information on the Java Message Service API is at:

- ❑ http://java.sun.com/products/jms/

Exercises

1. Write a message-driven bean that takes a word and writes it to `System.out`. Write a simple application that writes to a message queue to test the message bean. Remember to start the `j2ee` server using the `-verbose` option or to look in the server log to verify the bean is working.

2. Write a stateless session bean that implements the EJB Timer Service. Try using several of the different types of timers. Write an appropriate message to `System.out` to verify the timer is working.

C H A P T E R 12

Understanding Web Services   **531**

Developing Web Services in Java   **537**

Summary   **561**

Resources   **562**

Exercises   **562**

Web Services and JAX-RPC

In the previous chapter we wrapped up the main part of our discussion about Enterprise JavaBeans. This chapter, and the chapter following, will cover another mechanism that is used to enable distributed applications – **web services**.

In this chapter you will learn:

❑   What web services are

❑   Fundamental concepts regarding web services, including the web services protocol stack

❑   Some guidelines for when to use web services

❑   How we can enable web services using SOAP and JAX-RPC

❑   How to use J2EE SDK 1.4 tools to configure and deploy an application that contains web services

❑   Describing web services using WSDL

❑   What SAAJ is

❑   The three ways that a client can invoke web service methods

Understanding Web Services

A web service consists of functionality that is available to applications via protocols associated with the Web. Example protocols that are commonly associated with the Web are HTTP (which, as we saw previously, is used for transmitting requests and responses between web clients, such as browsers, and web servers), XML, and SOAP (we'll be looking at XML and SOAP a little later on in this chapter.) Using these protocols, an application can make use of the functionality provided by a web service. For example, a bookseller named Wrox might have a web service running on its web server that provides the ability to order books. We'll call this web service WroxBookService. An application could use this service when it needs to look up a price or order a book. This WroxBookService web service would have **operations**, each of which performs some functionality. For example:

❏ A `getPrice` operation could take the ISBN number of a book as input and would return the price of the book.

❏ An `orderBook` operation might take an ISBN and a credit card number, and process an order for a book, including having it shipped.

In the same way as the **WroxBookService** web service above, organizations and individuals can offer services to applications over standard, ubiquitous protocols such as XML, SOAP, and HTTP. The availability of web services over such protocols makes them an attractive choice for developing distributed applications, which can be composed of web services offered by other divisions in a company, or by other organizations.

For an example of some web services that are currently available, check out www.xmethods.com. This site is one of several that allow developers to post information about a web service that they have developed, including a description of the service and instructions on how to use it. To give you a flavor of the kinds of web services being developed, some interesting examples listed on this site at the time of writing include:

Web Service Name	Description
Air Fare Quote Search	Searches major airlines in real time to find the best available prices direct from their web sites.
BabelFish	Interface for AltaVista's Babelfish (language translator) service.
Bible Webservice	Retrieves Biblical text.
Delayed Stock Quote	20 minute delayed stock quote.
Domain Name Checker	Checks whether a domain name is available or not.
eBay Price Watcher	Checks current bid price of an eBay auction.
FedEx Tracker	Access to FedEx Tracking information
Generate Bar Codes	This service generates (Interleaved 2 of 5) Bar Code images.
Get Currency Exchange	Returns the value of a given number of units changed from one currency to another.
Great Circle Distance	Great circle distance between 2 points of longitude, latitude.
Image Converter	Convert from one type of image to another.

Web Service Name	Description
Shakespeare	Takes a phrase from the plays of William Shakespeare and returns the associated speech, speaker, and play.
USA Zip Code Information	Gets USA State Code, City, Area Code, Time Zone, Zip Code by State Code, or City, or Area Code.
Weather – Temperature	Current temperature in a given U.S. zip code region.

The ability for parts of a distributed application to communicate with each other, and call each other's methods, like web services, should be familiar to you from the EJB chapters earlier in this book. In fact, many standards have evolved that enable clients on one machine to invoke the operations or methods of a server on another machine. Examples of this are:

❏ Remote Procedure Calls (RPC). There are a few flavors of RPCs, including:

   ❏ Distributed Computing Environment (DCE) RPCs

   ❏ Sun RPCs (interestingly enough, Sun was a pioneer of RPCs in the early 1980s)

❏ Common Object Request Broker Architecture (CORBA)

❏ Distributed Component Object Model (DCOM)

❏ Java Remote Method Invocation (RMI), which enables EJBs

Each of these standards are excellent, but each are, to some degree, platform or programming language dependent. To enable a future in which any application can invoke the methods of any other application (governed by security policies, of course), we need a standard that:

❏ Is available with most of the popular programming languages

❏ Can be used on almost any hardware/operating system platform

❏ Uses communication protocols that are ubiquitous

❏ Encourages communication over ports that are not likely to have firewall issues

Web services promise to help us realize that future, as they meet all of the criteria listed above: web services can be created in Java, C++, C#, Visual Basic, and many other programming languages. They can be used on most, if not all, major hardware operating system platforms. In addition, they typically run over TCP/IP and HTTP, both of which are ubiquitous. Because of this wide availability, we can all write applications that offer method-based services, and we can expect to be able to call the methods of applications that others have written. These applications can be deployed within the confines of a company's intranet, extranet, or on the Internet.

The RPC model is one way of implementing web services. In this model, a web service application makes an interface available to clients on the network, very similar to the EJB session bean model. Client programs can then find and invoke methods of this interface as if it were residing on the same machine. The data communicated between the client and the web service is expressed using Simple Object Access Protocol (SOAP) and XML.

The other way of implementing web services is using a messaging model. Each application can send SOAP messages to another, without expecting a return value as a caller of a method would. The applications communicate asynchronously, as did the components of the message-drive beans example in the previous chapter. We'll focus most of our attention on the RPC model of web services.

Why Use Web Services?

The cross-platform nature of Java facilitates distributed applications running on multiple hardware and operating system platforms. If all of the components of a distributed application are written in Java, then using EJBs with Java RMI is a good choice. However, web services are a great choice for integrating applications that are written in various languages, because most major platforms have support for SOAP, which is the protocol used in web services for passing object data from one application to another. This enables, for example, an application developed in Java to use the web service operations of an application developed in Perl.

A subtler advantage to web services is that they typically use HTTP as an underlying communication protocol. Because of this, they can easily and naturally be implemented over the TCP/IP ports most commonly open in firewalls, for example 80, 8080, and 443. Ports 80 and 8080 are used for standard browser-to-web server HTTP traffic, and port 443 is used for encrypted, secure HTTP traffic.

Because web services are so conducive to interoperability, legacy system vendors can expose functionality so that other systems can have access. For example, many banks have web access to accounts, including the ability to perform transactions such as transferring money between accounts. But wouldn't it be nice to be able to use your personal finance software to perform these transactions in real time, no matter what institutions those accounts are in? If every bank had a common set of secure web services that wraps their account management systems, then that could be a reality.

The use of web services in personal finance brings up the important issue of security. Applications that share sensitive information with each other need to do so securely. This is addressed in web services in a similar manner to other web-based applications: that is, through the use of network traffic encryption and user authentication.

Let's take a look at an architectural view of web services, in the form of a protocol stack.

The Web Services Protocol Stack

The diagram below shows the protocols used in web services, from highest to lowest level, reading downward. We've omitted layers lower than HTTP, most notably the ones that employ TCP/IP and Ethernet technologies.

Layer	Technology
Service Discovery	UDDI
Service Description	WSDL
Messaging	SOAP
Encoding	XML
Transport	HTTP

Let's cover these protocols from the bottom up.

Transport Layer

The typical transport layer is Hypertext Transfer Protocol (HTTP), the protocol over which most Web traffic travels. As you may recall, HTTP was discussed in the context of servlets and JSPs, in Chapter 5. Web services can also be carried over e-mail messages, using Simple Mail Transport Protocol (SMTP).

Encoding Layer

All web service traffic is expressed in Extensible Markup Language (XML). For information on XML, see the *Resources* section at the end of this chapter or the Wrox book, titled *Beginning XML, 2nd Edition* (ISBN 1-86100-559-8).

Messaging Layer

All application data sent via web services is enclosed in Simple Object Access Protocol (SOAP) messages. SOAP is based entirely upon XML, and contains structures such as the SOAP envelope, and within that, the SOAP header and SOAP body. The SOAP body, for example, contains all of the instance data of the objects that are being transported. The following code is an example SOAP message for the `getPrice` operation of the fictional **WroxBookService** discussed previously.

```
<SOAP-ENV:Envelope
  xmlns:SOAP-ENV="http://schemas.xmlsoap.org/soap/envelope/"
  <SOAP-ENV:Body>
    <m:getPrice xmlns:m="http://ws.wrox.com">
      <isbn>1861008333</isbn>
    </m:getPrice>
  </SOAP-ENV:Body>
</SOAP-ENV:Envelope>
```

A Java application can use the API defined in the SAAJ (SOAP with Attachments API for Java) to create, send, and receive SOAP messages. This API is contained in the `javax.xml.soap` package, which is included in the J2EE SDK 1.4. As you'll see a little later, we'll be using a facility known as JAX-RPC that lets us develop at a higher level of abstraction. JAX-RPC uses the SAAJ API under the covers to produce and consume the SOAP message. You can learn more about SAAJ from the SAAJ 1.1 specification, which is available for download at the URL provided in the *Resources* section of this chapter.

Service Description Layer

The functionality provided by a given web service is described by the Web Services Description Language (WSDL). When using JAX-RPC (which will be covered later in this chapter), web services are implemented in Java, with WSDL using XML to describe the interfaces, methods, arguments, return values, and the URL of a web service. To get a feel for WSDL parlance:

❑   A WSDL **port** element is analogous to a Java **interface**.

❑   A WSDL **operation** element is analogous to a Java **method**.

❑   WSDL **part** elements (contained inside of message elements) are analogous to Java **arguments** and **return values**.

We'll see an example of a WSDL file a little later in this chapter.

Service Discovery Layer

Web services can be registered for use, and then discovered at run-time. For example, a client application seeking a web service that offers the functionality of a thesaurus could check to see which applicable web services are registered. This is known as Universal Description, Discovery, and Integration (UDDI). UDDI registries hold information about businesses and the web services that they offer. These UDDI registries are hosted by various vendors and are available on the Internet, but could also be located within a corporate intranet. A list of UDDI registries available on the Internet, as well as more information on UDDI, is available at http://www.uddi.org. There is also an API known as JAXR (Java API for XML Registries) that provides a uniform interface to registries such as UDDI. To learn more about UDDI and the JAXR API, please see the appropriate URLs in the *Resources* section of this chapter.

Emerging Layers

Some emerging layers of the web services stack deal with issues such as security, client identity, transaction coordination, web service user interfaces, and business process workflow. These are very important issues with regard to the use of web services in mission-critical applications.

Developing Web Services in Java

There are a number of toolkits that may be used to develop web services in the Java programming language. One such toolkit is the very popular open-source implementation of SOAP called Apache AXIS. AXIS is from the Apache Software Foundation (http://www.apache.org/), an organization that provides support for open-source projects.

Another such toolkit is the Java API for XML-based RPC (JAX-RPC), which provides a Java API for developing and implementing web services. JAX-RPC handles all the details of the SOAP layer, via SAAJ, enabling development in terms of remote procedure calls. JAX-RPC is available in the J2EE SDK 1.4 that we've been using to build and run the examples throughout this book.

SAAJ and JAX-RPC are also contained in the Java Web Services Developer Pack. The Developer Pack is a toolset for developing web service-related applications, and is meant to be used in conjunction with the J2SE (version 1.3.1_04 or later). It is available from Sun's Java web site at the link provided in the *Resources* section of this chapter. You do not need to download this pack for the examples in this book, because all of the required technologies are available in the J2EE SDK 1.4.

Understanding JAX-RPC

JAX-RPC is a remote procedure call-based programming model introduced in the J2EE 1.4 platform. Its purpose in life is to provide an API for Java applications to communicate with each other using the SOAP protocol. As illustrated below, the programming model of JAX-RPC is very much like EJBs and Java RMI in that the details of the underlying over-the-wire protocols are hidden behind **web service stubs**. A stub implements the same interface as the web service that exists remotely, and it communicates with a **web service tie** on the server. The tie calls the methods of a web service, and communicates the return value and any exceptions encountered back to the client through the stub.

> **Ties are also referred to as skeletons, a familiar term in traditional RPC programming.**

This interface that both the stub and the web service implements is known as the Service Definition Interface. The communication between the stubs and the ties is SOAP, typically over HTTP.

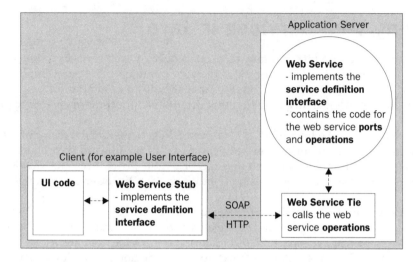

Developing Web Services Using JAX-RPC

Let's begin developing web services. Our first web service is going to be a very simple one; on par with a "Hello World!" application, named `SimpleService`:

Because this is the first web services example, and we haven't learned to build and deploy web services yet, we're going to create our code files now, and run them later. There are three Java source files and three XML files for this example.

These files should be organized in a subdirectory structure as shown below. Also shown in this structure are the three XML files that will be used in the build process. These three XML files are created by the application developer and will be used by the deployment and compile tools. We'll be creating these later in the chapter, or, along with the Java source code, they can be downloaded from the code download for this book.

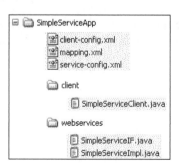

1. The first Java source file that we need to create is the web service interface for this example. The file name is `SimpleServiceIF.java` and it is represented as the Service Definition Interface (in the figure shown opposite):

```java
package webservices;

import java.rmi.Remote;
import java.rmi.RemoteException;

public interface SimpleServiceIF extends Remote {
  // the service methods
  public String getEchoString(String clientString)
    throws RemoteException;
}
```

2. The next file that we need to create is the class that implements the web service interface, `SimpleServiceImpl.java`:

```java
package webservices;

public class SimpleServiceImpl implements SimpleServiceIF  {

  // the service method implementations

  public String getEchoString(String clientString) {
    return clientString + " - from service";
  }
}
```

3. Now we need to create the file that will be the client we'll be using to test the web service, `SimpleServiceClient.java`:

```java
package client;

import webservices.SimpleServiceIF;
import webservices.SimpleService_Impl;

import javax.xml.rpc.Stub;

public class SimpleServiceClient {
  public static void main(String[] args) {
    try {
      Stub stub = (Stub)
          (new SimpleService_Impl().getSimpleServiceIFPort());
      SimpleServiceIF myProxy = (SimpleServiceIF)stub;
      System.out.println("got service!");

      // loop through the words
      for (int i = 0; i < args.length; i++) {
```

```
        String returnedString =
          myProxy.getEchoString(args[i]);
        System.out.println("sent string: " + args[i]
          + ", received string: " + returnedString);
      }
    } catch(Exception e) {
      e.printStackTrace();
    }
  }
}
```

This web service has one method, which takes a `String` as input. It concatenates the `String:" - from service"` to the input `String`, and returns the resultant `String`.

We'll build and run this example later in the chapter, but first we're going to examine how it all works.

How It Works

We have three Java source files to walk through here. We'll start with the Service Definition Interface, and then cover the web service implementation class, followed by the client. We'll examine the three XML files when we build the example.

The Service Definition Interface

The interface defined in `SimpleServiceIF.java` is the Service Definition Interface, which is used both at development-time and at run-time.

❑ At development time it will be used as input to generate the WSDL file. Recall that the WSDL file describes the interfaces, methods, arguments, return values, and the URL of a web service.

❑ At run-time it is the interface that is implemented by the stub and the web service implementation.

Our web service declares one method in its interface:

```
public String getEchoString(String clientString)
  throws RemoteException;
```

Since a web service is remote by definition, its interface must:

❑ Extend `java.rmi.Remote` and

❑ Declare that its methods throw `java.rmi.RemoteException`.

Supported Data Types

Notice that the getEchoString() method takes a String as input and returns a String. Because the arguments and return values of web services are described by WSDL, only Java types that can be represented by WSDL may be used in the method signatures of a JAX-RPC application. Fortunately, all of the Java primitive types and their associated wrapper classes are supported. As a refresher, these are:

Primitive Type	Wrapper Class (in **java.lang**)
byte	Byte
short	Short
int	Integer
long	Long
float	Float
double	Double
boolean	Boolean

Additionally, the following Java classes are supported:

Package	Supported Class
java.lang	String
java.math	BigInteger
	BigDecimal
java.util	Date
	Calendar
	Many of the collection classes, such as ArrayList and HashMap

Arrays of primitive types and classes listed above are supported as well. Classes whose fields are composed exclusively of JAX-RPC supported data types can be supported as well. For more details on this you can consult the JAX-RPC Specification, which is listed in the *Resources* section of this chapter.

The Web Service Implementation Class

The implementation of our web service is contained in `SimpleServiceImpl.java`, which implements the `SimpleServiceIF` interface. As you can see from the listing above, other than this fact there is nothing special about this implementation class. The JAX-RPC tools and runtime classes do the heavy lifting!

A Web Service Client

The client for our web service is the `SimpleServiceClient.java` code. The `main()` method takes an array of `String` arguments and loops through these arguments, calling the `getEchoString()` web service method with each one.

As explained previously, a client communicates with a web service method via stub and tie classes. In our code example, we use the `getSimpleServiceIFPort()` of a class named `SimpleService_Impl` to obtain a reference to a stub that implements the Service Definition Interface. In this case, the stub implements the `SimpleServiceIF` interface, and the reference is held in the variable named `myProxy`.

```
Stub stub = (Stub)
    (new SimpleService_Impl().getSimpleServiceIFPort());
SimpleServiceIF myProxy = (SimpleServiceIF)stub;
```

By the way, the `SimpleService_Impl` class and the stub classes that it returns are generated in the build process that we'll walk through soon.

Continuing on, the `getEchoString()` method of the stub class is then called, which communicates the argument via SOAP to the tie. This calls the web service implementation, which returns the value via the tie to the stub, and back to the client:

```
String returnedString =
    myProxy.getEchoString(args[i]);
```

The returned value ends up in the `returnedString` variable, which we print out just to prove that the round trip to the web service was achieved:

```
System.out.println("sent string: " + args[i]
    + ", received string: " + returnedString);
```

The Three Ways to Invoke Web Service Methods

There are actually three ways for a client to invoke the methods of a web service:

Probably the most common way, which the example above employed, is known as static stubs. It is also referred to as generated stubs. Using this model, the stubs are created at development time, which we'll see when we build the example shortly.

There is another model, known as **dynamic proxy**, in which the stub classes are created at runtime instead of during development. The Service Definition Interface, however, is created at development time. We'll walk through an example of this in the next chapter.

There is also a Dynamic Invocation Interface (DII) call interface model in which the client can call a web service for which it has no Service Definition Interface or stubs. This is much like Java reflection, in that method signatures are dynamically created and subsequently invoked. The SimpleCalculatorApp example, from Chapter 8, will be transformed into a web service example that employs the DII in the chapter following this one.

Let's take a macro view of a build and deploy process for web services, and then we'll apply it to this example.

The Essential Steps for Building and Deploying Web Services

You'll be using two tools supplied with the J2EE SDK 1.4. One of these tools, the Deployment Tool, has been used throughout this book already. The other one, wscompile, will be used to create the WSDL file and the client stubs. All of the J2EE SDK tools, including the ones we have just mentioned, are located in the bin directory of the J2EE SDK installation.

To create a web service using JAX-RPC with the J2EE SDK 1.4, you can follow these steps:

1. Create the Service Definition Interface and the web service implementation class in the Java programming language, and compile the source files.

2. Create the WSDL file with the wscompile command line tool.

3. Start the J2EE Server and create the J2EE EAR file with the Deployment Tool.

4. Create the WAR file and configure the web service with the Deployment Tool.

5. Create the application server-specific deployment descriptor with the Deployment Tool.

6. Run the Verifier Tool.

7. Deploy the web service.

8. Build the web service stubs classes.

9. Create the client in the Java programming language and compile the source files.

10. Run the web service client.

Let's apply the steps listed above to build and deploy the example.

Compiling the Java Source Files for the Web Service

To build the following example, we'll first compile the two `.java` files that define and implement our web service:

❑ `SimpleServiceIF.java` (in the `webservices` package)

❑ `SimpleServiceImpl.java` (in the `webservices` package)

Later, we'll also compile the `.java` file that provides the client functionality:

❑ `SimpleServiceClient.java` (in the `client` package)

To compile these Java files, set the `classpath` to:

❑ The current directory, and

❑ The `j2ee.jar` file that is in the `lib` directory of the Java 2 SDK, Enterprise Edition 1.4 (J2EE SDK 1.4) installation.

For example, on a default J2EE SDK 1.4 Windows installation, the `classpath` would be set correctly by using the following command:

```
> set classpath=.;c:\j2sdkee1.4\lib\j2ee.jar
```

With the directory that the client and webservices directories are rooted in (this example has used `SimpleServiceApp`) as the current directory, execute the following command from the command prompt:

```
> javac -d . webservices/*.java
```

The Java class files for the web service should end up in the same directory as the source files. We'll compile the client class in the *Compiling the Client* step.

At this point we need to create the WSDL file because it will, in turn, be used to create other files needed by this example.

Try It Out   **Create the WSDL File for the Simple Web Service**

The drawing shown below illustrates this step:

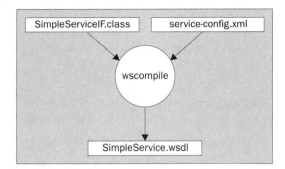

The inputs to this step are the `SimpleServiceIF.class` file that was created by the compile in the previous step, and the `service-config.xml` file shown below.

1. We need to create this XML file now and save it in the **SimpleServiceApp** root folder for our application, as shown in the diagram of the file layout, previously;

```
<?xml version="1.0" encoding="UTF-8"?>
<configuration
  xmlns="http://java.sun.com/xml/ns/jax-rpc/ri/config">
  <service
    name="SimpleService"
    targetNamespace="urn:simpleService"
    typeNamespace="urn:simpleService"
    packageName="webservices">
    <interface name="webservices.SimpleServiceIF"/>
  </service>
</configuration>
```

This `service-config.xml` file provides input to the `wscompile` tool, giving it some of the information that it needs to create the `SimpleService.wsdl` file. This information, as seen above, is the name of the web service, namespaces to be used in the WSDL file, the Java package name in which the web service classes reside, and the fully qualified name of the service definition interface.

2. To create the WSDL file, we'll use a command-line tool that comes with the J2EE SDK 1.4 named `wscompile`. This tool's purpose in life is to create WSDL, stub, and tie files. Here we'll just be using it to generate the WSDL file, which contains XML. To do this, with the current directory set as indicated above, type the following command:

```
> wscompile -define -nd . -classpath . service-config.xml
```

So, let's take a look at what we've accomplished here.

How It Works

This command takes the `service-config.xml` file shown above, and the interface defined in the `SimpleServiceIF.class` file, and it generates the `SimpleService.wsdl` file.

❑ The `-define` option tells the tool to read a Java RMI interface and create a WSDL file that defines a web service. In this case the RMI interface is in the `SimpleServiceIF.class` file as indicated by the `webservices.SimpleServiceIF` entry in the `service-config.xml` file.

❑ The `-nd` option indicates where to place any non-class files that are generated. In this case, the `SimpleService.wsdl` will be placed in the current directory.

❑ The `-classpath` option specifies where to find the input files.

Documentation on the `wscompile` tool is included in the J2EE SDK 1.4 installation.

An excerpt shown below of the generated `SimpleService.wsdl` file has an XML representation of the interface, method, parameters, and return types defined by the `SimpleServiceIF` interface. As previously noted, the nomenclature used in the WSDL file includes ports, operations, messages, and parts. For example, the `<operation>` element defines the `getEchoString` operation and the `<message>` elements define the parameters and return type of that operation:

```xml
<?xml version="1.0" encoding="UTF-8"?>
<definitions name="SimpleService"
             targetNamespace="urn:simpleService"
             xmlns:tns="urn:simpleService"
             xmlns="http://schemas.xmlsoap.org/wsdl/"
             xmlns:soap="http://schemas.xmlsoap.org/wsdl/soap/"
             xmlns:xsd="http://www.w3.org/2001/XMLSchema">
  <types/>
  <message name="SimpleServiceIF_getEchoString">
    <part name="String_1" type="xsd:string"/>
  </message>
  <message name="SimpleServiceIF_getEchoStringResponse">
    <part name="result" type="xsd:string"/>
  </message>
  <portType name="SimpleServiceIF">
    <operation name="getEchoString" parameterOrder="String_1">
      <input message="tns:SimpleServiceIF_getEchoString"/>
      <output message="tns:SimpleServiceIF_getEchoStringResponse"/>
    </operation>
  </portType>
  <service name="SimpleService">
    <port name="SimpleServiceIFPort" binding="tns:SimpleServiceIFBinding">
      <soap:address location="REPLACE_WITH_ACTUAL_URL"/>
    </port>
  </service>
</definitions>
```

Note that when you are developing a new web service, you can modify the `service-config.xml` (shown at the beginning of this step) to reflect the name of the web service, and the package and name of the interface class. As an example, if you were developing a web service named **WeatherService**, and the package name was `web_services`, your `service-config.xml` file would look something like this:

```xml
<?xml version="1.0" encoding="UTF-8"?>
<configuration
  xmlns="http://java.sun.com/xml/ns/jax-rpc/ri/config">
  <service
    name="WeatherService"
    targetNamespace="urn:weatherService"
    typeNamespace="urn:weatherService"
    packageName="web_services">
    <interface name="web_services.SimpleServiceIF"/>
  </service>
</configuration>
```

Now that the WSDL file has been created, we'll use the Deployment Tool to configure and deploy the web service.

Try It Out — Creating the J2EE EAR File

Let's go ahead and start up the application server that comes with J2EE SDK 1.4 because we'll be deploying our web service soon. To start it up, type the following command from your operating system prompt:

```
> j2ee
```

Now we'll use the Deployment Tool that comes with the J2EE SDK 1.4 to configure and deploy the web service. From the operating system prompt, please start up the Deployment Tool by entering the following command:

```
> deploytool
```

After the Deployment Tool starts up, we'll create the J2EE Enterprise Application Resource (EAR) file in which the application will be packaged. When everything is completed, the web service will be packaged in a web application resource (WAR) file, which we'll stick in our EAR.

Try It Out — Creating the WAR File and Configuring the Web Service

1. Start by creating a new Application EAR file, and name it SimpleServiceApp.ear, placing it in your `SimpleServiceApp` directory, and setting the display name to be SimpleServiceApp.

2. One of the files we'll be putting in the WAR file is `mapping.xml`, which is another configuration file. The code for this file is as follows:

```
<?xml version="1.0" encoding="UTF-8"?>
<!DOCTYPE java-wsdl-mapping PUBLIC
    "-//IBM Corporation, Inc.//DTD J2EE JAX-RPC mapping 1.0//EN"

"http://www.ibm.com/standards/xml/webservices/j2ee/j2ee_jaxrpc_mapping_1_0.dt
d">
<java-wsdl-mapping>
  <package-mapping>
    <package-type>webservices</package-type>
    <namespaceURI>urn:simpleService</namespaceURI>
  </package-mapping>
</java-wsdl-mapping>
```

Make sure you enter this code and save it before continuing.

3. Now we'll create the WAR file in which the web service classes and resources will be packaged. To do this, make sure that SimpleServiceApp is selected in the tree on the left. From the File menu choose the New menu item, and then the Web Application WAR menu item.

You will be asked by the wizard to choose where you want the WAR file to be placed. We're going to put it in our newly created SimpleServiceApp EAR file, so make the related choices that you see below. Also on this page is a place to enter the name for the WAR Display Name that you would like to appear in tools like this Deployment Tool. Let's call it SimpleServiceWar:

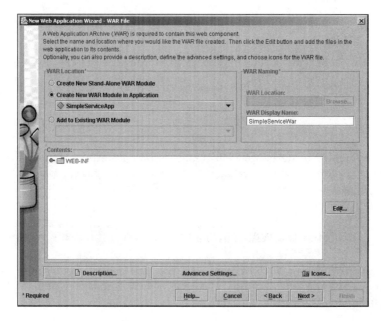

4. Next, click the **Edit** button on this page to pick the files that you want to put in the WAR file.In the **Available Files** panel of the dialog box shown below, navigate to the base directory of this **SimpleServiceApp** example. Choose the following files and click the **Add** button:

❏ The Service Definition Interface (`SimpleServiceIF.class`).

❏ The Web Service Implementation class (`SimpleServiceImpl.class`).

❏ The WSDL file (`SimpleService.wsdl`).

❏ The J2EE JAX-RPC mapping file (`mapping.xml`). The purpose of this file is to associate the Java package in which the web service class files are located with the namespace of the web service in the WSDL file. This is seen in the `<package-mapping>` element shown above.

Those four files should now appear in the **Contents of SimpleServiceWar** panel as seen below.

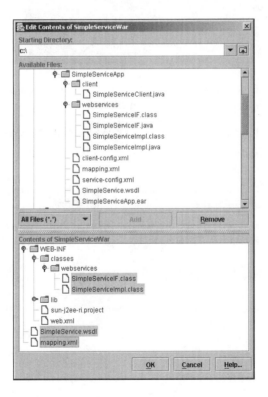

5. Closing the dialog box and clicking the **Next** button should make the page shown below appear. This page lets you choose the features that you want the web application to have. Here, because it is a web service, we'll indicate that we want it to be a **Web Services Endpoint**. For this example, none of the other features are necessary:

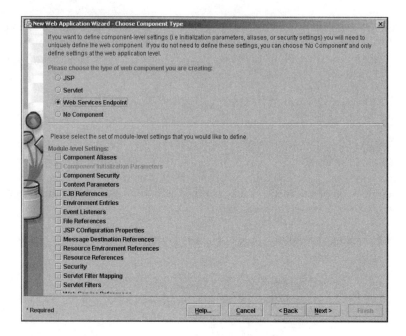

6. The next page of the wizard, shown below, lets you define the new web service. For this, we'll supply four pieces of information:

❑ Firstly, we'll indicate the name of the WSDL file (`SimpleService.wsdl`).

❑ Secondly, we'll indicate the name of the J2EE JAX-RPC mapping file (`mapping.xml`).

❑ The third piece of information that we'll supply to the page shown below is the name that we'll give the web service. **SimpleService** would be an appropriate name.

❑ Finally, we'll give it the name for the service that you would like to appear in tools like this Deployment Tool. Let's use the name **SimpleService** for this as well.

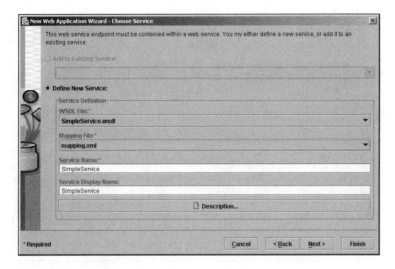

7. In the next page of the wizard, shown below, we'll enter information about the interface for the web service. There are five fields to fill out on this page:

❑ Service Endpoint Interface: An **endpoint** in web services parlance is the URL address of a web service. The Service Endpoint Interface that is implemented at the endpoint is what we've been referring to as the Service Definition Interface. The fully qualified name of this interface for our web service is webservices.simpleServiceIF, so choose that name from the drop-own list.

❑ WSDL Port Namespace and Local Part: These uniquely identify the web service port in the WSDL file, and associate it with the Service Endpoint Interface chosen above. Enter urn:simpleService and SimpleServiceIFPort, respectively.

❑ Port Component Name and Port Component Display Name: We'll use the class name of the Service Endpoint Interface for both of these fields, so enter SimpleServiceIF in each one.

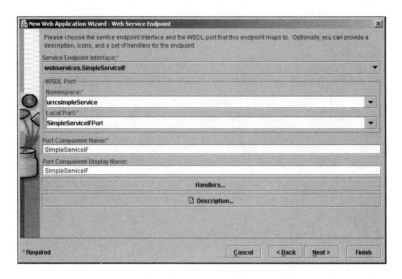

8. The next page of the wizard is shown below. In the Service Endpoint Implementation drop-down, you'll choose the fully qualified name of the Java class that implements the web service, in this case webservices.SimpleServiceImpl. The other fields will be loaded with default values as seen below, and we'll keep the defaults:

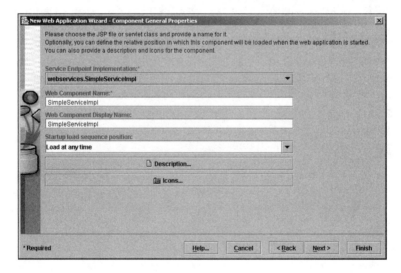

9. The last page of the New Web Application Wizard (not shown) shows the **Deployment Descriptor** for the WAR file that will be generated by the Deployment Tool. Click the Finish button to leave the wizard, and the screen should look like the one shown below:

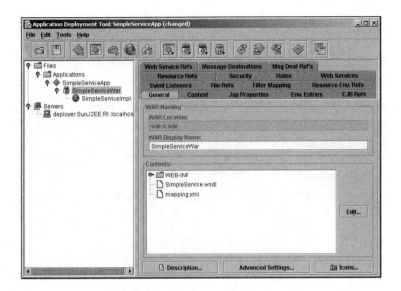

10. In the General tab of the page shown below, enter SimpleServiceImpl in the Web Component Display Name field if it isn't there already.

*Note: Even though that field was entered in the **New Web Application Wizard** a few pages earlier, this required field (and a couple of others we'll check shortly) didn't stick around in the beta version of the Deployment Tool that we are using. This is why we're verifying that they are there now. Hopefully, the final release of the Deployment Tool has this problem corrected.*

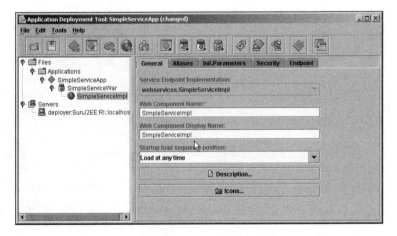

11. Now select the Aliases tab and we'll tweak some more. The Aliases tab, shown below, lets us assign an alias to our web service. The web service endpoint is a URL, and the alias that we enter will be part of that URL. As you'll see when we examine the `client-config.xml` file, the URL for our web service will be the following:

http://localhost:8000/simple-jaxrpc/simple

To assign the alias, click the **Add** button, and enter **/simple** in the row that appears in the **Component Aliases** panel:

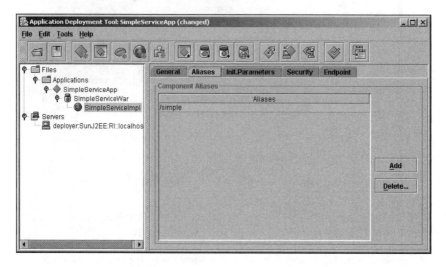

Now let's look at the **Endpoint** tab.

12. In the **Endpoint** tab shown below, enter **SimpleServiceIF** in the **Port Component Display Name** field if it isn't there already:

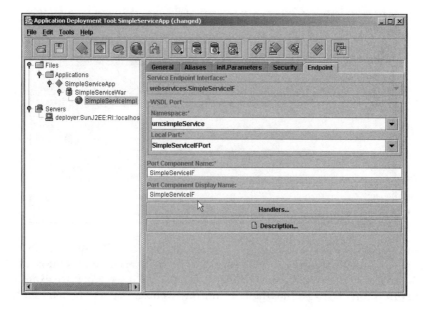

13. Then, in the tree in the left-hand panel, go ahead and select SimpleServiceWar, and click the **Web Services** tab. From the page shown below, select the SimpleService Service Name from the **Web Services** panel, and click the **Edit** button:

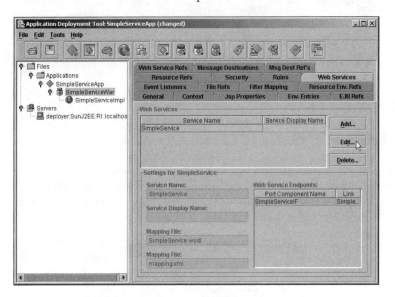

In the **Service Display Name** textbox shown below, enter SimpleService if it isn't there already, and click the **OK** button:

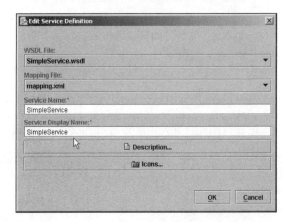

14. Now select SimpleServiceApp from the tree in the panel on the left, and select the **Web Context** tab in the panel on the right. In the **Context Root** column of the **Web Context** tab, enter simple-jaxrpc beside the SimpleServiceWar entry, as shown in the screenshot below. The **Context Root** is the base directory for its WAR file, so in addition to the alias that we defined above, simple-jaxrpc will become part of the URL for our web service endpoint: http://localhost:8000/simple-jaxrpc/simple

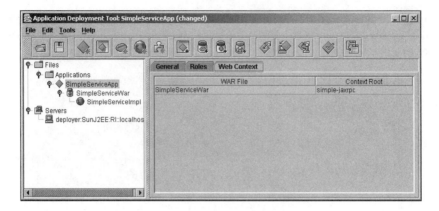

15. Now we're going to create a platform-specific deployment descriptor for the J2EE server. To do this, make sure that the SimpleServiceApp is selected in the left-hand panel. From the File menu choose the Deployment Settings menu item, and then the Create New File menu item:

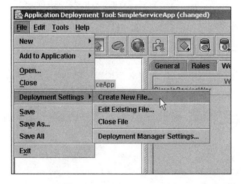

As shown below, a dialog box will be displayed, prompting you to enter the location that you want the platform-specific deployment descriptor to be placed in. We'll take all of the defaults in this dialog box and will close the dialog box by clicking OK:

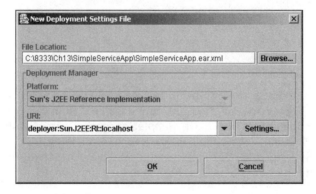

16. Navigate to the screen shown next by selecting the second node labeled Sun's J2EE Reference Implementation in the tree in the left-hand panel. It should appear just below the SimpleServiceWar node. You may have to expand nodes on the tree to see that particular one. You won't have to change anything in this screen now, but just take note that it is available if you want to see a list of Web Service Endpoints in the application:

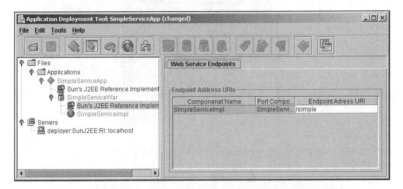

Close and save the platform-specific deployment descriptor by choosing the Deployment Settings menu item from the File menu, and then choosing the Close File menu item. You will be prompted to save the deployment descriptor with the Save Deployment Settings File dialog shown below, so click the Save button:

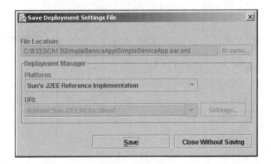

Also, it is very important to save the application, so at this point select SimpleServiceApp from the tree on the left, and select Save from the File menu.

Try It Out   Deploying the Web Service

Before we deploy, as a good housekeeping measure, we'll make sure that no other applications are deployed. There is no problem with having more than one application deployed at a time, but this will ensure that we don't have two of our example web services deployed with the same endpoint. To do this, select deployer:SunJ2EE:RI::localhost from tree in the left-hand panel to see the page shown below. If there are any rows in the Deployed Objects panel, select each row individually and click the Undeploy button.

1. To deploy the J2EE application that contains our web service, select SimpleServiceApp from the tree in the left-hand panel, and choose Deploy from the Tools menu as shown in the following screenshot:

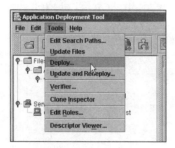

2. When the following dialog appears, click the OK button:

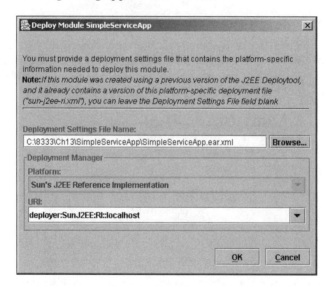

3. The following dialog will appear, and your SimpleServiceApp should successfully deploy, including the web service that we created. The web service is now ready for a client to invoke its one and only method. Click the Close button when it becomes enabled:

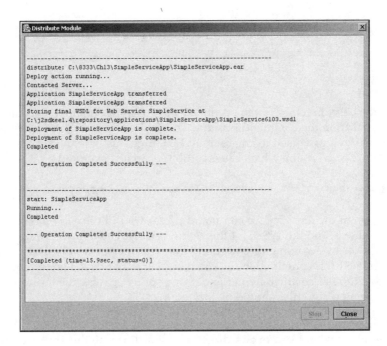

If you have any problems deploying, then follow the instructions in the *Troubleshooting the Deploy* section of Chapter 8.

After the web service is deployed, we'll turn our attention towards building and running the client.

Try It Out   Final Configuration and Test of the Web Service

Before we can compile the client application, we need to create the stub classes, because the client application is dependent upon them. Recall that the client calls methods of the stub, which communicates on its behalf via SOAP to the tie, which invokes methods of the web service. To create the stub classes:

1. Verify that your `classpath` is set as described in the *Compiling the Java Source Files for the Web Service* section earlier in this chapter.

2. With the base directory of the example (this explanation has used `SimpleServiceApp`) as the current directory, create a subdirectory named `stubs` (if it doesn't already exist). If it does exist, go ahead and delete everything within it for the sake of good housekeeping.

3. We need to enter the code for the last of our XML configuration files, `client-config.xml`. Enter the following code and save the file:

```
<?xml version="1.0" encoding="UTF-8"?>
<configuration xmlns="http://java.sun.com/xml/ns/jax-rpc/ri/config">
  <wsdl location="http://localhost:8000/simple-jaxrpc/simple?WSDL"
        packageName="webservices"/>
</configuration>
```

4. With the base directory of the example as the current directory, execute the following command from the command prompt. This is the same `wscompile` command-ine tool that we previously used to create the WSDL file. This time, however, we're using the `-gen:client` option, which causes stub files to be generated.

> **`wscompile -gen:client -d stubs -classpath . client-config.xml`**

This form of the `wscompile` command takes as input the `client-config.xml` file shown above, and the WSDL of the web service. It gets the WSDL from the deployed web service by accessing its endpoint URL with the string "?WSDL" appended to the end. This URL is contained in the `<wsdl>` element of the `client-config.xml` file. The `packageName` attribute in the `client-config.xml` file indicates what package the generated stub files should be located in.

As a result of the `wscompile`, the Java class files for the stub should be generated and placed in a new `webservices` directory subordinate to the `stubs` directory.

5. Now we can compile the client class, being careful to add the `stubs` directory to the `classpath`. To do this on a Windows platform, for example, the command would look like this:

> **`javac -classpath %classpath%;stubs -d . client/*.java`**

The Java class files for the client should end up in the same directory as the source files.

6. To run the client, as with the compile, we'll need the `stubs` directory on the `classpath`:

> **`Java -classpath %classpath%;stubs client.SimpleServiceClient bon jour`**

The `SimpleService` web service will be invoked once for each of the command-line arguments. If you run the client with the command line arguments shown above (`Hello` and `Jim!`), it should produce the following output:

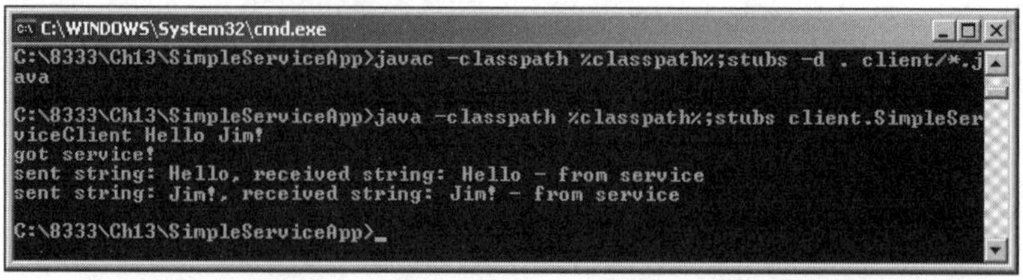

How It Works

Congratulations! You've created and invoked a web service. The web service Java code and XML files are pretty straightforward, but building and deploying can seem like a chore the first couple of times that you do it (as you may have noticed).

By the way, because web services are invoked via HTTP, you can ping a web service via a web browser. For example, if you enter the endpoint of the web service followed by "?WSDL", the server will respond by sending you the WSDL for the web service. To try this, paste the following URL in your web browser with the web service deployed:

```
http://localhost:8000/simple-jaxrpc/simple?WSDL
```

You may recall that this is the same URL that the `wscompile` tool used to get the WSDL for creating the client stubs.

Summary

In this chapter, we discovered that web services are a way to create distributed applications whose components communicate with each other over protocols associated with the Web. This application functionality can be offered via web services over the public Internet, or limited for use within a corporate intranet or extranet.

We saw that some of the advantages of web services are:

❑ They promote the development of distributed applications whose components are written in various languages, and deployed on various hardware and software platforms.

❑ They communicate over protocols and ports that are used by the Web, so they can be implemented relatively easily.

This chapter has also touched upon the fact that the availability of web services over the public Internet makes security, in the form of data encryption and user authentication, an important issue.

We then explored the web services protocol layers, which employ technologies such as HTTP, XML, SOAP, WSDL, and UDDI. An introduction to JAX-RPC was given, and web service concepts such as stubs and ties were explained in that context. Finally, we developed a simple web service and client, using the J2EE SDK 1.4 Deployment Tool and JAX-RPC implementation.

Now that we've explored web services and JAX-RPC, in the next chapter we'll cover some more topics germane to web services .

Resources

Here are some good resources for learning about XML:

- *Beginning Java 2 SDK 1.4 Edition, Wrox Press, 1-86100-569-5*
- *Beginning XML, Wrox Press, 1-86100-559-8*
- http://java.sun.com/xml/docs.html
- http://www.xml.org/
- http://www.xml.com/

You can learn more about JAX-RPC from the JAX-RPC Specification, which can be downloaded from the following page:

- http://java.sun.com/xml/downloads/jaxrpc.html

You can download the SAAJ specification from the following page:

- http://java.sun.com/xml/downloads/saaj.html

You can learn more about UDDI and the JAXR API from these web sites, respectively:

- http://www.uddi.org/
- http://java.sun.com/xml/jaxr/

The Java Web Services Developer Pack is available from Sun's Java web site on the following page:

- http://java.sun.com/webservices/webservicespack.html

Exercises

1. Write a JAX-RPC web service that takes a word and returns it spelled backwards.

2. Write a JAX-RPC web service that takes two numbers and a string operator value of "+" or "-". Apply this operator to the numbers.

CHAPTER 13

Implementing a Session Bean as a Web Service   565

Implementing a Stateful Web Service   580

Summary   597

Exercises   597

More J2EE Web Services Topics

The previous chapter gave us an introduction to web services, including concepts such as the web services protocol stack and the layers contained within. We discussed JAX-RPC and developed a web service application using the J2EE SDK 1.4, including the JAX-RPC implementation.

In this chapter, we'll cover more topics germane to developing J2EE web services, including how web services and EJBs play well together, additional JAX-RPC concepts, and some dynamic aspects of web services.

In this chapter you will learn:

- ❑ How to implement a session bean as a web service.
- ❑ How to develop **dynamic proxies** for web services.
- ❑ How to create a stateful web service.
- ❑ About the **JAX-RPC endpoint model**.
- ❑ How to use the **DII (Dynamic Invocation Interface)** to call web services dynamically.

We'll start by revisiting EJBs and take a look at how we can combine knowledge of EJBs with the deployment of web services.

Implementing a Session Bean as a Web Service

There is a relatively new capability in the EJB specification that provides for making the methods of a stateless session bean available via a **web service endpoint**. Note that the specification only requires that *stateless* session beans implement a **web service endpoint**, not *stateful* session beans. We do have a stateful web service example in this chapter, but it is implemented in a different way.

In the first example in this chapter, we'll be building on some of the techniques we've already learned. This example demonstrates how to take a stateless session bean and deploy it as a web service. In order to accomplish this we'll give the session bean a web service endpoint. Because we're dealing with an EJB that will become a web service, this example uses EJB concepts as well as web services concepts that we've learned in previous chapters:

❑ The EJB concepts, and some of the code for this example, come straight out of the *EJB Fundamentals* chapter. Specifically, we're going to use some of the session bean code and build process from the first *Try It Out* example, which was the *SimpleSessionApp* session bean example in Chapter 8.

❑ The web services concepts, and some of the code for this example, come from the previous chapter. We'll use some code and build process from the *SimpleServiceApp* example as well.

Recall that the *SimpleSessionApp* example referred to above is a stateless session bean that takes a `String` argument, concatenates the string: " – from session bean", and returns the resultant string. The *SimpleServiceApp* does essentially the same thing, except for the fact that it is a web service. Let's take a look the code that we'll borrow from each of these examples:

Try it Out   Creating a Web Service with a Session Bean

1. We'll start by using the session bean class code from the *SimpleSessionApp* example, which is in the Java source file, `SimpleSessionBean.java`:

```java
package beans;

import javax.ejb.SessionBean;
import javax.ejb.SessionContext;

public class SimpleSessionBean implements SessionBean {
    // the public business method. this must be coded in the
    // remote interface also.
    public String getEchoString(String clientString) {
      return clientString + " – from session bean";
    }

    // standard ejb methods
    public void ejbActivate() {}
    public void ejbPassivate() {}
    public void ejbRemove() {}
    public void ejbCreate() {}
    public void setSessionContext(SessionContext context) { }
}
```

Note that we're not going to use the session bean's **home interface** or **bean interface** classes. This is because the client in this example is a web service client. It will be invoking the methods of the **service definition interface** which is very similar to the **bean interface**, and it won't be using the **home interface** at all. Of course, you could leave those interfaces in, which would enable the deployed bean to be invoked via a web service client as well as via an EJB client. This is often a better approach, as it provides more flexibility as to how the session bean may be used.

2. The service definition interface is taken from the *SimpleServiceApp* example, `SimpleServiceIF.java`:

```
package webservices;

import java.rmi.Remote;
import java.rmi.RemoteException;

public interface SimpleServiceIF extends Remote {
  // the service methods
  public String getEchoString(String clientString)
    throws RemoteException;
}
```

3. The client for this example, `SimpleServiceClient.java`, is very similar to the client in the *SimpleServiceApp* example in the previous chapter: the basic difference is that we're going to take this opportunity to demonstrate how to use **dynamic proxies** mentioned in the previous chapter:

```
package client;

import webservices.SimpleServiceIF;

import java.net.URL;
import javax.xml.namespace.QName;
import javax.xml.rpc.Service;
import javax.xml.rpc.ServiceFactory;

public class SimpleServiceClient {
  public static void main(String[] args) {
    try {
      String serviceName = "SimpleBeanService";
      String urlString =
        "http://localhost:8000/simplebean?WSDL";
      String nameSpaceUri =
              "urn:simpleBeanService";
      String portName = "SimpleServiceIFPort";

      URL wsdlUrl = new URL(urlString);

      ServiceFactory serviceFactory = ServiceFactory.newInstance();
```

```
        Service jaxService =
          serviceFactory.createService(wsdlUrl,
                  new QName(nameSpaceUri, serviceName));

        SimpleServiceIF myProxy = (SimpleServiceIF) jaxService.getPort(
                  new QName(nameSpaceUri, portName),
                  SimpleServiceIF.class);

        System.out.println("got service!");

        // loop through the words
        for (int i = 0; i < args.length; i++) {
          String returnedString =
            myProxy.getEchoString(args[i]);
          System.out.println("sent string: " + args[i]
            + ", received string: " + returnedString);
        }
      } catch(Exception e) {
        e.printStackTrace();
      }
    }
  }
```

We'll also be using slightly modified versions of the service-config.xml and mapping.xml files from the *SimpleServiceApp* example that we created in the previous chapter. These files will be listed in the place where we build and deploy the example.

Let's go ahead and build the example, using a fusion of the session bean and web service build processes described below.

To build this example, we'll begin by following the process defined in the *Essential Steps for Building and Deploying EJBs* section of the *EJB Fundamentals* chapter. You'll also notice that a lot of the steps in this example are the same as in the previous chapter. We'll coach you through this here, pointing out variations as they come up.

Here are the steps that will be followed for building and running this example:

- ❑ Compile the Java source code
- ❑ Create the WSDL document
- ❑ Start the J2EE Server and create the J2EE EAR file with the Deployment Tool
- ❑ Create and populate the bean JAR
- ❑ Configure the web service
- ❑ Create the platform-specific deployment descriptor
- ❑ Run the Verifier Tool

❏ Deploy the web service

❏ Run the web service client

There are three Java source files in this example, and we'll compile all of them now, even the web service client. Do you remember why we didn't compile the client program in the previous web service example until later in process? It was because the static stubs first had to be generated due to the fact that the client depended upon them. In this example, we're going to demonstrate **dynamic proxies** which don't use static subs, so there are no dependency issues. Note that there is no relationship between this example being a session bean with a web service endpoint, and the client using a dynamic proxy. We could have just as easily used either of the other two client models (**static stubs** and **DII**) introduced in the previous chapter.

Here are the three .java files:

❏ SimpleSessionBean.java (in the beans package)

❏ SimpleServiceIF.java (in the webservices package)

❏ SimpleServiceClient.java (in the client package)

These files should be organized in the following subdirectory structure. Also shown in this structure are the two XML files that will be used in the build process:

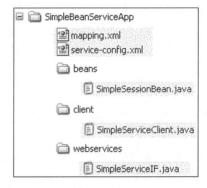

4. To compile these Java files, set the classpath to:

❏ The current directory, and

❏ The j2ee.jar file that is in the lib directory of the Java 2 SDK, Enterprise Edition 1.4 (J2EE SDK 1.4) installation.

For example, on a default J2EE SDK 1.4 Windows installation, the classpath would be set correctly by using the following command:

```
> set classpath=.;c:\j2sdkee1.4\lib\j2ee.jar
```

5. With base directory of the example as the current directory, execute the following commands from the command prompt.

```
> javac -d . beans/*.java
> javac -d . webservices/*.java
> javac -d . client/*.java
```

At this point we'll borrow a step from the **Web Services and JAX-RPC** chapter. Because our session bean will be a web service, it will need a WSDL document, and to create that document, we need a `service-config.xml` file. Here is the `service-config.xml` file that we're using as input to the `wscompile`:

```
<?xml version="1.0" encoding="UTF-8"?>
<configuration xmlns="http://java.sun.com/xml/ns/jax-rpc/ri/config">
  <service
      name="SimpleBeanService"
      targetNamespace="urn:simpleBeanService"
      typeNamespace="urn:simpleBeanService"
      packageName="beans">
      <interface name="webservices.SimpleServiceIF"/>
  </service>
</configuration>
```

6. Now, to create the WSDL, with the current directory set as indicated above, type the following command:

```
> wscompile -define -nd . -classpath . service-config.xml
```

This will create a file named `SimpleBeanService.wsdl` that we'll put in the bean jar shortly. Now, back to the session bean build process:

7. After starting the J2EE server and Deployment Tool, create an **Application EAR** file and name it SimpleBeanServiceApp.ear.

8. Invoke the **Edit Enterprise Bean Wizard** by selecting **File | New | Enterprise JavaBean JAR** from the menu.

In the **EJB JAR** page of the **Edit Enterprise Bean Wizard**, use SimpleBeanServiceJar as the **JAR Display Name**. Click the **Edit** button on that page, and add the following files to the **SimpleBeanServiceJar** panel shown in the dialog below.

- ❑ The session bean implementation class (`SimpleSessionBean.class`). Recall that for this example, we don't need the two interface files that are normally included in session beans

- ❑ The **service definition interface** (`SimpleServiceIF.class`) for the web service.

- ❑ The WSDL file (`SimpleBeanService.wsdl`) for the web service.

- ❑ The J2EE JAX-RPC mapping file (`mapping.xml`) for the web service. Here is the `mapping.xml` file that we're using for this example:

```
<?xml version="1.0" encoding="UTF-8"?>
<!DOCTYPE java-wsdl-mapping PUBLIC
    "-//IBM Corporation, Inc.//DTD J2EE JAX-RPC mapping 1.0//EN"
"http://www.ibm.com/standards/xml/webservices/j2ee/j2ee_jaxrpc_mapping_1_0.dtd">
<java-wsdl-mapping>
    <package-mapping>
        <package-type>beans</package-type>
        <namespaceURI>urn:simpleBeanService</namespaceURI>
    </package-mapping>
</java-wsdl-mapping>
```

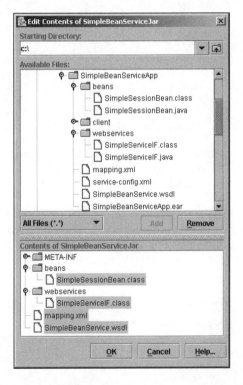

Since the session bean interfaces aren't needed, we won't choose them from the **General** page shown below. Do, however, remember to choose that the session bean is **Stateless**. Also, select `beans.SimpleSessionBean` from the **Enterprise Bean Class** drop-down, and enter `SimpleSessionBean` as the Display Name:

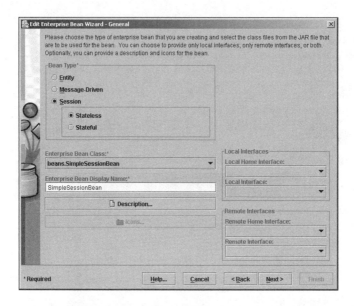

The more inquisitive among us will have clicked the dropdowns in the Remote Interfaces panel to see if those interfaces were available to be chosen. They're not available in the drop-downs because we didn't add them in the previous dialog (I had to check).

9. The next page in the Wizard, shown below, is a pivotal one. From it, we'll indicate that our session bean should be a web service, and we'll be led into some pages that we saw in the Creating the WAR File and Configuring the Web Service section of the Web Services and JAX-RPC chapter. To do this, select Yes in the Expose Bean as a Web Service Endpoint panel:

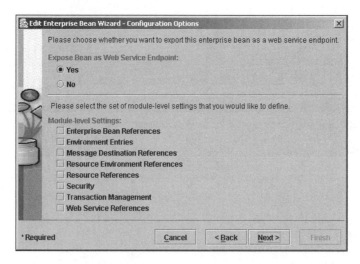

10. From the next page of in the Edit Enterprise Bean Wizard, shown below, select the WSDL File and `mapping.xml` file from the dropdown lists. Use SimpleBeanService for the Service Name and Service Display Name:

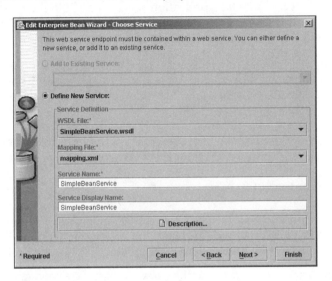

11. From the next page, shown below, select our **service definition interface** from the Service Endpoint Interface drop-down list. We'll use urn:simpleBeanService for the WSDL Port Namespace, and SimpleServiceIFPort for the WSDL Port Local Part. For a refresher on what these fields mean, refer to the *Creating the WAR File and Configuring the Web Service* section of the previous web services chapter. Enter SimpleServiceIF in the Port Component Name and Port Component Display Name fields:

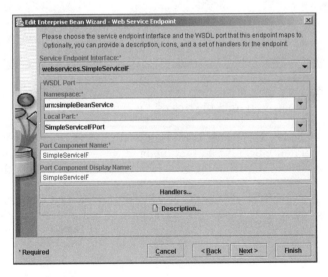

The last page of the Edit Enterprise Bean Wizard (not shown) contains an EJB JAR deployment descriptor with no home or remote interfaces defined.

12. The next step is to create the application server-specific deployment descriptor, which we do by selecting SimpleBeanServiceApp in the left-hand panel and choosing the File | Deployment Settings | Create New File menu item).

Navigate to the screen shown below by selecting the second node labeled Sun's J2EE Reference Implementation in the tree in the left-hand panel. It should appear just below the SimpleBeanServiceJar node. You may have to expand nodes on the tree to see that particular one.

13. In the Web Service Endpoints tab shown below, enter simplebean as the Endpoint Address URI. The complete URL for our web service will be:

```
http://localhost:8000/simplebean
```

It is not necessary to visit the JNDI Names tab and give the session bean a JNDI name. The reason for this is that we'll be using the web service endpoint, shown above, to locate the session bean rather than using JNDI.

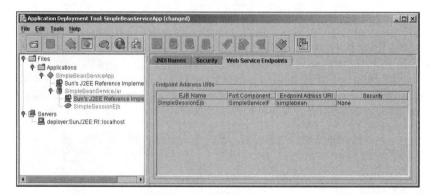

After saving the deployment descriptor, be sure to save the application by selecting SimpleBeanServiceApp from the tree on the left, and selecting Save from the File menu.

14. The last step before we deploy is to run the verifier tool (start by choosing the Tools | Verifier menu item). Be advised that the beta version that we used reported that several tests failed, shown in the screenshot below, even though the web service deployed successfully. These failed tests are caused by the fact that our session bean doesn't have any EJB interfaces, as discussed previously. Other than the failed tests seen below, when everything checks out in the Verifier Tool, we're ready to deploy!

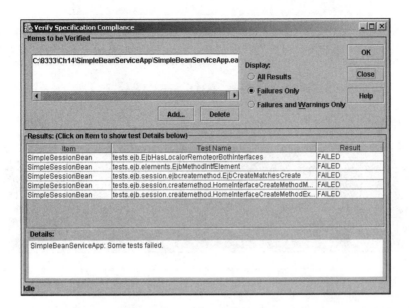

15. Deploy the application in the usual way (using the Tools | Deploy menu item). This causes the web service to begin running, listening for requests from clients:

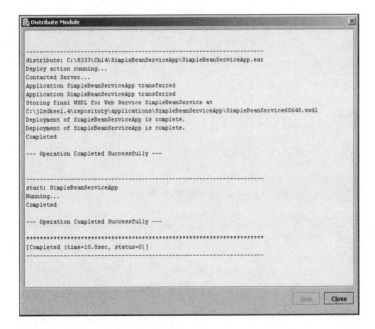

16. If you have any problems deploying, then follow the instructions in the *Troubleshooting the Deploy* section of Chapter 8.

17. We've already compiled our client class, and we don't need to build Stub classes here, because we're going to use **dynamic proxies**. So, to run the client, enter the following on the command line, including some arguments like the ones shown below:

> `java client.SimpleServiceClient faith hope love`

You should see the following:

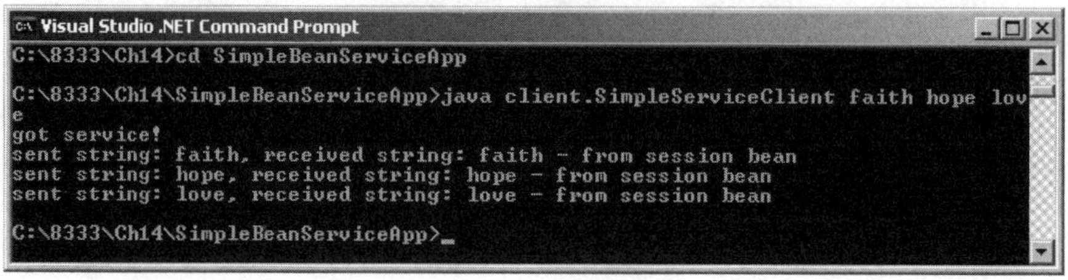

How It Works

The Deployment Tool took care of deploying the session bean in such a way that it may be accessed via a web service endpoint. Now we're going to examine the client code that dynamically accesses this web service without the benefit of a pre-existing client stub.

Let's revisit the Java source code for the web service client, `SimpleServiceClient.java`:

```java
package client;

import webservices.SimpleServiceIF;

import java.net.URL;
import javax.xml.namespace.QName;
import javax.xml.rpc.Service;
import javax.xml.rpc.ServiceFactory;

public class SimpleServiceClient {
  public static void main(String[] args) {
    try {
      String serviceName = "SimpleBeanService";
      String urlString =
        "http://localhost:8000/simplebean?WSDL";
      String nameSpaceUri =
                "urn:simpleBeanService";
      String portName = "SimpleServiceIFPort";

      URL wsdlUrl = new URL(urlString);

      ServiceFactory serviceFactory = ServiceFactory.newInstance();

      Service jaxService =
```

```
        serviceFactory.createService(wsdlUrl,
                new QName(nameSpaceUri, serviceName));

    SimpleServiceIF myProxy = (SimpleServiceIF) jaxService.getPort(
            new QName(nameSpaceUri, portName),
            SimpleServiceIF.class);

    System.out.println("got service!");

    // loop through the words
    for (int i = 0; i < args.length; i++) {
      String returnedString =
        myProxy.getEchoString(args[i]);
      System.out.println("sent string: " + args[i]
        + ", received string: " + returnedString);
    }
  } catch(Exception e) {
    e.printStackTrace();
  }
  }
}
```

Rather than generating a stub for our web service at build time, this client manufactures a stub at run-time. An advantage to this approach is that the location of the web service doesn't have to be known at build time (recall that in the *Building the Web Service Stubs* section of the previous chapter, the endpoint URL was specified in the `client-config.xml` file at build time). Rather, the endpoint URL of the web service can be supplied at run-time, perhaps passed in on a command-line or obtained from a database. A stub created dynamically at run-time is known as a **dynamic proxy**. Here is the statement that creates this dynamic proxy:

```
    SimpleServiceIF myProxy = (SimpleServiceIF) jaxService.getPort(
            new QName(nameSpaceUri, portName),
            SimpleServiceIF.class);
```

The `jaxService` variable contains a reference to an instance of the `java.xml.rpc.Service` class, which represents a web service. Its purpose in life is to create proxies that may be used to call the methods of the web service that it represents. We'll back up in a moment and explain how the `Service` instance was created, but for now let's discuss the `getPort()` method of the `Service` class. The `getPort()` method takes two parameters:

❏   The **qualified name** of the web service **port**, which as discussed previously is analogous to a Java interface. The qualified name is represented by the `QName` class in the `javax.xml.namespace` package, and consists of the values that we gave it in the **WSDL Port** panel of the **Web Service Endpoint** page of the **Edit Enterprise Bean Wizard**. Those values are defined in the following statements of our client program:

```
    String nameSpaceUri =
            "urn:simpleBeanService";
    String portName = "SimpleServiceIFPort";
```

❑ The **service definition interface**, which in this case is defined in
   `SimpleServiceIF.class`.

If there are problems creating the proxy, the `getPort()` method will throw a
`javax.xml.rpc.ServiceException`. As a result of the call to the `getPort()` method, the
variable named `myProxy` contains a proxy whose methods will invoke the methods of our web
service. As with the example in the previous chapter which used **static stubs**, the object that is
referred to by `myProxy` implements the `SimpleServiceIF` interface. Therefore, the following
code can be identical to the previous example even though the proxy was created in a
different manner.

```
String returnedString =
   myProxy.getEchoString(args[i]);
```

As promised, backing up a bit, let's take a look at how the instance of the `Service` class was
created. First off, there is a class in the `javax.xml.rpc` package named `ServiceFactory`
whose job is to create instances of the `Service` class discussed previously. The following
statements create a `Service` object for our web service:

```
ServiceFactory serviceFactory = ServiceFactory.newInstance();

Service jaxService =
   serviceFactory.createService(wsdlUrl,
           new QName(nameSpaceUri, serviceName));
```

The `newInstance()` method of the `ServiceFactory` class is a static method that returns an
instance of the `ServiceFactory` class. The `createService()` method of the
`ServiceFactory` object is then called, passing in a couple of arguments:

❑ An instance of the `java.net.URL` class that represents the URL of the WSDL
   document for our web service. This is how the resultant `Service` object knows the
   details of how to create the proxy, such as what web service **operations** (methods) are
   available. It is given this information dynamically from the WSDL document of the
   deployed web service. The WSDL URL is defined in the following statements of our
   client program:

```
String urlString =
   "http://localhost:8000/simplebean?WSDL";

URL wsdlUrl = new URL(urlString);
```

❑ The **qualified name** of the web service definition. This name consists of the values that
   we gave it in the **Service Definition** panel of the **Choose Service** page of the **Edit
   Enterprise Bean Wizard**. Those values are defined in the following statements of our
   client program:

```
String nameSpaceUri =
        "urn:simpleBeanService";
String serviceName = "SimpleBeanService";
```

If you want to display the WSDL of the deployed web service in your browser, you can do so by going to the following URL:

http://localhost:8000/simplebean?WSDL

By doing this you'll see the WSDL document, as shown below, that describes our web service so that the dynamic proxy can be created:

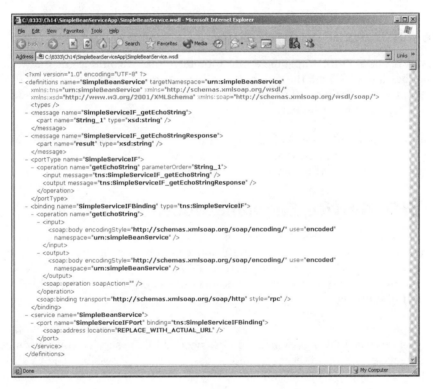

Notice that all of the **operations** are described, including parameters and return values. Notice also that three of the values from the WSDL document were passed into the `ServiceFactory.createService()` and `Service.getPort()` methods in order to identify the desired web service and port.

In this section we learned about, and walked through an example of, a stateless session bean that is exposed as a **web service endpoint**. We saw that the EJB specification enables us to use the now familiar EJB component model to create web services. This example also demonstrated how to use dynamic proxies to call a web service without having to generate stubs at build time.

579

In the next section, we'll learn how to create a web service that maintains state. In the process, we'll learn about the **JAX-RPC service endpoint model**, and how to use the **dynamic invocation interface** (DII) to call web services in an even more dynamic way.

Implementing a Stateful Web Service

In the *EJB Fundamentals* chapter, we demonstrated the concept of stateful session beans by creating a simple calculator whose session bean remembers a running total. In this section we're going to modify the calculator example by implementing it as a web service instead of a session bean.

Can Web Services be Stateful?

Web service *can* be stateful, but some application developers would argue that web services should not be stateful. Often, the rationale for this argument is that state is stored for a given user's session, and that there is currently no standard, interoperable way of associating SOAP messages with a particular session.

With that caveat in mind, we're going to go ahead and demonstrate the ability to create a stateful web service using JAX-RPC. In the process, we're going to introduce the **JAX-RPC service endpoint model**, which enables that functionality.

The JAX-RPC Service Endpoint Model

As discussed previously in this book, Java servlets and EJBs have lifecycles. As you know, Java applets have lifecycles as well. Each of these Java components, for example, is notified by their respective containers when they are first created. Web services enabled by JAX-RPC also have a life cycle, known as a **service lifecycle**. This **service lifecycle** is a feature of the **JAX-RPC service endpoint model**.

The current version of the JAX-RPC service endpoint model is underpinned by Java servlets. The underlying servlet layer provides facilities needed by the service endpoint model, for example, lifecycle method invocations and access to the HTTP session. The JAX-RPC service endpoint model has two major features:

❑ A **service lifecycle**, which consists of two methods: `init()` and `destroy()`.

❑ A servlet **endpoint context**, which exposes to the web service the context in which it is operating.

Both of these features are defined by interfaces in the `javax.xml.rpc.server` package. Let's explore these a bit.

The Service Lifecycle

A JAX-RPC web service may implement the `ServiceLifecycle` interface, which defines two methods that are called by the JAX-RPC runtime system at different points in the web service's lifecycle:

- ❑ When the web service endpoint is instantiated, the `init()` method will be called. As with the Java servlet lifecycle, implementing the `init()` method gives the web service an opportunity to initialize itself and connect to resources. Passed into this method is an object that represents the **endpoint context**, which will be discussed shortly.

- ❑ When the JAX-RPC runtime system decides that the web service endpoint is no longer required, it calls the `destroy()` method of the web service. As with the Java servlet lifecycle, implementing the `destroy()` method gives the web service an opportunity to release resources.

The Endpoint Context

When the `init()` method of a web service endpoint is called, a `java.lang.Object` is passed in that exposes the context in which it is operating. In a JAX-RPC implementation that is enabled by Java servlets, this object implements the `ServletEndpointContext` interface. According to the API documentation for the `ServletEndpointContext` interface, the JAX-RPC runtime system is required to provide appropriate session, message context, servlet context, and user principal information per method invocation on the endpoint class. The web service can use this object to do things such as:

- ❑ Get a reference to the `ServletContext` object. This is accomplished by calling the `getServletContext()` method, which we have already discussed back in Chapter 5.

- ❑ Find out about the user that is calling the web service. This can be performed by calling the `getUserPrincipal()` method. This returns an object that implements the `java.security.Prinicipal` interface. Please consult the J2EE API documentation for information on this interface.

- ❑ Get a reference to the `HttpSession` object, which was discussed when we covered servlets in Chapter 5. This object can be accessed via the `getHttpSession()` method. We'll use the `HttpSession` object in the upcoming stateful calculator example to maintain the state of a web service session.

Try it Out   Creating a Stateful Web Service

This example, similar to the calculator example in the Chapter 8, mimics some very simple operations on a calculator: adding, subtracting, and keeping a running total. To keep the running total we'll use features of the JAX-RPC service endpoint model that we just finished discussing. This example will also show how to use the third model that we discussed in the Web Services and JAX-RPC chapter of invoking a web service, known as **Dynamic Invocation Interface** (**DII**). Like dynamic proxy, this model does not use generated stubs. We'll also demonstrate the ability of JAX-RPC to carry exceptions thrown from the web service to the client.

Let's build and run the calculator web service example, and then we'll walk through the code.

You can use a subset of the ten-step process defined in the previous chapter to build and run this example. The *Building the web service stubs classes* step is omitted because we're not generating stubs at build time. Also, the separate *Compiling the client* step will be combined with Step 1. This is due to the fact that there are no stub classes for the client class to be dependent upon. Here are the steps that we'll use to build this example:

❑ Compile the Java source files.

❑ Create the WSDL file with the `wscompile` command line tool.

❑ Start the J2EE Server and create the J2EE EAR file with the Deployment Tool.

❑ Create the WAR file and configure the web service with the Deployment Tool.

❑ Create the application server-specific deployment descriptor with the Deployment Tool.

❑ Run the Verifier Tool.

❑ Deploy the web service.

❑ Run the web service client.

The Java source and XML files are organized in the following directory structure. Their listings appear in the text of this example. They also may be downloaded from the Wrox web site for your convenience:

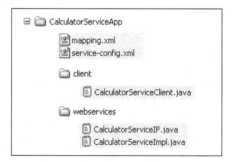

1. To compile these Java files, set the `classpath` to:

❑ the current directory

❑ plus the `j2ee.jar` file that is in the `lib` directory of the Java 2 SDK, Enterprise Edition 1.4 (J2EE SDK 1.4) installation.

For example, on a default J2EE SDK 1.4 Windows installation, the `classpath` would be set correctly by using the following command:

```
> set classpath=.;c:\j2sdkee1.4\lib\j2ee.jar
```

2. With the directory that the client and **webservices** directories are rooted in (this explanation has used `CalculatorServiceApp`) as the current directory, execute the following commands from the command prompt:

```
> javac -d . webservices/*.java
> javac -d . client/*.java
```

The Java class files should end up in the same directories as the source files.

3. Next we need to create the WSDL file. Here is the `service-config.xml` file that you'll use as input to the `wscompile`:

```xml
<?xml version="1.0" encoding="UTF-8"?>
<configuration
  xmlns="http://java.sun.com/xml/ns/jax-rpc/ri/config">
  <service
      name="CalculatorService"
      targetNamespace="urn:calculatorService"
      typeNamespace="urn:calculatorService"
      packageName="webservices">
      <interface name="webservices.CalculatorServiceIF"/>
  </service>
</configuration>
```

With the current directory set as indicated above, type the following command:

```
> wscompile -define -nd . -classpath . service-config.xml
```

4. Time to create the application! Start the J2EE server and the Deployment Tool. When creating the application EAR file (from the File | New | Application EAR menu item), name it CalculatorServiceApp.

5. So, the next step is to create the WAR file and configure the service. Here are the contents of the `mapping.xml` that you'll use in this step:

```xml
<?xml version="1.0" encoding="UTF-8"?>
<!DOCTYPE java-wsdl-mapping PUBLIC
    "-//IBM Corporation, Inc.//DTD J2EE JAX-RPC mapping 1.0//EN"

"http://www.ibm.com/standards/xml/webservices/j2ee/j2ee_jaxrpc_mapping_1_0.dtd">
<java-wsdl-mapping>
    <package-mapping>
        <package-type>webservices</package-type>
        <namespaceURI>urn:calculatorService</namespaceURI>
    </package-mapping>
</java-wsdl-mapping>
```

6. Start the New Web Application Wizard by choosing the File | New | Web Application WAR menu item. In the WAR File page of the New Web Application Wizard, enter CalculatorServiceWar as the WAR Display Name. Click the Edit button.

7. In the Available Files panel of the Edit Contents of CalculatorServiceWar dialog box, navigate to the base directory of this CalculatorServiceApp example. Choose the following files and click the Add button:

❏ The **service definition interface** (`CalculatorServiceIF.class`).

❏ The web service implementation class (`CalculatorServiceImpl.class`).

❏ The WSDL file (`CalculatorService.wsdl`).

❏ The J2EE JAX-RPC mapping file (`mapping.xml`).

8. In the Choose Component Type page of the New Web Application Wizard, indicate that we want it to be a Web Services Endpoint.

9. In the Choose Service page of the New Web Application Wizard you'll supply these four pieces of information:

❏ The name of the WSDL File: `CalculatorService.wsdl`

❏ The name of the Mapping File: `mapping.xml`

❏ The Service Name: CalculatorService

❏ The Service Display Name: CalculatorService

10. In the Web Service Endpoint page of the New Web Application Wizard, do the following:

❏ Choose webservices.CalculatorServiceIF from the Service Endpoint Interface drop-down list.

❏ In the WSDL Port Namespace and Local Part fields, enter urn:calculatorService and CalculatorServiceIFPort, respectively.

❏ Enter CalculatorServiceIF in the Port Component Name and Port Component Display Name fields.

11. In the Component General Properties page of the New Web Application Wizard:

❏ Choose webservices.CalculatorServiceImpl from the Service Endpoint Implementation drop-down.

❏ Verify that CalculatorServiceImpl is entered in the Web Component Name and Web Component Display Name fields.

❏ Verify that Load at any time is selected in the Startup load sequence position drop-down list.

12. Click the Finish button to leave the wizard. From the tree in the panel on the left, select CalculatorServiceImpl.

❑ In the General tab, enter CalculatorServiceImpl in the Web Component Display Name field if it isn't there already.

❑ In the Aliases tab, use the Add button to assign the /calc alias to the web service.

❑ In the Endpoint tab, enter CalculatorServiceIF in the Port Component Display Name field if it isn't there already.

13. In the tree in the left-hand panel, select CalculatorServiceWar, and click the Web Services tab.

❑ Select CalculatorService from the Web Services panel, and click the Edit button.

❑ In the Service Display Name text box, enter CalculatorService if it isn't there already, and click the OK button.

14. Select CalculatorServiceApp from the tree in the panel on the left, and select the Web Context tab in the panel on the right.

❑ In the Context Root column, enter calc-jaxrpc.

15. We now need to create the Application Server-Specific Deployment Descriptor. Perform this step in the usual way (by selecting CalculatorServiceApp in the left hand panel and choosing the File | Deployment Settings | Create New File menu item).

You don't have to do any configuration for this example. After saving the deployment descriptor, be sure to save the application by selecting CalculatorServiceApp from the tree on the left, and selecting Save from the File menu.

16. Before deploying, follow the instructions on running the Verifier Tool in the relevant section in Chapter 8. As explained in the previous chapter, the beta version that we used reported that the tests.web.ServletInterface test failed, even though the web service deployed successfully.

17. We're now ready to deploy the application. Select CalculatorServiceApp from the tree in the left-hand panel, and choose Deploy from the Tools menu:

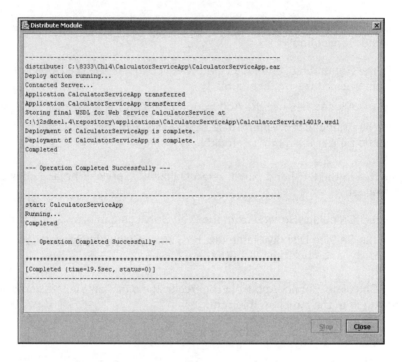

18. Finally, we need to run the client. Use the following command to run the client:

```
> java client.CalculatorServiceClient
```

To operate the calculator GUI, shown below, type a number into the textbox, press the = button, then enter a second number, select an operation (+ or –) from the drop-down, and click the = button. The running total will be displayed beside the **Calculator value** label. This calculator is no "Deep Thought" computer, but it did give me the answer 42 as a result of subtracting 58 from 100.

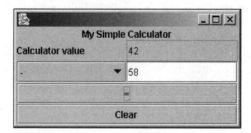

To demonstrate the ability to throw exceptions from the web service back to the client, an exception will be thrown and displayed in a dialog if the answer is a negative value, as shown below.

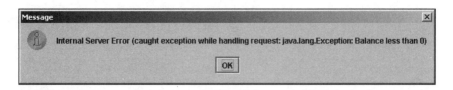

Also, you might want to start up a second calculator client to show that the state of the running total is kept by the web service for each calculator.

How It Works

To see how this example works, we'll first look at the Java source code for the web service interface, `CalculatorServiceIF.java`:

```
package webservices;

import java.rmi.Remote;
import java.rmi.RemoteException;

public interface CalculatorServiceIF extends Remote {
  // the service methods
  public void clearIt() throws RemoteException;
  public void calculate(String operation, int value)
    throws Exception, RemoteException;
  public int getValue() throws RemoteException;
}
```

The web service interface defines three methods that are implemented by the web service implementation, `CalculatorServiceImpl.java`:

```
package webservices;

import javax.servlet.http.HttpSession;
import javax.xml.rpc.ServiceException;
import javax.xml.rpc.server.ServiceLifecycle;
import javax.xml.rpc.server.ServletEndpointContext;

public class CalculatorServiceImpl
  implements CalculatorServiceIF, ServiceLifecycle {

  private ServletEndpointContext _endpointContext = null;

  // service lifecycle methods
  public void init(Object context) throws ServiceException {
    _endpointContext = (ServletEndpointContext) context;
  }

  public void destroy() { System.out.println("destroying"); }
```

```
    // the service business method implementations
  public void clearIt() {
    HttpSession session = _endpointContext.getHttpSession();
    session.setAttribute("balance", new Integer(0));
  }

  public void calculate(String operation, int value)
    throws Exception {
    // get the balance
    HttpSession session = _endpointContext.getHttpSession();
    Integer val = pluckValue();
    int bal = val.intValue();

    // if "+", add it
    if (operation.equals("+")) {
      bal = bal + value;
      session.setAttribute("balance", new Integer(bal));
      return;
    }

    // if "-", subtract it
    if (operation.equals("-")) {
      bal = bal - value;
      if (bal < 0) {
        throw new Exception("Balance less than 0");
      }
      session.setAttribute("balance", new Integer(bal));
      return;
    }

    // if not "+" or "-", it is not a valid operation
    throw new Exception("Invalid Operation");
  }

  public int getValue() {
    return pluckValue().intValue();
  }

  private Integer pluckValue() {
    HttpSession session = _endpointContext.getHttpSession();
    Integer val = (Integer) session.getAttribute("balance");
    if (val == null) {
      val = new Integer(0);
    }
    return val;
  }
}
```

Service Lifecycle and Endpoint Context

Before discussing the three methods that implement the CalculatorServiceIF interface, we're going to look at the code that pertains to the **JAX-RPC service endpoint model** discussed above. Recall that this model defines two methods in its **service lifecycle** that need to be implemented when the web service implements the ServiceLifecycle interface as this one does.

The first of these methods is the init() method. In this implementation we cast the **endpoint context** reference to a ServletEndpointContext and tuck it away into this web service's only instance variable:

```
public void init(Object context) throws ServiceException {
  _endpointContext = (ServletEndpointContext) context;
}
```

We'll use this **endpoint context** later to access the HTTPSession object in which we'll maintain the calculator's running total. Note that this method can throw a ServiceException, which is in the javax.xml.rpc package, if it has any problems initializing.

The other **service lifecycle** method is destroy(), in which we supply a nearly empty implementation. If we had, for example, connected to resources in the init() method that needed to be released, the destroy() method would have been an appropriate place to do that. An example resource would be a JDBC connection to a database.

The Implementation of the Calculator Web Service Interface Methods

The three methods of this web service that are defined in the CalculatorServiceIF interface, therefore having the ability to be called from the calculator client, are clearIt(), calculate() and getValue().

The clearIt() method clears the running total by setting it to the value of 0, as seen in the code below. It does so by getting a reference to the HttpSession object from the ServletEndpointContext instance that was supplied to the init() method earlier. It then sets a session attribute, arbitrarily named balance, to the value of 0. Recall that session attributes must be objects, which is why we're using the Integer wrapper class.

```
HttpSession session = _endpointContext.getHttpSession();
session.setAttribute("balance", new Integer(0));
```

The calculate() method takes two arguments, performs a calculation, and stores the result in the session. The two arguments are:

❑   An operator (either "+" or "-")

❑   The value to be added or subtracted from the running total

This calculate() method uses the private method named pluckValue() to get the running total from the session, returning 0 if it didn't exist, as shown below:

```
private Integer pluckValue() {
  HttpSession session = _endpointContext.getHttpSession();
  Integer val = (Integer) session.getAttribute("balance");
  if (val == null) {
```

```
      val = new Integer(0);
    }
    return val;
  }
```

If the result of a subtract operation causes the running total to be negative, an `Exception` is thrown, which is propagated to the client via the JAX-RPC runtime and SOAP:

```
if (operation.equals("-")) {
  bal = bal - value;
  if (bal < 0) {
    throw new Exception("Balance less than 0");
  }
  session.setAttribute("balance", new Integer(bal));
  return;
}
```

The `getValue()` method uses the `pluckValue()` method to supply the client with the current running total. For the client's convenience it converts the wrapped value stored in the session to a primitive type, as shown here:

```
public int getValue() {
  return pluckValue().intValue();
}
```

The Dynamic Invocation Interface (DII)

The client for this example calls the methods of the web service in a completely dynamic way. To demonstrate this, here is the Java source code for the client, `CalculatorServiceClient.java`:

```
package client;

import java.rmi.ServerException;
import javax.xml.namespace.QName;
import javax.xml.rpc.Call;
import javax.xml.rpc.ParameterMode;
import javax.xml.rpc.Service;
import javax.xml.rpc.ServiceFactory;

// general imports
import java.awt.*;
import java.awt.event.*;
import javax.swing.*;

public class CalculatorServiceClient extends JFrame
  implements ActionListener {

  private JButton _clear = new JButton("Clear");
```

```
private JButton _equals = new JButton("=");
private JTextField _topNumber = new JTextField("0");
private JTextField _bottomNumber = new JTextField("0");
private JComboBox _operator = new JComboBox();
private Call _call;

public CalculatorServiceClient() {
  // get the Call
  try {
    _call = this.getCall();
  }
  catch (Exception e) {
    e.printStackTrace();
  }

  // add the title
  JLabel title = new JLabel("My Simple Calculator");
  title.setHorizontalAlignment(JLabel.CENTER);
  getContentPane().add(title, BorderLayout.NORTH);

  // add the calculation panel
  JPanel calcPanel = new JPanel(new GridLayout(2, 2));
  calcPanel.add(new JLabel("Calculator value"));
  _topNumber.setEditable(false);
  calcPanel.add(_topNumber);
  _operator.addItem("+");
  _operator.addItem("-");
  calcPanel.add(_operator);
  calcPanel.add(_bottomNumber);
  getContentPane().add(calcPanel, BorderLayout.CENTER);

  // add the buttons
  JPanel buttonPanel = new JPanel(new GridLayout(2, 1));
  _equals.addActionListener(this);
  buttonPanel.add(_equals);
  _clear.addActionListener(this);
  buttonPanel.add(_clear);
  getContentPane().add(buttonPanel, BorderLayout.SOUTH);
  addWindowListener(new WindowAdapter() {
    public void windowClosing(WindowEvent e) {
      System.exit(0);
    }
  });

  setSize(300, 150);
  setVisible(true);
}

public void actionPerformed(ActionEvent ae) {
  // if equals was clicked, run the calculation
  if (ae.getSource() == _equals) {
    runCalculator();
```

```
      }

      // if clear was clicked, clear the calculator
      if (ae.getSource() == _clear) {
        clearCalculator();
      }
    }

    private Call getCall() throws Exception {
      ServiceFactory factory = ServiceFactory.newInstance();
      Service service =
        factory.createService(new QName("CalculatorService"));
      Call call = service.createCall();
      call.setPortTypeName(new QName("CalculatorServiceIF"));
      call.setTargetEndpointAddress(
        "http://localhost:8000/calc-jaxrpc/calc");
      call.setProperty(Call.SOAPACTION_USE_PROPERTY,
        new Boolean(true));
      call.setProperty(Call.SOAPACTION_URI_PROPERTY, "");
      call.setProperty("javax.xml.rpc.encodingstyle.namespace.uri",
          "http://schemas.xmlsoap.org/soap/encoding/");
      call.setProperty(Call.SESSION_MAINTAIN_PROPERTY,
        new Boolean(true));
      return call;
    }

    private void runCalculator() {
      try {
        // get the bottom value to be added to the calculator
        int operVal = 0;
        String textVal = _bottomNumber.getText();
        if (textVal != null) {
          try {
            operVal = Integer.parseInt(textVal);
          }
          catch (NumberFormatException nfe) { }
        }

        // get the operator
        String oper = (String) _operator.getSelectedItem();

        // invoke the service to calculate the new value
        Object[] calcParms =
          new Object[] { oper, new Integer(operVal) };
        _call.removeAllParameters();
        _call.setReturnType(null);
        _call.setOperationName(new QName("urn:calculatorService",
                                         "calculate"));
        _call.addParameter("String_1",
          new QName("http://www.w3.org/2001/XMLSchema", "string"),
          ParameterMode.IN);
        _call.addParameter("int_2",
```

```
                  new QName("http://www.w3.org/2001/XMLSchema", "int"),
                        ParameterMode.IN);
      Object ret = _call.invoke(calcParms);

      // invoke the service to display the new value
      Object[] getParms = new Object[0];
      _call.removeAllParameters();
      _call.setOperationName(new QName("urn:calculatorService",
                                      "getValue"));
      _call.setReturnType(
        new QName("http://www.w3.org/2001/XMLSchema", "int"));
      Integer getRet = (Integer) _call.invoke(getParms);
      _topNumber.setText(getRet.toString());
    }
    catch (ServerException se) {
      JOptionPane.showMessageDialog(this, se.getMessage());
    }
    catch (Exception e) {
      e.printStackTrace();
    }
  }

  private void clearCalculator() {
    try {
      // invoke the service to clear it out
      Object[] parms = new Object[0];
      _call.removeAllParameters();
      _call.setReturnType(null);
      _call.setOperationName(new QName("urn:calculatorService",
                                      "clearIt"));
      Object ret = _call.invoke(parms);
      _topNumber.setText("0");
      _bottomNumber.setText("0");
      _operator.setSelectedIndex(0);
    }
    catch (Exception e) {
      e.printStackTrace();
    }
  }

  public static void main(String[] args) {
    CalculatorServiceClient calcClient =
      new CalculatorServiceClient();
  }
}
```

Using the **dynamic invocation interface** (**DII**), the client doesn't need **static stubs**. You may recall that the **dynamic proxy** example didn't need **static stubs** either. Unlike **dynamic proxy** however, when using the **DII** the client doesn't even need a web service interface. In fact, it is possible to create a generic web service user interface that dynamically configures its functionality based upon the WSDL document of the web service with which it happens to be interacting.

As its predecessor in Chapter 8, this calculator client is a Java Swing application with GUI components and event handler methods. The client needs to call methods of the web service, so it creates an object that implements the `Call` interface of the `javax.xml.rpc` package. We'll dynamically configure this `Call` object to be able to use our calculator web service. The code that creates the `Call` object and performs this configuration is in our `getCall()` method which is called from the constructor, and progressively shown below.

As with the dynamic proxy example earlier in this chapter, a `ServiceFactory` is created. This `ServiceFactory` instance is then used to create an object that implements the `Service` interface that represents our `CalculatorService`:

```
ServiceFactory factory = ServiceFactory.newInstance();
Service service =
  factory.createService(new QName("CalculatorService"));
```

Now we'll create the `Call` object by calling the `createCall()` method of the Service interface:

```
Call call = service.createCall();
```

To configure the `Call` object for our calculator web service, we'll use methods of the `Call` object itself. First, as seen below, we'll tell it the name of the port type from the WSDL document:

```
call.setPortTypeName(new QName("CalculatorServiceIF"));
```

Next, we'll give the `Call` object the **web service endpoint** on which it will invoke methods.

```
call.setTargetEndpointAddress(
  "http://localhost:8000/calc-jaxrpc/calc");
```

The `Call` interface defines several constants, including the ones seen below, that can be used as properties. We'll set some properties of the `Call` object that specify that we'll be using SOAP and that provide some configuration. If you create a client that uses DII, you can use the following statements "as is":

```
call.setProperty(Call.SOAPACTION_USE_PROPERTY,
  new Boolean(true));
call.setProperty(Call.SOAPACTION_URI_PROPERTY, "");
call.setProperty("javax.xml.rpc.encodingstyle.namespace.uri",
    "http://schemas.xmlsoap.org/soap/encoding/");
```

Finally, as seen below, we'll tell the `Call` object that we want the client and the web service to maintain a session. This is very important in our case because as discussed previously, the calculator web service uses the `HttpSession` object associated with that session to store the running total on behalf of the client.

```
call.setProperty(Call.SESSION_MAINTAIN_PROPERTY,
    new Boolean(true));
return call;
```

Please note that the **static stubs** model provides for specifying that a session be maintained as well: you can call the _setProperty() method of the Stub interface to configure the Stub object, and one of the properties is Stub.SESSION_MAINTAIN_PROPERTY.

Using DII to Invoke Methods

Now that the Call object knows about the calculator web service, we'll begin invoking the web service's methods. When the "=" button is clicked on the calculator GUI client, two things are passed to the calculate() method of the calculator web service: The operator (either "+" or "-"), and the value to be added or subtracted from the running total. Because we don't have the benefit of a web service interface, we need to tell the Call object about the method that it is about to invoke. This is a very similar programming model to invoking methods using Java reflection. Let's progressively walk through some statements from the client's runCalculator() method that demonstrate this:

First, a java.lang.Object array is loaded with the arguments that will be passed into the calculate() method of the web service. Note that before the code snippet below is executed, the oper variable contains a String that represents the operation, and the operVal variable is an int that contains the value to be added or subtracted. The int must be wrapped in order to be able to live inside the Object array:

```
Object[] calcParms =
    new Object[] { oper, new Integer(operVal) };
```

Next, because we're going to reuse this Call object for invoking methods with different signatures, we'll do a little clean up: we'll remove the method parameters associated with the last method for which it was configured (if there was one).

```
_call.removeAllParameters();
```

Now we'll begin telling the Call object about the calculate() method of the calculator web service. The statement below says that it has no return type:

```
_call.setReturnType(null);
```

The following statement says that in the WSDL document, the namespace of the calculator web service is urn:calculatorService and the operation name is calculate:

```
_call.setOperationName(new QName("urn:calculatorService",
                                 "calculate"));
```

Now we'll tell the `Call` object that the `calculate()` method has two parameters. The first one is a `String`, and the second one is an `int`. The parameter types are represented by the types in the XML Schema specification, whose namespace is the URI in the snippet below. Note: Although normal programming practices would dictate putting literals like some of the ones below into constants, we've not followed that practice here for the sake of clarity.

```
_call.addParameter("String_1",
   new QName("http://www.w3.org/2001/XMLSchema", "string"),
   ParameterMode.IN);
_call.addParameter("int_2",
      new QName("http://www.w3.org/2001/XMLSchema", "int"),
            ParameterMode.IN);
```

To invoke the `calculate()` method, we'll pass the `Object` array that contains the arguments, which is referred to by the `calcParms` variable, into the invoke() method of the `Call` object:

```
Object ret = _call.invoke(calcParms);
```

Because our calculator web service maintains the running total, the client then calls the `getValue()` method of the web service to retrieve the running total and subsequently display it. The code below accomplishes this using the same techniques as we did to call the `calculate()` method.

```
Object[] getParms = new Object[0];
_call.removeAllParameters();
_call.setOperationName(new QName("urn:calculatorService",
                                "getValue"));
_call.setReturnType(
   new QName("http://www.w3.org/2001/XMLSchema", "int"));
Integer getRet = (Integer) _call.invoke(getParms);
_topNumber.setText(getRet.toString());
```

When the user presses the **Clear** button, the `clearIt()` method of the calculator web service is called, which sets the running total to 0. Because the `clearIt()` method has no parameters and no return value, configuring the `Call` object is more concise than usual, as shown below:

```
Object[] parms = new Object[0];
_call.removeAllParameters();
_call.setReturnType(null);
_call.setOperationName(new QName("urn:calculatorService",
                                "clearIt"));
Object ret = _call.invoke(parms);
```

As you can see, using the **dynamic invocation interface** is a little more work. It also can be harder to debug because the compiler can't help enforce that you're calling the web service interface methods correctly. DII can be invaluable, however, when coupled with Universal Description, Discovery, and Integration (UDDI) mentioned in the previous chapter. In that environment, web services are discovered dynamically, and often must be used without having a perfect understanding of their interfaces, therefore requiring dynamic invocation.

Summary

In this chapter, we continued covering some topics that are pertinent to web services in the context of J2EE:

❑   We demonstrated how to implement a session bean as a web service, giving it a **web service endpoint**. This provides the ability for a client written in virtually any language, running on most any platform, to be able to invoke the methods of EJBs.

❑   Two models that enable the client to dynamically deal with web services were explored: **dynamic proxies** and the **dynamic invocation interface** (**DII**). Both models allow flexibility by using a proxy created at run-time rather than a stub generated at build time. The DII model allows even more flexibility by not requiring a web service interface. Instead, it uses a model much like Java reflection to dynamically invoke web service methods at run-time.

❑   Covered also was the **JAX-RPC service endpoint model**, which defines a web service lifecycle and the ability for the web service to get in touch with its context. This enabled us to demonstrate a stateful web service, which was a modified version of the stateful session bean-based calculator from an earlier chapter.

Web services are a relatively new technology that has wide appeal in the Information Technology industry. It is far from being a mature technology, however, and we'll see much growth in the areas of development tools, deployment platforms, and web services-related standards. As this happens, developing mission-critical enterprise applications that utilize web services will become easier, to the point that the underlying web services infrastructure will become all but invisible to the developer. A great place to find out about developing standards surrounding web services is the World Wide Web Consortium (W3C) web site, which is http://www.w3.org. The W3C is the main policy-making body in the area of the Web, including web services.

Exercises

1.   Write a stateless session bean that takes a word and returns it spelled backwards. Implement it as a web service, and use static stubs for the client.

2.   Modify the previous exercise to use a dynamic proxy for the client.

3. Modify the previous exercise to use dynamic invocation interface (DII) for the client.

4. Write a stateful web service that takes one word at a time and appends it to the previous words received to make a sentence. Return the entire sentence each time a word is added.

CHAPTER 14

The J2EE Roadmap   602

Paths to Knowledge   607

J2EE Resources   614

Summary   617

Resources   617

Further J2EE Topics

Congratulations! You now have a good, solid background in J2EE! Together, we have studied JavaServer Pages, servlets, Enterprise JavaBeans, and web services, the core technologies that make up the Java 2 Enterprise Edition. Take a few moments away from your book and computer and see if you remember the real world. Throw away all those empty pizza boxes and high caffeine drink cans then get some fresh air and get reacquainted with the people around you.

Now that you have rested and recovered from total immersion in J2EE, it is time to take stock and ask one final question: "where do I go from here?" The title on the cover contained the word *Beginning*, which implies that there is still much more to learn, but as you may have noticed, there are few pages left in this book. This is because you now have a strong foundation in J2EE and can choose from many different paths. In this chapter, as well as the next, we'll briefly examine other parts of J2EE that you may want to explore and we'll also offer a number of strategies for approaching this broad subject. This chapter will briefly look at several additional technologies found within the J2EE specifications, then in the next chapter we will look at J2EE in the real world.

In both these chapters, we will be looking at the technologies at a very high level, covering them *very* quickly. You already have the basics and are ready to get to work with J2EE. The aim in these two chapters is to give you some familiarity with additional terms and technologies that you may encounter while interviewing for a job or when talking to your project manager. Look through these chapters, see what interests you, then spend some time researching these technologies.

In this chapter we will examine:

- ❑ The J2EE roadmap, incorporating the technologies we haven't studied in detail in this book

- ❑ Paths to obtaining more knowledge on the other areas of the J2EE platform

- ❑ J2EE resources to enable you to decide how to approach the task of getting yourself up to speed with what isn't covered in this book

The J2EE Roadmap

In addition to those topics explored in this book, the J2EE platform offers several other technologies and APIs that may be used to build enterprise applications. J2EE offers facilities for enterprise-wide directory services, messaging, mail, and integration with other distributed computing protocols, as well as management, administration, and deployment standards. Sorting out all of these technologies can be confusing and difficult though, so let's begin with a roadmap illustrating some of the topics you may want to pursue:

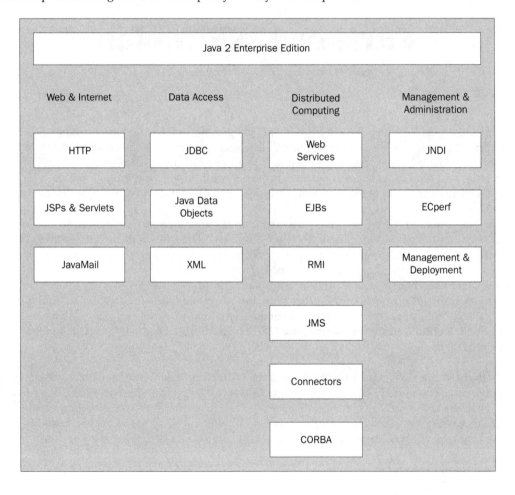

To help you understand all of the different technologies, the roadmap is divided into several general areas:

- ❑ Web & Internet
- ❑ Data access
- ❑ Distributed computing
- ❑ Management & administration

Many of these technologies address more than one category, but to simplify the discussion, each is listed only under their primary topic. The roadmap has also been simplified by consolidating those technologies already covered in this book into five general topics:

- ❑ JavaServer Pages
- ❑ Java DataBase Connectivity
- ❑ Enterprise JavaBeans
- ❑ XML
- ❑ Web services

The rest of this section will briefly discuss each technology, offering just enough information to explain its functions and roles in the scheme of J2EE and to whet your appetite for more study.

Web and Internet Technologies

As an enterprise platform, J2EE relies heavily on Internet and web standards for communications and user interface functions. As such, much of the J2EE standard is focused on technologies and APIs that support and simplify web development. We're going to run through these right now.

HTTP & Web Server Standards

This may seem somewhat obvious, but we often forget that J2EE includes basic web capabilities like HTTP and CGI. These form the foundation for much of the J2EE platform. At its core, J2EE defines requirements and standards that must exist within web servers and browsers for J2EE to function properly. As such, a basic knowledge of these standards is necessary to understand J2EE operations and this knowledge will be very helpful when it comes time to optimize your applications. Remember, HTTP has always been, and will always be, an evolving standard as it addresses new applications and devices. Keeping abreast of this technology is a must for all J2EE developers.

JavaServer Pages (JSP) & Servlets

By now, JSPs and servlets should be old friends and there is little more to say about this technology. This book covers these subjects extensively and offers a solid foundation so, at this point, practice is the best path to mastery. If you want to explore some advanced JSP and servlet subjects like large data transfers or JavaServer Faces (JSF), have a look at this link to Sun's web site http://java.sun.com/j2ee/javaserverfaces/.

JavaMail

The JavaMail API allows developers to generate and process e-mail messages from applications, servlets or JSPs. E-mail is one of those pervasive technologies that fit within just about any application from fill-in-the form web pages for customer feedback or service requests to sending messages to the developer when exceptions or errors occur within a web application. The JavaMail API offers a wide range of applications and is a must-have tool for all J2EE developers. More information can be found here http://java.sun.com/products/javamail/.

Data Access

The next category of J2EE technologies is data access. J2EE offers a wide range of tools and options for managing data from traditional database access through JDBC to using XML and directory services (covered in the management section below).

JDBC (Java DataBase Connectivity)

Although not technically a part of the J2EE standard, JDBC is fundamental to enterprise development. It has been covered in some detail within this book but as will be seen in the next chapter, there are a wide variety of commercial implementations and vendor standards that extend this technology in a number of ways. Explore your database and JDBC drivers for ways to exploit their features and optimize performance.

Java Data Objects (JDO)

In addition to JDBC, JDO offers an alternative approach to data access. JDO can generate objects and classes to represent database tables, views, and queries, as well as a variety of other data structures such as directories or file systems. JDO simplifies and standardizes data access throughout an enterprise and improves developer productivity.

XML APIs

As will already be familiar to the reader, J2EE provides a number of different APIs for accessing XML data structures. Over the past few years, XML industry groups have standardized data representations in many industries and fields of study. XML will continue to be a fundamental technology. And mastery of XML will be essential for all developers.

Distributed Computing

Distributed or enterprise computing is a group of technologies that bridge different platforms, from mainframes, workstations, wireless and embedded systems, into an interconnected whole. Using these tools, a hand-held PDA can execute program code that resides on a mainframe or workstation anywhere on (or off) the planet. Distributed computing is also the foundation for supply chain automation and legacy integration – all skills that are in high demand.

Web Services

Web services were covered extensively in this book and offer an excellent example of the power of distributed computing. Applying web services will be a challenge for years to come and will provide a rewarding career for many J2EE developers.

Enterprise JavaBeans (EJBs)

EJBs could be inserted into any of the categories, but fit best as a distributed computing technology. Although covered in detail in this book, the challenge to the new EJB developer is to learn how to use and optimize vendor implementations, and exploit the features and extensions that are available. The distributed nature of EJBs give the developer new ways to think about how to design and develop high-performance enterprise wide applications and business solutions. If EJBs are of interest to you, research the variety of architectural and design patterns and see how to apply them to your projects.

Remote Method Invocation (RMI)

Java's earliest distributed computing solution was the Remote Method Invocation (RMI) and it is still the foundation for many of the distributed Java APIs. RMI offers bare-bones remote method calls, opening up an object's methods to programs running on other machines on the network. RMI does have some restrictions that limit its use, primarily that RMI is a Java-only solution and cannot be used with other programming languages. Within a pure Java solution though, RMI is often a good choice for distributed computing.

Java Message Services (JMS)

In many applications, messaging is a much better solution than remote method calls or web services. A message is a one-sided procedure call where the first computer sends a message request, and the second computer runs the function when it has time to do so. As an example, an order entry system may receive an order. To fulfill the order, the order entry system sends a message to a warehouse to send the products to the customer. Once the order entry system sends the message, it no longer cares about the order, as it is now the fulfillment system's responsibility to ship the goods. The fulfillment computer can then process the order when it has time and, since there is no reply necessary, processing can occur whenever time permits. JMS defines a set of Java interfaces and APIs that allow access to messaging services that can be used to implement these asynchronous method calls. The specifications, documentation, and tutorials can be found on Sun's Java web site, at http://java.sun.com/products/jms/.

Connectors

Connectors are a specification for connecting J2EE applications with legacy systems, allowing developers to access these systems in JSPs or servlets. The legacy application is represented as an EJB, with access to properties and methods in a manner familiar to J2EE developers. For those interested in legacy integration, the connector specification will be a standard to watch.

Java IDL and CORBA

CORBA has long been a standard for distributed object computing and support is available for almost any programming language or platform in existence. IDL is the Interface Definition Language that CORBA uses to define properties and methods in a language-neutral manner. So, while RMI offers distributed computing in a Java-only environment, CORBA can provide distributed computing across a wide range of platforms. CORBA has been an industry standard for many years and will continue to be a stable technology for mixed platform integration.

Management and Administration

The final category on the roadmap is a set of APIs and technologies that offer management and administrative tools for the J2EE platform. These services include access to directories, benchmarking, management, and deployment. Although these technologies are not as critical to the J2EE developer as those listed above, the developer should have some familiarity with them and know their basic usage.

Java Naming and Directory Interface (JNDI)

Like HTTP, JNDI is fundamental to the J2EE platform and the basics were addressed in this book in the context of JDBC and EJBs, but JNDI also offers access to most industry standard directory services, both within the J2EE environment and on other enterprise platforms. Directories can store pointers to database servers, remote file systems, distributed objects, and a wide variety of other enterprise resources. Since JNDI can access LDAP, NDS, and Microsoft's Active Directory Services as well as most other industry standard enterprise directory services, JNDI can unlock a wealth of knowledge stored in these directories. Spend some time getting to know both the advanced capabilities of JNDI and the directory services on your network.

ECperf

The ECperf benchmark suite is a set of sample applications and documents for tuning and optimizing J2EE EJB and e-commerce applications. It is based on a supply chain application and provides a comprehensive discussion on performance issues, as well as a wealth of sample program code. Created using a community development approach, it was built with code from many different backgrounds and offers the new J2EE developer several perspectives on coding practices and design approaches.

J2EE Management and Deployment Specifications

In addition to specific technologies like EJBs and JNDI, the J2EE specifications also include interface definitions for access to industry standard deployment and management tools and protocols like SNMP (Simple Network Management Protocol). These standards offer management and administration of enterprise-wide resources from a single centralized application. A systems administrator can monitor and manage database servers, networks, and application servers from a single application anywhere on the network. As a J2EE developer, these APIs may be useful for performance monitoring or to automate deployment and configuration of new applications across a wide geographic area.

Other Technologies and APIs

This list was a very brief summary of those technologies and APIs that may be of interest to you as a beginning J2EE developer, but J2EE is a very broad subject and there is much more to learn. For a complete list of technologies, see the J2EE technology page on Sun's web site, at http://java.sun.com/j2ee/#technologies.

After viewing this list, you may wonder where to start, so let's next look at some of the major applications and fields of study where J2EE can be applied.

Paths to Knowledge

Hopefully, one or more of the topics listed above just jumped out and grabbed you and you are now running off to the bookstore or Internet to learn everything you can about your newfound passion! If so, best wishes, but please come back and finish this book – we still have a lot more to tell you. If you are still wondering which way to go, let's look at these subjects again from a different perspective, by surveying some of the computer and business applications where J2EE can be used.

So why approach it from the point of view of applications? J2EE was designed as a platform for building and deploying high-performance, large-scale enterprise applications, so each API and technology is targeted towards certain application types. Reversing this view, we can choose an application category then see which technologies are needed to build the project. Hopefully, one or more of these application categories will pique your interest and lead you on your chosen path:

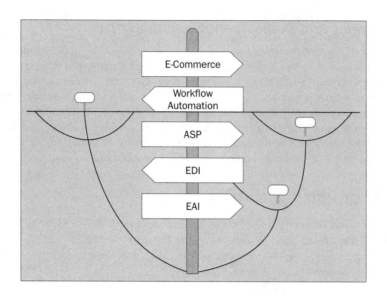

e-Commerce

Much of this book focused on how to build and deploy e-commerce solutions using J2EE, so this is already a familiar topic. Nevertheless, it is an important application and bears a second look. E-commerce applications include marketing, catalogs, order entry, customer service, and information retrieval. A customer could log onto the Internet at any time, or anywhere, with a desire to learn more about your company, request services or place orders.

This book offered a good foundation in e-commerce development but there is always more to learn. Explore those topics that fit your needs in greater depth. JSPs, servlets, JDBC, EJBs, and web services all form the foundation of e-commerce. You could also study sample code to learn new techniques, and then try them in your own environment. In addition, check out some of the following topics in this section.

Review J2SE APIs

J2EE provides a wealth of server-side tools, but e-commerce also relies heavily on client-side development. HTML, JavaScript, applets, and other client-side applications all originate from the web pages and JSPs on the server so expertise in these areas is essential for successful e-commerce deployment. In addition, take a look at J2SE's multimedia APIs for speech, sound, and video, and don't forget web-based wireless technologies.

Performance and Optimization

A key issue in e-commerce, and one that we will look at in more detail in the next chapter, is that of performance. In e-commerce, performance is money. During peak volume, the time from request to response dictates the number of transactions processed, the number of orders taken and the volume of products shipped. Bottlenecks limit business volume and drive customers away.

Performance begins and ends with good programming techniques so start off on the right foot. Study J2EE performance issues and get into the habit of programming for performance. Check out the literature and materials from Sun and other J2EE vendors (see next chapter). Study what happens inside JSP servers and EJB containers then alter your code to leverage this knowledge. Learn how to gather metrics and performance data then experiment with different coding styles and techniques.

Web Design and Human/Computer Interaction

One final topic, outside the domain of J2EE but extremely important is the subject of useability. Next to performance, usability is the key to success in e-commerce – especially on the consumer side. Surf the web to see what works well and what gets in the way. Survey the literature to understand the various theories, and then decide for yourself what makes sense and what doesn't. This is a subject that is still in its infancy and is far more art than science – everyone has their own personal preference.

Workflow Automation

Just as J2EE can offer high performance, scaleability, and rapid development for e-commerce applications, it can also be an excellent platform for corporate information solutions like workflow automation, business intelligence, data warehousing, or other large-scale business applications. Workflow automation applications are those that get the right information to the right person at the right time, streamlining business processes, and decision-making.

An example we are all familiar with is that of a help desk. An employee in San Francisco has a problem with an application on their desktop computer so they call the help desk. The help desk clerk records the problem and then saves it in a database, which triggers a routing function to send the problem to the appropriate person. It may be that the problem requires a service technician so the message is routed to the first available hardware person who looks into the problem. When he decides it is a software problem (they always do!), he annotates the report and it gets sent to a maintenance programmer in Chicago who follows up the problem. Since the software person thinks it is a hardware problem, it gets routed to a supervisor who knocks heads together until the two technicians resolve the problem.

As the example illustrates, workflow solutions often require databases, communications, decision-making, and messaging. Since databases have been covered already, let's concentrate on messaging, communications, and decision-making.

Messaging

In our example, messaging allows the help desk application in San Francisco to notify the bug-tracking program in Chicago that a problem exists. The J2EE developer may use JMS to send the message from one site to another, and then a message bean will catch the message and record the appropriate information into an entity bean where it is stored in the database. Messaging is a powerful technology for workflow automation in its ability to get information from one place to another. Since a message only needs to be sent in one direction, it can be fired then forgotten. The messaging software will ensure that it is sent as soon as physically possible. If the network is down, the messaging software will queue the traffic until it can be sent so messages always get to their destination.

Distributed Computing

In other cases, messaging may not be an acceptable solution. In our example, suppose the help desk clerk is located in St. Louis. He receives the call from San Francisco and diagnoses the trouble as a hardware issue. He needs to know immediately which of the hardware people in San Francisco are available to handle the problem, so the help desk application sends a remote request to the San Francisco application to see who is available. In this case, messaging is probably not a good solution since an immediate response is required.

Alternatives for distributed processing include Remote Method Invocation (RMI), which is the simplest as long as all applications are written in Java. EJBs are also a good alternative since they fit well in an object-oriented development model. Other alternatives include SOAP or CORBA when applications must tie together different platforms and languages.

Object-Oriented Analysis and Design

Finally, for those involved in workflow automation, a strong background in object-oriented analysis and design is a must. As we saw in our example, workflow applications tie complex business processes together over many different departments and geographic regions. Modeling these processes and communication flows requires strong analysis skills, knowledge of design patterns, and use of modeling tools.

Application Service Providers (ASP)

As development costs continue to grow and applications continue to increase in complexity, it becomes more difficult all the time to fund and develop in-house projects. The third party software market continues to grow and development work seems to be shifting from individual companies to software vendors.

One effective delivery model for third party software that seems to be gaining momentum is the Application Service Provider (ASP). Instead of shipping executable code directly to the customer, where they install it on their desktop machines or servers, software is accessed over the Internet or other private network. The software and databases are centralized at the vendor's site where administration, backup, and other traditional IT functions are handled by the vendor. The customer does not have to invest in servers, infrastructure, and IT staff to administrate and maintain the software and the vendor can provide better support and price the software based on customer usage. Some of the most familiar desktop software like Quick-Books and Turbo-Tax have shifted some or all of their business to the ASP model. You can now do accounting, run large-scale ERP and CRM applications, and even scan for viruses directly from a web site. Businesses also have moved many of their mission critical functions to ASP based vertical market packages.

Those interested in developing software for the ASP market need all of the skills listed in the e-commerce section above as well as a background in the areas that we are about to take a look at.

Database Technologies

Most business solutions require large persistent data stores and ASP is no exception. JDBC, JDO, and entity beans can all be used to store client data. In addition, strong database design and modeling skills are necessary to rapidly store and retrieve large volumes of data. EJBs can also play a strong role in developing flexible business objects.

Management and Deployment APIs

One of the sticky areas for the ASP vendor is in application and network administration. Most of the administration work is done by the vendor, but clients need to adjust network configurations, manage user and security access permissions and, in some cases, manage and tune databases. Fortunately, J2EE's management and deployment APIs solve many of these problems. Custom application administration programs can be built that provide limited access to system administration and management functions, restricting access to only those within the client's domain. Vendors cannot let clients touch other client's resources, but they do want to allow access within their own domain. The J2EE's management and deployment APIs offer great flexibility in this area.

Web Services

Finally, as the ASP market matures, vendors are finding that it is necessary to balance the workload between the client workstations and the servers. Performance and network bandwidth can be optimized by letting the client handle the user interface work, and then calling web services to complete the tasks. As we have seen throughout this book, web service technologies offer far more flexibility and clients can pick and choose the services they need.

EDI and Supply Chain Management

Electronic Data Interchange (EDI) is a set of mature technologies that allow businesses to send information to customers and suppliers. A manufacturer can order supplies, invoice customers and even request funds transfers over the Internet or private networks. With this infrastructure in place, the science of supply chain management has grown to automate every phase of the production cycle and distribution chains, optimizing costs through Just-In-Time (JIT) inventory and automated ordering.

As an example, a candle factory may need wax, wicks, dyes, scented oils, and packaging materials to make their candles. The production manager pulls up the application to schedule next week's production and is immediately presented with orders taken from his customers along with an aggregate total of the various products to make. He can then adjust these numbers to anticipate future demand or optimize production runs, and finalize the schedule. Once he has the schedule set, the application polls his suppliers for price and availability of raw materials then places orders on the wire. The suppliers then respond with invoices for the raw materials, which are routed to the accounting department for payment. Throughout this process, no paper is used and all transactions occur immediately.

To date, most EDI and supply chain applications have been based on legacy technologies, but as new vendors enter the market and the ASP model begins to take hold, J2EE will be chosen to implement many of these applications. We'll look at the technologies of interest in this arena right now.

XML

Although still slow to be adopted by the traditional EDI vendors, XML is emerging as a new standard for data exchange. The XML/EDI Group, a standards organization dedicated to promoting XML for EDI, has defined XML languages for all of the standard business documents and transmittals. With its self-descriptive data structures and flexibility to handle a wide variety of data formats, XML seems ideal for EDI. Its only drawback, and the reason for its slow acceptance is the amount of overhead needed for data tags, resulting in much larger data files and more bandwidth to transfer information. As compression techniques mature and bandwidth costs continue to drop, XML will gain a foothold in this industry.

In our candle factory example, the production program could use JAXP to format each of the purchase requests, then send them using JAXM. When a reply is received, XSLT scripts could be used along with JAXP to reformat them into a standard representation then parse them into a DOM structure and store them in the appropriate databases. Once the purchase requests are sent, the supplier can translate the request into their preferred format using another XSLT script.

JavaMail

So far, we have looked at EDI in its standard role as a framework for business-to-business e-commerce, but quite often, EDI has other roles, facilitating communications between two trading partners or transmitting data within a single organization. In these cases, the large industry standards are not always necessary and simple file transfers using FTP or e-mail are sufficient as the transport mechanism. In these cases, JavaMail can be used to implement a bare bones, cost-effective EDI solution. Once the two organizations agree on a standard data representation (XML or otherwise), the information can be saved as a file then sent using a call to the JavaMail API. On the receiving end, the file attachment is run through a simple application that processes the information and stores it in a database or other form.

Enterprise Application Integration (EAI)

One of the most critical initiatives that many large organizations are undertaking is the marriage of commercial applications, legacy systems, and e-commerce together into large integrated enterprise-wide systems. There are a number of forces driving EAI that have made this essential, including mergers and acquisitions, adoption of large commercial ERP, and CRM applications and the continued importance of e-commerce. At the same time, EAI leverages past technology investments by providing easy access to legacy systems either on the web or through new user interface applications.

EAI is a massive subject, tying together every phase of information technology, accessing diverse platforms and programming languages and many generations of technology. For the J2EE developer interested in EAI, there are some essential technologies you'd need to know.

Java IDL & CORBA

Crossing most common programming languages and hardware platforms, CORBA (the Common Object Request Broker Architecture) offers a language-neutral Interface Definition Language (IDL) and a set of standard services that allow programs to request services over a common network. By creating interfaces describing existing code, CORBA allows your Java programs (servlets, Java Beans, or EJBs) to call existing code on any platform. It is ideal for creating new user interfaces to legacy code or to bridge applications.

Connectors

New to J2EE 1.4 is the Connectors specification, which uses EJBs to represent legacy code. Again, it is ideal for creating new user interfaces to existing legacy applications or to integrate legacy processes into new workflow applications. EJBs offer the advantages of transactions, which ensure that all applications stay consistent and processes either complete successfully or fail as a whole. If a problem occurs somewhere in the transaction, all processes are rolled back as if nothing happened. EJBs also allow locking services to ensure that changes made within the process are not corrupted along the way by other users' concurrent access.

Other Technologies

Finally, developers interested in EAI need to have a broad base of understanding in a variety of technologies. The integrated application will span mainframes, client/server databases, legacy code, and a variety of networks and hardware platforms. Basic knowledge of these technologies is critical, even if it is just to talk to the mainframe developer. You will be amazed at the differences in terminology and you will often discover that you are both using different words to mean the same thing.

For programmers who have been in the industry a while, their background and knowledge of J2EE, combined with past experience, make them especially valuable. They can take the role of interpreter to bridge diverse backgrounds and intimate knowledge of the legacy applications will make interfacing between the two technologies easier.

Other Applications

In this section, we have looked at a few J2EE applications and the technologies needed to make them work. In addition to these, J2EE can fit into many other applications, providing server-side functionality to any Java application. One that comes immediately to mind is JINI and wireless applications where server-side processing and data storage will become critical. Wouldn't it be nice to let your refrigerator keep track of its own inventory and order its own groceries, or your car schedule its own service appointments? Add J2EE to JINI and let your imagination go wild.

Hopefully, you now have a good idea of where your interests lie and are ready to move forward with your pursuit of J2EE. There are many different sources of information and ways to go about your quest. In the next section we will examine some of these options.

J2EE Resources

Armed with the roadmap and a few suggested paths, it's now time to decide which way you want to go. It may be that what you learned in this book will be all you need for now, and that's fine, but if you need to learn more, here are a few resources that can help you get started:

- ❑ SDKs, documentation, and specifications
- ❑ Books and reference manuals
- ❑ Java periodicals
- ❑ Other sources

SDKs, Documentation, and Specifications

The first place to go, and the primary source for all J2EE technologies, is found in the SDKs and their supporting documentation and specifications. The SDK will provide the libraries, interfaces, and reference implementations that let you try them out yourself. Sun's documentation is usually pretty good (although it can take some time to get used to reading vendor documentation) and is often accompanied by tutorials and sample code to get you started. In many cases, this is all you need to get on your way and, thanks to the http://java.sun.com/ web site, the downloads are only a few mouse clicks away.

Although everyone has their own way of approaching new technology, my approach is to start by skimming the documentation – just enough to know where things are. Then, I study the sample code to see how the APIs and class libraries work. With that knowledge, I choose a simple problem and try my hand at writing some code of my own. My goal is usually not to become an expert on every possible function and class, but to learn just enough to do what I need to for my needs. I may never learn enough to become J2EE certified, but I can make it work. To me, that's what matters.

For those of you who do want to know everything there is to know about a specific technology, each API comes with a specification describing the technology in very fine detail. Reading specifications takes a special talent and supply of patience that I have never possessed, but there is a wealth of information hiding in there and much can be learned if you can cultivate this talent!

Sun has always been strongly committed to supporting their developers with downloads, documentation, specifications, tutorials, and other resources, usually free of charge, all easily accessed from their web site at http://java.sun.com. If you suffer from a slow dial-up connection, like me, you may also find their Java Jump-start program very helpful. Sun distributes much of their Java web site (including downloads) on a set of CD or DVD-ROMs for a relatively low subscription price. It saves download time and is accessible even when your wife or kids are on the Internet.

Books and Reference Manuals

These references hardly need mentioning since you are looking at one right now, but they need to be included to make this list complete. Aftermarket books like this one bring the SDKs, APIs, and specifications back down to earth, explaining difficult issues and pointing the way to tools and technologies that you may not otherwise discover on your own. My strong recommendation is to choose the big red books with the author's picture on the cover! The programmer-to-programmer approach makes them easy to understand and supplies lots of real-world sample code. In addition, Sun does offer a line of reference books covering all of their technologies and excerpts can often be found on their web site. Browse through your local library and bookstore, or go surfing to see what titles are available on your chosen subject.

Java Periodicals

The Java trade press is another place to go to find leading-edge material on J2EE topics. Most offer companion web sites with additional articles and program code. They also organize trade shows with seminars and vendor presentations where you can get in-depth information on your topic of interest.

Other Sources

In addition to the Sun web site and aftermarket books, there is a wealth of information available in print and on the Web. Here are some places to look:

❏ **Vendors** –Vendors who develop and market J2EE technologies publish their work on their web sites and trade publications. They sell training programs as well as conducting marketing presentations and other seminars where you can learn much about their technology offerings. Most also support local user groups where you can meet others with similar interests. More on these vendors can be found in the next chapter.

❏ **Industry and Trade Groups** – Trade groups like ACM (The Association for Computing Machinery) and IEEE (The Institute of Electrical and Electronics Engineers) publish a wealth of articles and research on all phases of computing technology. For those who enjoy reading academic writings or specifications, these publications can provide a wealth of material. Access is usually limited to group members but much of their material is available through libraries and university computer networks. There are also other technology specific trade groups like the XML/EDI group mentioned above that focus on industry applications to specific technologies.

❏ **Colleges and Universities** – Local universities and technical colleges offer a great alternative for those interested in classroom study or who are looking into certification programs. Although most courses are a little bit behind the curve when it comes to new technology, they are getting better. College and university libraries also stock books and trade publications that may be difficult to find from other sources and their on-line computer systems often offer access to professional organization publications (like ACM and IEEE) without having to pay their high subscription fees.

For more information on the topics listed above, see the reference list at the end of this chapter.

Summary

In this chapter, we have looked at a number of additional J2EE topics that you may want to explore. The focus of the chapter was to acquaint you with these technologies and offer a number of areas that you may find interesting as you further your J2EE career. Here is a brief summary:

- ❑ We examined a brief roadmap of the APIs and technologies available to you as a J2EE developer.

- ❑ We surveyed each of these technologies briefly to help you understand their uses.

- ❑ We looked at a number of technology applications and discussed how J2EE technologies can be used within the problem domain.

- ❑ We listed a number of resources to help you along your pursuit of J2EE mastery.

In the next chapter, we will look at what is happening in the real world where you will apply your J2EE skills. We will help you get acquainted with some of the vendors who build and market industrial-strength J2EE tools.

Resources

Here are some web sites that can help you begin to learn more on your chosen topic. Remember that this is just a starting point – the pleasure is in the journey!

General web sites of interest:

- ❑ Sun's Java web site – http://java.sun.com
- ❑ Sun's J2EE web site – http://java.sun.com/j2ee/
- ❑ Wrox web site – http://www.wrox.com

Java trade press sites:

- ❑ Java Developers Journal – http://www.sys-con.com/java/
- ❑ Java Pro – http://www.fawcette.com/javapro
- ❑ Java World – http://www.javaworld.com/

Industry groups:

- ❑ ACM – http://www.acm.org
- ❑ IEEE – http://www.ieee.org
- ❑ XML/EDI Group – http://www.geocities.com/WallStreet/Floor/5815/

CHAPTER 15

Reasons for Using Industrial-Strength J2EE	**620**
The Application Server Market	**623**
Supporting Roles	**628**
Competing Technologies	**634**
Summary	**635**
Resources	**635**

J2EE in the Real World

Welcome to the real world. In computer-speak, the *real world* is a mythical place populated by monsters called managers, users, customers, and vendors, where the things learned in the classroom don't always work the way they are supposed to, where costs and schedules prevent you from doing your work the right way, and where you, as a software developer, face your worst nightmares. In actuality, the real world is not usually quite that terrible and most of us do learn to live and thrive in its hostile environment.

The main difference between J2EE as covered in this book and J2EE in the real world is the requirements that have to be fulfilled by the applications we build. In this book, our most important requirement was *learning*. We needed tools that were easy to obtain, easy to use, and sample applications that were easy to understand. In the real world, the requirements are vastly different, with emphasis on performance, high availability, security, productivity, and other considerations. To meet these needs, J2EE application server and development tool vendors have stepped up to the plate with a host of products including application servers, integrated development tools, administration tools, and performance utilities.

In this chapter, we will briefly look at some of these real world considerations and the vendors and commercial tools that meet these needs. As J2EE developers, these are the tools you will use to build your real world applications.

The topics covered in this chapter include:

- ❑ Reasons for using industrial-strength J2EE
- ❑ Fully-featured servers
- ❑ JSP servers
- ❑ Development tools
- ❑ Testing and performance tools
- ❑ Other J2EE tools

Reasons for Using Industrial-Strength J2EE

The J2EE platform used in this book has been great as a teaching tool. The J2EE SDK, command line compiler, and the J2EE reference implementation are easy to use and can be downloaded at no cost to the budding enterprise application programmer, straight from the Internet. They work well to illustrate how J2EE works and can be used to build small applications, but they can be tedious and don't perform as well as the real world tools we will examine in this chapter.

A good analogy is that of carpenter tools. We can build a house using a hammer and a cross-cut saw and it will eventually get built. Consider how much faster and easier it would be to build the same house with a nail-gun and power saw though! They cost a little more, but the time saved is well worth the expense. The same is true with commercial J2EE tools. Real world application servers offer higher performance and easier administration, and can be complemented with development and deployment tools that allow you to build your J2EE applications faster and easier.

In addition to performance and ease of development, there are several other reasons for considering commercial J2EE products. These include:

❑   Fault-tolerance

❑   Scaleability

❑   Security

❑   Administration

❑   Developer Productivity

Performance

As we saw with the nail-gun analogy, *performance* is the primary reason for spending money on commercial tools. Performance is the need for speed in the time from request to response, transaction throughput, order entry, data retrieval, and all other processing needs. This same need for speed can be found throughout the entire development cycle, from inception to deployment; in the time it takes to code a servlet or EJB, and in the time it takes to get the application online.

Performance needs also vary between applications and, as such, vendors offer a range of choices in application server performance options. When comparing server products (at least in theory), the amount spent on a commercial application server will determine the performance that the product offers. Spending more on the server will increase the number of concurrent users accessing the application, speed up the time from request to response, and raise the level of performance. Of course, other factors apply too. Faster networks and server machines contribute even more to overall performance and the architecture and design of the application itself can easily make or break its ability to quickly respond to requests. These again, though, are a function of cost.

When considering a commercial application server, this balance between cost and performance will be the most important issue. It will also drive your decision of which J2EE technologies to use. Simple JSPs may be all that your application need, so a JSP server will host your application at a much lower cost. In other cases, the application could require more processing and complex business logic. In this case an EJB server may be a better choice. Other technologies such as messaging or support for web services may fit well in your application, and support for these technologies will affect your application server choices.

Fault-Tolerance

Second on the list of requirements for industrial-strength J2EE is the need for availability. Most applications must be available anytime/anywhere and downtime cannot be tolerated. Even in those cases where an application is only used during normal business hours, it must still be available during those times. Fault-tolerance and redundancy features solve these problems.

Fault-tolerance can be as simple as a consistent approach to J2EE exception handling or can be as complex as clustering, redundant back up servers and networks located in other parts of the world. Commercial vendors offer many solutions, both within the application server or as separate hardware and network solutions. Since we are only considering J2EE application servers here though, you can pursue external fault-tolerance issues on your own. We will only be looking at J2EE server issues in this section.

Fault tolerance begins with a good exception handling process that includes recovery and reporting. Recovery means that the application or server will not stop running when an error occurs. The server must attempt retries when network errors occur or when messages time out. Application errors also must be recovered and reported by the server when they occur. The server's administration tools should offer a flexible range of choices when errors occur, with options to ignore, log, or notify the administrator through on-screen messages, e-mails, or even a call to a pager. In addition to error handling, other fail-safe options include clustering and mirroring servers for both performance and fault-tolerance, and switching to alternate servers when serious exceptions occur or when it appears that network errors are causing problems.

Just as in the choices of performance, the options for fault-tolerance will vary depending on the cost and complexity of the server chosen. Different applications require different levels of fault-tolerance and vendors offer a wide range of choices. Basic exception handling is a must for all servers, but additional features should only be added if they are really needed.

Scaleability

All successful applications need room to grow. Applications that have begun life as a simple solution for a small workgroup can often grow to enterprise level. Scaleability is the ability to either add capacity within an existing server or provide alternative upgrades to manage growth. J2EE offers strong scaleability since it focuses on distributed computing, allowing multiple servers to work together on a single application. Commercial servers offer features like load balancing to route traffic among several servers to optimize performance and support redundancies the failure of one server will not bring down the application.

Also, since J2EE is a somewhat vendor-neutral platform, scaleability is not quite as major an issue as with other server choices. Note the word *somewhat*, though. Even though J2EE offers standards that define how the server performs, vendors do offer extensions and additional features to attempt to lock you into their products. Migrating to another vendor's server may not be as easy is it seems. As such, scaleability should be considered carefully when choosing your J2EE platform.

Security

With the wake of new internet worms and attacks targeted towards specific server platforms (like the recent SQL Server incident), it is imperative that your server vendor has a high level of expertise on security issues. The J2EE specification already has some excellent security features built in and we saw how these were implemented as we worked through the examples in this book. Security works on several levels though. In the Chapter 8, where we cover session beans, you saw how to implement application-level security, requesting user IDs and passwords that limit access to the session beans. Underneath this feature though, we have to know that the user and password repositories are secure, that no one can obtain this data and crack the passwords to subvert our application-level security. These same concerns have to be addressed at other levels too. Are the communications secure between client and server, can the encryption be cracked, have all the back doors been closed? This all comes down to a level of trust with your vendor.

When considering security, see what kind of commitment your vendor has towards these issues. Does the server support a number of different security models? A feature touted by several vendors is that of "pluggable" security models, allowing add-ins to enhance J2EE security. Check to see if they issue security bulletins that address and correct security problems. Also, don't rely completely on your application server vendor for a security solution. Security is a network-wide issue that encompasses firewalls, VPNs, anti-virus, data backup, and procedural issues.

Administration

In the J2EE community, one area where vendors distinguish themselves is in their administration tools. Here, ease of use is the key. These servers are complex applications in their own right and their user interfaces must provide tools for installing, testing and deploying new applications, tuning performance, managing directory services, linking to databases and handling the fault-tolerance issues described above. They also must do this on a host of different hardware platforms in a consistent manner.

Due to the complexity and high learning curve of these products, another issue here is the availability of talent. Learning these tools takes time so either finding or training administrators (as well as developers and testers familiar with these tools) must be considered in the choice of a server platform. One trend that simplifies administration is the move towards single vendor solutions, which combine application servers, database servers, directory services and, in some cases, even operating environments all from a single vendor. Within these products, a single administration console tool manages all servers. This speeds the learning curve and simplifies administration.

Developer Productivity

Finally, as our nail-gun analogy illustrated, a small expenditure in tools can go a long way toward getting a product out of the door. Along with application servers comes a full range of tools to enhance performance on the development side. Java compiler vendors offer Enterprise Java language versions with full-featured IDEs (Integrated Development Environments) suited to J2EE development. These include an integrated program editor, a high performance, optimized Java compiler, a debugger that handles both locally and remotely deployed programs, code profilers to optimize performance, deployment tools, and a host of other goodies to make J2EE development easier. Other vendors concentrate on tools to automate the design process, testing, performance monitoring, and deployment.

Getting to Know the Players

With these considerations in mind, it is time to start looking at some of the products and services available and meet the vendors who provide them. This is in no way a comprehensive list and the aim here is to acquaint you with the names of the companies and products available. As a J2EE developer, you should at least know what WebLogic Server is when talking to a prospective employer or your new project manager.

Just as we discussed all of the J2EE technologies in the last chapter with the aim of pointing you towards areas that you may want to explore, the same is true with these products and vendors. Check their web sites, read their sales literature and white papers. Almost every vendor offers trial versions either as Internet downloads or as low cost demos and these can provide a wealth of knowledge to the new J2EE developer. Choose one or more servers, load them onto your machine, and take them for a test drive. Try their sample applications and study the code for new programming techniques. Find out how to deploy some of the applications you built from this book and give them a try. The vendors want you to choose their products so they go out of their way to cultivate developers. Use this to your advantage.

The Application Server Market

Application servers come in a number of forms, from the full-featured everything but the kitchen sink variety to simple JSP and HTTP servers. In this section we will take a look at some of the major vendors so you can learn their names and get acquainted with their products. This will be a very quick survey, giving you enough information to understand their area of emphasis and a little of their background, but will not be a comprehensive buyer's guide in any way. The aim here is to introduce you to them (check the *Resources* section at the end of the chapter for URLs).

> One quick caution before we start. The industry is in the throes of consolidation, mergers, and acquisitions. Vendor and product names change without notice and products are bought and sold on a daily basis. In this section, we will try to highlight the industry leaders – those who have a solid, proven history in the market, but don't be surprised if things have changed by the time you read this!

In this section we will look at:

❑ Fully-featured servers

❑ JSP servers

❑ HTTP servers

Fully-Featured Servers

Our vendor survey will begin with the high-end products – the fully-featured application servers. These servers implement most, or all, of the features of J2EE, including servlets, JSPs, and EJBs, and support the web services standards. Most are multi-leveled products, offering a number of versions based on your feature and performance needs. Competition in this market is fierce so all vendors work hard to stay current with new standards. At the time of writing, most have committed to supporting J2EE 1.4 and are frantically working to get these features out of the door.

As with many mature technologies, the market seems to consolidate around two or three leading vendors and these products are no exception. Market share is largely revolving around three vendors with BEA's WebLogic Server leading, followed by IBM's WebSphere Server and Oracle's 9i Application Server. Several others still remain in the market, but as time goes on, most will either be absorbed by one of these three or will move on to other products.

In this section, we will look at these three dominant application server products in just enough detail to let you know their intended markets and distinguishing characteristics. For more information on any of these, see the reference list at the end of the chapter for links to their web sites.

BEA's WebLogic Server

BEA has been a major player in distributed computing for many years and is the leader in the J2EE application server market. As a software vendor, their focus is on products to support enterprise infrastructure and, as such, offer the best (and highest priced) server products of the three. As of this writing, BEA's most current release of their server is version 7.0, supporting every feature of J2EE version 1.3 as well as several of the 1.4 features such as connectors and web services. As a contributor to the J2EE standards, they have made a solid commitment to the standard and will most likely have a J2EE version 1.4-compliant release in the near future.

The WebLogic server runs on most server platforms including UNIX, Windows, Linux, and mainframe operating systems. Their focus is on high-end, high transaction, high-availability enterprise applications, offering clustering and load balancing for extended scaleability and fault tolerance. They feature pluggable security modules to tailor security to your application's needs and support SMTP and web-based administration tools so administration can be handled from anywhere on the network. The WebLogic server leads in market share with estimates between 35% to 45%, and rates highest in most industry group performance benchmarks. It is the high-end solution for those who need, and are willing to pay for, the highest performance.

IBM's WebSphere Application Server

As a hardware vendor, IBM's approach to application servers is a little different from that of BEA. Their focus is on offering support for their hardware platforms, so their WebSphere server is targeted towards mainframes, AS/400, and their network server platforms (including Windows and Linux). Even so, they have been active in the transaction monitor and messaging middleware markets for many years. As a result of this, they bring a wealth of experience to their application server products. Their position in the IT solutions market also gives them a large existing customer base that has contributed to their position as number 2 in the J2EE application server market.

Their WebSphere server (currently version 4.0 as of this writing) is not quite as current in its implementation of J2EE standards. They support all of J2EE version 1.2 as well as some of the web services features on 1.3 and 1.4, but IBM's emphasis is not bound tightly to J2EE. Their focus is on support for their existing proprietary transaction and middleware standards, as well as industry standards like CORBA. For those working on legacy or mainframe integration projects, WebSphere may be your best choice in web servers.

Oracle's 9i Application Server

Nipping at the heels of IBM, Oracle is quickly gaining market share with their 9i Application Server. Oracle is the industry leader in database server products and has taken advantage of their place in the market to promote their J2EE 1.3-compliant server. Oracle's product focuses on database integration, speed, and performance with advanced clustering and web caching features.

Their support for J2EE is about the same as BEA's (J2EE 1.3-compliant) and, at least in their marketing materials, they seem to have a commitment to maintaining J2EE standards. As with BEA, J2EE 1.4 will most likely be included in their next release. Other J2EE features include strong support for web services, XML and data integration. Their J2EE implementation is geared towards performance with some benchmarks out-performing WebLogic.

While Oracle may be relatively new to the application server market, they are an industry leader in database servers and vertical market applications. Add to this their strong suite of development tools and Oracle can offer one-stop shopping for a host of business solutions. For those who need to build data-intensive applications, Oracle is probably your best choice.

Other Choices

Of course the big three are not your only choices. There are other vendors who also offer great application server products and these may offer the best choice depending on your circumstances. Here is a quick run down of some of the other players.

Borland's Enterprise AppServer

Borland has been a leader in PC development products for many years but has always seemed to have had difficulty penetrating the server market. Their AppServer product competes well with the big three, supporting J2EE 1.3 as well as several other middleware standards. Its main advantage is tight integration with Borland's JBuilder Enterprise tools, which also now supports WebLogic. This server may be a great starting point for those already using JBuilder.

Iona's Orbix E2A J2EE Edition

Iona is an industry leader in the CORBA marketplace and has complemented their server (called an ORB in CORBA-speak) with a J2EE edition. Their implementation of J2EE is fully compliant with version 1.3 with strong focus on implementing current web services standards. Iona offers a comprehensive set of tools to integrate applications through CORBA and web services on almost any platform and any programming language. It is a strong choice for EAI and legacy integration.

JBoss

JBoss is an open source J2EE application server with many of the features of the high-priced industrial strength servers. It was developed by somewhere in the region of 100 programmers, contributing their efforts to produce a free implementation of the J2EE framework. Over the past three years, the project has grown to encompass all of the features needed for a complete application server. JBoss was implemented completely in Java and makes a great starting place for those new to J2EE.

Novell exteNd

Recently purchased from Silverstream, the Novell exteNd package includes development, deployment, and integration tools supporting WebLogic and WebSphere servers, as well as their own J2EE application server. Due to the transition from Silverstream to Novell, at the time of this writing, there was little information available about their J2EE capabilities. From what can be gathered from the information available, they appear to be promoting their tools much more aggressively than their server. Time will tell.

JSP Servers

For those who do not need all of the features and overhead of a J2EE application server, there are several servers that just provide servlet and JSP support. These servers have much smaller footprints, require less server resources and installation, and administration is much easier. Of course, they cannot be expected to handle the high traffic volumes and perform as well as the high priced, fully-featured servers described above, but many companies have found that these servers are all they need. So don't be surprised if you hear these names when talking with future employers or project managers.

Apache's Tomcat

Tomcat, part of the Jakarta project, the reference implementation for the J2EE servlet and JSP standard, is a popular platform for delivering Java servlets and JSPs from the Apache web server. Developed as an open source project, it is available on most UNIX, Linux, and Windows platforms. The Apache organization has been a leader in implementing web standards and offers strong performance at a very reasonable price (free). Release 5.x, (soon to be released at the time of this writing) supports Servlets 2.4 and JSP 2.0 standards.

MacroMedia's JRun

Another long time player in Internet development, MacroMedia offers the industry's leading commercial JSP server. With its strong set of development tools like DreamWeaver and its Flash animation tools, MacroMedia offers a strong presence in the market. Compared to the price of fully-featured J2EE servers, JRun offers a low cost alternative and, as we will see later in this chapter, JRun is available through many hosting service providers for a very low fee per month.

HTTP Servers

Although these are not really in the category of J2EE servers, the HTTP server is a dominant force in the market so these are products you should know. HTTP servers are the foundations that drive a large portion of the Internet and many of the products listed above rely on these servers for basic HTTP services. Let's look at them quickly.

Apache Web Server

The Apache web server is the dominant force in the market. It is an open source product and runs on almost any server platform. It is a bare-bones server that can be found on most Linux and UNIX systems and offers high performance at no cost.

Microsoft's Internet Information Services (IIS)

Microsoft's dominance in the desktop computing market cannot be ignored so we do have to mention IIS here. It does power many web sites and you will often see it running in conjunction with JRun or Tomcat. It also provides some good administration tools. It is included as part of the Windows NT and 2000 platforms.

Getting to Know the Servers

This has been a very brief discussion of the major J2EE application server products, and is intended to whet your appetite. We've covered things quickly here, just giving you enough information to get you started. If you want to learn more, the *Resources* section below lists web sites for both the vendors and their application server products. Check them out and learn more about each. There is a wealth of information, white papers, and downloads to get you started with any of them.

Supporting Roles

Although the servers are the foundation of a successful J2EE application, there are a number of other supporting roles that need to be filled to bring the project from inception to deployment. Tools are needed for development, testing, performance tuning, and deployment. Database servers are needed to host the persistent data and it often makes sense to let someone else administer the servers and networks where the application will be deployed.

Just as we saw in the server market, a small expenditure in these tools can reap strong benefits when building a J2EE application, relieving programmers from much of the work needed to build and test program modules and components. Testing tools can also alleviate much of the boredom and tedium, through automating endless repetitions of the same test cycles. As a new J2EE developer, you need to be familiar with these tools and be ready to dive in and start using them when you get into your development projects. Once you get used to these tools, you will be amazed at how much easier it is to build a J2EE application.

In this section, we will briefly look at some of the tools and products that make J2EE development easier. Again this is not a comprehensive review or buyer's guide, but just a brief introduction to some of the tools and concepts surrounding J2EE development. These tools include:

❑ J2EE integrated development environments (IDEs)

❑ Testing and performance tools

❑ Configuration management

❑ Database servers

❑ Service providers

J2EE Integrated Development Environments (IDEs)

Top on the list of tools for J2EE development is the Integrated Development Environment (IDE). While the command line compiler may be adequate for other development environments, the IDE is a mandatory tool for J2EE development. These enterprise suites, as they are called, can be horribly expensive (expect to spend over $1000 per user for commercial products), but you will reap rewards within the first month of development. While considering IDEs, also look to your application server vendor for development tools tied directly to their products. The one-stop shopping solution may lock your company into their product, but the gains in developer productivity may be worth it.

In this section, we will examine some of the features of the enterprise IDEs, then look at some of the products available.

IDE Features

If you have used a Java IDE or a similar tool for one of the other languages like C++ or Visual Basic, some of this will look very familiar, so please bear with us. All IDEs provide program editing, compiling, and debugging from a single screen. What makes the enterprise IDEs so powerful is their close integration with the J2EE servers. Let's begin by briefly examining the features available from the IDE:

❏ The basics – edit, compile, debug

❏ Coding automation

❏ Local and remote debugging

❏ Profiling

❏ Deployment

❏ Other tools

The Basics – Edit, Compile, Debug

What makes the IDE so powerful is that the editor, compiler, and debugger are tightly integrated into a single package. Write some code, compile it with a single keystroke and then, if any errors were found, the IDE moves your cursor on your editor window to the first error and lets you know the problem. From there, you step through the errors and fix them, then click the compile button again. Once clean, click the debug button and you can step through the code line by line, set breakpoints (stop when execution gets to a specific line) and set watches to inspect class properties or variables. All this is very powerful and should be familiar to most developers.

Coding Automation

Now let's move into the features that distinguish the J2EE enterprise IDEs. First on the list is coding automation. When we built the EJB examples, we first defined a home interface, a remote interface, and a bean file for each entity or session bean. You may have noted that much of this code is repeated in every bean, so why code it every time? Why not let the compiler build it for you? That's the first step to coding automation. Simply give the IDE the name of the bean, its type (entity, session, and so on), describe a few properties (like the source of the data if it's an entity bean), click finish, and look at all that code.

Now that the basic code is built, all you have to do is tell the IDE that you want a new property or method, and then enter the implementation code. It keeps track of the book-keeping – adding the proper interfaces and updating the deployment descriptors. If you find that a method was not really necessary, simply delete the method and the interface files will be changed automatically.

Coding wizards, as they are often called, automate many of the routine tasks involved throughout the development process. So much of the coding is repetition and there is no reason to spend time doing something a computer can do. These wizards are presented as a set of dialog boxes, asking for information that is then pasted into basic templates to create the skeleton programs and support files. The programming wizard also provides standardized code that looks similar no matter who does the programming so maintenance is easier and faster.

629

Local and Remote Debugging

Another advantage of the IDE is its tight integration between program editor and debugger. In an enterprise environment, code will be executing in many places at the same time. Your user interface executes directly on your workstation, servlets and JSPs are generated from the web server, EJBs may be running on another server, and database procedures somewhere else. Trying to debug all of these processes can be a complicated task, but the enterprise IDE keeps track of all of the threads and sessions throughout the network, not only tracking the processes, but also synchronizing your program code to these sessions, presenting you with program code and watch windows so you know what is happening when and where.

Of course, learning to track and debug all of these processes is difficult and the learning curve can be tough for someone just starting out, but the debugging and browsing windows are presented in a logical manner and skills are learned with practice. Nevertheless, remote debugging is a powerful tool and one that speeds up development.

Profiling

The profiler is a performance tool that tracks program execution, then lets the developer know how much time is spent executing each class and method. It can also profile memory and resource utilization, tracking system loads on each machine. Using these statistics, the developer can determine where to spend time optimizing code to speed up overall performance. At the highest level, it points towards those classes and methods where the work is done, where a small effort optimizing code will bring the highest benefit. At the detail level, it can be used to isolate slow algorithms, slow loops, or any other code segments that could be performing better.

The profiler can help immensely when optimizing code, but remember, optimization has to start at the design phase; choosing the technologies, data structures, and algorithms that fit best for the problem being solved. Waiting until the coding is done to optimize with profilers and such will not solve major performance problems. At the same time, if the design work was done right, the profiler can tune your code to make it lean and mean.

Deployment

Finally, given the amount of information collected by the wizards during development, things like the relationship between EJB interfaces and implementation files, how databases are linked to the entity beans, which beans are used in the JSPs and such, deployment can be handled with a few mouse clicks. There is no reason to go through all of the screens we used with the J2EE reference implementation's deployment tool. The IDE already knows this and can create deployment descriptors and the information needed to deploy the components. This eliminates the communication and confusion between the developers and administrators and ensures that everything goes into its proper place.

Commercial IDEs

With this background in mind, let's now look at the major players in the IDE market. Due to the complexity of these products, the choices are pretty slim. The trend seems to be for the server vendors to acquire and tailor the IDEs to their own products. This is not a bad thing since the vendor can tightly integrate their server into the development product, but at the same time, choosing a vendor's IDE may lock you into their product. So, in addition to the IDEs provided by the server vendors, here are a couple of independent products that support multiple servers.

Borland's JBuilder Enterprise

Borland has been a leader in the desktop language market since the earliest days of the PC, competing, and often beating, Microsoft on their own platform. This experience shows in all of their language products, and JBuilder Enterprise version 8 is no exception. JBuilder offers end-to-end development within a single application, building EJBs and XML applications using wizards and visual tools. Applications can be deployed, tested, debugged, and optimized on WebLogic, WebSphere, and several other application server platforms. With their recent partnership with WebLogic, this tight integration will get even stronger.

IBMs WebSphere Enterprise Studio

IBM's language expertise goes back even farther than Borland's; all the way, in fact, to the earliest computers. As such, they know how to deliver fast, highly optimized language tools. Directly coupled to the WebSphere server, this all encompassing IDE includes support for Java, EJBs, JSPs, web pages, and even COBOL and PL/1 (remember those?) development. The IDE supports strong team-based development and offers easy deployment, testing, and debugging for the WebSphere and other servers. For those interested in development on the WebSphere platform or for legacy integration, this may be the IDE for you.

Testing and Performance Tools

In addition to the tools available in the IDEs, debuggers like JProbe from Sitraka and automated testing tools like Parasoft's JTest can help ensure that applications are delivered clean and bug-free. These tools do not replace program validation and user testing, but they can automate the constant repetition of test cases and stress test your application. Here are a few of the tests that can be performed:

Code Validation

Code validation looks for possible programming errors that may not be caught by the compiler. It's almost like a grammar check on a word processor. It checks to ensure that the code conforms to its standards and warns the developer when there is a potential problem. This would include things like unreferenced local variables, infinite loops, and similar problems. But like a grammar checker, these errors should be taken with a grain of salt. Use the diagnostics as guidelines and don't spend too much time changing your code just to satisfy the validator.

Unit Testing

Tools like JTest can perform unit tests on each class and method by randomly throwing everything but the kitchen sink at it. These tests can quickly verify data validation and exception handling by trying to make them fail. They also ensure full code coverage, making sure that all of the code is exercised. They also allow you to select specific sets of parameters when random values don't make sense and ranges can be set on random data to ensure that the tests will conform to real-world conditions.

Test Case Automation

One of the most boring parts of testing is the constant repetition of test cases through the same code, over and over, as each problem is fixed. It's easy to skip tests once the test passes and take shortcuts to get back to finding and fixing problems. This is where the problems occur. Testing tools offer record/playback functions and scripting that allow you to run the test process once, and then repeat it over and over as each change is made. It will report and flag changes in results, so exceptions can be found quickly, relieving much of the drudgery. It also solves the problem of regression testing, ensuring that all functions already working are not broken by later changes.

Stress Testing

As development starts winding down, stress testing can be used to make sure that the application will keep running no matter what the load placed on it. The stress test simulates worst-case real world workloads on the application. What may work well in single user testing may completely break down when large volumes of users hit the application all at once. Problems in session tracking, concurrency, and capacity can all be isolated by these stress tests.

Code Optimization

Finally, one of the distinguishing characteristics of commercial compilers is their code optimization techniques. This is the ability of the Java compiler to "rewrite" the code to perform better. Many of the optimizations are low level, choosing the way methods are called or events are handled. Others actually change the source logic, like replacing a `for` loop into several repetitions of the same code. The IDEs often give you control, allowing you to decide which optimizations should be used. A little trial and error here can greatly increase performance.

Configuration Management (CM)

Although not a part of J2EE (so we'll cover this very quickly), configuration management is another one of those rude awakenings that you will encounter when you move into the real world, so it should be mentioned here. Configuration management is a process, as well as a set of commercial tools, that is used to manage and coordinate development efforts within a project team. It focuses your work towards specific assignments and ensures that developers don't overwrite each other's code. It is like concurrency management for developers. Since this is a huge subject and could take several books in their own right, we will try to cover only the basics here.

Configuration management tools can be huge and complex like Rational's ClearCase, or as simple as UNIX CVS (Concurrent Versioning System) or RCS (Revision Control System). Each supports a process combining some or all of the following features:

❑ **Requirements and problem tracking** – Monitoring what needs to be done and who will be doing it.

❑ **Version control** – Controlling and coordinating access of source code using check-out and check-in functions so developers don't step on each others code.

❑ **Integration or build management** – Managing the program build process and tracking what changes have been included in each build.

What makes CM a little overwhelming to the new developer is the knowledge that your name is attached to each work ticket and each module checked in. It's a little like Big Brother watching you, keeping track of everything you do. Used correctly though, CM is a powerful process that speeds development and delivers clean, reliable products. Used incorrectly, it can be your worst nightmare (if so, find another job as fast as you can).

As a developer, CM will keep you focused on the work that needs to be done, ensure that your work is not lost and help you to identify where changes have gone wrong. Code comparisons in the versioning tools will highlight your changes, letting you know what you did as well as subsequent changes by other developers. It can also be your friend (or enemy) during annual reviews, highlighting all of your hard work and professional successes. CM may seem like a lot of extra work but it can also be your best friend, if you learn to use it to your advantage.

> It may seem like we are moving farther away from J2EE and you're right, but as we move into the real world, we need to look at a few other products and tools that you as a J2EE developer will be using in your job. Depending on your work environment, you will probably work with CM, databases, and service providers almost as much as you do J2EE.

Database Servers

Hiding behind most J2EE applications is another tool almost as complex as the application server – the DBMS (Database Management System). Databases have been around since the early 1970s and there is a huge legacy of data stored on most enterprise networks. As a J2EE developer, it will most likely be your job to present this data in your applications so a basic knowledge of the DBMS is mandatory. Like CM, this is a huge subject. The basics have been covered earlier in this book, so we will just briefly mention some of the major database vendors and it will be your responsibility to go to their web sites (listed in the references below). Here are some of the major database vendors and their products:

❑ **Oracle 9i** – The long-time industry leader and the most flexible of the bunch.

❑ **Microsoft's SQL Server** – Highly used throughout the industry, it has the backing of Microsoft and offers a good price/performance option.

❑ **IBM's DB2** – One of the oldest relational databases and very popular in large mainframe applications.

❏ **IBM's Informix** – Another one of the originals, found on mainframe and UNIX platforms, recently acquired by IBM.

❏ **Sybase's Adaptive Server Enterprise (ASE)** – Another long-time industry standard, popular on UNIX platforms.

❏ **MySQL** – Open source, often used in conjunction with Tomcat or JBoss.

Downloads and demonstration CDs are available for most of these products and you may want to take some time to get familiar with one or two of them. See the *Resources* section at the end of the chapter for pointers to their web sites.

Service Providers

In many cases, it makes more sense to rent than it does to buy. This is also true for the low-end J2EE application servers. Internet service providers offer web hosting at relatively low monthly rates that can include JSP and servlet support as well as databases and other features. For this low monthly rate, you get shared use of one or more servers, faster networks, staffing to back up your data and make sure the server is always running, software development and consulting (at a price if you need it) and the use of their software to handle traffic reporting, e-commerce, and other functions. Of course, there is also a downside and most of the advantages can also be disadvantages. Prices rise as your traffic increases, you are sharing a server so other user's traffic may slow your processes down and, since they are doing the administration, you have no control over maintenance and downtime. Even so, a service provider can help a new application get off the ground and can help keep costs down for many applications.

Adjusting to the Real World

We covered a lot of ground in this section, and it must seem overwhelming for someone just starting out, but don't be too concerned. Your primary job is still to *build* J2EE applications. All of these products and tools are here to help you and make your job easier. As mentioned in the previous chapter, you don't have to know everything there is to know about every one of these tools; you only have to know enough to do your job. Focus on those features that you need and don't get overwhelmed with all the details. Remember, you don't need to know the internal theories of electricity and mechanics of how a nail gun works; you just have to hold it up to the board and pull the trigger! The same holds true with these tools. Open the IDE, start the wizard, answer the dialogs, and watch it build your code.

Competing Technologies

At the time this was written, vendors of all types were scrambling to be the new industry leader in web services and were frantically forming alliances and acquiring the tools to move them into the forefront of this new technology. BEA and Borland are cross-marketing each other's products, Novell purchased Silverstream, and IBM is in the midst of acquiring Rational. By the time this book is released, several product names may have changed or may be sold by different vendors.

Remember too that the web services market is not just a J2EE phenomenon. Vendors selling XML, CORBA and those pushing other distributed technologies (.NET anyone?) are also fighting for market share. As a J2EE developer, you may find yourself getting into other technologies, but don't abandon your work on J2EE. To me it's the best web services platform of the bunch, but be open to other technologies too.

One of the trends that I saw while writing this chapter was the move back to the "big vendor". Products that I planned to mention have disappeared off the face of the planet, being absorbed into one of the big development suites. In my mainframe days, each hardware vendor supplied proprietary products that did everything needed to build and deploy applications built on their platform. It appears that this trend is repeating. BEA, Oracle, IBM, and Microsoft are each trying to position themselves as one-stop shops for corporate development needs. In some ways this consolidation is good since tight integration simplifies development. At the same time, this trend could be harmful, stifling competition, locking customers into inferior products and limiting good new ideas. Only time will tell.

Summary

In this chapter we looked briefly at the vendors and products that drive the J2EE market and the concepts behind these products. Building industrial-strength J2EE applications is a daunting task, but the tools and technologies available make this much easier. To recap, in this chapter we examined:

- ❑ Reasons for an industrial-strength J2EE application server
- ❑ The major J2EE application server products
- ❑ JSP, Servlet, and HTTP servers
- ❑ J2EE integrated development environments
- ❑ Other tools and products to support J2EE development

Now that you know what the real world holds for you as an aspiring J2EE developer, it is time to start thinking about using your skills to make a living. The next chapter will discuss how to put your skills to work so you too can be a professional J2EE developer.

Resources

You can find out more information about any of the vendors or products mentioned in this chapter on the Internet, so here is a list of their URLs in the order presented in the chapter.

For more information on fully-featured servers, take a look at the following links:

❑   BEA's WebLogic server – http://www.bea.com/products/weblogic/server/index.shtml

❑   IBM's WebSphere server – http://www-3.ibm.com/software/webservers/

❑   Oracle 9i Application Server – http://www.oracle.com/ip/deploy/ias/

❑   Borland's Enterprise Application Server – http://www.borland.com/besappserver/

❑   Iona's Orbix E2A J2EE Edition – http://www.iona.com/products/appserv-j2ee.htm

❑   Jboss – http://www.jboss.org/

❑   Novell exteNd – http://www.silverstream.com/Website/app/en_US/Extend

Next up are the JSP servers:

❑   Apache Tomcat – http://jakarta.apache.org/tomcat/index.html

❑   MacroMedia's JRun – http://www.macromedia.com/software/jrun/

HTTP servers:

❑   Apache web server – http://httpd.apache.org/

❑   Microsoft IIS – http://www.microsoft.com/servers/

And now the J2EE integrated development environments (IDEs):

❑   JBuilder Enterprise Edition – http://www.borland.com/jbuilder/enterprise/index.html

❑   IBM WebSphere Enterprise Studio –
     http://www-3.ibm.com/software/ad/studioenterprisedev/demo/

Testing and performance tools:

❑   Parasoft JTest – http://www.parasoft.com/jsp/products/home.jsp?product=Jtest

❑   Sitraka JProbe – http://www.sitraka.com/software/jprobe/

Configuration Management Tools:

❑   Rational's ClearCase – http://www.rational.com/products/clearcase/index.jsp

❑   CVS – http://www.cvshome.org/

And finally, database servers:

❑ Oracle 9i – http://www.oracle.com/ip/deploy/database/oracle9i/

❑ Microsoft's SQL Server – http://www.microsoft.com/sql/default.asp

❑ IBM's DB2 – http://www-3.ibm.com/software/data/

❑ IBM's Informix – http://www-3.ibm.com/software/data/informix/

❑ Sybase's ASE – http://www.sybase.com/products/databaseservers/ase

❑ MySQL – http://www.mysql.com/

CHAPTER 16

Web Resources   639

Java Certification   642

The Jobs   644

Books from Wrox Press   645

First Steps in Your Java Career

The material in this book has provided you with a solid foundation to the workings of J2EE, and, to a certain extent, considering the size of J2EE, it has prepared you to begin developing enterprise-standard applications. As extensive as this material has been though, you can be assured that it is just the beginning. There are many resources available that will allow you to expand your knowledge, and many ways for you to prepare yourself for a career within this exciting field.

This chapter will take a look at some of those resources, both on the Web and in print, as they apply to Java in general and J2EE in particular, along with information about Java certifications, and even a quick look into the areas of job searching and ways to enter the J2EE workplace.

Web Resources

Although we don't often think of it in this way, one of the most complete and varied libraries in the world is the Internet. Of all the resources available to you, there are none to compare with the World Wide Web in terms of the complexity, immediacy, low cost, and the accessibility of information. The variety of material that can be accessed with your browser is incredible, both in terms of the quality (or lack thereof) and the range of topics. Much of this material is not only available for browsing, but also available to you far earlier than you could possibly obtain it from a book or periodical. In most cases, the only cost involved is your Internet access, which you probably have in place already anyway. It is particularly rich in resources for software developers, including those who use the technologies outlined in this book. Access to this treasure trove of resources is often little more than a few mouse clicks away.

In this section, we will take a quick tour of some of the most significant and useful web sites for J2EE developers. Remember, though, that the resources mentioned are by no means all that is available. From these sites, by simply following the Links section, you will gain access to far more material than can ever be fully absorbed. Also, note that many of the pages have a generous amount of advertising, both banner and display advertisements. Ignore these at your peril as they frequently herald new developments, tools, seminars, and trade shows, and other information targeted at the developer world: people like you!

Java and J2EE

The Internet is filled with sites about Java, sites that are using Java, and Java-related technologies. You wouldn't need to look for long to find all of the material needed to learn the basics of the language, or to learn enough to successfully challenge the Java certification exams, or even to find the information necessary to help you to build Java applications of all sizes and complexities.

The first and most obvious place to start when it comes to looking for more information on anything Java-related, must always be Sun Microsystems and their web site at http://java.sun.com. Sun has a wide range of information available for developers, including a tutorial site, http://java.sun.com/docs/books/tutorial/, which will guide a reader from simple beginnings through a broad range of Java technologies to some of the most complex available, offering hundreds of examples and dozens of lessons on particular topics.

When it comes to J2EE, Sun also provides a comprehensive tutorial, http://java.sun.com/j2ee/tutorial/1_3-fcs/, which, although it is billed as a beginner's guide, touches on all the many technologies that make up the J2EE platform, including EJBs, JSPs, Servlets, web clients, and custom tags. For the J2EE version 1.4, Sun includes a tutorial addendum at http://java.sun.com/j2ee/1.4/docs/tutorial/index.html.

Downloadable documentation has always been a key part of the many Java technology releases by Sun. For example, the following page, http://java.sun.com/j2ee/docs.html, allows you to select and download documentation on the full range of J2EE technologies, including general information, FAQs, SDKs, and the many specifications for the various platforms and APIs.

In a site that the company has titled Solutions Marketplace, located at http://industry.java.sun.com/solutions/, Sun Microsystems has assembled a virtual goldmine of the best services and products from around the Web for developers utilizing applications for the Java platform.

Another key site within Sun is the Developer Services page, http://developer.java.sun.com/, where everything is geared to providing Java developers with the latest information about the most recent technologies. You will need to sign up for free membership to the Developer Connection, which is required for access to much of the content there.

IBM also offers web sites that are heavy with resources for developers. Check out either the alphaWorks site at http://www.alphaworks.ibm.com/ or its parent developerWorks site at http://www-106.ibm.com/developerworks/ for an extensive range of excellent reading material regarding XML, web services, and Java technologies. Although much of the material is based around IBM's own products, there is a significant amount of information about a wide variety of emerging technologies to be found here too.

The internet.com web site (http://www.internet.com/home.html) confidently proclaims itself as the Internet industry portal. Some of its goodies are job search sites, forums, and news. Furthermore, within the internet.com world is a gem that should be book marked by every serious Java developer. The Java Boutique site (http://javaboutique.internet.com/) is packed with newsletters, free code and other downloads, discussion forums, relevant and up-to-date articles, and many other resources.

And let's not forget the massive quantity of superior Java-related material at the Café au Lait site, http://www.ibiblio.org/javafaq/– tons of news, FAQs, articles, and links to articles, and pages of every sort of Java information imaginable.

Among the hundreds of About sites available, there are several that offer a wide range of Java-related material, especially tutorials, many of them excellent. In addition to the primary Focus on Java page, http://java.about.com/, About has a site devoted specifically to J2EE (http://java.about.com/cs/j2ee/index.htm) that you should check out.

The jGuru site, http://www.jguru.com/, is another extensive web resource for Java developers, with its wide range of downloads, articles, news, and discussion forums. Perhaps its most fascinating page is the one containing a sweeping spectrum of FAQs about Java and Java-related technologies. The FAQ page (http://www.jguru.com/faq/index.jsp) goes far beyond core Java technologies and tools, to include client and server-side development, web services, certification, and methodologies.

The VPSource site at http://www.vpsource.com/programming-java.html is primarily (OK, almost exclusively) a huge page of Java-related links, from certification, news, FAQs and tutorials to code archives and job searching resources.

The Gamelan page (http://www.developer.com/java/) is another huge Java resource that is part of the wealth of material within the developer.com web site. Here, you will find up-to-date articles, developer news, discussion forums, and tutorials by some of the best writers on the Web.

Speaking of good Java tutorials, one of the most extensive sources of these is Dick Baldwin's web site, http://www.dickbaldwin.com/. Although he specializes in Java at all levels, he includes extensive material on such related topics as XML, JavaScript, Python, and even C#.

Among all the many good Java e-magazines that are available and that should be on the reading list of all serious developers, JavaWorld (http://www.javaworld.com/) stands out as one of the best. But don't stop with JavaWorld! Shop around, and select others that may be appropriate to your field of development.

Finally for this section, who says learning Java can't be a little fun, too? The good folks at JavaRanch (http://www.javaranch.com/) have built some excellent learning tools, especially for those who want to know if they are anywhere near ready to pass their certification exams. (Hint: don't try the exam until you get the silver horseshoe!)

> We've alluded to forums when talking about a variety of web sites but the following links are dedicated to them: **http://forum.java.sun.com**, **http://p2p.wrox.com/java/**, and **http://www.javaranch.com/**, as featured above. These are arenas for programmers to interact in, and ideal for finding answers that no other source has provided.

Non-Java Web Resources

The http://www.brainbuzz.com/ web site, which bills itself as "The Mother of all Tech Sites", is typical of the many places on the Internet where developers and other IT professionals can search for jobs. brainbuzz.com offers its members such services as cramming sessions and other resources for those seeking certification, job searching and job posting facilities for job seekers and, for employers, skills assessments, discussion forums, and a wide range of IT articles.

Another of the many good sites offering a pot-pourri of information, products and links, is ZDNet, http://www.zdnet.com/, which is an excellent place to start a search for IT information, especially relating to the Internet.

Java Certification

One of the best ways to prove our proficiency in a programming language, or in any other area for that matter, is to show off our certification in it. The question is, do we *really* need to be certified in order to be hired as a Java developer, or to be recognized by our peers as a credible developer?

Much of the response to that question depends on where we will be working. There are many highly skilled Java developers who have never gained a certification of any kind, and yet produce some of the finest applications in the business. And there are many employers who are far more interested in examples of a potential employee's work than in any certification that the employee might happen to hold. Passing a certification exam does *not* automatically make a skilled or useful developer.

On the other hand, passing a certification exam *does* prove that the candidate, at least at the time of taking the exam, had a significant grasp of the material required. If you are a holder of a Java certification, employers everywhere will know that you know at least enough to pass the exam. And let's face it, Java certifications, like most IT certifications, require a high level of knowledge and diligence to pass.

Perhaps a better question than "why?" is, "why not?" Nobody is going to reject us as a developer on account of our holding a certification! Certification provides a solid foundation on which we can build a career and a reputation as a developer.

Although there are other certifications that carry some weight, certification from Sun Microsystems are recognized worldwide. Sun Certification exams are not for the faint of heart – the SCJP (Sun Certified Java Programmer) exam is made up of 59 multiple-choice or short answer questions with a pass grade of 61%.

The following Sun Microsystems web page contains an extensive list of questions and answers about Java certification:

❏   http://developer.java.sun.com/developer/technicalArticles/Interviews/Certification2/

And this is Sun's Java Platform Certification web site for the United States, with links to other countries:

❏   http://suned.sun.com/US/certification/

There are many excellent books to help those preparing for their certification exams, just as there are many outstanding web resources. Fortunately, those web resources are the best sources of information about the books that should be used. Take a good look through the links on the web pages that follow, to see what reading material the experts recommend.

The JavaPrepare site, http://www.javaprepare.com/, has just about everything needed to help you prepare for the certification text, including tutorials, sample questions, FAQs, and links to other resources. Furthermore, the page of **Other Certification sites** is one of the best of its type that I have seen.

You will also find plenty of Java-related material in About's **Focus on Java** section, including a page at http://java.about.com/library/quizzes/blscjp.htm that contains a good mock exam, which is free as well!

Additionally, JavaCaps (http://www.javacaps.com/scjp_tutorial.html) is yet another site with valuable certification preparation material, including a page with a "final exam cramming" tutorial and JavaCoding (http://www.javacoding.net/) is an excellent general Java resource site, with prominent certification-related links.

There is also a site at http://www.jchq.net/ created by Marcus Green, a certified Java programmer with a genuine interest in helping others along the certification pathway. Here, in addition to extensive Java-related material, the site also has a mock exam and FAQ's about certification.

Also, don't forget the JavaRanch site at http://www.javaranch.com/, which we looked at earlier in this chapter for assistance with your Java certification.

For a realistic sense of what it's like to write the exam, check out the web site for Whizlabs, http://www.whizlabs.com/products/javawhiz/javawhiz.html, which has among its many products one called J@Whiz, which is a SCJP test simulator.

There are many other such web sites for more information on certification, many of which are intuitively named, such as http://java.certifiedprogrammer.com/ and http://www.jcert.org/. Try typing in various search terms into Google for example and you will find many other sites to read and gain information from.

The Jobs

For those of you who are reading this book to improve your skills in your current jobs, this section may seem to have limited relevance. However, it is worth remembering that the average length of stay in any one job is much lower for IT employees than for just about any other type of skilled workers. You may well be busy and secure today, but you might find yourself looking for a new position tomorrow either at your own or your employer's request.

You have two basic approaches to finding work in the development of J2EE applications: you can be reactive, or proactive, and both work. Don't expect a be-all-and-end-all guide on how to get the perfect Java job for yourself, by the way – it's going to require as much work as learning J2EE itself!

The **reactive** approach is to find the job advertisements, and respond to them wherever they are found. That means you need to access the various Java magazines and IT journals, and web sites of all types, many of which you have seen throughout this chapter, to sort through their advertisements for developers. It also means you need to look often and thoroughly through the jobs posted on appropriate Internet newsgroups, in newspapers and by employment-related agencies of all types. You will also need to check out, register, post your resume, and constantly browse the ads on one or more of the many IT job search web sites. The page at http://www.employment-job-search.net/default.asp?article=gooit2 is just one example of the many sites that the Internet offers for this purpose.

If you would prefer one that is specifically geared to the Java world, you should take a look at http://www.javajobsonline.com/. Again, you should use a good search engine such as Google to seek out those keys to unlock your new career.

And then there's the **proactive** approach, in which you take on the initiative, by locating the company or companies of your choice, and doing your own campaigning to become part of their J2EE development staff. Those who adopt this approach are generally far more successful and land far more rewarding positions than those who opt for the reactive approach. That's because the proactive job search requires a tremendous amount of initiative, imagination, and entrepreneurial spirit. And those are the attributes that always lead to success in any endeavor.

Although the scope of tackling a proactive approach is beyond this book, there are ten aspects of the challenge you need to consider. The first nine aspects are research, research, research, research, research, research, research, research, and research. It is impossible for you to know too much about your prospective employer. You will need to learn the company's history and its primary markets, its philosophies and approaches in the business world, the key players in the company, the company's major successes in recent months, ways in which your abilities will mesh with the company's approach to J2EE development, and much more. And don't forget to check out the company's financial status – even rats know better than to swim toward a sinking ship!

The tenth aspect is preparation. That means being able to convince the prospective employer that you are exactly what they need. In addition to having all the information about the company and yourself at your fingertips, make sure you have at least one J2EE project you can present. Nothing is more convincing than something that works. Even a simple project, well presented and well executed, can be captivating. The contents of this book have given you all the tools you need to develop such a project.

Books from Wrox Press

Now that we've examined the resources that are available on the Web as well as some certification and career issues, let's take a look at some of the books available from Wrox Press that should also help you to realize the direction you would like to take the skills you have gained from this book you are reading right now. Just as you have turned to Wrox Press to provide you with this introduction to J2EE, you can also turn to Wrox Press to provide you with some of the deeper elements of this technology.

The following listing of books is far from exhaustive; there are many other books that are available, and that will continue to be written, as the J2EE platform continues to evolve and expand its role in the development world. These books are representative of those that you will find useful, even essential, in your preparation to develop J2EE applications.

Take note that in each listing is a description, not only of the book itself, but also of a sample chapter that you can download by following the supplied URL. This will allow you to determine if the material within the book fits your current development needs.

Professional Java Server Programming J2EE 1.3 Edition

ISBN: 1-86100-537-7
Published: September, 2001
URL: http://www.wrox.com/books/1861005377.htm

Description

For developers working with J2EE, *Professional Java Server Programming, J2EE 1.3 Edition* is one of the most significant resources on the market. Even though we're now working with J2EE 1.4, the release of the 1.3 version helped J2EE to evolve into a more mature and sophisticated platform. This was the release that gave servlets events and filtering, that introduced a new XML syntax and custom tag enhancements to JSPs, and that significantly changed the CMP (container-managed persistence) model for EJBs. All of these enhancements carry on into the J2EE 1.4 version. *Professional Java Server Programming, J2EE 1.3 Edition* offers the professional approach to designing and building secure and scaleable n-tier J2EE applications.

Audience

Professional Java Server Programming, J2EE 1.3 Edition is a natural next step for Java programmers who are seeking to add to their basic knowledge of server-side Java technologies, and learn in greater depth about networking and web programming.

Sample Chapter

The sample chapter is Chapter 20, titled *The J2EE Connector Architecture*. This is an introduction to the J2EE Connector Architecture (JCA), which was a significant addition to the platform in version 1.3. The chapter looks at the JCA and how to develop J2EE Connector components that allow J2EE applications to integrate and interact with backend EIS (Enterprise Information Systems) resources.

Professional J2EE EAI

ISBN: 1-86100-544-X
Published: December, 2001
URL: http://www.wrox.com/books/186100544X.htm

Description

One of the key advantages of J2EE applications is their capability of integrating with different domains, architectures, and technologies, using Enterprise Application Integration (EAI). *Professional J2EE EAI* tells you how to create an integrated information infrastructure, using a variety of technologies, including XML, EJBs, CORBA, RMI-IIOP, and so on.

Audience

If you need to create integrated information systems, you should read *Professional J2EE EAI*. And now that you have covered the basics in this book, you have the background knowledge needed to grasp the methodology and process outlined in *Professional J2EE EAI*.

Sample Chapter

The chapter available on the URL above is Chapter 2, *Choices and Strategies*, and it reviews the general guidelines relating to the most important choices and strategies that we must be aware of before starting an integration project. It discusses how different types of integration may be relevant to different systems.

Expert One-on-One: J2EE Design and Development

ISBN: 1-86100-784-1
Published: October, 2002
URL: http://www.wrox.com/books/1861007841.htm

Description

This book offers a practical approach to using J2EE to make your applications simpler, not more complex. It will also show you how to solve some of the more common problems developers encounter with J2EE, and to avoid some of the expensive and time-consuming mistakes often made in J2EE projects.

Audience

If you are involved in any way in developing enterprise projects, you can benefit from reading *Expert One-on-One: J2EE Design and Development*, although some sections are primarily for architects and lead developers. You should have no difficulty building and understanding the sample application in the book, although you might want to refer to this book to help you get through some of the more involved sections.

Sample Chapter

The chapter provided at the above URL for this book is on *J2EE Architecture*, Chapter 1 from the book. It discusses the high-level choices in developing a J2EE architecture, and how to decide which part of J2EE to use to solve real problems.

J2EE Design Patterns Applied

ISBN: 1-86100-528-8
Published: June, 2002
URL: http://www.wrox.com/books/1861005288.htm

Description

This book is a guide to using patterns to create scaleable and secure J2EE applications. The focus of the book is on solving problems with patterns, and on creating strategies for implementing and deploying patterns within applications. You will learn how patterns can be applied to build a robust and manageable web tier, how patterns can be employed to improve your application's scaleability and performance, and how using patterns can help enable enterprise integration, among many other things.

Audience

Now that you are familiar with the J2EE platform, you can read *J2EE Design Patterns Applied* to learn how to exploit the power of patterns in your J2EE applications.

Sample Chapter

The chapter available for download from the above URL is Chapter 3, *Patterns Applied to a Persistence Framework*. It focuses on developing an application's data tier using a combination of common data-persistence design patterns and J2EE technologies. It defines persistence frameworks and outlines the design patterns that can be used to implement them, as well as what strategies to consider when building them.

Professional Java Servlets 2.3

ISBN: 1-86100-561-X
Published: January, 2002
URL: http://www.wrox.com/books/186100561X.htm

Description

Although Professional Java Servlet 2.3 deals with the Java Servlet 2.3 API that is part of the J2EE 1.3 version, it offers valuable information for developers seeking to incorporate servlets into their enterprise solutions. It addresses such key issues as security, scaleability and performance, and design. It also offers many example applications to show servlets in action.

Audience

If you want to apply your J2EE skills by developing real-world web components, you will find *Professional Java Servlets 2.3* an invaluable resource. You already should have the basic Java technology skills needed to launch into *Professional Java Servlets 2.3*; some XML experience would be helpful, but is not necessary.

Sample Chapter

The sample chapter available for this book is Chapter 5 *Session Handling*. It discusses the various methods for maintaining sessions, such as rewriting URLs, creating cookies and using hidden form fields, and how to use these mechanisms to help maintain state between requests in our web applications. It also shows how to use interfaces and classes from the Java Servlet API to create, destroy, and manipulate Java objects that can be used to create classes that listen for changes to the `Session` object.

Professional JSP Tag Libraries

ISBN: 1-86100-621-7
Published: April, 2002
URL: http://www.wrox.com/books/1861006217.htm

Description

The real power behind JSPs lies in the use of tag libraries. Tag libraries not only allow a clean separation between logic and presentation within web developments, but also promote reusability of web components. *Professional JSP Tag Libraries* will teach you how to create usable, maintainable, and flexible tags that will enable you to maximize the reusability of your code. This book covers all aspects of tag development, including design and best practices, as well as when it is best to use tags and when to use JavaBeans, and ways to replace scriptlets with tags.

Audience

If you are (or want to be) a web developer creating powerful and maintainable JSP applications, you will benefit from reading *Professional JSP Tag Libraries*. You should have a basic grasp of JSPs, some knowledge of sessions, and know how to use JavaBeans in pages in order to get the most out of this book.

Sample Chapter

A chapter on *Body Tags* is available at the above URL. This chapter looks at the `BodyTag` interface that can be implemented by custom tag handlers. We will see how it extends the functionality available over tags that implement the `IterationTag` interface. The chapter also shows why we would want to implement a tag with the `BodyTag` interface when the `IterationTag` interface would do, and it also introduces new methods that are part of the `BodyTag`'s lifecycle.

Professional Java Web Services

ISBN: 1-86100-375-7
Published: January, 2002
URL: http://www.wrox.com/books/1861003757.htm

Description

The Java world, through J2EE, offers a system for distributed, highly scaleable, and maintainable enterprise systems. In order to implement cross-application communication, all you need to do is add a web services layer, as you have already seen in the book. *Professional Java Web Services* explains the important technologies and specifications behind web services, including SOAP, WSDL, and UDDI. It also outlines the architecture of web services and explains how they can be used to enable existing J2EE applications.

Audience

If you need to gain a good grasp of web services, *Professional Java Web Services* will set you in the right direction. Make sure you have a fairly good grasp of both Java and XML before tackling it, though.

Sample Chapter

The sample chapter available to look at for this book is on Apache SOAP 2.2. This chapter takes a look at both the history and the future of the Apache SOAP project, explains how to install Apache SOAP, and how to develop a SOAP service and deploy it onto the Apache SOAP runtime environment. It also works through a sample application to show how it's done.

Professional Web Services Security

ISBN: 1-86100-765-5
Published: December, 2002
URL: http://www.wrox.com/books/1861007655.htm

Description

As web services move towards occupying an important role in the e-commerce world, it is becoming increasingly critical that web services meet the security requirements for e-business. This book tells you all about the evolving standards, concepts, and challenges in web services security, and how to implement web service applications that meet those standards.

Audience

If you are going to be working with web services, you will also need to know how to make them secure, so you will need the information contained within this book.

Sample Chapter

The sample chapter provided online for this book is on P3P (Platform for Privacy Preferences), which is a project of the World Wide Consortium (W3C). P3P provides a standard way for Web sites to encode their privacy policies in a format that can be retrieved and interpreted. Its goals are to meet the privacy expectations of consumers while allowing electronic commerce to operate. The chapter looks into the P3P specifications, how P3P works, how to deploy it on your web site, and what tools are available to use with it.

Professional Apache Tomcat

ISBN: 1-86100-773-6
Published: September, 2002
URL: http://www.wrox.com/books/1861007736.htm

Description

As we have already seen in this book, Tomcat is an open source web server that processes JavaServer Pages and Java servlets. Although, as we have noticed, the core Tomcat program is relatively simple, there are many enhancements that can be added to make the Tomcat package much more complex. In *Professional Apache Tomcat*, you will learn how to integrate Tomcat with the Apache HTTP server, how to set up database connectivity through JDBC, and how to make sure your web applications are secure. You will also learn some of the tools that can be integrated with Tomcat, such as Ant, for automatically building web applications, and Log4J, for advanced logging.

Audience

If you will be working with Java web applications, especially in any form of administrator role, *Professional Apache Tomcat* will be invaluable. It does, however, assume you know something about databases, XML, HTML, and networking principles.

Sample Chapter

The chapter available at the above URL is Chapter 7, on *Manager Configuration*. It examines the management tools available with Tomcat, which are tools that allow administrators to deploy web applications, to view deployed applications, and finally, to undeploy them.

APPENDIX A

Getting Tomcat   **655**

Binary Installation to Windows   **656**

Binary Installation to Linux/Unix   **657**

Source Installation   **658**

Running Tomcat   **658**

Installing Tomcat

Although you can use the J2EE 1.4 server for all the examples in this book, there is another server you can use for the examples in the JSP and servlet chapters. To be correct, this other server is actually the same one used by the J2EE server for JSPs and servlets, but you can install it in a standalone mode so that you can run JSPs and servlets without a running a full J2EE server. This server is named Tomcat, and when running in this mode, it is referred to as **Tomcat standalone**.

Getting Tomcat

Tomcat is a part of the Apache Jakarta Project. Copies of Tomcat can be obtained from the Apache web site at http://jakarta.apache.org/tomcat/index.html.

For most of the JSP and servlet examples, you will be able to use either of two versions of Tomcat. At the time this was written, the stable version of Tomcat was version 4.1.18. The alpha version was version 5.0. Which version of Tomcat you use depends on which features you need. Most of the JSP and servlet examples are based on the Servlet Specification 2.3 and JSP Specification 1.2; for these examples, you can use Tomcat 4.0 or any later version. However, a few of the JSP examples use features specified by the JSP Specification Version 2.0. For these examples, you must use Tomcat 5.0 or later. This is summarized below:

Servlet version	JSP version	Tomcat version
2.3	1.2	4.0 or later
2.4	2.0	5.0 or later

After deciding which version you want, follow the links on the Tomcat web page to the directory that contains the Tomcat binaries. For Tomcat 4.1, this means clicking the **Binaries** link under **Downloads** on the left of the main Tomcat page, and then clicking the link for Tomcat 4.1.xx, where xx is the current stable version number. You can also try going directly to the download directory using http://jakarta.apache.org/builds/jakarta-tomcat-4.0/release/.

Since Tomcat 5.0 was an alpha version when this was written, there was no direct link to the download files, however the files could be found at http://jakarta.apache.org/builds/jakarta-tomcat/nightly-5/.

It is, of course, possible that these locations might be changed by the time you read this. If so, you can still access the download directories using the links on the Apache Jakarta web site, and then navigate through the various download directories as needed.

If you are installing to Windows, you should download either the `.exe` or `.zip` files for the version you want. If you are installing to Linux you can download an `.rpm` file, a `.tar.gz`, or a `.zip` file. Other Unix versions will use the `.tar.gz` file. Finally, for any platform, you can download the full source of Tomcat and compile it yourself.

Also, note that you will need a version of Java 2 for Tomcat. The Tomcat web page recommends using Java 2 version 1.4 JDK. Check the Tomcat web page for the requirements for using earlier versions of the JDK. Ensure you have an environment variable named `JAVA_HOME` that points to your JDK installation on your machine.

Binary Installation to Windows

The simplest installation for Windows is to download the `.exe` distribution. This is an installation program that handles all of the installation tasks for you. Simply double-click the `.exe`, and the installer will run. The installer runs as a wizard, and for the most part you can simply accept the default options at each step. The installer will extract and copy all the files to their correct locations, and configure the environment variables for you. It will also create **Start** menu shortcuts for starting and stopping the server.

If you downloaded the zipped distribution file, start by extracting the files in the `.zip` archive to a directory. One good choice would be to unzip the files using the default directory name, `jakarta-tomcat-4.1.xx`, into the same location as your Java Standard and Enterprise development kit directories. For example, you might have the following directory structure in the root of your `C:` drive:

After unzipping the files, you will need to set the environment variables yourself. You need to create an environment variable named CATALINA_HOME which will point to the location of Tomcat. For example, if you installed Tomcat to the default directory as suggested, you would set CATALINA_HOME to C:\jakarta-tomcat-4.1.18. In Win 9x and WinME, you will do this through the autoexec.bat file. For WinNT and Win2000 this is done on the **System** dialog, which you can access via **Start | Settings | Control Panel** and choosing the **System** option. Then, select the **Advanced** tab, and click the **Environment Variables** button. Installing Tomcat this way does not create **Start** menu shortcuts, but you can access the startup.bat and shutdown.bat files for starting and stopping the server in the Tomcat /bin directory.

One other thing you need to do for Win 9x and WinME is to ensure there is enough environment memory. Navigate to the Tomcat /bin directory and right-click the startup.bat and shutdown.bat files, select **Properties**, then select the **Memory** tab, and finally, set the **Initial Environment** to 4096.

Binary Installation to Linux/Unix

If you downloaded the .tar.gz or .zip distribution file, start by creating a directory for the installation and extracting the files to that directory.

If you are using an RPM for Linux, create an installation directory and copy the RPM to that directory. The RPM can be installed using the rpm program with the name of the .rpm file. For example, to install Tomcat 4.1.18, the command would be

```
> rpm -iv tomcat4-4.1.18-full.1jpp.noarch.rpm
```

After installing the files, you will need to set an environment variable. The variable is named CATALINA_HOME and it will point to the location of Tomcat. For example, if you installed Tomcat to /usr/local/tomcat you would set the variable with this command in the bash shell:

```
> CATALINA_HOME=/usr/local/tomcat
> export CATALINA_HOME
```

If you are using a different shell, use the command that is appropriate for that shell. The scripts for starting and stopping the server are in the Tomcat /bin directory.

Source Installation

You can install and compile the source files of Tomcat if you are so inclined. However, this is not really necessary if all you want to do is use Tomcat as a server for JSPs and servlets. Since this book is about developing web applications, and not developing servers, we will not cover the steps in building a Tomcat server from sources. If you would like to explore this option, there are detailed instructions at http://jakarta.apache.org/tomcat/building.html.

Running Tomcat

After installing Tomcat, start the server using the start menu, batch file, or script file for your system. When the server is running, you can open a browser to the Tomcat web page at http://localhost:8080. If the Tomcat installation is successful, you should see a web page like this:

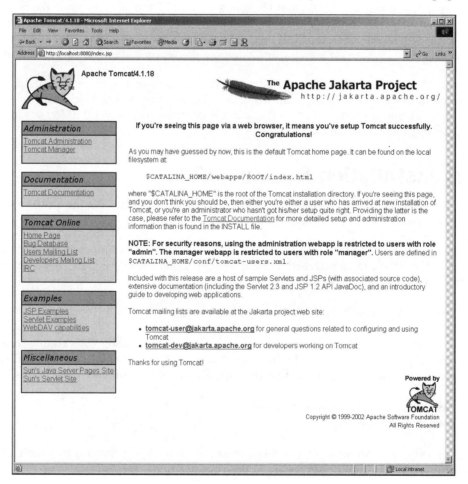

For the most part, if you follow these directions, you should have no problems installing Tomcat. If you do encounter any problems though, check your Java installation and ensure that the JAVA_HOME and CATALINA_HOME environment variables are set. If you are using Win 9x or WinME, ensure the environment memory space is set correctly as explained earlier. If that doesn't help, check the Tomcat web page at http://jakarta.apache.org/tomcat/index.html for documentation on installing and running Tomcat. This document contains additional troubleshooting steps that may help.

APPENDIX B

SQL   661

EJB QL   677

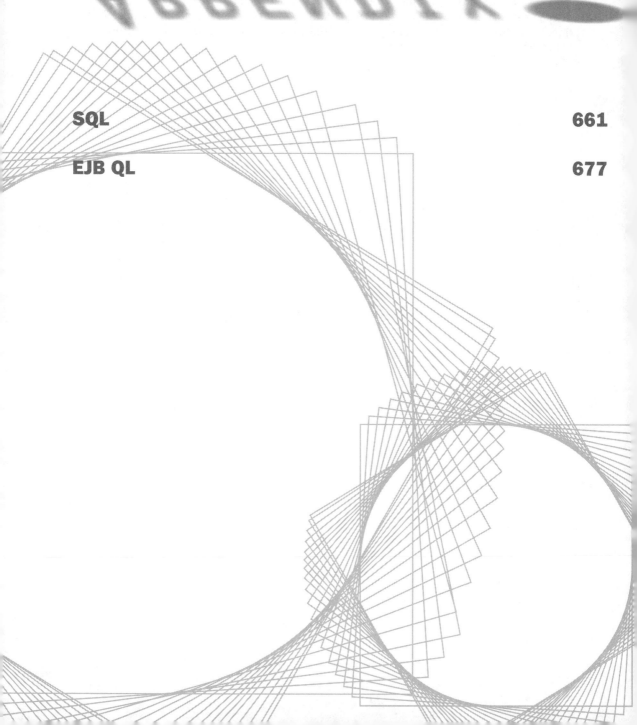

SQL and EJB QL

The **Structured Query Language**, **SQL**, and the **Enterprise JavaBeans Query Language**, **EJB QL**, are two techniques for accessing data that can be used in J2EE 1.4 programming. They are briefly introduced and summarized in this appendix.

SQL is relevant to data access techniques using JDBC, which was first introduced in Chapter 6, where we looked at several examples of how SQL code should be incorporated in your Java code. EJB QL provides an alternative data access methodology specific to Enterprise JavaBeans, which were covered in Chapters 8 to 11, and more specifically entity EJBs, which were described in Chapter 9.

SQL

SQL, the Structured Query Language, is a standardized query language for retrieving or updating data held in a relational database management system. At the time of writing, the current version of SQL is SQL99, sometimes referred to as SQL3.

> *SQL is a topic that merits a book to itself. This appendix covers selected topics only. For a full introduction to SQL see Instant SQL, by Wrox Press, ISBN: 1-86100-845-7.*

Many database management systems had proprietary methods of data retrieval and manipulation before SQL was disseminated, so database vendors provide somewhat variable support for SQL99. However, all the big name databases provide significant SQL99 support. It is important, nonetheless, that you check which aspects of SQL99 are supported by the database management system that you plan to use.

RDBMS products differ in how they handle *case*. Some products are case sensitive, for example in table names, whereas others are not. If there is any likelihood of you, or your client, wanting to transfer data to another product at a future date, it is a good idea to have a consistent naming scheme for tables, columns, and so on, in order that you don't end up with differing case in names in different parts of your code. That can cause problems, and much wasted time, when you switch products.

Similarly it is a good idea to adopt consistent use of case when writing SQL code. One convention, which you may recall from Chapter 6, is to use upper case for all SQL commands and lower case for table and column names. This style will be used in the code in this appendix. In addition, each clause of a SQL statement is expressed on a separate line, making the SQL code easier to read.

In practice, when working for a client, you will likely need to adopt the case convention in existing databases and code. When moving code from a non-case-sensitive RDBMS to a case-sensitive RDBMS be aware that code such as:

```
SELECT * FROM presidents
```

and:

```
SELECT * FROM Presidents
```

which will work identically in a non-case-sensitive RDBMS may cause difficult-to-diagnose problems in a case-sensitive RDBMS, depending on whether the table is named `presidents` or `Presidents`.

To understand the SQL approach to an RDBMS, we need to understand the objects and relationships that, conceptually, make up an RDBMS. A relational database provides a logical framework to allow the storage of pieces of data and the relational model includes a hierarchy of objects listed here:

❑ Clusters

❑ Catalogs

❑ Schemas

❑ Objects

❑ Columns

❑ Domain-defined data types and user-defined data types

❑ Rules and assertions

A **cluster**, as described in the SQL99 specification, broadly corresponds to an RDBMS product and is a named set of **catalogs** available in a SQL session. The SQL99 specification indicates that access permissions may be controlled at the cluster level, but some database vendors implement permissions only at the catalog level, which is described next, and at lower levels of the hierarchy.

A **catalog** is a uniquely named set of schemas. Some database products, for example Microsoft's SQL Server and Oracle, use the term **instance** to broadly correspond to a SQL99 catalog.

A **schema** is a uniquely named set of objects and data owned by an individual user.

Most usage of SQL takes place at the **object** level and below. Objects include tables, views, modules, and routines (such as stored procedures, which are used in Chapter 9).

SQL objects consist of one or, usually, more **columns**. A typical database table will consist of several columns, each of which contains, for each row, a piece of data of a particular **data type**. Data types may be domain-defined, which are standard SQL-recognized data types, or may be defined by a user, which are **user-defined data types**. Each piece of data in a column must comply with the constraints on its possible values imposed by the specified data type. Data types vary among vendors, but usually you will easily be able to identify a data type in any RDBMS, which corresponds to a SQL99 data type.

In the sections in this appendix, we will look primarily at how to use SQL to work with table objects, and to execute queries that select data from one or more columns in one or more tables. First, let's briefly look at the data types that are recognized in SQL99.

SQL Data Types

SQL data types are essentially **constraints** on the types of data that may be stored in a column and on *how* that data is actually stored in the RDBMS.

Careful consideration of what data types are appropriate is an important part of the analysis and design of a new database.

As with many aspects of RDBMS, the use of data types varies among RDBMS packages. Check the documentation to determine the precise rules.

String Data Types

String data is one of the most commonly used data types.

String data of fixed length is specified using the CHAR keyword. For example, to declare the last_name column as accepting text of exactly 20 characters in length we could write:

```
last_name CHAR(20)
```

Such declarations are used when creating columns for tables, as described in the next section. A CHAR declaration commonly is padded with spaces to the stated number of characters if the user-supplied string is shorter.

Commonly, a character string is declared to be of **variable length**. For example, to declare the last_name column as being a variable-length string up to 20 characters in length we could write:

```
last_name VARCHAR(20)
```

Some database packages use LONG, TEXT, or MEMO in place of VARCHAR. A VARCHAR is stored more efficiently than a CHAR in terms of disk space, but performance during sorts of VARCHAR data is likely to be slower. Some database systems don't allow indexes to be created on VARCHAR data types, which further impacts performance.

In addition, the NCHAR and NVARCHAR data types support multi-byte or Unicode characters.

All string data types, when referred to in SQL code, must be surrounded by paired apostrophes.

Numeric Data types

At the risk of stating the obvious, numeric data types store numbers. Think carefully about the likely extreme values that may need to be stored when deciding among the list of data types listed here:

Data type	Description
BIT	Single bit value, which can be 0 or 1
DECIMAL	Floating-point values with specified level of precision
FLOAT	Floating-point values
INT	4-byte integer value
REAL	4-byte floating-point value
SMALLINT	2-byte integer value
TINYINT	1-byte integer value

Check your RDBMS documentation to confirm which data types it supports.

In addition, many RDBMS store a MONEY or CURRENCY data type.

Date and Time Data Types

Date and time data types vary between RDBMS. Likely types include DATE, DATETIME, and SMALLDATETIME.

Binary Data Types

Binary data types can be used to store data such as graphic images. Support may include BINARY, LONG RAW, RAW, and VARBINARY data types. Again, it's a good idea to check the documentation of your RDBMS to confirm allowable byte length.

Working with Tables

Creating and manipulating tables is a relatively infrequent but essential use of SQL, since typically a table will be created once and then used with unchanged structure over extended periods of time. Changes to table structure, assuming that the database design has been well thought out, will be rare.

Creating a Table

In SQL a table is created using the CREATE TABLE statement. The general format for a simple CREATE TABLE statement is:

```
CREATE TABLE tablename
(
  columnDefinitions
);
```

If we wanted to create a table called presidents with four columns, last_name, first_name, birth_date and gender, we would use code like this:

```
CREATE TABLE presidents
(
    last_name VARCHAR(20) NOT NULL,
    first_name VARCHAR(20) NOT NULL,
    birth_date DATETIME NOT NULL,
    gender VARCHAR(6)
);
```

The CREATE TABLE statement causes an RDBMS to create a new table. The code in parentheses defines the columns to be created in that table. For each column, we declare the column name (note the use of all lower case), its data type, and permitted number of characters, and then specify, for example, whether or not it is allowed to contain NULL values.

Specifying Default Values

In some circumstances, you may find it useful to specify a default value for a column. In our presidents table we might want to acknowledge the historical situation and allow for future possibilities by including a gender column in the presidents table, with a default value of Male. We could do that using code like the following:

```
CREATE TABLE presidents
(
    last_name VARCHAR(20) NOT NULL,
    first_name VARCHAR(20) NOT NULL,
    birth_date DATETIME NOT NULL,
    gender VARCHAR(6)DEFAULT 'Male'
);
```

A default value can also be specified for columns that are marked as not accepting NULL values:

```
gender VARCHAR(6) NOT NULL DEFAULT 'Male'
```

Updating the Structure of a Table

If we have designed our tables with enough careful thought, the need to alter the structure of a table should be an infrequent one. However, SQL provides an ALTER TABLE statement for such situations. If we wanted to add a death_date column to our presidents table, we could do so using the following code:

```
ALTER TABLE presidents
ADD death_date DATETIME
;
```

Be aware that RDBMS products differ significantly in what alterations in structure they will allow. To avoid difficulties at a later date, it is good practice to take more care when designing the table structure when the data store is created.

Similarly, if you had created a column for death_date, and later decided you wanted to delete it, then you could remove it using the following code:

```
ALTER TABLE presidents
DROP COLUMN death_date;
```

Deleting a column is not something you will do often, nor is it something to do lightly. If you don't have a backup then once you drop the column, it and all of its data is gone forever! So be careful...

If you feel that you really want to carry out substantial restructuring of a table, it may be more appropriate to create a new table and use the INSERT SELECT statement (not described in detail in this appendix) to copy data from the existing table, verify that the desired data has copied, rename the original table and then rename the new table to the name of the original table. You can expect to need to recreate any stored procedures, indexes, and so on.

Deleting Tables

Deleting or dropping a table is also not something to be done lightly. The SQL syntax to drop our presidents table would look like this:

```
DROP TABLE presidents;
```

When you execute this statement, you probably won't see any confirmation dialogs, nor is there any way to undo the statement. Executing this statement will permanently remove the table and all of its data.

Handling Null Values

In a relational database, a value in a particular field (the intersection of a row and column) may contain a NULL value. A NULL value signifies an absent or unknown value. A NULL is *not* the same as an empty string, a sequence of space characters, or a value containing numeric zero.

When a column is created it can be specified as allowing or disallowing NULL values. In a table called presidents, we might want to specify that the death_date column is allowed to contain a NULL value (the default situation), since not all US presidents will have died at any selected time. On the other hand, we would likely want to specify that a last_name column and a first_name column are not allowed to contain NULL values (they should always contain data for each row in the database). We could achieve both desired constraints using the following code:

```
CREATE TABLE presidents
(
   last_name VARCHAR(20) NOT NULL,
   first_name VARCHAR(20) NOT NULL,
   birth_date DATETIME NOT NULL,
   death_date DATETIME
);
```

Let's move on to examine how we can use SQL to query existing tables and, later, to update data contained in such tables.

Selecting Data from Tables

Querying data in an existing table is likely to be the most common SQL task that you will carry out. Such SQL queries are based on the SELECT statement.

The simplest form of the SELECT statement is shown here:

```
SELECT * FROM presidents;
```

This selects all columns from the presidents table, as indicated by the * wildcard. Since there is no WHERE clause, all rows contained in the presidents table are retrieved.

If, as is more usual, you wish to retrieve selected columns from the presidents table, you use what is known as a *projection*. You simply replace the * wildcard by a comma-separated list of the columns you want to retrieve. Specifying selected columns is also likely to be a more efficient query than using the * wildcard. If you wanted to retrieve the last_name and first_name columns of the presidents table, you could do so using the following code:

```
SELECT last_name, first_name FROM presidents;
```

Filtering Data in Queries

In practice, it is unlikely that you will want to retrieve all rows from a table. In SQL, you can filter out unwanted rows by specifying those rows you do want to see using a WHERE clause in conjunction with a SELECT statement. For example, if we wanted to retrieve the rows that contained data concerning presidents Theodore Roosevelt and Franklin Roosevelt, we could use the following SQL:

```
SELECT * FROM presidents
WHERE last_name='Roosevelt'
;
```

The * wildcard signifies that all columns are retrieved from each row of the presidents table. The WHERE clause filters the results so that only those rows containing the value Roosevelt in the last_name column are retrieved.

The WHERE clause can use a number of operators in filtering data in addition to the = operator used in the preceding example. The following table shows the operators which can be used in a WHERE clause:

Operator	Description
=	Exact equality
<>	Inequality
!=	Inequality
<	Less than
<=	Less than or equal to
!<	Not less than
>	Greater than
>=	Greater than or equal to
!>	Not greater than
BETWEEN	Between two stated values (inclusive)
IS NULL	A NULL value

You will most probably have noticed that there is some duplication in the available operators. For example, we can use the ! > or <= operators to signify that values less than or equal to a specified value are to be included. As you may have guessed, this is another area where vendors may differ in which SQL syntax they support. Again, you will want to check the RDBMS documentation carefully.

If you wanted to select information about all US presidents except the two presidents Roosevelt you could use the following code:

```
SELECT last_name, first_name
FROM presidents
WHERE last_name <> 'Roosevelt'
;
```

Since the content of the last_name column is character data, we need to use paired apostrophes to delimit the value used in the WHERE clause. If the string value itself contains an apostrophe, then that will need to be escaped. The escape character varies between RDBMSs – in SQL Server the apostrophe is used while in Oracle the backslash is used.

Similarly, if you wanted to retrieve information about presidents whose birth year was between 1800 and 1900 inclusive, you could use code like the following:

```
SELECT last_name, first_name
FROM presidents
WHERE birth_year BETWEEN 1800 AND 1900
;
```

In this case, the value contained in the birth_year column is numeric so no delimiters are need for the values to which the BETWEEN operator is applied. Notice the AND keyword which is used in a WHERE clause of this type.

Sorting Data from Queries

Rows of data retrieved by an SQL query cannot be assumed to be in any particular order. If you want to sort the rows of data in a particular way you must specify the criteria for ordering the data by using an ORDER BY clause in conjunction with a SELECT statement.

If we wanted to select all columns of information about all US presidents from the presidents table and order them by last name we could do so using the following code:

```
SELECT * FROM presidents
ORDER BY last_name
```

The ORDER BY clause can be used together with the WHERE clause. For example, if the year of appointment was stored in an appointment_year column, we could display the surname and first name with the year of appointment of all US presidents whose surname begins with the letter R or later using the following:

```
SELECT last_name, first_name, appointment_year FROM presidents
WHERE last_name>'R'
ORDER BY appointment_year;
```

If we want to sort the rows returned by a query by more than one criterion, we can do so by combining the two columns in the order needed. In this example, the rows are ordered alphabetically by `last_name` and then by the `first_name`:

```
SELECT last_name, first_name
FROM presidents
ORDER BY last_name, first_name;
```

Where there is more than one US president with the same last name (Adams, Roosevelt, Bush) the ordering would be strictly alphabetical.

Wildcards and Regular Expressions

In addition to using the comparison operators described earlier, SQL provides facilities to allow you to retrieve data based on text *patterns*, similar to the pattern matching you can carry out using the regular expression support in Java.

The `LIKE` keyword allows text pattern searches. The `%` pattern matches zero or more text characters. So, to retrieve data from the `presidents` table about presidents whose last name begins with the letter B you could use the following code:

```
SELECT last_name, first_name
FROM presidents
WHERE last_name LIKE 'B%'
;
```

Notice that the text pattern is contained in paired apostrophes. The pattern `B%` matches any text string which begins with the upper case B, and that contains zero or more other characters. Therefore when that pattern is used to match the `last_name` column, which contains presidential surnames, data on all presidents whose surname begins with B is retrieved.

If we wished not to retrieve data on President Buchanan, but only on those whose surname begins with the characters "Bus", we could refine the search like this:

```
SELECT last_name, first_name
FROM presidents
WHERE last_name LIKE 'Bus%'
;
```

Data on both presidents Bush would be retrieved.

The underscore character, _, can also be used in text patterns and matches exactly one character. So, if we used a pattern like that in the following code:

```
SELECT last_name, first_name
FROM presidents
WHERE last_name LIKE 'Bu__'
;
```

We would retrieve the surname Bush. If the USA had had a president John Bull, then data on that fictional president would also be retrieved, since the pattern Bu__ matches any string that is exactly four characters long and begins with the characters Bu.

If you plan to use the LIKE keyword, then be aware that support for this keyword depends on the RDBMS package you use.

Some database management systems also explore fuller regular expression syntax, sometimes associated with the LIKE keyword, and sometimes, for example MySQL, using the REGEXP keyword.

If we wanted to retrieve data from a MySQL database on presidents whose surname begins with the letters K or R we could use the following SQL code:

```
SELECT last_name, first_name
FROM presidents
WHERE last_name REGEXP "^[KR]."
;
```

Notice the REGEXP keyword, and that the text pattern is, in MySQL at least, contained in paired double quotes. The ^ character at the beginning of the pattern indicates that the text pattern matches the beginning of the data and the square brackets indicate a **character class**. Any character in the character class that occurs at the beginning of the data in the column will match. The . metacharacter serves a similar function to the % character with the LIKE keyword. Regular expression support in your favorite database management system may not have the functionality that MySQL supports, or may use different metacharacters inside text patterns.

Calculated Fields

Many pieces of data are reported exactly as they are held in the data store. However, sometimes you will want to retrieve data that combines data from more than one column. SQL provides **calculated fields** to achieve that functionality. Calculated fields can be created by combining string or numeric values.

A **field** often means the same as a column, and does so in this case. Occasionally, in discussions of databases, you may meet the term field used to refer to the intersection of a particular row and column. That is not the usage in the term "calculated field".

For example, you might hold address data in separate columns but want to display a city, regional code, and postal code together in an address. SQL code to achieve that might look like the following:

```
SELECT city+ ', ' + regional_code + ', ' + postal_code
FROM address
;
```

The + operator in the `SELECT` statement concatenates the string values contained in the `city`, `regional_code`, and `postal_code` columns. Depending on the data type used to create the `city`, `regional_code`, and `postal_code` columns you may have to trim out space characters contained as padding in the named columns, using the SQL `RTRIM()` function:

```
SELECT RTRIM(city)+ ', ' + RTRIM(regional_code) + ', ' + RTRIM(postal_code)
FROM address
;
```

If you declared the columns to be of type `VARCHAR`, then there will be no padding space characters and the `RTRIM()` function will be unnecessary.

Calculated fields also allow us to perform simple mathematical calculations to produce calculated fields.

For example, you may want to display a product catalog with item price, tax rate, and tax rate information. In that case, you would want to use an **alias** for the calculated field. So, to fill the tax rate field we could use code like this:

```
SELECT product_name, product_code,
item_price, tax_rate,
item_price * tax_rate AS taxed_price
FROM product_catalog
WHERE status = 'current'
;
```

Notice the `AS` keyword in the `SELECT` clause. In the third line of the SQL code, the value of the `item_price` and `tax_rate` columns are multiplied together to produce a calculated field with the **alias** of `taxed_price`.

Most database management systems will support standard mathematical operations of addition, subtraction, multiplication, and division using the standard mathematical operators, +, -, *, and /. Of course, Java provides the syntax to carry out these and more complex calculations. The choice of whether you use SQL or Java to achieve any desired calculations will depend on your level of comfort with the two languages, as well as other factors.

SQL Functions

A number of functions can be used in SQL to manipulate character, numeric, or date/time data. In an earlier example, you saw the `RTRIM()` function, which can be used to remove padding space characters from character data columns of fixed width.

SQL functions can be used to extract part of a string (that is, a substring), to convert data types, return a number's ceiling, retrieve the current date, and so on. Unfortunately, the implementation and syntax of SQL functions varies greatly among database packages. If you are familiar with the corresponding Java functions, as you are likely to be if you are reading this book, it may well be more convenient to ignore the SQL functions in many situations where you are using JDBC. If you do decide to use SQL functions then be sure to carefully consult the documentation for the database management system in order to determine the appropriate syntax.

In practice, if you want your JDBC code to be portable, it is highly advisable to use the Java functions rather than the SQL functions. One exception to that general advice is SQL's aggregate functions, which are pretty uniformly supported by popular database management systems:

- ❏   AVG() – Returns the arithmetic mean value of a column

- ❏   COUNT() – Returns the number of rows which contain a value in a named column

- ❏   MAX() – Returns the largest value in a column

- ❏   MIN() – Returns the smallest value in a column

- ❏   SUM() – Returns the sum of the values in a named column

These SQL aggregate functions avoid the need to retrieve, perhaps across a slow network, all rows in a table and perform the corresponding calculations in Java. The retrieval and calculation of data is likely to be much more efficiently carried out by the database management system.

If you wanted to find the highest priced product in a product catalog you might use code like the following:

```
SELECT MAX(product_price)
FROM product_catalog
WHERE status = 'current'
;
```

Many other retrieval techniques are possible in SQL but those mentioned in the preceding sections will give you a start in how to use SQL syntax.

Inserting New Rows into a Table

As well as retrieving data, SQL can be used to insert new values in a database.

The most straightforward technique to insert data into a table is to insert a complete new row. This is done using the INSERT statement.

For example, in late 2000, we might have needed to add information about the election of the second president Bush. If the row contained data in last_name, first_name, and election_year columns, we add the information using code like the following:

```
INSERT INTO presidents
(last_name, first_name, election_year)
VALUES ('Bush', 'George', 2000)
;
```

If we also wanted to store a middle name but weren't (at the time) aware of the newly elected president's middle name we would need, to avoid ambiguity, to use an explicit NULL value, and we could do that using the following code:

```
INSERT INTO presidents
(last_name, first_name, middle_name, election_year)
VALUES ('Bush', 'George', NULL, 2000)
;
```

In the two preceding examples, each column was named. If you are totally confident of the ordering of column names, you can omit the column names, using code like the following:

```
INSERT INTO presidents
VALUES ('Bush', 'George', NULL, 2000)
;
```

Of course, if you make even a slight error in the ordering of column data then an error will be generated unless all columns happen to have compatible data types. Omitting column names increases the likelihood of data values being swapped around.

If we need to correct a mistake in an existing row we need to use a different technique using the UPDATE statement.

Updating Data in Tables

When you use UPDATE statements, be very careful to include a WHERE clause, and also make sure that the WHERE clause is appropriately tightly defined. If you omit the WHERE clause, then every row in the chosen table will be updated in the way defined. For example:

```
UPDATE presidents
SET middle_name = 'Walker'
;
```

This code would assign the middle name "Walker" to every US president in the table, which is not what we intended to do! The existing data for middle name for all presidents, whether NULL or an actual value, would be overwritten. You have been warned! Mistakes of this type make you very glad that you have a recent backup of your valuable data. You do have a recent, full backup, don't you?

The WHERE clause is used to ensure that the UPDATE statement is appropriately applied. Thus, we could change the middle name of the president elected in 2000 using the following code:

```
UPDATE presidents
SET middle_name = 'Walker'
WHERE election_year = 2000
;
```

The preceding code makes the reasonable assumption that only one president was elected in the year 2000.

Deleting Data from a Table

We are unlikely to want to permanently delete information from our `presidents` table, because it is of historical interest. However, in an e-commerce setting, we might choose to delete information about obsolete products. To achieve that you would use the DELETE statement.

Be very, very careful not to omit the WHERE clause in a DELETE statement. Look at this example:

```
DELETE
FROM product_catalog
;
```

This code has potentially just deleted all the data in every row in your `product_catalog` table. If you don't have a very recent, usable backup, you may want to start writing your resignation letter...

Suppose we wanted to delete a product with product ID of ABC123, we could use the following code:

```
DELETE
FROM product_catalog
WHERE product_ID = 'ABC123'
;
```

The WHERE clause confines the deletion to the specified row in the table.

Joins

A **join** is the combining of results from more than one table in a query. This is a crucial technique for RDBMS systems for all but simple queries. Let's consider how this works by reviewing the basics of relationships in an RDBMS.

Relational database tables each have a primary key, which uniquely identifies each row in the table. Suppose you had several orders from one customer over a period of time. It would be inefficient and error-prone to enter customer address data into each order individually. If order data was held in an `orders` table, then the corresponding customer data would be held in a `customers` table. A mechanism is needed to express the fact that a particular customer in the `customers` table is the customer for a particular order in the `orders` table. If the `customers` table contains a `customer_id` column that is the table's primary key, then we can create a `customer_id` column in the `orders` table as a foreign key. This expresses the fact that a particular order is linked to a particular customer.

Let's assume that we want to retrieve all orders for a particular customer. We will assume that an order can be made up of only a single type of product, and that the `orders` table contains the following columns: `order_id`, `product_id`, `product_quantity`, `customer_id`, and `order_date`. To simplify, we will assume that the `customers` table consists of `customer_id`, `customer_name`, and `customer_address` columns. We can use a `SELECT` statement similar to the following:

```
SELECT order_id, product_id, product_quantity, order_date, customer_name,
       customer_address
FROM orders, customers
WHERE orders.customer_id='ABC123'
AND orders.customer_id = customers.customer_id
;
```

This will retrieve all orders for the customer who has the ID of 'ABC123'.

The `SELECT` statement is similar to several you have seen earlier in this appendix, but notice that some of the columns are in the `orders` table, and some columns (`customer_name` and `customer_address`) are in the `customers` table. This is indicated by the `FROM` clause which specifies both the `orders` and `customers` tables. We need to filter the retrieved rows, so we do that using a two part `WHERE` clause. The first part of the `WHERE` clause specifies that we want data on the customer whose `customer_id` is 'ABC123'. The second part specifies that all retrieved rows from the `customers` table must have a `customer_id` column equal to the `customer_id` column in the `orders` table. This uses notation which will be familiar to you – a `.` separates the name of the table object from the name of the column object:

```
orders.customer_id = customers.customers_id
```

So far so good, but suppose we also want to retrieve price data, which is held in a separate `prices` table. We need a join that retrieves data from three tables. The following code will achieve that:

```
SELECT order_id, product_id, product_price, product_quantity, order_date,
       customer_name, customer_address
FROM orders, customers, prices
WHERE orders.customer_id='ABC123'
```

```
AND orders.customer_id = customers.customer_id
AND orders.product_id = prices.product_id
;
```

Notice the additional AND clause:

```
AND orders.product_id = prices.product_id
```

This clause expresses our desire to retrieve only products relevant to our query.

SQL allows us to construct joins from arbitrary numbers of tables.

EJB QL

Enterprise JavaBean Query Language, EJB QL, is a relatively new method of data access, having first been introduced in the EJB version 2.0 specification. In EJB version 1.1, vendors provided their own, non-standard query language for finder methods of entity EJBs, which meant that applications that used container-managed persistence had to be partly rewritten if they were moved from one vendor's EJB container to another.

The Enterprise JavaBeans query language, EJB QL, is used to define data queries for entity EJBs in a portable way. EJB QL is specified in the EJB specification (from EJB version 2.0 on), therefore all EJB 2.x implementations must conform to that specification. In that respect, EJB QL offers better portability than SQL, which, as mentioned in the first part of this appendix, is implemented in significantly varying ways on different database management systems.

EJB QL is a query specification language for the finder and setter methods of entity EJBs. EJB QL is confined to queries against in-memory objects, and thus, differs from SQL in that EJB QL cannot be used as a general purpose query against a database. Additionally, EJB QL queries must be defined properly if container-managed persistence is to work correctly. Each EJB QL query is specified in the ejb-jar.xml file, as will be described later in this section.

An EJB QL query consists of the following:

❑   A SELECT clause which specifies the type or values of objects to be selected

❑   A FROM clause which specifies the domain (or table) from which objects are to be selected

❑   An optional WHERE clause which is used to filter the results returned by the query

❑   An optional ORDER BY clause which is used to sort the data returned by the query

If you have read through the section on SQL in this appendix, you will likely recognize the similarities of the syntax between some of the SQL you were introduced to and the syntax of EJB QL.

677

A common form of an EJB QL query is:

```
SELECT OBJECT(variable)
FROM abstractSchemaName [AS] variable
[WHERE value comparison value]
[ORDER BY ...]
```

To understand how EJB QL works, let's think briefly about what an entity bean is.

An entity bean is a representation of data stored persistently in a database table. Data in an RDBMS is held in tables, and data in those tables can have relationships expressed using primary keys and foreign keys. Since entity beans represent data stored in database tables, it shouldn't be surprising that entity beans can similarly have corresponding relationships between them.

The relationships between entity EJBs are expressed in an XML deployment descriptor file. Typically, the EJB container will use the information in the deployment descriptor to create queries in a language such as SQL, which actually queries the data store.

The deployment descriptor file contains a `<relationships>` element for each entity enterprise bean which has relationships with other entity beans. Nested inside the tags of the `<relationships>` element are further elements which express where a particular piece of data is situated in the RDBMS (the `<cmp-field>` element is used for that when persistence is container-managed) and which express relationships among entity beans (the `<cmr-field>` element performs this function when persistence is container-managed).

An EJB QL query references entity beans by their name in the appropriate abstract schema. The mapping of abstract schema names to an entity bean takes place in the `ejb-jar.xml` deployment descriptor file. Inside each `<entity>` element there will be an `<abstract-schema-name>` element that is used for that purpose:

```
<ejb-jar>
 <enterprise-beans>
  <entity>
   <ejb-name>MyPresidentsEntityBean</ejb-name>
   ...
    <abstract-schema-name>
     MyPresidentsSchema
    </abstract-schema-name>
    ....
    <query>
     <query-method>
      <method-name>findBySurname</method-name>
       <method-params>
        <method-param>java.lang.String</method-param>
       </method-params>
     </query-method>
     <ejb-ql>
```

```
          <![CDATA[SELECT OBJECT(o) FROM MyPresidentsSchema AS o WHERE o=?1]]>
        </ejb-ql>
      </query>
      ...
    </entity>
  </enterprise-beans>
  ...
</ejb-jar>
```

In addition, query methods for an EJB inside the same `<entity>` element are described using the `<query-method>`, `<method-name>`, `<method-params>`, and `<method-param>` elements. The preceding code corresponds to a finder method named `findBySurname`, which takes a single `java.lang.String` parameter.

As you have seen, the `CDATA` section in the `ejb-jar.xml` file contains the actual EJB QL query:

```
<ejb-ql>
 <![CDATA[SELECT OBJECT(p) FROM MyPresidentsSchema AS p]]>
</ejb-ql>
```

The query is nested inside `<ejb-ql>` start and end tags. The `CDATA` section indicates to an XML processor that the content need not be well-formed XML, and is not to be processed as XML.

The EJB QL query shown will return all rows from the database object that corresponds to the `MyPresidentsSchema` abstract schema.

The SELECT Clause

The `SELECT` clause may contain an **identification variable**, which requires an `OBJECT` operator. A `SELECT` clause must not use the `OBJECT` operator to qualify path expressions (discussed later).

The `SELECT` clause can be filtered using a `WHERE` clause. If we wished to retrieve data only for presidents whose surname is 'Bush' we could use the following EJB QL query:

```
SELECT OBJECT(p)
FROM MyPresidentsSchema AS p
WHERE p.last_name = 'Bush'
```

Notice that the `FROM` clause associates the identifier variable p with the abstract schema name `MyPresidentsSchema`. The abstract schema name is specified in the deployment descriptor as you saw a little earlier.

The `WHERE` clause filters the query results so that only those results which match the supplied parameter are returned to the client.

Navigation Operator

In EJB QL the . operator is termed the **navigation operator**, which is similar to how objects are navigated in Java itself. The . operator allows us to navigate paths which are expressed in **path expressions**.

Input Parameters

You may use input parameters in an EJB QL query. The number of input parameters must not exceed the permitted number of parameters for the corresponding EJB finder method. An EJB QL query need not make use of all the parameters permitted by a finder method.

Each input parameter is indicated by a preceding literal ?, followed by an integer value beginning at 1. In other words the first two input parameters are expressed as ?1 and ?2 respectively.

In an earlier EJB QL example you just saw, a literal query could be constructed like this:

```
SELECT OBJECT(p)
FROM MyPresidentsSchema AS p
WHERE p.last_name = 'Bush'
```

Using an input parameter we can more flexibly construct the query as follows:

```
SELECT OBJECT(p)
FROM MyPresidentsSchema AS p
WHERE p.last_name = ?1
```

When an appropriate parameter is supplied, we can retrieve records for presidents with any specified surname.

Where there may be duplicate data, such as in the surnames of presidents we can use multiple parameters as appropriate. To retrieve data on the younger George Bush we could use the following query (assuming appropriate declaration of a second parameter in the deployment descriptor):

```
SELECT OBJECT(p)
FROM MyPresidentsSchema AS p
WHERE p.last_name = ?1 AND p.election_year=?2
```

Wildcards

You may use the LICE keyword together with the % and _ characters as described under SQL earlier in this appendix. As a recap, the % character stands for zero or more characters and the _ character stands for any single character.

Functions

EJB QL has string and numeric functions, which are listed below. All EJB 2.1-conformant EJB containers will support the following functions.

The string functions are:

- ❏ CONCAT(String, String) – Concatenates two strings and returns a String
- ❏ SUBSTRING(String, start, length) – Returns a String
- ❏ LOCATE(String, String [, start]) – Returns an int
- ❏ LENGTH(String) – Returns an int

The numeric functions are:

- ❏ ABS(number) – Returns an int, float, or double of the same data type as the argument to the function
- ❏ SQRT(double) – Returns a double
- ❏ MOD(int, int) – Returns an int

Aggregate Functions

EJB QL has the following aggregate functions: AVG(), SUM(), COUNT(), MAX(), and MIN(). The AVG() and SUM() functions must have a numeric argument. The other aggregate functions have an argument corresponding to the data type of the corresponding EJB field.

Values which contain NULL are eliminated before the aggregate functions are applied. The DISTINCT keyword can be used to eliminate duplicate values in conjunction with the EJB QL aggregate functions.

Using Relationships

We can use EJB QL to exploit relationships that are specified in the deployment descriptor.

Suppose we had an entity bean with abstract schema name ActsSchema, which contained information on all acts passed by the US Congress, and included information about which president was in office at the time. We could construct the following query:

```
SELECT OBJECT (p)
FROM MyPresidentsSchema AS p, IN (p.ActsSchema) AS a
WHERE a.president_surname = ?1
```

Notice the IN clause, which includes the syntax p.ActsSchema expressing that there is a relationship between the MyPresidentsSchema, identified by the identifier variable p and the abstract schema ActsSchema. Of course, if this is to work the necessary declarations for ActsSchema need to be present in the ejb-jar.xml deployment descriptor.

There is much more to EJB QL than has been explained in this brief description. Further information on EJB QL is contained in the EJB 2.1 specification, which can be downloaded from the Sun web site at http://java.sun.com/products/ejb/docs.html.

APPENDIX C

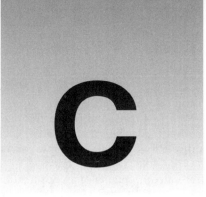

J2EE Glossary

Component

Definition – Essentially the building blocks of a J2EE application, components are specific software units, supported by a container, and configurable at deployment-time. The four types of components defined within J2EE are EJBs, web components, applets, and application clients.

Where used – In all J2EE applications.

Container

Definition – A software entity that provides services to components, including life cycle management, security, deployment, and runtime services. A container of a specific type of components, such as EJB, Web, JSP, servlet, applet, or application client, will provide the services its components need. For example, servlet containers will need to support HTTP as a protocol for requests and responses, while JSP containers need to provide the same services as servlet containers, plus an engine to interpret and process JSP pages into servlets.

Where used – In J2EE applications.

CORBA

Definition – Common Object Request Broker Architecture, CORBA, is a standard architecture for distributed object systems, a model specified by the Object Management Group. It allows a distributed, heterogeneous collection of objects to interoperate, regardless of platform or programming language.

Where used – In distributed object systems where language and platform-independence is critical.

Distributed Application

Definition – An application composed of a variety of components running in separate runtime environments, often on different platforms, and connected over a network. Distributed application types include two-tier (client-server), three-tier (client-middleware-server), and multi-tier or n-tier (client-multiple middleware-multiple servers).

Where used – Wherever different components of an application need to be connected to each other over a network.

Enterprise JavaBeans

Definition – A server-side component model for Java, a component architecture designed to enable developers to build and deploy scaleable, secure, multi-platform, business-critical applications that are object-oriented, reusable, and distributed. It allows the enterprise developer to focus on writing business logic without the need to write code that handles such tasks as transactional behavior, security, connection pooling, or threading, since the architecture delegates these tasks to the server vendor.

Where used – In distributed business applications that will operate on any server that provides the Enterprise JavaBeans APIs.

EJB Container

Definition – A container (see *Container*) for EJB components, providing a scaleable, secure, transactional environment in which enterprise beans can operate. It is the container that handles the object life cycle, including creating and destroying an object as well as handling the state management of beans. When a bean is installed in a container, the container provides an implementation of the bean's EJBHome interface and the bean's remote interface. The container will also make the bean's EJBHome interface available in JNDI, the Java Naming and Directory Interface. An EJB container is provided by an EJB or J2EE server.

Where used – In any distributed application that uses EJBs.

EJB Server

Definition – A collection of services and resources needed to support an EJB installation. These services include management of distributed transactions, management of distributed objects and distributed invocations on these objects, as well as low-level system services. Since the J2EE architecture assumes that an EJB container is hosted by an EJB server from the same vendor, it does not specify the contract between these two entities. Each EJB server may host one or more EJB containers.

Where used – In distributed applications that employ one or more EJB containers.

Java 2 Enterprise Edition (J2EE)

Definition – A platform that creates an environment for developing and deploying multi-tiered web-based enterprise applications. It allows developers to create standardized, modular components, and provides those components with a complete set of services, application programming interfaces (APIs), and protocols that automatically handle many of the details of application behavior, without the need for complex programming. J2EE adds to the features of the Java 2 Platform, Standard Edition by including full support for EJB components, Java servlets API, JavaServer Pages and XML.

Where used – In distributed transactional enterprise applications in which the developer needs to reduce the costs and time of development, and use the speed, security, and reliability of server-side technology.

Java IDL

Definition – The Java Interface Definition Language, IDL, is a technology for distributed objects, providing CORBA interoperability and connectivity capabilities for the J2EE platform. Similar to RMI (Remote Method Invocation), which supports distributed objects written entirely in the Java programming language, Java IDL enables objects to interact regardless of whether they're written in Java or another programming language. It uses CORBA's IDL to map Java to all other languages supported by CORBA.

Where used – In distributed applications in which objects written in Java will need to interact with objects that may be written in other programming languages.

JavaServer Pages (JSP)

Definition – A web technology that combines the tasks of page designing and programming. JSPs use template data, custom elements, scripting languages, and server-side Java objects to return dynamic content to a client. The developer writes the template data in HTML or XML, adding inline Java code, within special tags, to provide the dynamic content. These tags also allow JSPs to interact with Enterprise JavaBeans from a number of sources and display them. The beans can also be filled by using the input parameters of HTTP requests. Application servers compile JSPs into servlets.

Where used – To develop and maintain dynamic web pages that leverage existing business systems.

JDBC

Definition – An API that allows connectivity between J2EE applications and virtually any tabular data source. Typically, the data source is a SQL relational database (RDBMS), but the JDBC API also provides access to such data sources as flat files and spreadsheets.

Where used – Whenever a distributed application needs to access enterprise data.

Module

Definition – A software unit that is the smallest deployable and usable unit of J2EE components. It consists of one or more components of the same container type and one deployment descriptor that contains meta-information about the components. The three types of modules are EJB, web, and application client. Modules can be deployed as stand-alone units, assembled as packages of related components, or assembled into a single application module.

Where used – Throughout all J2EE applications.

Resource Manager

Definition – A J2EE component that manages the life cycle of a resource type. This primarily involves providing access to a set of shared resources, including connection pooling, transaction support, and network communication. A resource manager provides and enforces the ACID transaction properties (atomicity, consistency, isolation, durability) for specific data and operations. An example of a resource manager is a relational database, which supports the persistent storage of relational data. The resource manager typically operates in a different address space or on a different machine from the clients that access it.

Where used – In enterprise applications where data and other operational resources require life-cycle management.

RMI

Definition – Remote Method Invocation. A strictly Java-to-Java technology that allows an object running in one Java virtual machine to invoke methods on an object running in a different Java virtual machine. The JVMs can be on the same or on different hosts. The object in the first program can make a call on a remote object in the second program once it has obtained a reference to the remote object.

Where used – Wherever distributed applications will involve only Java technology from end to end, or where provision is made, such as through RMI-IIOP, for Java technology to operate seamlessly with other languages.

Servlet

Definition – A component-based Java program that provides a simple, consistent mechanism for extending and enhancing the functionality of a web server and for accessing existing business systems. Servlets generate dynamic content and interact with web clients using a request-response paradigm. They have access to the entire family of Java APIs. Since servlets are server and platform-independent, they allow the developer to select servers, platform, and tools of choice. Think of a servlet as a GUI-less applet that runs on the server side.

Where used – To enhance the functionality of a web server in accessing distributed enterprise systems.

Servlet Container

Definition – A container (see *Container*) that provides network services for sending requests and responses, as well as decoding requests, and formatting responses. Servlet containers are required to support HTTP as a protocol for requests and responses, but may additionally support other request-response protocols such as HTTPS.

Where used – Wherever servlets are part of a distributed application.

Secure Sockets Layer

Definition – A security protocol designed to enable private communications over a non-private network such as the Internet. It uses public key encryption and digital certificates to establish a secure connection between a client (such as a web browser), and a web server, to prevent eavesdropping or tampering with communications within and between distributed applications. Servers are always authenticated and clients are optionally authenticated. Web pages that are secured with SSL will likely display a 'closed padlock' or other symbol to indicate that SSL has been enabled. By convention, such web site address will start with https:// rather than the usual http://.

Where used – In virtually all distributed enterprise applications, especially those in which communications include private or sensitive material.

Transaction

Definition – An indivisible unit of work that modifies data while ensuring its integrity. A transaction encloses one or more program statements, all of which must either complete (a commit) or be rolled back, ensuring that the data always remains in a consistent state. When a transaction commits, the data modifications made by its statements are saved. If any of the statements within a transaction fail, the transaction rolls back, undoing the effects of all statements in the transaction. Transactions control the concurrent access of data by multiple users.

Where used – In any application in which data is modified.

Web Application

Definition – An application written to be deployed over the Internet. This includes not only those built with Java technologies such as JavaServer Pages and servlets, but also those built with non-Java technologies such as CGI and Perl. Distributable web applications use J2EE technology, written to be deployed in web containers distributed across multiple Java virtual machines running on the same host or different hosts.

Where used – Whenever a distributed application will be deployed over the Internet.

Web Container

Definition – A container (see *Container*) that provides a runtime environment for web components, including security, concurrency, life cycle management, transaction, deployment, and other services. A web container provides the same services as a JSP container plus a federated view of the J2EE platform APIs. A web container is provided by a web or J2EE server. A distributed web container is one that can run a web application that is tagged as distributable and that executes across multiple Java virtual machines running on the same host or on different hosts.

Where used – In any distributed application that includes web components.

Web Server

Definition – Software that provides a collection of services and resources for accessing the Internet, an intranet, or an extranet. A web server hosts web sites, provides support for HTTP and other protocols, and executes server-side programs. Within the J2EE architecture, a web server provides services, such as HTTP message handling, to a web container. Since the J2EE architecture assumes that a web container is hosted by a web server from the same vendor, it does not specify the contract between these two entities. Each web server may host one or more web containers.

Where used – Whenever web containers form part of an application, essentially whenever any part of the application involves a network.

XML

Definition – The eXtensible Markup Language (XML) is a universal syntax that allows developers to describe and structure data, independent of the application logic. Unlike HTML, which has fixed tags that deal mainly with style or presentation, XML tags are defined as needed. XML can be used to define unlimited languages for specific industries and applications. XML documents need to be transformed into a language with style tags under the control of a stylesheet before they can be presented by a browser or other presentation mechanism. Since XML and Java are both portable and extensible, they are an ideal combination for web applications.

Where used – In conjunction with J2EE technology, whenever an enterprise application needs to consume and generate information that is exchanged among different servers that run on varied system platforms.

INDEX

Index

A Guide to the Index

The ~ character is used to reduce the need to duplicate almost identical entries. For example destination/~Type properties refers to both the destination property and the destinationType property. The part which is replaced by the ~ is shown in normal (not italic) type.

The use of Xyz is to indicate that numerous options exist, as is the case for <jsp:xyzActionElements>.

Symbols

[] operator, EL, 128
_ (underscore character), SQL, 670
<jsp:xyzActionElements>
  see jsp:xyzActionElements.
9i application server
  see Oracle 9i application server.
9i database server
  see Oracle 9i database server.

A

ABS function, EJB QL, 681
abstract schema
  CMR (container-managed relationships), 447
  developing CMP entity beans, 403
action elements, JSP, 85
  using JavaBeans in JSP pages, 100
activation
  stateful session beans, 378
Adaptive Server Enterprise
  see Sybase Adaptive Server Enterprise.
Add Enterprise Bean References dialog
  creating EJB with local references, 425
  creating entity bean using CMR and EJB QL, 454
Add Relationship dialog
  creating entity bean using CMR and EJB QL, 459
Add Servlet Filter mapping dialog
  using filters, 235
addAnalyst method
  implementing façade design pattern, 498, 500
  loading database with CMP Field Data, 475
addBatch method
  batch updates, 277
  example using Statements, 283
  prepared statements, 303
addCookie method
  response object, 90

  session management with cookies, 222
addHeader method
  response object, 90
AddRating.java file
  using JSP and servlets with EJBs, 511
addStock method
  developing CMP entity beans, 411, 412
  loading database with CMP Field Data, 475
addStockRating method
  implementing façade design pattern, 497
  loading database with CMP Field Data, 474
administration tools
  commercial J2EE, 622
Aliases tab
  Application Deployment Tool window, 553
alphaWorks web site, 640
ALTER TABLE statement, SQL, 666
AnalystBean.java file
  loading database with CMP Field Data, 465
AnalystForm.jsp file
  using JSP and servlets with EJBs, 512
  using MVC architecture, 243, 251
AnalystVo.java file
  implementing façade design pattern, 492
Apache AXIS
  developing web services in Java, 537
Apache Tomcat
  see Tomcat.
Apache web server, 627
Applet class, 22
application context
  deploying web application in Tomcat, 84
Application Deployment Tool window
  Aliases tab, 553
  creating Deployment Descriptor, 556
  creating EJB with local references, 428
  creating entity bean using CMR and EJB QL, 458
  creating session beans, 363, 368
  creating WAR file, 548
  creating web service with session bean, 574
  defining classic tag handler, 160

Application Deployment Tool window (continued)
  deploying servlet to J2EE server, 191
  deploying web application in J2EE, 76
  deploying web service, 558
  developing BMP entity beans, 417
  developing CMP entity beans, 405
  Endpoint tab, 554
  example using data sources, 313
  testing J2EE installation, 47, 52
  using EJB Timer to invoke message bean, 523
  using filters, 233
  using JDBC from session bean, 479
  Web Services tab, 555
application object
  JSP implicit object, 93
application scope
  scope, JSP, 93
application servers
  administration using EJBs, 355
  commercial J2EE, 623
  description, 11
  HTTP servers, 627
  J2EE servers, 624
  JSP servers, 626
application structure
  packaging tag libraries, 146
applications
  enterprise applications, 11
applicationScope implicit object, EL, 129
architectures
  client-server, 15
  J2EE architectures, 31
  multi-tier architecture, 14
  MVC (Model-View-Controller), 237
  n-tier architecture, 31, 32, 33
  single tier, 15
  three-tier architecture, 17
  two-tier architecture, 16
ArrayList
  loading database with CMP Field Data, 473
AS keyword, SQL, 672
ASP (Application Service Providers)
  technologies required, 610
assignStock method
  loading database with CMP Field Data, 466, 475
asynchronous messages
  message-driven beans, 514
  using EJBs, 355
attribute element, JSP, 85
  <tag> element, 145
attributes
  getProperty element, JSP, 88
  include directive, JSP, 67
  page directive, JSP, 66
  setProperty action, JSP, 87
  useBean element, JSP, 86
autocommit
  transactions, 321, 322
AVG function
  EJB QL, 681
  SQL, 673

B

batch updates, 277
  prepared statements, 303
BEA
  J2EE implementation, 14
BEA WebLogic
  tag libraries, 175
BEA WebLogic server
  see WebLogic Server.
bean class, entity bean, 392
bean class, session bean
  creating stateful session bean, 379
  introduction, 359
  SimpleSessionBean.java file, 361
  specifying class names, 375
bean interface, entity bean
  introduction, 392
  making bean interface local, 430
bean interface, session bean
  creating stateful session bean, 379
  creating web service with session bean, 567
  introduction, 359
  SimpleSession.java file, 361
  specifying class names, 375
bean jar, 374
bean stub, 360
beanName attribute, jsp:useBean element, 86
BEGIN TRAN command, 321
BETWEEN keyword, SQL, 668
binary data type, SQL, 664
BMP (bean-managed persistence), 394, 415
body element, JSP, 85
body-content element, 144
BodyTag interface, 155
  classic tag handlers, 153
  tag handlers, JSP, 141
books from Wrox Press, 645
Borland
  J2EE implementation, 14
Borland Enterprise AppServer, 626
Borland JBuilder Enterprise IDE
  see JBuilder Enterprise IDE.
brainbuzz web site, 642
business components, 21
business rules tier/layer, 15

C

Café au Lait web site, 641
calculate method
  creating stateful session bean, 383
  creating stateful web service, 589
  invoking methods using DII, 595
calculated fields, SQL, 671
CalculatorServiceClient.java file, 590
CalculatorServiceIF.java file, 587
CalculatorServiceImpl.java file, 587

CalculatorXyz.java files, 378
CallableStatement object, 306
    Connection interface methods, 306
    placeholders, SQL, 308
    stored procedures, 349
careers, 644
catalog, SQL, 662
certification, 642
    mock exam web site, 643
CHAR keyword, SQL, 663
class attribute, jsp:useBean element, 86
    using JavaBeans in JSP pages, 101
classic tag handlers, 152
    body tag support, 163
    defining, 157
    tag handlers, JSP, 141
classpath
    building and deploying web services, 544
    communicating with databases, 271
    creating EJB with local references, 429
    creating entity bean using CMR and EJB QL, 453
    creating session beans, 363, 371
    creating stateful session bean, 380, 382
    creating stateful web service, 582
    creating web service with session bean, 569
    developing CMP entity beans, 400
    ensuring correct setting, 371
    example using Statements, 282
    testing web services, 559
clean up, JSP, 88
cleanupTable method
    transaction control, 331
clearBatch method
    batch updates, 277
clearIt method
    creating stateful web service, 589
    invoking methods using DII, 596
clearParameters method
    CallableStatement class, 309
    PreparedStatement class, 302
client code, session bean
    SimpleSessionClient.java file, 362
client communication
    using EJBs, 354
client-server architecture
    explained, 15
    J2EE client, 21
    server-side components, 21
close method, Connection class
    communicating with databases, 273
    connection pools, 312
    releasing database connection, 266
    releasing Statement objects, 278
    transactions, 322
cloudscape command
    communicating with databases, 271
    isql tool, 298
    JDBC protocol, 273
    stored procedures, 306
    testing J2EE installation, 41
Cloudscape database server
    documentation, 265
    starting, 41
    stopping, 42, 57
clustering, 14
clusters, SQL, 662

CMP (container-managed persistence)
    entity beans, EJBs, 393
    loading database with CMP Field Data, 461
    version 1.1 CMR support, 403
CMP entity beans
    deploying, 395
    Stock.java file, 396
    StockBean.java file, 397
    StockHome.java file, 398
    StockList.java file, 398
    StockListBean.java file, 398
    StockListHome.java file, 400
CMR (container-managed relationships), 447
    creating entity bean using CMR and EJB QL, 451
    developer convenience, 485
    entity beans, EJBs, 395
code
    downloading sample code, 6
coding
    IDEs, 629
Coldjava Bar Charts
    tag libraries, 175
collections
    creating entity bean using CMR and EJB QL, 459
columns, SQL, 663
comments, 70
commit method, Connection class
    ResultSet holdability, 294
    transactions, 320, 321, 323, 325
compilation error
    deployment problems, 60
components
    definition, 685
    distributed transactions, 332
    MVC application, 238
components, UML, 354
CONCAT function, EJB QL, 681
concurrency, 334
conditional actions
    core actions, JSTL, 168
config object
    JSP implicit object, 92
    JSP init parameters, 92
configuration management, 632
connecting to databases, 258
    see also JDBC.
    getConnection method, 264
    releasing connection, 266
    setting login timeout, 268
Connection class
    methods, 321
    transaction control, 322
connection factory
    using EJB Timer to invoke message bean, 526
Connection interface methods
    CallableStatement class, 306
Connection objects
    example using ResultSet object, 291
connection pools, 310, 311
    data sources, 350
    example using data sources, 312
    using close method, 312
connections
    data sources, 349
    distributed transactions, 332

connectors
Enterprise Application Integration, 613
overview of J2EE and related technologies, 606
consistency
transactions, 321, 323, 350
containers
definition, 685
deploying web application in Tomcat, 84
EJB container definition, 686
interfaces, 21
introduction, 21–23
servlet container definition, 689
web container definition, 690
content type, 190
contentType attribute
JSP page directive, 67
context-param element
deployment descriptors, 200, 202
core actions, JSTL, 167
cookie implicit object, EL, 130
Cookie object
session management with cookies, 222
cookies
session management, 221
session object, 92
session tracking, 220
CORBA (Common Object Request Broker Architecture)
definition, 685
Enterprise Application Integration, 613
overview of J2EE and related technologies, 606
web services, 533
core actions, JSTL
conditional actions, 168
formatting actions, 169
general-purpose actions, 167
iterator actions, 169
JSTL tag categories, 167
SQL actions, 170
COUNT function
EJB QL, 681
SQL, 673
create method
bean class, entity bean, 392
creating entity bean using CMR and EJB QL, 452
creating session beans, 372, 373
creating stateful session bean, 379
developing CMP entity beans, 408
home interface, entity bean, 391, 394
CREATE statement, SQL
example using Statements, 283
rows affected, 276
CREATE TABLE statement, SQL, 665
createSender method
using EJB Timer to invoke message bean, 526
createStatement method
creating Statement objects, 275
example using ResultSet object, 290
ResultSet holdability, 294
resultsets, 284, 285
cursors, 284
custom actions, JSP, 139, 140
introduction, 123
tag library, 140
customer support used in this book, 6

D

-d option, javac command, 363
data access tier/layer, 15
data sources, 310
connection pools, 350
connections, 349
example using, 312
parameters, 318
data types
SQL, 663
WSDL, 541
database connection management, 354
database servers, 633
testing J2EE installation, 41
database technologies
Application Service Providers, 611
DatabaseMetaData object
communicating with databases, 274
databases
batch updates, 277
communicating with databases, 269
connecting to databases, 258, 264
creating Statement objects, 275
Java API, 257
loading with CMP Field Data, 461
releasing connection, 266
using JDBC from session bean, 478
DataSource object, 311
date and time data type, SQL, 664
DB2, 633
DCOM (Distributed Component Object Model)
web services, 533
debugging
IDEs, 630
declarations
method definition, 70
scripting elements, JSP, 68
variables declared in, 70
default values, SQL, 665
DELETE method, HTTP request, 180
DELETE statement, SQL, 675
rows affected, 277
deleteRow method
updating ResultSet objects, 292
deleteStock method, 411
Deploy Module dialog
creating session beans, 369
deploying web service, 558
testing J2EE installation, 55
deployment
APIs, 611
IDEs, 630
servlet to J2EE server, 191
web application in J2EE, 81
web application in Tomcat, 82
web service example, 558
deployment descriptors, 199–204
create EJB using EJB QL find, 443
creating session beans, 367, 374
creating stateful session bean, 385
creating web service with session bean, 574
defining classic tag handler, 162

deployment descriptors (continued)
deploying servlet to Tomcat, 196
deploying web application in Tomcat, 82
developing CMP entity beans, 413
EJB local interfaces, 432
EJB QL, 681
element order, DTD, 84
exceptions, 105
filters, 229
loading database with CMP Field Data, 476
maintaining state with session object, 224
packaging tag libraries, 146
platform-specific descriptors, 375
root element, 200
running application after J2EE installation, 52
scripting elements, 124
sub-elements, 200
thread unsafe servlet example, 211
Tomcat, 159
using EL expressions, 134, 136
using MVC architecture, 248
<web-app> element, 200
Deployment Settings dialog
developing CMP entity beans, 406
Deployment Tool
building and deploying web services, 543
creating Deployment Descriptor, 556
creating J2EE EAR file, 547
creating session beans, 363, 364
creating web service with session bean, 576
developing CMP entity beans, 401
session bean stubs, 360
deploytool utility
defining classic tag handler, 160
deploying servlet to J2EE server, 191
deploying web application in J2EE, 76
deploying web application in Tomcat, 84
deployment problems, 60
J2EE 1.4 bug, 249
main window, 47
running application after J2EE installation, 46
using JavaBeans in JSP pages, 98
using JSTL, 173
description layer
service description layer, 536
description element
deployment descriptors, 200
design patterns
design problems, 528
implementing, 488
using in EJB applications, 487
destination, 526
destination/~Type properties
using EJB Timer to invoke message bean, 523
destroy method
Filter interface, 228
handling requests, 186
JAX-RPC service endpoint model, 580, 589
servlet lifecycle, 207
developer productivity
commercial J2EE, 623
developerWorks web site, 640
dialogs
see also windows; wizards.
Add Enterprise Bean References dialog, 454
Add Relationship dialog, 459

Add Servlet Filter mapping dialog, 235
Deploy Module dialog, 55
Deployment Settings dialog, 406
Distribute Module dialog, 376
Edit Contents dialog, 49, 427
Edit Contents of SimpleServiceWar dialog, 549
Environment Variables dialog, 39
Finder/Select Methods dialog, 437
New Deployment Settings File dialog, 53
Save Deployment Settings File dialog, 54
Servlet Filters dialog, 234
System Properties dialog, 39
Dick Baldwin's web site, 641
DII (Dynamic Invocation Interface)
creating stateful web service, 581, 590
invoking methods, 595
invoking web service methods, 543
directive elements
JSP elements, 66
discovery layer
service discovery layer, 536
display-name element
deployment descriptors, 200
DISTINCT keyword, EJB QL, 681
creating entity bean using CMR and EJB QL, 455
distributable element
deployment descriptors, 200
Distribute Module dialog
creating session beans, 370
creating stateful web service, 586
troubleshooting session bean deployment, 376
distributed applications
definition, 686
web services, 533
Distributed Component Object Model
see DCOM.
distributed computing
introduction, 13, 35
overview of J2EE and related technologies, 605
workflow automation, 610
distributed transactions
introduction, 331
transaction manager, 332
method call prohibitions, 333
two-phase commit, 333
doAfterBody method
BodyTag interface, 156
classic tag handler with body tag support, 165
defining classic tag handler, 161
TagSupport interface, 155
doBody element, JSP, 85
documentation
J2EE resources, 615
Document Type Definition
see DTD.
doEndTag method
BodyTag interface, 156
defining classic tag handler, 161
TagSupport interface, 153, 155
doFilter method
Filter interface, 228
FilterChain interface, 228
using filters, 236
doGet method
handling GET requests, 187
using MVC architecture, 251

doInitBody method
  BodyTag interface, 156
  classic tag handler with body tag support, 165
doPost method
  creating a servlet, 190
  handling POST requests, 187
  thread unsafe servlet example, 213
  using filters, 236
  using MVC architecture, 251
doQuery method
  example using ResultSet object, 290
doStartTag method
  BodyTag interface, 156
  classic tag handler with body tag support, 165
  defining classic tag handler, 161
  TagSupport interface, 153, 155
dot operator, EL, 128
  EJB QL SELECT method, 450
doTag method
  packaging tag libraries, 151, 152
  tag handlers, JSP, 142
downloading sample code, 6
doXXX methods, 187
DriverLoader class
  communicating with databases, 272
  example using Statements, 279
DriverManager class
  choosing between drivers, 262
  logging with, 274
drivers
  choosing between drivers, 261
  connecting to databases, 259
  getConnection method, 264
  loading, 262
  system property, 263
  type 1 driver, 259
  type 2 driver, 260
  type 3 driver, 260
  type 4 driver, 261
DROP TABLE statement, SQL, 666
DTD (Document Type Definition)
  deployment descriptor element order, 84
Dynamic Invocation Interface
  see DII.
dynamic proxies
  creating stateful web service, 581, 593
  creating web service with session bean, 567, 576, 577
  invoking web service methods, 543

E

EAI (Enterprise Application Integration)
  technologies required, 613
EAR (Enterprise Application Resource) file
  creating session beans, 364
e-commerce
  technologies required, 608
ECperf
  overview of J2EE and related technologies, 606
EDI (Electronic Data Interchange)
  technologies required, 612
Edit Contents dialog
  configuring web service, 549
  creating EJB with local references, 427

  creating session beans, 365
  creating web service with session bean, 571
  developing CMP entity beans, 401
  implementing façade design pattern, 504
  testing J2EE installation, 49
  using EJB Timer to invoke message bean, 522
Edit Enterprise Bean wizard
  create EJB using EJB QL find, 436
  creating EJB with local references, 426
  creating entity bean using CMR and EJB QL, 454
  creating session beans, 366
  creating web service with session bean, 571
  developing BMP entity beans, 416
  developing CMP entity beans, 402
  Transaction Management page, 456
  using EJB Timer to invoke message bean, 521
EJB (Enterprise JavaBeans)
  calling beans from beans, 357, 390
  calling beans from client, 358, 390
  choosing type of bean to use, 358
  container, 686
  definition, 686
  description, 353
  design patterns, 487
  EJB Server, 356, 686
  entity beans, 389–445
  introduction, 26, 27
  JavaBeans compared, 354
  local interfaces, 422
  overview of J2EE and related technologies, 605
  reasons for using, 354
  session beans, 356
  summarized, 34
  Timer Service, 516
  type, 366
  using JDBC with Enterprise JavaBeans, 478
  using JSP and servlets with EJBs, 507
  varieties of EJB, 356
EJB QL (Enterprise JavaBean Query Language), 434, 677
  aggregate functions, 681
  creating entity bean using CMR and EJB QL, 451
  DISTINCT keyword, 681
  entity beans, EJBs, 395
  find methods, 434
  FROM clause, 677
  input parameters, 680
  JDBC alternative, 485
  LIKE keyword, 680
  navigation operator, 680
  numeric functions, 681
  ORDER BY clause, 677
  SELECT clause, 677, 679
  SELECT method, creating, 449
  select methods, 434
  string functions, 681
  WHERE clause, 677
  wildcards, 680
ejbActivate method
  creating session beans, 374
  stateful session beans, 378
ejbCreate method
  bean class, entity bean, 392
  creating session beans, 373
  developing BMP entity beans, 419
  developing CMP entity beans, 409
ejbFindByPrimaryKey method
  developing BMP entity beans, 419

EJBHome interface
  creating session beans, 373
  session beans, 359
ejb-jar.xml file
  creating session beans, 375
  creating stateful session bean, 384
ejbLoad method
  developing BMP entity beans, 421
ejb-local-ref element
  deployment descriptors, 201
EJBObject interface
  session beans, 359
ejbPassivate method
  creating session beans, 374
  stateful session beans, 378
ejbPostCreate method
  developing CMP entity beans, 410
ejb-ref element
  deployment descriptors, 201
ejbRemove method
  creating session beans, 374
  developing BMP entity beans, 420
  developing CMP entity beans, 410
ejbSelectAnalyst method
  creating entity bean using CMR and EJB QL, 456
  loading database with CMP Field Data, 469
ejbStore method
  developing BMP entity beans, 421
ejbTimeout method
  EJB Timer Service, 516
  using EJB Timer to invoke message bean, 525
EL (Expression Language), 124–39
  implicit objects, 128
  introduction, 123
  literal values, 126
  operators, 126
  syntax, 125
  using EL expressions, 130, 131
emerging layers
  protocol stack, 536
empty operator, EL, 127
encodeRedirectURL method
  response object, 92
  session tracking with URL rewriting, 220
encodeURL method
  maintaining state with session object, 226
  response object, 92
  session tracking with URL rewriting, 220
encoding layer
  protocol stack, 535
endpoint context
  JAX-RPC service endpoint model, 580, 581, 589
Endpoint tab
  Application Deployment Tool window, 554
endpoints
  Service Endpoint interface, 551
  web service endpoint, 565
enterprise applications
  introduction, 11, 13
Enterprise AppServer
  see Borland Enterprise AppServer.
Enterprise Bean wizard
  creating session beans, 365
Enterprise JavaBeans
  see EJB.
entity beans, 389–445
  bean class, 392

bean interface, 392
  BMP (bean-managed persistence), 394
  calling beans from client, 358, 390
  choosing type of bean to use, 358
  CMP (container-managed persistence), 393
  CMP entity beans, 395
  CMR (container-managed relationships), 395
  create EJB using EJB QL find, 435
  creating EJB with local references, 424
  developing BMP entity beans, 415
  diagrammatic representation, 390
  EJB QL, 395
  home interface, 391
  introduction, 27, 357
  loading database with CMP Field Data, 461
  local bean interface, 392
  local home interface, 391
  primary keys, 395, 448
  relational databases, 357
  remote bean interface, 392
  remote home interface, 391
env-entry element
  deployment descriptors, 201
environment variables
  installing J2EE 1.4 SDK, 38
Environment Variables dialog
  installing J2EE 1.4 SDK, 39
errata in this book, 7
error pages
  servlet exceptions, 218
Error.jsp file
  using MVC architecture, 247
errorPage attribute
  JSP page directive, 67
error-page element
  deployment descriptors, 201
  servlet exceptions, 218
errors
  JSP, 105
exception object
  JSP implicit object, 93
exceptions
  deployment descriptor, 105
  JSP, 105
  page directive, 105
  servlets, 216–19
  summary, 253
  using EL expressions, 130
  using JDBC from session bean, 484
execute method
  CallableStatement object, 309
  creating Statement objects, 276
  transactions, 321
executeBatch method
  batch updates, 277
  creating Statement objects, 276
  example using Statements, 283
  prepared statements, 303
executeQuery method
  CallableStatement object, 309
  creating Statement objects, 276
  example using Statements, 284
  resultsets, 284
executeUpdate method
  CallableStatement class, 309
  creating Statement objects, 276
  example using Statements, 284
  transactions, 321

Expression Language
see EL.
expressions
scripting elements, JSP, 68, 70
exteNd
Novell exteNd, 626

F

façade design pattern, 505
implementing, 490
using in EJB applications, 488
factory design pattern
getFacade method, 506
failover, 14
fallback element, JSP, 85
FaqCategories class
creating JSP web application, 73
fault-tolerance, 621
fields
calculated fields, SQL, 671
file attribute
JSP include directive, 67
Filter interface
Filter API, 227
filter element
deployment descriptors, 200
Filter*Chain*/*~Config* interfaces
Filter API, 227
filtering data, SQL, 668
filter-mapping element
deployment descriptors, 200
filters, 227–37
deployment descriptors, 229
Filter API, 227
summary, 253
using filters, 231
find methods
create EJB using EJB QL find, 435
EJB QL, 434
home interface, entity bean, 394
findAllAnalysts method
loading database with CMP Field Data, 468, 473
using JDBC from session bean, 484
findByPrimaryKey method
create EJB using EJB QL find, 440
creating entity bean using CMR and EJB QL, 452
developing BMP entity beans, 419
developing CMP entity beans, 408
home interface, entity bean, 391
implementing façade design pattern, 497
finder methods
creating EJB QL SELECT method, 449
loading database with CMP Field Data, 471
Finder/Select Methods dialog
create EJB using EJB QL find, 437
creating entity bean using CMR and EJB QL, 455, 456, 458
findRatedStocks method
implementing façade design pattern, 495
findStockRatings method
loading database with CMP Field Data, 472
findUnratedStocks method
loading database with CMP Field Data, 474
<fmt.tld>

core actions, JSTL, 169
form encoded parameters, HTTP
request object, 90
formatting actions
core actions, JSTL, 169
forName method
loading drivers, 262
forums, 642
forward method
using request dispatcher, 240
forwarding requests
MVC application, 239
FROM clause, EJB QL, 677
functions
EJB QL, 681
SQL, 672

G

Gamelan page, 641
garbage collection
releasing Statement objects, 278
general-purpose actions
core actions, JSTL, 167
GenericServlet class, 186
GET method/requests, 181
creating a servlet, 189
diagram illustrating, 187
doGet method, 187
request method, 180
sending an HTTP request via telnet, 182
server response to requests, 184
get methods
relationships, 448
getAllAnalysts method
loading database with CMP Field Data, 473
using JDBC from session bean, 484
getAnalyst method
creating entity bean using CMR and EJB QL, 459
implementing façade design pattern, 496
loading database with CMP Field Data, 469
getArray method
reading data from resultsets, 286
getAttribute method
adding parameters to request, 241
persisting client information, 220
syntax, 91
using JavaBeans in JSP pages, 100
using MVC architecture, 251
getAttributeNames method, 91
get*BigDecimal*/*~Boolean*/*~Byte* methods
reading data from resultsets, 286
getCalculator method
creating stateful session bean, 383
getConnection method
communicating with databases, 273
connecting to databases, 264
drivers, 264
getConnection method, DataSource class, 311
getCookies method
session management with cookies, 222
getCreationTime method
session creation and lifecycle, 221
getDatabaseConnection method
developing BMP entity beans, 421

getDate/~Double method
reading data from resultsets, 286
getEchoString method
creating session beans, 372, 374
creating web service with JAX-RPC, 541
getEJBMetaData method
creating session beans, 373
getFacade method
factory design pattern, 506
singleton design pattern, 506
using JSP and servlets with EJBs, 514
getHeader method
HttpServletRequest object, 198
getHomeHandle method
creating session beans, 373
getHttpSession method
JAX-RPC service endpoint model, 581
getInitParameter method
thread unsafe servlet example, 213
getLastAccessedTime method
session creation and lifecycle, 221
getMaxInactiveInterval method
session creation and lifecycle, 221
getName method
session management with cookies, 222
getNamedDispatcher method
forwarding and including requests, 240
using MVC architecture, 251
getNextException method
connecting to databases, 268
getOutputStream method
using response object, 199
getParameter/~Map/~Names/~Values methods
creating a servlet, 190
reading methods of request object, 90
using request object, 196, 197
getPathInfo method
request object, 90
using JSP and servlets with EJBs, 514
using MVC architecture, 250
using request object, 198
getPort method
creating web service with session bean, 577, 578
getProperty element, JSP, 88
getProtocol method
using request object, 197
getQueryString method
using request object, 198
getRemoteAddr/~Host methods
using request object, 197
getRequestDispatcher method
forwarding and including requests, 240
getRequestedSessionId method
session management, 219
getServerName method
using request object, 197
getServletConfig method
handling requests, 186
getServletContext method
forwarding and including requests, 240
JAX-RPC service endpoint model, 581
getServletInfo method
handling requests, 186
getSession method
maintaining state with session object, 226
session management, 219
getStock method

create EJB using EJB QL find, 442
developing CMP entity beans, 411
getStockHome method
developing CMP entity beans, 411
getStockRatings method
implementing façade design pattern, 495, 496
loading database with CMP Field Data, 472
getStocks method
creating entity bean using CMR and EJB QL, 459
loading database with CMP Field Data, 466, 467
getter methods
bean class, entity bean, 392
creating entity bean using CMR and EJB QL, 452
developing BMP entity beans, 418
getUnratedStocks method
loading database with CMP Field Data, 473
getUserPrincipal method
JAX-RPC service endpoint model, 581
getValue method
creating stateful session bean, 383
creating stateful web service, 589
invoking methods using DII, 596
session management with cookies, 222
getValueObject method
implementing façade design pattern, 499
GUI applications
Swing, 11

H

HashMap
packaging tag libraries, 151
HEAD method
request method, 180
header/~Values implicit objects, EL, 129
holdability
ResultSet object, 294
home interface, entity bean
create method, 391
find method, 394
findByPrimaryKey method, 391
introduction, 391
making home interface local, 429
remove method, 391, 394
home interface, session bean
creating stateful session bean, 378
creating web service with session bean, 567
developing CMP entity beans, 411
introduction, 359
SimpleSessionHome.java file, 361
specifying class names, 375
home stub
session beans, 360
HTTP (HyperText Transfer Protocol)
do methods, 187
HTTP servers, 627
overview of J2EE and related technologies, 603
ports for HTTP traffic, 534
sending an HTTP request via telnet, 182
session management, 219
transport layer, 535
HTTP GET
see GET method/requests.
HTTP POST
see POST method/requests.

HTTP request parameters
request object, 89
HttpServlet class, 180, 186
creating a servlet, 189
HttpServletRequest object, 188
methods for reading header data, 198
session management, 219
HttpServletResponse interface
methods for responding to HTTP requests, 199
session tracking with URL rewriting, 220
HttpSession object
JAX-RPC service endpoint model, 581

I

IBM
J2EE implementation, 14
IBM WebSphere application server
see WebSphere application server.
IBMs WebSphere Enterprise Studio IDE
see WebSphere Enterprise Studio IDE.
icon element
deployment descriptors, 200
id attribute, jsp:useBean element, 86
IDE (Integrated Development Environments), 628
IDL (Interface Definition Language)
overview of J2EE and related technologies, 606
IIS (Internet Information Services)
HTTP servers, 627
implementation class
web services, 542
implicit objects, EL, 128
implicit objects, JSP, 89
application object, 93
config object, 92
exception object, 93
out object, 91
request object, 89
response object, 90
session object, 91
import attribute
JSP page directive, 67
IN operator, SQL
EJB QL SELECT method, 450
include directive, JSP, 66
attributes, 67
creating JSP web application, 72
using EL expressions, 138
include method
using request dispatcher, 240
including requests
MVC application, 239
info attribute
JSP page directive, 67
Informix, 634
init method
Filter interface, 227
handling requests, 186
initialization servlet lifecycle, 205
JAX-RPC service endpoint model, 580, 588
init parameters, JSP
config object, 92
initialization
JSP (Java Server Pages), 88
JSP lifecycle, 64

servlet lifecycle, 205
initParam implicit object, EL, 130
init-param element
deployment descriptors, 203
input parameters, EJB QL, 680
INSERT statement, SQL, 673
create EJB using EJB QL find, 438
rows affected, 276
insertRow method
updating ResultSet objects, 292
installing J2EE 1.4 SDK, 38
running application, 46
starting server, 42
testing installation, 41
instance variables
creating stateful session bean, 384
instantiation
JSP lifecycle, 64
servlet lifecycle, 205
interfaces
containers, 21
J2SE and J2EE, 13
local interfaces, EJB, 422
remote interfaces, EJB, 422
Service Definition Interface, 540
tag handlers, JSP, 141
internationalization-capable formatting
JSTL tag categories, 167
invalidate method
session creation and lifecycle, 221
invoke element, JSP, 85
invoke method
JspFragment interface, 143
packaging tag libraries, 152
invoking methods
using DII, 595
Iona Orbix E2A J2EE Edition
commercial J2EE servers, 626
isELEnabled attribute
page directive, JSP, 124
isErrorPage attribute
creating JSP web application, 75
JSP page directive, 67
isNew method
session creation and lifecycle, 221
isolation, 335, 350
concurrency, 334
isql tool, cloudscape command
prepared statements, 298
isRequestedSessionId*FromCookie/~FromURL/~Valid* methods
session management, 219
isScriptingEnabled attribute
page directive, JSP, 124
isThreadSafe attribute
JSP page directive, 67
IterationTag interface, 154
classic tag handlers, 153
defining classic tag handler, 161
tag handlers, JSP, 141
iterator actions
core actions, JSTL, 169
Iterator class, Java API
creating JSP web application, 73
iterator method
packaging tag libraries, 151

J

J2EE (Java 2 Platform, Enterprise Edition)
application deployment, 59
commercial J2EE, 619
components summarized, 34
cross implementation deployment costs, 14
definition, 687
deploying web application in J2EE, 76
EAR file, 543, 547
features, 31
IDEs, 628
installing J2EE 1.4 SDK, 38, 41, 46
introduction, 20
overview of J2EE and related technologies, 602
relation to J2SE, 12
services summarized, 34
specification, 14, 19
technology page, Sun web site, 607
web services, 565–98
J2EE servers, 623
starting, 42
stopping, 57
J2EE_HOME
setting environment variables, 40
J2SE (Java 2 Standard Edition)
relation to J2EE, 12
JAR (Java application ARchive) file
bean jar, 374
creating session beans, 364, 370
creating stateful session bean, 382
Java
database API, 257
developing web services in Java, 537
Java Boutique web site, 641
Java certification, 642
Java IDL
definition, 687
Enterprise Application Integration, 613
Java Server Pages
see JSP.
java.lang/~math/~util packages, 541
java.net.URL class
creating web service with session bean, 578
Java/J2EE tutorials
see web resources.
JAVA_HOME
setting environment variables, 40
JavaBeans
EJB compared, 354
using JavaBeans in JSP pages, 94
javac command
-d option, 363
creating entity bean using CMR and EJB QL, 453
creating stateful session bean, 380
creating stateful web service, 583
creating web service with session bean, 570
developing CMP entity beans, 401
implementing façade design pattern, 504
using EJB Timer to invoke message bean, 521
JavaCaps web site, 643
JavaMail
EDI and supply chain management, 613
overview of J2EE and related technologies, 604
JavaPrepare web site, 643
JavaRanch web site, 641

JavaScript, 25
JavaWorld web site, 641
JAXR (Java API for XML Registries)
service discovery layer, 536
JAX-RPC (Java API for XML-based RPC), 537
creating stateful web service, 581
creating WAR file, 549
creating web service with session bean, 570
developing web services in Java, 537
example creating web service, 538
JAX-RPC service endpoint model, 580
JAX-RPC service endpoint model
creating stateful web service, 588
implementing stateful web service, 580
summary, 597
JBoss
commercial J2EE servers, 626
J2EE implementation, 14
JBuilder Enterprise IDE, 631
JDBC (Java DataBase Connectivity)
connecting to databases, 258
definition, 687
DriverManager class, 262
drivers, 259
EJB QL alternative, 485
Java database API, 257
overview of J2EE and related technologies, 604
using JDBC with Enterprise JavaBeans, 478
JDBC protocol
cloudscape command, 273
JDBCClient class
communicating with databases, 273
JDBCManager class
example using Statements, 279, 282
JDBC-ODBC bridge
type 1 driver, 259
JDO (Java Data Objects)
overview of J2EE and related technologies, 604
jGuru web site, 641
JMS (Java Message Services)
JMS API, 515
message-driven beans, 514
overview of J2EE and related technologies, 605
JNDI (Java Naming and Directory Interface)
creating session beans, 368, 372
overview of J2EE and related technologies, 606
tag libraries, 175
jobs, 644
see also web resources.
joins, SQL, 675
JRun
JSP servers, 627
JSF (JavaServer Faces)
overview of J2EE and related technologies, 604
JSP (Java Server Pages), 63–120
action elements, 85
clean up, 88
comments, 70
creating web application, 71
custom actions, 139, 140
definition, 687
deploying web application in J2EE, 76
deploying web application in Tomcat, 82
deployment, 58
developing, 64
directive attributes/elements, 66

JSP (Java Server Pages) (continued)
elements, 66
see also scripting elements.
errors, 105
exception handling, 106
exceptions, 105
Expression Language (EL), 124–39
implicit objects, 89
initialization, 88
introduction, 24
JSP API, 102
JSP servers, 626
lifecycle, 64
method definition, 70
scope, 93
scripting elements, 68
Servlet API, 102
summarized, 34
tag handlers, 141
template data, 71
translated JSP, 103
translation and compilation, 102
using JavaBeans in JSP pages, 94
using JSP and servlets with EJBs, 507
variables, 70
JSP Standard Tag Library
see JSTL.
JSP translator
tags, 139
jsp:attribute/~body/~doBody/~fallback elements
action elements, JSP, 85
jsp:getProperty action
action elements, JSP, 88
attributes, 88
using JavaBeans in JSP pages, 101
jsp:invoke/~params/~plugin elements
action elements, JSP, 85
jsp:setProperty action
action elements, JSP, 87
attributes, 87
using JavaBeans in JSP pages, 101
jsp:useBean action
action elements, JSP, 85
attributes, 86
using JavaBeans in JSP pages, 101
jsp-file element
deployment descriptors, 202
JspFragment interface
invoke method, 143
tag handlers, JSP, 141, 143
jspService method
translated JSP, 104
jsptags.com
tag libraries, 175
JSTL (JSP Standard Tag Library), 166
categories, 167
introduction, 123
using, 170
JTA (Java Transaction API)
distributed transactions, 332

L

layers
multi-tier architecture, 14, 354
protocol stack, 535
LENGTH function, EJB QL, 681
lifecycles
JAX-RPC service endpoint model, 580
ServiceLifecycle interface, 581
servlets, 204
LIKE keyword
EJB QL, 680
SQL, 670
Linux
installing J2EE 1.4 SDK, 37
listener element
deployment descriptors, 201
literal values
Expression Language (EL), 126
local bean interface
entity beans, EJBs, 392
local home interface
entity beans, EJBs, 391
remote home interface compared, 430
local interfaces, EJB, 422
LocalAnalyst.java file
loading database with CMP Field Data, 467
LocalStock.java file
loading database with CMP Field Data, 469
LocalStockHome.java file
create EJB using EJB QL find, 439
loading database with CMP Field Data, 470
LOCATE function, EJB QL, 681
locking, 336
concurrency, 334
pessimistic locking, 337
logging
DriverManager class, 274
Login servlet
maintaining state with session object, 223
servlet lifecycle, 208
using filters, 231
login-config element
deployment descriptors, 201
lookup method
creating session beans, 368
getting DataSource object, 311

M

MacroMedia JRun
see JRun.
maintaining state
session object, 223
makeConnection method
using JDBC from session bean, 484

management APIs
  Application Service Providers, 611
  loading database with CMP Field Data, 467
mapping
  configuring web service, 549
  creating stateful web service, 583
MAX function
  EJB QL, 681
  SQL, 673
MEMBER OF operator, SQL
  EJB QL SELECT method, 450
message beans, EJBs
  choosing type of bean to use, 358
  introduction, 28, 358
  message-driven beans, 514
  using EJB Timer to invoke, 516
message-driven beans
  asynchronous messages, 528
MessageWriter session bean
  using EJB Timer to invoke message bean, 517
MessageWriterBean.java file
  using EJB Timer to invoke message bean, 520
messaging
  workflow automation, 610
messaging layer
  protocol stack, 535
messaging model
  web services, 534
methods
  invoking methods using DII, 595
Microsoft Internet Information Services
  see IIS.
Microsoft SQL Server
  see SQL Server.
middle tier
  see business rules tier/layer.
middleware component
  type 3 driver, 260
mime-mapping element
  deployment descriptors, 201
MIN function
  EJB QL, 681
  SQL, 673
MOD function, EJB QL, 681
model
  MVC application, 238
Model 1/Model 2
  MVC architecture, 237
module, 688
moveToCurrentRow method
  updating ResultSet objects, 294
moveToInsertRow method
  updating ResultSet objects, 292
multiple concurrent request threads
  thread unsafe servlet example, 212
multi-tier architecture, 14, 354
MVC (Model-View-Controller) architecture, 237–52
  MVC application, 238
  summary, 253
  using MVC architecture, 241
MySQL, 634

N

name attribute
  jsp:getProperty element, 88
  jsp:setProperty element, 87
name element
  <tag> element, 144
name-value pairs
  properties, 263
navigation operator, EJB QL, 680
New Application dialog
  creating session beans, 364
  deploying web application in J2EE, 76
New Deployment Settings File dialog
  creating Deployment Descriptor, 556
  creating session beans, 367
  deploying web application in J2EE, 81
  testing J2EE installation, 53
New Web Application wizard
  configuring web service, 549
  creating WAR file, 549
  deploying servlet to J2EE server, 191
  deploying web application in J2EE, 77
  testing J2EE installation, 48, 50
next method
  resultsets, 285
Novell exteNd
  commercial J2EE servers, 626
n-tier architecture
  deployment of layers, 18
  J2EE architectures, 31
NULL values, 287, 667
  setting, 302
numeric data type, SQL, 664

O

object-orientation
  workflow automation, 610
one-to-many relationship
  container-managed relationships (CMR), 448
operation element, WSDL
  service description layer, 536
operators
  EL, 126
  SQL, 668
optimistic locking, 344–49
optimization
  testing and performance tools, 632
OPTIONS method
  request method, 180
Oracle 9i application server, 625
Oracle 9i database server, 633
Orbix E2A J2EE Edition
  see Iona Orbix E2A J2EE Edition.
ORDER BY clause, EJB QL, 677
ORDER BY clause, SQL, 669
Orion EJB
  tag libraries, 175
out object
  JSP implicit object, 91

P

p2p.wrox.com, 8
packaging tag libraries, 146
Page cannot be displayed error
 deployment problems, 60
 problem starting J2EE server, 46
page directive, JSP, 66
 attributes, 66
 exceptions, 105
 scripting elements, 124
page scope
 scope, JSP, 93
pageContext implicit object, EL, 128
pageEncoding attribute
 JSP page directive, 67
pageScope implicit object, EL, 129
param attribute
 jsp:setProperty element, 87
param implicit object, EL, 129
params element, JSP, 85
paramValues implicit object, EL, 129
part element, WSDL
 service description layer, 536
passivation
 stateful session beans, 378
PATH
 setting environment variables, 40
pattern searching, SQL, 670
performance
 commercial J2EE, 620
 e-commerce, 608
 testing and performance tools, 631
persisting client information
 sessions, 220
pessimistic locking, 337–44
placeholders, SQL
 CallableStatement object, 308
 prepareStatement method, 300
 set methods, 301
platform independence, 14, 19
 n-tier architecture, 31
 prepared statements, 299
plugin element, JSP, 85
point-to-point messaging
 JMS API, 515
Port Component Name
 configuring web service, 551
port element, WSDL
 service description layer, 536
ports
 HTTP traffic, 534
POST method/requests, 184
 creating a servlet, 188
 doPost method, 187
 request method, 180
prepareCall method
 CallableStatement object, 307
prepared statements, 298–306
 example using, 303
PreparedStatement object
 creating, 299
 SQL statements/commands, 349
prepareStatement method
 PreparedStatement class, 299

presentation tier/layer
 multi-tier architecture, 15
primary key
 entity beans, EJBs, 395, 448
ProcessAnalyst.jsp file
 using MVC architecture, 244, 251
profiling
 IDEs, 630
programmer to programmer™, 8
properties
 name-value pairs, 263
Properties object
 connecting to databases, 265
property attribute
 jsp:getProperty element, 88
 jsp:setProperty element, 87
protocol stack
 web services, 535
publish/subscribe messaging
 JMS API, 515
PUT method, 180

Q

qualified name
 creating web service with session bean, 577, 578
queue
 JMS API, 515
 using EJB Timer to invoke message bean, 526

R

RatingsForm.jsp file
 using JSP and servlets with EJBs, 509
 using MVC architecture, 245, 251, 252
REGEXP keyword, SQL, 671
registerDriver method
 loading drivers, 262
registerOutParameter method
 CallableStatement class, 308
registration page
 using JavaBeans in JSP pages, 98
regular expressions, SQL, 670
relational databases
 access, JSTL tag categories, 167
 description, 257
 entity beans, 357
relationships
 see also CMR.
 creating entity bean using CMR and EJB QL, 459
 get methods, 448
 one-to-many relationship, 448
releaseSavepoint method
 Connection class, 322, 325
releasing Statement objects, 278
remote bean interface
 entity beans, EJBs, 392
remote home interface
 entity beans, EJBs, 391
 local home interface compared, 430
Remote interface
 RMI, 26
remote interfaces, EJB, 422

Remote Method Invocation
see RMI.
remove method
creating session beans, 373
home interface, entity bean, 391, 394
removeAttribute method
adding parameters to request, 241
session class, 91
request dispatchers, 240
request handling
servlet lifecycle, 207
request methods, 180
request object
JSP implicit object, 89
using JavaBeans in JSP pages, 94
using request object, 196
request scope
scope, JSP, 93
RequestDispatcher
forwarding and including requests, 239
requests
adding parameters to request, 241
forwarding and including requests, 239
JSP lifecycle, 64
requestScope implicit object, EL, 129
resource manager, 688
resource-env-ref element
deployment descriptors, 201
ResourceParams element
data sources, 318
resource-ref element
deployment descriptors, 201
resources, 614
see also web site references.
books from Wrox Press, 645
response object
creating a servlet, 190
encodeRedirectURL method, 92
encodeURL method, 92
JSP implicit object, 90
sendRedirect method, 92
using response object, 199
responses
server response to requests, 184
ResultSet interface, 284
ResultSet object
example using, 287
holdability, 294
updating, 292
resultsets, 284
prepareStatement method, 299
reading data from, 285
scrollable resultsets, 285
updatable resultsets, 285
RMI (Remote Method Invocation)
communicating with databases, 271
definition, 688
introduction, 26
overview of J2EE and related technologies, 605
RMI registry, 26
session bean stubs, 360
web services, 533
role-based authentication
using EJBs, 355
rollback method, Connection object
savepoints, 322
transactions, 322, 323, 325

RPC (Remote Procedure Calls)
web services, 533, 534
RTRIM function, SQL, 672

S

SAAJ (SOAP with Attachments API for Java)
messaging layer, 536
sample code
downloading, 6
sandbox, 46
Save Deployment Settings File dialog
creating Deployment Descriptor, 557
creating session beans, 368
testing J2EE installation, 54
savepoints
transactions, 322, 323
scalability
commercial J2EE, 621
J2EE architecture, 20
session beans, 356
schema, SQL, 663
scope attribute, jsp:useBean element, 86
scope, JSP, 93
scripting elements
deployment descriptor, 124
page directive, JSP, 124
scripting elements, JSP, 68
declarations, 68
expressions, 68, 70
scriptlets, 68, 69
scriptlets
method definition, 70
scripting elements, JSP, 68, 69
variables declared in, 70
security
commercial J2EE, 622
introduction, 31
security-constraint element
deployment descriptors, 201
security-role element
deployment descriptors, 201
SELECT clause, EJB QL, 677, 679
see also Finder/Select Methods dialog.
creating entity bean using CMR and EJB QL, 451
creating SELECT method, 449
finder methods compared, 485
select methods
EJB QL, 434
loading database with CMP Field Data, 469
SELECT statement, SQL, 667
developing BMP entity beans, 421
sendRedirect method
response object, 90, 92
servers
see application servers; database servers.
server-side components, 21
Service Definition Interface file
building and deploying web services, 543
creating WAR file, 549
creating web service with JAX-RPC, 539, 540
web service stubs, 537
service definition interface, session bean
creating web service, 567, 570, 578

service description/discovery layers
protocol stack, 536
Service Endpoint interface
configuring web service, 551
service method
handling requests, 186
request handling, servlet lifecycle, 207
service providers, 634
service-config.xml file
creating WSDL file with wscompile, 545
ServiceFactory object
creating stateful web service, 594
creating web service with session bean, 578
ServiceLifecycle interface
JAX-RPC service endpoint model, 581
servlet container, 689
Servlet Filters dialog, 234
servlet lifecycle, 253
servlet element
deployment descriptors, 201, 202
sub-elements, 202
servlet-class element
deployment descriptors, 202
ServletConfig object
initialization servlet lifecycle, 205
servlet-mapping element
deployment descriptors, 201, 203
servlet-name element
deployment descriptors, 202
ServletRequest interface, 196, 197
servlets, 179–254
see also HttpServlet class.
creating, 188
definition, 688
deploying JSP, 58
deploying servlet to J2EE server, 191
deploying servlet to Tomcat, 195
endpoint context, 580
error pages, 218
event logging, 208
exceptions, 216–19
handling requests, 186
HTTP servlets, 186
introduction, 23
JSP, 24
JSP Servlet API, 102
lifecycle, 204, 208
Login servlet, 208
servlet model, 185
summary, 34, 252
thread safe servlet, 214
thread unsafe servlet example, 209
threading, 208
using filters, 231
using JSP and servlets with EJBs, 507
using response object, 199
session beans, EJBs, 356, 358–85
bean class, 359
bean interface, 359
bean stub, 360
calling beans from client, 358
choosing type of bean to use, 358
creating, 360
developing CMP entity beans, 410
diagrammatic representation, 359
home interface, 359
home stub, 360

introduction, 27
scalability, 356
state, 356, 377 (see also stateful/stateless session beans)
troubleshooting deployment, 376
using JDBC with Enterprise JavaBeans, 478
session object
JSP implicit object, 91
maintaining state, 223
methods, 91
session management with cookies, 221
session tracking
cookies, 220
summary, 253
URL rewriting, 220
SessionBean interface
session beans, 359
session-config element
deployment descriptors, 201
sessions
persisting client information, 220
session creation and lifecycle, 221
scope, JSP, 93
session attribute, 67
session management, 219, 221
state management, 354
sessionScope implicit object, EL, 129
set methods
CallableStatement object, 308
placeholders, 301
using JavaBeans in JSP pages, 101
setAnalyst method
creating entity bean using CMR and EJB QL, 459
implementing façade design pattern, 496
loading database with CMP Field Data, 466, 469
setAttribute method
adding parameters to request, 241
persisting client information, 220
session object, 91
using MVC architecture, 250
setAutoCommit method, Connection class
transactions, 321, 322
setBodyContent method
BodyTag interface, 156
classic tag handler with body tag support, 165
setEntityContext method
developing BMP entity beans, 421
developing CMP entity beans, 410
setLogWriter method
logging with DriverManager, 275
setMaxAge method
session management with cookies, 222
setMaxInactiveInterval method
session creation and lifecycle, 221
setNull method
PreparedStatement class, 302
setProperty element, JSP, 87
setProperty method
connecting to databases, 265
setSavepoint method,
Connection class, 322
setSessionContext method
creating session beans, 374
using EJB Timer to invoke message bean, 525
setStocks method
creating entity bean using CMR and EJB QL, 459
loading database with CMP Field Data, 466, 467

setter methods
bean class, entity bean, 392
developing BMP entity beans, 418
setTickerSymbol ethod
developing CMP entity beans, 409
setup method
optimistic locking, 347
setValue method
session management with cookies, 222
setVariables method
classic tag handler with body tag support, 165
short-name element
<taglib> element, 144
SimpleService.wsdl file
creating WSDL file with wscompile, 545
SimpleServiceClient.java file
building and deploying web services, 544
creating web service with session bean, 576
SimpleServiceIF.java file
building and deploying web services, 544
creating web service with session bean, 567
SimpleServiceImpl.java file
building and deploying web services, 544
SimpleSession.java file, 361
SimpleSessionBean.java file, 361
creating web service with session bean, 566
SimpleSessionClient.jave file, 362
creating session beans, 371
SimpleSessionHome.java file, 361
SimpleTag interface
tag handlers, JSP, 141
single tier architecture, 15
singleton design pattern
StockListFacade class, 506
using in EJB applications, 488
sleep method
pessimistic locking, 343
thread unsafe servlet example, 213
SMTP (Simple Mail Transport Protocol)
transport layer, 535
SNMP (Simple Network Management Protocol)
overview of J2EE and related technologies, 607
SOAP (Simple Object Access Protocol)
messaging layer, 535
web services, 534
SOAP with Attachments API for Java
see SAAJ.
software vendors
see vendors.
Solaris SPARC 8 & 9
installing J2EE 1.4 SDK, 37
Solutions Marketplace web site, 640
sorting data, SQL, 669
specification
implementations, 14
J2EE resources, 615
sprocs
see stored procedures.
SQL (Structured Query Language), 661–77
AS keyword, 672
AVG function, 673
BETWEEN keyword, 668
binary data type, 664
calculated fields, 671
catalog, 662
CHAR keyword, 663
clusters, 662

core actions, JSTL, 170
COUNT function, 673
data types, 663
date and time data type, 664
default values, 665
filtering data, 668
functions, 672
joins, 675
LIKE keyword, 670, 671
MAX function, 673
MIN function, 673
NULL value, 667
numeric data type, 664
operators, 668
ORDER BY clause, 669
pattern matching, 670
PreparedStatement object, 349
REGEXP keyword, 671
regular expressions, 670
RTRIM function, 672
schema, 663
sending SQL commands to the database, 349
sorting data, 669
SQL Server, 633
String data type, 663
SUM function, 673
WHERE clause, 668
wildcards, 670
SQL statements, 275
ALTER TABLE statement, 666
CREATE statement, 276
CREATE TABLE statement, 665
DELETE statement, 277, 675
DROP TABLE statement, 666
INSERT statement, 276, 673
SELECT statement, 667
UPDATE statement, 277, 674
<sql.tld>
core actions, JSTL, 170
SQLExceptions
connecting to databases, 268
SQRT function, EJB QL, 681
SSL (Secure Sockets Layer), 689
Standard Actions
action elements, JSP, 85
Standard Tag Library
see JSTL.
startTimer method
EJB Timer invoking message bean, 518, 525
state
maintaining with session object, 223
stateChanged method
create EJB using EJB QL find, 442
stateful web service
creating, 581
implementing, 580
stateful/stateless session beans, EJBs, 377–85
choosing between, 377
Edit Enterprise Bean wizard, 366
introduction, 356
stateful session beans, 378
stateless session beans, 365, 565, 566
Statement objects, 275
creating, 275
example using, 279
example using ResultSet object, 291
releasing, 278

Stock.java file
developing CMP entity beans, 396
StockBean.java file
developing CMP entity beans, 397, 409
loading database with CMP Field Data, 468
StockClient.java file
developing CMP entity beans, 412
implementing façade design pattern, 501
loading database with CMP Field Data, 476
StockHome.java file
developing CMP entity beans, 398, 408
StockList.java file
create EJB using EJB QL find, 440
developing CMP entity beans, 398
implementing façade design pattern, 494
loading database with CMP Field Data, 471
StockListAdder.java file
creating entity bean using CMR and EJB QL, 453
implementing façade design pattern, 499
loading database with CMP Field Data, 461
StockListBean.java file
accessing local home interface, 430
create EJB using EJB QL find, 440
developing CMP entity beans, 398
implementing façade design pattern, 494
loading database with CMP Field Data, 471
using JDBC from session bean, 480
StockListException.java file
implementing façade design pattern, 492
StockListFacade class
implementing façade design pattern, 505
singleton design pattern, 506
using JSP and servlets with EJBs, 512
StockListFacade.java file
implementing façade design pattern, 490
StockListHome.java file
developing CMP entity beans, 400
loading database with CMP Field Data, 476
StockListServlet.java file
using JSP and servlets with EJBs, 508
using MVC architecture, 250
StockVo.java file
implementing façade design pattern, 493
stored procedures (sprocs)
callable statements, 306
CallableStatement object, 349
cloudscape command, 306
reasons for using, 306
transactions and, 325
stress testing
testing and performance tools, 632
string data type, SQL, 663
struts
tag libraries, 175
stubs
creating stateful web service, 593
creating web service with session bean, 577
invoking web service methods, 542
session beans, EJBs, 360
web service stubs, 537
stubs classes
building and deploying web services, 543
style conventions used in this book, 4
SUBSTRING function, EJB QL, 681
SUM function
EJB QL, 681
SQL, 673

supply chain management
technologies required, 612
support
customer support used in this book, 6
errata in this book, 7
p2p.wrox.com, 8
technical support in this book, 7
Swing, 11
Sybase Adaptive Server Enterprise, 634
System Properties dialog
installing J2EE 1.4 SDK, 39
system property
loading drivers, 263

T

tables, SQL, 665
deleting, 666
tag element
<taglib> element, 144
tag handlers, JSP, 141
classic tag handlers, 152, 157
interfaces, 141
packaging tag libraries, 147
Tag interface, 153
tag handlers, JSP, 141
tag libraries, 175
see also JSTL.
custom actions, 140
packaging, 146
Tag Library Descriptor
see TLD.
tag-class element
<tag> element, 144
taglib directive, JSP, 66
defining classic tag handler, 162
packaging tag libraries, 147
<taglib> element
sub-elements, 144
TLD (Tag Library Descriptor), 143
taglib element
deployment descriptors, 201
tags
JSP translator, 139
TagSupport interface
IterationTag interface, 154
Tag interface, 153
technical support in this book, 7
telnet
POST requests, 184
sending an HTTP request via telnet, 182
template data, JSP, 71
testing
testing and performance tools, 631
thin clients, 21
thin driver
type 4 driver, 261
this keyword
thread unsafe servlet example, 213
threading
servlets, 208
summary, 253
thread safe servlet, 214
thread unsafe servlet example, 209

tiers, application architecture
introduction, 14
three-tier architecture, 17
two-tier architecture, 16
ties
web service ties, 537
TimedObject interface
EJB Timer Service, 516
TimeIt session bean
using EJB Timer to invoke message bean, 516
TimeIt*Bean*/~*Tester*.java files
using EJB Timer to invoke message bean, 518
timeout
connecting to databases, 268
Timer/~*Service* interface
EJB Timer Service, 516
timer services
see EJB Timer Service.
TLD (Tag Library Descriptor), 143, 146, 152
classic tag handler, 164
creating scripting variables, 165
implementing JSTL, 166
JSTL categories, 167
tag handler class, 162
taglib directive, 162
tlib-version element
<taglib> element, 144
Tomcat
deploying servlet to Tomcat, 195
deploying web application in Tomcat, 82
deployment descriptors, 159
example using data sources, 317
JSP servers, 627
thread unsafe servlet example, 211
using EL expressions, 134
using JSTL, 173
using MVC architecture, 247
versions, 655
Tomcat installation, 655
Linux/Unix, 657
Windows, 656
topic property
packaging tag libraries, 151, 152
topics
JMS API, 515
TRACE method
request method, 180
transaction management
using EJBs, 354
transaction manager
distributed transactions, 332
method call prohibitions, 333
transaction support, 30
transactions, 320–34
autocommit status, 321
BEGIN TRAN command, 321
connection methods, 322
consistency, 321, 323, 350
definition, 689
isolation, 335
locking, 336
savepoints, 323
stored procedures and, 325
transaction control, 322, 325–31
transport layer
protocol stack, 535

troubleshooting
creating session beans, 376
try...catch... finally blocks
releasing database connection, 267
using EJB Timer to invoke message bean, 527
tutorials
see web resources.
two-phase commit
distributed transactions, 333
type attribute, jsp:useBean element, 86
TYPE_SCROLL_SENSITIVE
scrollable resultsets, 285

U

UDDI (Universal Description, Discovery and Integration)
service discovery layer, 536
UML (Unified Modeling Language)
bean classes and interfaces, 360
components, 354
entity bean classes and interfaces, 393
local interfaces, EJB, 423
underscore character, SQL, 670
UnicastRemoteObject class
RMI, 26
UPDATE statement, SQL, 674
developing BMP entity beans, 421
pessimistic locking, 337, 343
rows affected, 277
updateRow method
updating ResultSet objects, 292
updateStock method
developing CMP entity beans, 411
updateXyz methods
updating ResultSet objects, 292
URI (Uniform Resource Identifier), 181
testing J2EE installation, 56
URL (Uniform Resource Locator), 181
URL encoding, 181
URL rewriting
session tracking, 220
URL-encoded parameters, HTTP
request object, 89
usability
e-commerce, 609
useBean element, JSP, 85
user authentication
using EJBs, 355
user interface layer
see presentation tier/layer.

V

validation
testing and performance tools, 631
value attribute, jsp:setProperty element, 87
value object design pattern, 506
using in EJB applications, 488
variable element
<tag> element, 144
vendors
independence of vendors, 19
J2EE solutions, 14

verbose command
   problem starting J2EE server, 46
   starting J2EE server, 43
Verifier reports error
   deployment problems, 60
Verifier tool
   building and deploying web services, 543
   creating session beans, 369
   creating web service with session bean, 574
   troubleshooting session bean deployment, 376
Verify Specification Compliance window
   testing J2EE installation, 54
version command
   installation problems, 38
   installing J2EE 1.4 SDK, 38
view
   MVC application, 238
VPSource web site, 641

W

WAR (Web Archive) file
   building and deploying web services, 543
   creating, 548
   deploying J2EE to server, 59
   running application after J2EE installation, 48
web applications
   creating JSP web application, 71
   definition, 689
   session management, 219
web components
   which components are web components, 21
web container, 690
web resources
   see also web site references.
   certification, 642
   developers, 640
   forums, 642
   J2EE technologies documentation, 640
   J2EE tutorials, 640
   Java services and products, 640
   Java tutorials, 640
   job search sites, 641, 644
web server, 690
web service client, 542
web service endpoints
   configuring web service, 549
   creating Deployment Descriptor, 557
   creating stateful web service, 594
   creating web service with session bean, 579
   summary, 597
Web Service Implementation class, 542
   creating WAR file, 549
web service interface
   creating class implementing, 539
web services, 29, 531–62, 565–98
   Application Service Providers, 611
   building and deploying, 543–61
   configuring web service, 549
   creating client file for testing, 539
   creating stateful web service, 581
   creating web service with session bean, 566
   creating WSDL file with wscompile, 545
   deploying, 557
   developing in Java, 537

   endpoints, 565
   example creating with JAX-RPC, 538
   examples of web services, 532
   implementing stateful web service, 580
   invoking web service methods, 542
   protocol stack, 535
   reasons for using, 534
   standards enabling client to invoke, 533
   stubs, 537
   testing, 559
   ties, 537
web site references, 617, 636
   see also web resources.
   ACM, 617
   alphaWorks, 640
   Apache web server, 636
   BEA, 14
   Borland, 14
   Borland Enterprise AppServer, 636
   brainbuzz, 642
   Café au Lait, 641
   certification, 643
   Cloudscape database server, 265
   CVS, 636
   DB2, 637
   developerWorks, 640
   Dick Baldwin's web site, 641
   EJB QL, 682
   Gamelan page, 641
   garbage collection, 278
   IBM, 14
   IBM WebSphere server, 636
   IEEE, 617
   IIS, 636
   Informix, 637
   Iona Orbix E2A J2EE Edition, 636
   J2EE, 617
   J2EE patterns, 528
   J2EE technologies, 607
   Java, 640
   Java Boutique, 641
   Java on IBM, 640
   Java web sites, 617
   JavaCaps, 643
   JavaMail, 604
   JavaPrepare, 643
   JavaRanch, 641
   JavaWorld, 641
   JBoss, 14, 636
   JBuilder Enterprise IDE, 636
   JDBC-ODBC bridge, 259
   jGury, 641
   JMS (Java Message Services), 605
   JMS API, 528
   JRun, 636
   JSF (JavaServer Faces), 604
   JSP, 65
   JSP directive attributes, 66
   JSTL, 166
   JTA (Java Transaction API), 332
   MySQL, 637
   Novell exteNd, 636
   Oracle 9i, 637
   Oracle 9i application server, 636
   Parasoft JTest, 636
   Rational ClearCase, 636
   request methods, 181

RMI, 26
Sitraka JProbe, 636
SQL Server, 637
Sun, 617
Sybase Adaptive Server Enterprise, 637
tag libraries, 175
Tomcat, 636
Tomcat installations, 655
UDDI, 536
VPSource, 641
web services, 597, 640
web services examples, 532
WebLogic Server, 636
WebSphere Enterprise Studio IDE, 636
Whizlabs, 643
Wrox, 617
xmethods, 532
XML, 640
XML/EDI group, 617
ZDNet, 642
WebLogic server
commercial J2EE servers, 624
WebSphere application server
commercial J2EE servers, 625
WebSphere Enterprise Studio IDE, 631
welcome-file-list element
deployment descriptors, 201
WHERE clause
EJB QL, 677
SQL, 668
Whizlabs web site, 643
wildcards
EJB QL, 680
SQL, 670
windows
see also dialogs; wizards.
Application Deployment Tool window, 47
Verify Specification Compliance window, 54
wizards
see also dialogs; windows.
Edit Enterprise Bean wizard, 366
Enterprise Bean wizard, 365
New Web Application wizard, 48

workflow automation
technologies required, 609
Wrox
books from Wrox Press, 645
wscompile command line tool
building and deploying web services, 543
creating stateful web service, 583
creating web service with session bean, 570
creating WSDL file, 545
testing web services, 560
WSDL (Web Services Description Language)
creating WAR file, 549
creating web service with session bean, 570, 579
creating WSDL file with wscompile, 545
Port Namespace and Local Part, 551
Service Definition Interface, 540
service description layer, 536
testing web services, 560
WSDL URL, 578

X

XA prefix
distributed transactions, 332
xmethods
examples of web services, 532
XML (Extensible Markup Language)
definition, 690
EDI and supply chain management, 612
encoding layer, 535
introduction, 29
overview of J2EE and related technologies, 604
web services, 534
XML processing
JSTL tag categories, 167

Z

ZDNet web site, 642

wrox

Programmer to Programmer™

Registration Code: | 83331GCHO3789601 |

Wrox writes books for you. Any suggestions, or ideas about how you want information given in your ideal book will be studied by our team. Your comments are always valued at Wrox.

Free phone in USA 800-USE-WROX
Fax (312) 893 8001

UK Tel.: (0121) 687 4100   Fax: (0121) 687 4101

Beginning J2EE 1.4 – Registration Card

Name _____

Address _____

_____

_____

City _____ State/Region _____

Country _____ Postcode/Zip _____

E-Mail _____

Occupation _____

How did you hear about this book?

☐ Book review (name) _____

☐ Advertisement (name) _____

☐ Recommendation _____

☐ Catalog _____

☐ Other _____

Where did you buy this book?

☐ Bookstore (name) _____ City_____

☐ Computer store (name) _____

☐ Mail order _____

☐ Other _____

What influenced you in the purchase of this book?

☐ Cover Design ☐ Contents ☐ Other (please specify):

How did you rate the overall content of this book?

☐ Excellent ☐ Good ☐ Average ☐ Poor

What did you find most useful about this book? _____

_____

What did you find least useful about this book? _____

_____

Please add any additional comments. _____

_____

What other subjects will you buy a computer book on soon?

_____

What is the best computer book you have used this year?

_____

8333   Check here if you DO NOT want to receive support for this book ▮   8333

wrox

Programmer to Programmer™

Note: If you post the bounce back card below in the UK, please send it to:

Wrox Press Limited, Arden House, 1102 Warwick Road,
Acocks Green, Birmingham B27 6HB. UK.

Computer Book Publishers